JEHOVAH'S WITNESSES

JEHOVAH'S WITNESSES

◆

A Comprehensive and Selectively Annotated Bibliography

Compiled by Jerry Bergman

Introduction by Joseph F. Zygmunt

Bibliographies and Indexes in Religious Studies, Number 48

Greenwood Press
Westport, Connecticut • London

Library of Congress Cataloging-in-Publication Data

Bergman, Jerry.
   Jehovah's Witnesses : a comprehensive and selectively annotated
bibliography / compiled by Jerry Bergman ; introduction by Joseph F.
Zygmunt.
       p.   cm.—(Bibliographies and indexes in religious studies,
   ISSN 0742–6836 ; no. 48)
     Includes bibliographical references and index.
     ISBN 0–313–30510–2 (alk. paper)
     1. Jehovah's Witnesses—Bibliography.   I. Title.   II. Series.
   Z7845.J45B46   1999
   [BX8526]
   016.2899′2—dc21   98–37845

British Library Cataloguing in Publication Data is available.

Library of Congress Catalog Card Number: 98–37845
ISBN: 0–313–30510–2
ISSN: 0742–6836

First published in 1999

Greenwood Press, 88 Post Road West, Westport, CT 06881
An imprint of Greenwood Publishing Group, Inc.

Printed in the United States of America

The paper used in this book complies with the
Permanent Paper Standard issued by the National
Information Standards Organization (Z39.48–1984).

10 9 8 7 6 5 4 3 2 1

CONTENTS

ACKNOWLEDGMENTS

A project such as this involved a large number of people on five continents, many of whose suggestions and contributions were critical and appreciated. Foremost are Dr. Gordon Melton, Jim Parkinson, and Ken Raines. I am also very grateful to Dr. M. James Penton of Lethbridge University, Dr. Richard Singelenberg of the University of Utrecht, Dr. Edmund Gruss, William Chamberlin, Duane Magnani, Rodney Bias, Matthew Alfs, Mick Van Buskirk, Carl Hackensack, Dr. Robert Morey, Dr. Alan Rogerson, Dr. Melvin Curry, Rud Persson, Carl Olof Jonsson, and Dr. Joseph F. Zygmunt of the University of Connecticut.

And thanks must also be given to Gaetano Boccaccio, Dr. Regis Deriequebourg, Abe Dijkstra, Norman Hovland, Gary Shearer, Daniel Dykstra, Raymond Franz, James Caudle, Marge and Leonard Chretein, Marley Cole, David W. Bercot, Dr. Carl Thornton, Bettie and John Vauls, Jim Valentine, Richard Estes, and Richard Rawe for their hours of help, aid in locating hundreds of references, and, most important, their persistent encouragement. Many other persons cannot be noted because they are active Witnesses and listing their names may cause them to experience disciplinary action by the Watchtower. And mention must be made of my typists, Cathy Hern, Nancy Tucker, and Susan Schwarz, who struggled through the many drafts of this manuscript. And, most of all, thanks go to my wife Dianne and our four children, Aeron, Christine, Mishalea, and Scott, for their support and encouragement with this now three-decades-old project.

Introduction
by Joseph F. Zygmunt

As we approach the end of the twentieth century, both popular and scholarly interest in millennial prophecies seem to be undergoing something of a "revival." This style of thinking about religious as well as secular life has, of course, been a recurrent part of the historical scene and many different cultural traditions for centuries. From time to time it has erupted into more clearly visible, and sometimes dramatic, manifestations.

While millennial beliefs have varied among their many different advocates, their central tenets have commonly included a conviction that the established earthly social order is doomed to more or less imminent destruction and that it will be replaced, usually with the anticipated intervention of some supernatural agencies, by a radically contrasting system of existence, from which all evil and injustice will be banished. The expected "time of the end" and colossal transformation may be more or less specifically predicted, or it may remain more loosely defined simply as temporally proximate.

As such expectations mount and spread, and as the time of the grand collapse approaches, such shared convictions have motivated actions which often take deviant, even bizarre, and sometimes shocking forms in the eyes of outsiders. An example is the Heaven's Gate cult. On some occasions they have assumed a quasi-revolutionary stance, causing agitation and fervor, possibly even sparking challenges to the established secular political system as well.

Jehovah's Witnesses are only one among many groups which have promoted various versions of this ancient set of beliefs during the last century or so. The sect's extensive and fascinating history is well documented in Dr. Bergman's annotated bibliography, one of the best guides to the literature dealing with various aspects of the Watchtower's complex history since it was founded in Allegheny, Pennsylvania, in the early 1870s. This reference work covers not only the elaborate literature produced and circulated by the Witnesses themselves (an invaluable historical guide), but also a rich variety of studies, interpretations, and critical commentaries by others as well, a incomparably valuable source of clues to its changing status in the broader society.

Despite recurrently strong persecution and repression, even on the American scene, the group has managed not only to survive but, by 1997, to grow to a worldwide organization of some five million active believers in 233 countries. Over the years, many

occurred; yet the group's millennial faith remains as strong as ever, as does its enthusiastic promotion.

Scholars and others who share an interest in the sect's millennial beliefs and long-term historical development, will find this bibliography an indispensable source of valuable information.

Joseph F. Zygmunt, Ph.D.
Professor of Sociology Emeritus
University of Connecticut

References

Case, S.J. (1918). *The Millennial Hope.* Chicago: University of Chicago Press.

Cohn, N. (1957). *The Pursuit of the Millennium: Revolutionary Messianism in Medieval and Reformation Europe and Its Bearing on Modern Totalitarian Movements.* New York: Harper.

Lofland, J. (1966). *Doomsday Cult.* Englewood Cliffs, NJ: Prentice-Hall.

Rogers, P.G. (1966). *The Fifth Monarch Men.* London and New York: Oxford University Press.

Talmon, Y. (1968). "Millenarism." *The International Encyclopedia of the Social Sciences,* 10:349-362. New York: Macmillan and Free Press.

_____. (1962). "Pursuit of the Millennium: The Relation between Religious and Social Change." *Archives europeenes de sociologie.* 3:125-148.

Thrupp, S. L. (ed.) (1962). *Millennial Dreams in Action: Essays in Comparative Study.* The Hague: Mouton.

Watchtower Bible and Tract Society. (1997). *1997 Yearbook of Jehovah's Witnesses.* New York: Watchtower Bible and Tract Society.

Worsley, P. (1957). *The Trumpet Shall Sound: A Study of "Cargo" Cults in Melanesia.* London: MacGibbon & Kee.

Zygmunt, Joseph F. (1967). "Jehovah's Witnesses: A Study of Symbolic and Structural Elements in the Development and Institutionalization of a Sectarian Movement." Doctoral dissertation, University of Chicago.

_____. (1970). "Prophetic Failure and Chiliastic Identity" *American Journal of Sociology.* 75:926-948.

_____. (1972). "When Prophecies Fail: A Theoretical Perspective on the Comparative Evidence." *American Behavioral Scientist.* 16:245-268.

ABBREVIATIONS

WtBTS refers to the *Watchtower Bible & Tract Society*, the legal corporation of the Jehovah's Witnesses. This acronym is often used as a synonym for the Witness organization. Watchtower is now spelled Watchtower but was once spelled Watch Tower. Also the terms *The Society* and *The Organization* are both used by Witnesses to refer to the Watchtower organization

JW means a *Jehovah's Witness*, the most common term for the followers of the Watchtower Society. It is used to refer primarily to active followers but also refers to believers in the Jehovah's Witnesses' doctrine.

IBSA is the *International Bible Students Association*, another one of the many legal corporations the Watchtower Society has used in the past. The legal corporation of the British branch is the *International Bible Students Association*.

pb means paperback, and **hb** means hardback.

INTRODUCTION TO THE WATCHTOWER MOVEMENT

Virtually every household in most of the Western World has been visited by a Jehovah's Witness offering for sale a Watchtower book or a copy of the *Watchtower* or *Awake!* magazine. Many school children have had the experience of a fellow pupil's refusing to salute the flag for "religious reasons." Newspapers and magazines frequently carry stories about a Jehovah's Witnesses refusing to accept blood transfusions, celebrate the holidays, become members of the armed forces, attend college, vote, run for public office, sing the national anthem, or involve themselves in the political arena in other ways.

Among America's religions, the Witnesses in many ways stand markedly apart. They take pride in their separation from the cultural mainstream, both in their differences and in the fact that others perceive them as "different." To emphasize this contrast, instead of calling their meeting houses churches, they use the term "kingdom halls," and (except during the period from 1975 to 1981--see *The Watchtower*, 3-15-1981) all of their baptized members are legally ordained ministers. The Watchtower Society once insisted that their belief structure is not a religion and even once taught that "religion is a snare and a racket." During the 1930s and 1940s they even proclaimed that all religion was from Satan and the devil, while their belief structure alone was of God and therefore was simply "the truth," a term they still use today.

Few organizations can boast of as many "true believers" as the Watchtower Bible and Tract Society (the legal corporation of the Jehovah's Witnesses). Their growth until the "great disappointment of 1975" (when the end of this world was confidently expected) was phenomenal to say the least. From a handful in the 1880s they now have over five million hardcore adherents and thirteen million sympathizers (see the 1996 *Yearbook of Jehovah's Witnesses*, p. 41).

Witness Attorneys Argue Before the Supreme Court

The Witnesses, even though a relatively small sect, have been highly influential in shaping American society. Their court cases in regard to proselytizing and first amendment freedoms have been extremely important in molding constitutional law. Almost all contemporary freedom of speech and press cases and even the recent court decisions regarding pornography have relied heavily on the cases in which Jehovah's Witnesses were involved.

Edward Waite in his article, "The Debt of Constitutional Laws to Jehovah's Witnesses" (*Minnesota Law Review*, Vol. 28, No. 4, 1944), concludes that Jehovah's Witnesses have done more to guarantee basic freedoms than any other religious group in

America. They have taken 45 cases to the Supreme Court and were victorious in 36 of them (Walker 1990 see biography index for references). They have by this means not only forced the clarification of many freedom and human rights issues, but in at least two instances have forced the Court to reverse itself. While their battles with government have produced some vindication for them, the persecution continues today in different forms in spite of their many Supreme Court victories (Penton 1976).

Jehovah's Witnesses had their beginning in what is known as the Millerite tradition, an 1850s millennial movement. Historically, thousands of millennial movements have existed, and the modern movements have much in common with earlier ones. The modern movement of concern here began with William Miller, a Baptist layman and farmer (later a Baptist minister) who settled in New York after the War of 1812. For some time Miller was a Deist (one who believes that God created the universe and the laws which control it, then left it to run itself); but after a three- or four-year study of the Bible he became a believer. Miller also became convinced that the "end" was very near, prophesying that in about 1843 (later changed to October 22, 1844) Christ's second coming and the ushering in of the millennial reign of Christ would occur. The year 1844 passed, severely disappointing the thousands of people who had excitedly awaited this date to witnesses the beginning of the reign of Christ. The "great disappointment," as this date is now called, resulted in a multiplicity of new sects in America, one of which became the modern day Jehovah's Witnesses.

The various groups which broke off or were highly influenced by the movement started by William Miller, including the Watchtower Society, are consequently classified as part of the Adventist family (J. Gordon Melton *Encyclopedia of American Religions*) and include the Seventh-day Adventists. The Witnesses technically are an offshoot of the Second-day Adventist movement, and the Witnesses and the Seventh-day Adventists (the largest of the Adventist movements today) both came from the same religious line. C.T. Russell, the Society's founder, openly borrowed a great deal from and was highly influenced by the Adventist movement as a whole. He was originally a part of a group led by Jonas Wendell, an Advent Christian Church minister.

In 1831, Miller spoke at a revival at Dresden, New York, and soon after this date he proved to be in demand to the degree that within a year he was able to accept only about half of his speaking invitations. Miller's teachings attracted primarily Methodists, Baptists, and persons of other Protestant denominations. In 1833 he published his first book, *Evidences from Scripture and History of the Second Coming of Christ About the Year 1843 Exhibited in a Course of Lectures.* In 1839 Joshua Himes invited Miller to preach in his Boston church and was so impressed that he soon brought the new movement into national prominence. Himes, a man with much promotional and organizational talent, was active in publishing the movement's writings, including its first periodical entitled *Signs of the Times.*

Miller believed that the Bible was like a cryptic treasure map and that he had deciphered the "hidden Biblical chronology" which, by the proper interpretation of symbols, enabled one to discern the exact date of the "end of the age" or the end of this world. He made many assumptions, such as that some prophetic days are equal to a year but other days equal some other span of time, and that the prophetic Biblical passages in Daniel and Revelation apply specifically to the 1800s. He concluded from this that the date for the end of the present world and the coming of Christ was in 1843.

As the movement grew, although a large number of mainline churches supported it until about 1843, it encountered increasing opposition from the established churches. Many church laymen and ministers who joined the movement after 1843 were "disfellowshipped" (expelled from the church and not allowed to associate with any church members), an event which often resulted in even more publicity. This caused Miller's movement to crystallize after 1844 and separate itself from the other churches.

Although Miller was at first vague about the exact month of the end, etc., he finally decided upon "between March 21, 1843, and March 21, 1844." Certain natural events such as the appearance of a large comet in February of 1843 gave impetus to the movement. When March 21, 1844 came and went, many of his approximately 30,000 to 50,000 followers and sympathizers became disappointed and left the movement, but many others had come to firmly believe that Christ's return was in the near future.

Soon other dates were predicted, such as October 22, 1874 by Jonas Wendell. This new date came from the realization that a key period on the Jewish calendar was seven months long. After this date also failed, a number of churches and sects developed from the original group, including the Advent Christian Church, the Seventh-day Adventist Church, the Primitive Advent Church, Church of God, Abrahamic Faith, among others.

One of the offshoots of the Adventist movement was the Bible Students founded by "Pastor Russell," from which has sprung another approximately 200 splinter groups. Charles Taze Russell was born February 16, 1852, in Pittsburgh, Pennsylvania, of Scottish-Irish Presbyterian parents. His first exposure to Advent theology was in 1869. When just seventeen, Russell heard the teachings of Jonas Wendell and Rufus Wendell, both prominent Adventists. In 1876 he met an Adventist by the name of Nelson H. Barbour. Barbour learned from B.W. Keith, learned from Wilson's *Emphatic Diaglott* that the Greek word "parousia," usually translated "coming," could also mean "presence"--so that Christ might have actually returned in 1874 after all, only he was *invisible*! (See White 1967, p. 21.) Thus, Russell came to conclude that Jonas Wendell's 1874 prediction may not have been wrong after all.

In his book *The Hope of Christ's Second Coming* (1864), S.P. Tregelles explains the origin of this view, called the Secret Rapture teaching: "But when the theory of a secret coming of Christ was first brought forward (about the year 1832) it was adopted with eagerness: it suited certain preconceived opinions, and it was accepted by some as that which harmonized contradictory thought." In Volume II of *Studies in the Scriptures*, Study V, in a chapter entitled "The Manner of the Lord's Return and Appearing," Pastor Russell expressed his belief in this same idea.

Although Russell worked with Barbour for only a short time as coeditor (according to Barbour, in name only) of the *Herald of the Morning Magazine* and co-author (Russell wrote in a 1906 *Watchtower* it was mainly written by Mr. Barbour, and Barbour denied Russell's contribution) of *The Three Worlds or Plan of Redemption*, he was greatly influenced by Barbour. Russell was very concerned about the Adventist movement's prophetic failures, especially the 1874 error. Barbour's account of this period is as follows:

> This is the history in outline, of this movement, in which I have had part
> for more than fifty-five years. Many individuals have come in, and gone
> out; but the movement kept on, and every detail of the parable has thus far

been fulfilled to where the Bridegroom seems to be due; when they that are ready will go in with him to the marriage.

Of the leaders of the various factions who found themselves out of the movement, after the midnight cry; Eld. J. H. Paton, became interested in 1873-4, mainly by reading the papers I sent to him; and finally by hearing my lectures on these subjects; though he was an Adventist before that. C. T. Russell first became slightly interested by reading the *Herald of the Morning*, in 1875, but did not identify himself with the movement until the autumn and winter of 1876-7, through listening to lectures which I delivered during the Centennial, at St. George's Hall Phila., and in other places. Both men left the movement in 1878. C.T. Russell then, having been in the movement about eighteen months; felt competent to start a paper of his own. Since which he has remained faithful to just what he learned from me, prior to the "midnight," while we "ALL slumbered and slept." Namely that Christ came as King, in 1878; and [Russell] believes it because of the time arguments, as he then learned them from me. But he and his followers little know how imperfect and crude are the arguments as then presented, and on which they base their theory of Christ's presence; or that his coming as the lightning, the first stage of his coming forth, is all there is of the coming "of this same Jesus, as they SAW him go" (Barbour, *The Herald of the Morning* 1907, pp. 368-369).

During his early years Russell also worked with other Adventists and Bible students such as A.P. Adams, A.D. Jones, and John H. Paton (who later embraced universalism). Partly because Barbour incorrectly predicted April 1878 as the month when the church would ascend to Heaven, and because of doctrinal disagreements with him, Russell, Adams, and Paton withdrew their support from Barbour. They immediately began, primarily under Russell's leadership, their own journal, first named *Zion's Watchtower and Herald of Christ's Presence*. The first issue was published in July of 1879 and had a printing of 6,000 copies (this issue was reprinted later in a set of reprints). The 11 x 15 inch, newspaper-sized, eight-page journal listed J.H. Paton, W.I. Mann, B.W. Keith, H.B. Rice, and A.D. Jones as regular contributors.

Russell obtained Barbour's subscription list (without his permission, some claim) and sent a free copy to each *Herald* subscriber. Russell, in effect, began his movement as a mail-order publisher, and the printed page has played an important part in the movement ever since. According to Russell, the Watchtower Society itself was originally "nothing more than a publishing house," but in time became "God's organization, the only ark of salvation," and the Witnesses now believe that one must be firmly inside that ark to be saved.

For one reason or another, Paton and almost all of Russell's early followers eventually left his organization. The Watchtower movement, especially in its early history but still today, has always experienced a constant flow of individuals in and out of "God's organization." Called a revolving-door religion, relatively few persons have stayed for a long period of time. Periodic schisms and the departure of high-ranking members have plagued the sect from the beginning. The most recent large schism occurred in 1979 when Ray Franz, Ed Dunlop, and many other prominent Witnesses left. In the decade of 1976-1986 alone, over a million persons left.

By 1880 scores of congregations existed in most eastern states and several in the central states, all from the one small Bible study which Russell began in the early 1870s. *Zion's Watchtower Bible and Tract Society* was formed in 1881 and legally incorporated in 1884 with C.T. Russell as its first president. There were 50 full-time workers in 1888 (a number that grew to over one-half million by 1992). In 1909 the headquarters moved from Allegheny, Pennsylvania, to Brooklyn, New York, partly because Russell wanted to "start over" after several embarrassing episodes, including his "messy" divorce trial in Allegheny.

At first, the various groups were only loosely affiliated with Russell, and each "ecclesia" was largely independent. The ecclesias were loosely held together primarily by Watchtower representatives called "pilgrims." The structure gradually became more and more autocratic until today the Society owns all of the local property in many countries, and individual "congregations," as they are now called, exercise virtually no independence. They must strictly follow all of the instructions from the Watchtower Society. The "meetings," as their religious services are termed, are the same the world over with only very slight variations. Almost every congregation studies the same Watchtower lesson on the same Sunday and even sings the same songs.

Early Opposition from the Established Churches

Although Russell's basic theology came primarily from the Adventists, he also borrowed from other movements. He was influenced not only by the conservative churches but also the Universalists, the Unitarians, and even the Plymouth Brethren and the Mennonites. Russell vehemently insisted on the correctness of his teachings, and because his position on several major issues conflicted with the orthodox churches, many persons in the religious world intensely disliked him. The *Brooklyn Daily Eagle*, an influential eastern newspaper, constantly criticized Russell, his personal practices, his religion, and his followers. Some sample headlines illustrate the flavor of the attacks: "Girl Kissed Pastor and Sat on His Knee" (October 29, 1911), "Pastor Silent to His Wife for Months" (October 31, 1911), "Give Up Their Homes, Following Russellism" (December 26, 1911), "Russell's Latest Outburst" (May 1, 1912), "Sold House for $50.00 to Defy His Wife" (November 27, 1911).

Russell was at first simply one rather insignificant member of a large movement which consisted of many individuals, including some ministers from different denominations, especially the Lutheran and Calvinist branches of Protestantism. The majority of Russell's ideas came from such men as Storrs, William Miller, Siess, Paton, Adams, Barbour, and other prominent Adventists. Most researchers have been unable to find a single idea that Charles T. Russell contributed to the Adventist movement. These Protestant ministers were the real intellectual backbone of the movement. Although few stayed with him for any length of time, Russell learned much from these individuals until he was able to develop mature theological concepts.

The primary advantage Russell had was the money to widely propagate his message before the public. Yet, the Seventh-day Adventist part of the movement was more successful in gaining converts, partially because of Russell's inability to get along with people. Russell himself became one of the most prominent Adventists in part because he was one of the few men who had both the money (over three-quarters of a million dollars) and the drive and determination needed to propagate Adventist ideas. His success helps explain why this movement became permanently entrenched in the American religious scene.

Russell became famous (or more accurately infamous), however, not so much for what he believed but for what he did *not* believe. Among the orthodox Christian doctrines which he denied were the immortality of the soul, eternal hellfire, the Trinity, the bodily resurrection of Christ, the full deity of Christ (Christ was believed to be a lesser god, created by the father), the personality of the Holy Spirit, and the legitimacy of the Church and all its branches after the apostles died. An article in the *Advent Christian Times* of July 18, 1877, provides a good example of opposition to Russell:

> One N.H. Barbour, called Dr. Barbour, with his confreres, J.H. Paton and C.T. Russell, is traveling around the country, going everywhere that they can find Adventists, and preaching that Jesus has come secretly, and will soon be revealed and mingling in their lectures a lot of "Age-to-come" trash, all to subvert their hearers. They are not endorsed by Adventists, "Age-to-come" folks, or anybody else, yet having some money and a few sympathizers they will probably run awhile. They have been to Ohio and Indiana and are working westward. We are credibly informed that one of them boasted in Union Mills, Ind., a few days since, that they would break up every Advent church in the land. We guess not. Their whole work is proselytizing. The Lord never sent them on their mission. Give them no place, and go not near them or countenance them.

Russell's untimely and unexpected death on October 31, 1916, in Pampa, Texas, was a blow to the movement which should have been anticipated. His health was always somewhat poor, but, as he tended to feel his life was shielded by God, he evidently did not take care of himself and toward the end neglected necessary medical treatment. When he died, the organization was thrown into a turmoil which resulted in the formation of many large splinter groups, most which insisted on following Russell and not the Society's new president. Russell was seen by many of his followers as the faithful and discrete slave, God's only spokesman on earth today. The changes made in policy and doctrine after he died were so drastic that many scholars now consider the modern Jehovah's Witnesses to be an offshoot of the original movement which Russell started.

Today, several movements claim to be the "faithful" followers of Russell's teachings. These groups are in general called *Bible Students*. Russell was buried in United Cemetery in Millvale, Pennsylvania, near Pittsburgh, close to a large nearly ten-foot-high model of the Great Pyramid of Giza in Egypt with markings that make him appear more like an Egyptian Magus than a Christian, all of which is very embarrassing to Jehovah's Witnesses today (especially the cross and crown once commonly used).

Joseph F. Rutherford

Joseph Rutherford, who became the second president, was by far the most controversial of the Watchtower's five leaders. Born on November 8, 1869, in Morgan County, Missouri, near the town of Boonville. His parents, James Calvin Rutherford and Elona Strictlyn, were both Baptists. Rutherford showed an interest in law while still very young but his parents only allowed him to attend law school if he contributed to the wages for a hired hand needed to replace him on the farm. He financed his education at a local "academy" by learning shorthand and working as a court stenographer.

After two years of tutoring by a local judge, he was admitted to the state bar at the young age of 22 and started to practice with a small Boonville law firm. For several years he was a public prosecutor and also substituted (for four days) for the regular judge as was required of all of the prosecutors in the city. Since he was never elected or appointed a judge, the title "Judge Rutherford," which both Rutherford and his followers relished, is not accurate.

During this period Rutherford appealed a lower court conviction for "stealing" a cash register for his client (although it was actually more of a case of improper repossession) to the Kansas City Court of Appeals (October term 1896). The court ruled that Rutherford was wrong in taking possession of the cash register. In 1896, Rutherford campaigned for William Jennings Bryan and for the rest of his life adopted the collar-up style of dress in imitation and honor of Bryan.

Rutherford was first introduced to Russell's teachings when several female book peddler Witnesses (then called colporteurs) visited his law office in 1894 and sold him three Watchtower books. He did not formally join the movement, though, until 1906, at which time he wrote his first religious book, *Man's Salvation from a Lawyer's Viewpoint* (privately published). Russell soon utilized Rutherford, one of the few lawyers in the Society then, to defend him in many of the court cases in which he was involved. Rutherford was elected president in January of 1917.

One of the women who had called on Rutherford lived in an apartment above a Bible student named Malewski, an elderly woman who often gave her "lectures" against marriage (Malewski later got married anyway). Evidently the woman had married twice, and after both her husbands died, she had become a colporteur. Rutherford told them that since he had worked his way through college selling books and realized how difficult it was, he vowed never to turn down a book salesman. Although Rutherford purchased some of the publications, he did not read them until a few years later. Interestingly, the colporteurs stated that when they later returned, Rutherford had them stand at the same spot they had stood when they first placed the books.

The Arrests of Watchtower Officers

On April 6, 1917, the United States entered World War I, and conflicts over the war developed between the government and the Watchtower. The Society's stand on conscientious objection was part of the reason for the arrest and subsequent conviction of J.F. Rutherford and his close associates W.E. Van Amburgh, Alexander H. MacMillan, Robert J. Martin, Clayton J. Woodworth, G.H. Fisher, F.H. Robison, and Giovanni De Cecca (a warrant for the arrest of R.H. Hirsh was later issued on May 8, 1918). Those who opposed the Watchtower's religious ideas and doctrine were no doubt instrumental in their arrests and convictions. Interestingly, at their trial Rutherford said, "My individual inclination is to go into war, because that has been my ambition from youth |was| to lead an army" (*Rutherford v. United States* 1919 p. 993).

During the imprisonment of the eight Watchtower leaders in an Atlanta prison, C.H. Anderson acted as president, and J.F. Stephenson was secretary-treasurer. They moved the Watchtower offices to Pittsburgh on September 25, 1918, for slightly more than a year. At the Society's annual meeting on January 4, 1919, in Pittsburgh, J.F. Rutherford was reelected president and W.E. Van Amburgh as secretary-treasurer even though they were still in prison at the time. The others elected to the Board of Directors-- C.A. Wise (vice-president), R.H. Barber, W.E. Spill, W.F. Hudgins, and C.H. Anderson--were all free to carry out their responsibilities. When those imprisoned were released, R.H. Barber resigned, and was replaced by A.H. MacMillan.

While in prison, Rutherford organized "Bible study classes" among the inmates and began writing weekly letters to his growing number of followers. He also launched another magazine, *The Golden Age* (renamed *Consolation* in 1937 and, in 1946, *Awake!*), an act that was contrary to Charles T. Russell's last will and testament. In March of 1919 the case was appealed, and the defendants were released on March 26, 1919, pending a new trial. A new trial was ordered in May, but with the war over the government lost interest and *nolle prosequi* (dropped all charges) the case on May 5, 1920.

By this means Rutherford came to be seen as a martyr, and partly for this reason, at the first convention after his release (Cedar Point, OH, in 1919) the group was fired with new enthusiasm. Rutherford was soon to teach that each individual Witness must be an active minister, the first of many changes in Witness doctrine that he instigated. The prison experience had seriously affected Rutherford's health and caused him lifelong suffering, which was partially alleviated by moving to a warm climate (usually southern California) during the cold months. It also caused in him a lifelong hatred of the American government and especially the court system, a dislike which even alienated his only son, Malcolm.

A major long-standing problem of Rutherford's was his drinking. During a drinking spree at a motel in Canada, Bonnie Boyd reported that someone threw a beer bottle in the toilet, and the Society was forced to pay for damage to the floor and walls. The Dawn Bible Students had photographs of Rutherford while extremely drunk, with his face contorted.

Dignified and self-confident in his appearance, Rutherford, according to a contemporary newspaper account, "looked more like a senator than most senators." Although much in the news, he made far fewer public appearances than Russell and secluded himself for long periods of time at Beth-Sarim, a mansion in San Diego, California, which was donated to the Society in 1929 to house Abraham and the prophets upon their return to the earth (an event which was then believed to be imminent).

Rutherford died of uremia January 8, 1942, at Beth-Sarim at the age of seventy-two, a few weeks after an operation for cancer. He had requested burial on the property of Beth-Sarim, but this was not permitted under local ordinances. Five months later he was supposedly interred in Staten Island, New York (he was probably buried on the Beth-Sarim property). His wife, Mary M. Fetzer, crippled by polio, died on December 1962.

Rutherford's son, Malcolm G., was committed to his father's religion as a young man and was quite active in the movement for some time, even working as Russell's stenographer. Later Malcolm became disillusioned, partly due to his father's doctrinal changes, and eventually left the organization. His father's policies on patriotism evidently also bothered him. Malcolm served in the military from 1917-1919 and lived in California for 77 years until his death of coronary heart disease at age 96 on June 22, 1989 in Monrovia, California. According to his death certificate he had two years of college and his last occupation was as a court bailiff. Malcolm's wife preceded him in death.

Rutherford as the Leader of the Jehovah's Witnesses

Rutherford's writings were seen by his adherents as almost inspired. Hayden C. Covington, one of the most knowledgeable men in the movement then (vice president of the Society for several years and head of the Society's legal department for over two decades), in an interview with the author, stated that "God was writing through [Rutherford]" and he was "definitely inspired by God to do what he did." Covington asserted that Rutherford had absolute power over the organization, and the Board of

Directors "only rubber stamped his [Rutherford's] will and did nothing more and that's the way it should be."

During this interview, Covington also maintained that Rutherford was an extremely dynamic person, and once he made up his mind no one could change it. The "Judge" also "enjoyed a good physical fight." Covington's favorite example of this occurred at Madison Square Garden where Rutherford encouraged fistfighting with the "opposition" at a small riot after his talk. According to Covington, "Knorr [the man who became the Society's third president] ran like a gutless bastard." Covington's opinion of Knorr was further clarified during the interview. Covington claimed that after Rutherford died he himself received 99 percent of the votes for president, but Knorr convinced him to become vice president instead.

Several years later, Covington stated, Knorr also convinced him to resign from the vice presidency as well. In his own words, Covington stated that he was "the dope that put that bastard [Knorr] in office." Covington added, "I should have been smarter, for I didn't realize I was lying in bed with a snake. Knorr can't be trusted--he slithers around like a snake; he is a cobra." Until recently the Society has had trouble with most of their lawyers, and Olin Moyle and Covington were no exceptions. Covington was reputed to have argued with Knorr so loudly that you could hear them at it several rooms away until late into the night.

The "Judge" was a flamboyant, coarse, outspoken man who spent much of his time attacking all of the churches of Christendom. Except for some *Consolation* and *Golden Age* magazine articles, Rutherford himself wrote virtually everything published during his administration. He coined a number of phrases that Witnesses used for years, such as "millions now living will never die" and "religion is a snare and a racket." His forthright, bold personality often antagonized local government and religious authorities, and he delighted in ridiculing and criticizing his opponents in the pages of the *Golden Age* and *Consolation* (both journals make fascinating reading today).

A good illustration of his control is a case involving a Bethel Society headquarters coworker and editor of the *Golden Age* and *Consolation*, Clayton J. Woodworth. In an article written for *Consolation*, the pagan origin of the names of the months was mentioned and an alternative system was suggested by Woodworth. He felt that the Witnesses should utilize the names he coined instead of January, February, etc. In front of the entire Bethel family, Rutherford called Woodworth a "jack-ass," and Woodworth meekly responded, "I am a jack-ass" (see p. 1093 Olin Moyle transcript, 1944). This is typical of the strong language that Rutherford often used, not only in Watchtower publications but also in daily interaction with the Bethel family. He had a violent temper and could be exceedingly vengeful toward those who did not obey his whims. He saw himself as God's messenger, having authority without fear.

The Witnesses as a whole at this time were given to strong language, both in speeches and in their publications. This approach to other people and the Watchtower's strict political neutrality repeatedly caused difficulties with various authorities and resulted in a number of riots, arrests, beatings, and even murders (for some of the many examples see the 1940s ACLU booklets). As a result, in America, Canada, Nazi Germany, and many other countries the Witnesses hold the dubious distinction of being one of the most persecuted religious minorities in modern times. Probably few countries in the world have not banned or proscribed the work of the Witnesses at one time or another; in many countries, such as the former Soviet bloc nations and several Asian and South American nations, they were banned until recently.

The practice that probably caused the Witnesses the most problems with the state was their refusal to align themselves in any way with the national political or religious powers and institutions. A 1941 American Civil Liberties Union pamphlet entitled *The Persecution of Jehovah's Witnesses* stated, "Not since the persecutions of the Mormons years ago has any religious minority been so bitterly and generally attacked as the members of Jehovah's Witnesses....documents filed with the department of justice...showed over 335 instances of mob violence [occurred] in forty-four states involving 1,488 men, women and children."

The leading Witness attorney for years was Hayden Covington, who fought hundreds of cases from 1939 to 1960 and in his own words "worked 24 hours a day" on these cases. He was introduced to Rutherford for the first time in 1939 at an assembly. His opinion of Rutherford was that he was "a good lawyer, dynamic and capable." Soon thereafter Covington was called to serve at Bethel. He saw Rutherford as a person who knew how to organize, and felt "he was the greatest," a somewhat jovial but serious person who took full control. According to Covington, most people who knew Rutherford had a great deal of respect for him.

By the end of 1937, almost all of the adult male Witnesses (and many of the adult females) in Germany and the occupied countries--some estimate almost 10,000 people-- were in prisons or concentration camps. In America almost 4,000 were in prison for avoiding the military. Ironically, during World War II, Witnesses in the West were often accused of being German spies or pro-Nazis, yet in Nazi Germany some of Hitler's most outspoken foes were the Witnesses. Timothy White, in his book *A People for His Name,* stated that thousands of Witnesses in Germany were imprisoned, and "those in prison were treated extremely harshly, some losing their lives or being forcibly sterilized." Most Witnesses fearlessly went about their business and openly defied the Hitler government, even sending Hitler numerous telegrams informing him that "God was going to destroy" him if he "did not permit the Witnesses to continue their work."

In 1936 at a convention in Holland, it was announced that thousands of tracts explaining the Witness position and denouncing Hitler were to be distributed. No one, including the officials in Nazi Germany, knew the distribution date. On the twelfth of December at 5:00 P.M., 3,540 Witnesses began to go from door to door distributing the tracts. At 6:15 P.M. the S.S. began radio broadcasts to instruct the people not to accept them. The work was successfully completed by 7:00 P.M. the same day.

Several Nazi officials claimed that Hitler had a "love-hate relationship with the Witnesses," admiring them for the strength of their convictions and their determination to carry out what they believed was God's will; he often felt that many of them would make excellent Nazis. However, the Witnesses' obstinacy frustrated him more than that of any other group, except possibly the communists.

Doctrinal Changes
From the very start of his control, Rutherford's teachings differed from Russell's, and these differences increased as time progressed. Starting in about 1925, the war between Michael and the dragon, discussed in Rev. 12, and the 1260 days were reinterpreted so they were now literal. In 1926 the "abomination that maketh desolate"

was interpreted as the League of Nations, and in 1929 the Society's followers were told that they must put the Society first: if a conflict between the Society's teaching and the Earthly governments occurred, they were to obey the Watchtower. (They used Rom. 13 as the major text to support this.) This later led to the ruling that a Witness must refuse to salute the national flag of any country (an edict which caused conflicts and violence that did not climax in the United States until the 1940s).

By 1932 the number of Witnesses exceeded the total number that were believed to go to Heaven -- 144,000 -- so Rutherford created a new class, the "Jonadabs" (now called "great crowd" or "other sheep"). They were to participate in preaching about the destruction of Babylon, which was believed to be soon, and had the hope of an "Earthly reward"--everlasting life on Earth--and not a heavenly reward as did the 144,000. In 1935, the "Great Multitude" was reinterpreted to be an Earthly class. In 1938, it was proclaimed that only the Great Multitude would survive Armageddon and that they (and the dead and resurrected Jehovah's Witnesses) would procreate so as to fill the Earth during the Millennium (the 1,000-year reign of Christ).

In the 1930s it was first taught that Christ gave himself as a ransom--not for all people as formerly believed; but for Jehovah's Witnesses only, or at least only they would benefit from it. This last teaching was partially withdrawn by 1965 (the Sodomites and other people who were destroyed by God, it was now taught, could also benefit). To many, Rutherford and his Society were going into "outer darkness," but the Watchtower claimed that the changes were an example of "the light shining brighter and brighter unto the perfect day." Actually, they were often only examples of their many policy changes which did not indicate progress but rather a lack of knowledge or foresight.

Take for example what was taught regarding salvation of the Sodomites. The Watchtower Society's founder and first president, Charles Taze Russell, taught they would be resurrected (Zion's Watch Tower, July 1879, p. 8). However, in the June 1, 1952, Watchtower (p. 338), it was taught that the Sodomites would not be resurrected. Jehovah, by the use of His Holy Spirit, they taught, had corrected their thinking. Since the light is getting brighter and brighter, the 1879 views are now considered old light, actually error.

Then in 1965, the August 1 Watchtower (p. 479) argued that Russell was right after all; the Sodomites would, in fact, be resurrected. What was considered old light is now new light, but had not Jehovah corrected them in 1952? The June 1, 1988 Watchtower taught the Sodomites will not be resurrected but the Insight book Vol. 2, p. 985 again reversed their required beliefs and said they would be. This is important because they teach that Jehovah is personally directing the Watchtower Society (Watchtower, Nov. 1, 1956, p. 370). The Watchtower Society is so brash as to state they are "the only organization on earth that understands the 'deeper things of God!'" (Watchtower, July 1, 1973, p. 402).

A major issue during Rutherford's tenure was the matter of the appropriateness of having a centralized government over all Bible classes. This was a heated issue for years. In Russell's day, the various Bible study classes were autonomous: each class voted on its own elders and deacons, and on other class matters they only voluntarily cooperated with the Society. Then, starting in 1919 Rutherford appointed a "service director" for each class who at first was primarily to direct the "Golden Age work."

By 1920 he required detailed weekly reports from all class workers, and by 1932 he had stopped the appointment of elders by election and replaced the existing elders with a local "service committee" which was appointed by the Society. By 1938, he removed the last vestiges of autonomy: all classes were now fully controlled by the Society. Although Rutherford called his new system "Theocratic Organization," his many dissenters called it a ruthless takeover and the establishment of a dictatorship. Large numbers of prominent brethren left over this issue.

Numerous other dissensions occurred at this time and caused many members to leave. The great pyramid, a major doctrine of Russell's (see *Thy Kingdom Come*, 1903 edition, p. 313), was now declared to be of Satan (see "Satan's Bible and not God's" in the *Watchtower*, Nov. 15, 1928, p. 344). The Society also now stressed that, to serve God, all of his followers *must* go out and "sell books" to the public. The concept of personal character development was abandoned and later even declared a false doctrine. The Society claimed to be "God's exclusive channel of Truth," representing "God's visible organization on Earth," whose teachings were not to be questioned. Answers directly from the Bible were now banned in some local Watchtower classes. Many readily accepted these changes, but others dissented and left the Society even though personal reasons (such as a spouse or family involved in the movement) often made departure difficult. Still others believed that Rutherford was "smiting his fellow-servants" and that the Society was now part of Babylon (false religion). Such persons often joined one of the many splinter groups, but many left all formal involvement with religion.

Some of those who left the Society were able to withdraw quietly, but most were publicly "disfellowshipped." Many were anathematized and treated with indignation and animosity by their former brothers. Those who associated with various other Bible student groups were labeled by the Society as "evil servants" or "the evil servant class" (Matt. 24:48) until recently when the meaning of "evil slave" was modified to mean any person who accepts the Society's teachings but who does not cooperate with it.

Rutherford's first large "slogan" campaign began in 1918 and was "The World *Has* Ended--Millions Now Living Will Never Die." During the time of the "Millions" slogan, the Society emphasized that the Church would probably be complete and the Ancient Worthies (David, Moses, etc.) raised in 1925. After 1925 had passed, the study of time prophecy was discouraged. Even though 1975 marked a major failure, Armageddon still figures prominently in the Society's message. The next expectation is that it will come before the year 2000 (*The Watchtower*, June 1, 1990, p. 12, non-bound edition).

In spite of these problems, the Society slowly grew. The 1918 Watchtower office staff consisted of about ten persons, but in 1929 about 180 workers were at Bethel, a few more than in the last years of Pastor Russell's administration. Today the number is close to 2,500. Conventions held in New York in 1950 and 1953 filled Yankee Stadium, and in 1958 Yankee Stadium and the Polo Grounds together packed in a record one-quarter of a million Witnesses. In 1963 they drew 140,000 to the Rose Bowl in Pasadena, California (the same week Billy Graham was drawing an equivalent number to the Coliseum).

In 1915 the Memorial (partaking of the Lord's Supper) was celebrated by over 15,000 persons; from 1917 to 1920 it had around 20,000 participants, and in 1925, the date of the great prediction of the end, the number was over 90,000. After the 1925 prophecy failure, attendance declined for several years (in 1928 it was only 17,000). In 1942 the number was up to 141,000, and in 1957 it reached over one million for the first time. By 1992 over ten million attended the Memorial, and a large portion of these were overseas, but only about 9,000 partook of the emblems, indicating that they were of the heavenly class. This shrinkage of this group portends to Witnesses the closeness of Armageddon.

The Watchtower work in the 1930s was slowed or stopped in most countries until the war ended. The work in Germany was outlawed when Hitler came to power in 1933, and during this time the Society expended a great deal of effort in the West on winning a wide variety of legal cases, mostly related to the freedom to practice their brand of religion.

Following World War II, the Witnesses experienced spectacular growth which continued until shortly after 1975 when hundreds of thousands left the Watchtower Society after Armageddon failed to commence in that year. As should be clear by now, a continual problem with the Witnesses is prophetic failure. They have confidently announced Armageddon in 1914, 1918, 1925, c. 1972, and 1975; and each failed prophecy produced both disappointment and schisms (see Zygmunt in the May 1970 *American Journal of Sociology*).

The Watchtower and the Printed Page

The movement has always emphasized the importance of formal study, particularly the study of, first, Russell's writings, then Rutherford's, and today "the Governing body's." The movement was first called by some "Millennial Dawn Bible Students," and also "Bible Students" in addition to "Russellites," "Dawnites," and other names. In 1931, members became known as "Jehovah's Witnesses," a name selected by Rutherford to separate them from the Bible Student movement, those who still held to most of Russell's teachings.

The Bible Student groups as a whole, including contemporary Jehovah's Witnesses, have consistently stressed the importance of religious knowledge and study and have minimized the value of ritual, edifices, music, and poetry in their worship. One must study, they believe, to become approved by God. This requires publication, which partially explains the prodigious output not only of the Jehovah's Witnesses but also of many of the 200 or so different Bible Student groups formed during and since Russell's day.

Ironically, the Watchtower has opposed all higher education for almost a century, at first high school, then college. Of late, it has not been as critical of technical or trade school education as it was formerly. The Society's opposition to education is difficult to understand. According to Covington, Knorr disapproved of higher education because he did not have much formal education himself, barely graduating from high school. Covington also claimed that Knorr fired Colin Quackenbush (the editor of *Awake!*) because "he had brains."

Russell became famous not only for his prodigious output of literature but also for his widely syndicated newspaper column (which he paid newspapers to print) and his many speaking tours. By 1913, the newspaper syndications were in four languages and in 3,000 newspapers in the United States, Canada, and Europe.

The Witnesses have also not shied away from using the newest technology. The 1914 *Photo-Drama of Creation*, a multi-media presentation, first utilized color lantern slides (colored by hand) and phonograph records, all synchronized to present a coordinated photo-phone presentation. The "Photo-Drama" included music, a script to be read, a short motion picture of Russell at the beginning, and a total of two hours of film plus costumed skits of various biblical accounts used in some showings. It was presented in four parts (two hours each) and was viewed by some eight million people in many nations.

Portable phonographs were also popular with the Society during the 1930s and 1940s. The Witnesses asked householders if they would like to listen to a record, which was almost always a short talk by Judge Rutherford. In the 1930s and 1940s John Kurzen designed for the Watchtower a wind-up portable phonograph. The Watchtower built hundreds of these phonographs which the Witnesses carried door to door until the late 1940s. Engineers at Bethel (the Society's headquarters) even designed and manufactured a portable phonograph which could be played vertically while the cover was closed.

Radio was used extensively from the 1920s to the 1950s, and many of the Society's booklets during this time were printed radio broadcast messages. Rutherford was especially fond of phone and radio hookups so that he could speak at one convention and conventioneers in a dozen or so other assembly cities could simultaneously hear his presentation. He made his first radio broadcast in April 1922, and the first radio chain began in 1927 (the Detroit Convention tied together more than 100 stations). The Society built radio station WBBR in 1922 and operated it from 1924 to 1957. The peak radio work was during 1933 when 403 stations were broadcasting the Society's message. In 1937, except for WBBR, radio work was virtually abandoned in favor of portable phonograph work.

The Witnesses also utilized sound cars (automobiles or trucks equipped with loudspeakers) which drove around blaring the Watchtower message. Sound cars often operated in front of churches on Sunday in the hope that those in attendance would listen to the Witness message rather than to their minister's sermon.

For the first time in 1922 all Witnesses were required to go from door to door, not just the colporteurs as in the past. During the 1940s, Witnesses were trained to go individually from door to door with memorized oral presentations. The Society came to believe that this method was more effective than playing records, which had irritated many people. Many of Rutherford's records were bombastic and highly critical of the Catholic Church in particular, religion as a whole, and all earthly governments.

In 1943, a special training school for the Society's missionaries, the *Watchtower Bible School of Gilead*, was established. The school graduated two classes each year, and for most of its history that graduating class numbered around 100 students. After the 1975 failure, the size decreased markedly to as few as 25 students. Recently, special courses have been established for training congregational elders, branch personnel, full-time ministers, and single men with potential. These courses are held in various cities in the United States, Canada, and other countries.

Few religious organizations have been more preoccupied with the production and dissemination of religious literature than the Watchtower. Thousands of books, booklets, tracts, etc., have been published, many with printings in the multi-millions, and the "Truth book" of well over one-hundred million. Books printed by the Watchtower Society have achieved greater circulation than almost any others. First printings of three or four million are common, and twenty million or more copies of many Witness books and booklets are produced before they go out of print. The 192-page *"Truth* book" written by Raymond Franz and others made the *1983 Guinness Book of World Records* (p. 175) with 103 million copies in 116 languages by April 1982. For some unexplained reason, this entry was removed from the 1990 edition and replaced with the *Guinness Book of World Records* which by mid 1989 had surpassed 61 million copies. *The Watchtower* now has an average printing of almost nineteen million copies per bimonthly issue, and in 1996 it was printed in over 125 languages, more than any other existing journal.

The Watchtower As a Publisher

The Society's first printing press was a small job press set up in Brooklyn, New York, in 1909. Prior to this, all of their literature was printed by commercial firms, often those owned by Bible Students. During World War I, as a result of the imprisonment of the Watchtower's president and several of its officers, publication slowed almost to a standstill, although *The Watch Tower* magazine (in 1939 changed to *Watchtower*) was regularly published on schedule even then. The Watch Tower's "Tabernacle" building was liquidated, the Bethel headquarters closed, and the staff moved to Pittsburgh, Pennsylvania. In 1919 when the Society's officers were released from prison, the Brooklyn Bethel Home was reopened and again began producing literature. A rotary press was purchased in 1920 and installed in a building that the Society rented on Myrtle Avenue close to the existing Bethel Home.

In the latter part of 1921, the Witnesses began making their own metal printing plates and doing their own electroplating. Four years later, the Society expanded its printing operation and rented three floors of a building (including the basement) at 18 Concord Street in Brooklyn. The Society soon purchased some property on Adams Street, and in 1927 an eight-story factory was built at 117 Adams Street. Within ten years, a four-story addition was completed; in 1950 a nine-story addition was finished, and four years later a thirteen-story building was added. In the 1970s the large Brooklyn Squibb Building complex was purchased, a number of large apartments and printing facilities were built at Wallkill, New York, Canada, and elsewhere. In addition, large (and in some cases multi-million-dollar) assembly halls were built in many states in the United States, in Canada, and in Europe. The Society now has over seventy Web rotary presses and has the capacity to produce literature in about 200 languages.

The main Watchtower Farm at Wallkill, New York (1,700 acres) produces most of the food for the Bethel family in both the Brooklyn complex and on the farm itself. At Wallkill are over 800 head of cattle and pigs, a slaughter house, a smokehouse, and other facilities (all parts of the animals are used except blood, even the spleen and kidneys). In addition, a flock of over 4,000 chickens and 3,300 white leghorns lays an average of 2,700 eggs a day. Ninety-two cows produce over 420 gallons of milk, part of which goes into the ice cream, butter, and cheese made at the farm. The farm also has a cannery and a bakery where 700 or more loaves of bread and other foods are baked daily. The Society also owns a fruit farm in Washington, New Jersey, and a grain farm in South Lansing, New York (see *Harpers Magazine*, March 1973: "A Case of Self-Sufficiency" by Nadine Brozan).

International and National Conventions

The Witnesses are well known for their large conventions which serve to vividly show each Witness that there are many others like him- or herself. These conventions serve as tremendous publicity-generating events as well as important morale boosters for the Witnesses attending. For many Witnesses, these conventions are the high point of their summer. The first major convention was held in Chicago, Illinois, in 1893 and was attended by 360 persons with 80 baptized. After J.F. Rutherford and the other Watch Tower officers were released from prison in 1918, their first convention was at Cedar Point, Ohio, on September 1-7, 1919. The attendance exceeded 6,000 and about 200 were baptized. Rutherford also went to Europe the next year to revitalize the overseas work. The 1922 Cedar Point convention drew 18,000 to 20,000 with 144 baptized. The largest single convention to date was held in New York City in 1958 and required renting both Yankee Stadium and the Polo Grounds to hold the crowd. The Sunday peak attendance was 253,922 with 7,136 baptized. The year 1978 saw a set of international conventions which included hundreds of assemblies located in 45 countries that were attended by hundreds of thousands of persons.

Major Watchtower Beliefs

The Watchtower teaches that all 66 books of the Bible are the "inspired Word of God" and are historically accurate. They believe that, while many passages of the Bible are figurative, most of it is literal, and much of it can be used to predict future events. They refer to the New Testament as the *Christian Greek Scriptures* because they were first written in Greek, and the Old Testament the *Hebrew Scriptures* because most of them were originally written in Hebrew. Jehovah's Witnesses use the name "Jehovah" even though they recognize that the term is an improper translation because it is the commonly accepted English word for the tetragrammaton. They teach that a "proper Name" for God is important because of such Scriptures as Psalms 83:18 which says "that men may know that thou, whose name alone is Jehovah are the most high over all the earth" (KJV). They are not averse to using some other form, such as Yawa or Yahweh, but consider the term "God" a title; thus some specific name is to be preferred. They reason that the word "Jesus" is also not a correct translation of the original Hebrew ("Y'shua," "Joshua," or "Yehoshuah" is more accurate) but because "Jesus" is widely understood in English, it is preferred over the more correct "Yehoshuah."

The *Watchtower* stresses that Witnesses are to use the "language of the people," and "Jehovah" should be used because it is the most common English rendering of the term. In addition, because they have used "Jehovah" for some time, it would probably be difficult to change now. The name "Jehovah's Witness" comes from Isaiah 43:11: "ye are my witnesses saith Jehovah, and my servant whom I have chosen." This name was announced in 1931 at the Columbus, OH, convention.

The year 1878 and later 1914 were to have brought "the glorification of the saints," the end of the harvest (the witness work), and the beginning of the Millennium (the 1,000-year earthly rule by Christ). Since these events did not occur on either date, their teachings were reinterpreted to the effect that in 1914 the Gentile times (rule of worldly rulers) "legally" ended and a "period of trouble" began. Further, within one generation from 1914, everlasting peace would come to Earth in the form of a New World ruled by Christ, a prophesy that also failed. In recent publications the 1914 doctrine has been drastically downplayed.

Jehovah's Witnesses teach that God created Adam and Eve with a specific purpose in mind, namely to live forever on a paradise earth free from sin, suffering, and sorrow. Our first parents' sin temporarily interrupted God's plan, but provision was made through Christ to restore humankind to perfection. As a part of this restoration, Jesus established a church which started to become corrupt soon after the death of the last apostle of Jesus Christ, John, and in time completely fell away. At the time of the emperor Constantine, the church which Christ established became totally corrupt, and, although throughout history various small groups maintained allegiance to what they called "the truth," it was not fully restored until the late 1800s by Charles T. Russell.

Russell was "specifically guided by God," according to contemporary Witness doctrine, to restore the work and prepare the world for Armageddon, a decisive battle in which most all non-Jehovah's Witnesses are to be destroyed. After Armageddon, the "thousand year millennial reign of Christ" is to begin. The survivors will "clean up the earth" and restore it to paradise conditions. During this time both those who have never heard the message preached by the Jehovah's Witnesses and those who died faithfully will be resurrected to earthly life. Most of those resurrected during this time will remain faithful, but even during the reign of Christ a few will again "fall away," creating pockets of rebellion.

The final cleansing of the earth will occur at the end of the millennial reign of Christ when Satan will be let loose to tempt all of those who can be tempted, and then those who fall away will be destroyed. Those who survive this last test will be given "everlasting life" but not "immortality." The Witnesses teach that "immortality" is a state or condition in which one cannot die, but "everlasting life" is life which is conditional, based only upon the continual obedience of the individual. In other words, *everlasting life* means that one *could* live forever, but this is not guaranteed, whereas *immortality* means that one *cannot* die.

The Watchtower also teaches that there are two classes of believers, the heavenly one (which is limited to 144,000) and the earthly class (to which most Witnesses belong). The heavenly class will live in heaven with Christ and rule over the earth. This is to some degree "a higher calling," although most Witnesses claim that they would prefer to live on the earth. Part of the heavenly class, they believe, lived during Jesus' day, but most or many of its members lived during Russell's day and the remaining ones, less than 9,000, are believed to still be alive today.

During Russell's day, the "gathering" was limited to those in the heavenly class, but since the 1930s it has been taught that most of the new converts are part of a new class called "the great crowd" (the earthly class). Outsiders feel that this class came about because Witness numbers exceeded 144,000 because of the delayed end of the world. The Witnesses consider it imperative to spread the "good news of the kingdom" to as many as possible before Armageddon. In order to survive Armageddon, one must accept the message preached by the Witnesses, and, for someone to accept this message, it must be preached. If a Witness neglects to preach the message to someone and that person dies in ignorance, losing out on everlasting life, the one who neglected the preaching could also lose his or her life (a doctrine called *blood guilt*).

The Witnesses are very strict regarding moral behavior. They condemn adultery, fornication, masturbation, abortion, pornography, dirty jokes, swearing, singing or listening to worldly songs (especially religious hymns), celebration of traditional holidays, smoking, drinking (except in moderation), and the non-medical use of drugs.

The Congregation

Each local assembly of Jehovah's Witnesses is now called a *Congregation* (previously termed a "Church," then an "Ecclesia," and later a "Company"). The hierarchy and general structure within the Congregation has changed somewhat over the years, but the duties of offices have remained fairly similar. The Congregation organizes the proselytizing work, primarily the door-to-door activity, which is now almost a sacrament among the Witnesses in spite of its ineffectiveness and the antagonism it often arouses among those visited. Congregations doggedly continue to pressure individual Witnesses to pursue this unrewarding mode of proselytizing. However, this activity does generate income, and Witnesses today have almost totally neglected other methods of outreach (although in the past, as noted above, phonograph, radio, and film were utilized).

They have so far avoided the use of television, even though this medium is extremely effective. They have also strongly discouraged individual Witnesses from taking the initiative in developing new ways to proselytize and have insisted primarily upon formal "one to one contact" in the door-to-door activity. Individual Witnesses (many who have have been disfellowshipped as a result) are strongly discouraged from writing books or articles and producing films or television and radio shows, etc. Groups of Witnesses have recently tried to set up Witness schools and hospitals but have received no cooperation or encouragement from the Watchtower Society. The Society has solidified into a rigid mold in which it will probably continue for some time.

For years, each Congregation had a *Presiding Minister* (also called the *Presiding Elder* or *Overseer*) who was required to be male. One of his duties is to insure that all those Witnesses living in the congregation's territory are behaving according to the Society's strict, inflexible rules that cover almost every area of life. The head Elder has had many titles--at first he was called an *Elder*, then the *Company Head*, then later the *Company Servant*, the *Congregation Servant*, the *Congregation Overseer*, the *Presiding Overseer* and now the *Chairman of the Body of Elders*. He oversees most of the legal aspects of the Congregation, makes arrangements for "hour talk" speakers, and assigns different congregational duties to those he feels are qualified.

Now the Watchtower stresses that elders as a group are to run the Congregation. The vice president, or second in command, was at one time called the *Assistant Congregation Servant*, then *Field Overseer,* and now the *Service Overseer*. He is in charge of the Congregation if the Presiding Overseer is absent and is responsible for oversight of the preaching work, filing the door-to-door work reports, and keeping other records. The *Field Overseer* now also fulfills the duties of the *Bible Study Servant* who used to supervise, encourage, and sometimes work with individual publishers in conducting "Bible" studies based upon a systematic study of the Society's publications (scriptures are read primarily as "proof texts" to support the Society's teachings).

Another position is the *Secretary* who does the paperwork and reports. Once a month the secretary sends a report to the Society's branch office which eventually reaches the world headquarters in Brooklyn, New York. The *Secretary* serves as a "go-between" between the Society and the local congregation.

The *Literature Servant* (formerly called the *Stock Keeper* and later the *Literature*

Overseer) is the only person authorized to order literature from the Watchtower Society. This person stocks and pays for the literature that the congregation uses. The *Magazine Territory Servant* or *Overseer* orders the *Watchtower* and *Awake!* magazines for door-to-door use. The *Territory Servant* keeps track of the Witness territory concerns. The *Accounts Servant* (formerly called the *Treasurer*) counts the contributions and, under the direction of the *Chairman,* is responsible for paying for the Society's literature and other bills and maintaining the Congregation's bank account. These roles are combined in small Congregations, and in large Congregations new roles in addition to the above may be created for each position.

The United States and Canada, and most of the rest of the world, are divided up into "territories." The rest, called "unassigned territory," is worked by Congregations nearby during the summer and holidays. Each Congregation's area is divided into territories, usually a few city blocks, or large apartments, which can be canvassed in ten hours or so by a carload of Witnesses. Most congregations have one- to two-hundred territories, depending on the size of the Congregation and the number of persons living in the territory assigned to it.

Members "work" their territories by offering issues of *The Watchtower* and *Awake!* (which for years sold for a nickel each; as of 1981 for $.10, and in the late 1980s for $.25) or books (the Society's latest hardbound book or sometimes several Society books). A year's subscription to the *Watchtower* or *Awake!* was $1.00 from 1879 until a few years ago; as of 1981 subscriptions were $2.50 each or both for $5.00. Now, because of Supreme Court rulings requiring that religious publishing houses pay taxes on books sold, the publications are said to be free, while in fact the Congregation members pay the full cost, either directly or in conjunction with the donations requested for the literature given to the public.

Local Meetings

Since 1943, each Congregation established a *theocratic ministry school* (after 1976 called a *theocratic service school,* then again a ministry school). The 45-minute weekly meeting teaches Witnesses to present talks in front of an audience and indoctrinates them in the Witness history, theology, and world view. This school covers Biblical material in much the same way as theological seminaries but in far less depth. Subjects such as Biblical Greek, Biblical history, and other topics not directly part of Witness doctrine and teaching are largely ignored.

The school consists of four talks given by congregation members. The first one, prepared by a "spiritually mature" Witness, is fifteen minutes long. The second talk consists of a six-minute Bible highlights lesson and a six-minute Bible reading presented by a newer Witness. The last two talks or presentations are given at a table or the platform in front of the Congregation, by female Witnesses to another female Witness who plays the role of either a Bible Student, a householder, or a neighbor. Female Witnesses are forbidden to use the podium to address the Congregation except when relating experiences, because they are not allowed to directly teach the Congregation. Material for these talks is to be taken almost verbatim from various Society publications. Counsel (constructive criticism) by the *Theocratic School Overseer* is given after each talk in front of the Congregation.

The *Service Meeting* is usually on the same night as the Theocratic Ministry School and is also 45 minutes in length. The Service Meeting is designed to help each Witness present his or her message effectively in the door-to-door work. The *Service Overseer* (formerly called the *Field Overseer,* then the *Back Call Servant,* then the *Back Call Overseer*, and later the *Return Visit Overseer*) is in charge of helping Congregation members make return visits, bring follow-up literature or "call back" on persons who expressed an interest in the Witnesses and their message.

During the middle of the week (usually Tuesday) the Society has "book studies" (at one time called *Berean Classes*, a term from the Bible, Acts 17:10-11), which consist of a study of some specific *Watchtower* publication, usually a hardbound book. This study is led by a person called the *Book Study Conductor*.

On weekends, the Witnesses meet at the Kingdom Hall (where Congregational meetings are held) to arrange for door-to-door activity and, during the week, at the *Book Study houses* (held at the private home of a Witness). This meeting place was formerly called the *Contact Point*, later the *Service Center*, still later the *Rendezvous for Field Service*, and finally the *Meeting for Field Service*. Those who engage in full-time preaching work (their hours vary but usually range from 60 to 90 per month according to the type of "pioneering" missionary work) were first called *Sharp Shooters*, then *Colporteurs* (during the Colporteur stage, the primary goal was to sell books) and now *Pioneers*. There are two types of Pioneers, a *Regular Pioneer* and an *Auxiliary* (temporary) Pioneer (at one time called *Vacation Pioneers*).

The only meeting to which the general public is invited is usually on Sunday (commonly at ten o'clock in the morning); this was once called the *Hour Talk*, (it once was 55-minutes long) and is now called the *Public Talk*. As of 1978 this meeting consists of a 45-minute lecture given by an experienced baptized Witness. Since the advent of the elder system in 1975, only elders and ministerial servants are allowed to give hour talks at the local Congregation, and, except in unusual circumstances, only elders are allowed to give talks in other Congregations. These talks are generally little more than extemporaneous presentations of official Society materials. At one time, a one-page outline with a number of references to Society publications was followed; then a much more detailed outline of approximately four pages was followed almost word for word, and in the last few years a shorter two-page outline is again provided. Witnesses are not to deviate from this outline.

The *Watchtower Study* follows the Sunday public meeting and is conducted by the *Watchtower Study Conductor*, who also must be an Elder. It is conducted in a very formal but perfunctory manner. The Study Conductor for years read the questions printed at the bottom of *The Watchtower*, and after someone in the audience answers "correctly," the paragraph is "summarized" or read out loud by the Reader (the paragraph is now read first, then the questions are asked). This is the most important meeting of the week because *The Watchtower* is considered semi-inspired. For years a ten-minute break was allowed between the public talk and the Watchtower Study, but in an effort to keep people from leaving (usually more people attend the public talk because the Watchtower Study is rather boring, and one can read the magazine at home), this intermission was eliminated. Since the 1940s a song has been sung after the *Public Meeting* and also after the *Watchtower Study*, as well as before the Ministry School and the Service Meeting, which are now conducted back to back.

Directly above the congregational level in the administrative hierarchy is the *Circuit*

Overseer or *Servant* (at one time called *Zone Servant* and earlier *Pilgrim*) and above him is the *District Overseer* who has charge of several circuits. Next in the hierarchy is the *Branch Committee* with a chairman (once called the *Branch Overseer*, who supervises several districts. Above him is the *Zone Overseer.* Finally, the highest level, the Governing Body, is in charge of all the branches. This level is made up of the president, the vice president, and a number of other individuals (the number has been as high as seventeen and is currently twelve). The Circuit Servant is actually a representative of the Governing Body (or, at one time, a representative of the president of the Watchtower Society). All of these positions can be held only by males.

Congregations are visited about twice a year by the *Circuit Overseer* who supervises about twenty congregations. This official has regained much of his former status after having been reduced almost to the level of an elder in the Congregation. The Society has tried a number of techniques to ensure an efficient organization and, especially during the 1970s, has had considerable problems in this area. They are very organization-minded and are concerned primarily about cost efficiency and the development of an efficient, large-scale operation.

Nathan Homer Knorr

Nathan Knorr, the third president of the Society, was born in Bethlehem, Pennsylvania, on April 23, 1905. An average student, he graduated from Allentown, Pennsylvania, High School in June of 1923. He first associated with the Witnesses at age sixteen, became a Pioneer at age eighteen, and was called to Bethel headquarters on September 6, 1923, where he advanced rapidly. In 1932, he became general manager of the publishing office and plant. Two years later, at only 29, he was elected to the Board of Directors, and at 35 in 1940 he was appointed the vice president of the Society. He became president at 37 when Rutherford died in 1942 and remained in this position until June 7, 1977, when he died of a brain tumor at the age of 72.

Knorr had the reputation of being an astute businessman who worked extremely hard and expected others to do likewise. He is said to have run his workers "ragged" but generally did it with "never-failing good humor." Knorr's talents were predominantly in organization and business, and he was not noted as a theologian either inside or outside the movement. During his administration, the chief theologian was Fred Franz, assisted by several others.

Knorr was seen by some as a brown-noser who tried for years to win the favor of people like Rutherford in order to work his way up in the Society. When he became president, he had evidently changed for the worse. In the words of Ed Dunlop, a prominent Watchtower official for years and the registrar of the Society's Gilead School, "power corrupts and in the case of Knorr, power has corrupted him also" (personal interview April 19, 1981). Mr. Knorr had enormous power over millions of persons who had to obey him almost without question or be expelled, and he was vividly aware of his power. He was, for all practical purposes, the absolute ruler of the Society for years, although the 18-member Governing Body did have some input.

Although Knorr was friendly and enjoyed good humor and conversation, he was somewhat aloof. He often locked himself in his Brooklyn penthouse to do his work. Knorr could take a world tour anytime he wanted to, or do pretty much as he pleased as long as it did not upset the moral sensibilities of his followers (such as openly committing adultery). Members of the governing body had exclusive use of an automobile (Knorr usually had a new Buick each year which was passed down to lesser members of the governing body the next year). The car was washed, gassed, stored, and maintained in the Society's private garage in Brooklyn and was sometimes chauffeur driven.

Knorr was far less colorful than either Rutherford or Russell, and thus much less is known about him. He was moderate in habits and kept a low profile, rarely making the bombastic announcements for which both Russell and Rutherford were famous. Virtually nothing is known about his personal life. Knorr was a tall man (over six feet) and had a sister Isabel Knorr and no children. He was raised in the Dutch Reformed Church. Aside from various rumors about his personal life (he broke the Society's ban on marriage when he married Audrey Mock in 1953), he avoided most of the scandals of his predecessors. Like them, however, he spent a great deal of time traveling, supervising the growth of the Witnesses' growing world empire. Knorr was also partly responsible for the toning down of the Witness message and for the more conservative orientation which the Witnesses developed during his administration. He stressed theocratic education, and consequently set up the Gilead Bible School in 1943, a training place for elders.

Fred Franz

The fourth president, Frederick William Franz, was born in Covington, Kentucky, on September 12, 1893. He was considered by Witnesses to be a first-class scholar with a photographic memory. Franz was allegedly fluent in six languages (Greek, German, Spanish, Portuguese, Latin, and English). He was class valedictorian of Woodward High School and then spent two years at the University of Cincinnati (Sept. 1911 to May 1914) studying languages and theology intending to become a Presbyterian minister. After he was introduced to the Watchtower by reading a booklet by Edgar, he left school to enter full-time Witness work because of the confident expectation of Armageddon in 1914. He joined the Bethel staff in June 1920 and worked in the press room.

In 1926 he became part of the editorial staff and in 1945 became vice president of the Watchtower. The Society once claimed that he was offered a Rhodes Scholarship but turned it down to become a full-time minister for the Society (see A.H. MacMillan, p. 181, and the 1954 Scottish Douglas Welsh Trial, p. 175), but the official Ceil Rhodes records show that this claim is false (letter from William J. Barber 1981). In Franz' life story he states that although he was told that he had "been chosen to receive it," Franz claimed that he turned it down (*Watchtower* May 1, 1987 p. 24-25). Franz's sister and mother became Witnesses; his brother never converted and his father died an active Lutheran. His uncle Albert V. Franz was active for years but then left the Watchtower; and a nephew, governing body member Raymond Franz, was also active for most of his life but recently left as well.

In 1977 Franz became President of the Watchtower. For over 50 years, even during Knorr's presidency, Franz was the main intellectual driving force behind the Society. He *was* in many respects the Society, more powerful than any other individual. Unfortunately, extremely little is known about Franz as a person. His life was never accompanied by the scandals that were such an important part of the lives of both Russell and Rutherford. Franz and Knorr were very careful to conceal their life and any possible criticisms from the public, and their close associates have respected this wish.

In 1982, however, Raymond Franz, Frederick Franz's nephew and a longtime member of the governing body of the Witnesses, left because of a number of disagreements. Soon thereafter, he was disfellowshipped for eating a meal with his boss, ex-Witness Peter Gregerson. He has since written two books about his 35 years of experiences as a top-ranking Witness. Both works are extremely illuminating relative to the modern history of the organization and especially its current president and Governing Body. This is the first time since the 1917 split that a major high level administrator has left the Society and publicly criticized it.

Fred Franz never married, was quite retiring, read prodigiously, and spent much of his time in his room studying and writing. He was evidently somewhat absent-minded but was one of the very few Watchtower leaders who was respected by both friend and foe, although some Bethelites have referred to him as an egomaniac. According to Covington, he was "humble and easy until he learns which way the wind is blowing."

Franz died of a heart attack on December 22, 1992, at the age of 99 in Brooklyn Heights, New York. Seventy-two-year-old Milton G. Henschel immediately became the new president. He had been "ordained" a Watchtower minister on March 15, 1934, and had served as vice president since 1977. A third-generation Witness, he was born in Pomona, New Jersey in 1920, began house-to-house preaching at the age of eight, and was a full-time worker for the Watchtower at age fourteen. He now runs an organization that has an income of more than one billion-two hundred million dollars annually, owns more than thirty properties in the United States valued in excess of 186 million dollars, and has branch offices and property worth a total of possibly twice this in most every country of the world. The Watchtower is now run by the president and a governing body, which according to Jack Barr consists of five committees: **Personal**: 1. Gerald Grizzle. 2. Patrick Lafranca. 3. Ralph Walls. **Publishing**: 1. Richard Abrahamson. 2. Don Adams. 3. Robert Butler. **Service**: 1.Gerrit Losch. 2. William Van De Wall. 3. Robert Wollen. 4. Leon Wraver. **Teaching**: 1. Harold Jackson. 2. William Malenfant. 3. David Mercante. **Writing**: 1. Joseph Rames. 2. Robert Pruy. 3. Gene Smally.

The Division Used in This Bibliography

The rationale for dividing the literature in this bibliography into book, booklet, and tract sections is the nature of the literature on the Witnesses. It is helpful to separate books, booklets, and tracts because books are readily available while booklets and tracts are almost impossible to obtain except from private collectors or, at times, from better libraries. Most of the Witness and non-Witness tracts are brief and repetitive and of minor value to researchers. In addition, almost all tracts are purely of a proselytizing nature as are many of the booklets. Many of the books, on the other hand, are not theological but sociological and psychological studies and are far more useful to academics.

Sometimes a non-Witness tract or booklet contains a section on Jehovah's Witnesses, but these are relatively few and are listed under non-official tracts and booklets. The fact that only a section of the booklet discusses the Witnesses is also noted.

Our definition of a book, booklet, or tract was based primarily upon binding and size. **Tracts** are two, four, or six pages of folded and unstapled printed matter. **Booklets** are usually 10 to 25 pages, occasionally as many as 90 pages, and most always bound by saddle stapling. **Books** are perfect bound (glued) or stitched (sewn) and are usually from about 100 to 300 or more pages. Both hardbound and paperback books are included in the books category.

Although scores of indexes, bibliographies, persons, libraries, etc., have been consulted, some items have undoubtedly not been included in this work. Readers aware of additional references are strongly encouraged to contact the author.

Existing indexes were of limited usefulness in compiling this bibliography. For example, of the booklets listed in Chapter Three, fewer than five percent are listed in any of the standard indexes, and less than half of the books were listed in *Books in Print*. Many of the listings in this bibliography were obtained not only from indexes but also from library research and correspondence with researchers in this area.

A major weakness of this list is the result of lack of access to indexes of smaller, local publications and some publications which are not included in any of the standard library indexes. Many booklets and limited-circulation publications are produced locally and are not commonly available. The indexes of a large number of smaller journals were consulted; nonetheless, thousands of small, local publications, especially religious publications, have very limited circulations.

When this writer was at Bethel (the Society's world headquarters) in the mid-1960s, he made extensive notes of their library holdings. Much of that information is incorporated into this bibliography. Since then, while preparing this bibliography for publication, he contacted Bethel several times and was told the Watchtower Society was "not interested" in helping with this work. Spokesmen for the Society stressed that "it would not be profitable" to read either non-Witness publications or older Witness works.

Much of this material is available only through inter library loan. Few libraries, even large university libraries, contain, for example, more than four or five books on Witnesses, and almost none of the other material is publicly available. The "official" material is available primarily in private libraries and a very few large university theological libraries. One of the most complete collections belongs to the author, but other large collections are housed in the Institute for the Study of American Religion (ISAR), Dept. of Religious Studies, University of California, Santa Barbara, Santa Barbara, CA 93106; Witness Incorporated (c/o Duane Magnani, P.O. Box 597, Clayton, CA 94517); and Mike Castro (Box 2817, Providence, RI 02907) who has the largest collection of original Society material in the world. The Watchtower Society has a fairly large collection, although they may still be missing many important items because their library was confiscated in 1918 when the United States government partly outlawed them as an organization. It is rumored this material is stored in a government warehouse somewhere, but this is unlikely; it was probably destroyed. Although Watchtower is usually not cooperative with outsiders (and often insiders as well), for those who wish to write, the address of the Watchtower Society is 25 Columbia Heights, Brooklyn, New York 11201.

The Watchtower has several large libraries and at least three fairly complete sets of their official literature. One is available to the writing staff, another to the school of Gilead, and the third to the Bethel family members. In addition, at Bethel exists another locked library with very old and rare material, many non-Society publications, etc., which is available only to the governing body and some of their close associates.

In addition to its publications, the Watchtower Society has a large number of books in their libraries on religious, medical, and scientific topics, many of which are quite dated and most of which were willed to the Society. The Society also has a bound set of all their Supreme Court cases (about fifty) as well as most of the other court cases they have fought (hundreds). A large collection of anti-Society tracts, booklets, and books is available, but only by special permission to certain people. For example, William Schnell's books are listed in the library catalog, but the card entry says that they can be seen only by special permission--which is rarely granted, and then only to certain people. I would assume asking for these books would result in trouble for most Witnesses.

Much of this literature is extremely rare, and thus is fairly valuable. For a discussion of its value see "Witnesses to a New Area of Book Collecting" by this author, in *Book Collector's Market,* Vol. 4, No. 3, May-June 1;1979, pp. 1-9. The most comprehensive list of Watchtower literature, including various editions and the value, is available from Witness, Inc., address above.

Readers who are able to provide any further information on the entries or new entries are cordially requested to submit to the writer in care of Northwest State College, 22-600 State Rt. 34, Archbold, OH 43502. Also, since individual contact is the main source of information, information on possible mistakes that may have been made in classifying some of the material is greatly appreciated.

OFFICIAL WATCHTOWER BIBLE & TRACT SOCIETY LITERATURE

A very clear distinction exists between official and non-official literature. Although a few non-society publications have been accepted as semi-official, such as Marley Cole's *Jehovah's Witnesses, The New World Society*, and A.H. Macmillan's *Faith on the March*, Witnesses are discouraged from reading anything on religion not published by the Society except possibly concordances and Bible dictionaries. An active Witness may be criticized for publishing about religion *even* if the work is in agreement with the current teachings of the Society. Although Marley Cole's first book was approved by the Society and written in conjunction with the Society's editorial staff and Governing Body, his second book, *Triumphant Kingdom*, did not have this blessing, and thus sold very poorly. Few Witnesses knew of or read the book, and many would probably have declined to read it had they known it existed.

When attorney Victor Blackwell (*O'er the Ramparts They Watched*, 1976) and Professor James Penton (*Jehovah's Witnesses in Canada*, 1976), both lifelong Witnesses and both very active in defending the Witness movement, published books, they were both chastised by some. Although the reasons are complex, Penton was eventually forced out of the Movement as was Jay Hess, a very talented Witness apologist (for a history of Penton's case see Beverly 1986). Recently Matt Alfs was also alienated from the Witnesses. This attitude has existed since the early days of the Society. In the early 1900s A.B. Dabney of Virginia wrote a booklet entitled *Questions Answering Questions* that was totally in harmony with the Society's position at the time, but he felt pressured to withdraw it from circulation. In a letter to Russell, published in the April 1, 1911, *Watchtower* (p. 110), he stated:

> Owing to much literature being circulated by the opposition within our ranks ... I concluded it wise to discontinue the distribution of the *questions Answering Questions* booklet. Since then I have received many orders for these booklets from friends who are not advised of their discontinuance, and some do not understand why they are refused. I would thank you for the publication of this letter in the *Watch Tower*, notifying the friends of their discontinuance and my reason for this. Prayerful meditation on Mark 9:38-40 leads me to the conclusion that we can be workers in the Harvest, but must also be workers according to his will. The fact that the majority of the Lord's "little ones" now disapprove of the circulation [of] all literature other than that published by the Society, and my belief that the expression of the majority in such matters is the expression of the will of the Lord, are other reasons for its discontinuance. Feeling sure that all the

Lord's faithful ones ... may receive a greater blessing by the
discontinuance that by the circulation of the booklet, I remain

                                                                A.B. Dabney

It is unlikely that this letter was totally Mr. Dabney's idea, but it was probably
written at the encouragement of C.T. Russell. The message is clear: only the Society is to
publish literature.

Although the Society wants exclusive control of publishing, it will allow letter
writing--although some difficulties have been encountered in publishing letters in the
newspaper in defense of the Witnesses. Commercial publishing almost invariable spells
expulsion for a Witness today, as has been true during the entire history of the Society.
Witnesses view the literature that comes from headquarters as semi-inspired, the latest
installment of the Bible. Even the "mistakes" the Watchtower teaches are thought to be
part of God's plan to carry out Jehovah's purpose (such as a means to remove the weak or
"faultfinders").

Some Witnesses also sometimes believe that Jehovah "misleads" His people for
His own purposes. For example, the explanation for Rutherford's sometimes
embarrassing behavior, both in print and in person (especially his strong language,
drinking, and pugnacious behavior) is as follows: "God's organization needed a leader
like him during times of difficulties in the 1930s to the 1940s." Few Witnesses realize that
Rutherford's behavior *caused* many of their "difficulties."

Witnesses are even at times discouraged from general reading in the Watchtower
Society literature that is over two score years or older or so because it is viewed as "old
light." This in spit of the fact that their current index goes back to 1930 and they recently
reprinted the bound volumes back to 1951. Some have concluded that the reprinting was
primarily to make money, others that this is a contradiction. As each new president took
over, doctrines changed and the old literature was phased out. Rutherford's books soon
replaced those by Russell and today Franz's books have replaced Rutherford's. The last
of Russell's books were published by the Society in 1927 and were last circulated in 1932
(see the *Bulletin*, December 1, 1932) although some were still on the cost list as late as
1952.

Witnesses are especially discouraged from reading non-Witness religious
literature. They are taught that God's holy spirit directs only the Watchtower Society
which He uses to direct His people. All other religious organizations are of Satan, thus
reading material by persons in these organizations is like reading pornography or worse. It
is clearly inferred and believed by most Witnesses that their literature is inspired, and
consequently important to distinguish between literature which has the official seal of
approval, the Watchtower Imprimatur, and nonofficial literature.

This distinction was not as clear in the very early history of the Society as it is
today. Several other Bible students who wrote much of the early literature, such as Paton
and Barbour, later left Russell's group and began or continued their own ministry. Thus,
it is more problematic to determine what would be considered "official" literature,
especially from the 1870s to the early 1900s. The imprint of the Watchtower Bible and
Tract Society (in America, in the early years, Allegheny, PA, and later Brooklyn NY) or
inclusion in the official *Watchtower Bible and Tract Society Publications Index* from 1930
to 1960 usually indicated "official" literature. Also included in this section are the
publications sold by the Society and published with their approval, such as those edited by

L.W. Jones, M.D., an early active Bible Student who lived and practiced medicine in Chicago. Dr Jones, who was killed around 1930 in a car accident, later left the Watchtower and became a Bible Student. He also organized one of the first conventions of Bible Students. His daughter now lives in California, but is not active religiously. Another reason the Society does not use names for publications is because so many prominent persons left.

Much of the very early literature was written by Russell, and from 1917 or so until the early 1940s most all of the literature was written by Rutherford. During the Knorr administration (1942-1977) the writing was done by several different persons, especially F.W. Franz. On only a few of the works published in Russell's day is the author indicated. On the other hand, in the Rutherford era, at least for the booklets and books, the author is almost without exception most always listed (Rutherford himself). During both the Knorr and Franz (1977 to 1992) and the current administrations, works are listed only as "published by the Watchtower Bible and Tract Society."

The only books *not* included in this section which probably would be considered official Witness publications are *Jehovah's Witnesses: The New World Society* by Marley Cole, and *Faith on the March* by A.H. Macmillan, both of which were written with full approval of the Society and in cooperation with the Society by active Witnesses (the Society's staff actually did much of the writing and editing for both books) and were sold by the Society. In both cases, the Society wished to produce a Pro-Society book by a secular press. A number of other active Witnesses have written books favorable to the Society, but non of these has achieved their official approval, although they are occasionally quoted in the Society's literature. These works are listed in the nonofficial books section.

A. Books

Books Printed in the Russell and Early Rutherford Era (1877-to the early 1920s)

Barbour, Nelson H., and C.T. Russell. *Three Worlds and the Harvest of This World.* Office of the Herald of the Morning. Rochester, NY, 1877, 197 pp. (Photo reprinted by Witness, Inc.). (Eschatology, much on chronology, argues for the presence, not coming of Christ theology; also discusses God's plan of redemption).

Bond, M.R., ed. *Thy Word Is Truth.* c. 1920, 114 pp. (a selection from Russell's writings.

Paton, John H. *The Day Dawn; or The Gospel in Type and Prophecy.* Pittsburgh, PA: A.D. Jones, 1st ed. 1880, 334 pp., hb., pb. (The two later editions were not acceptable to Russell because Paton soon left Russell's group and made changes in the second edition). (Primarily covers the chronological arguments and last days speculation).

Russell, Charles Taze. *Food for Thinking Christians: Why Evil Was Permitted and Kindred Topics.* Sept. 1881, Zion's Watchtower, Pittsburgh, PA, 161 pp., Supplement to Zion's Watch Tower, Pittsburgh, PA. (On the second advent, the second chance, the second birth and salvation).

_____.*The Tabernacle and Its Teachings.* Feb. 1882, 97 pp., supplement to *Zion's Watch Tower*, Pittsburgh, PA. Revised as *Tabernacle Shadows of the "Better*

Sacrifices." Allegheny, PA: WtBTS, 1891; revised ed., 1899, 1908, 1911, 1914, 1915, 1916, 1919, 1920, 1924 and the 1889 edition was reprinted in Vol. 5 *Studies in the Scriptures*). The post 1899 edition added a chapter and later a scriptural index and an appendix. The last edition was 192 pp. (An extensive discussion of the temple and ark of the covenant).

_____.*Studies in the Scriptures.* First titled *Millennial Dawn*, published by Tower Pub. Co., Allegheny, PA, or WtBTS, Allegheny, PA, until 1907, thereafter titled *Studies in the Scriptures* (all published by the Watchtower Bible and Tract Society in Brooklyn, NY, although some list International Bible Student's Association as the publisher--another name the WtBTS uses). The *Millennial Dawn* editions were published in Allegheny, PA, and *Studies in the Scriptures* published in Brooklyn, NY. The *Studies in the Scriptures* are also called "Series" (Vol. I were all called Series I, etc.). The six volumes are still in print, reprinted by several of the Bible Student groups)

Vol. I, *The Divine Plan of the Ages.* Pittsburgh, PA: Zion's Watch Tower, 1886, 356 pp. (originally called *The Plan of the Ages*). (Mrs. Russell claimed she was the co-author of volume 1-4 a claim partly denied by Russell. The internal evidence indicates her claim may be correct).

Vol. II, *The Time Is At Hand.* Allegheny, PA: Tower Pub. Co., 1st ed. 1888, 366 pp.; 2nd ed. 1889, 387 pp. with index.

Vol. IV, *The Day of Vengeance.* Allegheny, PA: WtBTS, 1897, 672 pp. (retitled *The Battle of Armageddon* in 1912).

Vol. V, *At-One-Ment Between God and Man.* Allegheny, PA: WtBTS, 1899, 500 pp. (later editions bound with *Tabernacle Shadows*).

Vol. VI, *The New Creation.* Allegheny, PA: WtBTS, 1904, 752 pp.

_____. *What Say the Scriptures About Spiritism?* Brooklyn, NY: WtBTS, 1897, 126 pp., pb.

_____. *Outlines.* Pittsburgh, PA: WtBTS, 1909, 493 pp. (six booklets bound under one cover: *Chart Discourses, Our Lord's Return, Tabernacle Shadows,* Spiritism, *Hell*, and *Evolution*), hb. with the same cover design as the *Studies in the Scriptures.*

_____. *Pastor C.T. Russell's Articles for the Twelve Months: February 1911 to February 1912.* 1912, 60 pp. (reprinted from *Overland Monthly*, identical, only renumbered). (Probably each year was reprinted separately by the Overland Monthly.) See also Chicago Bible Student reprint.

_____. *Scenario of the Photo-Drama of Creation.* Brooklyn, NY: International Bible Students Association, 1914, Parts 1, 2, and 3, 196 pp. (reprinted by the Chicago Bible Students), pb., hb. Later edition bound separately in 3 volumes, also 3 parts bound in one volume. (Well illustrated history of the world showing God's plan.).

_____. *The Divine Plan of the Ages as Shown in the Great Pyramid.* Brooklyn, NY: WtBTS, 1915, 438 pp. (A special edition of *Studies in the Scriptures*, Series I, *The Divine Plan of the Ages*, with chapter 3 of *Thy Kingdom Come* [Series III] included.)

_____. *God's Chosen People.* 1915, 288 pp. (a reprint of Russell's articles printed in *Overland Monthly*, 1910-1915).

_____. *Pastor Russell's Sermons: A Choice Collection of His Most Important Discourses on All Phases of Christian Doctrine and Practice*, edited by L.W.

Jones. Brooklyn, NY: People's Pulpit Association, 1917, 804 pp. (reprinted by the Chicago Bible Students).

_____. *What Pastor Russell Said; His Answer to Hundreds of Questions*, edited by L.W. Jones. Chicago, 1914 and 1917, 776 pp., hb. (reprinted by the Chicago Bible Students).

_____. (Ed) *The Revelation of Jesus Christ According to the Sinaitic Text with Explanatory Notes and Comments.* Brooklyn, NY: WtBTS, 1918, 200 pp., hb.

_____. *What Pastor Russell Taught: On the Covenants, Mediator, Ransom, Sin Offering, Atonement,* ed. by L.W. Jones. Chicago, 1919, 298 pp. (reprinted by the Chicago Bible Students); original ed. 320 pp.

_____. *Tabernacle Shadows of the Better Sacrifices, A Helping Hand for the Royal Priesthood.* Pittsburgh, PA: WtBTS, 1919, 131 pp., pb. (Questions: 30 pp. bound with book: total of 161 pp.); Brooklyn, NY, 1920 ed. reset, totaling 182 pp., pb.

_____, ed. *The Watch Tower.* Brooklyn, NY: WtBTS, 1919. (Reprints of all major and most minor articles.) Vol. 1, 1879-1887, pp. 1-996; Vol. 2, 1888-1895, pp. 997-1908 ; Vol. 3, 1896-1900, pp. 1909-2748; Vol. 4, 1901-1905, pp. 2749-3692; Vol. 5, 1906-1910, pp. 3693-4732; Vol. 6, 1911-1915, pp. 4733-5820; Vol. 7, 1916 Je 15 1919, pp. 5821-6622 (including index).These reprints were reprinted up to Dec. 1916 (when Russell died) by the Chicago Bible Students.

Seibert, Gertrude W., and Hatie Woodward, compliers. *Daily Heavenly Manna for the Household of Faith.* Allegheny, PA: WtBTS, 1905, 386 pp.; enlarged ed. 1907 (later published in Brooklyn, NY);some eds. titled *Daily Heavenly Manna and Birthday Record.* Several bindings available. One printing was titled *My Friends --Their Birthdays and Autographs* (reprinted by the Dawn Bible Students and by the Chicago Bible Students).

Smith, J.G.(a pseudonym). *Angels and Women.* New York: A.B. ABAC Co., N.Y. 1924, 268 pp. (a revision of *Seola* by "J.G. Smith' Boston, Lee and Shepard Pub. 1878), introduction and appendix by WtBTS. (Edward Brenisen evidently revised the book. He was a long time associate of the Watchtower and also worked for W.B. Conkley, the primary printer for the Watchtower. ABAC, the publishing name given in the book, was a pseudonym which Edward Brenisen occasionally used. The book was also printed by the W.B. Conkley publishing company. Brenisen died in 1949 in Ashland, MA.)

Van Amburgh, William E. *The Way to Paradise.* Brooklyn, NY: IBSA, 1924, 1925, 256 pp. (A review of Watchtower theology for young people; much on the creation account and the fall and restoration of humankind).

Woodworth, Clayton J. *Bible Students Manual.* Pittsburgh, PA: WtBTS, 1909 and 1916, 654 pp. (all 5 parts bound in one volume). Many editions of this work exist. (Reprinted by the Chicago Bible Students)

> Part 1: Zion's Watch Tower and Dawn-Studies--Comments, 481 pp.
> Part 2: Instructor's Guide, 18 pp., compiled by Gertrude W. Seibert.
> Part 3: Berean Topical Index, 28 pp., compiled by Gertrude W. Seibert.
> Part 4: Difficult Texts Explained and Spurious Passages Noted, 14 pp.
> Part 5: (In the 1916 editions) Index to Scripture Citations in the Watchtower from
>   Jan. 1, 1908, to Jan. 1, 1916; 15 pp.
> Appendix: 98 pp. (including index). Total: 654 pp.

Woodworth, Clayton J., and George H. Fisher. *The Finished Mystery.* Brooklyn, NY: International Bible Students' Association (IBSA), 1917, 608 pp. (also available in deluxe pocket edition). The book was claimed to be the posthumous work of

Pastor Russell but Woodworth wrote the section on the book of Revelation and Fisher the section on the book of Ezekiel. This work was banned by the American and Canadian governments because of statements which were viewed as critical of the war effort. As a compromise the Society agreed to ask its members to tear out pp. 247-258, and thus many copies of this book lack these pages. The book was not accepted by many Bible students and was an important factor in the split that took place in 1917-1918.

_____. *The Finished Mystery.* revised ed. Brooklyn, NY: WtBTS, 1927, 380 pp. (contains only the book of Revelation discussion).

Books Written by Joseph Franklin Rutherford
(often called "Judge Rutherford," although he was never elected a judge)

Rutherford, J.F. *Man's Salvation from a Lawyer's Viewpoint.* Pub. by Author., 1906, 96 pp., hb. (Reproduced by Witness, Inc.) (Covers Rutherford's early theology).

_____. *Millions Now Living Will Never Die.* Brooklyn, NY: WtBTS, 1920, 128 pp., pb. (Includes the prophesy that 1925 will "witness the return of" the faithful (p. 88-89). Much criticism of business, religion, and government).

_____. *Talking With the Dead.* Brooklyn, NY: WtBTS, 1920, 156 pp., pb. (revised as *Can the Living Talk With the Dead?*126 p.). (A critique of spiritism and religion in general).

_____. *The Harp of God.* Brooklyn, NY: WtBTS, 1921, 384 pp., h.b.; also published in a smaller pocket edition. (Covers basic doctrine; creation, Jesus, the ransom, Christ's return). The 1928 edition was extensively revised, especially the chapter on Christ's return which removed all references to Russell as being the faithful and wise servant of Matt. 24).

_____. *Comfort for the Jews.* Brooklyn, NY: WtBTS, 1925, 128 pp., pb., hb. (About God's purpose for the Jews. The establishment of a homeland and other fulfillments of God's plan). This book was revised as *Restoration.* Brooklyn, NY: WtBTS, 1927, 127.

_____. *Deliverance.* Brooklyn, NY: WtBTS, 1926, 384 pp., hb. (Two different covers, identical contents). (An exposition of the divine plan for humanity).

_____. *Creation.* Brooklyn, NY: WtBTS, 1927, 368 pp., hb. (published in two different covers, identical contents). (A summary of God's purpose for humans contains their old 1799, 1874 chronology).

_____. *Government.* Brooklyn, NY: WtBTS, 1928, 368 pp., hb. (On the history, need, corruption and future of governments).

_____. *Reconciliation.* Brooklyn, NY: WtBTS, 1928, 368 pp., hb. (Explains how man will be reconciled to God).

_____. *Life.* Brooklyn, NY: WtBTS, 1929, 360 pp., hb. (Covers the way of salvation) an expansion of *Comfort for Jesus.*

_____. *Prophecy.* Brooklyn NY: WtBTS, 1929, 358 pp., hb. (Much on Satan vs. God's organization. This is the last major book that teaches the 1874 date system).

_____. *Light, Book One.* Brooklyn, NY: WtBTS, 1930, 350 pp., hb. (Covers Revelation 1-14 A review of Watchtower theology).

_____. *Light, Book Two.* Brooklyn, NY: WtBTS, 1930, 352 pp., hb. (A review of Watchtower theology covers Revelation, chapters 15-22 and Daniel 2).

_____. *Vindication, Book One.* Brooklyn, NY: WtBTS, 1931, 350 pp., hb. Also called *Vindication.* (On Ezekiel's prophecy, covers Ezekiel 1-24).

_____. *Vindication, Book Two.* Brooklyn, NY: WtBTS, 1932, 350 pp., hb. (On Ezekiel 25-39 mostly on prophecy).

_____. *Vindication, Book Three.* Brooklyn, NY: WtBTS, 1932, 384 pp., hb. (On Ezekiel 40-48, Zechariah 3 and Haggai 1-2 mostly on prophecy).

_____. *Preservation.* Brooklyn, NY: WtBTS, 1932, 384 pp., hb. (An exposition of the book of Esther and Ruth and the last days).

_____. *Preparation.* Brooklyn, NY: WtBTS, 1933, 384 pp., hb. (On the prophecy of Zechariah and the battle of Armageddon; a verse by verse "commentary").

_____. *ehovah.* Brooklyn, NY: WtBTS, 1934, 382 pp., hb. (On Watchtower theology).

_____. *Riches.* Brooklyn, WtBTS, 1936, 386 pp., hb. (On Watchtower theology).

_____. *Enemies.* Brooklyn, NY: WtBTS, 1937, 384 pp., hb. (A critique of Watchtower enemies--especially the churches, religion, and governments).

_____. *Salvation.* Brooklyn, NY: WtBTS, 1939, 384 pp., hb. (The basis of salvation).

_____. *Religion.* Brooklyn, NY: WtBTS, 1940, 384 pp., hb. (An "expose" of all religion, all which the Society teaches is corrupt except their own; also a verse by verse commentary on Joel).

_____. *Children.* Brooklyn, NY: WtBTS, 1941, 382 pp., hb. (A theology text for young people. This is the book that discouraged young Witnesses from marrying.)

Zurcher, Franz. *Kreuzzug gegen das Christentum.* Zurich-New York: Europe Verlag, 1938 214 pp. (Crusade Against Christianity). Translated into French as *Croisade Contra le Christianisme.* Paris: Editions Rieder 1939 210 pp. (Written by a Witness about the Witnesses in Nazi Germany, especially the concentration camps; listed by the Watchtower as an official publication).

Books Printed in the Franz-Knorr Era

The New World. Brooklyn, NY: WtBTS, 1942, 384 pp., hb. (Covers eschatology and apologetics.)

"The Truth Shall Make Your Free." Brooklyn, NY: WtBTS, 1943, 380 pp., hb. (A basic doctrinal book; covers the end times doctrine, and the role of the Watchtower as the savior during this time).

"The Kingdom Is at Hand." Brooklyn, NY: WtBTS, 1944, 380 pp., hb. (A basic doctrinal book and Watchtower doctrine as it relates to the last days).

Theocratic Aid to Kingdom Publishers. Brooklyn, NY: WtBTS, 1945, 382 pp., hb. (A homiletics and ministry school textbook; a section on Bible helps, translations and various religions).

"Equipped for Every Good Work." Brooklyn, NY: WtBTS, 1946, 382 pp., hb. (A homiletics and ministry school textbook; covers Bible languages, and each book of the Bible as to history contents and purpose).

"*Let God Be True.*" Brooklyn, NY: WtBTS, 1946, 320 pp., hb. (The basic Witnesses
    doctrine book, used until the revised edition replaced it in 1952; green cover;
    covers hell, trinity, the end of the world and the new world, the resurrection and
    Satan)

"*This Means Everlasting Life.*" Brooklyn, NY: WtBTS, 1950, 318 pp., hb. (A basic
    doctrine and soteriology textbook; much on the way of salvation)

What Has Religion Done for Mankind? Brooklyn, NY: WtBTS, 1951, 352 pp., hb. (A
    history of world religions, arguing that all are false and of Satan except the
    Watchtower; much on ancient religion)

"*Let God Be True.*" Revised ed. Brooklyn, NY: WtBTS, 1952, 320 pp., hb. (The basic
    Witness doctrine book, used for over 10 years)

"*Make Sure of All Things.*" Brooklyn, NY: WtBTS, 1953, 416 pp., hb. Revised in
    1957. (A reference book primarily of Scriptures listed under topics to support
    Witness doctrine)

"*New Heavens and a New Earth.*" Brooklyn, NY: WtBTS, 1953, 380 pp., hb.
    (Watchtower eschatology and "new world theology;" much on the basis for
    salvation).

Qualified to be Ministers. Brooklyn, NY: WtBTS, 1955, 384 pp., hb. Revised in 1967.
    (A homiletics and ministry school textbook; covers the Watchtower organization
    and gives a history of its development (p. 297-340).

You May Survive Armageddon into God's New World. Brooklyn, NY: WtBTS, 1955,
    380 pp., hb. (an eschatology text, also covers the basis of salvation).

Branch Office Procedure of the Watchtower, Bible And Tract Society of Pennsylvania.
    Brooklyn, NY: WtBTS, 1958, 158 pp., hb. Revised in 1965. (A procedural
    guide available only to branch offices, not the public or Witnesses in general.)

From Paradise Lost to Paradise Regained. Brooklyn, NY: WtBTS, 1958, 256 pp., hb.
    (A text of basic theology for children; covers all of the basic Witness doctrines;
    focusing on the end times theology).

"*Your Will Be Done on Earth.*" Brooklyn, NY: WtBTS, 1958, 384 pp., hb. (A history
    of God's dealings with humans; concludes God's earthly kingdom will soon be
    established).

Jehovah's Witnesses in the Divine Purpose. Brooklyn, NY: WtBTS, 1959, 315 pp., hb.
    (The most complete official history of the Watchtower Society; presented in a
    dialogue form; includes many references).

Kingdom Ministry School Course. Brooklyn, NY: WtBTS, 1960, hb. (A text for
    congregation servants and their assistants who attend the Kingdom Ministry
    School). Extensively revised in 1972

"*Let Your Name Be Sanctified.*" Brooklyn, NY: WtBTS, 1961, 384 pp., hb. (Argues
    the Watchtower is not man's, but God's organization, p. 338).

"*All Scripture Is Inspired of God and Beneficial.*" Brooklyn, NY: WtBTS, 1963, 352
    pp., hb. Revised in 1990. (A text on the contents of each book of the Bible, much
    on hermeneutics; includes sections on manuscripts, creationism, the Bible canon,
    archaeology and inspiration evidence).

"*Babylon the Great Has Fallen!*" Brooklyn, NY: WtBTS, 1963, 704 pp., hb.
    (Commentary on Revelation 14-22; and parts of Isaiah and Jeremiah. Primarily
    covers esoteric prophecy; includes much history as it relates to the final

outworking of God's plan).

"Make Sure of All Things: Hold Fast to What Is Fine." Brooklyn, NY: WtBTS, 1965, 512 pp., hb. (A revision of the 1953 *Make Sure* reference book).

"Things in Which It Is Impossible for God to Lie." Brooklyn, NY: WtBTS, 1965, 416 pp., hb. (also deluxe ed., smaller with thinner paper). (Covers general doctrine and the Watchtower end times theology).

Life Everlasting in Freedom of the Sons of God. Brooklyn, NY: WtBTS, 1966, 416 pp., hb. (also deluxe ed., smaller with thinner paper) (Doctrine and Witness eschatology).

Did Man Get Here by Evolution or Creation? Brooklyn, NY: WtBTS, 1967, 192 pp., hb. (A scientific critique of evolution and an argument for creationism).

"Your Word Is a Lamp to My Foot." Brooklyn, NY: WtBTS, 1967, 224 pp., hb. (An organizational policy text which serves as law for Witnesses).

The Truth That Leads to Eternal Life. Brooklyn, NY: WtBTS, 1968, 192 pp., hb. Revised in 1981. (A basic doctrine text for new Witnesses).

Aid To Bible Understanding. Brooklyn, NY: WtBTS, 1969, 544 pp., hb. (A to E only; a Bible encyclopedia covering Bible topics from the Watchtower viewpoint)

Is the Bible Really the World of God? Brooklyn, NY: WtBTS, 1969, 192 pp., hb. (A hermeneutics and apologetic text written to defend the inspiration of the Bible; one chapter on creationism).

Then Is Finished the Mystery of God. Brooklyn, NY: WtBTS, 1969, 384 pp., hb. (A verse by verse commentary on Revelation 1-13, focusing on prophesy and eschatology).

Theocratic Ministry School Guidebook. Brooklyn, NY: WtBTS, 1971, 192 pp., hb. Revised in 1992 (A homiletics text, mostly used as an instruction manual for public speaking)

"The Nations Shall Know That I am Jehovah'--How?" New York: WtBTS, 1971, 412 pp., hb. (The vindication of God's purpose for humankind).

Listening to the Great Teacher. New York: WtBTS, 1971, 192 pp., hb. (A book for parents to use to teach their children Watchtower doctrine)

Aid to Bible Understanding. New York. WtBTS, 1971, 1,696 pp. (A Bible encyclopedia and apologetics text covering religious topics from the Watchtower viewpoint, very similar to a standard Bible dictionary)

Paradise Restored to Mankind--by Theocracy. New York: WtBTS, 1972, 416 pp., hb. (How God's will will be done on earth).

Organization for Kingdom Preaching and Disciple Making. New York: WtBTS, 1972, 192 p., hb. (A policy manual).

God's Kingdom of a Thousand Years Has Approach. New York: WtBTS, 1973, 416 pp., hb. (Presents evidence to support their millennial kingdom teachings).

True Peace and Security--From What Source? New York: WtBTS, 1973, 192 pp., hb. (The basis of salvation; much on morals, conduct, and rules of living).

God's "Eternal Purpose" Now Triumphing for Man's Good. New York: WtBTS, 1974, 192 pp., hb. (The basis of salvation, the new world).

Is This Life All There Is? New York: WtBTS, 1974, 192 pp., hb. (The Watchtower teaching on the afterlife, hell, heaven and life in the new world).

Man's Salvation Out of World Distress at Hand! New York: WtBTS, 1975, 382 pp., hb. (Bible prophecy and the last days; much about the enemies of God's people).

Good News To Make You Happy. New York: WtBTS, 1976, 192 pp., hb. (A morals and Witness philosophy text; much on the Watchtower view of the new world).

Holy Spirit--The Force Behind the Coming New Order! New York: WtBTS, 1976, 192 pp., hb. (The holy spirit of the Watchtower and its role in bringing in the new world).

Your Youth--Getting the Most Out of It. New York: WtBTS, 1976, 192 pp., hb. (A text on the required lifestyle and morals for young Witnesses; covers school, sex, morals, dress, drinking, drugs, sports, music, dating, marriage, materialism and parents).

Branch Organization. New York: WtBTS, 1977. (Instructions to Branch Servants on policy)

Shining as Illuminators in the World. New York: WtBTS, 1977, 253 pp., hb. Revised in 1989 (The pioneer service school textbook, covers hermeneutics and policy).

Our Incoming World Government--God's Kingdom. New York: WtBTS, 1977, 192 pp., hb. (An eschatology text; covers the time of the end and the theocracy)

Life Does Have a Purpose. New York: WtBTS, 1977, 192 pp., hb. (Arguments for Witness last things theology and the paradise they envision).

Books Printed in the Franz Era

Making Your Family Life Happy. New York: WtBTS, 1978, 192 pp., hb. (The role of Witness wives, husbands, and children; covers discipline, communication, marriage and the later years).

My Book of Bible Stories. New York: WtBTS, 1979, 192 pp., hb. (A doctrinal text for children, to replace the *Paradise Lost* book; large type and many illustrations).

Choosing the Best Way of Life. New York: WtBTS, 1979, 192 pp., hb. (Witness moral and lifestyle requirements).

Commentary on the Letter of James. New York: WtBTS, 1979, 222 pp., hb. (A word for word commentary on James; one of the few Bible commentaries that the Watchtower has ever published).

Happiness--How to Find It. New York: WtBTS, 1980, 192 pp (A review of Witness social and moral teachings; covers spiritism, sex, family life, money, coping skills).

Let Your Kingdom Come. New York: WtBTS, 1981, 192 pp. (Witness doctrinal text, focusing on the Kingdom/New World teaching).

You Can Live Forever in Paradise on Earth. New York: WtBTS, 1982, 256 pp., Revised in 1989 also a pocket edition published. (Covers basic doctrine, the organization, Heaven, Hell and other topics; many pictures, most in color; for neophytes).

Watchtower Convention Sound Reinforcement Handbook. 1982. (A loose leaf technical book covering the use of a sound system at conventions).

Organized to Accomplish Our Ministry. New York: WtBTS, 1983. (A policy for publishers)

United in Worship of the Only True God. New York: WtBTS, 1983, 192 pp. (A review of Witness social and moral teachings; stresses the need to keep close to and follow God's organization on earth, the Watchtower).

Survival Into a New Earth. New York: WtBTS, 1984, 190 pp. (much color, a review of Witness new world doctrine, the end times teaching, the destruction of the old world).

Reasoning From the Scriptures. New York, WtBTS, 1985, 445 pp. Revised in 1989 (Replaces *Make Sure of All Things*; far more Watchtower commentary than *Make Sure*; this is closer to a short *Aid* book).

Life--How Did It Get Here; By Evolution or Creation? New York: WtBTS, 1985, 255 pp. (A text that attempts to refute evolution, much of the material comes from creationists literature; also argues that short-age creationism is unscientific and unscriptural).

True Peace and Security: How Can You Find It? WtBTS, 1986. 192 pp. (Covers God's Plan and the New World and how one can be part of God's plan).

Worldwide Security Under the Prince of Peace. WtBTS, 1986, 192 pp. (About the last days, Armageddon and why one must be in Gods organization to survive this battle.)

Insight on the Scriptures. 2 vol., Vol. I. Aaron to Jehoshus and Vol. II. Jehovah to Zuzim, 1988, 1,278 pp. each. (replaces the aid book, a Bible dictionary covering Witness doctrine and beliefs and the material often found in Bible encyclopedias)

Revelation--Its Grand Climax at Hand! New York: WtBTS, 1988. (Much color, well illustrated commentary on Revelation interpreted as referring primarily to Jehovah's Witnesses.

Questions Young People Ask. WtBTS, 1989, 318 pp. (Covers morals, sex, school, drugs; similar in content to *Your Youth* (1976).

The Bible; Gods Word or Man's. WtBTS, 1989, 192 pp. (Argues the Bible is Gods word and that Christendom does not follow it and often does not believe it).

Organized to Accomplish Our Ministry. 1989. Revised edition.

Mankind's Search for God. WtBTS, 1990, 384 pp. (A history and evaluation of the major religions; concluding that only the Watchtower teaches the truth; all others are false).

The Greatest Man Who Ever Lived. WtBTS, 1991, 400 pp. (A chronological review of the life of Jesus; much color; stresses moral teachings and doctrine).

Pay Attention to Yourselves and To All The Flock (Kingdom Ministry School Textbook). 1991, 158 pp. (A revision which consolidates the three booklets for elders issued under the same title in 1977, 1979, 1981. An elder who has taken the course may retain the book only as long as he continues to serve in that capacity, but if he loses his position, he must then turn over his copy to the elders in his local congregation!)

Family Care and Medical Management for Jehovah's Witnesses. WtBTS 1992. (Uses ring-binder format for updating and adapting material for different countries. Includes reprints of medical articles and Watchtower policy statements on the blood issue. Used by Hospital Liaison Committees and distributed to certain health care and legal professionals).

Jehovah's Witnesses Proclaimers of God's Kingdom. WtBTS, 1993, 749 pp. (A history of the Watchtower movement; well illustrated, much information, not always very accurate or honest).

Books printed in the Henshel Era

Knowledge that Leads to Everlasting Life. WtBTS, 1995, 191 pp. (Similar to the "truth" book a basis text to teach interested persons, focuses on the New World, covers basis Watchtower theology; much color).

The Secret of Family Happiness. WtBTS, 1996, 191 pp. (About how a family can be happy by applying Bible teachings)

B. Song, Hymn, and Poem Books
(most early song books contain the same songs)

Songs of the Morning. 1977, c. 67 pp.
Songs of the Bride. Allegheny, PA: Tower Pub. Co., 1879.
Poems and Hymns of Dawn (without music). Allegheny, PA: Tower Pub. Co., 1890, 1902, 495 pp.
Zion's Glad Songs for All Christian Gatherings, by M.L. McPhail. Allegheny, PA: Zion's Watchtower and Tract Society, 1900, 79 pp.
Songs of Comfort for All Christian Gatherings and the Home by M.L. McPhail C. 1910. Chicago, IL (published just before McPhail left the Society)
Hymns of Millennial Dawn (with music). Brooklyn, NY: WtBTS, 1905, 332 pp. (also 1909, 1915, 1916, 1924 eds.).
Zion's Glad Songs for All Christian Gatherings, by M.L. McPhail, 1908, 248 pp.
Poems of the Dawn. Brooklyn, NY: WtBTS, 1912, 286 pp. also a 1915 ed which included 38 new poems and dropped 21 poems, all by Gertrude Seibert, who was by then publishing her poems separately. Two major editions exist, the second edition added 215 pictures
Angelophone Hymns. New York: Angelico, 1916, 100 pp (contains hymn number 49-98; no known copy of Vol I exists (Hymns no 1-48).
Hymns of the Millennial Dawn (without music). Brooklyn, NY: WtBTS, 1924, 120 pp. (also 1905, 1915, 1916 eds).
The Coming of the Kingdom. by W. H. Pepworth. The hardback 1924 (third) edition of this poem carries a 1922 endorsement from J.F. Rutherford.
Kingdom Hymns. Brooklyn, NY: WtBTS, 1925, 63 pp.
Songs of Praise to Jehovah (with music). Brooklyn, NY: WtBTS, 1928, 300 pp.
Songs of Praise to Jehovah (without music). Brooklyn, NY: WtBTS, 1928, 143 pp.
Kingdom Service Song Book. Brooklyn, NY: WtBTS, 1944, also 1948 ed., 96 pp.
Songs to Jehovah's Praise. Brooklyn, NY: WtBTS, 1950, 62 pp. (also 1962 ed., pb.).
Singing and Accompanying Yourselves with Music in Your Hearts. Brooklyn, NY: WtBTS, 1966, 128 pp. (both paper and vinyl cover).
Sing Praises to Jehovah. New York: WtBTS, 1984, 225 pp. plus index, hb. (Changes in doctrine require a revision of songbooks).
Sing Praises to Jehovah. New York: WtBTS, 1991, (225 songs plus index; large print edition available).

C.   Yearbooks

In the first yearbook, *Yearbook of the International Bible Students Association with Daily Text and Comments, 1927,* contained data for the year 1926 and the daily text for the year 1927. With the new name Jehovah's Witness in 1931, the title of the yearbook likewise changed. Thus, from 1934 forward it was called *Yearbook of Jehovah's Witnesses.*

The yearbooks until 1986 contain roughly 260 pages of discussion of the worldwide Witness work; approximately eighty pages of what is known as the "year text," a quoted scriptural text; and finally, comments on this text from the previous year's *Watchtower*. The comments do not always closely relate to the scripture, but the commentator tries to create a relationship.

Until 1971, the first half of the yearbook included a report of the Witness work in each country, as well as the general discussion of the work worldwide. As of 1972 a history of the Watchtower work in a few selected countries, "Acts of Jehovah's Witnesses in Modern Times," is given instead. In the 1972 yearbook the history of the work in Argentina, Czechoslovakia, Dominican Republic, Nicaragua, Pakistan, Afghanistan, Taiwan, and Zambia is discussed. Such histories provide a more complete story of the work of the Witnesses in these countries than any other reference. Each year, a different group of countries is covered. After 1986 the daily text and comments have been issued separately from the yearbook and were titled *Examining the Scriptures Daily*.

D. Booklets and Brochures (General)

Bradford, W.H. *The Rich Young Man Whom Jesus Loved and Another Rich Young Man* 42 p. Reprint of a Memorial address for Charles Taze Russell published by the St. Paul Enterprise, the unofficial newspaper of the Bible Student movement for several years. Several special issues were widely used in tract distribution work including to try to defend Russell's character and theology. One was composed of his sermons and a special funeral number.

Dabney, A.B. *Questions Answering Questions.* June 1908, 60 pp., hb., pb. This booklet was written by an active follower of Russell but was later withdrawn although its author evidently continued to follow Russell (see the April 1, 1911, *Watchtower*, p. 110).

Fisher, George, and Clayton J. Woodworth. *The Parable of the Penny.* Scranton, PA, 1917, 6 pp. (A printed abstract from an address given at the Boston Convention, Aug. 4, 1917; also includes Vol. 7 corrections (almost a page) and other information about this controversial volume).

Herr, A.S. *A Letter to Major Whittle from the Berean Bible Class of Tiffin, Ohio.* 1898, 12 pp.

Lardent, J.C. and C.E. Stewart. *The School of the Prophets* published by the New Era Enterprise of St. Paul, MN. (previously called the *St. Paul Enterprise*). 1922 48 pp. plus a fold out chart on the Tabernacle. Although an official booklet on the order 'Hiram and Manda' it is referred to in the latest Society history book "Proclaimers" (page 247) because it was used extensively by Bible Students in the early 1920s for male public speaking training. This booklet contained a series of lessons on public speaking by J.C. Lardent (later a British Bible Student whose brother Fred also became a well known Bible Student) and a series of skeleton sermons including 'Millions Now Living' by C.E. Steward.

Land, Margaret Russell. *The Wonderful Story of God's Love.* 1908 16 pp (listed in the Watchtower's official bibliography). Not to be confused with "The Wonderful Story" (1891-2) a poem written by Russell's wife (see below). This booklet was a poem written by Russell's sister.

Manda, Sister. *How Hiram and Manda Found the Truth.* Washington, PA: Press of Observer Job Rooms, 1916, 26 pp. (An interesting booklet published by Hiram and Manda about how they became followers of Russell. The language and grammar are Southern Black: "When Hiram and me was married we didn't care

much about religion: we didn't seem to care for nobody but ourselves"--p. 1. See
St. Paul Enterprise Sept 19, 1916.

Russell, Maria. *The Wonderful Story.* 1892, 60 pp. (reprint of #8 Old Theology
Quarterly). Originally the long poem printed in Poems and Hymns of Dawn 1890.
The poem was evidently adapted from anothers work.

Siebert, Gertrude W. *In the Garden of the Lord.* Lahr, Buden, c. 1913.

Sweet Briar Rose. 1909, 8 pp.

Woodworth, Clayton J, and Gertrude W. Seibert. *Instructor's Guide and Berean Index.*
1907, 68 pp. Also a 1909 edition, 32 pp. St. Louis, MO (Additionally has index
to Towers; about the covenant, and includes a suggestive outline for an analytical
study of the covenants.)

Booklets by C.T. Russell

The Object and Manner of the Lord's Return. Pittsburgh, PA: 1877, 64 pp. Reprinted
(photographically reproduced in Cetnar, p. 101).
Three World Tract. 1876, 1877, 32 pp. First chapter of the book *The Three Worlds (see
Books)*.
Tabernacle Teachings. 1881.
The Tabernacle and Its Teachings, 1882, 96 pp., pb. (a supplement to the Watchtower)
Dr. Talmadge's View of the Dawn of the Millennium. 1890, 32 pp. (reprint of #4 Old
Theology Quarterly).
Thy Word Is Truth--An Answer to Robert Ingersoll's Charges Against Christianity.
1892, 32 pp. (reprinted in the July 15, 1906, *Watchtower*).(Reprint of #15 Old
Theology Quarterly).
A Conspiracy Exposed and *Harvest Siftings.* 88 and 32 pp. Bound together as a special
number of *Zion's Watchtower*, Vol. 15, No. 8, April 25, 1894 (Tower Pub. Co.,
Allegheny, PA). (A discussion of some early Watchtower schisms).
Outlines of the Divine Plan of the Ages. 1896, 47 pp.
What Say the Scriptures About Hell? 1896; new ed. 1911, 82 pp. A reprint of # 30 Old
Theology Quarterly.
What Say the Scriptures About Spiritualism? 1897 48 pp. (A critique of Spiritualism).
The Bible Versus Evolution. 1898, 48 pp. Reprinted in 1912 and called *The Bible
Versus Evolution Theory.* (A critique of evolution). A reprint of #43 Old
Theology Quarterly
Gathering the Lord's Jewels. 1899, 16 pp. (A reprint of #44 Old Theology Quarterly).
Which Is the True Gospel? 1900, 16 pp. (A reprint of #49 Old Theology Quarterly).
What Say the Scriptures About our Lord's Return! 1900.
Death Is the Wages of Sin and Not Eternal Torment. 1901, 32 pp. (A reprint of #53 Old
Theology Quarterly).
Epistle to the Hebrews. 1902, 48 pp. (some English, mostly in Yiddish). (A reprint of
#56 Old Theology Quarterly).
The Scriptures Teaching on Calamities and Why God Permits Them. 1902, 16 pp. (A
reprint of #57 Old Theological Quarterly).
Criticisms of Millennial Hopes and Prospects Examined. 1904, 32 pp. (Also found in
Vol. 1, *Studies in the Scriptures*, 1903 to 1920 ed.). A reprint of #64 Old
Theological Quarterly.
The Sin-Offering and the Covenants. Privately pub. at St. Louis, MO, 1907, 28 pp.;
reprinted. 1954, 32 pp.; reprinted by the Chicago Bible Students. (The Booklet
was taken from a stenographic report of a question meeting directed by Charles T.
Russell in St. Louis, MO, Aug. 11, 1907. It consists of audience's questions and
Russell's answers.)
What Do the Scriptures Say About Survival After Death? N.D. (about 1909), 64 pp.
Comforted of God. 1910, 48 pp. (Edited by Russell; contains poems, songs, short
stories, many illustrations, this booklet is not typical of Watchtower literature).
Die Stimme. (The Voice) 1910, 64 pp. A reprint in Yiddish of the Studies in the

Scriptures and news and reprints of Russell's sermons to the Jews.(See Watchtower reprints p.4743).

"Jewish Hopes"--Jerusalem--Restoration Prospects for God's Chosen People. 20 new pages and reprint of Chapter 8 from *Studies in the Scriptures*: "Thy Kingdom Come," pp. 243-300 (57 pp.). Total, 77 pp., 1910.

Charter of the Watch Tower, Bible and Tract Society. 1917, 12 pp. (Intra-organizational booklet).

An Open Letter to the People of the Lord Throughout the World. N.d., 1 p.

Suggestive Hints to New Colporteurs. 1912 and 1914. 16 pp.

Home and Office Rules 1916. (Rules for Bethel Service for Bethel workers)

Booklets by J.F. Rutherford

Rutherford, J.F. (All published in Brooklyn, NY) *A Great Battle in the Ecclesiastical Heavens.* Privately printed, 1915, 64 pp. (The British edition had the Watchtower's imprinter, included the same text except it lacked illustrations). (An apology on Russell, deals in detail with most of the morals and other non-doctrinal charges against him. Sold by the Society. The Society here tried to achieve an objective appearance, as *Faith on the March* by MacMillan, by not putting their imprinter on this booklet).

Harvest Siftings. Aug. 1, 1917, 24 pp.; Pt. 2, Oct. 1, 1917, 7 pp. (a booklet explaining Rutherford's views on several recent major Watchtower schisms).

Golden Age ABC. 1920, 32 pp. (An A.B.C. poetry book which is illustrated by scenes from the Photodrama of Creation. For Children).

The Bible on Hell. Brooklyn, NY: WtBTS, 1922, 96 pp.

World Distress--Why? The Remedy. Brooklyn, NY: WtBTS, 1923, 64 pp.

A Desirable Government. Brooklyn, NY: WtBTS, 1924, 64 pp. (On afterlife and the doctrine of Hell)

Hell: What Is It? Who Are There? Can They Get Out? Brooklyn, NY: WtBTS, 1924, 64 pp. (Argues hell is the grave only; similar to standard historical Witness teaching on the subject).

Comfort for the People. Brooklyn, NY: WtBTS, 1925, 64 pp. (On eschatology; argues the clergy are misleading the people).

Our Lord's Return: His Parousia, His Apocalypses, and His Epiphania. Brooklyn, NY: WtBTS, 1925, 64 pp. (Printed with two different covers; the contents are identical). (The standard Watchtower teaching on Christ's second coming).

The Standard for the People. Brooklyn, NY: WtBTS, 1926, 64 pp.

Where Are The Dead? Brooklyn, NY: WtBTS, 1927, 64 pp. (On the afterlife and the doctrine of hell).

Freedom for the Peoples. Brooklyn, NY: 1927, 64 pp.

Prosperity Sure. 1928, 64 pp. (Lambastes business, the clergy, and all governments; this booklet shows why the Witnesses were poorly regarded by outside society).

The Last Days. 1928, 64 pp. (On eschatology; shows the Society used many very different arguments then for the time of the end)

The People's Friend. 1928, 64 pp.

Judgment of the Judges. 1929, 64 pp. (Lambastes governments, preachers, politicians, financiers and commerce).

Oppression: When Will It End? 1929, 64 pp. (A critique of modern society and governments).

Crimes and Calamities: The Cause: The Remedy. 1930, 64 pp. (Shows the only remedy for the evil world and clergy is the Watchtower kingdom).

Prohibition and the League of Nations--Born of God or of the Devil, Which? 1930, 64 pp. (Rutherford, a drinker, condemned those who supported prohibition, especially the clergy).

War or Peace--Which? 1930, 64 pp. (In dialogue form, argues for Armageddon as the only solution to the world's problems; very anti-clergy).

Heaven or Purgatory. 1931, 64 pp. Also a revised 1932 edition. (A dialogue between a Catholic "Churchman" and "Christian," a Watchtower follower; concludes that Purgatory is a pagan doctrine, and only 144,000 will go to heaven).

The Kingdom: The Hope of the World. 1931, 64 pp. Also revised in 1932 edition. (The talk in which the new name *Jehovah's Witnesses* was announced, and the rationale for using this name).

Cause of Death. 1932, 64 pp. (A review of Watchtower theology).

Good News. 1932, 64 pp. (On the resurrection).

Home and Happiness. 1932, 64 pp. (Covers a variety of topics).

What You Need. 1932, 64 pp. (On the kingdom, the resurrection, and other topics).

Liberty. 1932, 64 pp. (A critique of religion and modern society).

Health and Life. 1932, 64 pp. (Covers eschatology and the millions will never die prophesy).

Keys of Heaven. 1932, 64 pp. (Shows only the Watchtower has the keys to heaven).

Who Is God? 1932, 64 pp. (Covers God, Satan, the kingdom and other topics).

The Final War. 1932, 64 pp. (Armageddon and last days theology).

What Is Truth? 1932, 64 pp. (Focuses on eschatology).

Where Are the Dead? 1932, 64 pp. (reset reprint of 1927 ed.).

Hereafter. 1932, 64 pp. (On hell, heaven, purgatory and the purpose of humankind).

Dividing the People. 1933, 64 pp. (Discusses the work of the Watchtower which will cause all good persons to leave Christendom).

Escape to the Kingdom. 1933, 64 pp. (A critique of the clergy and how the kingdom will solve mankind's problems).

Intolerance. 1933, 64 pp. (Discusses the Watchtower's view of Witness persecution, blames the clergy and governments).

Bethel Home Rules and Regulations. c. early 1930s, 24 pp. (Inter-organizational).

The Crisis. 1933, 64 pp. (Lambastes the American government and discusses the

Watchtower's conclusions as to why Witnesses were persecuted then).

Angels. 1934, 64 pp. (Covers the purpose, nature and role of Angels).

Beyond the Grave. 1934, 64 pp. (Reviews the hope for humans in the new heavens and which the Watchtower then taught was to come very soon).

Favored People. 1934, 64 pp. (On Jews, rulers, and the righteous).

His Vengeance. 1934, 64 pp. (About Armageddon which was expected then soon).

His Works. 1934, 64 pp. (A review of God's purpose for humans).

Righteous Ruler. 1934, 64 pp. (A critique of the clergy and the last day).

Supremacy. 1934, 64 pp. (Claims big business put America into war, and that "democracy has perished," p. 33).

Truth: Shall It Be Suppressed? Or Will Congress Protect the People's Rights. 1934, 64 pp. (On the persecution of Witnesses; focuses on the Catholic church).

Why Pray for Prosperity? Why Famine Threatened? The True Answer. 1934, 31 pp. (Shows the only answer to the world's problems then is the theocracy).

World Recovery? 1934, 64 pp. (Condemns the clergy and commerce; concludes only Jehovah's organization will bring recovery from the great depression of 1929 and other problems).

Government--Hiding the Truth--Why? 1935, 64 pp. (Argues that all governments are of Satan).

Universal War Near. 1935, 64 pp. (On Armageddon).

Who Shall Rule the World? 1935, 64 pp. (Argues that Satan rules the world and God will soon establish His rule).

Choosing Riches or Ruin: Which Is Your Choice? 1936, 62 pp. (on why the Watchtower is the only hope of mankind).

Protection from Those Who Seek to Hurt or Destroy Me--How Can I Find It. 1936, 64 pp. (Condemns all the churches, which it is argued, are of Satan).

Armageddon: The Greatest Battle of All Time--Who Will Survive? 1937, 64 pp. (A critique of Christendom; on eschatology and soteriology)

Safety, Comfort. 1937, 64 pp. (Two speeches given by Rutherford on contemporary topics).

Introducing the Kingdom Message in Your Language. 1937, 32 pp. (a one-page proselytizing message printed in 31 languages).

Uncovered: Things Which Have Deceived Millions to their Hurt Now Exposed for Your Protection. 1937, 64 pp. (An expose of Christendom and its false teachings).

Cure. 1938, 32 pp. (Mostly a critique of Christendom).

Face the Facts and Learn the Only One Way of Escape. 1938, 64 pp. (A diatribe against the Catholic and other churches).

Warning. 1938, 64 pp. (A warning that Armageddon "the great storm" will "soon break").

Freedom or Romanism. 1938, 64 pp. (This publication was printed in Australia by IBSA, Strathfield N.S.W. This work is mostly about the attempts, both successful and unsuccessful, to prevent J.F. Rutherford from speaking in Australia, see 1983 yearbook, p. 63).

Fascism or Freedom. 1939, 64 pp. (Argues the Catholic Church is behind Hitler, and that he persecutes Jews because Jesus Christ was a Jew; this booklet makes fascinating reading today).

Government and Peace (bound with *Victory*, pp. 34-64). 1939, 64 pp. (Condemns all governments and all churches).

Conspiracy Against Democracy. 1940, 64 pp. (About the persecution against Jehovah's Witnesses).

Judge Rutherford Uncovers Fifth Column. 1940, 32 pp. (Mostly a diatribe against the Catholic Church; written to answer a newspaper's questions).

Refugees. 1940, 64 pp. (Teaches that all living good people will leave the churches and join God's organization which is the Watchtower).

Satisfied. 1940, 32 pp. (On Christ's second coming).

End of Nazism. 1940, 32 pp. (In spite of its title, it is primarily a condemnation of Catholicism and Christendom).

Militarism; How It Will Be Forever Destroyed. (Historical Building, Norristown, PA: published by *Associated Bible Students*) 12pp., c. 1940. (God's kingdom in the new world will prevent war).

End of Axis Powers--Comfort All That Mourn. 1941, 32 pp. (How the theocracy will soon take over).

God and the State. 1941, 32 pp. (Written to deal with the flag salute issue).

Theocracy. 1941, 64 pp. (About the persecution of Witnesses).

Booklets Printed in the Knorr Era
(most by Fred Franz, Raymond Franz, Nathan Knorr or other governing body members)

Hope for the Dead, for the Survivors in a Righteous World. 1942, 64 pp. (About hell, afterlife and the new world theology).
Peace--Can It Last? 1942, 32 pp. (Concludes peace will soon be interrupted by Armageddon).

Fighting for Liberty on the Home Front. 1943, 32 pp. (About the persecution of the Witnesses).

Freedom in the New World. 1943, 32 pp. (About the persecution of the Witnesses).

Course in Theocratic Ministry. 1943, 32 pp. (An early ministry school text).

One World, One Government, 1944, 32 pp. (Shows the Catholic church and all governments will soon be replaced by the theocracy).

Religion Reaps the Whirlwind. 1944, 62 pp. (Argues that Christendom is of Satan).

The Coming World Regeneration. 1944, 32 pp. (About Armageddon and the new world).

Testimony Booklet. 1944.

Presenting This Gospel of the Kingdom. 1943. (For use with 'Course in Theocratic Ministry'). 56 pp. Printed by WtBTS in England. (A series of articles with index reprinted from *Consolation* magazines No. 590-615, which were not available in England during the war. Evidently used in many other countries as well.)

The Kingdom of God Is Nigh." 1944, 32 pp. (The 1914 teaching and Watchtower last days theology).

The "Commander to the Peoples." 1945, 32 pp. (About the end of this system).

The Meek Inherit the Earth. 1945, 32 pp. (On the soon to be here Armageddon and the new world).

"Be Glad Ye Nations." 1946, 64 pp. (Much on 1914, and the coming new world).

"The Prince of Peace." 1946, 64 pp. (Speeches given at assemblies on the world conspiracy against God's people (meaning the Watchtower) and why this conspiracy will fail).

The Joy of All the People, 1947, 32 pp. (On the new world hope).

The Watchtower Story. 1948, 16 pp. (About the Watchtower movement and its major offshoots in Africa, especially the indigenous Watchtower movement that has been part of social upheaval there).

The Permanent Government of All Nations. 1948, 32 pp.

The Kingdom Hope of All Mankind. 1949, 32 pp. (Argues only the Watchtower is the hope of humans).

Can You Live Forever in Happiness on Earth? 1950, 32 pp. (On eschatology, and the new world theology).

Evolution versus the New World. 1950, 62 pp. (A critique of evolution similar in content to most creationist's literature, about half the booklet is on eschatology)

Will Religion Meet the World Crisis? 1951, 32 pp. (Concludes only the Watchtower has God's favor, all other religions are of Satan).

God's Way Is Love. 1952, 32 pp. (Designed especially for Catholics, using only their Bible translations; discusses God's purpose for humans, why evil exists, etc.).

Dwelling Together in Unity. 1952, 32 pp. Revised in 1974, 1982, and 1989. (Rules for living at Watchtower headquarters).

After Armageddon--God's New World. 1953, 64 pp. (On eschatology; argues Armageddon is soon)

Basis for Belief in a New World. 1953, 64 pp. (On eschatology and apologetics)

"Preach the Word." 1953, 32 pp. (A one-page proselytizing message in 31 languages.)

This Good News of the Kingdom." 1954, 32 pp. (A review of Witness theology and last days teachings).

Counsel to Watchtower Missionaries. 1954. Revised 1974 32 pp (Information for W.T. Missionaries about laws, health and the problems of living in a foreign country. It must be signed for to indicate agreement and must returned when the person leaves their assignment.)

"This Good News of the Kingdom." 1954 revised in 1965, 32 pp.

Christendom or Christianity--Which One Is "the Light of the World?" 1955, 32 pp. (A critique of all non-Witness Christian religions).

What Do the Scriptures Say About "Survival After Death?" 1955, 94 pp. (On spiritism, hell, heaven, eschatology, demons, the soul).

World Conquest Soon by God's Kingdom. 1955, 32 pp. (On the last days eschatology).

Manual of Theocratic News Service. 1956. 32 pp. (One copy issued per congregation).

Healing of the Nations Has Drawn Near. 1957, 32 pp. (On Watchtower last days eschatology and Armageddon).

Aprenda a leer y escribir (Learn to Read and Write Spanish). 1958, 64 pp.

God's Kingdom Rules--Is the World's End Near? 1958, 32 pp. (A critique of the U.N., all governments and the teaching on Armageddon).

"Look! I Am Making All Things New." 1959 and 1970, 32 pp. A new 1986 revised edition was 9" x 11" and added much color, 32 pp. (A review of Witness eschatology).

When God Speaks Peace to All Nations. 1959, 32 pp. (On Armageddon).

Security During the "War of the Great Day of God the Almighty." 1960, 32 pp. (How one can survive Armageddon).

Jehovah's Witnesses and Blood Transfusions, The Facts. 1960. 12 pp. (Published in Australia to deal with cases such as that of a baby that died because his parents refused a blood transfusion.)

When All Nations Unite Under God's Kingdom. 1961, 32 pp. (On Armageddon and the end of this world).

Sermon Outlines. 1961, 32 pp. (A list of Scriptures grouped under topics that Witnesses use to proselytize others).

Blood, Medicine and the Law of God. 1961, 62 pp. (A Watchtower attempt to justify their earlier position on blood transfusion which has cost the lives of thousands of persons).

Kingdom Service Questions. 1961, 64 pp. (Contains rules and guidelines for the congregation judicial committee; one per congregation issued).

Take Courage--God's Kingdom Is at Hand! 1962, 32 pp. (Shows how bad conditions were in 1962 and how only the Watchtower has the answers).

The Word"--Who Is He? According to John. 1962, 64 p. (An anti-trinitarian argument and a defense of the Witness version of the doctrine of the Christ)

Living in Hope of a Righteous New World. 1963, 32 pp. (A review of Watchtower new world theology).

When God Is King over All the Earth. 1963, 32 pp. (Argues all governments are corrupt and only the Watchtower theocracy has the answers to modern problems).

Peace Among Men of Good Will or Armageddon--Which? 1964, 32 pp. (Watchtower new world theology).

World Government on the Shoulder of the Prince of Peace. 1965, 32 pp. (Watchtower new world theology).

Jehovah's Witnesses. 1966, 32 pp.

What Has God's Kingdom Been Doing Since 1914? 1966, 32 pp. (About the evidence and the importance of 1914).

Kingdom Ministry School Course. 1966, 32 pp. (A revised booklet issued to attenders of the reduced two week kingdom ministry school; the school was originally four weeks; contains space for notes).

Rescuing A Great Crowd of Mankind Out of Armegeddon. 1966, 32 pp. (On eschatology and Watchtower last days theology).

Man's Rule About to Give Way to God's Rule. 1968, 32 pp. (On eschatology and last days theology).

Learn to Read and Write. 1967, 64 pp.

Saving the Human Race in the Kingdom Way. 1970, 32 pp. (Last days theology).

When All Nations Collide, Head On, With God. 1971, 32 pp. (On eschatology and last days theology).

Divine Rulership--The Only Hope of All Mankind. 1972, 32 pp. (On eschatology and last days theology).

Divine Victory--Its Meaning for Distressed Humanity. 1973, 32 pp. (Last days theology).

Human Plans Failing as God's Purpose Succeeds. 1974, 32 pp. (On eschatology and last days theology).

A Secure Future--How You Can Find It. 1975, 32 pp. (On eschatology and last days theology).

Is There a God Who Cares? 1975, 32 pp. (On last days theology).

One World, One Government, Under God's Sovereignty. 1975, 32 pp. (Last days theology).

There Is Much More to Life. 1975, 32 pp. (On evidence for creationism and last days theology).

Du ar ju ett Jehovas vittne farjag fraga dej Jarfalla. Sweden, 1976, 16 p. (A history and summary of beliefs). *You are of course a Jehovah Witness* (second booklet).

Pay Attention to Yourselves and to All the Flock. 1977, 96 pp. Second part issued in 1979 and the third in 1981. The three booklets were revised extensively and published in 1991. (A Kingdom Ministry School textbook for elders only; see 1991 edition note).

Jehovah's Witnesses and the Question of Blood, 1977, 64 pp. (tries to justify the Watchtower's stand on blood transfusions which has cost thousands of lives).

Bible Topics for Discussion. 1977, 32 pp. (Replaced the 1961 *Sermon Outlines,* with some revisions).

Jehovah's Witnesses in the Twentieth Century. 1978; revised ed. 1979 and another revised ed in 1989, 32 pp. (A brief, official history of the Watchtower Society; many photographs).

Unseen Spirits: Do They Help Us? or Do They Harm Us? 1978, 32 pp. (About the harm of spiritism and related practices).

The Path of Divine Truth Leading to Liberation. 1980. 32 pp (Argues all paths don't lead to God; the focus of this discussion is on eastern religions).

Pay Attention to Yourselves and to All the Flock. Third booklet, 1981.

In Search of a Father. 1982 32 p (Designed to proselytize to Buddhists by a story designed to interest Buddhists in the Watchtower).

Dwelling Together in Unity. 1982. 32 pp

Enjoy Life on Earth Forever. 1982, 32 pp. (A full color booklet for new or interested persons; outlines Watchtower doctrine and prohibitions).

From Kurukshetra to Armageddon. 1982. 32 pp. (Designed to proselytize Hindus).

Good News for All Nations. 1982 32 pp, 64 pp. A one-page message printed in 64 languages; replaces above outdated 1953 edition which is similar.

The Time for True Submission to God. 1983, 62 pp. (The need to accept Watchtower teachings: directed at Muslims).

School and Jehovah's Witnesses. 1983, 32 pp. (Covers the many Witness school prohibitions and why they exist).

The Divine Name that Will Endure Forever. 1984, 32 pp. (On the history and use of the term Jehovah).

Questions que les gens se posent au sujet des Témoins de Jéhovah 1985 (Questions people are asking about Jehovah's Witnesses) 32 pp. (About Witness beliefs).

Should You Believe in the Trinity? 1989. 32 pp. (7" x 9") (Much color, a review of the Watchtower doctrine of Christ).

Centennial of the Watchtower 1884-1984. 1984 32 pp. (color, short history of WT.).

The Government that Will Bring Paradise. 1985 32 pp. (A full color comic book style review of Watchtower last days theology).

Jehovah's Witnesses--Unitedly Doing God's Will Worldwide. 1986. (A full color illustrated short history of the Watchtower, stressing its international activities).

Missionary Counsel Booklet 1985 (Replacing the earlier booklet of 1954 and 1974. This was was further revised in 1988.

Victory Over Death, Is It Possible for You? 1986 32 pp. (To proselytize Hindus).

Our Problems--Who Will Help Us Solve Them? 1990 32 pp. (Written for Hindus).

How Can Blood Save Our Life? 1990, 32 pp. (Much color; a grossly unethical attempt to convince readers that blood transfusions are against the law of God and often if not usually, medically harmful; many gross distortions of fact).

Spirits of the Dead. Can They Help You or Harm You? Do They Really Exist? 1991, 32 pp. 7" × 9". (color; review of Watchtower teaching on spirits, demons, the occult and angels).

How Did Life Begin on Earth? (Turkish) 1991.

Will There Ever Be A World Without War? 1992, 32 pp., 7" × 9". (On Watchtower eschatology designed to interest Jews).

Why Should We Worship God in Love and Truth? 1993 32 pp.

Jehovah's Witnesses in Greece 1993 16 pp 7' x 9' much color (published in English) (A short history of the Watchtower in Greece).

Jehovah's Witnesses in Hungary 1993 (In Hungarian).

Jehovah's Witnesses in the Czech Republic. 1993 (In Czech)

Why Should We Worship in Love and Truth? 1993. (Designed for Hindus).

Planned Giving to Benefit Kingdom Service Worldwide 1994 (A legal manual for those who wish to donate or lend money to the Society).

When Someone You Love Dies. 1994, 32 pp., 7"x9" color. (On dealing with grief, the New World).

What Does God Require of Us? 1996. 32 pp. (Designed as the most basic source to teach interested persons, even more basic than the 1995 *Knowledge* book, and to be translated in a large number of languages).

Aplique-se a' Leitura e a' Escrita. 1996 (Apply yourself to Reading and Writing-- Portuguese edition--published in Brazil-128 pp.

What is the Purpose of Life? How Can You Find It? 1993, 32 pp., 7"x9" color. (On Watchtower teachings on New World, validity of Bible and Creationism, and a condition of "Christendom").

Jehovah's Witnesses and Education. WtBTS, 1995, 32 pp., 7"x9". (Designed to give to teachers of Witness children; covers birthdays, holidays, flag salute, nationalism, and other common school conflicts; much color; replaces the 1983 booklet. A new edition was needed due to many changes in policy in this area, likely as a result of custody battles).

What Does God Require of Us? WtBTS, 1996, 32 pp. (Designed as the most basic text to teach interested persons, even more basic than the *Knowledge* book of 1995, and produced to be used in many languages with most cultures).

E. Question Booklets (Used for group study of Watchtower publications)

Berean Studies on the Divine Plan (Vol. 1). 1912 and 1915, 44 pp. (1911 ed. called *Berean Questions in "Studies in the Scriptures" on The Divine Plan of the Ages*, 48 pp.).
Berean Studies on The Time Is at Hand (Vol. 2). 1912, 1913, 1915, 48 pp.
Berean Studies on They Kingdom Come (Vol. 3). 1912, 43 pp.
Berean Studies on The Day of Vengeance (Vol. 4). 1912, 40 pp. (also entitled *Berean Studies on the Battle of Armageddon*).
Berean Studies on The At-One-Ment Between God and Man (Vol. 5). 1910, 86, pp. (1915 ed., 60 pp.).
Berean Questions on Tabernacle Shadows of the Better Sacrifices. 1917, 40 pp. (also bound with lined paper). (Also Called *Berean Studies on the Tabernacle*, Pittsburgh, PA, 1910, 44 pp.; 1919, 32 pp)
Berean Studies on The New Creation (Vol. 6). 1914, 72 pp.
Berean Studies on "The Finished Mystery" (Vol. 7). 1919, 88 pp.
Questions on Deliverance. 1927, 59 pp.

Model Study No. 1. 1937, 64 pp. (one ed. is entitled only *Model Study*).
Model Study No. 2. 1939, 64 pp.
Model Study No. 3. 1941, 32 pp.
"Children" Study Questions. 1942, 64 pp.
"The New World" Study Questions. 1942, 64 pp.
"The Truth Shall Make You Free" Study Questions. 1943, 64 pp.
"The Kingdom Is At Hand" Study Questions. 1944, 64 pp.
Questions on the Book: "Babylon the Great Has Fallen! God's Kingdom Rules!" 1964,
    96 pp.
Questions on the Book: "Then Is Finished the Mystery of God." 1969, 64 pp.
Study Questions for the Book: "Then Is Finished the Mystery the Word of God." 1969,
    64 pp.
Study Questions for the Book: Is the Bible Really the Word of God? 1978, 16 pp.
Study Questions for the Book: Is This Life All There Is? 1979, 16 pp.

F. Legal Tracts and Booklets (All published at Brooklyn, NY)

General Rules for Edition and Proofreading. 1925

The Watchtower Radio Stations WORD and WBBR. 1925-26. (Listed as a brochure in
    the Society's official bibliography).

Instructions for Translators and Proofreaders. 1927.   Listed in Society's official
    bibliography under this date.

Loyalty--Questions and Answers on Whose Servant?; Saluting a Flag; last Days. 1935,
    32 pp. (Watchtower policy on flag salute).

Liberty to Preach, by J.F. Rutherford. 1929, 16 pp.
*Information by the People's Pulpit Association, To the Honorable Federal
    Communications, Broadcasting Division.* 1934. (Listed as a brochure in the
    Society's official bibliography).

In Rebuttal--To the Honorable Federal Communications Commission, Broadcast Division.
    1934. Listed as a brochure in the Society's official bibliography).

Christianity is Not Free in the United States of America. 1936. (Listed as a brochure in
    the Society's official bibliography.

Christianity is Not Free in Lagrange, Georgia. 1937. (Listed as a brochure in the
    Society's official bibliography).

Liberty to Preach, by Olin R. Moyle. 1939, 26 pp. (revised ed. of the original by J.F.
    Rutherford, 16 pp.). (The legal case for Witness rights to proselytize).

Advice for Kingdom Publishers. 1939, 16 pp. (Information to help Witness avoid arrest,
    and how to respond if arrested).

Neutrality (from Nov. 1, 1939, *Watchtower*). 1939, 32 pp. (Official Watchtower stand
    on war).

Jehovah's Servants Defended. 1941 32 pp. (The legal case for Witness rights).

This Fight For Freedom. 1941. 16 pp. (Published in Australia as an immediate reaction to
    the Witnesses being banned as an illegal organization there in January 1941.
    Contains much historical, legal material).

Jehovah's Witnesses: Who Are They? What is Their Work? 1942. Listed as a booklet in
    the Society's official bibliography.

Course in Theocratic Ministry. The small print British war edition has 72 pages.

Organization Instructions. 1942, 29 pp.; 1945, ed. called *Organization Instructions for the Kingdom Publisher,* 47 pp. (Watchtower policy manual for publishers).

Advice for Kingdom Publishers. 1942, 16 pp. (British edition of 1939 U.S. booklet, with update on British situation to 1942).

Will You Judge Between Us? 1943. Published in Denmark. (See Watchtower Yearbook 1993, page 101).

Freedom of Worship. 1943, 64 pp. (Witness "preaching work" policy and recommendations and legal/court rulings).

Briefing and Arguing Appeals, by Hayden C. Covington. 1944, 36 pp.

Canada's Need for a Written Bill of Rights. c. 1947, 26 pp. (Imprinted only with "Watchtower Bible and Tract Society.")

Counsel on Theocratic Organization for Jehovah's Witnesses. 1949, by Hayden C. Covington, 64 pp. (Revised organization instructions, 1942).

Defending and Legally Establishing the Good News, by Hayden C. Covington. 1950, 96 pp. (A legal brief of cases and logic used to defend the Witness's right to preach).

United States of America Selective Service System. 1950, 64 pp. (Reviews the law relative to Witnesses and the draft, and advice to male Witnesses facing the draft in America).

Procedures of Jehovah's Witnesses Under Selective Service, by Hayden C. Covington. 1953, 30 pp. (A revision of the above).

Working Together in Unity. 1953, 32 pp. (Listed in the Society's bibliography. A booklet on grammar, style, proof-reading symbols etc. for writers of Society copy.

Preaching Together in Unity. 1955, 64 pp. (A revision of the 1945 organization booklet).

Preaching and Teaching in Peace and Unity. 1960, 62 pp. (A major revision of the 1955 preaching booklet).

Memorandum on Procedure of Jehovah's Witnesses Under Selective Service, by Victor V. Blackwell. 1964, 94 pp. (A revision of the 1953 booklet).

Convention Organization 1937 32 pp. (magazine size).

Preparing for Child Custody Cases. C. 1980, 64 pp. (A booklet designed to help Witnesses facing child custody court cases deal with common objections to Witness lifestyle. Several revisions. This booklet has produced much controversy because it advocates that Witnesses lie to the court. Reprinted by Witness Inc.).

A Letter to International Bible Students. March 1, 1918. (A tract supplement on the harvest siftings subject written by Rutherford).

Order of Trial. 1933, 2 pp. (Confidential instructions for Jehovah's Witnesses who are arrested and face a court appearance. Updated periodically. Instructions for 1939 are four pages.)

To the Police Department of the City of _____. 1939, 1 p. (An open letter to local police departments informing them of canvassing work in the area for purposes of avoiding conflict with opposers).

Law Abiding. 1940, 2 pp. (Mentioned in *Informant*, Nov. 1940. See *Jehovah's Witnesses in the Divine Purpose*, p. 251)

G. Magazines

The *Watchtower* with its slight title changes is the official doctrine magazine; the *Golden Age* later called *Awake!* are more secular journals designed to proselytize more discreetly.

1. The Watchtower (*Zion's Watchtower and Herald of Christ's Presence*. July 1879-Dec. 15, 1908. Named *The Watchtower and Herald of Christ's Presence* Jan. 1, 1909-Dec. 15, 1938. Named *The Watchtower and Herald of Christ's Kingdom* Jan. 1, 1939-Feb. 15, 1939. Named *The Watchtower Announcing Jehovah's Kingdom* March 1, 1939-to date. Canadian issue of Watchtower published by 'Jehovah's Witnesses of Canada' in 1945 when 'Watchtower' was banned. Called *Your Word is Truth*).

2. The *Awake!*

   The Golden Age. Oct. 1, 1919-Sept. 22, 1937. Edited by Clayton J. Woodworth and published by Woodworth, Hudgings, and Martin, 12365 Broadway, NY. Vol. 1, No. 1, to Vol. 1, No. 14; then at 35 Myrtle Ave., Brooklyn, until March 1, 1922; and 18 Concord St., NY, until Feb. 9, 1927 and thereafter at 117 Adams St., Brooklyn, NY. Renamed *Consolation* in Oct 6 1937 Also an Australian edition was published, most issues were pocket sized; different in content from the USA edition; printed locally when the Watchtower was banned in Australia. Evidently close to 100 issues were printed). Called*Awake!* Aug. 22, 1946 to date.

3. *Papers Published in the Early 1900's*

   Bible Student Monthly. Vol. 1, No. 1, (Feb. 1909) to Vol. 9, No. 12 (Dec. 1917). (In 1911, Issue 13 and 14 were printed. In 1914 two different editions of Vol. 6, No. 1, were printed: in the first the lead article was "End of World in 1914"; the second had "Battering Down the Walls of Hell." Early issues were reprints of *People's Pulpit Magazine.* (E.W. Hek edited this for several years). The title *Bible Students Monthly* was later included in a short-lived British series published by IBSA in 1920 called '*The Golden Age and Bible Students Monthly*'. Australia continued using the title *People's Pulpit* into the 1920's (or at least revived the title then). One Australian *People's Pulpit* (volume 14, number 12) dated December 1, 1923 features a Judge Rutherford talk that mentioned (and pictured) the Brooklyn Tabernacle--which was long gone by this time.

   People's Pulpit. Vol. 1, No. 1 (Feb. 1909) to Vol. 5, No. 1 (Jan. 1913). (Most of the material in this tract was reprinted in the *Bible Student Monthly.*)
   Everybody's Paper. Vol. 1, No. 1, to Vol. 4, No. 12. (Very similar to *Bible Student Monthly* in format and content; often the same articles were reprinted in this format which was used to advertise public lectures.)
   The Broadcaster. Vol. 1, No. 1, Aug. 14, 1924 to Vol. 2, No. 58, Sept., 17, 1925 Published weekly, usually 2 pages of short news articles and one longer religious article. Editor was F.E. Houston, 18 Concord St. Brooklyn, NY. (A short Bible Student Monthly).

H. Newsletters

1) *Bulletin* (Watchtower Bulletin from 1917 to July 1, 1931; thereafter *Bulletin for Jehovah's Witnesses* until Aug. 1935). 1917 to 1935, usually 2 pp. From 1913 to 1919 this bulletin was a typed 2 to 4-page letter.

Morning Messenger. 1918, (Canadian).
Special Colporteur Bulletin: Winter Edition. 1928, 16 pp.
This Kingdom Gospel Must Be Preached. 1929, 16 pp.
Bulletin: Special Colporteur Edition. C. 1930, 16 pp.
Bulletin: Special Supplement (England) Electrical Transcription. Sept. 1933, 6 pp.
Presenting "This Gospel of the Kingdom." c. 1940, 16 pp. Printed in Australia.
Suggestions from Colporteurs 1918, 8 pp. Watchtower size.
Suggestions for Workers Special Bulletin. May 1929, (16 pp.) contains a picture of
how to make a 'canvassing jacket'.
This Kingdom Must Be Preached December 1929.
Your Work with Transcription Machines 1933, 4 pages.
Building a Home on Wheels 1934, 8 pp. Instructions on how to build your own
trailer for pioneer work (includes text and plans).

2) *Director.* Sept. 1935 to June 1936, usually 2 to 4 pp. Monthly.

3) *Informant.* July 1936 to Aug. 1956, usually 2 to 4 pp. (special issues Aug.-Sept.
    1936, March-July 1938, and March 1939). Monthly.

4) *Kingdom Ministry.* Sept. 1956-Dec. 1975, usually 4 to 8 pp, changed to *Our
    Kingdom Service.* Jan. 1976 to 1982, usually 4 to 8 pp. monthly. Changed to
    Our Kingdom Ministry 1982 to date, 4 to 8 pp. monthly.

In addition to the official Bulletin-Director-Information-KM series, in the 1920's and
    1930's many larger congregations published their own four page monthly
    newsletter, including the following:

The News of Jehovah's Witnesses (Published in Philadelphia c. 1925 to at least 1933)
The Scope of the Ecclesia at New York (Published in New York c. 1925 to at least 1931).
The Outlook of the London Company (Published in London c. 1928-at least 1933).

I. Tracts

I. Kingdom News Series

   1. *Religious Intolerance--Pastor Russell's Followers Persecuted Because They Tell
      the People the Truth.* March 15, 1918.

   2. *The Finished Mystery and Why Suppressed-.* April 15, 1918. 2 pp. (Concludes
      the clergy were a major factor behind the 7th volume suppression; also covers the
      history of this publication).

   3. *Two Great Battles Raging--Fall of Autocracy Certain--Satanic Strategy Doomed to
      Failure.* May, 1918, 2 pp. (On Satan's world and his activities today).

   4. *Attempt to Wreck Garden Assembly--The Facts--An Open Letter to Mayor La
      Guardia.* July 1939, 4 pp. (On the attempt of the Catholic hierarchy to break up a
      Witness meeting and the press's response).

   5. *Can Religion Save the World Disaster?* Oct. 1939, 2 pp. (Concludes "religion has
      always been the institution of persecution and crime" and is a snare and a racket).

   6. *Tie of Darkness-Isaiah 60:2.* July 1940, 2 pp. (A condemnation of "religion,"
      especially Christendom with "headquarters in Vatican City").

   7. *Do You Condemn or Wink at Unspeakable Crimes?* Oct. 1940, 2 pp. (About
      Witness physical persecution).

   8. *If the Bill Becomes Law.* April 1941, 2 pp. (Opposes bills that attempt to control

politically incorrect speech).

9. *Victories in Your Defense.* Aug. 1941, 2 pp. (About favorable Witness court decisions).

10. *Life in the New Earth Under New Heavens.* Feb. 1942, 2 pp. (Concludes only the Watchtower has the answers to the World's problems).

11. *The People Have a Right to the Good News Now.* Sept. 1942, 2 pp. (Concludes we are very near the grand realization of that New World).

12. *The Last War Wins the Peace Eternal.* April 1943, 2 pp. (About Armageddon and the new world coming in "the immediate future").

13. *Education for Life in the New World.* March 1944, 2 pp. (About the soon to come new world).

14. *Overcoming Fear of What Is Coming on the Earth.* Nov. 1944, 2 pp. (Argues that "religion" has misinformed people about God's plan).

15. *World Conspiracy Against the Truth.* Feb. 1946. (Argues that the U.N., the Catholic and other churches are part of a conspiracy against the Watchtower).

16. *Is Time Running Out for Mankind?* Sept. 1973, 4 pp. (Argues that world problems and chronology portend that the end is very near).

17. *Has Religion Betrayed God and Man?* Dec. 1973, 4 pp. (Concludes all religion except the Watchtower is false, and is soon to be destroyed).

18. *Government by God, Are You for It--Or Against It?* May 1974, 4 pp. (Contrasts the worst of human governments with the Watchtower's picture of God's government).

19. *Is This All There Is to Life?* Nov. 1974, 4 pp. (On the biology of aging and God's promised everlasting life).

20. *Would You Welcome Some Good News?* May 1975, 4 pp. (The New World of the Watchtower).

21. *Your Future: Shaky? or Secure?* Nov. 1975, 4 pp. (On the New World solution to problems).

22. *How Crime and Violence Will Be Stopped.* 1975, 4 pp. (The problem and solution to crime).

23. *Why So Much Suffering--If God Cares?* 1976, 4 pp. (The problem of suffering).

24. *The Family--Can It Survive?* 1976, 4 pp. (Problems the family faces and some solutions).

25. *Why Are We Here?* 1977, 4 pp. (The purpose of life as per the Watchtower's beliefs).

26. *Relief from Pressure--It is Possible?* 1978, 4 pp. (The Watchtower's solution to the major social and life problems).

27. *What Has Happened to Love?* 1979, 4 pp. (The psychological need for love).

28. *Hope for Ending Inflation, Sickness, Crime, War.* 1980, 4 pp.

29. *Is A Happy Life Really Possible?* 1981, 4 pp. (A promo for the book *Happiness*).

30. *Is Planet Earth Near the Brink.* 1981, 4 pp. (A list of problems and the Watchtower resolution, let God solve them).

31. *Are We Nearing Armageddon?* 1982, 4 pp. (About what Armageddon is).

32. *A United Happy Family--What is the Key?* 1983, 4 pp.(stresses Watchtower teachings is the key)

33. *Life--How Did It Get Here; By Evolution or by Creation?* 1985, 4 pp. (argues in support of creationism)

34. *Why Is Life So Full of Problems?* 1995, 4 pp. (Reviews world problems and blames non-Watchtower religion and secularism, argues that the only solution is the Watchtower).

35. *Will All People Ever Love One Another?* 1997. 4 pp. (On Modern War and the Watchtower's solution).

Promotion of Christian Knowledge Tracts (Actually booklets published in Pittsburgh, PA. in 1919, designed to introduce outsiders to Watchtower beliefs).

1. *Where Are the Dead?* 16 pp.; 2. *What Is the Soul?* 16 pp. (A critique of the immortality of the soul doctrine); 3. *Calamities--Why Permitted.* 16 pp.; 4. *Spiritism Is Demonism.* 16 pp.; 5. *Christian Science.* 16 pp. (A critique of Christian Science); 8. *The Rich Man in Hell.* 16 pp. (Argues that Hell is the grave); 9. *Weeping All Night.* 16 pp.; 10. *Do You Believe in the Resurrection?* 16 pp.; 11. *The Liberty of the Gospel.* 16 pp.; 12. *The Dawn of a New Era.* 16 pp.; 13. *Demons Infest Earth's Atmosphere.* 16 pp. (On Watchtower view of demonism); 14. *Comforting Words of Life.* 16 pp.; 15. *Golden Age at the Door.* 16 pp. (On eschatology); 16. *Why God Permits Evil.* 16 pp.; 17. *Joyful Message for the Sin-Sick.* 16 pp.; 18. *Gathering the Lord's Jewels.* 16 pp.; 19. *Earth to Be Filled with Glory.* 16 pp.; 20. *Our Responsibility as Christians.* 16 pp.; 21. *Thieves in Paradise.* 16 pp.; 22. *The Bruising of Satan.* 16 pp.; 23. *Predestination and Election.* 16 pp.; 24. *Do You Know?* 16 pp.; 25. *Is the Soul Immortal?* 16 pp.

Old Theology Quarterly, Allegheny, PA: WtBTS (some are booklets)

1. *Do the Scriptures Teach That Eternal Torment Is the Wages of Sin?* April 1889, 32 pp. (same as No. 53).

2. *Calamities--Why God Permits Them.* Oct. 1889, 32 pp.

3. *Protestants Awake! The Spirit of the Great Reformation Dying. How Priestcraft Now Operates.* 1889, 32 pp. (same as No. 61). (Argues that the Protestant church no longer has God's favor).

4. *Dr. Talmage's View of the Dawn of the Millennium.* Jan. 1890, 32 pp.

5. *Friendly Hints on Bible Study and Students' Helps.* 1890, 21 pp., plus 13 pp. of price list.

6. *The Scripture Teaching on the Hope of the Groaning Creation.* 1890, 31 pp.

7. *The Wonderful Story of Wisdom, Love and Grace Divine* Oct. 1890, 32 pp. (A poem, 156 verses. Also available in leatherette cover with 15 illustrations, 1891).

8. *The Wonderful Story.* Illustrated. Dec. 1890, 32 pp.

9. *Swedish translation of No. 1.*

10. *A Broad Basis for True Christian Union--Contend Earnestly for The Faith Once Delivered to the Saints.* Aug. 1891, 8 pp.

11. *Tabernacle Shadows of Better Sacrifices.* Illustrated. Oct. 1891, 104 pp.

12. *The Divine Plan of the Ages For Human Salvation, Why Evil Was Permitted.* Jan. 1892, 16 pp. (same as Nos. 62, 74).

13. Norwegian translation of No. 1.

14. *Bible Study and Needful Helps Thereto.* July 1892, 4 pp. (same as Nos. 27, 54). (An advertisement for Russell's books).

14a. *A Dark Cloud and Its Silver Lining.* July 1892, 4 pp.

15. *Thy Word Is Truth; An Answer to Robert Ingersoll's Charges Against Christianity.* Oct. 1892, 32 pp. (same as Nos. 16, 71).

16. *Thy Word Is Truth.* Jan. 1893, 44 pp. (same as Nos. 15, 71) .

17. *Purgatory, The Scripture Teaching on.* July 1902, 16 pp. (same as No. 58).

18. *Did Christ Die as Man's Representative, Or As His Substitute?* October 1893, 6 pp.

19. Dano-Norwegian translation of No. 14.

20. Swedish translation of No. 14.

21. *Do You Know?* April 1894, 8 pp. (same as No. 66). (A review of doctrine).

22. *The Scripture Teaching Concerning the World's Hope.* 1894, 32 pp. (same as No. 59). (On eschatology).

23. German translation of No. 21.

24. *Friendly Hints on Bible Study and Students' Helps.* Dec. 1894, 15 pp., 17 p. catalog.

25. *The Only Name--A Criticism of Bishop Foster's New Gospel.* Jan. 1895, 16 pp.

26. Swedish translation of No. 21.

27. *A Dark Cloud and Its Silver Lining* (poem by John G. Whittier). April 1895, 4 pp. (same as Nos. 14, 54).

28. *Why Are Ye Last To Welcome Back the King?* July 1895, 32 pp. (same as No. 60).

29. Dano-Norwegian translation of No. 21.

30. German translation of No. 28.

30. Extra. *Wait Thou Upon the Lord* (Poem by George M. Bills). Oct. 1895, 2 pp. (same as No. 51).

31. *Millennial Dawn* (Letter of withdrawal from Babylon, dated Nov. 1, 1895).

32. *What Say the Scriptures About Hell?* 1896, 79 pp. (same as No. 55).

33. Dutch translation of No. 1, 1896.

34. German translation of No. 1, 1896.

35. Swedish translation of No. 1, 1896.

36. *Awake! Jerusalem, Awake!* Jan. 1897, 2 pp. (by G.M. Bills, primarily Scriptural quotes that relate to Israel's return to Palestine).

37. *How Readest Thou?* April 1897, 2 pp.

38. *The Hope of Immortality.* July 1897, 2 pp.

39. *What Say the Scriptures About Spiritism?* Oct. 1897, 119 pp. (see p. 312 for reprint).

40. *What is the Soul?* Jan. 1898, 16 pp. (A critique of immortality doctrine).

41. *Must We Abandon Hope of a Golden Age?* April 1898, 8 pp.

42. *Crosses True and False.* July 1898, 12 pp. (On doctrine).

43. *The Bible versus the Evolution Theory.* Oct. 1989, 48 p.

44. *Gathering the Lord's Jewels.* Jan. 1899, 16 pp.

45. *The Wonderful Story.* April 1899, 60 pp.

46. *The Good Shepherd and His Two Flocks.* July 1899, 8 pp. (The early teaching of the two class view).

47. Swedish translation of No. 40.

48. *What Say the Scriptures About Our Lord's Return, His Parousia, Apocalypses and Epiphania?* Jan. 1900, 80 pp.

49. *Which Is the True Gospel?* April 1900, 16 pp.

50. German translation of No. 49. Sept. 1900.

51. *Heathendom's Hope Future Therefore Wait Thou Upon the Lord.* Oct. 1900, 2 pp. (same as No. 30-Extra).

52. *Food for Thinking Christians, Our Lord's Return: Its Objective, The Restitution of All Things Spoken.* Jan. 1901, 16 pp. (printed both with and without a cover).

53. *The Scriptures Clearly Teach the Old Theology that Death is the Wages of Sin, and Not Eternal Torment.* April 1901, 32 pp. (same as No. 1).

54. *A Dark Cloud and Its Silver Lining.* July 1901, 4 pp. (same as Nos. 14, 27).

55. *What Say the Scriptures About Hell?* Oct. 1901, 82 pp. (same as No. 32).

56. *Epistle to the Hebrews.* Jan. 1902, 64 pp. (mostly Yiddish, some English; discusses God's plan for the Jews).

57. *The Scriptures Teaching on Calamities and Why God Permits Them.* April 1902, 16 pp. (same as Nos. 2, 73).

58. *Purgatory.* July 1902, 16 pp. (same as No. 17) (A critique of the Catholic teaching on purgatory).

59. *The World's Hope.* Oct. 1902, 16 pp. (same as No. 22).

60. *Why are Ye the Last to Welcome Back the King?* Jan. 1903, 16 pp. (same as No. 28).

61. *Protestants Awake!* April 1903, 16 pp. (same as Nos. 12, 74).

62. *The Divine Plan of the Ages for Human Salvation: Why Evil Was Permitted.* July 1903, 15 pp. (same as Nos. 12, 74).

63. *Christ's Death Secured One Probation or Trial for Life Everlasting to Every Man.* Dec. 1903, 32 pp.

64. *Criticisms of Millennial Hopes and Prospects examined.* Jan. 1904, 32 pp.

65. *Tabernacle Shadows of the Better Sacrifices.* Oct. 1904, 131 pp. (same as No. 11).

66. *Do You Know?* July 1904, 8 pp. (same as No. 21).

67. (Unknown)

68. *Increasing Influence of Spiritism.* Jan. 1905, 16 pp. (same as No. 75). (Condemns hypnosis, telepathy, spiritism and related--uses many case histories and newspaper accounts).

69. Pt. 1: *Christendom in Grave Danger!* April 1905, 4 pp.
    Pt. 2: *Study to Show Thyself Approved Unto God.* April 1905, 4 pp.
    Pt. 3: *Refrain Thy Voices from Weeping.* April 1905, 4 pp.
    Pt. 4: *Hope for the Innumerable Non-Elect.* April 1905, 4 pp.

70. Pt. 1: *Cheerful Christians!* July 1905, 4 p.
    Pt. 2: *Divine Predestination in Respect to Mankind.* July 1905, 4 pp.

71. *"Thy Word Is Truth,"* An Answer to Robert Ingersoll's Charges Against Christianity. Oct. 1905, 32 pp. (same as Nos. 15, 16).

72. *To Hell and Back! Who Are There. Hope for the Recovery of Many of Them.* Jan. 1906, 4 pp.
    Pt. 2: *The Oath-Bond Covenant.* Jan 1906, 4 pp.
    Pt. 3: *Selling the Birthright.* Jan. 1906, 4 pp.
    Pt. 4: *The Great Prison-House.* Jan. 1906, 4 pp.

73. *Calamities--Why God Permits Them* (same as Nos. 2, 57).

74. *The Divine Plan.* July 1906, 8 pp. (same as Nos. 12, 62).

75. *Spiritism Is Demonism! It's Increasing.* Oct. 1906, 8 pp. (same as No. 68).

76. Pt. 1: *Earthquakes in Prophecy.* Jan. 1907, 4 pp.
    Pt. 2: *"Tongues of Fire."* Jan. 1907, 4 pp.
    Pt. 3: *"In the Evil Day."* Jan. 1907, 4 pp. (also printed in *Pastor Russell's Sermons*, pp. 286-302 entitled *"Wolves in Sheep's Clothing"*).
    Pt. 4: *Filthiness of flesh and Spirit.* Jan 1907, 4 pp.

77. Pt. 1: *God's Unspeakable Gift.*
    Pt. 2: *What Would Satisfy Jesus for His Travail of Soul at Calvary?* Oct. 1907, 4 p.

78. Pt. 1: *Physical Health Promoted by Righteousness.* July, 1907, 4 pp.
    Pt. 2: *Jesus, The World's Great Sin-Bearer.* July, 1907, 4 pp.

79. Part 1: *The Lost Key of Knowledge.*
    Part 2: *What Would Satisfy Jesus For His Travail of Soul at Calvary?*

80. Part 1: *Are You of the Hopeful or of the Hopeless.* October, 1907, 4 pp.
    Part 2: *7 Women Desire One Husband.*
    Part 3: *The Millennial Morning Is Dawning.* January 1908, 4 pp.
    Part 4: *The Ransom Price Paid For Sinners Guarantees A Millennial Age of Restitution.*

81. Part 1: *Gathering The Lord's Jewels.* 4 pp.
    Part 2: *The Hope of Immortality.* 4 pp.

82. *What Is The Soul.*

83. *An Open Letter to a Seventh-day Adventist.*

Miscellaneous Tracts (listed according to date or approximate date)

Arp. B. 1886, 1 p. (advertisement for *The Plan of Ages,* a commendation by C.T.Smith).
Once in Grace Always in Grace. N.d., 2 pp (late 1800's).
Self Denial and Cross-Bearing Conditions. N.d., 2 pp (late 1800's).
"The Word Was Made Flesh"--Luke 2:1-16. N.d., (late 1800's) 2 pp.
"O Come Let Us Sing Unto the Lord: Let Us Make a Joyful Noise Unto the Rock of Our Salvation." N.d., 2 pp. (an advertisement for *Poems and Hymns of Millennial Dawn*).
To Bible Students of All Denominations, and All Lovers of Truth and Righteousness. 1912, 1 p. (a letter dated June 15, 1912, which criticizes Rev. I. M. Haldemann and his views of C.T. Russell's teachings).

The Case of the International Bible Students Association. 4 pp. (about the Society's view of the imprisonment of seven Watch Tower leaders by the U.S. government on June 21, 1918, for sedition, written by E.D. Sexton).
To Whom Work is Entrusted. 1919.
Response to "Reconciliation Bulletin." London, England: Watchtower Press, Jan. 26, 1921, 4 pp.
Proclamation--A Challenge to World Leaders. 1922, 2 pp. (resolution of the International Bible Student Association adopted at Cedar Point, Ohio, Sept. 10, 1922).
Proclamation--A Warning to All Christians. 1923, 2 pp. (resolution of the International Bible Student Association adopted at Los Angeles, CA on Aug. 15, 1923; against war, all churches, and a discussion of Armageddon).
Ecclesiastics Indicted--Civilization Doomed. 1924, 2 pp.
Message of Hope--World Reconstruction. 1925 2 pp. (resolution of the International Bible Student Association adopted at Indianapolis, IN on Aug. 29, 1925).
World Powers Addressed. 1926, 2 pp. (special edition of the *Golden Age*; lecture given at London, England, on May 30, 1926; about the closeness of the end and against the League of Nations which is "nothing but darkness").
Testimony to the Rulers of the World. 1926.
Do You Want to Know What's Wrong with the World? c. 1931, 2 pp.
Letters to Franklin D. Roosevelt. 1938, 4 pp. (open letters to the American President from Olin R. Moyle, legal counsel for the WtBTS. The letters of Nov. 9 and Dec 1, 1938, are critical of the Catholic hierarchy).
It Must Be Stopped! 1940, 4 pp. (an expose of the Canadian government's persecution of the Jehovah's Witnesses; printed in Toronto, Canada).
Resolution. 1941, 1 p. (adopted at 1941 Convention against Olin R. Moyle for his anti-Watchtower activities).
"Now Let the People Hear." N.d., 2 pp.
Jehovah's Witnesses: Their Position. London, England: Watchtower Press, July 21, 1942, 4 pp.
Good-Will Letter No. 1. 1943, 2 pp. (letter to interested parties on Watchtower teachings, and a capsule review of the book *The New World.*

Good-Will Letter No. 2. 1943, 2 pp. (similar to Letter No. 1 with slight variations).
Good-Will Letter No. 3. 1943, 2 pp. (similar to Letter No. 1 with slight variations).
Good-Will Letter No. 4. 1943, 2 pp. (similar to Letter No. 1 with slight variations).
Quebec's Burning Hate for God and Christ and Freedom Is the Shame of All Canada.
      1946, 4 pp. (similar to *It Must Be Stopped!*, 1940).
Canada Lifts Ban on Jehovah's Witnesses. C. 1945, 7 × 9, 24 pp., printed by Empire
      Printing and Pub., Co.
Quebec, You Have Failed Your People. 1946, 4 pp. (similar to *It Must Be Stopped!*,
      1940).
*Regret and Protest by American Convention-Hosts over Religious Discrimination Against
      Visiting Witnesses of Jehovah.* 1950, 4 pp. (Discusses the Department of Justice
      ruling made on June 29, 1950 curtailing visits of person from foreign countries
      who were "extreme pacifists" thus "thousands of Jehovah's Witnesses were
      detained at points of entry").
Blood Transfusion: Why Not for Jehovah's Witnesses? 1977, 4 pp. (written for members
      of the medical profession on why Witnesses do not accept blood transfusions).
How Has Christendom Failed all Mankind? 1958 4 pp (a resolution by the Watchtower
      on its role in God's plan).

Door-to-Door Tract Set

1. *What Do Jehovah's Witnesses Believe?* 1951, 6 pp. (Brief outline of basic beliefs).
2. *Hell Fire--Bible Truth or Pagan Scare?* 1951, 6 pp. (Argues that Hell is the grave).
3. *Jehovah's Witnesses, Communists or Christians?* 1951, 6 pp. (Argues the charge that
      they are communists is false).
4. *"Awake From Sleep!"* 1951, 6 pp. (The last days and 1914 doctrine).
5. *Hope for the Dead.* 1952, 6 pp. (On the resurrection).
6. *The Trinity--Divine Mystery or Pagan Myth?* 1952, 6 pp. (A summary of the
      Watchtower arguments against the trinity).
7. *How Valuable Is the Bible?* 1952, 6 pp. (Apologetics for the inspiration of the Bible).
8. *Life in a New World.* 1952, 6 pp. (New world theology).
9. *The Sign of Christ's Presence.* 1953, 6 pp. (Last days theology).
10. *Man's Only Hope for Peace.* 1953, 6 pp. (Last days theology).
11. *Which Is the Right Religion?* 1953, 6 pp. (Concludes only the Watchtower is true).
12. *Do You Believe in Evolution or the Bible?* 1953, 6 pp. (Defends creationism).
13. *How Has Christendom Failed All Mankind?* 1958, 4 pp.
14. *Why You Can Trust the Bible.* 1987 6 pp. (On the Bible, science and prophecy)
15. *What Do Jehovah's Witnesses Believe?* 1987, 6 pp. (Some of the major doctrines).
16. *Life in a Peaceful New World.* 1987, (T-15-E). 6 pp. (A colorful summary of the
      Watchtower's teaching on the new world after Armageddon).
17. *What Hope for Dead Loved Ones?* 1987, 6 pp. (On the state of the dead and the
      hope of the new world).
18. *A Peaceful New World. Will It Come?* 1991, 6 pp. (About the New World)
19. *Jehovah's Witnesses. What Do They Believe?* 1992, 6 pp. (Covers God's kingdom
      doctrine).
20. *Will This World Survive?* 1992, 6 pp. (Argues we are in the last days).
21. *Comfort for the Depressed.* 1992, 6 pp. (Discusses how one can deal with
      depression).
22. *Enjoy Family Life.* 1992, 6 pp. (Gives a history of the family and its Scriptural
      ideal).
23. *Who Really Rules the World?* 1992, 6 pp. (Argues that Satan rules the world).
24. *You Had a Visitor.* C. 1977, 2 pp. (A tract to leave at the door of not-at-homes).
25. *How to Find the Road to Paradise.* 1990.

Kingdom News, British Issues (different subjects then found in USA editions)

No. 6. *Which will give you freedom--Religion or Christianity?*
No. 7. *Religionists devise mischief to destroy Christians.*
No. 8. *Jehovah's Mandate to his servants--Witness against Papal Rome, etc.*

No. 9. *To the people of Scotland--Where does the church of Scotland stand?*
The Year of the Jubilee--Millions now living, etc. 1925, 4 pp. including local talk.
Deliverance postal study course--6 color letter cards. 1926.
Statement--Jehovah's Witnesses in Germany and Britain. 1939. 1 pp.
Information on Jehovah's Theocratic Government. 1939. 4 pp. (invitation to *Salvation* book study).
Catholic--Fascist menace in Britain. 1939, 4 pp.
Resolution (Golders Green hippodrome) 1941, 2 pp.
Children study course--set of 3 tracts. 1941.
Judge Rutherford and Empire News. 1941, 4 pp. (Published by 'Kingdom News').
To all lovers of freedom--warning! 1942, 4 pp.
Feed my sheep. 1942. 4 pp. (Instructions for the new work).
Will it be possible to shock the world? 1945. 4 pp.
Rendering of scriptures compared. 1963. 4 pp.
Impossible to Lie (folder). 1966. 4 pp.
Life and Liberty. 1967. 4 pp. (Life Everlasting book folder).
Would you like to understand the Bible? 1968. 4 pp. (Truth book folder).
What do you really know about God? 1972. 4 pp. (Know Jehovah book folder).
A visit to Watchtower House (London). c. 1972. 4 pp.
Not at home leaflet no. 2--*Alive and Healthy Forever.* late 70s n.d.

J. Bibles

The Watchtower Society has distributed various translations of the Bible. When the Society was first incorporated in 1881, it used the name *Watch Tower Tract Society* and in 1896 *Watch Tower Bible and Tract Society* to emphasize its goal of distribution Bibles as well as publishing books and tracts on the Bible. Although the Society did not print Bibles on its own presses for many years, in 1896 it commissioned the printing of Rotherham's New Testament, 12 Ed. Revised. In 1901 the Society commissioned a special printing of the Holman Linear Bible which contained the Authorized and Revised Versions of the Old and New Testaments, arranged to compare the readings of the two versions. In the margins were references to the five volumes of the *Studies in the Scriptures*, *Tabernacle Shadows*, and *Zion's Watchtower* 1895-1901. By April of 1901 the first 1,000 copies were shipped out of the Society's headquarters, and by 1903 the entire edition of 5,000 copies was sold.

In 1902 the Watchtower obtained the plates for the *Emphatic Diaglott*, first published in 1864 by Benjamin Wilson, a newspaper editor from Geneva, Illinois. Although the Society owned the plates, it was not until December 21, 1926, that the *Emphatic Diaglott* was printed on the Society's own presses. The story of how this occurred is as follows: Benjamin Wilson (or Professor Wilson) was first approached by Charles Taze Russell who wanted to purchase the Diaglott. Benjamin Wilson was then in serious financial trouble and was consequently looking for a buyer for his work. He did not want Russell to print it, though, and refused to sell the rights for his work to him. Russell then approached a third party who in turn purchased it from Wilson. When Wilson found the devious method Russell used to obtain his work, he publicly stated that there were numerous errors in the Diaglott, and that he was going to complete a revised edition. It is not known whether or not he ever completed his new work.

On September 18, 1942, the first complete Bible printed on the Society's presses was released, the complete King James Version. Thirty-five thousand copies were distributed at the local assembly that year, and since then a total of 700,000 copies of the Watchtower edition have been sold.

After negotiation and final arrangement with the publishers of the American Standard Version in 1944, the Watchtower Society was able to purchase the use of the plates, and added an extensive, specially-prepared appendix written by the Society. This edition was for years the most popular Witness Bible, primarily because it used the name Jehovah in 6,823 places, or each time it was thought to occur in the original Hebrew Scriptures. This version was used until it was replaced by the New World Translation in the late 1950s.

Since 1946 the president of the Society had been making arrangements to produce a new translation. On September 3, 1949, at Bethel headquarters the existence of a "New World Bible Translation Committee" was formally announced at the joint meeting of the Board of Directors of the Pennsylvania and New York operation. The committee had already turned its completed translation over to the control of the Watchtower Bible & Tract Society. On February 9, 1950, the translation committee completed its foreword, and the translation of the Greek Scriptures (New Testament) was immediately published.

Subsequently, the Hebrew Scriptures were translated and published in five installments until the entire Bible was completed in 1960 (5 volumes). A large-type complete edition with footnotes was published in 1961, and later several revisions of the entire work were completed and released in small-print versions. This translation has drawn much criticism, primarily because of its "slanted" rendering of various Scriptures which relate to doctrines such as trinity, hell-fire, immortality of the soul, etc., and the fact that it is somewhat awkward in places. The several revisions have corrected some of the grammatical and other problems, but the major problems remain.

In spite of the criticism, the Society has endeavored to produce a workable, useful translation. When this writer was at Bethel in the mid-60s, during one of his many long days in the Bethel library, he uncovered several boxes of letters concerning the drafts of the translation between Fred W. Franz, the head of the translation committee, and the well-known university of Chicago translator Edgar J. Goodspeed. From these letters I concluded that Goodspeed and several other eminent scholars had greatly contributed to the final product. Subsequent attempts to obtain copies of these letters in the historical archives at the University of Chicago (where Goodspeed deposited most of his letters, etc.) uncovered only a couple of vague letters. Subsequent attempts to obtain copies from the Watchtower Society have failed; my letters of inquiry were not answered.

Joseph B. Rotherham (translator). *The New Testament Newly Translated and Critically Emphasized.* Twelfth ed., revised, 1896. Printed commercially with Watch Tower imprint, Brooklyn, NY: WtBTS. First printed in 1872.

The New Testament, by Constantine Tishendorf, Special Edition for ISBA (WtBTS 13-17 Hicks St. Brooklyn NY) About 1902.

Watchtower edition of *The Holy Bible* (King James Version) bound with *Berean Bible Teacher's Manual.* Brooklyn, NY: WtBTS, 1907© by James Pott & Co.), other material useful for the Bible Students. (See *Berean Bible Teacher's Manual* for further details.) This edition titled *Bible Students Edition* and released in 1907.

Holman Linear. A.J. Holman Co., Philadelphia, PA, and Allegheny, PA: WtBTS. (The first Watchtower Bible with extensive notes by Russell; only 5,000 printed).

The Emphatic Diaglott. trans. by Benjamin Wilson, Brooklyn, NY: WtBTS. 1902 (various eds., the latest in 1942). First published by Fowler and Wells in 1864. First Watchtower printing Dec. 21, 1926. They purchased the plates in 1902.

Concordant Version The Sacred Scriptures, ed. and trans. A.E. Knoch. Los Angeles, CA: Concordant Publishing Concern, 1919, 78 pp. This edition was specifically printed for Rutherford, and advertised as such in the *Watchtower*. When Rutherford found out that a number of prominent Bible Students had left his organization and joined Knoch's organization, he refused to fulfill his contract with Knoch. This Knoch was forced to sell this edition through his organization.

Authorized Version (*King James Version*). 1942; The Old Testament, 824 pp.; The New Testament and Watchtower Concordance, 328 pp.; total pp. 1,152.

American Standard Version © 1901 by Thomas Nelson and Sons . First printed by the Society with its own footnotes in 1944, the Old Testament, 1,002 pp.; the New Testament, 288.; Concordance, 100 pp.; total pages are 1,390.

The New World Translation of the Christian Greek Scriptures. 1950 (revised ed. 1951), 800 pp. Translated into German French, Spanish, Portuguese, Italian, Dutch.

New World Translation of the Hebrew Scriptures. Vol. 1 (Genesis to Judges), 1953, 864 pp.Vol. 2 (Samuel to Ester), 1955, 718 pp. Vol. 3 (Job to Ecclesiastes), 1957, 511 pp. Vol. 4 (Isaiah to Lamentations), 1958, 408 pp. Vol. 5 (Ezekiel to Malachi), 1960, 480 pp.

New World Translation of the Holy Scriptures. 1961 (revised ed., 1970 and 1981) 1984, 1,468 pp.; large-print cd. with new footnotes, 1971, 1,371 pp.). This is the standard Witness Bible, 1,468 pp. Translated into numerous languages

New World Translation of the Holy Scriptures. 1963, Vols. 1 through 5 of the Hebrew Scriptures and the Greek Scriptures bound together in one volume, 3,646 pp., with extensive notes. Brooklyn, NY: WtBTS. The large print edition was published in 1971 and this version has been revised about a dozen times.

Kingdom Interlinear Translation of the Greek Scriptures. 1969, 1,180 pp. (Contains both the Greek and English. Appendix includes comments on specific verses and a discussion of Watchtower interpretations).

The Bible in Living English, trans. Steven T. Byington. 1972, 1,596 pp. (How the Society obtained this version is unknown. Byington was very critical of the New World Translation. Includes extensive marginal notes to each book).

The New World Concordance to the Bible. Printed at the Australian Branch, Strathfield, New South Wales, 1940, 374 pp. (Includes a section on Watchtower doctrine and policy and a 37 page list of proper names and their meaning).

Comprehensive Concordance of the New World Translation of the Holy Scriptures. 1973, WtBTS, NY, 1,275 pp. (Includes most all words that were used in the Watchtower New World Translation).

K.   Miscellaneous

Special Watchtower Supplement. July 1, 1879, 1 p.

Charter of *Zion's Watchtower Tract Society.* Nov. 12, 1884, on file at the Recorder of Deeds, Allegheny County, PA, 6 pp. (handwritten by C.T. Russell).

Berean Studies on Character Development. C. 1900, 28 pp. Interleaved with blank pages for personal notes. (Similar format to official Berean Studies booklets, but no publisher. Printed in Glasgow. Reprint of series of questionnaires in Watchtower from March 1905 to October 1906.

Russell, C.T. Typed Copy of sermon delivered at Bible House Chapel, Arch St., Allegheny, PA.Sunday, June 1, 1902, 7 pp. Saturday, Sept. 21, 1902, 7 pp.

The Messenger of Laodicea. 1919, 11 pp. (souvenir folder with pictures of Charles T. Russell at different points in his life; the pictures are also in the *Watchtower reprints; the folder also gives Russell's background).*

Your Work with Transcription Machines. C. 1935, 4 pp. (Service instructions).

L. Indexes (all published in Brooklyn, NY)

Since 1966, the Society has issued each year an index covering all of the previous year's publications. After four or five years these are usually replaced by hardbound indexes covering several years. All indexes include a subject and scriptural index for all of the official publications published during the year the index covers.

Watch Tower Publications Index 1930-1960. 1961, 380 pp.*1961-1965.* 1966, 254 pp. *1966-1970.* 1971, 335 pp. *1971-1975.* 1976, 201 pp. *1976-1980.* 1981, 285 pp.*1930-1985.* 1986, 1133 pp.*1930-1985.* 1990 Ed. 1,113 pp. (revised).*1986-1990.* 1992, 574 pp.*1986-1988.* 1989, 205 pp.*1986-1989.* 1990, 256 pp. *1990-1995*, 256 pp

M. Convention Reports

Chicago (World's Fair Convention). 1895. Published 1901 to 1903; no known copies. St. Louis, MO. Convention 1904, 20 pp.
Souvenir [notes from] *Watchtower Bible and Tract Society's Convention, Kingston, Jamaica.* 1905.
Souvenir [notes from] *Watchtower Bible and Tract Society's Convention, Niagara Falls, NY.* 1905, 34 pp.
Souvenir Report of the Asbury Park, New Jersey and St. Paul, Minnesota Conventions, 1906, 107 pp.
Souvenir Report of the Manchester Convention, Manchester, England. 1906-1907, 56 pp. (Mostly reprints of talks including Hemery, John Edgar, James Hay, and B.H. Barton).
Souvenir Notes from Watchtower Bible and Tract Society's Conventions of Believers in the Atoning Blood of Christ, Indianapolis, Indiana; Niagara Falls, New York; and Norfolk, Virginia. 1907, Pt. I, 73 pp.; Pt. II, 206 pp.
Souvenir Notes of Watch Tower Convention at Cincinnati, Ohio. 1908, 152 pp.
On to Victory; Watch Tower Bible Student's Convention, Put-In-Bay Island, Ohio. 1908, 168 pp.
Souvenir Report, Annotto Bay, Jamaica. 1908, 47 pp.
Souvenir Notes Bible Students' Convention, Nashville, Tennessee. 1908, 144 pp.
Souvenir Notes Bible Students' Convention, Various U.S. Cities. 1909, 256 pp. C.T. Russell and a number of Bible Students traveled the south, west, and northwest by train. Conventions were held at each stop.
Glasgow, Scotland. *Convention Report.* 1909, 66 pp.
Souvenir Notes Bible Students' Conventions. Brooklyn, NY, 1910, 299 pp.
Souvenir Notes Bible Students' Conventions. Various U.S. Cities. 1911, 312 pp. A transcontinental tour by train of the United States. The general convention was held at Mountain Lake Park, MD.
Souvenir Notes Bible Students' Conventions, Around the World Tour. 1912, 391 pp.
Souvenir Notes Bible Students' Conventions, Various Cities. 1913, 392 pp. The general conventions were held in Madison, WI; Springfield, MA; and Asheville, NC. General conventions in foreign countries were held in Toronto, Canada; London, England; and Glasgow, Scotland.

Souvenir Notes Bible Students' Conventions. 1914.
Souvenir Notes Bible Students' Conventions, Oakland and San Francisco, CA. 1915,
    180 pp. This report includes a 48-page supplement: The Rutherford-Troy Debate,
    Los Angeles, CA (The debate was photographically reprinted in Cetnar, pp. 101).
Supplement to the Souvenir Convention Report. 1915, 222 pp.
Souvenir Notes Bible Students' Conventions, Various U.S. Cities. 1916, 331 pp.
IBSA Souvenir Convention Report, Seattle WA. 1916, 65 pp.
Souvenir Report, Pittsburgh, PA. 1919, 64 pp.
The Messenger. Toronto, Canada, July 18 to 26, 1927, 40 pp. (four 8-page sections and
    a booklet on the Society's headquarters in Toronto, dated Feb. 19, 20, 22, 25).
The Messenger. Detroit, MI. 1928, July 31 to Aug. 6.
The Messenger. Columbus, OH, 1931 40 pp. (five 8-page sections dated July 25, 26,
    28, and 30).
*Supplement to Consolation: Report of the Convention of Jehovah's Witnesses for the
    Northwest.* Vol. XIX, No. 491. Seattle, WA, 1938, 32 pp.
The Messenger. Various cities worldwide, 1938, 64 pp.
The Messenger. Various cities worldwide, 1939, 32 pp.
The Messenger. Various cities worldwide, 1940, 64 pp.
Report of the Jehovah's Witnesses Assembly, St. Louis, MO. 1941, 80 pp.
Report on the Leicester (England) Convention. 1941, 32 pp.
Report of the New World Theocratic Assembly of Jehovah's Witnesses. Various cities
    worldwide; Cleveland, OH key city, 1942, 32 pp.
Supplement to Consolation. Various cities worldwide, 1943, 64 pp.
Consolation. Various cities worldwide; Buffalo, NY, key city, 1944, 40 pp.
The Messenger. Cleveland, Ohio, 1946 (five 8-page sections dated Aug. 5, 7, 9, 10, 11,
    and one 48-page section dated Aug. 12), 88 pp.
Report of the Theocracy's Increase Assembly of Jehovah's Witnesses. New York, 1950
    (four 16-page sections dated Aug. 1, 2, 3, 6, and one 32-page section dated Aug.
    8), 96 pp.
Report of the "Clean Worship" Assembly of Jehovah's Witnesses. Wimbly Stadium,
    London, England, 1951, 32 pp.
Report of the New World Society Assembly of Jehovah's Witnesses, New York City.
    New York, 1953 (four 16-page sections dated July 21, 23, 24, and 26, and one
    32-page section dated July 28), 96 pp.
Kongreß. "Triumphierendes Königreich." 1955, 8 pp. (German Assembly).
1958 Report of the Divine Will International Assembly of Jehovah's Witnesses. New
    York, 1958, 112 pp.
*Report on "Everlasting Good News" Assembly of Jehovah's Witnesses Around The
    World.* Various cities worldwide, 1963, 192 pp.
Convention News. Vol. 1, No. 1. Toronto, Canada, 1966. 8 pp.
Convention News. Vol. 2, No. 1. Montreal, Canada, 1966, 8 pp.
1969 Report "Peace on Earth" International Assembly of Jehovah's Witnesses. Various
    cities worldwide, 1969, 32 pp.
Peace on Earth--International Assembly. Yankee Stadium, 1969, 32 pp.
The Approaching Peace of a Thousand Years. Melbourne, Australia, 1969, 32 pp.

N. Articles by C.T. Russell in *Overland Monthly*

(A monthly literature magazine published in California). All of the following have been
    reprinted by the Chicago Students in *What Pastor Russell Wrote*)

"Battle of Armageddon." Vol. 62, Oct. 1913, pp. 402-411.
"Be Content with Your Wages." Vol. 60, July 1912, pp. 94-96.
"Bishop-Apostles' Costly Mistake." Vol. 67, March 1916, pp. 256-260.
"Changes of Creeds Necessary to Federation for Baptists, Adventists and Disciples."
    Vol. 61, March 1913, pp. 296-300.
"China's Prayer to One of Messiah's Kingdoms." Vol. 57, May 1911, pp. 548-551.
"Christendom in Great Danger." Vol. 63, March 1914, pp. 306-309.
"Church Militant's Surrender to the Church Triumphant." Vol. 59, Ap. 1912, pp. 386-

389.
"Church's Birth Due Now: World's Due Later--During Millennium." Vol. 66, Nov.
    1915, pp. 456-460.
"Church's Hope--the World's Hope." Vol. 68, Oct. 1916, pp. 332-336.
"Civil Baptism in France." Vol. 58, Nov. 1911, pp. 429-431.
"Clean Thing Out of an Unclean." Vol. 58, July 1911, pp. 86-89.
"Conditions of Acceptable, Effective Prayer." Vol. 67, April 1916, pp. 344-348.
"Creed Smashings Necessary for Federation." Vol. 61, Feb. 1913, pp. 195-198.
"Divine Plan of the Ages." May 1917-April 1918: Vol. 69, pp. 425-430, 538-542; Vol.
    70, pp. 90-94, 205-209, 300-305, 392-396, 495-499, 586-590; Vol. 71, pp. 87-
    97, 165-169, 252-256, 353-361.
"Divine Program." Feb. 1909-Jan. 1910: Vol. 53, pp. 85-88, 239-243, 349-354, 452-
    457, 548-554; Vol. 54, pp. 108-113, 193-199, 245-252, 400-405, 511-516, 567-
    569; Vol. 55, pp. 126-130.
"Episcopalian, Catholic, Lutheran: What These Creeds Surrender to Enter the Church
    Federation Proposed." Vol. 61, April 1913, pp. 400-404.
"Every Idle Word." Vol. 60, Sept. 1912, pp. 303-308.
"Exposition of the Justice of the Day of Vengeance." Vol. 65, March 1915, pp. 284-287.
"Famine in the Land." Vol. 62, Aug. 1913, pp. 201-204.
"Fatal Ambition--Noble Ambition." Vol. 63, June 1914, pp. 626-630.
"Financial, Ecclesiastical and Social Shakings." Vol. 65, Jan. 1915, pp. 95-98.
"Finished Mystery." Vol. 71, May 1918, pp. 447-451.
"God in the Home." Vol. 63, Feb. 1914, pp. 200-201.
"God's Chosen People." Feb. 1910-Jan. 1911: Vol. 55, pp. 227-231, 323-329, 414-
    420, 539-543, 622-627; Vol. 56, pp. 98-101, 238-244, 333-336, 427-432, 523-
    527, 615-618; Vol. 57, pp. 86-89.
"God's Justice and Love Perfectly Poised." Vol. 67, May 1916, pp. 432-436.
"Golden Age at Hand." Vol. 66, Dec. 1915, pp. 542-545.
"Golden Rule." Vol. 61, Jan. 1913, pp. 89-93.
"Great White Throne:" Day of Judgment Misunderstood." Vol. 62, July 1913, pp. 97-
    100 (reprinted in Vol. 64, July 1914, pp. 102-104).
"Greatest Thing in the Universe." Vol. 58, Dec. 1911, pp. 539-540.
"How and What to Fight." Vol. 64, Aug. 1914, pp. 216-220.
"Imminence of Christ's Kingdom." Vol. 64, Oct. 1914, pp. 216-220.
"Immortality of the Soul." Vol. 57, April 1911, pp. 431-435.
"Infant One Hundred Years Old to be Electrocuted." Vol. 57, March 1911, pp. 334-339.
"Is Christian Science Scriptural?" Vol. 66, Oct. 1915, pp. 269-273.
"Is Christian Science Reasonable??" Vol. 66, Oct. 1915, pp. 2363-367.
"Japanese Complimented." Vol. 59, June 1912, pp. 580-583.
"Jehovah's Saintly Jewels." Vol. 68, Sept. 1916, pp. 262-264.
"Jesus Died a Human--Raised a Spirit Being." Vol. 65, May 1915, pp. 482-485.
"Jews Not to Be Converted to Christianity." Vol. 58, Aug. 1911, pp. 171-175.
"Joyful Message for the Sin-sick." Vol. 59, Feb. 1912, pp. 174-178.
"Man's Fall from Divine Favor." Vol. 63, Jan. 1914, pp. 93-96.
"Messiah's Fast Approaching Kingdom." Vol. 64, Sept. 1914, pp. 316-319.
"Miraculous Birth of Jesus." Vol. 64, Nov. 1914, pp. 517-520.
"Nations Weighed in the Balances." Vol. 68, Nov. 1916, pp. 428-430.
"New Day Dawns." Vol. 65, April 1915, pp. 383-386.
"Observations on Conditions in the Orient." Vol. 60, Nov. 1912, pp. 503-506.
"Our Lord's Return." Vol. 60, Dec. 1912, pp. 600-606.
"Pains of Hell Explained to Us." Vol. 62, Sept. 1913, pp. 302-306.
"Paradise Better Than Honolulu." Vol. 59, March 1912, pp. 235-238.
"Pastor Russell and the Monitor." Vol. 58, Sept. 1911, pp. 261-267; Vol. 58, Oct. 1911,
    pp. 315-320.
"Pseudo Apostles of the Present Day." Vol. 67, June 1916, pp. 514-517; Vol. 68, July-
    August 1916, pp. 78-82, 174-176.
"Refrain Thy Voice from Weeping and Thine Eyes from Tears." Vol. 60 Oct. 1912, pp.
    399-404.
"Reign of the Messiah." Vol. 59, May 1912, pp. 479-483.
"Reply to Cardinal Gibbons' Sermon." Vol. 57, Feb. 1911, pp. 186-191.
"Sabbath Day." Vol. 62, Nov. 1913, pp. 512-517.

"Satan the Murderer--Murderer to Die." Vol. 63, May 1914, pp. 521-524.
"Satan's Ambition--Jesus' Ambition." Vol. 63, April 1914, pp. 409-413.
"Songs of the Night." Vol. 59, Jan. 1912, pp. 78-80.
"Sowing to Self and Sin--Reaping Corruption." Vol. 67, Feb. 1916, pp. 174-176.
"Three Men and Two Women Whom Jesus Loved." Vol. 64, Dec. 1914, pp. 616-620.
"Thrust in Thy Sickle." Vol. 61, May 1913, pp. 509-512.
"True Church." Vol. 62, Dec. 1913, pp. 610-613.
"Twenty Billion Slaves to Be Freed." Vol. 67, Jan. 1916, pp. 84-88.
"Two Escape from Hell--No Torment There!" Vol. 66, July 1915, pp. 87-91.
"Two Salvations." Vol. 61, June 1913, pp. 611-613.
"Value of Ideals to Church and World." Vol. 66, Aug. 1915, pp. 1750178.
"Weeping All Night." Vol. 60, Aug. 1912, pp. 189-193.
"What Is a Christian? What Are His Standards?" Vol. 65, June 1915, pp. 569-573.
"World That Was, Present Evil World and the World to Come." Vol. 57, June 1911, pp. 664-668.
"World-wide Theocracy." Vol. 65, Feb. 1915, pp. 190-194.

O. Articles by and about C.T. Russell in *Herald of the Morning* (Russell was assistant editor, the editor was N.H. Barbour).

"The Prospect." Vol. 7, No. 1, July 1878, pp. 11-15. (An explanation of the expectations of Russell that failed to materialize, the first of many failures).

Letter to C.T. Russell by Mrs. S.L. Slagle. Vol. 7, No. 1, Aug. 1878, p. 31. (She thanked Russell for new light).

"The Atonement." Vol. 7, No. 3, Sept. 1878, pp. 39-40. (Response by Barbour (p. 40-43) who argues that the substitution doctrine is "false" (p. 41). This was the beginning of the end of Russell's and Barbour's relationship, and is a good example of the minutia that produces hate so common in many religions. Paton responded in the Vol. 7, No. 4, Oct. 1878 issue, p. 56 which takes issue with both Russell and Barbour. Barbour's response to Paton is on pp. 56-58. Articles appeared on this topic as late as Feb. 1879, pp. 39-40.).

"Holiness." Vol. 7, No. 4, Oct. 1878, pp. 62-63. (Russell discusses the Doctrine of Holiness).

"The Prophetic Conference." Vol. 7, No. 6, Dec. 1878, pp. 83-84. (Russell ideas on the last days).

"Rich Man and Lazarus." Vol. 8, No. 1, Jan. 1879, pp. 9-10. (He argues here that this account is a parable and not literal).

"The Sabbath." Vol. 8, No. 1, Jan. 1879, pp. 14-16. (A discussion of the Biblical sabbaths).

"Your Vote Wanted." Vol. 8, No. 2, Feb. 1879, p. 40. (Russell here is putting out feelers about a new paper, which began in July and was called *Zion's Watchtower*).

"The New Paper." Vol. 8, No. 3, March 1879, p. 42. (Russell reports only a few persons wrote him in support of a new paper, thus claims that he abandoned the project unless he heard from a "great many more").

"Conversion and Holiness." Vol. 8, No. 4, April 1879, pp. 64-66. (On the process of conversion--Barbour's reply on p. 66).

Remarks by N.H. Barbour (about C.T. Russell's proposal of new paper). Vol. 8, No. 5, May 1879, pp. 83-87. (Barbour notes that Russell stated to him that "full fellowship no longer obtains between you and I" p. 87. Another response by Barbour on this topic was in Vol. 9, No. 2, Aug. 1879, pp. 27-28, 71-72, 93-94).

P. Articles by C.T. Russell in *The Bible Examiner* (Edited by George Storrs).

"Gentle Times: When Do They End?" Vol. 21, No. 1, Oct. 1876, pp. 27-29.
"Coming Events Cast Their Shadows Before." Vol. 21, No. 6, March 1877, pp. 181+.

Material Associated With the Russell Movement

As a tremendous amount of early religious material influenced Russell, it is difficult to compile an exhaustive list. None of Russell's doctrines were original with him, and most of them were openly accepted (or at least commonly discussed) by the Millerites, the early Adventists, and especially the Second Adventists. For an index of some of these works see *The Millerites and the Early Adventists; An Index to the Microfilm Collection of Rare Books and Manuscripts* (University Microfilms, Ann Arbor, Michigan, 1978, 65 pp.).

The works listed below are mostly by persons who were at one time close associates of Russell. It must be remembered, however, that from the founding of the Watchtower Bible and Tract Society in 1879 until his death in 1916, Russell was the Watch Tower Bible and Tract Society, and wrote virtually all of the booklets and pamphlets produced by the Society, although much of the material in the *Watchtower* itself was also written by his wife, John Paton, and others. Russell had full authority in all doctrinal matters, however, he was heavily influenced by the writings and personalities of George Storrs, Jonas Wendell, Nelson Barbour, John Paton, George Stetson, Joseph A. Seiss, and many others.

A. Important Pre-Watchtower or Contemporary Literature

(This material was highly influential in the development of Russell's views).

Adams, A.P., ed. *The Spirit of the Word.* Vol. I (reprint of the first 12 issues of the magazine, March 1885 to Feb. 1886). Corona, CA: Scripture Studies Concern, n.d., 157 pp., hb.

Barbour, Nelson. *Evidences for the Coming of the Lord in 1873: or the Midnight Cry.* Rochester, NY: D.T. Cooper, 1871, 99 pp. Some of Barbour's followers are still living; although because Russell left Barbour in 1878, the literature helps us understand the source of Russell's beliefs. Modern Barbourite works include *A Review*, and Hobbs and Hobbs, listed below.

_____. *Washed in His Blood.* Rochester, NY: Unique Book Co., 1907, 511 pp.

_____. *A Review / God's Wisdom Versus Man's Wisdom.* Dayton, OH: Christian Fellowship Associates, 1968, 81 pp.

Bickersteth, Rev. Edward (Rector of Watton, Herts.) *A Practical Guide to the Prophecies, with reference to their interpretation and fulfillment, and to personal edification.* 7th edition, London, Seeley, Burnside and Seeley, 1854. (Suggests 7 out. Refers back to Habershon's work).

Birks, T.R. *First elements of Sacred Prophecy.* London: William Edward Painter, 1843.

Blain, Jacob. *"Death Not Life: or the Destruction of the Wicked (commonly called annihilation). Established, and Endless Misery Disproved, by a Collection and Explanation of All Passages on Future Punishment to Which is Addenda Review of Dr. E. Beecher's Conflict of the Ages, and John Fosters Letter.* 7th ed. Buffalo: Pub. by author, 1857.

Brown, John Aquila. *The Even-Tide; or, The Last Triumph of the Blessed and Only Potentate, The King of Kings, and Lord of Lords; Being a Development of the Mysteries of Daniel and St. John and of Prophecies respecting the renovated Kingdom of Israel.* London, England: J. Offer, et al., 1823, 2 Vols. (On the end of the world and Christ's second advent).

Dunn, Henry. *The Destiny of the Human Race, a Scriptural Inquiry.* England, 1863.

Elliott, E.B. *Horae Apocalypticae:* or, *A Commentary on the Apocalypse.* 1st Ed 1844. London, England: Seeley, Jackson and Halliday, 1862, 4 Vols. (This work was important in Barbour's research. The 1st edition (page 1429) gives 606 BC to 1914 AD as one explanation for the 'seven times'. From the 4th edition onwards, (1851) 606 BC is mentioned, but the comment about 1914 is omitted.)

Farrar, Dr. F.W. *"Eternal Hope."* London, England: Macmillan, 1878.

_____. *"Mercy and Judgment."* London, England: Macmillan, 1904.

Grew, Henry. *The Divine Testimony Concerning the Son of God.* Published by author, 1842.

_____. *Future Punishment, Not Eternal Life in Misery but Destruction.* Philadelphia: Stereotyped at Moorbridge's Foundry, 1850.

_____. *The Intermediate State.* Philadelphia: For sale by the author and H.L. Hastings, 1844.

Guinness, H. Grattan. *The Approaching End of the Age.* 2nd ed. London: Hodder and Stoughton, 1879, 695 pp.

Habershon, Matthew. *A Dissertation on the Prophetic Scriptures chiefly those of a chronological character; showing their aspect on the present times, and on the destinies of the Jewish nation.* 1st edition, London, James Nisbett 1834. (Focuses on the 'times of the Gentiles' ending in 1843-44 or 1873-74, concluding the 'time of the end' expired in 1919).

_____. *An Historical Exposition of the Prophecies of the Revelation of Saint John; showing their connection with and confirmation of those of Daniel and of the Old Testament in general; particularly in their most important aspect on the present times.* Two volumes. London, James Nisbett and Co. 1844. (Works out 'times of Gentiles' from 676-7 BC to 1844 AD "the present year" and also 601 BC to 1919 AD "Seventy-five years from the present".)

Hobbs, A.E., and I.J. Hobbs. *Hope for All Mankind.* Auckland, New Zealand: Reliance Printing, 1920, 169 pp.

Jukes, Andrew. *The Restitution of All Things.* Pub. by author, 1867.

Martin, J.L. *The Voice of the Seven Thunders: or, Lectures on the Apocalypse.* 7th ed. Bedford, IN: James M. Mathes, 1874, 330 pp., hb.

Miller, William. *Evidence from Scripture and History of the Second Coming of Christ,*

About the Year 1843: Exhibited in a Course of Lectures. Troy, NY: Kember & Hooper, 1836. Also 1842 ed. Boston: Joshua Himes, 300 pp.

Moncrieff, Wm. Glen. *Dialogues on Future Probation.* C. 1840s.

_____. *Dialogues on Future Punishment.* 1848.

Newton, Thomas. *Dissertations on the Prophecies.* Northampton, MA: William Butler, 1796.

Seeley, Robert Benton. *An Atlas of Prophecy: Being the Prophecies of Daniel and St. John with a simple exposition, and A Series of Maps and Charts, exhibiting their fulfillment in the history of the Church and of the World.* London, Seeley's 1849. (Suggests on page 9 that the 'seven items' started from the commencement of Nebuchadnezzar's reign in BC 606 or 607, and would terminate 2520 years later in AD 1914. Acknowledges the influence of E. B. Elliott).

Seiss, Joseph A., D.D. *The Parable of the Ten Virgins in Six Discourses.* Philadelphia, PA: Smith English and Co., 1862.

_____. *The Last Times and Great Consummation.* Philadelphia, PA, 1863.

_____. *The Apocalypse.* Philadelphia, PA: Smith English and Co., 1865.

_____. *A Miracle in Stone of the Great Pyramid of Egypt.* Philadelphia, PA: London Christian Office, 1877, 250 pp. Reprinted in 1973 by Multimedia Publishing Corp. of Blauvelt, NY. The reprint is titled *The Great Pyramid: A Miracle in Stone* and has a new introduction by Paul M. Allen.

_____. *The Gospel in the Stars.* Philadelphia, PA: J.B. Lippincott, 1885.

Smith, Worth. *Miracle of the Ages: The Great Pyramid.* Holyoke, MA: The Elizabeth Town Co., 1934, 160 pp., hb.

Smyth, Piazzi. *Our Inheritance in the Great Pyramid.* London, England: Daldy, Isbister & Co., 1877. A third ed. reprinted by Steiner Books of Blauvelt, NY, in 1977, 626 pp., hb., pb. A fourth ed. reprinted (under the title *The Great Pyramid: Its Secrets and Mysteries Revealed*) by Bell Publishing Co. of New York in 1978 with a new foreword, 676 pp., hb.

_____. *The Glory of the Great Pyramid Found in England's Coming Glories* (fourth volume of the series "Identifications of the Anglo Saxons with Lost Israel"). Revised ed., by Edward Hine. New York: James Huggins, 1880, p. 222-230.

Snow, S.S. *The Book of Judgment Delivered to Israel by Elijah the Messenger of the Everlasting Covenant.* New York: G. Mitchell, 1848, 432 pp., hb.

Wellcome, Isaac C. *History of the Second Advent Message and Mission, Doctrine and People.* Boston, Mass: Advent Christian Publication Society, 1874, 707 pp.

Wendell, Elder J. (Jonas). *The Present Truth or Meat in due Season.* published by author, Edenboro, PA, 1870, 48 pages. (Highlights 1873 as the end of Daniel's '1335 days' and predicts the coming of Christ in the clouds before 1880. Jonas was a former editor of *The Crisis* and the man who first interested Russell in the Second Adventist movement in 1849.)

Wendell, Rufus. *The New Testament of Our Lord and Savior Jesus Christ.* Albany, NY: Pub. by author, 1882, c. 564 pp.

B. Magazines That Played an Important Role in Russell's Movement

Adams, A.P., ed. *The Spirit of the Word.* Beverly, MA: Droweht Pub. Co. monthly, 16 pp., March 1985 to Vol. 19, No. 12, 1903.

Advent Chronicler and Tent Reporter. Buffalo, NY: 1843 to about 1844 (no known copies remain).

Barbour, Nelson H., ed. *The Midnight Cry.* 1871-1873 (a most important paper. From 1873 to 1874 this was called The Midnight Cry and the Herald of the Morning. In 1875 it was renamed *The Herald of the Morning.* until 1903.

Fitch, Charles, ed. *Second Advent of Christ.* Cleveland, OH: c. 1843, 4 pp. (no known copies).

Fleming, L.D., ed. *The Kingdom at Hand.* Rochester, NY: 1843.

Grant, Miles, ed. *The Crisis.* N.d. (Advent Christian Church Journal). Published 1854-1952. Miles Grant was editor (or co-editor) from 1856-1876 except in 1861 when Rufus Wendell was editor. Barbour evidently also wrote for it in the 1860's--it details his expulsion from the Advents (*World's Crisis*, March 31, 1875, page 100). Also contained letters from George Stetson showing he held meetings in Allegheny which Charles T. Russell likely attended, and obituaries for Jonas Wendall and George Stetson, the latter using the term Brother Russell.

Gross, H.H., ed. *Sure Word of Prophecy.* Albany, NY, 1845.

Herald of Life and the Coming Kingdom. 1862-1882, Springfield, MA, New York: Life and Advent Union.

Himes, Joshua V., and S.S. Snow, eds. *True Midnight Cry.* Haverhill, MA, 1844.

Himes, Joshua V., et al., *Signs of the Times.* Boston, MA: 1840-1844 (continued as *Advent Herald*).

_____. *Southern Midnight Cry.* New York, 1844 (no issues located).

_____. *Advent Herald and Signs of the Times Reporter.* Boston, MA, 1849 to 1873.

Hutchison, Richard, and C. Green, eds. *Voice of Elijah.* Montreal, Canada, semi-monthly, 1843-1844.

Jacobs, Enoch, ed. *The Coming of Christ.* New York, 1843.

Jones, A.D., ed. *Zion's Day Star* (later called *Day Star*). Oct. 1881-1894?, monthly. Jones worked closely with Russell for several years.

Jones, Henry, and C.D. Fleming, eds. *Second Advent Witness.* 1842, 32 pp. per issue (no known copies).

Litch, Josiah, ed. *Philadelphia Alarm.* 1844 (no known copies).

_____. *Trumpet of Alarm.* Philadelphia, PA, 1844-1845 (no known copies).

Marsh, Joseph, ed. *Christian Palladium.* Union Mills, NY, 1832-1846.

Rice, H.B., ed. *The Last Trump.* 1879.

Seiss, Joseph (Ed). *The Prophetic Times* Philadelphia. (1863-1881) Name changed to *The Prophetic Times and Watchtower* in 1875. (in 1876 its title was changed to *The Prophetic Times and Watch Tower*). From volume 8, Number 12, December

1870 the main article 'Prophetic Times' page 183 said "as the times of the Gentiles are coexistent and coeternal with the Jewish dispersion, they must consequently end in AD 1914."

C. The Works of George Storrs

George Storrs was born on December 13, 1796, in Lebanon, New Hampshire, and died December 28, 1879, at Brooklyn, New York. He published parts of his autobiography in his journal *The Bible Examiner*, and the final issue, published in March 1880 by his only daughter, Hattie Storrs with the assistance of his widow, gives a complete biography.

C.T. Russell became aware of Storrs' work through Jonas Wendell in about 1869. In 1874 Storrs visited and preached at the small group at Allegheny and evidently met Joseph Lytel Russell for the first time then. George Storrs conducted a personal Bible study with Charles Russell who adopted many, if not most, of his views. Storrs was raised as a Calvinist and in 1825 involved himself with the Methodist Church, traveling, lecturing, and preaching (especially against slavery). His position on slavery (pro abolition) created conflicts (the Methodists were opposed to slavery but also opposed abolition work because they felt it was a "radical response") and thus in 1840 under pressure he withdrew from the church. Eventually, partially because of the influence of a pamphlet written by Henry Grew that he found on the floor of a railroad coach, he came to believe that the soul was mortal (thus denying the doctrine of inherent immortality). In 1842 he first heard the views of William Miller, many which he accepted for a short time. In 1843 he began *The Bible Examiner* which influenced C.T. Russell a great deal, and for which he wrote several articles.

In time, Storrs altered his ideas about the resurrection, the state of the unsaved, and other theological concepts and again had to change his religious association. He became president and editor of the *Life and Advent Union* but in 1871 he again went out on his own. He now held that Christ's ransom would benefit *all* mankind because both the saved and the unsaved would be resurrected after Armageddon. Thus, because Russell was closely connected with the entire Adventist movement and highly influenced by George Storrs, a listing of some of Storrs' important works appears below. In fact, both C.T. Russell and Russell's father, Joseph Lytel Russell, supported Storrs financially.

When Storrs died, Russell states in the January 1880 *Watchtower* "the news of Brother Storrs' death (December 28, 1879) reached us too late for insertion in the last issue...he was...a faithful servant...we mourned the loss of a friend and brother in Christ...." A number of Storrs followers believed that the "mantle' of God's spokes person was passed from Storrs to Russell partly because Russell's magazine began just as *the Bible Examiner* was ending. One major difference between Storrs and Russell was that Storrs was definitely a Trinitarian, although he printed an article in *The Bible Examiner* which indicated that the Holy Spirit was not a person but the power of God. For an excellent review of the Miller movement from which Storrs and C.T. Russell broke off, see Clara Endicott Sears, *Days of Delusion* (Boston: Houghton Mifflin Co., 1927).

Storrs, George. *Mob Under Pretense of Law, or the Arrest and Trial of Rev. George Storrs at Northfield, N.H.* Concord, N.H.: E.G. Chase, 1835, 24 pp.

_____. *Six Sermons of the Inquiry, Is There Immortality in Sin and Suffering?* New York, 1842, 167 pp. (200,000 copies were published from 1842 to 1861) Reprinted by Goodrich.

_____. *The Bible Examiner: Containing Various Prophetic Exposition.* Boston: Joshua V. Himes, 1843, 136 pp., hb. (Most articles are a reprint from *The Midnight Cry*; much on chronology).

_____. *An Inquiry: Are the Souls of the Wicked Immortal?* In three letters. Montpelier, VT: Privately printed in 1841.

_____. *The Wicked Dead or Statements, Explanations, Quirks, Answered, and Exposition of Texts Relating to the Destiny of Wicked Men.* New York: The Herald of Life, 1870.

_____. *A Vindication of the Government of God Over the Children of Men, or the Promise and Oath of God to Abraham.* New York: pub. by Author 1874.

_____. *An Inquiry: Are the Souls of the Wicked Immortal? in Six Sermons.* Philadelphia, PA: Albany W. and A. White, 1847, 64 pp.

_____. *The Gospel Hope.* New York, 1851, 85+ pp.

_____. *The European War, or the Position and Prospects of the Papal Roman Power and the Napoleon Dynasty as Indicated in Scripture Prophecy.* New York, 1859, 34 pp.

_____. *The French Empire.* N.p., 1859, 4 pp.

_____. *The Unity of Man: or Life and Death Realities.* New York, n.d., 122 pp.

_____. *The Gospel Faith.* New York, n.d., 12 pp. Also he published *God Is Love; Devil--Satan--Demons; The Divine Dispensations; The Essential Baptism.*

Magazine

The Bible Examiner. Vol. 1, No. 1, to Vol. 23, No. 10, 1843 to 1880. Suspended publication Jan. 1, 1858, to Jan. 1860 and from Aug. 1863 to Sept. 1871; 1843-1844 issued at Brooklyn, NY, from 1845 to 1853 at Philadelphia, PA, from 1853 on at Brooklyn, NY. About a total of 350 issues were published.

D.   The Works of John H. Paton

Probably one of the most important and influential early Bible students associated with C.T. Russell was John H. Paton. Paton, the son of David Paton and Christiana Woodburn, was born April 7, 1843, at Galston, Scotland, and died on September 6, 1922, at Almont, MI. John and his wife, Sara Elizabeth Wilson, had six children.

Paton was involved in the Baptist Church until he encountered the ideas of the Adventists. His new ideas resulted in his disfellowshipping from that church, and he eventually affiliated himself with C.T. Russell. He supplied much of the impetus for the early Watchtower movement, and was highly influential in formulating early Watchtower doctrine. Paton had joined the Advent Christian Church with N.H. Barbour in about 1873 and was Barbour's assistant editor until June 1879 and continued to work with him after this (See *Herald of the Morning* June 1880 pp. 193-194), soon after 1879 became Russell's assistant editor. When Russell became acquainted with Barbour, he also became a close friend of Paton's.

Paton continued to write for the *Watch Tower* magazine (most of his articles are signed J.H.P. and he was listed on the inside cover as a regular contributor for a number of years) until 1881 when he split with Russell over several areas including the meaning of Christ's ransom. He then had a serious falling out with Russell. The first edition of his book *Day Dawn* was accepted as an official *Watch Tower* Publication, but the second and third editions were revised and were *not* accepted by Russell, and his followers were discouraged from buying or reading them. According to White (see Books about Witnesses), Russell arranged for Paton to write *Day Dawn* and for Jones to publish it.

Paton's leaving resulted in a great division in the early Watchtower because, aside from Russell, he was the most prominent Bible student of the time. Paton was to deviate even further from Russell's doctrine; he even accepted the idea of universal salvation of all mankind, sometimes called "Universal Reconciliation" or "Universalism." After Paton broke with Russell (his last article was published in the June 1881 *Watch Tower*) he began an ambitious publishing career, producing numerous books, booklets, and a monthly magazine for many years. Paton called his concern the *Larger Hope Publishing Company* ("larger hope" referring to his belief that many more were to be saved than most people believed). Although he was active in printing his literature and served as an itinerant preacher for a number of years (his personal diaries discuss his many activities in Michigan, Indiana, Ohio and nearby states), he never built up a large organization, and his ministry stopped when he died. He wrote his life story in 1915, a 19 page document he never published.

Several of Paton's relatives are still scattered in Almont, MI, Toledo, OH, and around the United States, but few of them know much about his important contributions to the early Watch Tower Society. Most know only that he was a newspaper and book publisher and that he was also a minister. Paton was the last of Russell's five original co-workers to break away (Jones, Adams, and Barbour had already split with Russell), and his work left an important mark on the Society, especially its chronology which concludes we are in the last days, and his basic theology, much of which is still accepted even today.

Publications by the Larger Hope Publishing Company (Almont, Michigan)

Books

Paton, John H. *The Day Dawn or the Gospel in Type and Prophecy.* Pittsburgh, PA: A.D. Jones, 1880, 334 pp., hb. (4,000 copies printed). This work was accepted as an official Watch Tower publication and the revised editions were regarded as heretical.

_____. *The World's Hope.* 1880 to Aug. 15, 1916, semi-monthly, 16 pp. Paton was one of the founders of the Watchtower Society.

_____. *The Day Dawn or the Gospel in Type and Prophecy.* 2nd ed. Almont, MI: The Larger Hope Publishing Co., 1882.

_____. *Moses and Christ.* Almont, MI: The Larger Hope Publishing Co., 1888, 222 pp., hb. (3,000 copies printed). Also a second and third edition were printed.

_____. *The Day Dawn or Gospel in Type and Prophecy.* 3rd ed., Almont, MI: The

Larger Hope Publishing Co., 1890, 399 pp.

_____. *The Perfect Day.* Almont, MI: The Larger Hope Publishing Co., 1892, 240 pp., hb. (3,000 copies printed).

_____. *The Great Revelation or God's Love, Purpose and Plan.* Almont, MI: The Larger Hope Publishing Co., 1896, 95 pp., hb. (Some copies include *Moses and Christ*).

_____. *Souvenir of Our Visits to Scotland and England.* Almont, MI: The Larger Hope Publishing Co., 1897, 126 pp. (A readable story account of Paton's visit to their country of origin and their experiences).

_____. *Paton Family History.* Almont, MI: privately printed, 1905, 412 pp., hb. (A detailed history of the family; contains many letters and much information on the family's religious beliefs).

_____. *John H. Paton: Autobiography.* Almont, MI: The Larger Hope Publishing Co., 1915. (On universal salvation and the destiny of the wicked).

Stray, Ermina C. *The Golden Link or The Shadow of Sin, A Story of Our Times.* Almont, MI: The Larger Hope Publishing Co., 418 pp., hb.

Booklets

Paton, John H. *The Atonement; Its Nature, and Extant.* Almont, MI: The Larger Hope Publishing Co., 1989, 96 pp. (On the purpose of Christ's death on the cross).

_____, and Thos. Williams. *The Paton-Williams Debate.* Chicago, IL: Advocate Publishing House. 1906, 38 pp. (A debate between Paton and Williams, a Christadelphian, on Universalism and the state of the unsaved). Reported by Pearl A. Power.

Articles Published by John H. Paton in *Herald of the Morning.* "Not of the World." Vol. 7, NO. 2, Aug. 1878, pp. 25-26; Extracts from Letters. Vol. 7, No. 2, Aug. 1878, p. 28; "Euphrates." Vol. 7, No. 3, Sept. 1878, pp. 37-39, "Light and Fellowship." Vol. 7, No. 4, Oct. 1878, pp. 54-55, "The Atonement." Vol. 7, No. 4, Oct. 1878, p. 56, "Atonement." Vol. 7, No. 6, Dec. 1878, pp. 89-91, "Thoughts on Law." Vol. 8, No. 1, Jan. 1879, pp. 10-11, "The Kingdom." Vol. 8, No. 2, Feb. 1879, pp. 31-32, "Exhortation." Vol. 8, No. 6, June 1879, pp. 95-97.

E. The Works by the Edgar Brothers (Glasgow, Scotland)

The Edgar brothers were active Bible students who wrote a great deal about the Great Pyramid "The Bible in Stone." John Edgar was a medical doctor (obstetrics and gynecology) and a long time associate of Russell. He was born in 1862 in Glasgow and educated in science and medicine, and died on June 9, 1910, at the age of 48 of acute appendicitis (see the *Watchtower* of July 15, 1910). He was appointed one of the surgeons to the Royal Samaritan Hospital for Women in 1896. The whole family-- including John's sons, Jack and Stanley and his wife Grace--later left the Society, but their pre c. 1928 publications were accepted as semi-official.

His conversion story is of much interest. While working in the hospital, a Mrs. Sarah Ferrie was sent to Dr. Edgar for a mental examination at the request of a neighbor. The neighbor was concerned that she had a mental disorder because she had said that she believed that Christ had returned, as was the Witness teaching then. Dr. Edgar, a Presbyterian at the time, not only concluded that she was mentally sound, but listened to her explanation as to why she believed that Christ had returned and found it convincing. Soon Sarah Ferrie returned with two other Witnesses, Jesse Hemery and a Mr. Houston. Hemery became the Watchtower branch office director for many years, although he left the Society and started another group in 1951, now called the *Goshen Fellowship*.

Not long after Dr. Edgar found an opportunity to read the *Divine Plan of the Ages* on a trip to the far north of Scotland and became convinced that Russell teachings were valid. He soon began devoting more time to the work of the Bible Students than his medical career, and was one of the first elders to be elected by the Glasgow class, publishing a number of booklets which became quite popular in Russell's movement. Many, though, covered subjects which Russell did not discuss, and some introduced ideas which were not fully in harmony with Russell's movement. The memoirs of Dr. John Edgar below discuss in detail his life and work.

Books

Edgar, John, and Morton Edgar. *The Great Pyramid, Passages and Chambers.* Vol. 1. Glasgow, Scotland: Bone & Hulley, 1910, 1913, 1923, 410 pp., hb.; also quality pocket edition (1910; 301 pp.). Reprinted by Berean Bible Students.

_____. *The Great Pyramid, Passages and Chambers.* Vol. 2. Glasgow, Scotland: Bone & Hulley, 1913, 329 pp., hb.; also quality pocket edition; also London, England: The Marshall Press, 1924, 310 pp., hb. Reprinted in 1976 by Berean Bible Students.

Edgar, Morton. *The Great Pyramid, Its Scientific Features: Part I of 1914 A.D. and the Great Pyramid.* Glasgow, Scotland; Maclure, MacDonald & Co., 1924, 217 pp., hb. Reprinted by Berean Bible Students in 1976.

_____. *The Great Pyramid, Its Time Features: Part II of 1914 A.D. and the Great Pyramid.* Glasgow, Scotland: Bone & Hulley, 1924, 180 pp., hb. Also published by Maclure and MacDonald, Glasgow.

_____. *The Great Pyramid, Its Spiritual Symbolism.* Glasgow, Scotland: Bone & Hulley, 1924, 137 pp., hb.

_____. *An Open letter on Bible Chronology* c. 1936 26 pages. (Written to defend Russell's chronology and attack the 1954 AD date for the second advent).

Booklets
(Most of these were reprinted by the Berean Bible Students in one volume).

Edgar, John. *Where Are the Dead?* Glasgow, Scotland: Hay, Nisbet and Co., Ltd., 48 pp.; another ed. c. 1909, 70 pp., hb., pb. (reprinted in 1949. Covers hell, the judgment, the resurrections, and God's plan for humankind. This was the booklet that interested Fred Franz in the Bible Student movement.)

_____. *Socialism and the Bible.* Glasgow, Scotland: Hay, Nisbet and Co., Ltd., n.d. [c. 1908].

_____. *A Tree Planted by the Rivers of Water.* Glasgow, Scotland: Hay, Nisbet and Co. Ltd., c. 1909, 32 pp., hb., pb.

_____. *The Preservation of Identity in the Resurrection.* Glasgow, Scotland: Hay, Nisbet and Co. Ltd., c. 1909, 24 pp., hb., pb.

_____. *Abraham's Life History: An Allegory.* Glasgow, Scotland: Hay, Nisbet and Co. Ltd., c. 1090, 42 pp., hb., pb.

Edgar, Minna. *Memoirs of Aunt Sarah.* Glasgow, Scotland, n.d., 60 pp., hb., pb.

_____. *Memoirs of Dr. John Edgar.* Glasgow, Scotland: Hay, Nisbet and Co. Ltd., n.d., 60 pp., hb., pb. (About Dr. Edgar's early life, his medical training, his conversion, his work for the Watchtower in Glasgow and his death; much information on the early history of the society in Scotland).

Edgar, Morton. *Faith's Foundations, Also Waiting on God.* Glasgow, Scotland: Hay, Nisbet and Co. Ltd., c. 1920, 66 pp., hb., pb.

_____. *Prayer and the Bible.* Glasgow, Scotland: Nisbet and Co., Ltd., c. 1920, 66 pp., hb., pb.

_____. *The Great Pyramid and the Bible.* Glasgow, Scotland: Hay, Nisbet and Co., Ltd., c. 1920, 50 pp., hb., pb. (A summary of how the Great Pyramid is God's record in stone, a Bible record to confirm the Bible as taught by Russell at the time).

_____. *Mythology and the Bible.* Glasgow, Scotland: Hay, Nisbet and Co. Ltd., n.d., 48 pp.

_____. *1914 A.D., and the Great Pyramid.* Glasgow, Scotland: Hay, Nisbet and Co. Ltd., n.d., 48 pp.

_____. *Abraham's Life History--An Allegory Mythology and the Bible Faith's Foundations.* Glasgow, Scotland: Hay, Nisbet and Co. Ltd., n.d., 48 pp.

_____. *The Restoration of Israel.* Glasgow, Scotland: Bone & Hulley, c. 1920, 19 pp.

_____. *The Pyramid Portrayal of Creation.* Glasgow, Scotland: Bone & Hulley, 1923, 64 pp.

_____. *The Great Pyramid.* Glasgow, Scotland: Hay, Nisbet and Co., c. 1925, 8 pp.

_____. *The Great Pyramid Portrayal of Creation.* Lantern Lecture. 1923, 63 pp.

_____. *The Great Pyramid Witness and the Biblical Plan of Salvation.* Glasgow, Scotland: Bone & Hulley, c. 1929, 19 pp., pb. (Swedish ed.: *Stora Pyramides Vittnesbord och Bibelns Fralningsplan*). Refutation of Rutherford's Nov. 15, 1928, *Watchtower.*

_____. *An Open Letter on Chronology.* N.d. 28 pp. Morton Edgar.

_____. *The Original Appearance of the Great Pyramid.* N.d. 8 pp. Morton Edgar.

F.   Material Related to the 1917 Crisis Following Pastor Russell's Death

These papers are related to the ongoing set of charges, refutations, and countercharges from 1917 to 1919 concerning Watchtower management problems and the seventh volume of *Studies in the Scriptures,* listed according to date of publication.

Pierson, A.N. Resolution of the Board of Directors of the Watchtower Bible and Tract

Society. Brooklyn, NY, July 17, 1917. Signed by A.N. Pierson, W.E. Spill, W.E. Van Amburgh, J.A. Bohnet, A.H. MacMillan, Geo. H. Fisher. Later inserted on first page of *Harvest Siftings* (below).

Wright, J.D., A.I. Ritchie, I.F. Hoskins, and R.H. Hirsh. Circular. Brooklyn, NY, July 27, 1917, 4 pp.

Rutherford, Joseph F. *Harvest Siftings.* Brooklyn, NY, August 1, 1917, 24 pp.

Pierson, A.N., et al. "Open Letter to Boston Conventioneers." Boston, MA, Aug. 4, 1917, by A.N. Pierson, J.D. Wright, A.I. Ritchie, I.F. Hoskins, R.H. Hirsh. Reprinted on p. 23 of *Light After Darkness* (below).

Philadelphia Ecclesia. Letter to J.F. Rutherford, also "sent to each member of the Board." Philadelphia, PA, Aug. 5, 1917. Published in *Light After Darkness* (below), p. 20.

Woodworth, C.J. *The Parable of the Penny.* Undated. Issued in the middle of Aug. 1917. (Tract), 6 pp.

McGee, Francis H. *An Open Letter to the Shareholders of the Society.* Freehold, NJ. Aug. 15, 1917. Published on pp. 15-19 in *Lotte After Darkness* (below), p. 10. Written to "Messrs. Pierson, Ritchie, Wright, Hoskins and Hirsh."

Fason, F.G. *Auditor's Letter to Shareholders.* 13 Cranberry St., Brooklyn, NY, Aug. 20, 1917. Published on p. 15 of *Light After Darkness* (below).

Cook, Frank F., and Charles R. Cos. Letter. Published "*In Behalf of the Truth and Christian Liberty*" Undated; later than Aug. 22, 1917, 2 pp.

Hemery, Jesse. "*Harvest Siftings Reviewed," itself reviewed.* 1917. 12 pp.

Ritchie, A.I., J.D. Wright, I.F. Hoskins, and R.H. Hirsh. *Light After Darkness: A Message to the Watchers, Being Refutation of Harvest Sifting.*

Rutherford, Joseph F. *Harvest Siftings, Part II* Brooklyn, NY, Oct. 1, 1917, 8 pp.

_____. "The Penny." *the Watchtower.* Brooklyn, NY, Oct. 1, 1917. Reprints, pp. 6149, 6150.

_____. "Charges Answered." *The Watchtower.* Brooklyn, NY, Oct. 15, 1917. Reprints, p. 6154.

_____. "The History and Operations of Our Society." *The Watchtower.* Brooklyn, NY, Nov. 1, 1917. Reprints, pp. 6161-6165.

Johnson, Paul S.L. *Harvest Siftings Reviewed.* Nov. 1, 1917, 20 pp. Later republished by the author in *Merariism* (1938), pp. 7-96.

Kuehn, E.O. "An Open Letter to the People of Lord Throughout the World and a Petition to Bro. Rutherford and the Four Deposed Directors of the W.T.B. & T. Society." Undated; issued Nov. 1-15, 1917, 3 pp. Signed by 156 members of the Brooklyn, NY, Ecclesia. Sent to the public with *Facts for Shareholders* (below).

Richie, A.I., J.D. Wright, I.F. Hoskins, and R.H. Hirsh. *Facts for Shareholders of the Watchtower Bible Tract Society.* Brooklyn, NY, Nov. 15, 1917, 16 pp.

Rutherford, J.F. "Some Reasons Why." *The Watchtower.* Brooklyn, NY, Nov. 15, 1917. Reprints, pp. 6166-6171.

_____. "Questions Relating to Voting." *The Watchtower.* Brooklyn, NY, Nov. 15, 1917. Reprints, p. 6173.

_____. "Privileges Now Great." *The Watchtower.* Brooklyn, NY, Dec. 1, 1917. Reprints, pp. 6184, 6185.

_____. "Important Notice." *The Watchtower.* Brooklyn, NY, Dec. 15, 1917. Reprints, pp. 6181.

_____. Referendum Vote." *The Watchtower.* Brooklyn, NY, Dec. 15, 1917. Reprints, pp. 6184, 6185.

Pierson, Andrew. "Vice President's Statement." *The Watchtower.* Brooklyn, NY, Jan. 1, 1918. Reprints, pp. 6197, 6198.

Rutherford, J.F. "Annual Meeting of Shareholders." *The Watchtower.* Brooklyn, NY, Jan. 15, 1918. Reprints, pp. 6201-6204.

_____. "Seeking to Cause Division" and "Our Reply." *The Watchtower.* Brooklyn, NY, Jan. 15, 1918. A published letter from "GMK" plus and official statement. Reprints, p. 6204.
_____. "Two Classes in the Church." *The Watchtower.* Brooklyn, NY, Feb. 15, 1918. Reprints, pp. 6211-5215, 5 pp.

_____. "Qualifications of Elders." *The Watchtower.* Brooklyn, NY, March 1, 1918. Reprints, pp. 6222, 6223.

_____. "A Warning to the Church." *The Watchtower.* Brooklyn, NY, March 1, 1918. Reprints, pp. 6222, 6223.

Wright, J.D., R.G. Jolly, P.S.L. Johnson, I.F. Hoskins, and R.H. Hirsh. "A Letter to International Bible Students." Brooklyn, NY, March 1, 1918, 4 pp.

Rutherford, J.F. "Sowers of Discord Among Brethren." *The Watchtower.* Brooklyn, NY, March 15, 1918. Reprints, pp. 6224, 6225. Subtitle of "The Great Shaking Now in Progress." March 15, 1918. Reprints, pp. 6223-6226.

_____. "Resolution of Loyalty." *The Watchtower.* Brooklyn, NY, March 15, 1918. Reprints, pp. 6227, 6227, Philadelphia Ecclesia, PA.

McGee, Francis H. "Not in Harmony." *The Watchtower.* Brooklyn, NY, March 14, 1918. Reprints, p. 6227.

The Bible Standard and Herald of Christ's Kingdom. Vol. 1, No. 1, Aug. 15, 1918, 16 p. Only this sample issue. Limited distribution July 26, 1918. Members of the issuing committee were Wright, Jolly, Johnson, Hoskins, and Hirsh.

Resolution of the Philadelphia Church, Philadelphia, PA. Aug. 18, 1918. Published in *Another Harvest Siftings Reviewed* (below), p. 11.

Johnson, Paul S.L. *Another Harvest Siftings Reviewed.* Philadelphia, PA, Aug. 22, 1918, 12 pp. by Paul S.L. Johnson with endorsement of R.H. Hirsh and R.G. Jolly. Essentially republished by the author in *Gershonism* (1938), pp. 89-131.

Wright, J.D. *The Committee Bulletin.* No. 1, Aug. 1918, 8 pp. by J.D. Wright, I.F. Hoskins, P.L. Greiner, F.F. Cook, I.I. Margeson, F.H. McGee, H.C. Rockwell.

McGee, Frances. H. "A Brief Review of Brother Johnson's Charges." Undated; accompanied the Aug. 1918 *Committee Bulletin* (above), 4 pp.

Rutherford, J.F. "Interesting Questions." *The Watchtower.* Brooklyn, NY, Sept. 1, 1918. Reprints, p. 6322.

Wright, J.D., I.F. Hoskins, P.L. Greiner, F.F. Cook, I.I. Margeson, F.H. McGee, and H.C. Rockwell. *The Committee Bulletin.* No. 2, Sept. 1918, 8 pp.

McGee, Francis. "A Timely Letter of Importance to All the Brethren." Freehold, NJ, Sept. 10, 1918, 8 pp. Accompanied the Sept. 1918 *Committee Bulletin* (above).

Wright, J.D., I.F. Hoskins, P.L. Greiner, F.F. Cook, I.I. Margeson, F.H. McGee, and H.C. Rockwell. *The Committee Bulletin.* No. 3, Oct. 1918, 8 pp.

Wright, J.D. *Charter of Pastoral Bible Institute, Inc.* Signed by the Directors, Nov. 20, 1918; J.D. Wright, I.I. Margeson, P.L. Greiner, H.C. Rockwell, I.F. Hoskins, F.H. McGee, E.J. Pritchard. Published by Paul S.L. Johnson in *The Present Truth,* March 17, 1919, pp. 55, 56, and *Gershonism,* 1938, pp. 188-195.

"Re-Election and Proxies." The Watchtower. Pittsburgh, PA, Dec. 1, 1918. Reprints, p. 6366.

The Herald of Christ's Kingdom. No. 1, Dec. 1, 1918. The Pastoral Bible Institute. Editorial Committee of Five. First issue of regular monthly.

"Resolution." Dec. 1, 1918. The Philadelphia Ecclesia. Published by Paul S.L. Johnson in *The Present Truth,* Dec. 9, 1918 (Below), p. 24.

Johnson, Paul S.L., ed. *The Present Truth and Herald of Christ's Epiphany.* Philadelphia, PA, No. 1, Dec. 9, 1918, 24 pp.

Rutherford, J.F. "Varied Experiences a Blessing." *The Watchtower.* Pittsburgh, PA, Dec. 15, 1918. Reprints, p. 6367, Dec. 15, 1918.

Johnson, Paul S.L., ed. *The Present Truth and Herald of Christ's Epiphany.* Philadelphia, PA, No. 2, Dec. 24, 1918, 8 pp.

_____. Letter to the Philadelphia Ecclesia. *The Present Truth,* March 17, 1919, pp. 59, 60, and *Gershonism,* 1938, pp. 215-217.

Wright, J.D. *A Brief Review of Brother Johnson's Charges.* Bayonne, NJ, privately printed 1918.

G. Publications Protesting Current Watchtower Practices and Doctrine

This group of papers is by individuals protesting various practices of the Society. Chris Christensen wrote two "pronouncements" (1974-1975) protesting the current harsh and what he considered unjust disfellowshipping practices. He called for open meetings in disfellowshipping cases so as to allow other Witnesses to be present as well, and other changes in the current system to be more like the secular judicial system, among other organizational changes. These papers were very well written and caused much dissension in the Witness congregations in the United States, Canada, Europe, and Australia. Ironically, scores of disfellowshippings occurred as a result of these pronouncements.

Christensen, a highly respected younger Witness who had made several contributions to the Society's publications before he wrote his tracts, was soon disfellowshipped. He had been having a number of discussion meetings with several Witnesses, and the Circuit Overseer and others objected.

Christensen took the Society to court, claiming, among other things, that the Society did not follow its own procedure rules and that he was unjustly disfellowshipped. The courts, while acknowledging the validity of his claims, declined to rule in his favor, partly because they concluded that the disfellowshipping occurred outside the secular court's jurisdiction and that the state has no authority over these kinds of church affairs.

The Olin Moyle letter is quite important in that it was printed to protest certain allegedly immoral practices of the Society, and it resulted in the Society's publishing several articles against Moyle. Moyle brought suit for slander and won $30,000 in damages (later reduced on appeal to $15,000; see the section on Moyle).

The Walter Salter and Harvey Fink tracts are also important in that both Fink and Salter were well-known Witnesses, and their leaving caused no little discussion. The booklets by Weinz, Pawling, Gigliotti, etc., are primarily resignation letters distributed to a large number of persons or printed in semi-tract form and then distributed.

Alfandari, M. *We Bear Witness!* N.d., 2 pp., typed.

Amboy, Charles. *Response to the Pronouncements.* 1975, 13 pp., typed.

Bundy, Walter H., ed. *Studies in the Scriptures.* Los Angeles, Cal.: Concordant Publishing Concern, c. 1920, 160 pp., pb.

Christensen, Chris. *A Pronouncement: Concerning Justice for Jehovah's People.* 1974, 11 pp., typed and printed. Sent to thousands of Witnesses in the United Stated, Canada, Europe, and Australia.

_____. *The Second Pronouncement Concerning Justice for Jehovah's People.* 1975, 20 pp., typed and printed. Sent to thousands of Witnesses in the United States, Canada, Europe, and Australia. This paper caused many persons to leave the Society and also caused many internal problems.

Fink, Harvey H. *An Open Letter to Jehovah's Witnesses.* 1940, 2 pp. Fink was a prominent Witness and a Zone servant. In this 2-page typeset tract, he briefly outlines why he left the Society.

Fleming, Harold. *Observation.* 1975, 4 pp. Attempts to resolve some of the problems raised by the pronouncements.

Gigliotti, Carman. *The Watchtower Society and Jehovah's Witnesses--The Big Lie.* N.d., 4 pp.

Gula, Michael. *Did the Watchtower Society Prophesy That Armageddon Would Occur in 1914?* N.d., c. 1978, 2 pp.

Inqui, Louis (Samuel). *Warning: Jehovah's Witnesses?* N.d., 1 p. The purpose of this letter, sent to thousands of Kingdom Halls in the United States, is not clear.

McGee, Ingram A. (pseudonym). "The Organizational Crisis in the Watchtower Society Following Russell's Death. Watchtower Presentations Corrected." March 1979, 38 pp., unpublished manuscript typed.

McKinney, Carlespie. *The Glorification of the Holy Ones--Its Timing & Nature.* 1975, 8 pp. A discussion which attempts to answer some of the questions raised in the Pronouncements.

Moyle, Olin R. *Information Vital to Jehovah's Witnesses.* 1940, 4 pp., typeset letter. See also publications and discussion under *The Bible Examiner*, Section 4, below.

Pawling, James W. *Resignation Letter.* Jan. 1976, 18 pp., mimeographed.

Reed, Joseph. *The Wild Beast.* 1977, 10 pp. (A discussion of prophecy in the Book of Revelation and current Witness problems).

_____. Untitled (about disfellowshipping). Rosedale, B.C., Canada, n.d. (c. 1977), 4 pp.

_____. (about the situation in Malawi). N.d., (c. 1978), 3 pp.

_____. *Daniel the Prophet, the "Two Witnesses" of Revelation and Jehovah's Witnesses on 1980, where Do They All Fit In?* Rosedale, B.C., Canada: pub. by author, 1980, 8 pp.

_____. "The Great Tribulation" and "Kingdom Against Kingdom." Part II. Rosedale, B.C., Canada: pub. by author, April 1981, 16 pp.

_____. *Hello Richard* (about disfellowshipping). Rosedale, B.C., Canada, Oct. 1981, 12 pp.

Salter, Walter F. *Letter to J.F. Rutherford.* Toronto, Ont., Canada, 1937, 4 pp. (see also publications under Walter Salter directly below).

Weinz, John. *John Weinz to Jehovah's Witnesses.* 1941, 8 pp. Discusses why John Weinz left the Witnesses.

Wysong, Randy et al. *Questions.* 1975, 20 pp. Reprinted as *A Personal Letter from a Presiding Overseer, To All Jehovah's Witnesses in Good Standing.* 28 pp.; also as *Dear Brothers and Sisters,* 13 pp.

H. Walter Salter's Publications

Walter Salter became a member of the International Bible Student Association in about 1913. In 1918, the President, J.F. Rutherford, asked him to direct the work in Canada as the Canadian general manager (today called the branch head or overseer). Disagreements soon occurred over continual changes in doctrine and the teachings of things such as "was it appropriate to 'lie' if the work of the Watchtower Society could thereby be furthered," etc. In addition, Salter was somewhat independent; as his wife put it, "always he expressed his own convictions but not always were they letter perfect with the Watchtower, though he was never really out of line with it." For a number of years, though, Salter was able to express his views without any problems.

In time, rumors circulated that Walter himself was somewhat autocratic and hard to get along with, and behaved "improperly" toward female Bethel members. These charges, however, were never proved. Finally, in the winter of 1935-1936, unknown to Salter, Rutherford sent several persons to travel with him and "report on what he said in his lectures" (letter from Mrs. Salter, Jan. 30, 1974; also *The Watchtower,* 1939, p. 120). On the basis of these reports, in May 1936, Rutherford "abolished the office of Canadian General Manager quite suddenly, consequently, Salter was out of his position" (letter from Mrs. Salter). Rutherford then appointed Chapman as head of the Canadian branch.

For a period of nine months thereafter, Salter continued as a "class worker" with the Toronto Bible class. But his continued study alienated him from the Witnesses and eventually, in February 1937, he wrote an article stating that Christ had not returned in 1874 as taught at that time by the Society. At Rutherford's instigation, he was immediately disfellowshipped by the Toronto class for, interestingly, holding beliefs that are accepted today by Witnesses. Most of his beliefs are summarized in his book, *Truth As I See It.*

Salter's leaving caused quite a commotion in the Watchtower Society, partly because he was well known and highly respected throughout Canada, and the Canadian branch was then one of the largest. It was evident that the situation affected Rutherford greatly, so much so that several *Watchtower* and *Golden Age* articles were written about the situation. Some of these articles did not refer to Salter by name, but they unquestionably identified him. See *The Watchtower* (May 5 1937, pp. 159, 207; and 1939, pp. 117-126) and *Golden Age* (1937, pp. 498-507, 594-597) all which directly or indirectly condemned Salter. Fortunately for the *Golden Age* writer (probably Clayton J. Woodworth) Salter did not take legal action as did Olin Moyle.

After he left the Society, Salter spent the rest of his life doing independent Bible research and publishing various articles. Although he never formally started a group of his own, many agreed with his views and read his publications. He remained close to the Witness theology, but departed on some major points (he evidently embraced the theory of universal salvation). He died in April 1970 at the age of 86.

Book

Truth As I See It. Haliburton, Ont., Canada, 1959, 128 pp., pb. (A summary of Salter's views, especially those in contrast to the Society).

Tracts

Letter to J.F. Rutherford. Toronto, Ont., Canada, April 1937, 4 pp. A typeset copy of a letter to Rutherford in which he explains why he left the Society. He discusses Rutherford's lavish spending on penthouses, his 16-cylinder automobiles, and his $75,000 mansion (a fortune in 1937). Salter also offers an excellent discussion on the failure of the 1924 and 1925 prophecies.
Our Lord's Return to Israel. Los Angeles, CA: Concordant Publishers, n.d., 4 pp.
What Constitutes One a Christian? Haliburton, Ont., Canada, n.d., 1 p.
My Blind Servant. Haliburton, Ont., Canada, n.d., 1 p.
Christ the Seed of Promise. Haliburton, Ont., Canada, n.d., 1 p.
Christianity. Haliburton, Ont., Canada, n.d., 1 p.
Many False Christs; Matt. 24:11, 24. Haliburton, Ont., Canada, n.d., 1 p.
Israel, God's Chosen. Haliburton, Ont., Canada, n.d., 1 p.
The Kingdom of God Is at Hand--Jacob at War! Haliburton, Ont., Canada, n.d., 1 p.
Rightly Divide. Haliburton, Ont., Canada, n.d., 1 p.
Workers of Iniquity. Haliburton, Ont., Canada, n.d., 1 p.
Faith. Haliburton, Ont., Canada, n.d., 1p.
Perilous Times Shall Come. Haliburton, Ont., Canada, n.d., 1 p.

G. J. Salter (Mrs. Walter Salter)

Booklets

A Few Thoughts on the Scriptures. Haliburton, Ont., Canada, 1982, 51 pp.
The Human Paternity of Jesus Demonstrated. Haliburton, Ont., Canada: G.J. Salter Pub., 1983, 25 pp.

Tracts

He As God Sitteth in the Temple of God. Haliburton, Ont., Canada, n.d., 1 p.;
The Source and the Solution. Haliburton, Ont., Canada, n.d., 1 p.;*Christ and Moses.*
Haliburton, Ont., Canada, n.d., 1 p.;*Man's Destiny.* Haliburton, Ont., Canada, n.d., 1
p.;*Babylon.* Haliburton, Ont., Canada, n.d., 1 p.;*God.* Haliburton, Ont., Canada, n.d.,
1 p.;*The Coming World Government.* Haliburton, Ont., Canada, n.d., 1 p.;*Hope and
Expectation.* Haliburton, Ont., Canada, n.d., 1 p.;*Truth vs. Religion.* Haliburton, Ont.,
Canada, n.d., 1 p.;*World Government.* Haliburton, Ont., Canada, c. 1983, 1 p.;*Who
Are the Khazar Jews?* Haliburton, Ont., Canada, 5 pp.;*The Invisible God.* Haliburton,
Ont., Canada, 1985, 6 pp.

I. Maria Frances Russell (Mrs. C.T. Russell)

In 1879 Russell married Maria Frances Ackley, whom he met at one of his Bible
classes. She was a bright, petite, attractive well educated woman, and wrote many of the
early *Watchtower* articles and large sections in the *Studies in the Scriptures* . She was also
a director and served as secretary and treasurer for the Watchtower for many years, and
also as an associate editor of the Watchtower. Their major split came in 1897 after 18
years of marriage. After Mr. and Mrs. Russell separated, (no absolute divorce was ever
granted) she wrote several tracts on her views and on her side of the split with her
husband. She also wrote two books, both which advocated women's rights The 1975
Yearbook report on their divorce, which cost the movement thousands of followers, is as
follows:

> ... at C.T. Russell's funeral at Pittsburgh in 1916 ... Anna K. Gardner, whose
> recollections are similar to those of others present, tells us this: "An incident
> occurred just before the services at Carnegie Hall that refuted lies told in the paper
> about Brother Russell. The hall was filled ... and then a veiled figure was seen to
> walk up the aisle to the casket and to lay . . on it. . . . a bunch of lilies of the
> valley, Brother Russell's favorite flower. There was a ribbon attached, saying, 'To
> My Beloved Husband.' It was Mrs. Russell. They had never been divorced and
> this was a public acknowledgement."

Mrs. Russell was also reported as being in the funeral cortege that followed the coffin to
the grave side (letter from William Abbott to his wife published in the *St. Paul Enterprise*,
Volume 7, Number 17, November 14, 1916. Evidently C. T. Russell actually reviewed
her book 'The Twain One' in the *Pittsburgh Leader* (October 13, 1906 and in the magazine
section of October 14, 1906). Russell, as recorded in his 'divorce trial' transcript, was
asked by a reporter about Maria's work, and a newspaper article was the result. (see
transcript from the April 1907 hearing). Maria was reported to have spent her last years
being cared for by her niece Mabel Packard and died in 1938. (Maria's sister, Emma, was
Joseph Lytel Russell's second wife, and their daughter Mabel, born 1882 married Richard
Packard). The Packard family evidently inherited Maria's unpublished manuscripts.

Books

This Gospel of the Kingdom. Allegheny, PA, privately printed, 1906, 100 pp. (Mrs.
    Russell's doctrinal ideas; covers the harvest, last days, the kingdom and topics
    related to the end and Christ's return).

The Twain One. Allegheny, PA. Privately printed, 1906, 100 pp. (About religion and women's rights; focuses on women's role in marriage, and the scriptural family).

BOOKS, MANUSCRIPTS, TRACTS AND NEWSLETTERS

This section is divided into books, dissertations, booklets, chapters of books, tracts, unpublished manuscripts, newsletters, reviews, and court cases. All of this material specifically discusses Jehovah's Witnesses, although a few of these works may also cover the offshoots of the Watch Tower or related groups. Aside from the publications issued by the offshoots themselves, there is very little literature about these groups.

Although this section is not exhaustive, an effort has been made to list all of the more important literature and almost every book about the Witnesses from 1879 to 1992. Most of the literature listed is in the compiler's personal library. Some references, however, were obtained from secondary sources, and for this reason the citations are sometimes incomplete. Much of this literature is rare and extremely difficult to find. Only about one-hundred copies of Timothy White's important classic, *A People for His Name*, were printed, and this is one of the best scholarly books about the Witnesses ever written.

To obtain references for this bibliography, the author visited dozens of large libraries throughout the United States, Canada, and Europe and has corresponded with several score of authors of books or articles about the Witnesses. He has also consulted the Watchtower Society's libraries in Brooklyn, Toronto, London, Paris, and the Netherlands.

A. Books

This section includes most all books specifically about Jehovah's Witnesses published from their founding in 1879 to date. Also included are most of the foreign-language books about the Witnesses, including those published in Turkish, Russian, Spanish, French, German, Swedish, and other languages. A book is defined here as printed matter of generally more than 90 pages that is perfect bound (glued, as a phone book) or sewn (the more quality books). Both hardbound and paperback books were included. Except those in other alphabets, such as Russian and Chinese, the titles given in this section were exactly as listed on the book cover. All non-English alphabet titles were translated by the Library of Congress or the author into English letters. Also, titles of most of the foreign-language books were translated into English, with the translated title given after the publication data.

Of these books, almost all were written either by former Witnesses or non-Witnesses who oppose the Society, and the tone or viewpoint of most is anti-Watchtower. Most of these works concentrate on Witness doctrine, and as a group are greatly repetitious. Only eighteen were authored by Witnesses who were still active in the movement when they wrote--the volumes by Anonymous, Alfs, Blackwell, Buckley, Byatt, Carr, Cole, Dahl, Dalgleish, Felderer, Hess, Macmillan, Penton, Reppas, Stafford, Walter, White and Zucher.

Of these, all of the authors except Macmillan (who died shortly after he completed his book), and as far as I know Buckley, Byatt, Carr, Cole (actually Cole's book was a joint effort with the Watchtower, the Society being the final authority) Dahl, Dalgleish, Reppas and Stafford experienced a falling out with the Watchtower soon after their work was published. As discussed, the Watchtower has historically manifested very little tolerance toward those who write books, even if they are extremely favorable to the Watchtower point of view and are doctrinally "correct."

The first Cole book, *Jehovah's Witnesses: The New World Society* was written to facilitate a pro-Society book being placed in public libraries and sold to the general public. The Society openly advertised and marketed this work. Cole's other five books were written on his own, and even though they are also all pro-Society, they were far less successful then his first, primarily because the Society did not "authorize" or publicize them. Although the second book created some difficulties for Cole with the Society, he is still an active Witness. In addition, Cole wrote a number of articles in magazines such as *Nation, Color,* etc., which are blatantly pro-Watchtower and, interestingly, pro-education. Cole has taken great pains in both his book *Triumphant Kingdom* and his other writings to picture Witnesses as intelligent, well-educated, informed, aware persons, and some who hold high positions in secular society. His third book, *Living Destiny,* is an excellent translation of the story of Christ from the four Gospels, but sold poorly compared to his first book. His last book published in 1997 is the story of his life.

Although most items are annotated, the title is often indicative of the tone and scope of the work. About 80% of the works are primarily theological, and although all of the English-language books except those written by Witnesses mentioned above are essentially critical of the Watchtower movement, the works by authors that include Beckford, Czatt, Felderer, Manwaring, Stevens, and Rogerson are somewhat neutral, but more sociological and historical than theological.

Many excellent academic studies are now in print, mostly by sociologists and political scientists. Recommended are the works by Manwaring, Pike, Stevens, Rogerson, Harrison, Beckford, Stevenson, White, and the 1945 classic by Stroup, which was in print until recently. Also useful, especially for those with a theological background, are the works of Gruss and Sadlack and the classics by Schnell. The theological works are often difficult for the layman to follow, even those with a good background in Biblical studies.

Book reviews are listed under the name of the book's author, not the reviewer, since in a number of cases the reviewer is not known, and generally one is more likely to be aware of the name of the author of the book being reviewed than of the reviewer's name.

Alfs, Matthew. *Concepts of Father, Son and Holy Spirit.* Minneapolis, MN: Old
Theology Book House, 1984, 104 pp. Pp. 62-73 specifically discusses the
Witnesses. (On the history of the trinity and related doctrines written when Alfs
was an active Witness. Alfs favors the Watchtower position in this very well done
work. This is the first volume of a two-volume series.)

_____. *The Evocative Religion of Jehovah's Witnesses.* Minneapolis, MN: Old
Theology Book House, 1990, 518 pp. (An extremely well-referenced work--224
pages are text, and 294 pages are notes and index--little discussion of doctrine,
much of history, the custody and blood issues, their stand on war, the flag salute,
etc.)

Algermissen, Konrad. *Christliche Sekten und Kirche Christi.* Hannover, J. Giesel,
1925, 532 pp. (Christian sects and churches of Christ). (in German).

_____. *Die Internationale Vereinigung Ernster Bibleforscher.* Hannover: J. Giesel,
1928, 78 pp. (The International Union of Serious Bible Researchers).

Allgeier, Arthur. *Religiöse Volksströmungen der Gegenwart. Über die "Ernsten
Bibelforscher," und andere.* Freiburg, Herder und Co., 1924, 154 pp. (Modern
religious movements. About the "Earnest Bible Students" and others). (in
German).

Amaya, Ismael E. *Los Falsos Profetas de Jehová: La Verdad Acerca de los Testigos de
Jehova.* Buenos Aires, Argentina: Methopress, 1964, 150 pp. (The false
prophets of Jehovah) (Covers mostly doctrine and some history, from an
Evangelical world view).

Anonymous. *1,000 Years Well Spent: 1942-1946.* 1947, 112 pp., pb. (About the
Jehovah's Witnesses war resistors in the Chillicothe, Ohio Federal Prison; written
by a Witness about their prison experience).

Aros, Robert. *Beyond Courage* (with Rob Ternan). 277 pp. (About a witness family that
was shipwrecked for 28 days in the South Pacific. First told in the Sept. 1983
Readers Digest).

Arrinda, Donato, et al. *Testigos de Jehova.* Berriz, Vizcaya: pub. by author, 1977, 157
pp. (Jehovah's Witnesses).

Arzamazov, Vasilli Petrovich. *The True Face of Jehovah's Witnesses.* Irkutsk: Siberian
Publishing House, 1964, 160 pp. (in Russian).

Assenbergh, S.P. van. *De valse godsdienst der Jehovah's Getuigen.* Dordrecht, Van den
Tol, 1976, 136 pp., Dutch, 4th printing. (The false religion of the Jehovah's
Witnesses).

Axup, Edward J. *The Jehovah's Witnesses Unmasked.* New York: Greenwich Book
Publishers, 1959, 77 pp., hb. (A critique of the standard 1950s Watchtower
books such as "Let God Be True" from a fundamentalist's view. The book has
many errors.)

Barefoot, Darek. *Jehovah's Witnesses and the Hour of Darkness; Occult Subversion and
Blind Faith in the Watchtower Society.* Grand Junction, CO: Grand Valley Press,
1992. (The story of Barefoot's conclusion that occult drawings were hidden in
Watchtower publications and his disfellowshipping for trying to bring this to the
Watchtower's attention).

Barkley, Betty. *Jehovah's Garden* 40 pp. (Poetry written by a Witness for a Witness; on
Watchtower Theology).

Barnes, Peter. *Out of Darkness Into Light.* San Diego, CA: Counter Cult Ministries, 1984, 138 pp. (An excellent review of Watchtower history and doctrine by a former high level Watchtower official, a circuit overseer turned Evangelical Christian).

_____. *A Jehovah's Witness Finds the Truth in Jesus Christ.* Equippers, Inc., 1985, 138 pp.

Barnett, Maurice. *Jehovah's Witnesses: History, Organization, Doctrines and Deity of Christ.* Vol. I. Cullman, AL: Printing Service, n.d., (c. 1975), 96 pp., pb. (A well written history and critique of Watchtower doctrines; includes many photocopies or reprints of key Watchtower documents).

_____. *Jehovah's Witnesses: Nature of Man, Death, Resurrection, Dual Classes, Eternal Punishment.* Vol. II. Cullman, AL: Printing Service n.d. (c. 1975), 91 pp., pb. (Refutes major doctrines, Also includes a photocopy of *Life and Death* by Alexander Campbell, 1930, 48 pp., which deals with Witness doctrine).

Barney, Dan. See Quidam, Roger in this section.

Barrett, Arthur, and Duane Magnani. *From Kingdom Hall to Kingdom Come.* Clayton, CA: Witness, Inc., 1982, 79 pp., pb. (A critique on doctrine and history, includes many photocopies of Watchtower publications).

Bartoshevish, Eduard Mikhailovich. *In the Name of Jehovah God.* Moscow: State Publishing House of Political Literature, 1960, 158 pp. (In Russian).

_____. *Jehovah's Witnesses.* Moscow: Political Publishing House (Library of Contemporary Religions), 1969, 216 pp. (In Russian).

Beckford, James A. *The Trumpet of Prophecy.* A Sociological Study of Jehovah's Witnesses. Oxford, England: Basil H. Blackwell, 1975, 244 pp., hb.; New York: Halsted Press, 1975. (An excellent sociological study of the Witnesses based on Beckford's Ph.D. thesis; covers history, organization structure, the life of Witnesses and some doctrine.)

Beijer, Erik. *Falska Profeter: Ett ord om "Jehovas Vitten."* Stockholm, Sweden: Bolm and Soner Baktrycheri AB, 1948, 84 pp. Reprinted by Svenska Kyrkans Diakonistyrelses Bokforlag of Stockholm, Sweden, 1955, 95 pp., pb. (False Prophets: A Word on "Jehovah's Witnesses") (In Swedish) (Covers history, doctrine, life style, and the many prophetic failures of the Watchtower).

Beproeft de Geesten. *Hedendaagsch stromingen op religieus gebied.* 2nd ed. Amsterdam, Uitgeverij Holland, 1939, 349 pp. (Prove the Spirits. Present-days streamings and dominions)

Bergman, Jerry, *Jehovah's Witnesses and Kindred Groups: A Historical Compendium and Bibliography.* New York: Garland Press, 1984. (A comprehensive bibliography of literature by and about the Watchtower and its many offshoots.)

_____ (Ed). *Jehovah's Witnesses I: The Early Writings of J.F. Rutherford.* Sources for the Study of Nonconventional Religious Groups in Nineteenth-and Twentieth-Century America. New York: Garland Press, 1990. (A reprint of many of the major booklets authored by Rutherford.)

_____ (Ed). *Jehovah's Witnesses II: Controversial and Polemical Pamphlets.* Sources for the Study of Nonconventional Religious Groups in Nineteenth-and Twentieth-Century America. New York: Garland Press, 1990.(A reprint of some of the more important critiques of the Watchtower.)

_____. *The Mental Health of Jehovah's Witnesses,* Clayton, CA: Witnesses Inc.,

1986. (A study of the mental illness problems of the Witnesses; includes many case histories, a review of the literature.)

_____. *Zur seelischen Gesundheit von Zeugen Jehovas.* Germany: Druck Bielefeld. 80p. 1991.

_____. *Jehovah's Witnesses and the Problem of Mental Health.* Introduction by Dr. Carol Thornton, Prof. of Psychology, GMI, Flint, MI. Clayton, CA: Witnesses, Inc., 1992, 342 pp. (An extensive study of the mental health problems of the Witnesses and why mental health and crime are serious problems).

_____. *Jehovas Zeugen und das Problem der seelischen.* München: Claudius Verlag, 1994, . Translated by Dr. Helmut Lasarcyk. 88p. German (Jehovah Witnesses and the Problem of Mental Health)

_____. *Blood Transfusions: A History and Evaluation of the Religious Biblical and Medical Objections.* Intro. by Dr. Robert Finnerty. Clayton, CA: Witness Inc., 1994, 208p. Cover by David Merrick.

_____. *I Testimoni De Blutransfusion.* München: Claudius Verlag, 1995.

_____. *I Testimoni De Geova E La Salute Mentale.* Introduction by Dr. Maurizio Antonello, Psicologo (psychologists) Roma: Edizioni Dehoniane 1996. pp. 394. Largely a translation of *Jehovahs Witnesses and the Problem of Mental Health.*

Beverly, James A. *Crisis of Allegiance: A Study of Dissent Among Jehovah's Witnesses.* Burlington, Ontario, Canada, Welch pub. Co. Inc., 1986, 142 pp. (A detailed account of the Feb. 1981 disfellowshipment of Dr. James Penton and the resulting major schisms in the Watchtower that occurred primarily in Canada. The author is a college professor interested in religious affairs.)

Bjernstad, James. *Counterfeits at Your Door.* Glendale, CA: A Division of G/L Publications, 1979, 160 pp. (Discusses both Mormons and Jehovah's Witnesses; some good material but many inadequacies; basically discusses theology from an evangelical position.)

Blackwell, Victor V. *O'er the Ramparts THEY Watched.* New York: Carlton Press, 1976, 246 pp., hb. Revised edition 1983, 234 pp. (Monette, MO: Stoups Mfg. Co.). (In the new edition, many corrections were made and several sections revised. An excellent history of the Witnesses many legal battles. The author is a Witness attorney who was active in many of the cases he reviews.)

Blanche, Bernard. *Les Temoins De Jehovah Un siecle d'histoire.* Paris: Desclee de Brouwer, 1987. (Jehovah's Witnesses; A Century of History) (in French) (A scholarly history of the Watchtower movement in general, focusing on its activities in France).

Bond, M.R. *Thy Word Is Truth.* Abington, MA, 1905, 114 pp.

Botting, Heather and Gary Botting. *The Orwellian World of Jehovah's Witnesses.* Toronto, Canada: University of Toronto Press, 1984, 213 pp. hb., pb. (Extensive comparisons between the Orwell's book *1984* and the Witnesses. Adapted from a Ph.D. thesis in Anthropology done by Heather at the University of Alberta, Canada. Gary was a professor of English, and was terminated due to his defense of freedom of speech in Canada; he is now an attorney. Both Gary and Heather were raised Witnesses).

_____. *Fundamental freedoms and Jehovah's Witnesses* Calgary; University of Calgary Press 1993, 214p. (Covers mostly the Canadian history of the many Watchtower conflicts with the government; provides much insight, partly because of the author's background as a witness.)

Bowman, Robert M. *Jehovah's Witnesses, Jesus Christ, and the Gospel of John.* Grand
Rapids: Baker Book House, 1989, 165 pp., pb. (A critique of the Witnesses
doctrines that contradict evangelicals.)

_____. *Understanding Jehovah's Witnesses; Why They Read the Bible the Way They
Do.* Grand Rapids: Baker Book House, 1991, 165 pp. (A study of Watchtower
Hermeneutical theory, their use of the divine name in the New World Translation).

Bowser, Arthur. *What Every Jehovah's Witness Should Know.* Denver, CO: B/P
Publications, 1975, 65 pp., pb. (A critique of the Watchtower view of Christ, the
soul, Satan and the trinity).

Bradley, M.C., ed. *Criticisms of Pastor Russell and the International Bible Students
Association.* Elmhurst, IL: Elmhurst Press, Inc., 1914, 82 pp., pb. (Written in
support of Russell, and Russell's doctrines and person, much excellent material
which shows that many of the attacks against Russell were often unethical and just
plain wrong).

Bregning, Poul. *Jehovas Vidner Under Anklage.* Kobenhaven: Hans Reitzel, 1966, 248.
(Jehovah's Witnesses Under Pressure) (in Swedish). (Covers early history and
scandals, doctrine and social factors).

Briem, Efraim. *Jehovas Vittnen.* Stockholm, Sweden: Bokforlaget Natur Och Kultur,
1944; 2nd ed. 1951, 79 pp., pb. (Jehovah's Witnesses). (In Swedish). (Covers
early history, scandals, doctrine and social factors).

Brown, Jim, Darlene Miller and Steve Cannon. *Jesus Loves the Jehovah's Witness.*
Scottsdale, AZ: Christian Communications, Inc., 1976, 86 pp., pb. (Critiques
Witness doctrine; all three authors are evangelicals, Miller is an ex-Witness;
focuses on the Arian controversy and the trinity today.)

Buckley, J.A. *Second Century Orthodoxy.* Cornwall, Great Britain: pub. by author,
1978, 115 pp., hb. (Buckley is a Witness; about the early Christians and their
similarity to modern Witnesses)

Busch, Johannes. *Das Sektenwesen unter besonderer Berüchsichtigung der Ernsten
Bibelforscher.* Hildesheim: Verlag Fr. Borgmeyer, 1929, 359 pp. (The Nature of
Religious Sects with Special Consideration of the Jehovah's Witnesses).

Byatt, Anthony. *Building a Theocratic Library.* 1997. Malvern, Wores: Golden Age
Books. 80 pp. (Self Published by a Witness as a guide to books for Witnesses).

_____. *New Testament Metaphors: Illustrations in Word and Phase.* Edinburgh: The
Pentland Press.1995. (A dictionary of the meaning of new testament illustrations
by an active Witnesses, although this is not obvious)

Callwood, June. *Jim; A Life With AIDS.* Canada: Lester and Orpen Denny's Publ.,
1988, 310 pb. (The story of a Canadian Witness who, on the surface, had an ideal
Witness marriage and life, but his unhappiness forced him to leave his wife, and
come out of the closet. He eventually contracted AIDS, and became the longest
AIDS patient then to survive in Canada.)

Carr, Firpo W. *A History of Jehovah's Witnesses: From a Black American Perspective,*
Hawthorne, CA: Scholar Technological Institute of Research, 1993, 470 pp. plus
index. (Tries to show that the Watchtower was not biased against blacks in its
history, many case histories, much on Michael Jackson and other black
entertainers; bluntly pro Watchtower and often poorly researched.)

_____.*The Divine Name Controversy.* Corporate Pub. Services. Fremont, CA: 1991, 246 pp., Vol. 1. (presents the case for a "hidden code in the Hebrew text regarding" the name Jehovah. Much history about Carr's personal life.)

_____.*Search the Sacred Name* Aurora. MO Stoops Pub. Co. 1993, 177 pp. (An autobiography account of Carr's life and his search for the pronunciation of YHWH much on his trip to the old USSR and other countries.)

Carter, Nickie. *Grand Horizon.* Aurora, MO. Stoops Pub. Co. 1993 pb.127 pp. (About Ruth Johnson, a former W.A.S.P. WWII Airforce pilot who later in life became a Jehovah's Witness.) She earned her pilots license at 16 and had an "obsession for flying." Also covers her disfellowshipping and some of the problems in the Watchtower

Cetnar, William, and Joan Cetnar. *Questions for Jehovah's Witnesses.* Phillipsburg, NJ: Presbyterian and Reformed Pub. Co., 1983, 72 pp. (By use of photocopies the authors confirm many ethical and doctrinal problems of the Watchtower; much material not found elsewhere).

Chretien, Leonard and Marjorie Chretien. *Witnesses of Jehovah.* Eugene, OR: Harvest House, 1988, 219 pp. (An excellent critique of the Watchtower movement from an evangelical standpoint by two ex-Witnesses; well documented and much history included similar in content to their movie by the same name.)

Church, Gene. *No Man's Blood.* Fullerton, CA: Institute of Bloodless Medicine and Surgery, 1982, 268 pp. (A pro-Witness work about the life of Ron Lapin, M.D. a non-Witness who has found a unique niche in surgery doing bloodless surgery on Witnesses; also covers the history of bloodless surgery, and the problem of blood transfusion and the Witnesses).

Cline, Ted. *Questions for Jehovah's Witnesses and Select Sermon Outlines.* Phoenix, AZ: Gospel Lighthouse Publ. Co., 1975, 74 pp., pb. (An outline of a fundamentalist critique of Witness doctrine.)

Coffey, John Francis. *The Gospel According to Jehovah's Witnesses.* Melbourne, Australia: The Polding Press, 1979, 173 pp., pb. (Covers primarily doctrine--the Trinity, atonement, resurrection, after-life, the second coming--but also blood transfusions and war, all from an evangelical framework.)

Cole, Marley. *Jehovah's Witnesses: The New World Society.* New York: Vantage Press, 1955, 229 pp., hb. (Sold 100,000 copies in 1955 alone, and was in top ten best sellers list. Cole is a Witness; covers history, life-style, famous Witnesses, the Witnesses court cases and doctrine. Also proves that President Eisenhower's parents were Witnesses; Cole includes a good review of many of the major court cases.) (German translation) *Jehovas Zeugen. Die Neue-Welt-Gesellschaft. Geschichte und Organisation einer Religionsbewegung.* Frankfurt am Main: Pyramiden Verlag, 1956, 248 pp. (in German).

_____. *Triumphant Kingdom.* New York: Criterion Books, 1957, 256 pp., hb. (A follow-up to his first book, stresses the Witnesses successes, their lifestyles and history.)

_____. *Jehovah's Witnesses--The Global Kingdom,* Knoxville, TN, Proguides, 1985, 340 pp., (A reprint of Cole's 1955 book with five chapters from Triumphant Kingdom and a new appendix "We got ready for 1975" which shows the disappointment of Witnesses in the 1975 prediction).

_____. *Living Destiny; The Man From Matthew, Mark, Luke and John.* Knoxville, TN: Proguides, 1984, 245 pp. (A well done combined paraphrase of the four gospels, focusing on the life of Christ slanted to Witness theology).

_____. *David.* Aurora, MO. Stoops Manufacturing. (The Story of King David and how his life can help us understand our role in society).

_____. *The Harvest of our lives.* Aurora, MO: Stoops Pub. Co. pb.1997, 155 pp. (An autobiography of Cole's life and his writing) Much excellent material about his 1st book and the Watchtower's role in this project. Much more honest then one would expect from a book written by an active Witness.

Conner, W.T. *The Teachings of "Pastor" Russell.* Nashville, TN: Sunday School Board of the Southern Baptist Convention, 1926, 68 pp. (The author is professor of systematic theology at Southwestern Baptist Theological Seminary).

Countess, Robert H. *The Jehovah's Witnesses New Testament.* Phillipsburg, NJ: Presbyterian and Reformed Co., 1982, 135 pp. (An extensive review of the New World translation. Much discussion and criticism of their use of Jehovah in the New Testament.)

Crocetti, Giuseppe. *I Testimoni de Geova un Dialogo e un Confronto Partendo dalla Bibbia.* Balogna, Italy: EDB Publishers, 1978, 239 pp. (The Jehovah's Witnesses: A Dialogue of a Confrontation Based on the Bible.).

Curry, Melvin D. *Jehovah's Witnesses: The Millenarian World of the Watchtower.* New York: Garland Publishing Inc. 1992. 247 pages.

Czatt, Milton Stacey. *The International Bible Students: Jehovah's Witnesses.* Scottsdale, PA: Mennonite Press, 1933, 45 pp., No. 4, Yale Studies in Religion. (An excellent study which is a summary of the author's Yale University Ph.D. dissertation on the Witnesses).

Dahl, Ragna with Mary Ellen Gilliland. *Seasons in the Sun.* Dillon, CO: Alpenrose Press, 1986 166 pp. pb. (The story of a Norwegian Fjord woman who eventually became a Witness in the early 1930s and her experience under the Nazis and later in America.)

Dalgleish, George. *Bad Blood.* Winnipeg, Canada: Pennefather Publ., c. 1988, 218 pp, hb. (This book is irresponsible, the legal disclaimer not withstanding; Dalgleish, a Witness, implies blood transfusion is of far more harm than help in most cases).

D'Amigo, G. et al. *Dio e Geova: Confronto con i Testimoni de Geova.* Revised by Guiseppe Sacino. Napoli, Italy. Edition Dehoniane, 1975, 107 pp. (God and Jehovah: Confrontation with the Jehovah's Witnesses).

D'Angelo, Louise. *The Catholic Answer to the Jehovah's Witnesses: A Challenge Accepted.* Meriden, CT: Maryheart Catholic Information Center, 1981, 177 pp. (A Catholic defense of the attacks on Catholism by the Witnesses. One of the very few works written by a Catholic for Catholics.)

Danyans, Eugenio. *Preceso a la "Biblia" de los Testigos de Jehova.* Tarrasa, Spain: CLIE, 1971, 256 pp., pb. (The Process of the Bible by Jehovah's Witnesses). (Much of this work is on the Trinity and Christ, also covers the 144,000 and the Holy Spirit doctrine).

Deberty, Leon. *Kitawala.* Elisabethville, Belgian Congo: Editions Essor du Congo, 1953, 277 pp. (in French). (A historical novel about the Kitawala in Central Africa. The Kitawala is an offshoot of the Watchtower and is indirectly connected with it; also discusses the Watchtower itself).

Dencher, Ted. *The Watchtower Heresy versus the Bible.* Chicago: Moody Bible Institute, 1961, 160 pp., hb. (A critique primarily of Witness doctrine by an ex-Witness)

_____. *Why I Left Jehovah's Witnesses.* Great Britain: C. Tinling and Co., 1966, 222 pp., pb.; revised ed., Fort Washington, PA: Christian Literature Crusade, 1980, 238 pp. (A history and critique of Watchtower doctrine by a former Witness)

Devore, Steve and Steve Lagoon. *Blood, Medicine and the Jehovah's Witnesses: The Hidden History of the Watchtower's position on the Blood Issue.* Witness Inc., Clayton, CA, 1995. (An extensive discussion primarily on the Watchtower advocacy of quack medical treatment, focusing on blood and their inconsistency and many changes in this area.)

Doyon, Josy. *Hirten ohne Erbarmen (10 Jahre Irrweg mit den "Zeugen Jehovas" Sonderausg.)* Zürich; Zwingli Verlag, 1966, 332 pp., Shepherds Without Mercy: 10 Years on the Wrong Path with Jehovah's Witnesses). (An expose by an ex-Witness; much of the text is a personal biography).

_____. *Ich war eine Zeugin Jehovas: Bericht über einen Irrweg.* 2nd ed. Hamburg, Germany: Siebenstern Taschenbuch Verlag, 1975, 155 pp., pb., (I Was a Jehovah's Witness: Account About a Wrong Way.) (Revised ed. of the 1966 *Hirten ohne Erbarmen* book).

_____. *Herders zonder erbarmen Tien jaren Jehovah's Getuige: verslag van eer dwaaltocht.* Third ed. Baarn, Ten Have, 1975, 204 pp. (Shepherds without mercy. Ten years a Jehovah's Witness: a report of a wandering) .

Duggar, Gordon E. *Jehovah's Witnesses--Not Just Another Denomination.* Smithtown, NY: Exposition, 1982, 124 pp. (An ex-Witness physician tells why he resigned and some of the conclusions of his research on Witness history and doctrine)

_____. *Jehovah's Witnesses; Watchout for the Watchtower!* Grand Rapids, MI: Baker Book House, 1985, 124 pp. (A slight revision of the above work)

Duncan, Homer. *Heart to Heart Talks with Jehovah's Witnesses.* Lubbock, TX: Missionary Crusader, 1972, 156 pp., pb. (Spanish ed., *Los Testigos de Jehova ante la Biblia,* same publisher, 1975, 118 pp., pb.). (A critique of their doctrine-- the trinity, Hell fire, the soul, the second coming--from a fundamentalist's worldview)

Eason, Jean H. *A Jehovah's Witness Finds the Truth.* Worthville, KY: Love Agape Ministries Press, 1983, 117 pp., pb. (A story of one person's experience as a Witness; written like a novel).

Eaton, E.L. *The Millennial Dawn Heresy.* Cincinnati, OH: Jennings and Graham, 1910, 153 pp. Reprint, Aberdeen, Scotland: Impulse Publ., 1972, 119 pp., hb. (Eaton was a prominent Methodist pastor; he critiques primarily Witness doctrine).

Elle, Di Ci (Ed). *Cruto nostro Dio e nostra Sperantza i Cristiani di fronte ai testimony di Geord* Tornio, 1986, 176 pp. (Critiques primarily doctrine)

Engelland, Hans. *Die Zeugen Jehovas/Die Neuapostalischen.* 2nd expanded ed. Hamburg, Germany: Frieda Weigand, 1969, 64 pp., pb. (The Jehovah's Witnesses/ The New Apostles. The first 35 pages are about Jehovah's Witnesses, which discusses their general beliefs and history).

Farr, Alfred Derek. *God, Blood and Society.* Aberdeen, Scotland: Impulse Publ., 1972, 119 pp., hb. (This is the only full length objective secular work on the Witnesses' religious objection to blood transfusion issue. An excellent, well-documented work by a blood medical technologist which vividly shows the tragedy of the Watchtower view on blood).

Felderer, Ditlieb. *The History of Jehovah's Witnesses.* Taby, Sweden: pub. by author, 1971, 269 pp., pb. (Covers primarily the attacks on C.T. Russell (the miracle wheat, his knowledge of Greek) and shows that his detractors were not always ethical in their attacks nor were they above board either; Felderer tends to write in the style of 1930s Watchtower; he was eventually forced out of the movement).

Felipe del Ray, Pedro de. *¡El reino de Dios empezo en 1914! (y el inminete fin del mundo en Armageddon). ¿realidid o fraude? ¿politica o religion?* Madrid: Felipe del Ray Pub., 1974, 493 pp. (The Kingdom of God Began in 1914--and the Imminent End of the World in Armageddon--Reality or Fraud? Politics or Religion?)

Fetz, August. *Weltvernichtung durch "Bibelforscher" und Juden.* München: Deutscher Volksverlag, 1925, 164 pp. (World Destruction by the Bible Researchers [Jehovah's Witnesses] and Jews).

Fijnvandraat, J.G. *Jehovah's Getuige, mag ik ook iets zeggen?* 3rd pr. Vaassen, Medema, 1987, 135 pp. (Jehovah's Witness, may I also say something?)

Fields, Karen. *Revival and Rebellion in Colonial Africa.* Princeton, NJ: Princeton Univ. Press 1985 285 pp. (A sympathetic account of the Watchtower movement in Africa and the many conflicts that existed between the Watchtower and the local government and religions; A very revealing history).

Finnerty, Robert U. *Jehovah's Witnesses on Trial.* Phillipsburg, NY: Presbyterian and Reformed Publishing 1993 164 pp. (A well documented work by a medical doctor arguing that the Witnesses have dishonestly portrayed the early Christian teachings on doctrine and that they did not teach the basic doctrines that the Watchtower now teaches.)

Floyd, Shelby C. *An Examination of Jehovah's Witnesses.* 320 pp?, 11 chapters.

Fogerson, Dewey. *The Witnesses' Jehovah; A study of the term 'Jehovah' in the Watchtower's version of the New Testament.* Pub. by author, Carlsbad, NM, 1983, 100 pp. (From a thesis on the use of "Jehovah" in the Christian Greek Scriptures Translation of the Witness' New Testament; discusses some history and doctrine).

Forrest, James Edward. *Errors of Russellism: A Brief Examination of the Teachings of Pastor Russell as Set Forth in His "Studies of the Scriptures."* Anderson, IN: Gospel Trumpet Co., 1915, 277 pp. (A critique of Watchtower doctrine and teachings)

Franz, Raymond. *Crisis of Conscience: The Struggle Between Loyalty to God and Loyalty to One's Religion.* Atlanta: Commentary Press, 1983, 375 pp. (Franz was a former member of the governing body, thus this book gives insight into the Watchtower and information found nowhere else. A must for a student of the Watchtower).

_____. *In Search of Christian Freedom.* Atlanta: Commentary Press, 1991, 732 pp. (An encyclopedic work that covers the social world of Witnesses and the policy and history of the Watchtower; little on doctrine, much insight on the Watchtower).

Freistühler. *Die Zeugen Jehovas: eine Dokumentation über die Wachtturmgesellschaft.* (The Witnesses of Jehovah. A documentation about the Watchtower Society). Schwerte (Ruhr), 1971, 317 pp. (in German).

Freyenwald, Dr. Jonak Hans Von. *Die Zeugen Jehovas: Pioniere für ein Jüdisches Weltreich; die Politischen Ziele der nationalen Vereinigung Ernster Bibelforscher.*

Berlin, Germany, 1936, 104 pp., pb. (The Jehovah's Witnesses: Pioneers for the Jewish World King Power: The Political Goals of the International Union of Jehovah's Witnesses.) (Jonak stresses the Watchtower's support for "God's kingdom" is actually an effert to undermine the Nazi state, and why they should be banned).

Garbe, Detlef. *Zwischen Widerstand und Martyrium, Die Zeugen Jehovas im 'Dritten Reich'* Munchen: Oldenbourg Verlag. 1993, 577 pp. (Between Resistance and Martyrdom' the Jehovah's Witnesses in the 'Third Reich.') (The most extensive study ever completed on the Witnesses under Nazism. Garbe shows that the Watchtower's account about Witnesses in Nazi Germany is not always very accurate.) (In German)

Garcia, Jóse Luis. *Los Testigos de Jehova: A la Luz de la Biblia.* Tarrasa, Spain: Talleres Graficos de CLIE, 1976, 358 pp., pb. (Jehovah's Witnesses in the Light of the Bible). (Covers primarily doctrine but includes some history).

Gazhos, V.F. *Peculiarities of the Ideology of Jehovahism and the Religious Consciousness of Sectarians.* In materials of the MSSR (Moldavian Soviet Socialist Republic). Under the editorship of candidate of philosophical science V.N. Yermuratsky. Kishinev, 1969, 92 pp. (in Russian).

Gebhard, Manfred. *Die Zeugen Jehovas: Eine Dokumentation über die Wachtturmgesellschaft.* Schwerte, Ruhr: Verlag Hubert Freistuhler, 1971, 317 pp., hb. (Jehovah's Witnesses: A Documentation about the Watchtower Society). (An anti-witness work that includes much documentation, and photocopies of many confidential Watchtower files taken when the East Germans seized the branch in Magdeburg in 1950; much material in this work is found nowhere else).

Gérard, Jacques E. *Les Fondements Syncretiques du Kitawala.* Bruxelles, Belgium: Centre de Recherche et d' Information Socio-Politiques C.R.I.S.P. (rue du Congress 35). Bruxelles, Belgium: Le Livre Africain, 1969, 120 pp., pb. The Foundations, and history of events of the Watchtower. (About the Watchtower and its offshoots in Africa, covers history, doctrine, organization and social factors).

Gerasimenko, Vladimir Kuzmich, et al. *From an Alien Voice.* Travriia, USSR: Simferopol Pub. House, 1975, 104 pp. (in Russian)

Geyraud, Pierre. *Les Petites Eglises de Paris.* Paris: Emile-Paul Freres, 1937. (The Small Religions of Paris).

Giron, Jose. *Los Testigos de Jehova y Sus Doctrinas.* Miami, FL: Editorial Vida, 1954. 5th ed. 1972, 128 pp., pb. (The Jehovah's Witnesses and Their Doctrines). (A critique of doctrine by an evangelical Christian).

Graebner, Theodore. *War in the Light of Prophecy, "Was It Foretold?"* St. Louis, MO: Concordia Pub. House, 1941, 143 pp. p. 8, 13-14, 20-21, 35-36, 73, 99-113, 130-133. (effectively argues against the chiliastic teachings of the Russellites, and the other fundamentalist churches. Shows how date-setting and "end-times" prophesy has proved disastrous, especially those related to 1914 and World War I).

Gregori, Aldo. *I Testimoni di Geova Dottrina ed Errori.* Pesaro, Italy: STEP, 1967, 96 pp. (The Jehovah's Witnesses' Doctrine and Errors). (A history and critique of the Watchtower doctrine from a Catholic worldview).

Greschat, Hans-Jürgen. *Kitawala: Ursprung, Ausbreitung und Religion der Watchtower-Bewegung in Zentralafrika.* Marburg, Germany: Elwert, 1967, 128 pp., pb. (Jehovah's Witnesses: Origin, Expansion, and Religion of the Watchtower

Movement in Central Africa). (in German) (An excellent historical--sociological study of the Watchtower movement in central Africa).

Grigg, David H. *Do Jehovah's Witnesses and the Bible Agree?* New York: Vantage Press, 1958, 250 pp., hb. (A theological review from the viewpoint of a Seventh-Day Adventist, thus primarily those doctrines are discussed in which Adventists disagree with Witnesses).

Gruss, Edmond Charles. *Apostles of Denial: An Examination and Expose of the History, Doctrines and Claims of the Jehovah's Witnesses.* Nutley, NJ: Presbyterian and Reformed Publ. Co., 1970, 324 pp., hb., pb. (An extensive history of the Watchtower by a former Witness, this work is based on his Master's thesis; much well-documented material).

_____. *The Jehovah's Witnesses and Prophetic Speculation.* Nutley, NJ: Presbyterian and Reformed Publ. Co., 1972, 131 pp., pb., 2nd ed. 1975. (Specifically reviews the Watchtower system of chronology and their history of date setting, especially 1975; a well-documented classic).

_____. *We Left Jehovah's Witnesses--A Non-Prophet Organization.* Nutley, NJ: Presbyterian and Reformed Pub. Co., 1974, 169 pp., pb. (reprinted by Baker Book House of Grand Rapids, MI, 1975). (A set of short histories of persons who left the Watchtower, their experiences and why they resigned. Very interesting cases and a very readable text. Limited doctrine is reviewed, many personal experiences of the inhumanity of the Watchtower are included, some very tragic ones).

_____. and Leonard Chretien. *Jehovah's Witnesses; Their Monuments to False Prophecy.* Clayton, CA: Witness, Inc. 1997. 307 pp pb. (81/2 x 11") (A well documented history of the Watchtower involvement in Pyramidology, Beth-Shan and Beth-Sarim).

Gustafsson, Axel. *Vittnar Jehovas Vittnen falskt? En Stridsskrift.* Stockholm: Gummesson, also Falkoping,1955, 83 pp. (Are Jehovah's Witnesses False Witnesses?) (in Swedish) (A critique of Watchtower teachings).

Harris, Doug. *Awake! To the Watchtower.* Twickenham, England: Reachout Trust, 1988, 254 pp., pb. 1992 Revised edition 376 pp. pb. (A critique of Witness doctrine from an evangelical world-view; also covers history, failed prophesy, the blood issue, and related). Many extensive quotes from Watchtower publications.

Harrison, Barbara Grizzuti. *Visions of Glory: A History and a Memory of Jehovah's Witnesses.* New York: Simon and Schuster, 1978, 413 pp., hb., pb, abridged edition reprinted by Robert Hale, Pub. in London. (An excellent study of the Witnesses by one who was the President's assistant and a proofreader at Bethel; much inside information found nowhere else).

_____. *An Accidental Autobiography.* Boston: Houghton Mifflin Co. 1996, 396 pp. pb. (Contains much excellent material about the Witnesses as a social movement and their problems).

Hartog, John, II. *Enduring to the End: Jehovah's Witnesses and Bible Doctrine.* Schaumburg, IL: Regular Baptist Press, 1987. (A critique of the history and doctrines, covers each of the ten areas of systematic theology).

Heinzmann, Gerhard. *Lehren die Zeugen Jehovas die Wahrheit? Fragen und Antworten.* (Teach the Witnesses of Jehovah the truth? Questions and Answers). Asslar, Herold Schriftenmission, 1988, 96 pp. (in German).

Hérbert, Gérard, S.J. *Les Témoins de Jéhovah Essai Critique d'histoire et de doctrine.* Montreal: Les Editions Bellarmin, 1960, 341 pp. (The Jehovah's Witnesses, a critique of their history and doctrine).

Herle, Nelson A. Jr. *The Trinity Doctrine Examined in the Light of History and the Bible.* 1983, 208 pp. (An attempt to defend the Watchtower by an active Witness; self published).

Hermann, Friedrich Wilhelm. *Bibelforscher oder Bibelfalscher?* Kossel: Verlagshaus der Deutschen Baptisten, J.G. Oncken, Nachf, 1925, 114 pp. (Bible Researchers or Bible Falsifiers?).

Hess, Jay. *Jehovah's Witnesses are Not False Prophets.* c. 1985, pub. by author, 72 pp (the author was an active Witness when he wrote this, and was since forced out of the movement).

Hewat, Elizabeth Glendinning Kirkwood. *Meeting Jehovah's Witnesses: A Study of Jehovah's Witnesses in Scotland and Elsewhere.* Edinburgh, Scotland: Saint Andrew Press, 1967, 93 pp., pb. (A sympathetic review of Witness beliefs; much information on their work in Scotland).

Hewitt, Clide E. *Midnight and Morning.* Charlotte, NC: Venture Books, 1983. 326 pp. (A review of Advent Christian history and those who influenced C.T. Russell.)

Hewitt, Joe. *I Was Raised a Jehovah's Witness.* Denver, CO: Accent Books, 1979, 191 pp., pb. (Hewitt's story in the Witnesses and how he got out; includes much critical evaluation of their doctrine).

Hickman, Richard. *The Psychology of Jehovah's Witnesses; Reflections of Twenty-five Years.* Worthville, KY: Love/Agape Ministries Press, 1984, 150 pp. Revised ed., 1985, 108 pp. (A psychological-sociological analysis of the Watchtower and how it affects members adversely. Hickman is an ex-Witness and has been very active in publishing in academic journals).

Hoekema, Anthony. *Jehovah's Witnesses.* Grand Rapids, MI: W.B. Eerdmans Pub. Co., 1972, 140 pp., pb. (Updated from the section on Witnesses from *The Four Major Cults;* covers mostly doctrine, has a chapter on history and authority).

Hohenberger, A. *Jehovas Zeugen oder Jünger Jesu Christi?* Schweinfurt, Evangelisch Lutheriches Pfarramt, 1948, 160 pp. (Jehovah's Witnesses or disciples of Jesus Christ?). (in German).

Holzapfel, Heribert. *Die Sekten in Deutschland.* München, Verlag J. Rofel & J. Bustet, 1925, 133 pp. (The sects in Germany). (in German).

Horowitz, David. *Pastor Charles Taze Russell: An Early American Christian Zionist.* Philosophical Library, 1986, 160 pp. hb., pb. 2nd revised ed. Shengold, Pub., N.Y., 1990. (Much of this material was reprinted from United Israel Bulletin. Horowitz, a Jew, is extremely sympathetic to Russell and his modern followers, but not to the Jehovah's Witnesses).

Hudson, A.O. *Bible Students in Britain; The Story of a Hundred Years.* Hounslow, Middlesex: Bible Fellowship Union, 1989, 200 pp, pb. (A detailed history of the Russell movement in Britain, both before and after it broke off from the Watchtower, written by a Bible Student; includes much history found nowhere else).

Hudson, John Allen. *Russell-White Debate.* See Rowe, F.L.

Hull, Daniel.W. *Letters to Elder Charles T. Russell.* Pub. by author, Olympia, WA: 1910, 128, pb. (A critique of Russell's view of spiritualism. Hull was the pastor of the Progressive Spiritualist Society, reprinted in Bergman (Ed.) p. 23-150)

Iarotski, Petro Lavrentiiovych. *The Anticommunism of the Jehovah's Witnesses: Social and Political Doctrine.* Kiev, USSR: Dumka Pub. House and the academy of Sciences of the Ukrainian S.S.R., 1976, 214 pp. (Ukrainian).

_____. *The Crisis of the Jehovah's Witnesses: A Critical Analysis of the Ideology and Evolution of a Commonplace Religious Confession.* Kiev, USSR: Dumka Pub. House and the Academy of Sciences of the Ukrainian S.S.R., 1979, 301 pp. (Ukrainian).

_____. *The Evolution of Contemporary Jehovah's Witnesses.* Kiev, USSR: Izdatelstvo Politicheskoi Literatury Ukrainy, 1981, 143 pp. (Ukrainian).

Jabrah, Ibrahim. *The Truth About the Jehovah's Witnesses: An Extension of the Jewish People.* Cairo, Egypt: Almahabbah Library, 1976, 68 pp. (Arabic).

Jackson, Latoya. *Latoya: Growing up in the Jackson Family.* New York Dutton Book 1991 pgs. 21, 31, 36, 40, 52-57, 88-90, 93, 110, 112, 119, 120, 129, 133, 134, 136, 143, 144, 196-200, 227, 232, 257. (About the Jackson family, all which were raised Witnesses; An excellent inside story of the effects of their teachings. None of the children stayed with the movement.)

Jaron, Pierre. *Les Témoins de Jéhovah devant la Bible.* Dammarieles-Lys: France Editions S.D.T. (Signe des temps), 1969, 64 pp. (Jehovah's Witnesses Compared to the Bible) (Covers some history; primarily a critique of Witness doctrine).

Jasmin, Damien. *Les Temoins de Jehovah.* Montreal, Canada: Les Editions Lumen, 1947, 189 pp. (The Jehovah's Witnesses). (Written from a Catholic viewpoint, much excellent information about the history of Witnesses which shows that they are openly anti-Catholic).

Jonsson, Carl Olof. *The Gentile Times Reconsidered.* Lethbridge, Canada Good News Defenders (Ed. by M.James Penton) 1983, 226 pp. Revised and reprinted by Commentary Press, Atlanta, 1986, 228 pp. (An excellent extensive, scholarly Review of Witness chronology, showing why the critical date 1914 is wrong).

_____. *Bledfragån; Blodförbudit I Bibeln och Bloottranfusionerna Göteborg Cklförlaget* 1993 62 pp. (The blood prohibition in the Bible and Blood Transfusion. An excellent review of the scriptural and medical argument against transfusion; shows the Watchtower is dishonest and totally without foundation in this doctrine.)

Jonsson, Carl Olof and Herbst Wolfgang. *The Sign of the Last Days; When?* Atlanta, Commentary Press, 1987, 272 pp. (Documents extensively that the "last days" teaching of the Watchtower is not supported by the facts of history).

Joosten, H.W.A. *Zi jn zij God's Getuigen?* Heiloo, Kinheim-Uitgeverij, 1956, 117 pp. (Are they God's Witnesses?) (in Dutch).

Kaplan, William. *State and Salvation: The Jehovah's Witnesses and Their Fight for Civil Rights.* Toronto: University of Toronto Press, 1989. (An excellent well documented history of Jehovah's Witnesses in Canada, focusing on their civil liberties struggles; based on a Ph.D. thesis done at Stanford University).

Kaufmann, Robert. *Millenarisme et Acculturation.* Bruxelles, Belgium: 1'Universite Libre de Bruxelles, 1964, 134 pp. (in French).

Kennedy, Jimmy and Marilyn Kennedy. *Something to Laugh About.* 210 pp. (The life stories of two professional comedians who become Jehovah's Witnesses).

Kirban, Salem. *Jehovah's Witnesses: Doctrines of Devils.* No. 3. Chicago: Moody Press, 1972, 78 pp., pb. (Covers doctrine, history and lifestyle, which are critiqued from the fundamentalists worldview).

Knaut, Horst. *Propheten der Angst: Berichte zu Psychopathology. Trends d. Gegenwart: eine kritische Analyse.* Kempfenhausen Schultz Pub., 1975, 231 pp. (Prophets of Fear: Reports on Present Psychopathology Trends: A Critical Analysis).

Konik, Vasillii Vasilevich. *The "Truths" of the Jehovah's Witnesses.* Moscow: Politizdat Pub. House, 1978, 111 pp. (in Russian).

Köppl, Elmar. *Die Zeugen Jehovas: Eine psychologische Analyse.* Arbeitsgemeinschaft für Religions--und Weltanschauungsfragen. Innsbruch, 1985, 226 pp, (The Jehovah's Witnesses; A Psychological Analysis).

Lambert, O.C. *Russellism Unveiled.* Port Arthur, TX: O.C. Lambert & Sons, 1940; reprinted by Firm Foundations Publ. House, Austin, TX, n.d., 111 pp., pb. (A short history and critique of early Watchtower beliefs, including hell, trinity, soul, eschatology and related).

Lanzoni, D. Giuseppe. *I Testimoni di Geova.* Faenza, Italy: Societa Tipografica Taentina, Vol. I, 1952, 125 pp.; Vol. II, 1953, 143 pp.; Vol. III, 1953, 194 pp., pb. (The Jehovah's Witnesses) (An extensive critique of Witness doctrine by a Catholic professor) (in Italian).

Lavaud, M. Benoit *Sectes Modernes et Foi Catholique.* Paris: Aubier, 1954, pp. 15- 198. (Modern Sects and Catholic Faith) (in French).

Leech, Ken. *True Witness/The Amazing Story of British Detective Leech, Searching for the Truth, Escapes from the Clutches of "False Witness" into Glorius Liberty of Gospel.* Winona Lake, IN: Christian Witness Crusades, c. 1979, 152 pp. (Ken Leech was a former policeman in England who became a Witness. He tells of his involvement in both police work and the Witnesses; the book reads like a novel).

Levnin, Viktor Nikolaevich. *The Brothers of the Brooklyn Apostles (Concerning the Jehovah's Witnesses and Their Activity in the Stavropol Region).* Stavropol: Knizhno Izdatelstvo Pub. House, 1978, 87 pp. (in Ukrainian).

Lingle, Wilbur. *Approaching Jehovah Witnesses In Love; How to Witness Effectively Without Arguing.* Fort Washington, Penn,, Christian Literature Crusade 1994, 240 pp. (An easy to follow set of questions and answers about Jehovah's Witnesses; mostly doctrine, some history, a general review.)

Long, Norman. *Social Change and the Individual.* Manchester, England: Manchester University Press, 1968, 245 pp. (pp. 6, 37-38, 76-71, 126, 129, 155-156, 191- 199, and chapter 8 Religion and Social Action, pp. 200-245) (A study of the major positive role the Watchtower beliefs have played in the development of a rural Zambia community).

Loofs, Friedrich. *Die "Internationale Vereinigung Ernster Bibelforscher."* Leipzig, Germany: J.C. Hinrichs' sche Buchhandlung, 1921, 60 pp. (The International Union of Serious Bible Researchers) (in German).

Lovaillier, Midge. *A Hand in the Darkness.* Published by author 1992 45 pp. pb. (about the author's experience as a Jehovah's Witness and how she got out and became a Christian).

Macgregor, Lorri. *What You Need to Know About Jehovah's Witnesses.* Eugene, OR: Harvest House, 1992, 136 pp, pb. (A manual intended to help Christians convert Witnesses; the focus is on doctrine).

Macmillan, A.H. *Faith on the March.* Englewood Cliffs, NJ: Prentice-Hall, Inc., 1957, 243 pp. hb. (Written by an active Witness in conjunction with the Watchtower writing staff. A helpful but non-objective work which covers primarily history;

much about Mr. Macmillan's own experiences).

Magnani, Duane. *The Collector's Handbook of Watchtower Publications.* Clayton, CA: Jehovah's Witnesses Books, 1980, 165 pp., pb. (A listing of all "official" Watchtower literature, its rarity, etc. Includes many different editions of most works and a description of the major works) Revised in 1997.

_____. *Watchtowergate.* Clayton, CA: Jehovah's Witnesses Books, 1980, 345 pp., pb.

_____. *Where is Michael?* Clayton, CA: Jehovah's Witnesses, 110 pp.

_____. *Who Is the Faithful and Wise Servant?* Clayton, CA: Jehovah's Witnesses Books, 1979 ed. 32 pp., 1981, 79 pp. (Discusses the older Watchtower teaching that Charles Russell was the "faithful and wise servant. Shows beyond a doubt that the Society taught for years that Russell was viewed as "that servant").

_____. *Dialogue with Jehovah's Witnesses.* Clayton, CA: Witness Inc., 1983, 563 pp. (2 vols.). (A critique of Watchtower teaching on major doctrines--trinity, authority, salvation, the use of Jehovah, flag salute, holiday prohibition, and their string of false prophecies, p. 395-548).

_____. *Bible Students? Do Jehovah's Witnesses Really Study the Bible? An Analysis.* Clayton, CA: Witness, Inc., 1983, 220 pp. (A study of authority and the Watchtower; contains over one-hundred photocopies of old Watchtower literature for documentation).

_____. *The Watchtower Files: Dialogue with a Jehovah's Witness.* Minneapolis, MN: Bethany House Publishers, 1985. (A well-written extensively documented--with many photocopies of Witness material--critique of the Watchtower by an ex-Witness).

_____. *The Kids Go To Work,* Vol. 1. *Cruel and Unusual Punishment.* 354 pp, Vol. II, *Saleskids.* Clayton, CA: Witness, Inc. 442 pp., 1986. (Documents with hundreds of photocopies of original Watchtower publications showing that Witness children are forced to have a very unusual, not always healthy childhood).

_____. *The Heavenly Weatherman; A Look at a God Who Doesn't Know All Things--The God of Jehovah's Witnesses.* Clayton, CA: Witness, Inc., 1987, 326 pp. (A critique of the Watchtower view of God documented by many photocopies of the Watchtower publications).

_____. *Danger at your Door.* Clayton, CA: Witness, Inc., 1987, 392 pp (Documentary evidence for the film *Witnesses of Jehovah.*)

_____. *Refutation of Preparing for Child Custody Cases.* Clayton, CA: Witness, Inc., 1988, 274 pp. (Refutes by use of photocopies of original Watchtower publications the Watchtower's claims in their child custody booklet).

_____. *A Problem of Communication; Witnessing to Jehovah's Witnesses.* Clayton, CA: Witness Inc., 1988, 106 pp, pb. (A handbook on how to win Witnesses to Christ).

_____. *Another Jesus; Proving the Bodily Resurrection of Christ to the Jehovah's Witnesses.* Clayton, CA: Witness, Inc., 1990, 401 pp., pb. (Argues for the bodily resurrection of Christ and against the Witnesses teaching of a spiritual resurrection).

_____, and Arthur Barrett. *Eyes of Understanding.* Clayton, CA: Witness, Inc., 1980, 78 pp.; revised ed., 1981, 56pp. (Reviews the many failed Armageddon prophecies. Includes many photocopies of old Watchtower literature for documentation).

Malik, Joseph, and Elizabeth Taze Malik. *Beyond the Watchtower.* New York: Vantage Press, 1982, 295 pp. (The Maliks are former Witnesses. This work is a creative reinterpretation and a unique critique of Watchtower theology; includes much personal history).

Mann, W.E. *Sect, Cult and Church in Alberta.* Toronto: University of Toronto Press, 1962.

Manwaring, David Roger. *Render unto Caesar: The Flag-Salute Controversy.* Chicago: The University of Chicago Press, 1962, 320 pp., hb. (This is a revision of Manwaring's Ph.D. thesis on the flag issue, and is the most complete scholarly study ever done on this issue. It is thoroughly documented with 169 pages of notes; Manwaring's wife was a Witness, thus his interest).

Margot, Jean Claude. *Les Temoins de Jehovah.* Paris: Editions Delachaus et Niestle. (The Jehovah's Witnesses) (in French).

Martin, Walter, and Norman Klann. *Jehovah of the Watchtower.* Grand Rapids, MI: Zondervan Publishing House, 1953, 201 pp., hb. (Revised and updated by Moody Press of Chicago, 1974, 221 pp., pb.) Numerous editions of this book have been published; Italian edition, *Il Geova della Torre di Guardia,* Napoli, Italy: Edizione Centro Biblico, 1967, 250 pp. (A critique of the Watchtower--doctrine, history, lifestyle, and leaders--by two Baptists ministers).

Mason, Doug. *Witnessing to the Witnesses.* Australia: Pub. by author. (Pt. I), 63 pp., n.d. (c. 1974); *And All That* (Pt. II), 129 pp., n.d., *the Trinity* (Pt III), 112 pp., n.d., pb. (An extensive history and critique of the Watchtower society's major doctrines).

_____. *Witnessing The Name.* Australia: Pub. by author. (A scholarly discussion about the Watchtower use of Jehovah in their New Testament) 1986, 66 pp.

_____. *Jehovah in the New World Translation.* Australia, Pub. by author, 1981, 1985, 118 pp. (An in-depth study of the Watchtower's arguments in favor of using the word Jehovah for God in the Greek Scriptures; concludes they have no basis from the language or theology for this practice; also much information on the New World Translation).

McKinney, George D. *The Theology of the Jehovah's Witnesses.* Grand Rapids, MI: Zondervan Publishing House, 1962, 130 p., hb. (A critique of Witness doctrine from an evangelical prospective, showing that their expectations for the end have proved wrong. McKinney is a Black minister of the Church of God in Christ).

_____. *The Jehovah's Witnesses.* San Diego, CA: Production House, 1975.

McRoberts, Steve. (pseudonym) *Falling in Truth: The Education of a Jehovah's Witness*("F-I-T") Privately produced c. 1979. 732 pages. A novel in which a young man wanting to be an elder has a series of meetings with an old elder, who knew Russell, and who plays the devil's advocate on the Watchtower's history and doctrines. Written by an ex-Witness, who was in Brooklyn Bethel in 1975-76.

Meffert, Franz, Dr. *Bibelforscher und Bibelforschung über das Weltende; 5 Vorträge über die sogenannten Ernsten Bibelforscher,* 2nd ed. Freiburg: Caritasverlag, 1925, 149 pp. (The Jehovah's Witnesses and Bible Study on the End of the World; 5 Lectures About the Ernest Bible Students . A critique of Witness eschatology; an excellent work showing their expectations for the end have proved wrong).

Melinder, J.D. *I Brytningstider, En Studie i Modärn kättarförföljelsa*. Härnösand: Berea-
Förlaget, 1925, 144 pp. (In Difficult Times: A Study of a Modern Heretic). (An
extensive critique of Russell's doctrines and beliefs).

Miller, Ralph T. *Jehovah's Witnesses; Victims of Deception*. Assonet MA, Comments
from the Friends. 1995, 144 pp. (By a former Witness and retired police captain--
the author was a Jehovah's Witness for 30 years.)

Mitchell, N.J. *Evolution and the Emperor's New Clothes*. 1985, 255 pp. Self published
(A critique of evolution by a Witness).

Morey, Robert A. *How to Answer a Jehovah's Witness*. Minneapolis, MN: Bethany
Fellowship, 1980, 109 pp. (A brief review of Witness teaching and the
conservative Evangelical response, much on Watchtower failed prophesy and the
trinity).

Moskalenko, Aleksei Trofimovich. *Contemporary Jehovah's Witnesses*. Novosibirsk,
USSR: "Science." Siberian Division, 1971, 227 pp. (in Russian). (A history and
critique).

Muller, Albert. *Meet Jehovah's Witnesses: Their Confusion, Doubts, and Contradictions*.
Pulaski, WI: Franciscan Publ., 1964, 115 pp., pb. (A Catholic critiques major
doctrines that conflict with Catholicism, including those related to God,
resurrection, the Pope, date setting).

Munters, Quirinus J. *Rekrutering als raeping: Sociologische Overwegingen met
Betrekking tot het Missionaire Handelen*. Meppel, Holland: J.A. Boom en Zoon,
1970, 216 pp., pb. (Recruiting as a Calling; Sociological Consideration of
Missionaries) (in Dutch). An excellent sociological study of the missionary
enterprise (Pt. 1) and Pt II is on the Witnesses, focusing on their missionary work;
a summary is given in English).

Neidhart, Ludwig. *Die Zeugen Jehovas*. (The Witnesses of Jehovah). Altenberge, Soest,
CIS-Verlag, 1986, 200 pp. (in German).

Nelson, Wilton M. *Los Testigos de Jehova: Quineses son y lo que Creen*. Mexico: Casa
Bavtista de Publicaciones, 1949. Revised ed., 1976, 130 pp., pb. (The Jehovah's
Witnesses: Who They Are, and What They Believe) (in Spanish). (Covers
primarily doctrine).

Newton, Merlin Owen. *Armed with the Constitution: Jehovah's Witnesses in Alabama
and the U.S. Supreme Court 1939-1946*. Univ. of Alabama Press, 221 pp.
(Covers the Witnesses role in changing first amendment Jurisprudence, focusing
on the Alabama--based U.S. Supreme court cases, *Jones v. Opelika* and *Marsh v.
Alabama*.)

Nobel, R. *Falschspieler Gottes. Die Wahrheit über Jehovas Zeugen*. Hamburg: Rasch &
Röhring, 1985, 237 pp. (God's false player. The truth about Jehovah's
Witnesses). (in German).

Nova, Alex. *Who's That Knocking at My Door*. Poughkeepsie, NY: pub. by author,
1978, 108 pp., pb. (Covers primarily the trinity, and closely related topics; a
critique from an evangelical world view).

Nyman, Aaron. *Astounding Errors: The Prophetic Message of the Seventh-Day
Adventists and the Chronology of Pastor C.T. Russell in the Light of History and
Bible Knowledge*. Chicago: pub. by author, c. 1914, 419 pp. (especially useful
are pp. 3, 297-343). (A critique of the whole Adventist movement, focusing on
their chronology and eschatology contradictions and problems. A rare but

extremely important volume).

Oakley, Debbie, and Helen Ortega. *Mom and Me: Twenty Years Jehovah's Witnesses.* New York: Vantage Press, 1978, 82 pp., hb. (An account of the twenty years the author spent as a Witness, includes much insight on why people become Witnesses and the inhumanity of the organization).

Paffrath, Tharsicius. *Die Sekte der Ernsten Bibelforscher.* Paderborn: Bonifatius-Druckerei, 1925, 176 pp. (in German) (The Sect of the Jehovah's Witnesses).

Palotay, Sandor. *Tevedesek ut jan: a Jehova Tanui.* Budapest: Magyarorszagi Szabedegyhazak Tanosca (The Council of the Free Church of Hungary), 1977, 63 pp. (On the Road of Mistakes: Jehovah's Witnesses) (in Hungarian).

Papa, Günther. *Ich war Zeuge Jehovas. Enthüllungen eines ehemaligen mitarbeiters und Missioanrs der Watchtower Bible and Tract Society.* Aschaffenburg, West Germany: Paul Pattloch Verlag, 1961; 5th ed. 1975, 162 pp., pb., German. (I Was a Jehovah's Witness. A disclosure of a former co-worker and missionary). (A personal account of one man's experience in the Watchtower; much excellent personal information).

_____. *Die Wahrheit über Jehovas Zeugen: Problematik? Dokumentation.* Rottweil, Germany: Neckar Verlag Aktuelle Texte, 1979, 190 pp., pb. (The Truth About Jehovah's Witnesses: Problems and Documentation). (Includes much history, also covers doctrine and the Witness conflicts with the state) (in German).

Penton, M. James. *Jehovah's Witnesses in Canada.* Toronto, Canada: Macmillan, 1976, 388 pp., hb. (A very sympathetic, well documented history of the Watchtower's legal troubles in Canada and their Canadian history in general; this work partly resulted in the author's expulsion from the movement).

_____. *Apocalypse Delayed; The Story of Jehovah's Witnesses.* Toronto, Canada: University of Toronto Press, 1985, 432 pp. (One of the most complete sociological-historical studies of the Witnesses, done by a 5th generation Witnesses who spent his entire life of about fifty years in the movement. Well-documented, very balanced and covers some doctrine).

Pike, Royston. *Jehovah's Witnesses: Who They Are, What they Teach, What They Do.* New York: Philosophical Library; London: Watts Co., 1954, 140 pp., hb. (A journalistic account of the movement, covers some doctrine, and intended for the general public, fairly sympathetic).

Platt, F.G. *A Chapter in My Life.* London, England; pub. by author, n.d., 75 pp., pb. (The author tells of his life as a Witness in England from a young man until 1945; he spent a total of forty years as a full-time Witness).

Pollina, Sergio. *Il Popolo Dell' Apocalisse, Storie Di Ordinaria Utopia.* Tipse: Vittorio Vento 1993, 160 pp. (On a wide variety of topics on the Witnesses by an ex-Witness.) [Italian]

Potashov, Konstantin Ivanovich. *Why I Broke with the Jehovah's Witnesses.* Uzhgorod, USSR: Karpati Pub. House, 1978, 63 pp. (in Ukrainian).

Quick, Kevin R. *Reasoning with Jehovah's Witnesses.* Hyde Point, NY, 1986, 76 pp. (A critique of Watchtower teaching on the nature of God, man and salvation and eschatology).

_____. *Pilgrimage through the Watchtower.* Grand Rapids: Baker Bookhouse, 1989. (A personal account of a young man's experience in the Watchtower and why he left; much information on the Watchtower and its teachings).

Quidam, Roger D. (pseudonym for Dan Barney). *The Doctrine of Jehovah's Witnesses: A Criticism.* New York: Philosophical Library, 1959, 117 pp., hb. (Pp. 1-110 are poetry, pp. 110-117 are prose; this book requires a good knowledge of philosophy, and the Witnesses but reading it is well worth the effort. A critique from a secular humanist's world view).

Redeker, Charles F. *A Confirmation of the True Bible Chronology.* Pub. by author, Detroit, MI, 1971, 93 pp. (An excellent in-depth study of the Watchtower's vs. C.T. Russell's chronology. Also has a section on the Great Pyramid; Redeker is a Bible Student).

Reed, David A. *Jehovah's Witnesses: Answered Verse by Verse.* Grand Rapids: Baker Book House, 1986, 139 pp., pb. (A response to many of the Witness teachings, covers mostly doctrine).

_____. *How to Rescue Your Loved One from the Watchtower.* Grand Rapids: Baker Book House, 1990, 2nd pr., 168 pp, pb. (A well-documented work focusing on how one can critically review the Watchtower's past and current contradictions).

_____. *Index of Watchtower Errors.* Grand Rapids: Baker Book House, 1990, 138 pp., pb. (A list of quotes from the Society's own publications showing the Watchtower's many errors, contradictions and changes).

_____. *Behind the Watchtower Curtain; The Secret Society of Jehovah's Witnesses.* Southbridge, MA: Crowne Pub. 1989, 150 pp, pb. (An excellent critique of Watchtower social teachings, disfellowshipping, their treatment of children, censorship and related).

_____. *Worse then Waco.* Stoughton, MA: Comments from the Friends. 1993, 144p. (An excellent review of the Watchtower medical quackery and the results of their policy focusing on the blood transfusion ban and the past organ transplant prohibition; many case histories are included.)

_____. *Jehovah's Witness Literature A Critical Guide to Watchtower Publications.* Grand Rapids, MI: Baker Book House 1993 207 pp. (An extensive annotated guide to many Watchtower publications from 1879 to date; much excellent historical information).

_____. *"No Blood."* Assonet, MA: Comments from the friends. 1995, 144 pp. (A "novel" about a Jehovah's Witness boy who needs a transfusion to stay alive, but his Jehovah Witness parents block it, and a court battle results. In the end, the boy won and received the needed treatment.)

_____. *Answering Jehovah's Witnesses Subject by Subject.* Grand Rapids: Baker Book House, 1996, 247 pp., pb. (The Watchtower's beliefs on a wide variety of topics focusing on their many errors, contradictions and changes).

_____. *Blood on the Altar; Confessions of a Jehovah's Witness Minister.* Amherst, NY: Prometheus 1996 285 pp. (A part autobiography account of Reeds life as a Witness, why he left and the tragedy of the blood prohibition rule).

_____. *Jehovah-Talk; The Mind Control Language of Jehovah's Witnesses.* Grand Rapids, MI: Baker Books 1977 158 pp. pb. (A dictionary of Watchtower terms and Why they use the special vocabulary called "J.W.ese").

Reppas, Thanasis. *So As Never to Know War.* Athens, Greece, 1979, 356 pp. (About the injustice, prison and court experiences of Greek Witnesses; written by a Greek Witness attorney).

Rhodes, Ron. *Reasoning from the Scriptures with Jehovah's Witnesses.* Eugene, OR:

Harvest Horse Pub. 1993, 437 pp. (a well written, extensively documented work that covers mostly doctrine, the trinity, hell, the soul, the Holy Spirit, heaven and the unique Watchtower doctrine on blood transfusion prohibitions.)

Robertson, William. *The I.B.S.A. or Russellites in Prophecy.* Edinburgh, Scotland: Bible Student Publishing Co., c. 1922, 128 pp.; 1923 ed., 192 pp.

Robinson, J.L. *The Truth About Jehovah's Witnesses.* New York: Carlton Press, 1969, 45 pp., hb. (A very poor book; the author has only superficial knowledge of the Witnesses; covers the trinity, soul, hell, blood transfusion and eschatology).

Rogerson, Alan Thomas. *Millions Now Living Will Never Die.* London, England: Constable and Co., 1969, 216 pp., hb. (This is one of the best books ever written on the Witnesses. Rogerson (Ph.D., Oxford) was raised a Witness, and has done a great deal of research. This extremely well-reasoned and researched work is based on his Ph.D. thesis at Oxford).

———. *Millionenen die nu leven zullen nooit sterven: een beschouwing over de Jehovah's Getuigen.* Baarn, Bosch & Keuning, 1971, 221 pp. (Millions who now are living will never die: a considering about the Jehovah's Witnesses, a revision and translation of the above work) [Dutch ed.]

———. *Viele von uns werden niemals sterben: Geschichte und Geheimnis der Zeugen Jehovas.* Hamburg: Furche Verlag; Zürich; Theologischer Verlag, 1971, 228 pp. (in German).

Rondelle, H.K. la. *De profetische aanspraken van het Wachttorengenootschap. Een onderzoek naar de grondstructuur van de Koninkrijksboodschap van de Jehovah's Getuigen.* Den Haag, Veritas, 1964, 201 pp. (The prophetic claims of the Watchtower Society. An examination to the basic principles of the Kingdom message of the Jehovah's Witnesses).

Roper, Wayne and Norma. *Weekend Miracle.* Erin Ontario, Canada: The Boston Mills Press. 64 pp. (The story of the quick-build Kingdom Halls, a team of hundreds of witnesses who build a Kingdom Hall in a weekend; many black and white and color photographs. The authors evidently are not Witnesses, but are very sympathetic).

Rosen, Fred. *Blood Crimes.* New York, NY: Pinnacle Books, Kensington Pub. 1996 335 p. (About the skinhead murders by 3 boys all which were raised Witnesses; shows the critical importance of the J.W. faith and teachings in the crime).

Rosenthal, Stanley. *One God or Three?* Fort Washington, PA: Christian Literature Crusade, 1978, 94 pp.

Ross, Edward Eugene. *Jehovah's Witnesses: A Study and Analysis.* N.d., 94 pp.

Roundhill, Jack. *Meeting Jehovah's Witnesses.* Guilford, London: Lutterworth Educational, 1973, 40 pp., pb. (A good review of what the Watchtower teaches and an excellent reasonable analysis of their teachings and history).

Rowe, F.L., ed. *Russell-White Debate.* Cincinnati, OH: F.L. Rowe, 1908, 196 pp., hb. (reprinted by Campbell's Bookshelf of Magadore, OH, c. 1975). (The transcript of the Feb. 28, 1908 debate between Russell and Reverend L.S. White, a Church of Christ, on such topics as Hellfire, the Trinity, etc.).

Sabiers, Karl. *Where Are the Dead?* Los Angeles, CA: Christian Pocket Books, 1959, 190 pp., pb. (Swedish ed.: *Var ar de doda?* Orebro, Seden, 1970) (This work is primarily a critique of the Witnesses' view of Hell. The author quotes Rutherford extensively).

Sadlack, Emil, and Otto Sadlack. *The Desolations of the Sanctuary*. St. Louis, MO: Pastoral Bible Institute, 1930 (1st English ed., original edition in German, 1928), 314 pp., hb., pb. (An excellent, detailed doctrinal refutation of select early Rutherford teachings that conflict with those of C.T. Russell by two of Russell's followers. The authors were active in the Watchtower in Russell's day, and left because they could not accept Rutherford's many changes).

Sagau, Antonio M. *Testigos de Quien?* Publicaciones Portavoz Evangelico, 1963, 4th ed. 1974, 108 pp., pb. (Witnesses of Whom?) (in Spanish) (Covers primarily doctrine from an evangelical world view).

Saleeby, Abdallah Assed. *Truth Triumphant: or Falsehood Stripped of Its Mask*. Norfolk, VA: pub. by author, 1919, 145 pp., hb. (A critique of Watchtower teaching on the soul, hell, angels, the trinity and salvation by an evangelical Christian).

Santos, Jose Estevao dos. *A Verdada Sobre las Testemunhas de Jeova*. N.p.: pub by author, 1975, 196 pp. (The Truth About Jehovah's Witnesses) (in Spanish).

Scheurlen, Paul. *Die Sekten der Gegenwart und neurre Weltanschauungsgebilde*. Stuttgart: Qaell-Verlag der Evang. Gesellschaft, 4. Auflage, 1930, 440 pp. (The Sects of the Present and New World) (in German).

Schlegel, Fritz. *Die Wahrheit über die Ernsten Bibelforscher*. Vol. I. Freiburg: Kehl Eckmann W. Rh., 1922, 252 pp. (The Truth About the Serious Bible Researchers (Jehovah's Witnesses) (in German).

_____. *Die Teufelsmaske der Ernsten Bibelforscher; Propheten und Pioniere gewaltsamen Umsturzes*. Vol. II. Neckargemund, 1925, 217 pp. (The Devil's Mask of the Serious Bible Researcher: Prophets and Pioneer of the Violent Overthrow of the World).

Schnell, William. *Thirty Years a Watchtower Slave*. Grand Rapids, MI: Baker Book House, 1956, 207 pp., hb., pb. (2nd ed. reprinted in 1973, pb.) (Dutch: *Dertig jaar in de greep van Jehovah's Getuigen*. Groningen, Haan, 1958, 240 pp. (Thirty years in the grasp of the Jehovah's Witnesses) (German translation: *Falsche Zeugen stehen wider mich. 30 Jahre Sklave des Wachtturms*) Konstanz, Christliches Verlags Anstalt, 1960, 190 pp. (A detailed history of the Watchtower by an ex-Witness; covers much material about the situation in Germany; Schnell was a Zone servant in Ohio, thus has much information on the inner workings of the Watchtower).

_____. *Into the Light of Christianity*. Grand Rapids, MI: Baker Book House, 1959 (reprinted in 1976), pb. Reprinted with corrections as Jehovah's *Witnesses Errors Exposed*. 1985, pb.211 pp.(A critique of the Watchtower doctrines; especially Hell, trinity, soul; some history).

_____. *Christians Awake!* Grand Rapids, MI: Baker Book House, 1969, 157 pp., pb. (tells how Christians can Witness for Christ using the Jehovah's Witnesses as a reference point).

_____. *How to Witness to Jehovah's Witnesses*. Grand Rapids, MI: Baker Book House, 1975. 157 pp., pb. (A reprint of *Christians Awake!* above).

Scott, Frank Earl. *Armageddon and You*. Portland, OR: Metropolitan Press, 1972, 124 pp., pb. (An ex-Witness dentist argues that the Watchtower has more truth than any other religion; in this work he predicted Armageddon will start on Sept. 6, 1970 and will end on Oct. 21, 1970).

_____. *Revelation of Mysteries.* Portland, OR: Metropolitan Press, 1972, 124 pp., pb. (Concludes that Jehovah's Witnesses alone are the Scripturally approved Christians during our last generation; he concluded in this book that Armageddon will come April 7, 1974, and end on June 3, 1974).

Segaud, Evelyne. *Confessions d'un ancien temoin de Jehovah.* Paris: Pensee Universelle, 1976, 215 pp. (The Confessions of a Former Jehovah's Witness).

Shields, T.T. *Russellism or Rutherfordism: The Teachings of the International Bible Students, Alias Jehovah's Witnesses, in the Light of the Holy Scriptures.* Grand Rapids, MI: Zondervan Publ. House, 1934, 106 pp. (2nd ed. 1942, 99 pp., pb.) (A Baptist pastor in Canada critiques Watchtower doctrines; includes much interesting history, originally a series of sermons).

Skjerpe, Olav. *Jehovas Vitner--Hven laever de?* Oslow, Norway: Stavanger Nomi Forlag, 1970, 134 pp. (God's Witnesses: Who Are They?) Swedish ed., *Jehovas Vitten och vad de lär.* Stockholm, Sweden: Aktiebolaget Tryckmans, 1971, 125 pp., pb. (Jehovah's Witnesses and What They Teach) (in Swedish) (Covers history and doctrine).

_____. *Jehovas Vittnen och Vad de Lär.* Stockholm, Sweden, 1971, 125 pp.

Spadafora, Francesco. *Testimoni de Geova, Avventisti, Millenaristi.* Rovigo: Istituto padano di arti grafiche, 1951, 123 pp. (The Jehovah Witness, Adventists, and Millennialists) (in Italian).

_____. *Pentecostali e Testimoni di Geova.* Rovigo: 1st. pandano di arti grafiche, 3rd ed., 1968, 298 pp. (Pentecostals and Jehovah's Witnesses) (A critique of Witnesses and the Pentecostals by a Roman Catholic).

Spier, II.J. *De Jehovah's Getuigen en de Bijbel.* Kampen: J.H. Kok, 1971, 192 pp., 1982 ed, 220 pp. (Jehovah's Witnesses Against the Bible) (Much excellent information found nowhere else, covers history, doctrine and lifestyle).

Springmeier, Fritz. *The Watchtower & the Masons; A Preliminary Investigation.* Published by Author Portland, OR 1992 242 pp (An attempt to document the influence of the Masons on the Watchtower Society).

Stafford, Greg. *Jehovah's Witnesses Defended; An Answer to Scholars and Critics.* Huntington Beach, CA : Elihu Books 1998 273 pp. (A Witnesses attempts to defend Watchtower teaching and mistakes; focuses on doctrinal issues, especially the trinity)

Stanley, Joel. *The Patriarch and the Prodigal Son: What I Witnessed as a 'Jehovah's Witness.'* Springfield, MA: Pub. by author, 1983, 148 pp., 2nd ed. 1984. 175 pp. (An interesting, lively, biographical account of Stanley's experience as a Witness and the injustice that he faced).

Sterling, Chandler W. *The Witnesses: One God, One Victory.* Chicago: Henry Regnery Co., 1975, 198 pp., hb. (An excellent history and review of the Witness' beliefs which is marred by many mistakes, most of which are minor).

Stevens, Leonard. *Salute! The Case of the Bible vs. the Flag.* New York: Coward, McCann and Geohegan, Inc., 1973, 159 pp., hb. (A history of the Gobitis case and the flag salute cases in general).

Stevens, W.C. *Why I Reject the Helping Hand of Millennial Dawn.* New York: Alliance Press, Nyack, NJ, 1920? 156 pp. (Stevens was at the Missionary Institute).

Stevenson, W.C. *Year of Doom: 1975.* London: Hutchinson and Co., 1967, 209 pp., hb. (published in U.S. as *Inside Story of Jehovah's Witnesses,* Hart Publ. Co., 1968, 209 pp., hb.) (An excellent critique of the history and practices of the movement by a former Witness overseer who left Cambridge in 1956 to become a full-time minister. He left the Watchtower movement in 1965).

Stroup, Herbert Hewitt. *The Jehovah's Witnesses.* New York: Columbia University Press, 1945, 180 pp., hb. (reprinted in 1967 by Russell and Russell of New York). (This is the first extensive sociological study of the Witnesses; much information found nowhere else; it is now a classic, and it is an imperative read for further study).

Süsskind, Eckhard von. *Zeugen Jehovas. Anspruch und Wirklichkeit der Wachtturm-Gesellschaft.* Neuhausen, Stuttgart, Hänssler, 1985, 128 pp. (Tagesfragen, 16) (Witnesses of Jehovah. Claims and reality of the Watchtower Society) [German]

Tanyu, Hikmet. *Yehova Sahitleri.* Ankara, Turkey: ELIF Matbaacitite, 204 pp., (Jehovah's Witnesses) [Turkish]

Thomas, Frank W. *Masters of Deception.* Grand Rapids, MI: Baker Book House, 1972, 158 pp., pb. (A critique of Watchtower doctrine--the soul, trinity, hell, justified lying--by a fundamentalist).

Thomas, Stan. *Jehovah's Witnesses and What They Believe.* Grand Rapids, MI: Zondervan Publishing House, 1967, 159 pp., hb. (A former Canadian Witness and "Servant." Thomas covers history, doctrine, and lifestyle; he is now an Evangelical).

Tomsett, Valerie. *Released from the Watchtower.* Birkenhead, England: Willmer Brothers, Ltd., 1971, 128 pp., pb. (An ex-Witness tells of her experience in the Watchtower and how and why she left; a very readable, well-written work).

_____. *Watchtower Chaos.* London, England: Lakeland Publ., 1974, 112 pp., pb. (Covers doctrine, but much material on sociological-psychological aspects of the society).

Trombley, Charles. *Bible Answers for Jehovah's Witnesses.* Broken Arrow, OK: Expositor Publications, 1966, 110 pp., pb. (A history of the Watchtower and a critique of their major doctrines by an ex-Witness now a Pentecostal minister and the head of Trombley Ministries).

_____. *Kicked out of the Kingdom.* Monroeville, PA: Whitaker House, 1974, 184 pp., pb. (Trombley's account of how he was disfellowshipped in part for believing in faith-healing; written in novel format. Trombley is now the head of a large international charismatic ministry).

Trost, Alex, ed, *Jehovah's Witnesses: Alternatives to Blood Transfusion in Adults.* Self published c. 1972, 603 pp. (A collection of articles from medical journals which relate to the blood transfusion issue).

_____. *Jehovah's Witnesses: Alternatives to Blood Transfusions in Minors.* N.d.: Self published c. 1972, 601 pp.

_____. *Jehovah's Witnesses: Alternatives to Blood Transfusion.* Self published, 1973, 603 pp. (A selection of articles from the previous two volumes).

Twisselmann, Hans Jürgen. *Vom, "Zeugen Jehovas" zum Zeugen Jesu Christi.* B. Gießen, Basel,: Brunnen Verlag, 1961, 116 pp., pb.; 3rd ed. 1972. (From *Jehovah's Witnesses to Jesus Christ's Witnesses*) (A critique of Witness' doctrine and policy from an Evangelical world view) (Twisselmann is an ex-Witness).

_____. *Die Wahrheit, die frei macht: zum Thema "Jehovas Zeugen."* *Anfragen Antworten-Alternativen.* Gießen, Basel: Brunnen Verlag, 1985, 147 pp. (The truth that makes free: to the theme "Jehovah's Witnesses." Information, answers, alternatives). (in German).

TWMC. "The Report" Montgomery, AL, privately printed 1994 176pp. (An extensive discussion of the corruption and erroneous teachings in the Watchtower by a group of witnesses who wish to reform the Watchtower).

Van Buskirk, Michael. *The Sandcastle of the Jehovah's Witnesses.* Santa Ana, CA: Caris, 1975, 172 pp., pb. (A critique of Witness doctrine, includes many photocopies of incriminating Watchtower publications).

Vaz, Antonio Luiz. *As Testemunhas de Jeov'a.* Braga, Portugal: Braga-Editora, 1967, 132 pp. (A critique of Witness doctrine and beliefs). (In Spanish).

Verrier, Chanoine Henri. *L'Eglise devant les T'emoins de Jehovah.* Raismes (Nord): Wattel, 1956, 230 pp. (Position of the Church on Jehovah's Witnesses).(In French).

Volksströmungen. *Religiöse Volksströmungen der Gegenwart. Vortrag über die "Ernsten Blbelforscher," Okkultismus und die Anthroposophie R. Steiners.* Freiburg, Herder & Company, (Present days religious movements. Lecture about the "Earnest Bible Students," occultism and the Antroposophy of Rudolf Steiner). 1924, VII, 14 pp. (in German).

Walter, Paul H. *A Small Voice Crying in the Wilderness.* Los Angeles: Great Western Book Publ. Co., 1962, 160 pp. (A work by an active Witness in favor of the Society. This volume is very rare--no known original copies are left; uses primarily secular arguments to argue for the validity of Witness teaching; much history and current events covered; written in line with Marley Cole's books).

Ward, Haywood D. *Poems About You and People You Know.* Baltimore, MD: American Literary Press, 1994, 136 pp. (Poems by a Jehovah's Witness for Jehovah's Witness. Published for "common everyday people.")

Warne, Joan and Doug. *For Jehovah's Witnesses With Love.* Kailua, HI: Pub. by author, 1982, 152 pp. (A personal account of two ex-Witnesses, many Scriptures used to refute the Watchtower).

Warren, Russell A. *Outnumbered; Exploding the Myth of 144,000 .* Published by the author Eagle Creek, OR. c. 1984 94 pp. (A critic of the 144,000 doctrine).

Watters, Randall. *Thus Said the Governing Body of Jehovah's Witnesses.* Manhattan Beach, CA: pub. by author, 1981, 107 pp. 1995 revised edition 200 pp. (A collection of Watchtower publications, photocopies and reprints from various secular sources, collected to refute some of the Watchtower's major claims. Many examples of the Watchtower's misquoting are given).

_____. *Defending the Faith.* Manhattan Beach, CA: Bethel Ministries, 1970, 176 pp., pb. (A dictionary format of common evangelical responses to Watchtower beliefs; covers everything from the cross to the trinity; an excellent reference).

_____. *Refuting Jehovah's Witnesses.* Manhattan Beach, CA: Bethel Ministries, 1978 219 pp., 1987, 173 pp, pb.Ed (A companion book to the above; the same format).

_____. *Letters to the Editor Book One 1983-1989.* Manhattan Beach, CA: Bethel Ministries 1994 88 pp. (A collection of letters published in *Free Minds*, mostly from ex-Witnesses; very revealing as to the Watchtower's history and problems).

Weis, Christian. *Zeugen Jehovas, Zeugen Gottes? Eine Hilfe zür Kritik.*
        Auseinandersetzung mit der lehre des Wachtturmgesellschaft. Salzburg: Müller,
        Verlag Sankt Peter, 1985, 112 pp. Book 2 1995 148 pp. (Witnesses of Jehovah,
        Witnesses of God? A help to critical explanation of the doctrines of the
        Watchtower Society). (in German).

Werge, Asger Dan. *Kirke Kontra Kaelter.* Kobenhavn, Denmark: Eget Forlag, 1952,
        157 pp. (The Church Against the Cults) (in Danish).

Whalen, William J. *Armageddon Around the Corner.* New York: John Day Co., 1962,
        259 pp., hb. (An excellent general history of the Witnesses by a Catholic layman;
        critical but sympathetic).

White, Timothy (pseudonym for Anthony Wills). *A People for His Name: A History of
        Jehovah's Witnesses and an Evaluation.* New York: Vantage Press, 1967, 418
        pp., hb. (This is one of the most well-researched and documented of all the works
        in this section; Wills has a Ph.D. from Stanford; he covers the history, doctrine,
        policy and their contradictions).

Wilson, Bryan. *The Social Dimensions of Sectarianism.* Oxford: Claredon Press 1990
        (Much on the Witnesses but also covers other sects; chap 8 is a survey of Belgian
        Congregations (p. 149-175 and Chapter 2 is on the conflicts between sects and the
        state p. 25).

Wilting, Joseph Riket. *Som ikke kom; 40 ar bak Jehovah's Vitners pretige fasade.*
        Norway forlaget Ny Vision. (In Danish).

Wisdom, William N., and L.W. Jones. *"The Laodiciean Messenger": His Life, Works
        and Character; The Memoirs of Pastor Russell.* Chicago: The Bible Student's
        Bookstore, 1923, 332 pp. (About the life and teachings of C.T. Russell and his
        movement. Aside from the Horowitz's work, this is the only book written about
        Russell's life and works. Covers scandals, the Great Pyramid of Giza, the
        photodrama of creation, the persecution; much of this material is from the
        Watchtower; also includes phrenology evaluations).

Wisse, A.P. *De Jehovah's Getuigen aangelklaagd; een onthullend verhaal.* 4e druk.
        Kampen, Kok, 1984, 143 pp. (The Jehovah's Witnesses accused; a revealing
        story. 4th pr.).(In Dutch)

Wright, Gerald. *New World Translation: Perversions and Prejudice.* Fort Worth, TX:
        Star Bible and Tract Corp., 1975, 80 pp. pb. (Reprinted in Bergman 1990 p.263-
        342)

Wunderlich, Gerd. *Jehovas Zeugen, die Paradies-Verkäufer. Erfahrungen auf einem
        Irrweg.* (Jehovah's Witnesses, the Paradise-sellers. Experiences about a wrong
        way). Munchen, Claudius Verlag; Aschaffenburg, Pattloch, 1983, 2nd ed, 1985,
        231 pp. (in German).

B. Master's Theses and Ph.D. Dissertations

Of all the works on the Witnesses, the most objective and in many ways the most
useful are the 63 Ph.D. dissertations and Master's theses. About half of these deal fairly
objectively with the Society's history or with various psychological and sociological
aspects of the movement. The most exhaustive is Zygmunt's Master's and Ph.D. theses
(his Ph.D. thesis is three volumes--978 pages--and is the most complete history available).
Also highly recommended are Beckford's, Czatt's, and Manwaring's (a 765-page

discussion of the flag-salute cases, the most extensive work ever done on this issue) theses. Also very useful are the theses of Rogerson, Stroup, and Sprague (an excellent history, it contains long discussions of the Witnesses as people, and was accepted for a Ph.D. in Sociology at Harvard in the 1940s).

A number of the theses are in political science (see Kernaghan, Kim, and Richards), and about half of the works are theological; the theses of Curry, Morey, Gruss, Goodrich, and Lapides are all excellent. Other extremely useful works are Cumberland (an excellent history which contains much of the same information that Zygmunt does, but is far briefer and more succinct), Elhard (a good review of the flag-salute cases in America), and Hellmund (an excellent review of the Witnesses in Germany).

Arasola, Kai Jaakko. "The End of Historicism. Millerite Hermeneutic of Time
    Prophecies in the Old Testament." D.Th.Diss--Upsala Universitet (Sweden),
    1989 226 pp. (Miller had fifteen Biblical "proofs" that the second Advent that was
    to occur in 1843. His views were critical in developing Watchtower doctrine).

Assimeng, John Maxwell. "A Sociological Analysis of the Impact and Consequences of
    Some Christian Sects in Selected African Countries." Oxford University,
    England, 1968; see especially pp. 97-214. (Ph.D. diss.) (An excellent well-
    documented study of the Watchtower in Africa in the 1900s to the 1950s).

Baron, Rev. Michael. "A Critical Examination, in the Light of the Catholic Doctrine, of
    the Key Teachings of the Jehovah's Witnesses." Catholic University of America,
    Washington, DC, 1956. (Doctor of Sacred Theology, D.D. diss.)

Beckford, James A. "A Sociological Study of Jehovah's Witnesses in Britain."
    University of Reading, Reading, England, 1972, 892 pp. (Ph.D. diss.)

Bergman, Jerry. "Community and Social Control in A Chiliastic Religious Sect: A
    Participant Observation Study." Bowling Green, OH, Master's thesis, 1985, 265
    pp. (About the social network of the Witnesses and why people join and the social
    rewards they receive as a result of membership).

Botting, Heather D. "The Power and the Glory: The Symbolic Vision and Social Dynamic
    of Jehovah's Witnesses." University of Alberta, Edmonton, Alberta, Canada,
    1982, ? pp. (Ph.D. diss.)

Brackenridge, Douglass. "A Study of the Jehovah's Witnesses' Interpretation of the
    Scriptures Relevant to the Person of Jesus Christ in the Light of Historic
    Christianity." Xenia College, Pittsburgh, PA, 1959, 81 pp. (Master's thesis)

Brose, Alberta Jeanne. "Jehovah's Witnesses: Recruitment and Encultration in a
    Millennial Sect." Riverside, CA: University of California, 1982, 246 pp. (An
    excellent participant observation sociological study of one congregation in
    California) (Ph.D. diss.) (Stresses multicausal theory of recruitment and
    inculturation).

Burski, Ulrich von. "Die Zeugen Jehovas: Die Gewissensfreiheit und das Strafrecht."
    Freiburg im Breisgau, 1970, 181 pp. (Ph.D. diss.) (The Jehovah's Witnesses:
    Freedom of Conscience and the Criminal Law) (About the blood transfusion
    issues and state-church conflicts. Also covers their history and select teachings;
    includes several case histories).

Cahill, Susan Neunzig. "Passions of Memory: The Religious Theme in American Women
    Writers Autobiographies Since 1945." (Ph.D. Diss)--Fordham University, 1995
    368 p. (A Study of the religious background of five culturally diverse American

women writers including Barbara Grizzuti Harrison, a prominent ex-Witness.

Cohn, Werner. "Jehovah's Witnesses as a Proletarian Sect." New School for Social
Research, NY, 1954, 98 pp. (Master's thesis). (A study of Witness social-
economic life and theology as related to their total social status).

Cobreros Mendazona, Eduardo. "Compulsory Medical Treatments and Right to Health.
Systematic Study of The Italian Law and Spanish Law." Ph.D. Diss.--Universidad
Del Pais Vasco/Euskal Herriko Unibertsitatea (Spain), 1987 878 pp. (The first part
the study of the regulation of compulsory medical treatment under Italian law is
carried out. The second part of this study is dedicated to Spanish law. At the
beginning of the second part, article 43 of the 1978 Constitution is studied.
Particular attention is paid to the study of the problems arising from the Witnesses
denial of needed blood transfusions)

Côté Pauline. "Transactions Politiques et Collectivites Sacrales: Le Cas des
Charismatiques et des Temoins de Jéhovah," Ph.D. dissertation in social sciences
Université Laval, Quebec, Canada, 1988, 356 pp. (100 pages of notes; an
extensive sociological study of the Witnesses in Canada and the world). (Political
Transactions and Sacred Collective: The Case of the Charismatics and the
Jehovah's Witnesses)

Council, William Thomas, III. "Jehovah's Witnesses: The Study of a Christian
Bureaucratic Structure." B.A. honor's thesis, the University of North Carolina at
Chapel Hill, 1972.

Cronn-Mills, Daniel David. "A Social Construction of Reality Evident in the Discourse of
Jehovah's Witnesses." (PH.D. Diss) The University of Nebraska-Lincoln, 1994
278 p. (Explores how the contextual reality of Jehovah's Witnesses influences
their lives and their social reality. The Witness' reality is composed of three
separate worlds--Satan's, the Witness', and Jehovah's World. Witness' reality is
composed of three primary themes, visual, family, and foundation.)

Cross, Sholto. "The Watchtower Movement in South Central Africa." Oxford
University, Oxford, England 1973. (Ph.D. diss.)

Cumberland, William. "A History of the Jehovah's Witnesses." University of Iowa,
Iowa City, IA, 1958, 309 pp. (Ph.D. diss.) (An excellent well-documented study
focusing on their early history; does not cover much doctrine, contains much
material found nowhere else).

Curry, Melvin Dotson, Jr. "A Linguistic and Theological Evaluation of the New World
Translation." Wheaton College, Wheaton, IL, 1963, 127 pp. (Master's thesis)

_____. "Jehovah's Witnesses: The Effects of Millenarianism on the Maintenance of a
Religious Sect." Florida State University, Tallahassee, FL, 1980, 317 pp. (Ph.D.
diss.) (An excellent study on the millennial movement; specifically Russell's and
Rutherford's interpretations carried out within the framework of Roy Wallis'
reformation).

Czatt, Milton. "The International Bible Students Association: A Critical Study in
Contemporary Religion." Yale University, New Haven, CT, 1929, 356 pp.
(Ph.D. diss.) (One of the first major studies on the Watchtower; a must for a
historical perspective).

Dericquebourg, Regis. "Les Témains de Jéhovah, dynamique d'un groupe religieux et
rapport á L'institution essai de description psychosocilogique d'une secte." 1979
Ph.D. Thesis, Paris Sorbonne Univ., under Professor Jean Séguy. (The J.W.s
Dynamics of a Religious Group and Relation to the Institutional Testing of
Psychosocial Logic of a Sect.)

Dye, Elsa Maria. "Sectarian Protestantism: Another Dimension--The Case of Jehovah's Witnesses." The University of San Diego, San Diego, CA, 1968, 132 pp. (Master's thesis) (A six month exploratory, participant observation study of one congregation of Witnesses; the author found that Witness socialization produced behavior patterns congruent with middle class standards).

Elhard, D. Wayne. "The Brooks, Alberta, National Anthem Controversy." Baylor University, Waco, TX, 1976, 150 pp. (Master's thesis) (A history of the Witnesses flag salute conflicts and legal battles in Canada).

Fogerson, Dewey. "The Use of the Term 'Jehovah' in the New World Translation of the Christian Scriptures. (Master's thesis)

Goodrich, Arthur Reddington. "Soteriology in Jehovah's Witnesses." Dallas Theological Seminary, Dallas, TX, 1955. (Master of Theology thesis)

Gruss, Edmond Charles. "Apostles of Denial." Talbot Theological Seminary, Biola College, La Mirada, CA, 1961, 307 pp. (Master's thesis) His book of the same name is a revision of this thesis.

Hellmund, Dietrich. "Geschichte der Zeugen Jehovas (In der Zeit von 1870 bis 1920) mit einem Anhang; Geschichte der Zeugen Jehovas in Deutschland bis 1970." Theological faculty of the University of Hamburg, Hamburg, Germany, 1972, 340 pp. (Ph.D. diss.) (The History of the Jehovah's Witnesses from 1870 to 1920 in the appendix a History of the Jehovah's Witnesses in Germany to 1970).

Henson, Alan. "A Critique of the Doctrine of Hell in the Theology of the Jehovah's Witnesses." 59 pp.

Horrell, John Scott. "Isms versus a Biblical Doctrine of the Trinity." Dallas Theological Seminary, Dallas, TX, 1977. (Master of Theology thesis).

Jaffe, Clella Iles. "An Ethnography of a Rural Elementary School District Containing Three Types of Minority Students." Ph.D.Diss--Oregon State University, 1990. 187 p. (A modified ethnography study of a rural elementary school located in North Marion County, Oregon. This country is the site of Hispanics who work mainly in agricultural-related jobs. Jehovah's Witnesses comprise a cognitive minority whose belief system sets them apart from mainstream society. Children from these groups attend the small, local school, bringing varying cultural backgrounds, values, and perspectives to their environment).

Jansma, Lammert G. "Melchiorieten, Munstersen en Batenburgers. Een sociologische analyse van een millennistische beweging uit de 16e ceuw." Buitenpost, Lykele Jansma, 1977. 348 p. 22 cm Met bibliogr. en reg. 163315, Proefschrift Rotterdam. (Dissertation, University of Rotterdam, Ph.D. dissertation in the Social Science)

Kaplan, William. "The World War Two Ban of the Jehovah's Witnesses in Canada: A Study in the Development of Civil Rights." Stanford University, 1988 (J.S.D diss.) (This was revised and published as a book, which see).

Kernhagen, William David Kenneth. "Freedom of Religion in the Province of Quebec with Particular Reference to the Jews, Jehovah's Witnesses and Church-State Relations, 1930-1960." Duke University, Durham, NC, 1966, 363 pp. (Ph.D. diss.) (A study of religious freedom in Quebec which is 99 percent Catholic; covers the mob violence and court cases against the Witnesses during the 1930s to the 1960s).

Kim, Richard Chong Chin. "Jehovah's Witnesses and the Supreme Court--An Examination of the Cases Brought Before the United States Supreme Court

Involving the Rights Claimed by Jehovah's Witnesses, from 1938-1960."
University of Oklahoma, Norman, OK, 1963, 395 pp. (Ph.D. diss.) (An
excellent, well documented study of cases that the Watchtower brought to the
American Supreme court on the flag salute, public proselytizing, the draft and
related cases).

Klose, L.V. "The Cults and Sects in the Los Angeles Area." The University of Southern
California, Los Angles, 1940. (Master's thesis).

Kunhikannan, Palangadan. "A Down East Fishing Community: The Progress of
Transformation (Maine)." (Ph.D. Diss)--State University of New York at Stony
Brook, 1984 367 p. (A detailed ethnographic description of a small fishing
community in Maine which grew from a single Church to which all residents
nominally belonged. The major religious activity now centers on two relatively
new institutions, the Church of God (Pentecostal) and the Jehovah's Witnesses).

Lapides, Louis S. "The Jehovah's Witnesses and Jesus Christ." Talbot Theological
Seminary, Biola College, La Mirada, CA, 1977, 45 pp. (Church History Course
thesis) (A scholarly critique of the Witness views of Christology).

Maeson, William August. "Jehovah's Witnesses Decisions in the United States Supreme
Court as an Empirical Test Involving Yinger's Application of the Iron Law of
Oligarchy to Religious Movements." Indiana State University, Terre Haute, IN,
1968, 58 pp. (Master's thesis) (Found that Witnesses had a higher Supreme Court
win ratio than all other groups he compared).

Manwaring, David Roger. "The Flag Salute Litigation." The University of Wisconsin,
Whitewater, WI, 1959, 765 pp. (Ph.D. diss)

McDowell, Joshlin. "An Examination of the Jehovah's Witnesses' Doctrine of the
Creation of Christ Based upon Proverbs 8:28, Colossians 1:15 and Revelation
3:14." Dallas Theological Seminary, Dallas, TX, 1966, 90 pp. (B.A. thesis)

McLean, David Leslie. "History of the Jehovah's Witnesses: A Study in Biography,
1870-1962." McMaster University, Hamilton, Ont., Canada, 1963, 155 pp.
(B.A. thesis) (A history of the Watchtower divided into three sections, Russell,
Rutherford, and Knorr; a fair critique by a divinity student).

McNally, John Aloysius, III. "The Right to Die: Non-consenting Adult Jehovah's
Witnesses and Blood Transfusions." Cornell University, 1970 (M.A. thesis) 80
pp. (A study of the Witness prohibition on blood transfusions from the legal and
human rights standpoint; concludes that they have a right to take their own life for
this reason).

Morey, Robert A. "How to Witness to a Jehovah's Witness." Westminster Theological
Seminary, Philadelphia, PA, 1979, c. 100 pp. (Ph.D. diss).

Newman, Stephen Lee. "The Jehovah's Witnesses' Use of the Greek New Testament in
Relation to the Doctrine of the Deity of Christ." Dallas Theological Seminary,
Dallas, TX, 1976. (Master's thesis)

Newton, Merlin Owen. "Preach the Gospel Unto Every Creature: Jehovah's Witnesses
Alabama and the U.S. Supreme Court 1939 - 1946, Tuscaloosa, AL (Ph.D.
Diss.), University of Alabama, 1992, 345 pp. (An extensive study of two key
U.S. Supreme Court decisions and the persons behind them.)

Potter, Robert. "The Eschatology of the Jehovah's Witnesses." England. (M.A. thesis)

_____. "Social Psychological Study of Fundamental Christianity." Sussex University,
England, 1985. (Ph.D. diss.)

Ramos, Jose Carlos. "A People Waiting for Salvation: A Biblical Evaluation of Watchtower Christology and Soteriology with Suggested Strategies for the Evangelization of Jehovah's Witnesses." Andrews University, 1984, 222 pp. (Ph.D. diss.) (A critique of Watchtower theology from a SDA perspective, focusing almost totally on their doctrine of Christ Christolog and Soterbiology).

Reed, Jerold Franklin. "A Componential Analysis of the Ecudorian Protestant Church." Doctor of Missions Thesis--Fuller Theological Seminary, School of World Mission, 1974. 230 p. A Compential Analysis of the Ecuadorian Protestant Church is a study of over fifty factors relating to the internal-growth of the Protestant Church in Ecuador and shows how these factors effect its expansion growth. The Jehovah's Witnesses and the Mormons are included.

Richards, Claud Henry. "Jehovah's Witnesses" A Study in Religious Freedom." Duke University, Durham, NC, 1945, 166 pp. (Ph.D. diss).

Rogerson, Alan Thomas. "A Sociological Analysis of the Origin and Development of the Jehovah's Witnesses and Their Schismatic Groups." Oxford University, Oxford, England, 1972, 302 pp. (Ph.D. diss). (A must for a student of Watchtower history and sociology).

Sack, Ursula Hilde. "Case Studies of Voluntary Defectors from Intensive Religious Groups." University of Southern California, 1983. (Ph.D. diss), 294 pp. (One of the three cases she uses for her research is a Witness. Much excellent material on the attraction of intensive religious groups such as the Witnesses).

Salzman, Donald M. "A Study of the Isolation and Immunization of Individuals from the Larger Society in Which They Are Living." University of Chicago, Chicago, IL, 1951, 244 pp. (Master's thesis). (An excellent sociological study of the Witnesses focusing on lifestyle and organization).

Schwartz, Miriam Elaine. "The Jehovah's Witnesses: A Sect in Society." Liberal Arts College of the City of New York, 1954. (Honors Essay, B.A. thesis).

Scritchfield, Lois Fern. "Jehovah's Witnesses; Espit de Corps and Morals." Washington, University St. Louis, MO, 1947. (A.M. thesis) (No known copy of this work has survived).

Sprague, Theodore Wentworth. "Some Problems in the Integration of Social Groups with Special Reference to Jehovah's Witnesses." Harvard University, Cambridge, MA, 1942, 446 pp. (Ph.D. diss). (An invaluable study of the Witnesses in the United States in the late 1930s and early 1940s; much of the research was obtained from individual interactions with Witnesses).

Stroup, Herbert Hewitt. "The Jehovah's Witnesses." New School for Social Research, NY, 1950, 256 pp. (Ph.D. diss). (This diss was revised and published as a book, which please see).

Stryckman, Judith. *Les mécanismes de cohésion dans une secte établie: une observation participante des Témoins de Jéhovah Thèse de l'Université de Laval,* 1972. (The Mechanisms of Cohesion in an Established Sect; A Participant Observation of the J.W.s from the University of Laud.)

Weber, Herbert. *Religioese Mobilitaet. Religioese Sondergemeinschaften Und Katholische Kirche: Am Beispel Von Jehovas Zeugen* (Mobility In Religious Communities. Special Religious Communities (Sects) and The Catholic Church: An Example of the Jehovah's Witnesses) Ph.D. Diss.--Universitaet Wein (Australia), 1990. (In German). (Small religious communities have many social advantages to meeting people's needs and this is why many people are converting to these communities. The Witnesses are investigated as an example of religious mobility. Conversations to and out of them show both the attraction and the inconsistency of the Witnesses.)

Williams, Joel Stephen. "Ethical Issues in Compulsory Medical Treatment: A Study of Jehovah's Witnesses and Blood Transfusion." Baylor University, 1987. (Ph.D. diss). (A review of the issues, cases and history of the transfusion ban).

Zellner, William Wesley. "Of Another World: The Jehovah's Witnesses." South Dakota State University, 1981. (Ph.D. diss). 124 pp. (A study of how and why Jehovah's Witnesses recruit and retain new members; many comparisons of the Witnesses to the Moonies; concludes that the group's social characteristics are more important than the group's message).

Zygmunt, Joseph F. "Social Estrangement and the Recruitment Process in a Chiliastic Sectarian Movement." University of Chicago, Chicago, IL, 1953, 396 pp. (Master's thesis). (This work is critical to understanding the movement; a study of what attracts people to Witnesses and the techniques of recruitment that they use).

_____. "Jehovah's Witnesses: A Study of Symbolic and Structural Elements in the Development and Institutionalization of a Sectarian Movement." University of Chicago, Chicago, IL, 1967, 978 pp. (Ph.D. diss). (The most complete historical-sociological study of the Witnesses ever done on the Witnesses; a must for a serious researcher, fairly sympathetic to the Witnesses).

C. Booklets

Works in this section are stapled, soft covered, have fewer than 96 pages, and, except as noted, are completely devoted to Jehovah's Witnesses. Booklets, being briefer than books, are more limited in scope, often reflecting less research and investigation. Some are very poorly done. About 90% of the booklets in this section are theological in nature, and about 90% of these were written specifically to denounce the Witnesses, mostly concentrating on theological criticisms against the Witness' view of the trinity, hell, the soul and eschatology from an Evangelical perspective.

The Russian works (of which there are over a dozen in this section) are generally critical not only of the Witnesses but of religion in general, the Witnesses simply being one example of the shortcomings and inadequacy of organized religion. The Soviet booklets contain excellent information not found elsewhere, although they tend to rely heavily on secondary sources and the accuracy of their sources is sometimes questionable (and in many cases the source is not given).

For the person not interested in extensive research, the booklets are excellent, quick sources but are not as freely available as the books. Most libraries keep books longer than booklets, and the same is true of individuals. Many booklets give a good review of the Witnesses and their beliefs and discuss the problems of these beliefs. Theological discussions highly recommended are those of Bale, Bruce, Kern, and Kneedler. In this section the only contemporary booklets written by Witnesses are the two by Bremer, which are quite dated (published in the 1940s by the author) and two by Stockdale (one contains an excellent discussion of the approximately 5,000 Witnesses imprisoned during World War II; most were imprisoned because of their "total objector" stand, i.e., they refused to perform either combat or noncombat duty in the service.

The only booklets in the Russell era in favor of the followers of Russell are those by Bradford. Most of the nonofficial booklets of this era are listed in the various sections under Bible Students. All the other works are by persons who are neutral toward or opposed to the Witnesses. Two useful booklets are by the Dawn Book Supply, one in favor of Russellism, the other opposed to modern-day Witnesses (much of the literature by the offshoots either discusses the offshoot itself or, if it discusses the Witnesses, tends to be critical of certain teachings).

Excellent booklets for historical study are those published by the American Civil Liberties Union. Several excellent discussions of the controversial stand on blood transfusions taken by the Witnesses appear in Bergman, Montague, and the first work listed under Christadelphian Publications. Extremely useful booklets for historical research, although written primarily about Witness theology, include those by Cook, Pollock, Wiley, Rideout, Ross, Shield, Shaddick, and Swift. An excellent critique from a Seventh-Day Adventist's view is the work by Price and from the Catholic view, those by Rumble.The non English language material is listed according to the guidelines followed in the other sections.

Abel, Ron W. *Christadelphianism: Of God or Men? A Christadelphian Reply to the August, 1962 Watchtower Article.* Privately printed, c. 1963, 33 pp. (A well done critique of the Watchtower's attempt to criticize Christadelphians).

Åberg, Thorsten. *Vad är Jehovas Vitten.* 1961, 18 pp.

Ackland, Donald F. *False Witnesses: An Indictment of "Jehovah's Witnesses."* Stirling, Scotland: Stirling Tract Enterprise, 1958, 24 pp. (A critique of Russell's and Rutherford's works).

Algermissen, K. *Die Internationale Vereinigung Ernster Bibelforscher.* (The International Bible Students Association). Hannover, J. Giesel, 1928, 78 pp., (the 1949 ed. is 43 pp.) (in German).

Alpha and Omega Ministries. *The Watchtower Society and the Name Jehovah.*

Alred, Guy Alfred. *Armageddon, Incorporated.* Glasgow, Scotland: Strictland Press, 1941, 24 pp.

American Civil Liberties Union. *The Persecution of Jehovah's Witnesses.* New York, 1941, 24 pp. (Includes many case histories and the background of the persecution).

_____. *Jehovah's Witnesses and the War.* New York, Jan., 1943, 36 pp. (About the persecution of Witnesses during World War II)

_____. *In Defense of Our Liberties.* New York, 1944.

_____. *Liberty on the Home Front.* New York, July 1945.

_____. *Liberty Is Always Unfinished Business, 36th Annual Report, 1955/56.*

_____. *Justice for All, 37th Annual Report, 1956/57.*

Andibur, Miron Vasil'evich. *Before the Judgment of the People.* Abakan: Khakass Book Publishing House, 1963, 109 pp. (in Russian).

Ankerberg, John and John Weldon. *The Facts on Jehovah's Witnesses; Answers to the 20 Most Frequently Asked Questions About the Watchtower Society.* Eugene, OR: Harvest House Pub., 1988, 48 pp. (Covers theology, the New World Translation, prophecy, the Watchtower's deficient scholarship and world view).

Appel, H. *Biblische Wahrheit so oder so. Von den Irrtümern der Zeugen Jehovas.*
Berlin, Evangelische Verlags Anstalt, 1950, 15 pp. (Biblical truth like this, like
that! About the errors of the Witnesses of Jehovah). (in German).

Ardill, G.E. *Millennial Dawnism; Unscriptural, Pernicious, Soul Destroying.* New
Evangelization Society of New South Wales, c. 1920 (A critique of Watchtower
beliefs and doctrine from an evangelical world view).

Aydin, Ali Arslan, and Hüsyin Atay. *Yehova Sahidlerinia.* Anakara, Turkey, 1973, 55
pp. (Jehovah's Witnesses.)

Baaren, J.I. van *Jehovah's Getuigen, bi jbels of on-bi jbels?* Amsterdam, Stichting
Moria, 1986, 48 pp. (Jehovah's Witnesses, Biblical or non-Biblical?)

Baker, G. *Bijbel of Wachttoren?* Amsterdam, G. Bakker, 1946, 16 pp. (The Bible or the
Watchtower?) (By an ex-Witness). (A critique of doctrine).

Bakker, H. *Jehovah's Getuigen ontmaskerd.* Wageningen, Veenman, 4th printing,
1946, 16 pp. (Jehovah's Witnesses unmasked). (Critiques primarily Russell's
teachings).

Bales, James D. *Jehovah's Witnesses?* Dallas, Texas: Gospel Teachers Publication,
1978, 96 pp. (A critique of the Watchtower from Adam to Zionism, almost one-
hundred topics are listed in alphabetical order).

Ballard, Frank. *Why Not Russellism?* London: Charles H. Kelly, n.d.

Ballew, Harold. *God's Name is Not Jehovah.* Royal Oak, MI, published by author,
1979, revised 1983, 24 pp. Discusses the origin of the word "Jehovah" for God,
and argues that Jesus is God).

Barkley, Betty. *Jehovah's Garden* Privately published 40 pp. 1980's.

Barmhartigheid en geen offerande. *Ni jmegen, Informatie-Centrum,* z. j. 32 pp. (Mercy
and no offering) (Against blood transfusion).

Bartley, Colm J.S. *Searching for the Deep Things of God; A Letter of Concern to My
Brethren.* Lethbridge, Alberta, Canada: Christian Koinonia International, 1982,
32 pp. (A scholarly critique of the Watchtower doctrine of Christ's return).

Bautz, Friedrich Wilhelm. *Die "Zeugen Jehovas." Eine Darstellung ihrer Geschichte und
Lehre und ihre Beurteilung im Lichte der Bibel.* (The "Witnesses of Jehovah." A
description of their history and teachings and also their judgment in the light of
their history and teachings and also their judgment in the light of the scriptures).
Witten (Ruhr), Bundes-Verlag, 1949, 24 pp., 1955 ed. 31 pp. (in German).

_____. *Dsie Zeugen Jehovas: Worte der Aufklarung und Abwehr.* (The Witnesses of
Jehovah: words to clarify and defend). Gladbeck, Schriftenmissions-Verlag, 2nd
ed. 1971, 31 pp. (in German).

Beck, William F. *A Dialog About the Jehovah's Witnesses' Bible, "The New World
Translation."* St. Louis, MO: Concordia Publishing House, 1965, 13 pp. (A
critique of how the NWT renders scriptures that relate to the trinity and deity of
Christ doctrines).

Beijer, Erik. *Jehovas Vittnen.* Stockholm: pub. by author, 1950. (Jehovah's Witnesses)
(In Swedish)

Bergman, Jerry. *Watchtower Congregations: Communion or Conflict?* Santa Ana, CA:
CARIS Press, 1978. 8 pp.

_____. *Religious Objections to Blood Transfusions: A History and Evaluation.* Los Angeles, CA: CARIS Press, 1979. 22 pp.

_____ *Jehovah's Witnesses and Blood Transfusions.* St. Louis, MO: Personal Freedom Outreach, 1981, 20 pp. (A history of this teaching, and the many problems with it, both medical and theological, and the results of the teaching.)

_____. *Jehovas Zeugen und Bluttransfusionen.* (Jehovah's Witnesses and Blood Transfusions.) An extensive revision of the above. (German). 1986

_____. *The Watchtower Cult's Effect on the Human Mind.* Great Britain, International Publications, 1985. 8 pp.

Berry, Harold J. *Witnessing the Cults.* Lincoln, Neb: Good News Broadcasting Association, 1974, 14 pp. (General discussion on cults and how to convert them from an Evangelical view).

Best, J. "Big Business in Religion Being a Scathing Criticism and Exposure of the Origin and Methods of American Book-selling Corporations." Ballarat, Australia: Baxter & Stubbs Printers, c. 1930s, 16 pp. (Much historical focus on Rutherford's critiques of governments, especially the British empire; also critiques doctrine from a Catholic world view).

Bezuglov, Anatoli Alekseevich. *Coming Out of the Darkness.* Moscow: State Publishing House of Juridical Literature, 1960, 44 pp. (in Russian)

Bias, Rod. *"They Shall Know That a Prophet Was Among Them."* Pub. by author, Jan. 1975, 8 pp. (also revised edition, June 1975, slightly different). (Covers several topics, including failed prophecy, Christ's deity).

_____. *Jesus Christ: The Firstborn of All Creation.* Pub. by author, March 1975, 8 pp. (also revised ed., slightly different). (On the deity of Christ and the 1954 Walsh case).

_____. *Why Do Jehovah's Witnesses Have Complete Unity?* Pub. by author, July 1975, 8 pp. (A section of the 1954 Scotland Walsh trial).

_____. *Who Really Is the "Faithful and Discreet Slave?"* Pub. by author, July 1975, 8 pp. (Covers the faithful and discreet slave doctrine; Is Jesus God)

Biederwolf, Dr. William Edward. *Russellism Unveiled.* 1st ed. Chicago: Glad Tidings Pub. Co., 1910, 28 pp. Reprinted by Wm. B. Eerdmans Co., Grand Rapids, MI, 1920 and 1949, 28 pp. (A critique of Russell's major doctrines, the trinity, hellfire and others).

Biemond, L. *Jehova's Getuige, luister eens! Een ernstig woord tot de Jehova's Getuigen.* Utrecht, R.P.J. Kuijsten, (1962), 48 pp. (Jehovah's Witness, listen for a moment! A serious word to the Jehovah's Witnesses).

Bilusack, Royce. *Reasoning With the Scriptures.* New Liskeard, Ont., published by author, c. 1984, 20 pp. (A scholarly study of the Holy Spirit, shows the Watchtower's research is superficial and deficient, much of the booklet is on Greek grammar).

Bilz, Jakob. *Die Ernsten Bibelforscher und ihre Behauptungen.* In the 12th book of 'Hirt und Herde." Freiburg: Beiträge zur zeitgemaßen Seelsorge: Verlagsburh-handlung Herder & Co., 1924, 29 pp. (The Serious Bible Researchers and Their Contentions.)

B., J.H. *Pastor Russell's Position and Credentials.* New York: Loizeux Bros., n.d.

Black, James, D.D. *New Forms of the Old Faith.* London, England: Nelson & Sons, 1948.

Blandre, Bernard. *Des Adventistes A Russell (1843-1882) Bulletin de l'association detude et d'information sur les movements religieux* Gutenberg" Pierron No, 59-61 March-May 1985 48p (covers the Adventists background of Russell's movement).(In French).

_____. "Temains de Jehovah" a special issue of *Movements Relieux* Mai-Juin 1985. (Covers topics from the blood transfusion issue to custody matters).

Blennow, Hugo. *Sanningen Om Jehovas Vittner.* Kallinge: Eginostiftelsens Forlag, 1956, 16 pp. (The Truth About the Jehovah's Witnesses) (Covers history and doctrine).(In German).

Bodine, Jerry, and Marian Bodine. *Witnessing to the Witnesses.* CA: Christian Research Institute, 43 pp. (Photostats covering false prophecy, the doctrine of the Trinity, the deity of Christ, resurrection, hell).

Boerwinkel, F. *Jehovah's Getuigen. Beknopt overzicht van hun geschiedenis en leer.* (Driebergen, Veritas, 1957), 20 pp. (Jehovah's Witnesses. Brief survey of their history and teachings).

Boiarskii, Fedor. *Prophets: A Sketch.* Alma Ata: Kazakh State Publishing House of Artistic Literature, 1960, 12 pp. (in Russian.)

Bolchuk, Myroslav. *Who Are the Jehovah's Witnesses.* Kiev, 1957, 89 pp. (in Russian).

Bommert, Otto. *Wider Millennium-Tages-Anbruch oder wie C.T. Russell das Kreuz Christi vollstandig zunichte machte.* Westfalen: Verlagshaus der deutschen Zeitmission in Geisweid, 1924, 3 Auflag, 16 pp. (Against the Millennial Dawnites or How C.T. Russell Completely Destroyed the Cross of Christ).

Borst, Ernst Martin. *Was ich Ihnen sagen möchte. (Herausgegeben von der Arbeitsgemeinschaft für religiöse Fragen e.v Regensburg).* (Published by the Labor community for religious questions e.v. Rensburg). Lahr-Dinglingen, Verlag der St. Johannis-Druckerei Schweickhardt (What I like to say to you.) (part of the "Ausgage in der Schriftenreihe Glaube und Vertrauen") or Publication in the faith and confidence series) (in German).

Bos C.G. et al. *Dwalingen, sekten en stromingen; acht schetsen.* (Barneveld), Ned. Bond van Gerefeormeerde Jeugd-verenigingen, (1983). 60 pp. Mistakes, sects and streamings; eight outlines. (in Dutch).

Bowman, Robert M. *Jehovah's Witnesses* Grand Rapids, Mi Zondervon Pub House 1995 85 pp. (An outline of primarily Witness doctrine and the scriptural objections to their beliefs).

Bowser, Arthur. *Bible Study Course on Jehovah's Witnesses.* Denver, CO: Accent Books, 1975, 28 pp. (A study booklet to help the reader understand Witnesses and what they teach).

Bradford, W.H. *An Answer to Dr. Gray.* St. Paul, MN: St. Paul Enterprises, 1900(?), 47 pp. (Bradford was a follower of Russell).

_____. *The Rich Young Man Whom Jesus Loved and Another Rich Young Man, A Memorial Address for Pastor C.T. Russell.* St. Paul, MN: St. Paul Enterprises, 1916, 42 pp.

Branson, Ron. *Jehovah's Witnesses (4 parts).* North Hollywood, CA: The Albert Sheet Publication Ministry #37-40, n.d., 16 pp.

Brauenlich, Paul. *Die Ernsten Bibelforscher als Opfer bolschewistischer Religionsspötter.* Leipzig: Verlag M. Heinsius Nachfolger; Eger U. Sievers, 2nd ed. 1926, 40 pp., 1947 ed. 29 pp. (The Jehovah's Witnesses as Victims of Bolshevist Religious Mockers).

Bremer, J.C. *In Defense of the Despised "Sect."* Metropolis, IL: J.C. Bremer Printing Service, Feb. 12, 1944, 14 pp. (Published by an active Witness. Many excellent newspaper quotes; the focus is primarily on the Witnesses persecution due to the flag issue).

_____. *By Their Fruits Ye Shall Know Them.* 2nd ed. (revised). Metropolis, IL: J.C. Bremer Printing Service, n.d., 25 pp. (Published by an active Witness in response to the booklet "Jehovah's Witness" by F.E. Mayer; tries to refute the booklet section by section).

Brooks, Keith L. *The Spirit of Truth and the Spirit of Error.* Los Angeles, CA: Christian Fundamentals League, n.d.

_____. *Prophetic Program of Judge Rutherford.* Los Angeles, CA: American Prophetic League, Inc., n.d., 12 pp.

_____. *Prophetic Program of Jehovah's Witnesses.* Los Angeles, CA: American Prophetic League, Inc., n.d., c. 1945, 12 pp. (Critiques major and minor doctrines).

Brown, C.H. *Jesus Is Jehovah.* Bible Truth Publishers, 1963, 30 pp. (Argues by scripture comparisons that Jesus is another name for Jehovah and that the Watchtower teaching on this topic is erroneous).

Brown, Jim. *Jesus Loves the Jehovah's Witnesses.* Scottsdale, AZ: Christian Communications, 1976, 86 pp.

Bruce, F.F., and J.W. Martin. *The Deity of Christ.* Manchester, England: North England Evangelical Trust, 1964, 24 pp.

Bruder-dienst. *Wir wollen Wahrheit und Klarheit.* Itzehoe, Germany, 8 pp. (We Want Truth and Clarity).

Buisman, Wolfram. *Das Evangelium und die "Zeugen Jehovas."* (Gospel and the Witnesses of Jehovah). Berlin, Christlicher Buch-und Zeitschriften Verlag, 1947, 29 pp. (in German).

Bunzel, Ulrich. *Die Ernsten Bibelforscher. In alle Wahrheit."* Berlin: Krazverlag des Christlichen Zeitschriftenvereines, 1928, 32 pp. (The Ernest Bible Students Nos. 14 and 15 of the series of booklets) [German]

Burganger, Karl (pseudonym for Carl Jonsson). *The Watchtower Society and Absolute Chronology.* Lethbridge, Alberta, Canada: Christian Fellowship International, 1981, 28 pp.; revised ed. 1982, 28 pp. (A study of the 1914 date which resulted in a book on this topic, concludes 1914 is totally without scholarly foundation).

Burrell, Rev. Maurice C. *Jehovah's Witnesses.* London, England: Church Book Room Press, Ltd., 1960, 20 pp. (also 1968 ed.).

_____. *The Person and Work of Christ in Two Modern Deviationist Religions-- Jehovah's Witnesses and Christadelphians.* Bristol, England, 1962.

Burridge, J.H. *Pastor Russell's Date System and Teaching on the Person of Christ.* New York, c. 1911, 30 pp. (Covers history and critiques the Watchtower view of the trinity and heaven and hell).

_____. *Pastor Russell's Position and Credentials and His Methods of Interpretation.* New York, c. 1911, 32 pp.

_____. *Pastor Russell's Teaching on the Coming of Christ.* New York, c. 1911, 31 pp.

Butt, Steve. *A Christian Letter.* Portland, ME: Published by Author, 1982, 16 pp. (Argues salvation is from God, not an organization).

Cabeen, Tom. *Does God Work Through An Organization?* Pub. by author: Fairfield, CT, 1992, 24 pp. (An excellent discussion showing that God works through individuals; Cabeen was a Bethel staff member from 1968 to 1980).

Campbell, John. *A Manual on Counseling Jehovah's Witnesses.* John Ritchie Ltd. Kilmarmock, England. 1994 34 pp. (covers mostly doctrine from an evangelical perspective, focusing on the trinity and the basis of salvation).

_____. *Why Christians Cannot Accept the Teachings of Jehovah's Witnesses,* 17 pp.

Carty, Charles. *Freak Religion: An Expose of the Witnesses of Jehova.* Pub. by author, 1939.

Catalfamo, Margaret. *From Jehovah's Witness to Witness for Christ Jesus.* Victoria, Australia: Standfast Pub. Co., 1980, 56 pp. (A testimony of the author, a Witness for twenty-five years, and some reasons for accepting the trinity, and rejecting the 144,000 and other beliefs).

Central Board for Conscientious Objectors Bulletin. London, England, July 1941-Sept. 1946. April 1942 (issue 26) "The position of Women C.O.s" (accounts of women Witnesses imprisoned) and article 'Jehovah's Witnesses: The Facts'. September 1943 "The Case for Stanley Hilton" (The whole 12 page booklet is on this one Witnesses case).

Cetnar, William. (Ed). *Is This God's Organization?* Kunkletown, PA: published by author 1983, 77 pp. (Includes a photo reprint of the J.F. Rutherford versus Rev. John H. Troy debates (46 pp.), C.T. Russell's 64 p. *Object and Manner of Our Lord's Return,* originally published in 1877 and several other reprints).

Chery, H.Ch. *L'Offensive des Sectes.* Paris: Les Editions du Cerf, 1954. (The Offensive Position of the Sects).(In French).

Christadelphians. *Who are God's True Witnesses?* Erith, Kent: Erith Displays Ltd., c. 1980, 20 pp. (Argues that Christadelphians, not Witnesses, are God's true people and that the Watchtower beliefs are "almost wholly unscriptural" even though the two groups are probably more alike than any other sects).

Chretien, Leonard. (Ed) *Witnesses of Jehovah.* LaJolla, CA: Good News Defenders, 1987. 24 pp. (A collection of articles on Watchtower doctrine.)

_____. "Jehovah's Witnesses Refuted by the Bible." *Herald of the Coming Age,* Vol. 20, No. 3. Victoria, Australia: The Clyde Press, Oct. 1969, 48 pp. Revised, and printed as Vol. 31, No. 2, Aug. 1982, 16 pp.

Clark, Rev. C. Leopold. *Russell, Rutherford and Heresies of Jehovah's Witnesses.*

Clyne, Harold W. *A Word About Jehovah's Witnesses.* Palmerton North, New Zealand: Argosy Industrial Photos (1st ed. 1971), 1975, 30 p. (The writer, a retired journalist, left the Watchtower in 1970 after thirteen years involvement, and became a Bible Student; in this work he discusses his reasons; much on the negative changes that Rutherford, the second president, brought about).

Coenders, H. and P. Coenders. *In geest en in waarheid aanbidden!* Nijmegen,

Informatie-Centrum, ca. 1979, 12 pp. (Worshiping in spirit and truth!)

Colinon, Maurice. *Faux Prophets et Sectes d'aujord'hue.* Paris: Librairie Plon, 1953. (False Prophets and Sects of Today) (in French).

_____. *Le Phenomene des Sectes au XX Siecle.* Paris: Librairie Artheme Fayard, n.d. (The Phenomenon of Sects in the 20th Century) (in French).

Conner, W.T. *The Teachings of "Pastor" Russell.* Nashville, TN: Sunday School Board of the Southern Baptist Convention Publishers, 1926, 68 pp. (Conner, a professor of Systematic Theology at Southwestern Baptist Theological Seminary in Fort Worth, TX, reviews Russell's Theology and critiques it from a Baptist position.)

Cook, Charles C. *All About One Russell.* Philadelphia, PA: Philadelphia School of the Bible, n.d., 24 pp. (republished by Bible Institute of Los Angeles, Los Angeles, CA, n.d., c. 1900, 48 pp.

Concerned Bible Student. "An Open Letter to Bible Students." Summitt, Ill: c.1995. 28 pp. (An excellent review of early Watchtower history and the Bible Student movement.)

_____. *More Data on "Pastor Russell."* New York: pub. by author, n.d., 32 pp. (A follow-up on the above booklet; includes responses by Russell).

Cooke, A.E. *Jehovah's Witnesses.* Toronto, Canada: United Church Publishing House, 1948.

Cooksey, N.B. *Russellism Under the Searchlight.* Cincinnati, OH: Abingdon Press, 1916, 68 pp.

Cooper, G.H. *Millennial Dawnism or Satan in Disguise.* Swengel, PA, n.d., 10 pp.

Coveney, Maurice. *Jehovah's Witnesses: Do They Have the Truth?* Kelowna, B.C., Canada: pub. by author, n.d., 7 pp. (Many illustrations which effectively communicate the doctrinal problems of the Watchtower).

_____. *"Are You Truly Making Sure of All Things?"* Kelowna, B.C., Canada: Goodwill Printers, 1980, 64 pp. (Reprints of letters about Jehovah's Witnesses, some by Witnesses, and Mr. Coveney's response).

Crain, C. *"Millennial Dawn" Teaching on the Person of Christ.* New York: Loizeux Brothers, Bible Truth Dept., n.d., c. 1900 (reprinted in Bergman, 1990 p 5-22) 15 pp. A critique of Russell's teaching on Soteriology.

Crawford, William. *"Battle" of Armageddon Not Biblical.* Sun City, CA: pub. by author, n.d., 55 pp. (Argues that the Battle of Armageddon concept is based on a forgery, specifically improperly adding the word "battle" to the scripture in Rev. 16:16).

Crompton, Robert. *"Counting the Days to Armageddon; Jehovah's Witnesses and the second Presence of Christ."* Cambridge; James Clark & Co. 1996 160 pp. (A history of the Watchtower prophesy failures, well documented. The author is a former Witness, now a Methodist Minister in England).

Cross, P.G. *Russellism.* Cincinnati, OH: Standard Publishing, n.d.

Curran, Edward Lodge. Rev. *Judge "for four Days" Rutherford.* Brooklyn, NY: International Catholic Truth Society, 1940, 32 pp. (A strong critique of Rutherford, the person and his teachings from a Catholic view).

Custer, Stewart. *Do Jehovah's Witnesses Contradict the Bible?* Greenville, SC: Bob
    Jones University Press, 1975, 12 pp. (Critiques the Watchtower view of the
    trinity, salvation, hell, and their spiritual return of Christ doctrine).

Cutting, Curtis R. *Why I Left Jehovah's Witnesses.* Minneapolis, MN: Osterhaus
    Publishing House, n.d., 19 pp. (Includes the author's testimony; much
    discussion and criticism of Witness doctrine).

Dagon, Gerard. *Petites Eglises et Grandes Sectes.* Paris, 1962. (Small Religious
    Groups and Large Sects) (in French).

_____. *Petites Eglises de France Saverne.* (Little Churches of France) 1969. (in
    French).

_____. *Les Sectes en France.* N.d. (Sects in France) (in French).

Davidson, J.L. *Debunking "Jehovah's Witnesses:" A Written Discussion with the Cult of
    Jehovah's Witnesses.* Conroe, TX: pub. by author, c. 1970, 50 pp. (A written
    debate with Davidson, Church of Christ, and Ross Yerkes, a Witness, on the
    major doctrines).

Davies, Rupert Eric. *Jehovah's Witnesses: Is Their Witness True?* London, England:
    Epworth (Foundry Pamphlets No. 11), Aug. 1958, 14 pp.

Dawn Book Supply, The. *When Pastor Russell Died.* 1951, 53 pp.

_____. *The Teaching of Jehovah's Witnesses Examined.* London, England, c. 1971,
    16 pp. (A brief critique of basic Witness doctrines from a Christadelphian world
    view).

Deitsch, Martin. *Die Sekte der Ernsten Bibelforscher im Lichte der Vernunft und der
    Heiligen Schrift.* Heidelberg, Evang. Verlag, 1925, 55 pp. (The sect of the
    "Earnest Bible Students" in the light of practical reason and the Holy Scriptures).
    (in German).

Delleman, Th. *Jehovah's Getuigen.* Amsterdam, De Lichtdrager, (1961), 40 pp.
    (Jehovah's Witnesses) (in Dutch).

Demchenko, Mykola Stpanovych. *Who Are Jehovah's Witnesses?* Moscow, 1958. (in
    Russian).

Dencher, Ted. *Jehovah's Witnesses and John 8:58.* Sharon, PA: pub. by author, n.d.,
    16 pp. (A critique of the Watchtower view of Jesus).

_____. *Should I Become a Jehovah's Witness?* Sharon, PA: pub. by author, n.d., 16
    pp. (A brief critique of Witness doctrine).

_____. *An Alarming Situation for Jehovah's Witnesses.* Fort Washington, PA:
    Christian Literature Crusade, 1974, 28 pp. (A critique of the Watchtower teaching
    on the Deity of Christ).

_____. *I Wouldn't Believe in the "Trinity" If It Wasn't for the Watchtower Bible.*
    Sacramento, CA: Alpha-Media, 1977, 11 pp. (Argues that the trinity can be
    proved in the Watchtower's own translation).

_____. *Is This an "Aid to Bible Understanding?"* Sharon, PA: pub. by author, n.d., 8
    pp. (A useful critique of the lack of scholarship in the Watchtower aid book).

Der Ernsten Bibelforscher. Zürich: NZN-Verlag, 1922, 30 pp. (The Jehovah's
    Witnesses) (in German).

Deutsch, Martin. *Die Sekte der Ernsten Bibelforscher.* Heidelberg: Evangelischer Verlag, 1925, 55 pp. (The Sect of the Jehovah's Witnesses) (in German).

D'Haene, Daniel. *Praise the Lord, I Am Saved.* Sacramento, CA: Ted Dencher Publications, n.d. (c. 1976), 32 pp. (The story of an ex-Witness and his experiences in the Watchtower, much on the Watchtower failed prophecy).

Diaz, Edwin. *¿Testigos de Jehova o Testigos de Santanás?* West New York, NJ: Alex Books, 39 pp. (Witnesses of Jehovah or Witnesses of Satan?).

Dicks, J. *Leben unsere Toten? Auf diese und andere Fragen eine Katholische Antwort an die "Zeugen Jehovas." (Are our dead ones in life? On these and other questions a Catholic answer to the "Witnesses of Jehovah.")* Konstanz, Freiburg/Schweiz, Kanisius Verlag, 1951, 29 pp. (in German).

Dieterle, S. *Wer ist ein Ernster Bibelforscher? Worte zur Besinnung.* (Who is one Earnest Bible Student? A word to come to senses). St. Gallen 1925, Zollikofer & Cie: Buchhandlung der Evangelische Gesellschaft, 22 pp. (in German).

Diocese Anglican de I'LL, Maurice, Port Louis. *Les T´emoins de Jehovah un court récit de l'histoire des croyances ainsi que des méthodes d'une secte etrange, traduit de l'anglais.* Port Louis, Mauritius· Almadina Press, n.d. (Jehovah's Witnesses; A Brief Review of the Sects in the Anglean diocese of the Isle Maurice. The History, Beliefs, Methods of a Foreign Sect) (in French).

Dixon, A.C. "Russell" Under the Searchlight. London, England: Marshall, 1935.

Doev, Azgirel Batcherievich. *Under the Cover of Religion.* Frunze, USSR: Kirghizia (Atheists Library), 1964, 43 pp. (in Russian).

Doherty, J.E. *Jehovah's Witnesses.* Li Gourian, MO: Li Gourian Pamphlets, 1961, 22 pp. (Covers mostly history and the life of a Witness).

Dollinger, Ingo. *Die Zeugen Jehovas und das Zeugnis der Heiligen Schrift.* Donauwörth, W. Germany: Verlag Ludwig Auer Cassianeum 1965, 64 pp. (The Jehovah's Witnesses and the Witness of the Holy Scripture.) (in German) (A critique of Witness doctrine and history by a Catholic scholar).

Dönges, Emil. *Wider die Irrlehren der Ernsten Bibelforscher.* Dillenburg: Verlag der Geschwister Dönges, 1925, 22 pp. (Against the False Teachings of the Jehovah's Witnesses). From a Roman Catholic viewpoint.

_____. *Die Sekte Jehovas. 3 Mose 23 im Lichte des Evangeliums.* Neue Auflage. (The sect of the Jehovah's. Leviticus 23 in the light of the Gospel. New Edition). Dillenburg, Geschwister Dönges, 1925, 90 pp. (in German).
Dorosh, Ievmen Kyrylovych. *Types of Brooklyn Corporations.* 1966, 117 pp (in Ukrainian).

Dorsteen, T. *Jehovah's Getuigen. Een overzicht van hun leer, hun methoden en de gevolgen van deelname aan het Wachttorengenootschap.* (Hilversum), Radioomroep V.A.R.A., 1982, 56 pp. (Jehovah's Witnesses. A survey of their dogmas, their methods and the adventure of taking part in the Watchtower Society).

Downie, Henry. *The Annihilation of Jesus Christ or "Millennial Dawnism" Unveiled.* London, England: 14 Paternoster Row, A. Holness, n.d.

Duncan, Homer. *A Concise History of the Jehovah's Witnesses.* Lubbock, TX: Missionary Crusader, n.d., 8 pp. (Covers Russell, Rutherford and Knorr).

_____. *Armageddon in 1975?* Lubbock, TX: Missionary Crusader, n.d., 12 pp.

_____. *Did Jesus Return in 1914?* Lubbock, TX: Missionary Crusader, n.d., 60 pp. (A critique of Watchtower eschatology).

_____. *Doctrines of Jehovah's Witnesses.* Lubbock, TX: Missionary Crusader, n.d.

_____. *Five Themes That Transcend the Range of Human Understanding.* Lubbock, TX: Missionary Crusader, n.d., 23 pp. (Critiques the Watchtower's teaching of the trinity, and salvation).

_____. *Is It Not Strange That....* Lubbock, TX: Missionary Crusader, n.d., 7 pp. (Critiques Watchtower view of the deity of Christ).

_____. *Jehovah's Witnesses and the Deity of Christ.* Lubbock, TX: Missionary Crusader, n.d., 54 pp. (A critique of the Witness view of Christ).

_____. *Maliciously Misrepresenting the Holy Spirit.* Lubbock, TX: Missionary Crusader, c. 1965. 18 pp.

_____. *On the Wrong Train.* Lubbock, TX: Missionary Crusader, n.d., 18 pp. (A general discussion of why the Watchtower is a false cult).

_____. *Questions the Jehovah's Witnesses Cannot Answer.* Lubbock, TX: Missionary Crusader, n.d., 8 pp., reprinted revised version, 8 pp. (Covers the Deity of Christ, and John the Baptist's role).

_____. *Satan's Strategy.* Lubbock, TX: Missionary Crusader n.d.

_____. *The Doctrines of the Jehovah's Witnesses Compared with the Holy Scriptures.* Lubbock, TX: Missionary Crusader, c. 1973, 64 pp. (Critiques Watchtower teaching on the deity of Christ, the bodily resurrection of Christ, Hell and others).

_____. *The Jehovah's Witnesses and the Second Coming of Christ.* C. 1976, 45 pp. A revision of *Did Jesus Christ Return in 1914?* (Covers the many problems with the 1914 doctrine and Watchtower chronology in general).

_____. *The Jehovah's Witnesses Are Right!* Lubbock, TX: Missionary Crusader, n.d., 14 pp. (Also 8 p. edition). (Contrasts the Watchtower with fundamental Christianity).

_____. *Who Is a Christian?* Lubbock, TX: Missionary Crusader, n.d.

_____. *Who is Your Teacher? Watchtower Society or the Word of God?* Lubbock, TX: Missionary Crusader, n.d., c. 1975. (Argues that the Witnesses follow the Watchtower, not the Bible).

_____. *Why I Love Jehovah's Witnesses.* Lubbock, TX: Missionary Crusader, 1972, 23 pp. (A personal plea for Witnesses to evaluate their faith).

_____. *Reason: Is the Watchtower Bible and Tract Society Jehovah's Theocratic Organization?* Lubbock, TX: Missionary Crusader, International Publications c.. 1972 32 pp. (Discusses doctrine) (A critique of the Watchtower's view of Christ).

_____. *I am not an Ex-Jehovah's Witness; Therefore You Can Read This Without Fear.* n.d. 16 pp. (Covers a variety of minor doctrines).

Ebner, Friedrich. *Die soqgenannten "Zeugen Jehovas."* Trient, Erzbischöfliches Ordinariat, 1952, 23 pp. (The so-called "Witnesses of Jehovah.") (in German).

Elliot, Phillip. *Jehovah's Witnesses in the First and Twentieth Centuries.* Stirling, Scotland: Stirling Tract Enterprises, n.d., 24 pp. (Argues that the early Christians and the Watchtower teachings on major doctrines are radically different).

Engelder, Th. *Popular Symbolics.* St. Louis, MO, 1934.

Engelland, H. *Die Zeugen Jehovas.* (The Witnesses of Jehovah). Hamburg, Agentur d. Rauhen Hauses, 1961, 31 pp. (in German).

Ernste Bibelforscher, Die. *Katholische Antworten auf verschiedene Bibelfragen.* Zürich: NZN-Verlag, n.d., 30 pp. (the Catholic Answer to Different Bible Questions) (in German).

Fardon, A.H., and A.J. MacFarland. *Jehovah's Witnesses: Who Are They? What They Teach.* Chicago, IL: Moody Bible Institute, 1941, 23 pp.

Farkas, John R. and Pat Zarpentine. *Watchtower Bible and Track Society Teachings. Have They Changed?.* St. Louis, Personal Freedom Outreach, 1992, 38 pp. (Proves with photocopies that many major doctrines have changed).

Felix, Rev. Richard. *Rutherford Uncovered.* Pilot Grove, MO: Our Faith Press, 1937, 35 pp. (A critique of Rutherford's "Uncovered" booklet which is a criticism of the Catholic church; much excellent background on Rutherford found nowhere else).

Fellowship Baptist Church. *Who are Jehovah's Witnesses?* Lexington, KY: 1975, 22 pp. (Critiques the 144,000 concept, and the claim that the Watchtower belief system predates Russell).

Fennell, W.G. "Reconstructed Court and Religious Freedom." *New York University Law Quarterly,* 1942 (paper).

Fetz, August. *Der grosße Volks-und Weltbetrug durch die Ernsten Bibelforscher.* 4th ed. Hamburg: Verlag Arthur Gotting, 1924, 40 pp. (The Great Deception of the People and the World by Jehovah's Witnesses) (in German).

F.F.B. and W.J.M. *The Deity of Christ.* Manchester, England: North of England Evangelical Trust, 1964, 24 pp.

Fiebig, Paul. *Die Bibelauslegung der "Internationalen Vereinigung Ernster Bibelforscher" geprüft.* 2nd ed. Berlin: Wichern-Verlag, 1925, 32 pp. (The Bible interpretation of the International United Serious Bible Researchers proved) (in German).

Fisch, Rudolf. *Die "Ernsten Bibelforscher" entlarvt Neue Bearbeitung des Flugblattes: Die Rettung der Welt: geschieht sie durch Jesus Christus oder durch Russells Tausendjahrreich?* Elberfeld, Licht und Leben Verlag (Buchhandlung der Evangelische Gesellschaft), 1925, 31 pp. (The "Earnest Bible Students" exposed. New revision of the pamphlet "The saving of the world: shall that happen by Jesus Christ or by Russell's Millennium?) [German]

Fisk, Samuel. *Confronting "Jehovah's Witnesses."* Brownburg, IN: Biblical Evangelism, 1975, 24 pp. (In dialogue format, the author critiques the Watchtower's view of the resurrection, 1914, the 144,000 and Hermeneutics).

Floyd, Shelby G. *An Examination of the Jehovah's Witnesses.* Greenwood, IN: Pulpit Publications, 1977, 76 pp. (Covers history (p. 3-22) and critiques the Watchtower view of the trinity (p. 22-76)

Fox, Craig. *Error Never Desires to Be Investigated.* Easton, PA: pub. by author, c. 1983, 32 pp. (A set of 289 questions which are used to illustrate the extent of Watchtower changes and inconsistencies).

Gardiner, Ronald. *I Was a Jehovah's Witness.* Santa Ana: CA: CARIS, 1978, 12 pp. (A personal account of how the author became a Witness and why he eventually left).

Gascoin, E. *Les Religions Inconnues.* Paris: Librairie Gallimard, 1928 (The Little Known Religion) (in French).

Gaskill, Bonnie, and Toni Jean Alquist Meneses. *We Left the Watchtower for Jehovah!* Seattle, WA: Trinity Printing, 1979, 47 pp. (An account of why the authors left the Watchtower; consists of many letters sent to the Watchtower on the Watchtower's shortcomings and doctrinal problems).

Gauss, J.H. *God's Truth v. Man's Theories.* St. Louis, MO: Faithful Words Publishing Co., 1948.

Gazhos, V.F. *The Characteristics of J.W. Ideology and the Religious Conscience of the Sect's Members Based on the Material in the M.S.S.R.* Ed. V.N. Ermuratski. Keshinev, Moldavlin. SSR, 1969, 92 pp. (in Russian).

Geppert, W. *Die Zeugen Jehovas. "Ernste Bibelforscher" im Zeichen der Schlange.* Neuffen/Württ, Sonnenweg Verlag, 1952, 40 pp. (The Witnesses of Jehovah. "Earnest Bible Students" in the sign of the Serpent). (Schriftenreihe Irrläufer frommer Sehnsüchte und religiöser Leidenschaften) (in German).

Gerasimets, Aleksei Sergeevich. *The Truth About the Organization of Jehovah's Witnesses.* Irkutsk: Irkutsk Book Publishing House, 1960, 53 pp. (in Russian).

_____. *For Us Not According to the Path of the Jehovists.* Ed. I.P. Pentykhov. Irkutsk, 1960, 67 pp. (in Russian).

_____. *A Criticism of the Ideology of Contemporary Jehovah Witness Faith.* Scientific Leader N.A. Reshetinikov. Irkutsk: 1965, 20 pp. (in Russian).

Gerecke, Karl. *Die Gotteslästerungen der Ernsten Bibelforscher.* Leipzig: Verlag Adoplf Klein, 1931, 51 pp. (The Blasphemy of the Jehovah's Witnesses).

Gerstner, John H. *The Teachings of the Jehovah's Witnesses.* Grand Rapids, MI: Baker Book House, 1960, 31 pp. Originally appeared as Chapter 3 in *The Theology of the Major Sects.* (A critique of history and doctrine).

Gilbert, Dan. *Spiritual Bolshevism: The Truth About the Teachings of Jehovah's Witnesses.* Washington, DC: Christian Press Bureau, 1945, 75 pp. Revised and published as *Jehovah's Witnesses.* Grand Rapids: Zondervan Printing Co., 1946, 75 pp.

Gillentine, E.C. *Russellism or Jehovah's Witnesses vs. Christianity and the Bible.* Arkansas: Sunday School and Training Course Literature of the American Baptist Association, 1954, 32 pp.

Giselsson, Emanuel. *Sen till vad I Horen! En Varning fur Jehovas Vittnens Propaganda.* Hasselholm, Sweden, 1958, 32 pp. (Pay Attention to What May Be Heard: A Warning About the Propaganda of the Jehovah's Witnesses) (in Swedish). (A critique of Watchtower doctrine and beliefs).

Godbey, William B. *Russellism.* Zarephath, NJ: Pillar of Fire, 1918, 38 pp. (An indirect obtuse critique of Russell's ideas and philosophy).

Goedelman, M. Kirt (Ed.). *Jehovah's Witnesses Exposed.* St. Louis: Personal Freedom Outreach, 1989, 38 pp. (A collection of articles on doctrine and the blood issue).

Good News Publishers. *Do You Know...What These Religions Teach?* Chicago, IL: n.d., (pp. 10-11 on Jehovah's Witnesses).

Gray, James M. Rev. *The Errors of "Millennial Dawnism."* Chicago, IL: The Bible Institute Colportage Association, 1920, 24 pp. (Critiques Russell's teaching on salvation, Christ, eschatology and their view of the Bible, reprinted in Bergman, 1990 p. 197-188) critiques the basic doctrine of Russell such as Christ, future life, salvation, the church and others.

Greaves, Arnold E. *That Servant.* New York: privately published, 1932, 32 pp. A booklet about C.T. Russell.

Grieshaber, Erich, and Jean Grieshaber. *The Watchtower Doors Begin to Open.* Santa Clara, CA: pub. by authors, 1976, 10 pp. (The author tells how and why he left the Watchtower).

_____. *Redi-Answers on Jehovah's Witnesses Doctrine.* Santa Clara, CA: pub. by authors, 1979, 51 pp. (An outline developed to respond to the major Witness beliefs; many Scriptures listed).

_____. *Expose of Jehovah's Witnesses.* Santa Clara, CA: pub. by authors, n.d., 90 pp.

_____. *False Prophecy Packet.* Santa Clara, CA: pub. by authors, n.d. (Photocopies of some Watchtower cover ups).

Groot, J. de. *Wie zijn de Jehova's Getuigen en wat leren zij?* Oosterend (NH), Stork-Texel, (1982), 47 pp. (Who are the Jehova's Witnesses and what do they teach?)

Grudinin, Nikolai Nikolaevich. *The Jehovah Witness Faith and Children.* Irkutsk: Eastern-Siberian Book Publishing House, 1965, 50 pp. (in Russian).

Gruindon, Kenneth, and David Nicholas. *Why a New World Translation of the Holy Scriptures? A Frank Analysis of Jehovah's Witnesses.* Minnesota, c. 1977, 39 pp.

Gustafsson, Axel. *Jehovas Vittnen avslojas?* Gummessons, 1958, 48 pp. (Jehovah's Witnesses) (in Swedish).

Gustafsson, Ingmar. *Tro på villovägar.* Falkoping, Sweden, 1975, 48 pp. (Belief in Freewill; Jehovah's Witnesses, Transcendental Meditation, and the Scientology Church) (in Swedish) (p. 5-27 covers primarily history and teachings of the Watchtower).

Gutfleisch, Richard. *Der internationale Verein Ernster Bibelforscher; Eine Kritik.* Karlsruhe: Badenia-Verlag und Druckerei, 1922, 22 pp. (The International Society of Bible Researchers; a critique) (in German).

Haack, Friedrich-Wilhelm. *Jehovas Zeugen.* München, Germany: Evangelischer Presseverband für Bayern, 1973, 42 pp; 1975, 44 pp., 1985, 55 pp. (Jehovah's Witnesses).

Haensli, Ernst. *Bibel gegen Wachtturm.* Augsburg, Winfried Werk GmbH., 1961, 40 pp. (The Bible against the Watchtower) (in German).

Haldeman, Isaac Massey. *Millennial Dawnism: The Blasphemous Religion Which Teaches the Annihilation of Jesus Christ.* New York: Charles C. Cook Publications, c. 1910, 80 pp.

_____. *Two Men and Russellism.* New York, c. 1915, 63 pp. (A dialogue which attacks the Watchtower doctrines of hell, the trinity, the soul and others)

_____. *The New Religion or Athenian Culture and Christianity.* New York: Charles C. Cook Publications, 1910, 30 pp. (Haldeman, a Baptist pastor, in this work argues for the immorality of the soul doctrine, critiques modernism, and defends historic Christianity).

_____. *What Russellism or Millennial Dawnism Teaches.* Chicago: Bookstall, n.d., c. 1920, 11 pp. (A discussion and critique of what the Watchtower taught at the turn of the century).

_____. *The History of the Doctrine of Our Lord's Return.* New York: pub. by author, n.d., 40 pp. (Argues for a pre-millennial return, much history of this view is given).

_____. *A Great Counterfeit or the False and Blasphemous Religion Called Russellism.* New York: Charles C. Cook, 1915.

Hammund, T.C. *What Is Millennial Dawn Theory?* London: Charles J. Thynne, n.d.

Harding, William. *Cults, No. 1: Jehovah's Witnesses.* Faith Theological Seminary, n.d., 18 pp. (A critique of Watchtower teaching on the trinity, salvation, Christ and hell).

Hart, Alf. A. *Notes on the Finished Mystery.* Adelaide, Australia: pub. by author, 1919, 42 pp. (Objections to the 7th vol. from a Bible Student point of view; shows much of it is in opposition to Russell's teachings).

Hartzler, J.E. *Heresy of Russell and Russellism.* Scottsdale, PA: Mennonite Publ. House, n.d.

Haug, Karl. *Die Ernsten Bibelforscher, auch Millenniumsleute oder Russellianer genannt.* Lorch: Verlag Karl Rohm, 1923, 16 pp. (The Serious Bible Researchers, Also Called Millennial Dawnites or Russellites) (in German).

Haynes, Carlyle B. *Why I Am Not a Russellite.* Warburton, Victoria, Australia: Signs Publication Co., 1920, 8 pp.

Hearn, Roy J. *Handbook on Materialism. A Discussion of the Question: Does Man Have an Immortal Spirit?* Crossville, TN: (Box 211), n.d.

Hedegård, David. *Adventister, Russellianer och Efraims budbärare.* Stockholm: Svenska Missionsforbundet Forlag, 1929, 47 pp. (Adventists, Russellites and Ephraim's Messenger) (A critique of Russell's major doctrines and teaching). (in Swedish).

_____. *Jehovas Vittnen (Kring Jehovas Vittnen?).* 1930?, reprinted in 1958. (Jehovah's Witnesses) (in Swedish).

Heemstede, Katholieke *Getuigen, van Jehova.* Actie in Nederland, 1951, 24 pp. (Witnesses of Jehovah).

Heemstede, Uitgave. *Getuigen van Jehova.* Actie "Voor God." 1955, 20 pp. (Witnesses of Jehovah).

Heer, Johannes de. *De Verderfelijke Dwalingen der Jehova's Getuigen.* Driebergen, Het Zoeklicht, pb. 30 pp. (The pernicious errors of the Jehovah's Witnesses. Third enlarged printing). (A critique of Russell's and Rutherford's major teachings).

_____. *Achter de schermen der Jehova's Getuigen.* Driebergen, Het Zoeklicht, 1946, 61 pp. (Behind the fences of the Jehovah's Witnesses. Fourth enlarged printing) (in Swedish).

Heide, E. von der. *Die Zeugen Jehovas.* (The Witnesses of Jehovah). (Gladbeck, Schriftenmissions Verlag, 1954, 40 pp. (in German).

Heimbucher, Dr. Max. *Was sind denn die Ernsten Bibelforscher für Leute.* (Zugleich eine Aufklärung über das "tausendjahrige Reich" Christi. (What are than those "Earnest Bible Students" for people? At the same time an clearing-up about the "thousand year." Regensburg, Verlagsanstalt: G.J. Manz, 1923, 85 pp. (in German) (Millennium of Christ).

_____. *Was sind denn die Ernsten Bibelforscher für Leute.* Regensburg: G.J. Manz, 3rd ed. 1927, 85 pp. (What Kind of People Are the Jehovah's Witnesses?) (in German).

Help Jesus. *The False Prophet.* Kent, England: Help Jesus, n.d., 10 pp.

_____. *The 144,000: Who Are These?* Kent, England: Help Jesus, n.d., 10 pp.

Herold Verlag. *An einen Zeugen Jehovas. Von einem frohen Christen.* Frankfurt/Main, Herold Verlag, 1978 (To a Jehovah's Witness from a cheerful Christian). 18 pp. (A critique of the Watchtower from a evangelical world view)

Hewitt, P.E. *Russellism Exposed.* Grand Rapids, MI: Zondervan Publishing Co, 1941, 60 pp. (A critique of Russell's major doctrines, including trinity, soul, hell, 1914, soul-sleep, justification, resurrection).

Heydt, Henry J. *Jehovah's Witnesses and Their Translation.* New York: American Board of Missions, n.d., 19 pp. (A critique of the Watchtower translation from a theological standpoint)

Hicketheir, C. Robert. *Are Jehovah's Witnesses Really His Witnesses?* Darby, PA: pub. by author, n.d., 16 pp.

Hingston, W.H. *"Jehovah's Witnesses" Exposed.* Toronto, Canada: Garden City Press Co-Operative, n.d., c. 1950, 49 pp. (The author is a Roman Catholic Priest; a general critique of the Watchtower; concludes that this strange movement will eventually disappear).

Hobbs, A.G. *False Testimony of "Jehovah's Witnesses."* Fort Worth, TX: Hobbs Publications, 1955, 20 pp. (A critique of major doctrines and the Watchtower's prophetic failures).

Hodd, Eugene V. *L'Eglise et les Sectes.* Paris: Societe Centrale d'Evengelisation, 1941. (The Church and the Sects).

Hodges, Tony. *Jehovah's Witnesses in Central Africa.* Report No. 29. London, England: Minority Rights Group, 1976, 16 pp.

_____. *Jehovah's Witnesses in Africa.* Rev. ed. London: Minority Rights Group, 1985.

Hohenberger, Adam. *Christus und sein Reich nach der Entstellung durch die Ernsten Bibelforscher.* Leipzig: Sonderabdruck aus "Pastora Iblätter," herausgegeben von Lich. E. Strange 68, Jahrgang Heft 5, Kommissionsuerlag C.L. Ungelenk in Dresden, 1926, 20 pp. (Christ and His Kingdom after the Creation According to the Serious Bible Researchers) (in German).

_____. *Ernste Bibelforscher als Jehova's Zeugen im Kample gegen die Christliche Kirche* Germany: Buchdruckerei, 1932, 24 pp. (The Ernest Bible Researchers or Jehovah's Witnesses, and Their Fight Against the Christian Church) (A critique of the Watchtower's critique of the churches).

Holmlund, W.A. *A Substitute Gospel.* Vancouver, B.C., Canada, 1965, 23 pp.

Home Bible Studies. *Blood Transfusion; Is it Sinful; A reply to Jehovah's Witnesses.* London: The Plantation Press, c. 1980, 12 pp. (Shows the Jewish and Christian law does not condone condemning blood transfusions).

Hoornstra, Jean, ed. *The Millerites and Early Adventists: An Index to the Microfilm Collection of Rare Books and Manuscripts.* Ann Arbor, MI: University Microfilms International, 1978, 65 pp. (Includes an excellent subject index and a list of literature, much of which was critical in Russell's theological development).

Hopkins, Dick. *A Letter to the Watchtower Society.* Dublin, CA: pub. by author, 1981, 54 pp. (A critique of the Watchtower view of the Trinity).

Hopkins, L.H.C. *I.B.S.A. or Russellism.* Toronto, Canada: Ryerson Press, United Church, n.d.

Hunt, Marion Palmer. *The Exposure of Millennial Dawnism.* Louisville, KY: Pentecostal Publishing Co., 1934, 62 pp.

Iatsenko, Borys Ivanovych. *Servant of the Yellow Devil.* N.p., 1963, 56 pp. (in Ukrainian).

Il'in, Victor Andrilovych. *The Prophets of Armageddon.* Kiev, 1961, 36 pp. (in Ukrainian).

Jackson, Dennis R. *From Darkness to Light: The Testimony of a Converted Jehovah's Witness.* Lubbock, TX: Missionary Crusader, 1972, 21 pp. (The story of the author's becoming a Witnesses, his disillusionment, and why and how he left).

Jackson, Wayne. *Jehovah's Witnesses and the Doctrine of the Deity of Christ.* Stockton, CA: pub. by author, 1979, 24 pp. (Critiques the Watchtower teaching on Christ).

_____. *The Battle of Armageddon.* Stockton, CA: pub. by author, c. 1978, 12 pp. (Critiques the Watchtower view of Armageddon).

Jacquemin, Suzanne. *Les Prophetes des Derniers Temps.* Paris: Editions du Vieux Colombier, 1958. (The Prophets of the Last Days).(In French).

James, H.H. *Blood Transfusion: Is It an Unscriptural Practice?* Reprint. Hastings, New Zealand, 1961, 14 pp.

Jehovah's Witnesses. Port Louis, Mauritius, France: n.p., n.d.

Johnson, Andrew E. *Jehovah's Witnesses--Witnesses with False Evidence.* Lincoln, NE: Good News Broadcasting Co., 1973, 15 pp. (Covers history, the trinity and salvation).

Johnson, Bo. *Något om Jehovas Vitten och deras Verksamhet.* Lund, Sweden, 1975, (Something About the Jehovah's Witnesses) (Covers history, organization, teachings, doctrine).(in Swedish).

Johnson, Maurice. *8 Kinds of Death.* N.p.: pub. by author, n.d., 13 pp. (A critique of various teachings about the afterlife including the Jehovah's Witness's).

Johnson, Thomas Cary. *Russellism.* Richmond: Presbyterian Commission of Publications, c. 1920, 64 pp. (A critique on Russell's person and doctrine).

Jolly, Raymond G. *The Teachings of Jehovah's Witnesses Examined in the Light of the Scriptures."* Philadelphia: Laymen's Home Missionary Movement, n.d., 36 pp. (A critique of the Watchtower by an offshoot group that agrees with most of the

Watchtower doctrine and its minor doctrines, especially the works of Rutherford).

_____. *A Message for "Jehovah's Witnesses."* Philadelphia: Laymen's Home Missionary Movement, n.d., 7 pp. (Points out some reasons this group separated itself from the Watchtower).

Jonsson, Carl Olof. *Supplement to the Gentile Times Reconsidered; Refutation of Criticism and Additional Evidence.* Danville, CA: Odeon Books, 1989, 60 pp.

Joosten, H.W.A. *De Jehova-Getuigen.* 's-Hertegenbosch, Geert Groote Genootschap, 1957, 52 pp. (The Jehovah-Witnesses) (in Dutch).

Judah, J. Stillson. *Jehovah's Witnesses.* Philadelphia, PA: Westminster Books, 1967, 11 pp. (Critiques history and doctrine).

Juelsson, Gunnar. *Jehovas Vitten; i liuset av Guds ord Sweden Affarstryckeriet Broby.* 1976, 34 pp. (Covers nineteen areas of doctrine and practice; the author is an evangelical).

Kaiser, Fr. *Wer sind die sogenannten Ernsten Bibelforscher? Die verderblichen Irrlehren der Internationalen Vereinigung Ernster Bibelforscher (I.V.E.B.) auch Millenniums Tagosanbruchleute genannt--biblisch beleuchtet.* What are the so called "Earnest Bible Students?" Witten-Ruhr: Bundesverlag, 3rd ed. 1924, 40 pp. (The pernicious heresy of the International Association of Earnest Bible Students (I.B.S.A.)--also styled as Millennial Dawn-people--illuminated by Scriptures). (in German).

_____. *Die Irrlehren der Internationalen Vereinigung Ernster Bibelforscher.* (The false doctrines of the Internationale Association of Earnest Bible Students). Neukirchen (Kr. Moers), Missionsbuchhandlung Stursberg & Co., 1924, 29 pp. (in German).

_____. *Zions Wachtturm-oder Millennium-Tagesanbruchlehren.* (Zion's Watchtower or Millennial-Dawn-Teachings). Witten (Ruhr), Bundes Verlag, 1920. (in German).

Katholische, Carinthia Aktion. *Die Sekte von die Bibelforschern. Widerlegung ihrer Irrlehren.* (The sect of the Bible Students and a defense against their false doctrines). Klagenfurt, 1938, 47 pp. (in German).

Kaufmann, Robert. *Millenarisme et Acculturation.* Bruxelles, Belgium: L'Institut de Sociologie de l'Universite de Bruxelles, 1, 1964. (Millenarianism and Acculturation) (in French).

Kaul, Arthur O. *Are Jehovah's Witnesses God's Witnesses?* St. Louis, MO: Concordia Tract Mission, n.d., 9 pp. (Covers the trinity, hell, deity of Christ and the soul).

Kern, Herbert. *How to Respond to the Jehovah's Witnesses.* St. Louis, MO: Concordia Publishing House, 1977, 38 pp. (Covers history, the trinity, salvation and the recreation doctrine).

Kim, Rev. Kwan Suk. *A Critical Evaluation on the "Jehovah's Witnesses."* Korea: Christian Literature Society of Korea, 1963, 34 pp. (in Korean)

King, Ernest H. *Why Russellism? Being a reply to Dr. Ballard's 'Why not Russellism?'* Peterborough, England, pub. 1917, 31 pp.

Kirby, Gilbert Walter. *Jehovah's Witnesses.* London, England: Crusade Reprints, 1957, 12 pp. (A critique of Witness doctrine's including the deity of Christ, the trinity, the cross, prophecy and the social implications to the church of the movement).

Kneedler, William Harding. *Christian Answers to Jehovah's Witnesses.* Chicago:

Moody Bible Institute, 1953, 64 pp. (Italian edition: *Risposte dei Cristiani ai Testimoni ki Geova*. Napoli, Italy: Edizioni Centro Biblico, 1966, 32 pp). (Covers prophecy, date setting, Christ's return and resurrection, grace, the millennium and other topics).

Knights of Columbus. *Some Bible Beliefs Have to Be Wrong!* St. Louis, MO: Knights of Columbus, 1963, 28 pp. (Covers history, and critiques doctrine--the trinity, afterlife, hell, the Bible, and others).

Köhler, Ludwig. *Was sagen wir zu den Ernsten Bibelforschern?* Ein Vortrag, Zürich. Art Institute Orell, Fussli, 1924, 24 pp. (What Do We Say About the Jehovah's Witnesses?) (a lecture in German).

Krawielitzki, Martin. *Bewußte Bibelfälscher ("Internationale Vreinigung Ernster Bibelforscher."* Bad Blankenburg, Thür. Wald, Buchdruckerei und Verlag "Harfe," 1928, 15 pp. (Conscious Bible-falsifiers (International Association Earnest Bible Students.") (in German).

_____. *Die Internationale Vereinigung Ernster Bibelforscher.* Bad Blandenberg: Thur. Wald, Buchdruckerei und Verlag "Harfe," 1930, 16 pp. (The International Association of Bible Researchers) (in German).

Kuijt, P. *Geloof ze niet. (Lezing over Jehova's Getuigen).* (Gouda, Stichting ter lening van de bijzondere noden van studerenden aan de Chr. Kweekschool op Geref. grondslag) (Don't believe them; a lecture about Jehovah's Witnesses) (in Dutch).

Kuptsch, Julius. *Aufklärung über die Ernsten Bibelforscher.* Tilsit: J. Reylaender u. Sohn, 1927, 47 pp. (Enlightenment About the Serious Bible Researchers) (in German).

Lackner, O.; J. Meister; and H. Hagenau. *Die Bibel und die sogenannten Ernsten Bibelforscher.* Kassel: Christliche Traktatgesellschaft, 1924, 15 pp. (The Bible and the So-called Serious Bible Researchers) (in German).

La Haye, Tim F. *Jesus, Who Is He? An Open Letter to Jehovah's Witnesses.* San Diego, CA: Scott Memorial Baptist Church, c. 1965, 16 pp. (A response to the Watchtower booklet, *"The Word" Who is He According to John?).*

Larrigan, Karen. *Is the Kingdom Interlinear Translation Reliable?* Nelson, B.C. Canada MacGregor Ministries 1993 16 pp. discusses various changes and contradictions in various Watchtower translations).

Langrehr, Wilhelm. *Die Ernsten Bibelforscher und wir.* Witten-Ruhr: Evangelischer Presseverlag, 1925, 16 pp. (The Serious Bible Researchers and Us) (in German).

Lanzoni, Giuseppe D. *I Testimoni di Geova (errori-donfutazione).* Faenza: Biblioteca "S. Carlo Borromeo" del Seminari di Faenza, 1952. (The Jehovah's Witnesses--Errors and Confusions) (in Italian).

Lapin, Ron. *Institute of Bloodless Medicine and Surgery.* Norwalk, CA: 1985, 28 pp. (A booklet about the institute which includes reprints from magazines and newspapers about its work and results).

_____. *A Time to Choose.* Norwalk, CA: Practice Associates Medical Group, 1988, 12 pp. (About the bloodless medical institute, its services and programs for Jehovah's Witnesses).

Lash, Gustav. *Die Internationale Vereinigung der Ernster Bibelforscher und die Evangelische Kirche.* Strassburg: Buchhandlung der Evangelischen Gesellschaft, 1921, 20 pp. (The Serious Bible Researchers and the Protestant Church) (in

German).

LeCabellec, M. *The Jehovah's Witnesses and the Christian Faith.* Lorient Bulletin, Jan. 1976, 32 pp.

Lenfest, Edna T. *Charles Taze Russell 1852-1916.* Acton, Maine, n.d., 8 pp. (Lenfest was a Bible Student, and this tract is in favor of Russell).

Lewis, Gordon R. *The Bible, the Christian, and Jehovah's Witnesses.* Philadelphia, PA: Presbyterian and Reformed Publishing Co., 1966, 30 pp. (The author is a professor of theology at Conservative Baptist Theology Seminary in Denver; a critique of Watchtower history and doctrine).

Lienhardt, Hans. *Ein Riesenverbrechen am deutschen Volk und die Ernsten Bibelforscher* (*Jüdischer Weltherrschaftsplan*). (A great crime to the German People and the Earnest Bible Students). (Jewish plan of world dominion). Weissenberg i.
Bayrn, Großdeutscher Verlag, 1925, 46 pp. (in German).

Lindsay, Gordon. *What About Jehovah's Witnesses?* Dallas, TX: Christ for the Nations, 1974, 66 pp. (Covers both history and doctrine, the trinity, hell, the soul and other major doctrines).

Lloyd, George S. *Witnesses out of the Bottomless Pit.* Melbourn, Victoria Australia, c. 1930s, 20 pp. (A critique of history and doctrine; uses a large number of quotes from Watchtower publications which the author then critiques).

Lockyer, Herbert. *Jehovah's Witnesses Exposed.* Grand Rapids, MI: Zondervan Publishing Co., 1954, 32 pp. (Critiques history and major doctrines).

Loofs, Friedrich. *Die "Internationale Vereinigung Ernster Bibelforscher."* Leipzig: J.C. Hinrichs Buchhhandlung, 1918, and 1921, 60 pp. (The International Union of the Serious Bible Researchers) (in German). (A well-documented history and a critique of Watchtower doctrine).

MacCarty, William. *1914 and Christ's Second Coming.* Washington, DC: Review and Herald Publishing Assoc., 1975, 64 pp. (An excellent critique of the Watchtower's teaching on 1914 and the whole issue of Christ's second coming by a Seventh-Day Adventist).

MacGregor, Keith, and Lorri MacGregor; artwork by Jack Bundy. *The Watchtower Fairy Tale of Jesus Christ.* Vancouver, B.C., Canada: MacGregor Ministries, 1980, 10 pp. (A cartoon story critique of Watchtower teachings and doctrine).

MacGregor, Keith. *Fractured Families: Living with a Jehovah's Witness in Your Home.* Nelson British Columbia, Canada: 1994. 14 pp. (Covers how a divided household strains a marriage and how the Witness contributes to the problem.)

MacGregor, Lorri. *The Pagan Roots of Jehovah's Witnesses.* Nelson, British Columbia, Canada: 1990. 32 pp. (Covers the Pyramid, the Zodiac, Spiritism and Occult Teaching of the Watchtower.)

_____.*The Witness at You Door.* Nelson, British Columbia, Canada: 1989. 14 pp. (Mostly on Christ's Deity.)

_____. *We are the Prophets of Jehovah God, A reply to the "Awake" Magazine, March 22, 1993.* Nelson, British Columbia, Canada: 1994. 22 pp. (Covers Watchtower Prophecy failure.)

_____. *Brighter Light?* Nelson, British Columbia Canada: 1994. 16 pp. (A brief review of Witness Doctrine changes and prophecy failures.)

_____ *Jehovah's Witnesses and the Question of Blood.* Nelson, British Columbia, Canada: 1994. 18 pp. (A good brief review of some of the major problems with the Watchtower blood doctrine.)

Magnani, Duane. *Eyes of Understanding: Watchtower Armageddon Prophecies Examined.* Clayton, CA, 1972, 36 pp.; 2nd ed. 1977.

_____. *Who Is the Faithful and Wise Servant? A Study of Authority over Jehovah's Witnesses.* Clayton, CA: Witness, Inc., 1979, 33 pp.

_____, and Arthur Barrett. *Witnessing to Jehovah's Witnesses: How to Lead a JW to Christ in One Meeting.* Clayton, CA: Witness, Inc., 1979, 66 pp. (Shows how to convince Witnesses that their major doctrines are in error).

Main, C.F. *Notes on "The Finished Mystery."* Melbourne, Australia: Bible Students Tract Society, 1919, 43 pp. (A critique of the 7th volume from a Bible student standpoint).

Mansfield, H.P., ed. *Blood Transfusion Does Not Violate Bible Teaching* (West Beach, S. Australia). *The Herald of the Coming Age.* (An excellent refutation of the Watchtower teaching on blood) a reprint from *Herald of the Coming Age,* Vol. 16, No. 2, Aug. 1965 (revised ed. Vol. 24, No. 5, June 1974), 16 pp. Christadelphian Publications.

_____, ed. *"Jehovah's Witnesses" Refuted by the Bible.* Victoria, Australia: The Clyde Press, n.d., 16 pp. (reprint of *Herald of the Coming Age,* Vol. 20, No. 3, Oct. 1969, pp. 33-48) revised edition Aug. 1982. (Critiques Watchtower teaching on 144,000 Israel, Satan, bodily resurrection of Christ, and Jesus' invisible second coming teaching).

Martin Sanchez, Benjamin. ¿Quienes son los Testigos de Jehova? Zamora, Monte Casino, 1971, 47 pp. (Who are the Jehovah's Witnesses?) (in Spanish).

Martin, Walter R. *The Jehovah's Witnesses.* Grand Rapids, MI: Zondervan Publishing House, 1957. (An extensive critique of the Watchtower doctrine; Dr. Martin was a Baptist)

_____. *Jehovah's Witnesses and the Trinity.* N.p., n.d., c. 1975, 11 pp. (A critique of the Watchtower teaching on the trinity).

_____. *What About Jehovah's Witnesses?* Minneapolis, MN: Bethany Fellowship, 1969?, 32 pp.

Mathis, J. J.W. *A Review of Russellism Et Cetera, Et Cetera* pub. by author Arlington, TX 1916 67 pp. pp.1-43 on Russell p 44-66 (On Eddyism, now known on Christian Science covers primarily major doctrines, mostly a critique.)

Matzke, J. *Ernste Bibelforscher?* Katholische Aktion, 1935, 32 pp. (Earnest Bible Students?) (in German).

Mayer, F. E. *Jehovah's Witnesses.* St. Louis, MO: Concordia Publishing House, 1942 (revised 1957), 52 pp. (Critiques major doctrines; salvation, the ransom, hell, and covers date-setting failure, and eschatology).

Maynard, John Albert. *"Russellism."* London: S.P.C.K., 1926, 31 pp.

McCarty, Skip. The *Jehovah's Witnesses.* Boise, ID: Pacific Press 1987 31 pp (covers the Watchtower from the SDA orientation; much a 144,000, the trinity, and the deity of Christ).

McCluskey, Neil G. *Who Are Jehovah's Witnesses?* New York: The American Press, 1956, 17 pp. (reprinted from *America Magazine,* Nov. 19, 1955, pp. 204-208). (A brief history of the Watchtower organization; covers some doctrine).

McLean, W.T. *Isms, "Heresies, Exposed by the Word of God."* Grand Rapids, MI: Zondervan Publishing House, n.d., 29 pp. (Chapter 2, p. 12-15 "Millennial-Darwinism" covers Russellism, history, and major doctrines).

Mellows, F. *Russellism, the Latest Blasphemy, or "Millions-now-living-will-never-die-ism."* London: C.J. Thynne, 1921, 24 pp. (Vol. 4 of Substitutes for Christianity.). (an extremely rare booklet--the only known copy is at Princeton University--covers Witness chronology, refutes their teaching that "the new world era is to be set up in 1925" and their eschatology).

Metzger, Bruce M. *The Jehovah's Witnesses and Jesus Christ.* Princeton, NJ: Theological Book Agency, n.d., 21 pp. (reprinted from *Theology Today,* April 1953, pp. 65-85). (A scholarly critique of the Watchtower view of Christ and the trinity).

Meyenberg, Albert. *Uber die sogenannten Ernsten Bibelforscher, Geschichte, Lehre und Kritik.* Luzern: Räber und Cie, 1924, 19 pp. (About the so-called Serious Bible Researchers).

Mianecki, P. *Zeugen Jehovas?* (Witnesses of Jehovah?). Berlin: Morus Verlag, 1949, 31 pp. (Morus Kleinschriften, 1) (in German).

Miksch, L. *Die Ernsten Bibelforscher. Mit einen Anhang: Die Gerichtsverhandlung in St. Gallen wegen der Frage: Werden die "Ernsten Bibelforscher" mit Amerikanischen Judengeld fur ihre Zersetzungsarbeit bezahlt?* Lorch: Verlag Karl Rohm, 1925, 40 pp. (The Ernest Bible Students. Within the appendix: The court treatise of St. Gallen about the question: Do the "Earnest Bible Students" use American Jews' money for their disruption work?) (dislocating work). (in German).

Miller, Stephen. *Misguiding Lights?* Kansas City, MO:Beacon Hill Press. 1991. Chapter 3 "Jehovah's Witnesses" pp. 20-29 by Kurt Goedelman.

Moffitt, Jerry, ed. *Jehovah's Witnesses."* Thrust (Austin, TX: Southwest Church of Christ), Vol. 1, No. 1, 1979, 40 pp. and Vol. 1, No. 2, 1980, pp. 41-90. (Covers the trinity, salvation, hell, 1914, eschatology, blood transfusions and the *New World Translation*).

Montague, Havor. *Watchtower Congregations: Communion or Conflict?* Santa Ana, CA: CARIS, 1978, 8 pp.

_____. *Jehovah's Witnesses and Blood Transfusions.* Santa Ana, CA: CARIS, 1979, 21 pp.

Moore, T.W. *Millennial Dawn: Teaching and Errors.* 4th ed., c. 1910, Scotland Christian Literature, 24 pp. (A critique of doctrine; second advent, Christ, salvation and other doctrines; argues against some doctrines no longer taught by the Watchtower).

Mosemann, J.H. *Russell's Hell Vs. The Bible Hell.* c. 1914.

Moskalenko, Aleksei Trofimovich. *Who Are Jehovah's Witnesses?* Moscow: "Knowledge" (The All-Union Society for the Propagation of Political and Scientific Knowledge) (Editions, Series 2, No. 29), 1959, 32 pp. (in Russian).

_____. *The Sect of Jehovah's Witnesses and Reactionary Substance (Essence).* Moscow: "University," 1961, 76 pp. (in Russian).

Mott, Johannes Raleigh. *Bibelforscher und Gebet im Kammerlein, zur Forderung des geistlichen Lebens.* Woltersdorf b. Erkner, Jugendbund-Buchhandlung, 1928, 32 pp. (Bible Students and prayer like the Ethiopian Eunuch desire for spiritual life). (in German).

Moyer, Robert L. *The Rich Man in Hell and the Blasphemous Trinity.* Minneapolis, MN: Osterhus Publishing House, 1946, 29 pp. (Refutes the view that the rich man account is a parable, argues that hell is a locality, and conscious persons suffer there for eternity).

Mulder, M.H. *De Getuigen van Jehova--een ziekte van onze tijd.* Heerlen, Winants Uitgeverij, 1946, 32 pp. (The Witnesses of Jehovah--an illness of our days).

Müller, Anton. *Die Ernsten Bibelforscher und die letzten Dinge.* 12 Vol. of the series *"Hirt und Herde."* N.d., 23 pp. (The Serious Bible Researchers and the Last Things).

Munro, W. Fraser. *The Facts About Jehovah's Witnesses.* Toronto, Canada: The Board of Evangelism and Social Service, The United Church of Canada, c. 1955, 8 pp. (A critique of Witness doctrine and a brief history).

Murray, Wm. W., M.D. *Millennial Hopes and Prospects.* Richmond, VA: The Williams Printing Co., 1903, 16 pp.

National Service Board for Religious Objectors. *Statements of Religious Bodies on the Conscientious Objector.* Dec. 1951; revised Aug. 1953.

Nelson, Wilton. *Jehovah's Witnesses.* Chicago: Moody Press, c. 1955, 15 pp.

Nicole, J. *Les Témoins de Jéhovah ont-ils raison?* Edition Emmaüs, 1806 St. Légier, 1970. (The Jehovah's Witnesses, are they right?)

Nielsen, John R. *An Open Letter to the Jehovah's Witnesses.* St. Louis, MO: Concordia Tract Mission, n.d., 9 pp.

Nightengale, L. *Millennial Dawn--The Story of Jehovah and His Witnesses.* Adelaide: Summer's Press, 1986.

Nijmegen Informatie Centrum. *Zij hebben hun religie onderzocht!* Nijmegen, Informatie-Centrum, z.j., 12 pp. (They have their religion examined) (in Dutch).

_____. *Zij zagen uit naar 1975!* Nijmegen, Informatie-Centrum, z.j., 12 pp. (They looked to 1975) (in Dutch).

Nitzschke, K. *Die Zeugen Jehovahs. Eine Kritik.* (The Witnesses of Jehovah. A Critical considering). Berlin, Christlicher Buch-und Zeitschriften Verlag, 1949, 48 pp. (in German).

O'Brien, John A. *Light on Jehovah's Witnesses.* Huntington, IN: Sunday Visitor, Inc., n.d., 29 pp. (A Catholic critique of the Watchtower history; covers Russell (p. 1-10), Rutherford (p. 10-16), and Knorr (p. 18-20)).

O'Hair, J.G. *Millions Now Dying Will Never Live, A Scriptural Investigation of Russellism.* Chicago: pub. by author, n.d., c. 1920, 21 pp.

Ongman, John. *Varningsrop I Affallstider; Nagra af Tidens villfarelser framstalda I Biblisk Belysning.* Örebro; forfattarens Eget Förlag, 1910, 62 pp. (A critique of Watchtower and Adventist doctrines by an evangelical).

On the Watch (Australia). *What the Watchtower Does Not Tell You.* 19 pp.

Othmalm, Erick. *Bibelns lära om Gud.* Orebro, Sweden, 1975. (The Bible's Teaching on God) (in Swedish). (A critique of Watchtower doctrines including God, Jesus and the trinity).

Our Hope Publication Office. *How Pastor Russell Died.* New York, n.d.

_____. *How Russellism Subverts the Faith.* New York, n.d.

_____. *Date System and Teaching on Christ.* New York, n.d.

Passeleco, P. *De dwalingen van de Getuigen van Jehovah (het Katholieke standpunt).* Oosterhout, St. Paulus Abbe, (1957), 30 pp. (The Mistakes of the Witnesses of Jehovah (from the Catholic standpoint), edited by C. Levison) (in Dutch).

Pastoral Care. *Jehovah's Witnesses, Are You Free?* Van Nuys, CA, n.d., c. 1970, 22 pp. (Argues the Watchtower is a false prophet and that Witnesses follow the Watchtower, not God).

Personal Freedom Outreach. *Jehovah's Witnesses: The Christian View.* St. Louis, MO, 1978, 19 pp. This booklet is to accompany the slide set produced by *Personal Freedom Outreach.*

Petersen, Mark E. *Some Helps Regarding Jehovah's Witnesses.* Salt Lake City, UT: Mormon Missionary Manuals, n.d., 32 pp. (On the resurrection; the author does not understand Witness doctrine).

_____. *"Questions About the Jehovah's Witnesses,"* in *Peter and "The Rock."* Salt Lake City, UT: Mormon Missionary Manuals, n.d., pp. 12-26. (Covers the nature of God, titles and related).

_____. *Christ, Jehovah and the Witnesses."* Salt Lake City, UT: Mormon Missionary Manuals, 32 pp. (Argues that Christ and Jehovah are the same person).

Pfeil, Carl. *Jesus, Jehovah, and "the New World Translation:" A Study of the Deity of Christ in the Jehovah's Witness Translation of the Bible.* Renton, WA: Family Bible Fellowship, 1976, 20 pp., 2nd ed. 1978, 20 pp (A critique on the NWT translation of the Scriptures, that relates to the trinity)

Piette, Christian. Enlightenment on the Jehovah's Witnesses, Biblical literature edition 479 chaussee de Turbrze, Braine 1 Alleud, Belgique.

Pile, William. *Mistakes Jehovah's Witnesses Make.* Los Angeles, CA: Good News Publishers, 1968 (packet of 13 tracts--total of 56 pp).

Plantation Press. *Blood Transfusion: Is It Sinful?* Lisburn, N. Ireland, 1985?, 11 pp.

Pollock. A.J. *Examination of Judge Rutherford's Books.* New York, n.d., 15 pp.

_____. *How "Pastor" Russell Died.* New York, n.d.

_____. *Millennial Dawnism: Briefly Tested by Scripture.* London, England: Central Bible Truth Dept., 1917, 23 pp. (Quotes Russell, then attempts to refute him).

_____. *Jehovah's Witnesses Exposed by Scripture.*

_____. *"Jehovah's Witnesses" and Judge Rutherford's Books: An Exposure.* London, England: Central Bible Truth Dept., 1942, 16 pp. (A critique of doctrine, the 1914 predictions, and Watchtower teachings. Reprinted in Bergman,1990 pp.151-188).

Prakh'ie Borys Semenovych. *The Jehovah's Witnesses.* Odessa, USSR: Library of

Atheism, 1959, 13 pp. (in Ukrainian).

Price, Ernest B. *God's Channel of Truth--Is It the Watchtower?* Mountain View, CA: Pacific Press Publishing Assoc., 1967, 112 pp., German ed. *Gottes Kanal der Wahrheit, ist es der Wachtturm?* Zurich, Advent Verlag, 1972, 142 pp. (In story form, Price argues against Watchtower doctrines that Seventh-day Adventists disagree with. Reprinted in Bergman, 1990 p.343-352)

_____. *Our Friends: The Jehovah's Witnesses.* Victoria, Australia: Lay Activities Department of Victorian Conference of Seventh-Day Adventists, n.d., c. 87 pp., 1985 ed. revised and enlarged, 60 pp. (Uses a large number of photocopies of Watchtower publications to show the problems, changes, and inconsistencies of Watchtower doctrine).

_____. *What the Watchtower Does Not Tell You.* Victoria, Australia: Lay Activities Department of Victorian Conference of Seventh-Day Adventists, n.d, 17 pp.

Proctor, W.C. *An Answer to Latest Slogan or Russellism, Pamphlets on the Second Advent.* London: Thynne and Jarvis, 1926, 1925.

Putnam, C.E. *Jehovah's Witnesses: Russellism, Rutherfordism--Are They God's Prophets?* Randleman, NC: n.p., n.d., 6 pp.

Quaisser, G.S. und K.M. Undergmann. *Dreiunddreitβig Jahre Irrlehre im Names Jehovas.* (Thirty three years false doctrine in the name of Jehovah). Berlin, z.u., (ca. 1961), 15 pp. (in German).

_____. *Göttes Konigreich herrscht--Ist das Ende der Welt nahe? oder Fasse Mutt-Gottes Konigreich ist Nah! Welches von beiden ist die Wahrheit?* ("God's Kingdom Rules--Is the world's end near?" or "Take courage--Gods Kingdom is at hand!" Which of both is the truth?) Berlin, z.u., (ca. 1961), 16 pp. (in German).

Reed, David. *Radio Free Watchtower.* Stoughton, MA: Christians, 1981, 12 pp. (Reed is an ex-Witness and in this work he tells some of the reasons why he left them).

_____. *Out of the Watchtower Into What?* Stoughton, MA: Comments from the friends, 1984, 16 pp. (Discusses the problem of leaving the Watchtower and what Christianity is).

_____. *Leading Jehovah's Witnesses to Christ.* Stoughton, MA: Comments from the Friends, 1985, 16 pp. (Discusses why persons become Witnesses and how they reason; very well done).

_____. *I Was a Jehovah's Witness Elder."* Assonet, MA: Comments from the friends, 1986, 16 pp. (A personal account of a couple that left the Watchtower and why).

_____. *Proclaimers answered page by page.* Assonet, MA: Comments from the Friends, 1994, 40 pp.

_____. *New light Index. Bible Abuse--How JWs Misuse Scripture.* Assonet, MA: Comments from the Friends, 1994, 40 pp.

_____. *Witnessing Tips--Reach out to JWs.* Assonet, MA: Comments from the Friends, 1994, 40 pp.

_____. *Dictionary of 'J.W.ese.'* Assonet, MA: Comments from the Friends, 1995, 44 pp.

_____. *JWs a Cult? Pyramids, pictures and prophecies prove it.* Assonet, MA: Comments from the Friends, 1995, 40 pp.

_____.*WT Stake vs. Christian Cross.* Assonet, MA: Comments from the Friends, 1995, 60 pp. (Written by Carolyn Pemberton)

_____. *1914 Generation Prophecy proves false.* Assonet, MA: Comments from the Friends, 1996, 40 pp.

_____. *Ministry on the Internet.* Assonet, MA, 1996, 40 pp. (About setting up a web site dealing with the Watchtower)

_____. *More Verse by Verse Answers for JWs.* Assonet, MA: Comments from the Friends, 1996, 40 pp.

Reid, R.J. *How Russellism Subverts the Faith.* New York, n.d., (c. 1920), 69 pp. (A critique of Russell's doctrine and teachings by an evangelical).

Rekemchuk, Aleksandr Evseevich. *A Double-Depth* (Documentary Novel). Moscow: Siktivkar Komi Book Publishing House, 1958, 53 pp. (in Russian).

_____. *The Double Depths of "Jehovah's Witnesses," A Documentary Story.* Moscow: State Publishing House for Political Literature, 1959, 43 pp. (in Russian).

Remberger, F.X. *Zeugen Jehovas oder Zeugen Christi?* München, Pfeiffer, 1955, 71 pp. (Witnesses of Jehovah or Witnesses of Jesus Christ?) (in German).

Renker, Z. (pseudonym for Ferdinand Krenzer). *Unsere Bruder in den Sekten.* Limburg, Lahn Verlag. (Taschenbücher für wache Christen). (Our brothers in the sects).(In German).

Riemer, M. *Die Neuzeitlichen Sekten und Häresie in ihren verhältnis zur Kirchenh in Deutschland.* Gutersloh, F. Berthelsmann, 1926, 79 pp. (The new-days sects and heresy in their relations to churches in Germany). (in German).

Ridout, George Whitefield. *The Deadly fallacy of Russellism of Millennial Dawnism.* Louisville, KY: Pentecostal Publishing Co., n.d., 20 pp.

Riley, W.B. *Mistakes of Millennial Dawn.* Los Angeles, CA: Bible Institute of Los Angeles, Viola Book Room, n.d.

Rinman, John. *"Russelliamismen" Sken och Verklighet.* Stockholm: Evang. Fosterlands Stiftelsens Förlags, 1915, 32 pp. (Truth and Light on Russellism). (A critique of Russell's beliefs and doctrines). (In Swedish)

Ripley, Francis J. *The Witnesses of Jehovah.* London, England: Catholic Truth Society, n.d., 24 pp.

Rockwood, Perry. *Jehovah's Witnesses Examined in the Light of the Word of God.* Halifax, N.S., Canada, n.d., 21 pp. (Critiques the Watchtower's view of Christ, Hell, and the trinity).

Rogozniak, Nikolai. *We Cannot Be Silent. An Open Letter, Published in the Newspaper "Eastern Siberian Truth," No. 22 from 26 January, 1963, to Members of the Organization, "Jehovah's Witnesses" (Nikolai Rogozniak, Nikolai Khamei, Vasilii Pron).* Irkutsk, 1963, 14 pp. (in Russian).

Rohkohl, Pastor. *Wer hat recht? Eine Auseinandersetzung mit den Ernsten Bibelforschern.* (Who Is Right? An Explanation of the Serious Bible Students). Berlin: Evangelischer Presseverband, 1924 and 1928, 34 pp.

Ross, Rev. J.J. *Some Facts and More Facts About the Self-styled "Pastor" Charles T. Russell.* Philadelphia, PA: Philadelphia Presbyterian Board; Los Angeles, CA:

Bible Institute of Los Angeles, 1912, 50 pp. (A history of some of Russell's legal troubles and court cases; much important material). Reprinted in Barnett, above.

_____. *Some Facts About the Self-styled "Pastor" Russell.* New York: C.C. Cook, n.d.

Ross, K.N. *Jehovah's Witnesses.* London, England: S.P.C.K., 1954, (2nd ed. 1962), 10 pp. (A critique of the Watchtower view of Hell, the trinity and other doctrines).

Rowell, J.B. *The Death of Our Lord.* N.p., n.d., 60 pp.

_____. *The Deity of Jesus Christ Our Lord.* Victoria, BC, Canada: Hebden Printing Co., 1955, 39 pp. (A critique of the Watchtower view of Christ and the trinity).

Ruiz, Agustin. *Los Testigos de Jehova: Coleccion de Doctrinas Modernas.* 1966 (also 1976 ed). (The Jehovah's Witnesses: A Collection of Modern Doctrines) (in Spanish) (Critiques primarily the trinity, and eschatology from an evangelical worldview).

Rumble, Leslie. *The Anti-Immortals: A Reply to the Rationalists, Jehovah's Witnesses, Adventists, and Christadelphians.* St. Paul, MN: Fathers Rumble and Carty, n.d., 32 pp. (A Catholic critiques several sects which the author largely treats as a unit).

_____. *The Incredible Creed of Jehovah's Witnesses.* St. Paul, MN: Fathers Rumble and Carty, c. 1963, 31 pp. British ed., London, England: Catholic Truth Society, 1963, 24 pp. (A critique of the Witnesses from the Catholic viewpoint focusing on doctrine; also covers lifestyle, the last days and the effect of these teachings on Witnesses).

_____. *Jehovah Witness.* St. Paul, MN: Fathers Rumble and Carty, n.c., 32 pp. (Covers history and some doctrine, relies on reason to critique Witness)

Russell, O.B. *The Errors of Russellism.* N.p., 1934.

Sanchez, Benjamin Martin. *¿Quines son los Testigos de Jehova?* Zamora: Monte Casino, 1971, 47 pp. (Who are Jehovah's Witnesses?) (A critique of Watchtower beliefs by a Catholic professor of Biblical studies).

Sanders, E.L. *A Critique of the Jehovah's Witnesses.* Langley, B.C., Canada: Apostolic Church of God., n.d., 40 pp.

Sander, J. Oswald, and J. Stafford Wright. *Some Modern Religions.* London, England: The Tyndale Press, 1956, 72 pp.

Sandt, George W. *Another Pious Fraud or The Story of Russellism.* Philadelphia, PA: General Council Publication House, 1913, 31 pp. (A Lutheran minister critiques both Russell as a person and his basic teachings).

Scheurlen, Paul. *Die Sekten der Gegenwart und neuere Weltanschauungsgebilde.* Stuttgart: Quell-Verlag der Eveng. Gesellschaft, 1923. (The Present Sects and Their New World View) (in German).

_____. *Das Kleine Sektenbüchlein.* Stuttgart, z.u., 1933, 96 pp. (The little sects booklet) (in German).

Schevchenko, Vladimir Ivanovich. *The Prophets of Fire and Doom.* Moscow: "Knowledge" (Read, Comrades! Series), 1961, 34 pp. (in Russian).

Schmiedel, Paul. *Pilatus uber Jesus bei den Ernsten Bibelforschern.* Zürich: Art Institute Ovell Füssli, 1924, 15 pp. (Pilatus on Jesus by the Jehovah's Witnesses) (in

German).

Schnell, William J. *Another Gospel*. Seattle, WA: The Life Messengers, n.d., 32 pp. (Sections from Schnell's book *Thirty Years a Watchtower Slave*).

_____. *Who Are Jehovah's Witnesses?* Youngstown, OH: Espositer, n.d, 8 pp. (A brief review of history and doctrine).

Scott, Frank Earl. *Son of Man Revealed*. Wallace, ID: pub. by author, 1973, 32 pp. (The author, evidently an ex-Witness, predicted Armageddon on Dec 2, 1977 in this booklet).

Shadduck, B.H. *The Seven Thunders of Millennial Dawn*. Astabula, OH: Homo Publishing Co., 1928, 32 pp. (An excellent critique of Russell and Rutherford's person and teachings).

Shaw, Lloyd. *Points to Ponder*. 2nd ed. privately printed 32 pp. (A collection of poems, many deal with the creation and creator; written for and by a Jehovah's Witness).

Sheldon, Henry Clay. *Russell's Ventures in Adventism*. New York: Methodism Book Concern, 1921, 31 pp. (An excellent critique of Russell's eschatology and his view of the millennium).

Sherrill, Dave. *"Quick Quotes from the Watchtower."* Sioux City, IA. Cult Research and Evangelism 1995 68 pp. (An index of Watchtower quotes arranged by subject; helpful to show how Watchtower teachings have changed).

_____. *The Deity of Christ and the Jehovah's Witness' New World Translation*. Sioux City, Ia Cult Research and Evangelism 1994 16 pp. (Presents evidence for Christ's Deity as found in the Watchtower's own translation).

Shields, T.T. *Russellism, Rutherford: The Teachings of the International Bible Students in the Light of Holy Scripture*. Grand Rapids, MI: 1934, 106 pp.

_____. *Russellism or Rutherfordism in the Light of the Holy Scriptures*. Toronto, Canada: The Gospel Witness, 1946, 72 pp. (Critiques Russell's teaching on Christ, the second coming, and political involvement. Reprinted in Bergman,1990 pp.189-262)

Siedenschnur, Günther. *Kleiner Sekten-Katechismus*. (Little sect catechism). Gütersloh, Verlag Kirche und Mann, 1954, 32 pp. (in German).

_____. *Die "Zeugen Jehovas." Eine Handreichung für Evangelische Christen*. (The Witnesses of Jehovah. A hand book for Evangelical Christians). Hannover, Lutherhaus Verlag, 1990, 15 pp. (in German).

_____. *Wer sind die Zeugen Jehovas?* (Who are the Witnesses of Jehovah?). Gütersloh, Verlag Kirche und Mann, 1955, 32 pp. (in German).

Sinhung, Chonggyo Munje Yon'guso. *Research Report of Jehovah's Witnesses*. Seoul, Korea: New Religious Research Institute, 1978, 25 pp. (in Korean).

Smith, R.T. *Jehovah's Witnesses: Millennial Dawnism or Russellism and Rutherfordism--What Do They Teach?* Philadelphia, PA: n.d., 8 pp.

Smith, W.A. *The Search for Truth--A True Life Story*. Melbourne, Australia: Berean Bible Institute, n.d., 35 pp. (A Bible student tells his life story, from 1900 to 1940 or so, and of their beliefs in contrast to the Watchtower).

Soldiers of Christ. *The Doctrines of the Jehovah's Witnesses Contrasted to the Bible and the Historic Christian Faith.* Six Lakes, MI: The Soldiers of Christ, 1976, 60 pp. (An outline of Watchtower teaching in contrast to historic Christianity on the trinity, man, Satan, the soul, hell death, the resurrection and the last things).

Sonderegger, H. *Gespräch mit dem Zeugen Jehovas.* Zürich, Zwingli Verlag, 1960, 63 pp. (Das offene Wort, 25) (Conversation with the Witnesses of Jehovah). (In German).

Spier, H.J. *Getuigen van Jehova of van den Anti-Christ? Ons antwoord.* Groningen, Jan Haan, 1945, 22 pp. (Witnesses of Jehovah or of the Anti-Christ? Our Answer). (A theological critique of the Watchtower). (In Dutch)

_____. *Getuigen van Jehova of van de Anti-Christ?* Delft, Van Keulen, 1951, 32 pp. (Witnesses of Jehovah or of the Antichrist? 3th ed., 4th is 48 pp.).(In Dutch).

Spritzer, Jenny. *Ich War Nr 10291.* Verlag Darmstädter Blätter, Haubachweg 5 D-6100 Darmstadt Germany. 2nd Ed., 1980. Jehovah's Witnesses, p. 63-65.(I Was Number 10291) (About Auschwitz). (In German).

Sprung, Renate (pseudonym for Rosemarie Richter). *Gefangnis ohne Mauern: Wir waren Zeugen Jehovas.* Ostfildern: Schwabenverlag, 1977, 71 pp. (Prison Without Walls: We Were Jehovah's Witnesses) (In German).

Staehelin, Ernst. *Was haben wir von den Ernsten Bibelforschern zu halten?* Basel: F. Reinhardt, 1925, 32 pp. (What Do We Think About the Serious Bible Researchers?) (In German).

Stallmann, Heinrich. *Die Internationale Vereinigung Ernster Bibelforscher Zur Aufklärung und Warnung.* Zwickau: Verlag des Schrift-vereins, 2nd ed., 1925, 32 pp. (The International Union of Serious Bible Researchers) (in German).

Starkes, M. Thomas. *Armageddon's Army: The Jehovah's Witnesses.* Atlanta, GA: Home Mission Board, 1976, 12 pp. Reprinted from *Home Missions Magazine,* March 1975. (A brief review of history and doctrines).

Stephens, Carl. *Light on the Tower: Are They Really Jehovah's Witnesses?* Texarkana, TX: Bogard Press, 1977, 54 pp.

Stevens, Edward. *The Watchtower Society: Its Origin, Doctrine and Destiny.* Riverside, CA: c. 1960, 18 pp.

Stevens, Grover. *Jehovah's Witnesses Answered.* Lubbock, TX: Stevens Publications, n.d., 37 pp. (An outline responding to major Witness doctrine from a fundamentalist's world view).

Stevens, W.C. *Argument of Millennial Dawn.* Los Angeles, CA: Biola Book Room, Bible Institute of Los Angeles, n.d.

_____. *Why I Reject the Helping Hand of Millennial Dawn.* n.d., 121 pp.

Stilson, Max. *How to Deal with Jehovah's Witnesses.* Grand Rapids, MI: Zondervan Publishing House, 1962, 61 pp. (This poorly done work is mostly on doctrine).

Stockdale, William. *Jehovah's Witnesses in American Prison.* Putnam, CT: The Wilda Press, 1946, 27 pp. (A review of the Witness' experience in prison for opposing the draft and war).

_____. *The Government Is the Criminal.* Putnam, CT: The Wilda Press, 1947, 79 pp. (Written by an active Witness and highly sympathetic to the Witness situation).

Stover, Gerald L. *"Ye Shall Know the Truth"--An Expose of "Jehovah's Witnesses."* Ontario, Canada: Kitchener Printing Service, 1945, 50 pp. (Critiques Watchtower doctrine).

Strauss, Lehman. *An Examination of the Doctrine of "Jehovah's Witnesses."* New York: Loizeaux Brothers, 1942, 47 pp. (also titled *An Examination of the Teachings of Jehovah Witnesses*). (A Baptist critique of the Watchtower doctrines of the trinity, the deity of Christ, the atonement, the deity of the holy spirit, hell and eternal punishment).

Sturmann, Walter E. *The Jehovah's Witnesses and the Bible.* Tulsa, OK: Univ. of Oklahoma, 1955, 31 pp. (This review is an objective study, and includes a background of the Witness; focuses on doctrines; 12 pages on the Witness' translation).

Stump, J. *Russellism.* Philadelphia, PA: United Lutheran Publishing, 1923.

Suarez, Fernandez. *Los Falsos Testigos de Jehová.* Mexico: Casa Bautista de Publicaciones, 1962 (also 1975 ed.), 46 pp. (The False Witnesses of Jehovah) (A critique of Witness doctrine by an evangelical). (In Spanish).

Sundström, Erland. *Jehovas Vittnen på fammarsch, Religions--sociolgiska Institute.* Forsknings--rapport, No. 133 (1976:5), Oct. 1976, 25 pp. (Jehovah's Witnesses on the March) (in Swedish) (A history and a discussion of the growth of the Watchtower in Sweden).

Swarbrick, Fred. *Witnessing to Jehovah's Witnesses.* Belfast: Great Joy Publications, 1988, 4th ed., 20 pp. (Covers soul, sleep, Hell, and the trinity doctrines).

Swartz, Frank. *A Close Look at the Jehovah's Witness Bible.* Little Rock, AK: The Challenge Press, 1974, 32 pp. (A comparison of the NWT with the King James Bible on Scriptures relating to the trinity, and salvation).

Swift, John McIntosh. *Jehovah's Witnesses: A Brief Account of the History, Beliefs, and Methods of a Strange and Widespread Organization.* Oxford, England: A.R. Mowbray & Co., 1942, 16 pp. (Covers history, lifestyle and sociology of the Witnesses).

Talbot, Louis T. *Jehovah's Witnesses and the bible.* Findlay, OH: Dunham Publishing Co., 1957, 48 pp. (Covers history, critiques major doctrines; also covers Dawnites).

_____. *What's Wrong with Jehovah's Witnesses?* Findlay, OH: Dunham Publishing Co., 1957, 48 pp.

Tanis, Edward J. *What the Sects Teach.* Grand Rapids, MI: Baker Books, 1958, 89 pp. (One section on the Witnesses).

Target, G.W. *The Black Plague--Russellism.* Great Britain: Holiness, n.d.

Thomas, Fred W. *Should Jehovah's Witnesses Ridicule or Fear Hell?* Vancouver, B.C. Canada: pub. by author, n.d., 24 pp. (A critique of the Watchtower view of Hell).

_____. *The Bible Answers: Jehovah's Witnesses' Ridicule of Hell.* Minneapolis, MN: Osterhus, n.d., 30 pp. (A critique of the Watchtower view of hell and the soul; an extensive revision on of the above).

Thorell, Folke. *Lögn Profeter: En Saklig undersökning angaende Jehovas Vittnen och deras lära.* Stockholm, Sweden: Normans Forlag, 1955, 40 pp. (False Prophets: A Factual Research About the Jehovah's Witnesses and Their Doctrines) (Covers history and doctrine).(in Swedish).

_____. *Tio Religionssurrogat:* Folke, Thorells Forlag. Orebro, 1973, 49 pp. (Ten
Religious Surogates). (A critique of 10 religious sects, including the
Watchtower). (in Swedish).

Thorton, Carl L. *The Shifting Sands of Witness Belief.* Published by Author Flint, Mi
1996 19 pp. 81/2 x 11 (This is a chapter from the authors forthcoming book *A
Psychologists View of Jehovah's Witnesse*s. Covers Watchtower's Constant
doctrinal shifts called "new light")

Thurston, Herbert. *Jehovah's Witness, Judge Rutherford.* Catholic Truth Society,
London, 1956.

Tipton, S.R. *The Jehovah Witnesses Versus the Bible.* N.p., n.d.

Tisch, Rudolf. *Die Ernsten Bibelforscher entlarvt.* Elberfeld, Licht und Leben Verlag,
1924, 32 pp. (The Earnest Bible Students uncovered). (in German).

Tolle, James M. *An Expose of Jehovah's Witnesses.* Fullerton, CA: Tolle Publ., c.
1957, 29 pp. (earlier ed. San Fernando, CA, 19 pp.). (Critiques the major
doctrines, the Watchtower view of Christ, the resurrection, and the nature of man).

Torhorst, Arnold. *Die Ernsten Bibelforscher als Propheten des nahen Weltendes.*
Potsdam: Stiftungsverlag, 1925, 12 pp. (The Jehovah's Witnesses: Prophets of
the latest World's End).

Tovarystvo, Diia Poshyrennia. *The Society for the Spread (Development) of Political and
Scientific Knowledge in the Ukraine.* Chernivetske, 1959, 42 pp. (in Ukrainian).
Revised as: *The Society of Znannia (knowledge) in the Ukraine RSR: Why Do
Jehovah's Witnesses Follow?* Ed. E. Cherozok and O. Guber. 1959, 42 pp.

Tucker, W. Leon. *What Is Russellism? Commonly Called Millennial Dawn.* Los
Angeles, CA: Serial Tract Publishing Co., c. 1910, 29 pp. (A critique of
Russell's major doctrines, especially the trinity).

Twisselmann, Hans-Jürgen. *Die "Zeugen Jehovas" Erwählte oder Verführte?* Witten-
Ruhr, West Germany: Bundes Verlag, 1967, 32 pp. (The Jehovah's Witnesses:
Chosen or Deceived?) (Covers history and doctrine). (In German).

_____. *Als Zeugen Jehovas erlebt erlitten und Erzählt.* Witten Ruhr, West Germany,
n.d. (As Jehovah's Witnesses Experienced and Suffered). (Letters, reports, and
confessions) (In German).

_____. *"Zeugen Jehovas" brauchen Antwort.* N.p., n.d. (Jehovah's Witnesses Need
Answers) (In German).

_____, ed. *Alles--nur Kein Blut! Menschenleben opfern um religioser Grundsätze
willen? Verlangt das der christliche Glaube?* Itzehoe, Germany, n.d., 23 pp.
(All--But No Blood. To Sacrifice for the Sake of Religious Principles? Does the
Christian Creed Require That?) (An excellent discussion of the blood issue).(In
German).

United States Holocaust Memorial Museum. *Jehovah's Witnesses.* c. 1996. Washington
D.C. 20 pp. (About the Witnesses experience in Nazi Germany).

Valisevich, Ivan Stepanovich. *The Religious Sects--Baptists and Jehovah's Witnesses.*
2nd supplemental ed. Irkutsk: Irkutsk Book Publishing House, 1958, 84 pp. (in
Russian).

Van Buskirk, Michael. *The Scholastic Dishonesty of the Watchtower.* Santa Ana, CA: CARIS, 1975, 22 pp. (revised 1976 ed., 48 pp.) (Shows how the Watchtower misquotes or inaccurately quotes to prove their theology).

_____. *Examining the Watchtower Society: The New World Translation, A Perfect Score of 64, Why?* Santa Ana, CA: Caris, n.d., 8 pp.

_____. *Examining the Watchtower Society: 1975 Yearbook of Jehovah's Witnesses "Something Special?"* Santa Ana, CA: Caris, n.d., 8 pp.

Verhoeven, A. *Jehova's Getuigen in het licht van de Bijbel.* Amsterdam, Stichting Moria, (1982), 87 pp. (Jehovah's Witnesses in the light of the Bible) (in Dutch).

Verrier, Chanoine Henri. *L'Eglise devant les T'emoins de Jehovah.* Raismes, France: Les Editions Polyglottes, 1957. (The Position of the Church and Jehovah's Witnesses) (in French).

Verwoert, G.J. *Een schokkende ontdekking!* Cuyk, Eigen beheer, z.j., 40 pp. (A shocking discovery!). (by an ex-Witness) (In Dutch).

Vink, D. *Jehova's Getuigen.* Haarlem, Eigen beheer, 1950, 10 pp. (Jehovah's Witnesses). (by an Ex-Witness). (In Dutch)

Voerman, J. *Is dit de waarheid die tot eeuwig leven leidt?* Deel 1. Nijmegen, Informatie-Centrum, z.j., 64 pp. (Is this the truth that leads to eternal life? Part 1) (In Dutch).

_____. *Is dit de waarheid die tot eeuwig leven leidt?* Deel 2. Nijmegen, Informatie-Centrum, z.j., 64 pp. (Is this the truth that leads to eternal life? Part 2) (In Dutch).

_____. *Is dit de waarheid die tot eeuwig leven leidt?* Deel 3. Nijmegen, Informatie-Centrum, z.j., 64 pp. (Is this the truth that leads to eternal life? Part 3) (In Dutch).

Voke, Rogerd. *Be Not Deceived.* Roodeport, Transvaal, South Africa: Transo Press, n.d., 36 pp.

Walkem, Charles William. *Jehovah's Witnesses: An Expose.* Los Angeles, CA: pub. by author, 1943, 32 pp. (Critiques history and major doctrines including eschatological and Christological, much name-calling).

Walker, C.C. *Has Christ Come? The Truth About the Parousia, Apokalupsis, and Epiphaneia, as Against Some Errors of Russellism.* Birmingham, England: "The Christadelphian," 1915, 16 pp. (A critique of Russell's teaching on Christ's second coming).

_____. *"A Ransom for All:" The Bible Doctrine of Ransom or Redemption in Opposition to the Errors of Universalism and Russellism.* Birmingham, England: "The Christadelphian," 1937, 24 pp. (Argues against a universal resurrection).

Wallace, William. *To the Jehovah's Witness Caller.* Athens, AL: C.E.I. Pub. Co., n.d., 18 pp.

Wallis, Arthur. *Jesus of Nazareth--Who Is He?* Christian Literature Crusade, 1959.

Walters, Wesley, and M. Kurt Goedelman. *Jehovah's Witnesses.* Downers Grove, IL: Inter-Varsity Press, 1983, 32 pp. (A good critique of Watchtower doctrine and a review of their history).

Warren, Thomas B., ed. *"Jehovah's Witnesses."* Memphis, TN: Getwell Church of Christ, Vol. 6, No. 1, Oct. 1974, *Spiritual Sword*, 48 pp. (A set of articles critiquing the Watchtower view on baptism, Christ, man, the trinity, sin, salvation and eschatology).

Wassink, A. *The Bible and Jehovah's Witnesses.* Grand Rapids, MI: Faith, Prayer and Tract League, n.d., c. 1920, 16 pp. (Refutes Russell's views on salvation, second probation, 1914, the soul and Jesus).

Watchtower Bible Studies. *What Jehovah Wants His Witnesses to Know in the Watchtower Translations: New World Interlinear Translation of the Greek Scriptures.* Cleveland, TN: 1977, 56 pp. (Shows the Watchtower's own translation contradicts their theology).

Welsh, Harold E. *Do Jehovah's Witnesses Have a Personal Relationship with Jesus Christ?* South Gate, CA: Christian Publications, n.d., 25 pp. (Defends the deity of Christ, critiques the Witness view of salvation; argues against the use of Jehovah or Jehawh).

Westby, Wayne. *Christ's Witnesses.* Rose Valley, Saskatchewan, Canada: privately printed, n.d., 8 pp.

Westwood, Tom. *Jehovah's Witnesses the True and the False.* Glendale, CA: pub. by author, n.d., 32 pp. (A scriptural critique of Witness theology).

Whalen, William J. *Jehovah's Witnesses.* Chicago: Clareton Publications, 1975, 25 pp. (revised ed. 1978, 32 pp. (A brief review of Witness history and teachings by a Catholic layman).

_____. *Jehovah's Witnesses.* Chicago, IL: Clareton Publishers, 1978, 32 pp. (Covers history, and some doctrine).

_____. What About Jehovah's Witnesses? n.p. n.d., 32 pp. (Covers history and doctrine; by a Catholic layman).

Wheeler, Gerald. *Is God a Committee?* Nashville, TN: Southern Publishing Association, 1975, 47 pp. Deals only with Witness beliefs, not the people directly.

Whitaker, Harry. *Why I am Not a Jehovah's Witness.* Birmingham, England: Christadelphian Auxiliary Lecturing Society, n.d., 8 pp.

Whyte, Lloyd. *Witnessing to the Witness.* Atlanta, GA: Home Mission Board, Southern Baptist Convention, 1973, 16 pp.

Wilhelm, Friedrich. *Die Zeugen Jehovas. Worte der Aufklarung und Abwehr.* Gladbeck, Schriftenmissions Verlag, 1968, 31 pp. (The Witnesses of Jehovah. Words of clarification and defense). (in German).

Williams, Thomas. *Russellism Refuted.* Chicago: Advocate Publishing House, n.d., c. 1905, 48 pp. (A critique of many of Russell's less controversial doctrines by a Christadelphian, a group that is actually fairly close to Russell in doctrine).

Wimbish, Dr. John S. *What Is a Jehovah's Witness?* Murfreesboro, TN: Sword of the Lord Publishers, 1956, 22 pp. (A harsh critique of the Witnesses and their history and major doctrines).

Windle, Charles P. *The Rutherford Racket.* Chicago, IL: Iconoclast Publishing Co., 1937. 30 p (Covers Rutherford's prophecies, background, interpretation of Scripture and attacks on the churches). Reprinted by Witness Inc.

Winnipeg Free Press. *Constitutional Freedom in Peril: The Jehovah Witnesses' Case.* Winnipeg, Canada, 1954, 23 pp. (A sympathetic review of Witness' persecution in Canada mostly relating to nationalism).

_____. *Rights and Citizenship: The Threat to Our Freedom.* Winnipeg, Canada, 1954, 8 pp. (An address by Victor Sifton, Chancellor of the University of Manitoba on the problem of Witness persecution in Canada).

Wolff, Richard. *Do Jehovah's Witnesses Follow the Bible?* Lincoln, NE: Back to the Bible Broadcast, 1959.

Woods, A. *Tremendous Truth from the New World Translation.* Phoenix, AZ: pub. by author, n.d., 31 pp. (Argues that the NWT teaches hell, trinity, salvation now, and salvation by faith).

Wright, Gerald. *Perversions and Prejudices of the New World Translation.* Fort Worth, TX: Star Bible Tract Society, 80 pp. (A critique on the NWT where it relates to Watchtower teaching on the trinity, the soul, the kingdom, baptism and communion).

Zellner, Herold T. *Behold, He Cometh.* Nazareth, PA: pub. by author, n.d., 20 pp. (Critiques the Watchtower view of Christ's second coming).

_____. *Each Day for a Year.* N.d., 4 pp. (Critiques the day-year theory as applied to the 1914 date).

_____. *57 Reasons Why I Believe in the Bodily Resurrection of Jesus Christ.* Nazareth, PA: pub. by author, n.d., 16 pp. (Argues for the physical resurrection of Christ).

_____. *The Church of God.* Nazareth, PA: pub. by author, n.d., 8 pp. (Critiques the Watchtower ideas on the 144,000).

_____. *The Gateway into God's Kingdom.* Nazareth, PA: pub. by author, n.d., 15 pp. (Critiques the Watchtower teaching on the 144,000).

_____. *Who Is That Faithful and Wise Servant?* Nazareth, PA: pub. by author, n.d., 19 pp. (Critiques the servant doctrine of the Watchtower and the 144,000 teaching).

Zwaal, F.C. *De dwaalleer der z.g. "Jehovah-Getuigen."* Aalten: De Graafschap, 1947, 32 pp. (The false doctrine of the so called Jehovah-Witnesses) (in Dutch) (A critique of the major doctrines of Witnesses).

D. Chapters and Sections of Books

All entries in this section are full-length chapters or sections about Witnesses or the Watchtower. Much of it the material in this section excellent, but unfortunately is generally inaccessible, because most standard indexes and bibliographies do not tap this source. This list was compiled primarily through extensive library research of indexes, the help of fellow researchers, and consulting the various books written on the Witnesses. About half of these entries discuss theological issues. The others contain information relative to the Witnesses' influence on various governments (mainly in Africa, America, and Europe) and their various political involvements, mostly relative to personal freedoms (especially freedom of the press, of speech, the right to not salute the flag, and to proselytize from door to door, in parks, and with the use of loudspeakers).

Although only a fraction of the material about Witnesses in books is included here, an attempt has been made to list some of the more common as well as some of the more extensive references. For this reason, this section is less exhaustive than any other in this book. The sections about Witnesses that are very brief are included because of their importance or significance to their history. A number of these works also include extensive discussions of the Witnesses. Margrete Buber's book *Under Two Dictators*, about her experiences with Witnesses in the concentration camps in the Soviet Union and Germany, discusses the Witnesses extensively throughout. Burber, not a Witness herself, covers both her experiences with them and her observations about those that she met in the camps during World War II. Other excellent references which deal with the Witnesses in concentration camps are those by Luchterhand, Kogan, and Bettelheim.

Books that are recommended for a general understanding of the witnesses include those by Braden, Clark, Kolarz (an expert discussion of the Witnesses in the old USSR), and Davies. An excellent discussion and criticism of the Witnesses' belief, held until the late 1920s, that the Great Pyramid of Giza is the "bible in stone," God's hidden communication about the end of the age--the current time in history--and various important events in history (which, in retrospect, are easily interpreted) is by Gardner. Also very useful are the works by Gruss (a review of the Witnesses' theology from the evangelical standpoint), Gerstner provides a very useful review of the Witnesses' theology and Hoekema (includes a detailed discussion of the some of the problems of the Witnesses' doctrines of the soul, Jesus, hellfire, and the trinity).

References written by active Witnesses including those by Knorr (most of Knorr's references are in various encyclopedias) and by the new Watchtower president, Melton G. Henschel. An excellent historical source is Hoffman, who includes in his book, *Jungle Gods*, a chapter about "Thomas, son of God," an early Watchtower convert who caused havoc in Africa and left several score dead. Concerning the African situation in general, the most useful references are Shepperson and Rotburg. From a sociological perspective, the often quoted works by Bryan Wilson, Yinger, Zaretsky, Beckford, La Faye, Maesen, and Lanternari are the most helpful.

Aalders, C. *Lot en illusie. Hedendaagse bewegingen en stroomingen.* Amsterdam, Uitgevers Maatschappij Holland, 1939, 174 pp. pp. 159-160: Jehovah's Getuigen. (Jehovah's Witnesses) (Fate and illusion. Present day movements and trends). (in Dutch).

Abel, Ron W. *Wrested Scriptures.* Pasadena, CA: Geddes Press, c. 1974, pp. 57-67, hb.

Abrams, Ray H. *Preachers Present Arms.* New York: Round Table Press, Inc., 1933, pp. 135, 182-185, 218-219, hb.

Adair, James, and Ted Miller, eds. *We Found Our Way Out.* Grand Rapids, MI: Baker Book House, 1964 (reprinted in 1975).

Adam, Phillip. *Adam Versus God.* Melbourne, Victoria, Australia: Thomas Nelson, 1985, 192 pp., pb. (A critique of all religions, one section (pp. 74-77) is on Witnesses and is very critical of their entire world view).

Ahlstrom, Sydney E. *A Religious History of the American People.* New Haven: Yale University Press, 1972.

Aletrino, L. *Vijftien ontmoetingen; geestelijke stromigen in Nederland.* Amsterdam, Scheltema & Holkema, 1955, 116 pp., pp. 62-67: Jehovah's Getuigen. (Jehovah's Witnesses) (Fifteen meetings; spiritual trends in The Netherlands). (in Dutch).

Alexander, David, ed. *Eerdman's Handbook to the bible.* Grand Rapids, MI: William B. Eerdman's Publ. Co., 1973, p. 79.

Algermissen, Konrad. *Konfessionskunde.* Hannover: J. Giesel, 1930, 845 pp. (Church, communion, knowledge study of Denominations) pp. 853-863. *Die Bibelforscher und Sekten* (The Bible Students sect).

_____. *Christian Denominations.* St. Louis, MO: B. Herder Book Co., 1945, pp. 875-880.

_____. *The Christian Sects.* London: Burns and Oates, 1962.

Ambrose, Stephen E. *The Supreme Commander.* Garden City, NY: Doubleday & Co., 1970, p. 187. (About Eisenhower's Witness background).

Anderson, Christopher. *Michael Jackson; Unauthorized.* New York: Simon and Schuster 1994 p. 27-28, 51-52, 89, 117, 122-124, 146-147, 169, 199, 218, 237, 238, 245. (About Jackson ; much on his Watchtower background and the major influence it had in his life.)

The Australian Encyclopaedia. Vol. V. Sydney, Australia: Halstead Press, c. 1958, pp. 125-126.

Back, Marcus. *They Have Found a Faith.* Indianapolis, IN: Bobbs-Merrill Co., 1946, Chapter 2, "Jehovah's Witnesses," pp. 22-56. (A well-written sympathetic discussion of Witness' faith and practice, much in dialogue form).

_____. *Faith and My Friends.* New York: Bobbs-Merrill, 1951, 302 pp. (About the small American sects including several that are similar to the Witnesses).

_____. *Strange Sects and Curious Cults.* New York: Dodd, Mead and Co., 1961, pp. 3, 114-124.

Backman, Milton V. *American Religions and the Rise of Mormonism.* Salt Lake City, UT: Desert Book Co., 1970, pp. 377-387.

_____. *Christian Churches of America: Origins and Beliefs.* Provo, UT: Brigham Young University Press, 1976, Chapter 16, "The Watchtower Bible and Tract Society," pp. 175-184.

Baker, H. *Stroomingen en sekten van onzen tijd.* Utrecht, Kemink & Zoon, 1924, 132 pp. pp. 109-113: De Russellisten. 1939 ed. 202 pp. and p. 171-176 on Russell. (The Russellites) (Trends and sects of our time). (in Dutch).

_____. *Onder buitenkerkelijken, Sekte-menschen en Anderen.* Wgeningen, Veenman, 1935, 184 pp. pp. 156-174; Jehovah's Getuigen. (Jehovah's Witnesses) (Among the unchurched people, sect people and others). (in Dutch).

_____. *Stroomingen en sekten van onzen tijd.* Utrecht, Kemink & Zoon, 1939, 202 pp. pp. 171-176: Jehovah's Getuigen. (Jehovah's Witnesses) (Trends and sects of our time) (in Dutch).

Ball, Howard. *Judicial Craftsmanship or Fiat?* Westport, CT: Greenwood Press, 1967, Chapter 4, "The Flag Salute Cases," pp. 66-102.

Bandman, Elsie and Bertram. *Bioethics and Human Rights.* Boston: Little, Brown, 1978, pp. 16, 55, 169, 228, 232, 272, 321, (on the blood transfusion issue).

Barber, Holis W. "Religious Liberty v. Police Power: Jehovah's Witnesses" in *Outside Readings in Sociology,* Ed. E.W. Schuler, pp. 439-442, Reading 53.

Barker, A.J. *Prisoners of War.* New York: Universe Books, 1975, p. 116. (Notes Witnesses were more vocal against World War II than World War I).

Barker, Lucius. *Freedom, Courts, Politics: Studies in Civil Liberties.* Englewood Cliffs, NJ: Prentice-Hall, Inc., 1965, pp. 220-221.

Barmenkov. A. *Freedom of Conscience in the USSR.* Moscow: Progress Pub., 1983, pp. 71; 121-125 (very useful material on the Witnesses in the USSR).

Barrett, David. *Schism and Renewal in Africa.* Oxford, England: Oxford University Press, 1968, pp. 25, 57-58.

Barth, Alan. *Prophets with Honor.* New York: Alfred A. Knopf, 1974, Chapter V, "Freedom of Mind and Spirit Must Be Preserved," pp. 108-130 and "Minersville School District," Appendix D, pp. 224-228.

Bartoschevich, E. M. "Jehovah's Witnesses" in *The Great Soviet Encyclopedia.* New York: Macmillan, Inc., 3d ed., Vol. 10, 1976, p. 523.

Bartz, W. *Falsche Propheten: Jehovas Zeugen. Die Neuapostolische Gemeinde. Die Siebenten-Tags-Adventisten. Die Mormonen* (Kirche Jesu Christi der Heiligen der Letzten Tage). Überarbeitete Auflage. Trier, Paulinus Verlag, 1963 pp. (False prophets: Jehovah's Witnesses. The New-Apostolic Church. The Seventh Day Adventists. The Mormons (Church of Jesus Christ of the Saints of last days) (in German).

Baskin, Alex. *The American Civil Liberties Union Papers.* Stony Brook, NY: published by author, 1971 (lists ACLU files).

Bates, Ernest Southerland, ed. "Russell, Charles Taze" in *Dictionary of American Biography,* Vol. VIII. New York: Charles Scribner & Sons, 1935, 1963, p. 240.

Baumann, Thomas. *Kensington-Talmade.* San Diego, CA: privately printed, 1984, 196 pp., Chapter 13, on Judge Rutherford, pp. 132-135.

Beckford, James A. "The Embryonic Stage of a Religious Sects' Development: The Jehovah's Witnesses" in *Sociological Yearbook of Religion in Great Britain,* ed. Michael Hill, Vol. 5, 196 pp. 11-32. London: SCM Press Ltd., 1972.

_____. "The Contrasting Types of Sectarian Organization" in *Sectarianism: Analysis of Religious and Non-Religious Sects*, ed. Ray Wallis. London: Peter Owen Ltd., 1975, pp. 70-85; New York: John Wiley & Sons, 1975.

Beesley, Winfield. *Evangelism Unmasked.* NJ: Independent Publications, n.d., p. 31.

Beier, Lucinda. *Mormons, Christian Scientist, Jehovah's Witnesses.* London: Ward Lock Educational. 1981 48p (chapter 3 "Jehovah's Witnesses" pp. 34-46) (A short history of the Watchtower, covers some doctrine).

Benoit, Jean Paul. *Denominations et Sectes.* Paris: Librarie Protestante, n.d., (Denominations and Sects).

Benson, Purnell Handy. *Religion in American Culture.* New York: Harper & Bros., 1960, pp. 120-121, 614, 615, 669, 671, 691. (A brief review of the Watchtower history and several Witness court cases).

Benware, Paul N. *Ambassadors of Armstrongism.* Nutley, NJ: The Presbyterian and Reformed Publishing Co., 1975, pp. 30-32.

Berenbaum. Michael. (Ed) *A Mosaic of Victims; Non-Jews Persecuted and Murdered by the Nazis.* New York: New York University Press.,1990 Christine King Chapter 18 "Jehovah's Witnesses under Nazism." pp.188-193 and Ruediger Lautmann Chapter 20 " Jehovah's Witnesses and Political Prisoners." 244 pp.

Berendsen, A. *Vrouwenkamp Ravensbrück*. Utrecht, W. de Haan, 1946, 208 pp. pp. 78-79: Jehovah's Getuigen. (Jehovah's Witnesses) (Woman's camp Ravensbruck) (in Dutch).

Bergman, Jerry. "Jehovah's Witnesses and Blood Transfusions," in *Jehovah's Witnesses*, Vol. II; *Controversial and Polemical Pamphlets*, New York, NY: Garland Publishing, 1990, pp. 453- 633.

_____. Introduction to *Jehovah's Witness*, Vol. I. *The Early Writings of J.F. Rutherford*. New York, NY: Garland Publishing, 1990.

_____. Introduction to *Jehovah's Witnesses*, Vol. II. *Controversial and Polemical Pamphlets*. New York, NY: Garland Publishing, 1990.

_____. "The Adventists and Jehovah's Witness Branch of Protestantism" Chapter 3 in *America's Alternative Religions,* Albany, NY: State University of New York University Press, edited by Professor Timothy Miller, Professor, University of Kansas. 1995, pp. 33-46.

_____. "Jehovah's Witnesses" in *The Encyclopedia of New Religions, Cults, and Sects*. Ed. by James R. Lewis. New York: Promethus 1998.

Berkauwer, G.C. *The Person of Christ*. Grand Rapids, MI: Wm. B. Eerdmans Pub., Inc., 1954, "The Deity of Christ," pp. 155-192.

Berkelback Van Der Sprenkel, S.F.H.J. *Hedendaagsche Adventistische stroomingen*. Baarn, Hollandia-Srukkerij, 1923, 36 pp. (p. 27 on Russell) (Present day Adventist trends).

Berry, Harold. *Examining the Cults*. Lincoln, NE: Back to the Bible Pub., 1977, 1979, Chapter 4, "Jehovah's Witnesses: A Twisted Testimony," which covers primarily doctrine, pp. 45-59.

Bestic, Alan. *Praise the Lord and Pass the Contribution*. London, England: Cox and Wyman, Ltd., 1971, pp. 217-237, 251 and p. x (Chapter 12, "The End of the World Is Nigh").

Bettelhcim, Bruno. *The Informed Heart; Autonomy in a Mass Age*. Glencoe, IL: The Free Press of Glencoe, Illinois, 1960, pp. 20, 119, 122-123, 182, 190, 280. (An excellent discussion about the Witness experience in the concentration camps in Germany by a psychotherapist).

Dickel, Alexander. *The Supreme Court and the Idea of Progress*. New York: Harper Torchbooks, 1970, pp. 105-106.

Bills, Alex V. "The History of the English Bible: Studies of Translation and Translators, Versions and Publication." Unpublished manuscript, Garden City, KS, n.d.

Bischöfliches Seelsorge Amt. *Die Oxfordgruppenbewegung. Die Zeugen Jehovas.* Rottenburg am Neckar, 1949, 11 pp. (Handreichungen fur die Seelsorge, 5) (The Oxford group Movement. The Jehovah's Witnesses) (in German).

Blanke, F. *Kirchen und Sekten. Führer durch die religiösen Gruppen der Gegenwart.* Zürich, Zwingli Verlag, (1955), 152 pp. pp. 98-99: Zeugen Jehovas. (Jehovah's Witnesses) (Churches and sects. Guide through the religious present day groups) (in German).

Blanshard, Paul. *God and Man in Washington*. Boston, MA: Beacon Press, 1960, pp. 21, 51, 53, 57, 62-63, 67-69. (Covers several Witness court cases, Blanshard is very critical of religion as a whole).

_____. *Religion and the Schools: The Great Controversy.* Boston, MA: Beacon Press, 1963, p. 21-22 (on Witness Religious Freedom).

Blessing, William L. *Outer Space People and Inner Earth People.* Denver, CO: House of Prayer for All People, 1965, 1973, p. 146.

Bloesch, Donald G. *The Reform of the Church.* Grand Rapids, MI: William B. Eerdmans Publishing Co., 1970, p. 139.

Bloom, Harold. *The American Religion: The Emergence of the Post-Christian Nation.* New York: Simon & Schuster, 1992. Chapter 9 "Jehovah's Witnesses: Against the American Religion" p. 159-170; also p. 30, 39, 71, 145, 147-148, 150-157, 258. (An historical critique of the Witness movement, concludes they are among the most bizarre of American Religions and characterizes many of their writings as pathological).

Boa, Kenneth. *Cults, World Religions and You.* Wheaton, IL: Victor Books, 1972 (reprinted in 1977), Chapter 12, "Jehovah's Witnesses," pp. 73-80. (Mostly a critique of doctrine).

Bociurkiw, Bohdna R., and John W. Strong, eds. *Religion and Atheism in the U.S.S.R. and Eastern Europe.* Toronto, Canada: University of Toronto Press, pp. 60, 74, 85, 89, 126, 130, 136, 147, 361. (Covers the persecution of Witnesses in the old USSR).

Bodensieck, Julius. *Isms New and Old.* Columbus, OH: The Book Concern, 1938. 111 pp. One chapter on Russellism pp. 65-73. A good critique of Russell's writings.

Boehm, Eric H. *We Survived: Fourteen Histories of the Hidden and Hunted of Nazi German.* Santa Barbara, CA: CLIO Press, 1966, pp. 27, 137, 208. (Several personal accounts of Witnesses).

Boerwinkel, F. *Kerk en secte's* Gravenhage, Boekencentrum, 1956, 272 pp. pp. 216-217, 240-263: Jehovah's Getuigen. (Jehovah's Witnesses) (Church and sect) (in Dutch).

Bonlecou, Eleanor. *Freedom in the Balance.* Westport, CT: Greenwood Press, 1978. (In general, covers many cases J.W.'s were involved in).

Booth, Joseph. *Africa for the African.* Baltimore, MD: 1897. (Booth was a follower of Russell for several years).

Borovoy, A. Alan *When Freedoms Collide.* Toronto, Canada; Lester and Orpen. 1988 p 46-47, 52-53 (about Watchtower government conflicts).

Bosmajian, Haig. *Freedom of Expression.* New York: Neal-Schuman, Pub., 1988, 118 pp. (1, 4, 9-10, 16-18, 32, 48-49, 65-67) (A discussion of Witness free speech cases).

Bourdeaux, Michael. *Religious Ferment in Russia.* London: Macmillan, 1968, pp. 148-149; New York: St. Martin's Press, 1968. (About a Witness who committed murder, evidently due to emotional problems).

Braden, Charles S. *These Also Believe.* New York: Macmillan, 1949, 1960, Chapter 10, "Jehovah's Witnesses," pp. 358-384.

_____. "Jehovah's Witnesses" in *Twentieth Century Encyclopedia of Religious Knowledge,* Vol. 1, pp. 444-445.

Breese, Dave. *Know the Mark of Cults.* Wheaton, IL: Victor Books, 1975, pp. 37, 41, 48, 83, 113, pb., 128 pp. (Covers primarily Witness and similar group doctrines from an evangelical orientation).

Brock, Peter. *Pacifism in the United States.* Princeton, NJ: Princeton Univ. Press, 1968, pp. 18, 860-866, 918, 948.

_____. *Twentieth-Century Pacifism.* New York: Van Nostrand Reinhold Co., 1970, pp. 34, 45, 111, 165, 175, 180, 199-207.

Brockhaus, Der Große. *Handbuch des Wissens in Zwanzig Bänden.* Leipzig, Brockhaus. 5th Vol., 1930, pp. 656-657 "Ernste Bibelforscher" (Earnest Bible Students) (The Great Books. Handbook of science in twenty volumes) (in German).

Bromley, David and Anson Shupe. *Strange Gods; The Great American Cult Scare.* Boston: Beacon Press, 1981, 24 pp, pb., p. 9, 18, 25, 155, 211, 220, cover Witnesses (A sympathetic treatment of cults by two sociologists).

Brooks, Keith. *The Trinity: Must We Believe It?* Chicago: Moody Press, n.d., p. 2.

Brown, A.C. *Translations of the English Bible: Revisions and Versions--A Reference Guide.* Oak Park, IL, c. 1970, pp. 41-42, 51.

Brown, Mark M.D. (Ed) *Emergency! True Stories from the Nations E.R.'s.* New York: Willard 1946 p. 56-58. "A Blood Mess" by Lowrence M. Linett, M.D. (About a man who was shot and the ER doctors believed he was a Witness due to a "blood" card in his wallet. He was for this reason not given needed blood. It turned out he stole the wallet and was not a Witness).

Brown, W. Gordon. *Pagan Christianity.* Toronto, Canada: Toronto Baptist Seminary, first ed. Aug. 1933, revised ed. Jan. 1946, pp. 170-180.

Bruce, F.F. *The English Bible: A History of Translations.* New York: Oxford Univ. Press, 1961, 1970, p. 184.

Bryditzki, Victor V. *The Selling of Jesus.* Chino, CA: Chick Publ., 1985. (The author tells about his involvement in the Watchtower and what it did to his family).

Buber, Margarete. *Under Two Dictators.* London, England: Gollancz, 1940 (also published by Dodd, Mead & Co. in New York, n.d.), pp. 185-186, 201, 204, 213, 218-238, 246-249, 255, 256, 259, 261-262, 265, 271, 274, 277, 279, 280, 317-318.

Buell, Raymond Leslie. *The Native Problem in Africa,* Vol. 1. New York: Macmillan Co., 1928, pp. 242-243, 246-249.

Burrell, Maurice, and J. Stafford Wright. *Some Modern Faiths.* London, England; InterVarsity Fellowship, 1974, pp. 19-36 and 58-69.

_____. *Whom Then Can We Believe?* Chicago: Moody Press, 1976, pp. 16-34, 66-67, pb. Chapter 2, "Jehovah's Witnesses." (Briefly covers their history and reviews their beliefs).

Busch, Johannes. *Das Sektenwesen, unter bes. Berücks. d. "Ernsten Bibelforscher." Entstehung, Ausbreitung und Haüptirrtumer, sowie Widerlegung und Abwehr der modernen Sektiererei.* Hildesheim, F. Borgmeyer Verlag, 1930, 359 pp. (That sectarism, particular the Earnest Bible Students. Origin, development and major errors, also refutation and defense to the modern sectarianism) (in German).

Butter, Stephen H. *Legal Rights to Draft Deferments.* Cleveland, OH: Centre House Publishing, Inc., 1971, pp. 92-93, 122-123.

Butterworth, George. *Churches, Sects and Religious Parties*. London, England: Society for Promoting Christian Knowledge, 1936, Part III, Chapter 6, "Judge Rutherford," pp. 137-141.

Butterworth, John. *Cults and New Faiths*. Elgin, IL: David C. Cook Pub., Co., 1981, 62 pp., Chapter 18, "Jehovah's Witnesses," pp. 18-21. (A sympathetic factual review of Witness lifestyle and beliefs).

Buzzard, Lynn, and Samuel Ericsson. *The Battle for Religious Liberty*. Elgin, IL: David Cook Pub., Co., 1982, pp. 65-68, 72, 100, 251-252.

Candee, Marjorie (ed.). *Current Biography*. "Knorr, Nathan H(omer)." New York: H.W. Wilson Co. 1957, pp. 310-312.

Cantor, Norman L. "A Patient's Decision to Decline Life-Saving Medical Treatment: Bodily Integrity Versus the Preservation of Life." Chapter 27 in *Ethics in Medicine*, ed. Stanley Joel Reiser et al. Cambridge, MA: MIT Press, 1977 pp. 156-168, 199.

Carlson, Ron and Ed Decker. *Fast Facts on False Teachings*. Eugene, OR: Harvest House Pub. 1994 255 pp (Chapter 8 Jehovah's Witnesses p. 117-132).

Case, Shirley Jackson. *The Millennial Hope: A Phase of War-Time Thinking*. Chicago: The University of Chicago Press, 1918, p. 253. (Argues against the millennism theology of C.T. Russell, the Adventists and others. A must to understand the Watchtower today; includes an excellent history of millennialism).

Cawley, Clifford C. *The Right to Live: The Position of the Law When Religious Dogma Opposes Medicine*. South Brunswick, Canada: A.S. Barnes and Co., 1969, 303 pp. (Deals with Jehovah's Witnesses, Christian Science, and other religions; the section on the Witnesses is primarily about the legal issues around blood transfusions).

Chamberlin, Eric Russell. *Antichrist and the Millennium*. New York: Saturday Review Press/ E.P. Dutton Co., 1975, "October 1975," pp. 167-195.

Chapman, Anthony J., and Hugh C. Foot. *Humour and Laughter: Theory, Research and Applications*. London, England: Wiley, 1976, p. 73.

Chêne, Evelyn Le Mauthausen. *The History of a Death Camp*. London: Methuen 1971 p. 40, 130-131, 181-190 (about the Witness experience in the Nazi camps).

Christelijke. *Christelijke Encyclopedie*. (Christian Encyclopedia. 6 Vols). Kampen, Kok. Vol. 4, 1959, pp. 38-39: Kok, A.B.W.M. Jehova's Getuigen. (in Dutch).

Clark, Elmer. *The Small Sects in America*. Nashville, TN: Abingdon Press (revised ed. 1965), pp. 45-47, 256 pp., hb., pb. (A brief review of history and doctrine of the small American sects).

Clark, Ernest, Ruth Stockton, and Reppie Jones. "Jehovah's Witnesses." in *Foxfire 7*, pp. 139-169. Paul F. Gillespie, ed. Garden City, NY: Anchor Press/Doubleday, 1982.

Colson, Elizabeth, and Max Gluckman, eds. *Seven Tribes of British Central Africa*. Manchester, England: Manchester University Press, 1959, p. 235.

Concordia Cyclopedia. "Russellism" (1927 ed.).

Congressional Record, May 4, 1918, p. 6052, Senator Overman, Vol. 56, Part 6, pp. 6050-6054.

Conway, J.S. *The Nazi Persecution of the Churches: 1933-1945.* New York: Basic Books. 1968, pp. 195-199, 200-201, 371, 373, 413 n.61, 450. (Covers the history of the Nazi persecution of the Witnesses).

Coombs, J.V. *Religious Delusions* Cincinnati: The Standard Pub. Co., 1904, Chapter 14, Russellism, pp. 195-206.

Cooper, Lee R. "Publish" or Perish: Negro Jehovah's Witness Adaptation to the Ghetto." In *Religious Movement in Contemporary America,* pp. 700-721. I.I. Zaretsky and M.P. Leone, eds. Princeton, NJ: Princeton University Press, 1974. (An excellent study of a Witness congregation in a Philadelphia Black ghetto; much information on the Watchtower and race).

Cornell, Julien. *Conscience and the State.* New York: John Day Co., 1944, pp. 67, 68, 135. Reprinted New York: Garland Pub. Inc., 1973.

Coulter, Carol. *Are Religious Cults Dangerous?* Dublin and Cork: The Mercier Press, 1984, 108 pp. Chapter 6, "An Irish Cult Grows Up: The Jehovah's Witnesses," pp. 68-76. (An excellent review of the disaffection and schisms which began in 1975 due partly to the 1975 failure and the work of Raymond Franz, John May, Martin Merriman and others).

Cox, Archibold. *The Court and the Constitution.* Boston: Houghton Mifflin Co., 1987, pp. 178, 189, 198, 210, 372-373. (Discusses Witness' court cases; much on the flag case).

Craig, Samuel. *Christianity, Rightly So Called.* Philadelphia, PA: Presbyterian and Reformed Publishing Co., 1957, pp. 6, 252.

Creighton, Helen. *Law Every Nurse Should Know.* Philadelphia: W.B. Saunders Co., 1975, pp. 145-149.

Croall, Jonathan. *Don't You Know There's a War On? The People's Voice 1939-45.* London, England: Hutchinson Radius c. 1970s (*The Jehovah's Witness* by Ernest Beavor pp. 158-160).

Cross, Sholto. "A Prophet Not Without Honor: Jeremiah Gondwe" in *African Perspectives, ed. Christopher Allen and R.W. Johnson.* Cambridge, MA: Cambridge University Press, 1970, pp. 171-184, 187.

_____. "Independent Churches and Independent States: Jehovah's Witnesses in East and Central Africa." In *Christianity in Independent Africa,* pp. 304-15. Ed. E. Fashole-Luke, 1978.

Cumberland, William. "The Jehovah's Witness Tradition." Chapter 17 in *Caring and Curing.* Ed. by Ronald Numbers and Darrel W. Amundsen, New York: Macmillan, 1986, pp. 468-485. About Jehovah's Witnesses and medicine; much specifically on the problem of blood transfusion, but also covers the Witnesses and medicine in general .

Cunha, Silva E. *Movimentos Associativas no. Africa Negra, Ministero do Ultramar Lisboa.* 1956 (one chapter on the Watchtower Society).

Cushman, Robert E. *Civil Liberties in the U.S.* Ithaca, NY: Cornell University Press, 1956.

Davies, Horton. *The Challenge of the Sects.* Philadelphia, PA: The Westminster Press, 1961, pp. 99-110, pb. (Chapter 7 on Jehovah's Witnesses covers history, lifestyle, doctrine and beliefs).

_____. *Christian Deviations* (revision of *Challenge of the Sects*). Philadelphia, PA:

Westminster Press, 1961, pp. 64-73, pb. British ed. of SCM Press Ltd., London.

Dedek, John F. *Contemporary Medical Ethics.* New York: Sheed and Ward, Inc., 1975, pp. 13, 17.

Delleman, Th. *Tussen kerk en tegenkerk. Enkele godsdienstige bewegingen en religieuze gemmenschappen binnen en buiten de ruimte der kerk.* (Between church and opposite-church. Some religious movements and streamings inside and outside the church). Aalten, Uitgeverij de Graafschap, 1957, 183 pp. pp. 181-183: Jehovah's Getuigen (Jehovah's Witnesses) (in Dutch).

De Moor, U. *Leur Combat.* Paris, n.d. (Their Struggle) One Chapter on Kitawala. (In French)

Dennnett, H. *A Guide to Modern Versions of the New Testament.* 1966, "The New World Translation," pp. 111-113.

Dershowitz, Alan M. *Chutzpah.* New York: Touchstone, 1991 p. 48, 327-328 (about the prejudice against Witnesses).

Dicks, Henry V. *Licensed Mass Murder.* New York: Basic Books, Inc., 1972, pp. 228-229. (Argues the S.S. could resist German orders to act as hangman).

Douty, Norman F. *Another Look at Seventh-day Adventism.* Grand Rapids, MI: Baker Book House, 1962, pp. 62, 70, 182, hb.

Driel, L. and I.A. Kole. *Kerken, Sekten en Sromingen.* 5th Printing, Kampen, Kok, 1980, 224 pp. pp. 97-106, 217-223: Jehovah's Getuigen (Jehovah's Witnesses) (Church, sects and trends) (in Dutch).

Drinan, Robert. *Religion, the Courts and Public Policy.* New York: McGraw Hill, 1963, 261, pp. 20, 76-77, 190-193.

Drury, Robert L., and Kenneth C. Ray. *Essentials of School Law.* New York: Appleton-Century-Crofts, 1967, pp. 147-148.

Duncan, Homer. *The King Is Coming.* Lubbock, TX, n.d., p. 14.

Dunn, Bryan R. "The Death's Head and the Watchtower: Jehovah's Witnesses in the Holocaust Kingdom," pp. 155-172 in *Holocaust Studies Annual, Vol. 2, The Church's Response to the Holocaust.* Ed. by Jack Fischel and Sanford Pinsker Greenwood, FL: Penkevill Publ. Co. 1986, (An excellent review of the history of Witnesses persecution in Nazi Germany).

Duthie, Alan S. *Bible Translations and How to Choose Between Them.* Exeter, Great Britain: Paternoster Press, 1985. (Various references favorable to *Kingdom Interlinear* and Byington translations)

Einbinder, Harvey. *The Myth of the Britannica.* New York: Grove Press, 1964, p. 67.

Eisenhower, Dwight D. *At Ease: Stories I Tell to Friends.* Garden City, NY: Doubleday and Co., Inc., 1967, pp. 305-306. (Dwight discusses his mother's Witness background).

Ellwood, Robert S. "Jehovah's Witnesses." In *Abingden Dictionary of Living Religion,* Nashville, TN, 1981, pp. 377-378.

Emerson, Thomas I. *Toward a General Theory of the First Amendment.* New York: Vintage Books, 1963, pp. 65, 136, 137-141.

Eerste Nederlandse Systematisch Ingerichte Encyclopedie. (First Dutch Systematic Arranged Encyclopedia). Amsterdam, E.N.S.I.E. Vol. 10, 1952, p. 675: Jehova's Getuigen (in Dutch).

Eerste Nederlandse Systematisch Ingerichte Encyclopedie. (First Dutch Systematic Arranged Encyclopedia). Amsterdam, E.N.S.I.E. Vol. 11, 1959, p. 32: Jehova's Getuigen (in Dutch).

Encyclopedie van de godsdiensten, kerken en sekten. Amsterdam, Elsevier, 1978, 303 pp. pp. 161-162: Jehovah's Getuigen (Encyclopedia of religions, churches and sects) (in Dutch).

Encyclopedie van het Christendom in twee delen. (Encyclopedia of Christianity in two volumes). Amsterdam, Elsevier, 1955, Protestants deel, pp. 442-443: Jehoavh's Getuigen, 1956, pp. 464-465: Jehova's Getuigen (in Dutch).

Encyclopedia of Russia. "Jehovah's Witnesses." New York: Macmillan, 1972, Vol. 10, p. 244.

Encyclopedia of World Biography. "C.T. Russell" by Charles Wetzel. New York: McGraw-Hill, 1973, Vol. 9, p. 332.

Ernst, Morris L. *The Great Reversals; Tales of the Supreme Court.* New York: Weybright and Talley. 1973. (Covers the two Witnesses that were reversed by the Supreme Court. Chapter 10 " New Light on Old Freedoms" pp. 136-142.

Facey, Roy A. ed. *International Church Index* (Doctrinal) 'Jehovah's Witnesses' (chapter prepared by the public relations department of the Watchtower, London pp. 140-157).

Feig, Konnilyn G. *Hitler's Death Camps; The Sanity of Madness.* New York: Holmes & Meir Pub. 1979 P. 24-25, 51, 139

Ferguson, Charles W. *The Confusion of Tongues; A Review of Modern Isms.* Garden City, NY: Doubleday, Doran & Co., 1928, Chapter 4 is on Russellism, pp. 63-88, 464 pp., hb. (Primarily history, critical of Russell's movement).

Festinger, Leon, Henry W. Riecken, and Stanley Schachter. *When Prophecy Fails: A Social and Psychological Study of a Modern Group that Predicted the Destruction of the World.* New York: Harper & Row, Pub., 1956.

Field, G.C. *Pacifism and Conscientious Objection.* Cambridge, MA: Cambridge University Press, 1945, pp. 16-17, 98.

Fields, Karen Elise. *Revival and Rebellion in Colonial Central Africa.* Princeton, NJ: Princeton University Press, 1985. (Much of this work deals with the Watchtower in Africa)

Fischel, Jack and Stanford Pinsker. *The Churches' Response to the Holocaust.* Greenwood, FL: Penkevil, 1986. (See Brian Dunn above).

Fisher, C. William. *Why I Am a Nazarene.* Kansas City, MO: Nazarene Publishing House, 1958, Chapter 4, pp. 70-90, pb. Revised ed., 1969. (Primarily a critique of Witness doctrine--the trinity, hell, soul and eschatology).

Flint, David. *The Hutterites: A Study in Prejudice.* Toronto, Canada: Oxford University Press, 1975, p. 66.

Franz, Frederick W. "Jehovah's Witnesses" in *Britannica Book of the Year,* 1978, pp. 127, 610. The same article was revised each year to date: 1979, pp. 600-601, 1980, p. 600, 1981, p. 598, 1982, pp. 599, 606.

Freedman, Max (Ed.) *Roosevelt and Frankfurter; Their Correspondence* 1928-1945. Boston: Little, Brown and Co. 1967 p 669-701 (Quotes Roosevelt's opinions on Jehovah's Witnesses and the Flag Salute Controversy).

Freeman, Hobart E. *Every Wind of Doctrine.* Claypool, IN: Faith Publications, 1974, pp. 91-94, hb. (A brief critique of Witnesses; Freeman was head of the Faith Assembly in Indiana which does not believe in the use of medicine; about 125 deaths out of their congregation of 2,000 have been attributed to this teaching).

Friedman, Ina R. *The Other Victims. First -Person Stories of Non-Jews Persecuted by the Nazis.* Boston: Houghton Mifflin, 1990, 214 pp. Chapter 4 'Elizabeth's family: Twelve Jehovah's Witnesses Faithful Unto Death', pp. 47-59. (Story of the Witness Kusserow family which was featured in the video "Purple Triangles" produced by British TV and sold by the Watchtower).

Friedman, Phillip. "Was There an 'Other Germany' During the Nazi Period?" in *Yivo Annual of Jewish Social Science*, Vol. 10. New York: Yivo Institute for Jewish Research, 1955, pp. 111-113. (About why Witnesses were persecuted, and their relationship with Jews).

_____, and Tadeusz Holuj. *O'swiecim.* Warsaw: Spólka Wydawnicza "Ksiazke," 1946, 308 pp. (summaries in French, Russian, and English, pp. 291-308. Includes documents both in their original German and in Polish translation pp. 163-164. Pp. 179 to 186 is a discussion of the July 15, 1943 letter by Ernst Kaltenbrunner regarding Nazi policies concerning Jehovah's Witnesses.

Froom, Leroy Edwin. *The Conditional Faith of Our Fathers.* Washington, DC: Review and Herald Pub. Assoc., 1954, 2 Vol., A history of the Adventist movement.

_____. *The Prophetic Faith of Our Fathers.* Washington, DC: Review and Herald Pub. Asoc., 1950, 4 Vol.

Fuller, Edmund and David Green. *God in the White House.* New York: Crown Publ. 1968, pp. 212. (On Eisenhower's religious background--he was raised a Witness).

Gaebelein, A. C. *The Work of Christ.* New York: Our Hope, 1913, pp. 60-61.

Gann, L.H. *A History of Northern Rhodesia.* London, England: Chatto and Windus, 1964, pp. 168-170, 230-237, 300-303.

Gardner, Martin. *Fads and Fallacies in the Name of Science* (originally published in 1952 under the title *In the Name of Science*). New York: Dover, 1957, pp. 181-182; also Chapter 15, "The Great Pyramid," mostly about Russell's ideas.

Garraty, John (Ed.). *Quarrels That have Shaped the Constitution.* New York: Harper and Row, 1966.

Garrison, Winfred. *Unassimilable Varieties of Religious Expression.* New York: Harper and Brothers, 1933, p. 293.

Gaustad, Edwin Scott. *Dissent in American Religion.* Chicago: University of Chicago Press, 1973, pp. 114-117.

_____. *Historical Atlas of Religion in America.* New York: Harper and Row, 1969, pp. 115-118.

_____, ed. *The Rise of Adventism.* New York: Harper and Row, 1974, pp. 200, 204.

Gaylin, Willard. *In the Service of Their Country: War Resisters in Prison.* New York: Viking Press, 1970, pp. 179, 192, 269-273, 315, 327.

Gelder, B. van. *Zoekers naar waarheid. Een inleiding tot de zogenaamde sekten, godsdienstige bewegingen en stromingen in Nederland.* Leiden, Sijthoff, 1963, 176 p. pp. 69-74, 165-171: Jehovah's Getuigen (Jehovah's Witnesses) (Seekers for truth. An introduction to the so-called sects, religious movements and trends in The Netherlands) (in Dutch).

Gerecke, Karl. *Deutsch-Kritischer Gottesgeist...* (German Critical religions/spirits). Leipzig Klein Verlag, 1931, 161 pp. pp. 162-199: Die Gotteslasterungen der "Ernsten 'Bibel-forscher'; Ihr Alttestamentischer Tod; Ihr tötlicher Christushaß. The blasphemy of the Earnest Bible Students; Their Old Testamentic dead; Their deadly Christ-hate (in German).

Gerstner, John H. *The Theology of the Major Sects.* Grand Rapids, MI: Baker Book House, 1960, pp. 11, 13, 29-39, 130-134, 153-169, pb. (Chapter 3 "Jehovah's Witnesses" covers history and doctrine).

Gilespie, Paul F. *Forfire Seven.* 1982. (Discussion of religious denominations in America including JWs).

Goldberg, George. *Reconsecrating America.* Grand Rapids, Eerdmans, 1984, pp. 19-34, 53-55, 82-84.

Goldberg, Louis and Eleanore Levenson. *Lawless Judges.* New York: Negro Univ. Press 1969 303 pp. (Discusses early Watchtower cases)

Goode, Erich. *Deviant Behavior.* Englewood Cliffs, NJ: Prentice-Hall, 1978, p. 78.

Gorovitz, Samuel, ed. *Moral Problems in Medicine.* Englewood Cliffs, NJ: Prentice-Hall, Inc., 1976, pp. 196, 230-241.

Gray, James M. *Satan and the Saint: The Present Darkness and the Coming Light.* Chicago, IL: 1909. One chapter on Jehovah's Witnesses.

Great Soviet Encyclopedia, Vol. 10. New York: Macmillan, Inc., c. 1970, p. 523. An American translation of Russian edition entitled *Bol'shaia Sovetskaia Entsiklopediia,* ed. A.M. Prokhorov.

Grote Winkler Prins Encyclopedie. Amsterdam, Elsevier. Vol. 10, 1970, pp. 378-379: Jehovah's Getuigen (Great Winkler Prins Cyclopedia in twenty volumes) (in Dutch).Vol. 12, 1981, pp. 167: Jehovah's Getuigen.

Grundler, Johannes. *Lexickon der Christlichen Kirchen und Sekten. Unter Berück - sichtigung der Missionsgesellschaften und zwischenkirchlichen Organisationen,* (Lexicon of Christian Churches and Sects, with Respect to Missions-Societies and Middle-Course-Churches and Other Movements). Wien, Herder & Co., 1961, 2 Vol. No. 1551 Jehovah's Witnesses (Zeugen Jehovas); No. 0239 Amis de L'Homme (Groupe Suisse) ; No. 0335 Associated Bible Students (England); No. 0827 Dawn Bible Students Association; No. 0941 Elijah Voice Society; No. 1213 Freie Bibelgemeinde e.V. (Germany); No. 1344 Head Church of God's Students Bible in Christ Natives; No. 1637 Laymen's Home Missionary Movement; No. 2949 Pastoral Bible Institute; No. 2262 Servants of Yah; No. 2576 Watchtower Movement (Central Africa) (in German).

Grunfeld, Dayan I. *The Jewish Dietary Laws.* New York: Soncino Press. 1972 2 vol.

Gruss, Edmond. *Cults and the Occult in the Age of Aquarius.* Nutley, NJ: The Presbyterian and Reformed Publishing Co., 1974, pp. 5, 7-13, 131-132, pb.; 23nd ed. 1980, Revised, pp. 5, 9-16. Gruss is an ex-Witnesses; he did a masters thesis on the Watchtower.

_____. *The Ouija Board: Doorway to the Occult.* Chicago: Moody Press, 1975, revised 1994 Methen, NJ Presbyterian and Reformed 210 pp. (No direct reference to the Witnesses).

Gun, Nevin. *The Day of the Americans.* New York: Fleet Pub. Corp., 1966, 41 pp.

Gwatkin, H.M. *The Arian Controversy.* New York: Longmans Green & Co., Inc., n.d. (about 1890). (About early movement that held many of the same ideas as the Witnesses on Christ and the Trinity).

Haack, Friedrich Wilhelm. *Grossmark der Wahrheiten. Ausschnitte aus dem religiösen angebot unserer zeit.* Witten und Berlin, Eckart Verlag, 1969, 230 pp. (Possession of truths. A general view about religions from our time) (in German).

Hammerschmidt, Ernst. *Grundriß der Konfessionskunde.* (Basic principles of the confessions-knowledge). Innsbruck, Wien, München, Tyrola Verlagsanstalt, 211 pp. (in German).

Handboek bij de Bijbel. Den Haag, Voorhoeve, 1985, 678 pp. (Handbook on the Bible) (p. 80: Nieuwe Wereld-Vertaling van de Heilige Scrift; New World Translation of the Holy Scriptures) (in Dutch).

Hanbuch, Religiöse Gemeinschaften, Freikirchen, Sondergemeinschaften, Sekten, Weltanschauungsgemeinschaften, Neureligionen. (Handbook of religious communities, free-churches, special-communities, sects, worldview-communities, new religions). Gütersloher Verlagshaus Gerd Hohn, 1979, 840 pp. pp. 441-453 Zeugen Jehovas (Jehovah's Witnesses); pp. 454-462 Tagesanbruch (Dawn Bible Students); pp. 463-469 Freie Bibelgemeinde (Free Bible Students); pp. 755-766 Kitawala (Watchtower Movement Central Africa) (in German).

Handwörterbuch. *Die Religion in Geschichte und Gegenwart. (Handworterbuch für Theologie und Religionswissenschaft.* (Religion in history and modern time. Handbook for theology and religion science). Tübingen, J.C.B. Mohr, 1957-1965, 7 Vol. (6th Vol. Band, 1962, S. 1903-1906: Zeugen Jehovas (Jehovah's Witnesses) (in German).

Hardon, John A. *The Protestant Churches of America.* Westminster, MD: The Newman Press, 1956, pp. 297-302, hb.

Harrison, J.F.C. *The Second Coming: Popular Millinarianism.* 1780-1850. London: Routledge, 1979.

Hart, Stephen. *What Does the Lord Require?* N.Y. Oxford University Press. 1992 253 pp hb p. 35-38, 45-75, 77, 90-95, 105, 123, 128, 131-134, 141 (One of the persons researched was a Witness, much of their social policy and beliefs discussed).

Hayes, Denis. *Challenge of Conscience: The Story of the Conscientious Objectors of 1939-1949.* Reprint of original, New York: Garland Publishing, 1972, pp. 25-27, 48, 54, 83, 107-111, 170-175, 242-245, 254-256, 268-269, 274-275, 353, 374.

Hayward, Max, and William Fletcher, eds. *Religion in the Soviet State.* London, England: Pall Mall Press, 1969. (Reviews the problems the Watchtower had under communism)

Hebert, Gerard. "Jehovah's Witnesses" in *The New Catholic Encyclopedia,* Vol. 7. New York: McGraw-Hill Book Co., 1967, ed., pp. 864-865.

Hefley, James and Marti. *By Their Blood; Christian Martyrs of the 20th Century.* Grand

Rapids, MI: Baker Book House, 1979, p. 447. (On Witness persecution in Malawi).

Heley, A. "Jehovah's Witnesses' Worship" in *A Dictionary of Liturgy and Worship, ed., J.G. Davis.* New York: Macmillan Co., 1972, pp. 206-207.

Henschel, Milton G. "Who Are Jehovah's Witnesses?" in *Religion in America*, ed. Leo Rosten. New York: Simon and Schuster, 1963.

Hershey, L.B. *Legal Aspects of Selective Service.* Jan. 1, 1963. Rev. ed., pp. 21-23; Jan. 1, 1969. Rev. ed., pp. 24-27. Washington, DC: U.S. Government Printing Office.

Hesselgrave, David. *Dynamic Religious Movements.* Grand Rapids, MI: Baker Book House, 1978, Chapter 9, "Jehovah's Witnesses" by Wilton Nelson and Richard Smith, pp. 137-199.

Heuzeroth, Günther. *Unter der Gewaltherrschaft des National-Sozialismus: 1933-1945; Dargestelt an den Ereignissen im Oldenburger Land* (Hrsg. Universitat Oldenburg, Zentrum für Pädag. Berufspraxis, Oldenburg, (durch) Günther Heuzeroth. (Under the despotism of the National Socialism: 1933-1945; described the events in Oldenburger Land. Published by the University of Oldenburg, department of pedagogy and occupations praxis Oldenburg. 5 volumes. Vol. 3: Verfolgte aus religiösen Gründen. (Persecution for religious grounds). 1985, 214 pp. (in German).

Hexham I. "Jehovah's Witnesses" p. 577-578 In *Evangelical Dictionary of Theology* Grand Rapids, MI. Baker Book House, 1984.

Hills, Margaret T. *The English Bible in America.* New York: The American Bible Society, 1962, pp. 410, 416-417. (Discusses the Watchtower translation)

Hochhuth, Rolf. *The Deputy.* Trans. Richard and Clara Winston. New York: Grove Press, Inc., 1964, pp. 152, 305-306. (About why Witnesses were persecuted in Nazi Germany).

Hoekema, Anthony A. *The Four Major Cults.* Grand Rapids, MI: William B. Eerdmans Co., 1963, Chapter 5, Jehovah's Witnesses, pp. 223-360, 432-435, hb. (A scholarly critique of Witness doctrine, includes some history, published as a separate book).

Hoekstra, E.G. en M.II. Ipenburg. *Wegwijs in gelovig Nederland. Een alfabetische beschrijving van Nederlandse kerken en religieuze groeperingen.* (A guide in faithful Netherlands. An alphabetical description of Dutch churches and movements). Kampen, Kok, (1987), pp. 279, pp. 113-114: Jehovah's Getuigen (in Dutch).

Höess, Rudolf. *Commandant of Auschwitz.* (Translated by Constantine FitzGibbon) New York: Popular Library, 1959, pp. 61, 78-82, 126, 201; London: Weidenfeld and Nicolson, 1959; New York: World Pub. Co., 1959, pp. 75, 95-99, 149-151, 237. (Much excellent material by a Nazi leader on the Witnesses in Nazi Germany).

Hoffman, Carl von. *Jungle Gods.* New York: Henry Holt and Co., 1929, pp. 42-67, 283, 284, hb. (Much information about the work of Russell's followers in early 1900 Africa; one chapter on Thomas, Son of God, and the scores of lives lost due to his work).

Hook, Sidney. *Religion in a Free Society.* Lincoln, NE: Univ. of Nebraska Press, 1967, pp. 95-97.

Hopkins, Joseph. *The Armstrong Empire.* Grand Rapids, MI: William Eerdmans, 1974, pp. 98, 109, 127, 129, 184, 207, 220-221.

Hudson, Winthrop S. *Religion in America.* New York: Charles Scribners Sons, 1965, 1973, pp. 347-350.

Huestis, Douglas W., Joseph Bove, and Shirley Busch. *Practical Blood Transfusion.* Boston, MA: Little, Brown and Co., 1969, pp. 363-364 (on Witness cases).

Hurbon, Laënnec. "New Religious Movements in the Caribbean." In *New Religious Movements and Rapid Social Change,* pp. 146-176. James A Beckford, ed. Paris, Sage Publications/ UNESCO, 1986.

Hutten, Kurt. *Die Glaubenswelt des Sektierers. Anspruch und Tragödie.* Hamburg, Furche Verlag, 1965, 129 pp. (The beliefs world of the sectarians. Claim and tragedy) (in German).

_____. *Was glauben die Sekten? Modelle, Wege, Fragezeichen.* Stuttgart, Quell Verlag, 1965, 144 pp. (What do the sects believe? Examples, indicators, questions) (in German).

_____. *Seher, Grübler, Enthusiasten, Sekten und Religiöse Sondergemeinschaften der Gegenwart.* Stuttgart, Quell Verlag, 1966, 800 pp. pp. 75-130: Jehovas Zeugen. (Jehovah's Witnesses; pp. 131-135: Vereinigungen Freier Bibelforscher. (Free Bible Students Moments) (Prophets, dreamers, enthusiasts, sects and religious particular movements in modern time) (in German).

_____. *Iron Curtain Christians.* Translation by Walter Tillmanns of *Christen hinter dem Eisener Vorhang.* Minneapolis, MN: Augsburg Publ. House, 1967, pp. 81-83, 255. (Covers the history and persecution of Witnesses behind the iron curtain).

Ingham, Kenneth. "Korea" in *Britannica: Book of the Year, 1974,* p. 397-398.

_____. "Malawi" in *Britannica: Book of the Year,* 1974, p. 444.

_____. "Malawi" in *Britannica: Book of the Year, 1976,* p. 500.

Irons, Peter. *The Courage of Their Convictions.* New York: The Free Press, 1988, 420 pp., hb. (Chapter 1 is on the Gobitis flag salute case, pp. 13-36). (Provides a good, sympathetic review of the case).

Irvine, William C. *Heresies Exposed.* New York: Loizeaux Brothers, 12th ed., 1942, pp. 149-153, pb. First ed." *Timely Warnings,* 1917; 2nd ed.: *Modern Heresies Exposed,* 1919; 3rd ed.: *Heresies Exposed,* 1921, revised 1927, 1929, 1930, 1935. (Chapter on Russellism and Jehovah's Witnesses; a critique of their Christology, last days beliefs, and eschatology).

Jacquet, Constant H., Jr. and Alice M. Jones, eds. *Yearbook of American and Canadian Churches, 1990.* Nashville: Abingdon Press, 1991.

Jansma, Lammert G. and P.G.G.M. Schulten. *Religieuze bewegingen.* Den Haag, Martinus Nijhoff, 1981,284 pp., Chapter 9 (pp. 195-200): Zygmunt, Joseph F. Prophetic failure and chiliastic identity: the case of Jehovah's Witnesses. (Religious movements) (in Dutch).

Johnson, Thomas Cary. *Some Modern Isms.* Richmond, VA: Presbyterian Committee on Publ., 1919, "Russellism, One of the Most Insidious of the Modernisms," pp. 96-156.

Jong, L. de. *Het Koninkrijk der Nederlanden in de Tweede Wereldoorlog 1939-1945 's-*

Gravenhage, Martinus Nijhoff, 1969-1988, 13 Vol. Vol. 1: pp. 555: Dossier Jan Jansen. (Jehovah's Witnesses file Jan Jansen); Vol. 4: pp. 89: Jehovah's Witnesses; Vol. 5: pp. 685-687: Jehovah's Witnesses; Vol. 7: pp. 344, 1031, 1041, 1047: Jehovah's Witnesses; Vol. 8: pp. 18-19, 83-84, 217 (note), 250, 551-554, 577, 591, 604(note); Vol. 10b: pp. 832; Vol. 11b pp. 105 (note). (The Kingdom of the Netherlands in the Second World War 1939-1945) (in Dutch).

Jongendijk, J.W. *Geestelijke leiders van ons volk en hun kerken, stromingen en sekten.* Gravenzande: Eurpeese Bibliotheek, 1962, 202 pp. pp. 142-149: Jehovah's Getuigen. (Jehovah's Witnesses) (Spiritual leaders of our people and their churches, streamings and sects) (in Dutch).

_____. *Wat gelooft uw burrman?* (What does your neighbor believe?) Wageningen: Zomer & Keuning, 208 pp. pp. 90-101: Jehovah's Getuigen. (Jehovah's Witnesses) (in Dutch).

Kalb, E. *Kirchen und Sekten der Gegenwart.* (Churches and sects in this modern time). Stuttgart: Buchhandlung der Evangelical Gesellschaft, 1905, 576 pp.

Kater, Michael H. "Die Ernsten Bibelforscher im Dritten Reich." *Vierteljahrhefte für Zeitgeschichte.* Jan 17, 1969, pp. 181-218. (The Jehovah's Witnesses in the 3rd Reich). (A detailed account of the Witnesses under Hitler).

Katholieke Encyclopedia. (Catholic Encyclopedia). Amsterdam: Uitgeversmij Joost van den Vondel. Vol. 21, 1954, pp. 290-292: Russellisten. (Russellites). (in Dutch).

Kauper, Paul C. *Religion and the Constitution.* Baton Rouge: Louisiana State Univ. Press, 1964, pp. 15, 26, 32, 88, 92.

Keen, Clarence. "Jehovah's Witnesses" in *Darkness vs. Light.* Hayward, CA: The Regular Baptist Press, 1953, pp. 63-67.

Kellett, Arnold. *Isms and Ologies, A Guide to Unorthodox and Un-Christian Beliefs.* London, England: Epworth, 1956, New York: Philosophical Library, 1965, p. 10, and Chapter 6, "Jehovah's Witnesses," pp. 53-62 in both editions.

Kersten, Felix. *The Memoirs of Doctor Felix Kersten.* Garden City, NY: Doubleday & Co., 1947, Chapter 7, "1942: Concentration Camps and other matters" pp. 113-132. (About Witness inmates who worked for Kersten).

King, Christine Elizabeth. *The Nazi State and the New Religions: Five Case Studies in Non-Conformity.* New York: The Edwin Mellen Press, 1982, pp. vii, ix, z, 12-19, 24-26, 37, 47, 49, 50-67, 70-78, 83, 91-95, 102, 107, 109, 110-112, 123, 130-137, Chapter 6, 181, ff, 192, 203 ff. (An excellent study of how Christian Scientists, Jehovah's Witnesses, Latter-Day Saints, and Seventh-Day Adventists fared under Nazism; only Jehovah's Witnesses suffered major persecutions; she includes much excellent material).

_____. "The Case of the Third Reich." In *New Religious Movements. A perspective for Understanding Society.* Ed. by Eileen Barker studies in Religion. Vol. 3: 1982. 125-139 and 389 pp. (An excellent summary of the Witness experience in Nazi Germany; also covers other movements.)

_____. "Jehovah's Witnesses Under Nazism." In *A Mosaic of Victims: Non Jews Persecuted and Murdered by the Nazis.* Ed. by Michael Berengaum. Albany: State University of New York Press, 1990. pp.188-193 Chapter 18, 320 pp.

Knorr, Nathan Homer. "Jehovah's Witnesses of Modern Times" in *Religion in the Twentieth Century* by Vergillius Ferm. New York: The Philosophical Library, 1948, pp. 380-392.

_____. "Jehovah's Witnesses" in *Britannica: Book of the Year, 1974,* p. 588; *1975,* p. 591; *1976,* pp. 590-591; *1977,* pp. 500, 530, 570.

_____. "Jehovah's Witnesses" in *Colliers Encyclopedia.* New York: Macmillan Ed., 1979, pp. 534-535 (updated by Herbert Stroup and later written by Jim Penton).

_____. "Jehovah's Witnesses" in *Encyclopedia Americana,* Vol. 16, 1977 ed., p. 11; and Vol. 16, 1981 ed., p. 11. Danbury, CT: Grolier, Inc.

Kogon, Eugene. *The Theory and Practice of Hell.* New York: Octagon Books, Inc., 1st ed. 1950, 1973, pp. 41-45, 55, 122, 123, 273, hb., pb. (An excellent review which covers the Witnesses in the Nazi concentration camps).

Kok, A.B.W.M. *Waarheid en dwaling. Enkele secten en bewegingen.* Amsterdam, c. 1945, 361 p. pp. 57-88: Jehovah's Getuigen. (Jehovah's Witnesses) (Truth and error. Some sects and movement) (in Dutch).

_____. *Verleidende geesten.* Kampen, J.H. Kok, 1948, 192 pp. (Temptational spirits) (in Dutch).

Kolarz, Walter. *Religion in the Soviet Union.* New York: Macmillan, 1966, Jehovah's Witnesses, pp. 338-344. (A good review of why Witnesses have thrived in the old USSR and a history of their work there).

Konefsky, Samuel J. *Chief Justice Stone and the Supreme Court.* New York: Macmillan Co., 1946, pp. 215-234, 270-272.

Kubo, Sakae, and Walter Specht. *So Many Versions.* Grand Rapids, MI: Zondervan Publ. Co., 1975, pp. 88-106.

Kurland, Philip B. *Religion and the Law.* Chicago: Aldine Publ. Co., 1961; 2nd Ed. 1962, pp. 74.

Kyle, Richard. *The Religious Fringe; A History of Alternative Religions in America.* Downers Grove, IL: Intervarsity Press. 1993 467 pp. See especially pp. 11, 26, 37, 56, 90, 93, 98-99, 148, 150, 155-160, 329-330, 343, 366, 371-373.

Laendecker, L. *Religien en conflict. De zogenaamde sekten in sociologisch perpectief.* Meppel, Boom, (1967), 356 p. pp. 135-136: Jehovah's Getuigen (Jehovah's Witnesses) (Religion and conflict. The so-called sects in sociological perspective) (in Dutch).

La Fave, Lawrence. *Psychology of Humor: Humor Judgments as a Function of Reference Groups and Identification Classes.* New York: Academic Press, Inc., 1972, pp. 195-210.

Land, Sipke van der. *Wat bezielt ze...? Het nieuwe boek over sekten.* (What inspires them...? a new book about sects). Kampen, J.H. Kok, (1976), 119 pp. pp. 97-111, 117-119: Jehovah's Getuigen (Jehovah's Witnesses) (in Dutch).

_____. *Wat bezielt ze? Hanboek van sekten, stromingen en bewegingen.* Kampen: J.H. Kok, 1984, 419 pp. (What inspires them? Handbook about sects, trends and movements) (in Dutch).

Landis, Benson Y. *Religion in the United States.* New York: Barnes & Noble, Inc., 1965, pp. 31-32, 82, 105.

Lane, Christel. *Christian Religion in the Soviet Union; A Sociological Study.* Albany, NY: State University of New York Press, 1978, pp. 81-86, 161-191, 220-232. (An excellent summary of the Witnesses as persons in the old Soviet Union).

Langbein, Hermann. *Against All Hope: Resistance in the Nazi Concentration Camps 1938-1945.* New York: Continum, 1996, 502 pp. 4, 178-181, 325. (About the Witness in the Nazi concentration camps).

Lanternari, Vittorio. *The Religions of the Oppressed: A Study of Modern Messiah Cults.* New York: Alfred A. Knopf, 1963, pp. 11, 28-31, 35, 44-45, 54-55, 73, 134, 164, 195, 307, 309, 311 (original Italian edition, 1960).

Larson, Bob. *Larson's Book of Cults.* 428 pp. Wheaton, IL: Tyndale House Pub., 1982.

Larson, Martin A., and C. Stanley Lowell. *Praise the Lord for Tax Exemption: How the Churches Grow Rich--While the Cities and You Grow Poor.* New York: Robert B. Luse, Inc., 1969, pp. 68-192.

_____. *The Religious Empire: The Growth and Danger of Tax-exempt Property in the United States.* New York: Robert B. Luce, Inc., 1976, pp. 124, 192, 237-238.

Lash, Joseph. *From the Diaries of Felix Frankfurter.* New York: W. W. Norton Co. 1975 pp. 366 (Discusses Frankfurter's opinions on the Watchtower flag salute cases pp. 68, 70, 225, 234-235.

Lee, Charles M. *The Vatican, the Kaiser and the World War.* Aurora, CO: Menance Pub. Co., 1918, p. 67. Quotation from the Oct. 15, 1898, *Watchtower,* p. 302.

Lehmann, D. A. *Christians in the Copperbelt.* 1961. London: SCM Press. 308 pp. (Covers the Watchtower in Africa).

Leinwand, Gerald. *The Draft.* New York: Pocket Books, 1970, pp. 33, 35.

Lewis, Gordon. *Confronting the Cults.* Nutley, NJ: Presbyterian and Reformed Publ. Co., 1966.

Lewis, Jack P. *The English Bible/From KJV to NIV: A History and Evaluation.* Grand Rapids: Baker Book House, 1981.

Lewy, Guenter. *The Catholic Church and Nazi Germany.* New York: McGraw-Hill Book Co., 1964, p. 43. (Shows that some Catholic churches cooperated in the persecution of Witnesses).

Lincoln, C. Eric. *The Black Muslims in America.* Boston: Beacon Press, 1961, p. 13.

Linderholm, Emanuel. *Pingströrelsen Dess Foruttnigar och uppkomst.* Stockholm: Albert Bonniers förlag, 1924, (Section on "Russellianismen" pp. 190-203. (A critique of Watchtower history and theology).

Lippy, Charles H. "Millennialism and Adventism" in *Encyclopedia of the American Religious Experience: Studies of Traditions and Movements.* Vol. II:831-44. Eds. Charles H. Lippy and Peter W. Williams. New York: Charles Scribners Sons, 1985.

Lipset, Seymour Martin. "Three decades of the Radical Right" in *The Radical Right.* Ed. by Daniel Bell. Garden City, NY: Anchor Books, 1964, 435 pp. (Shows a high level of dislike by society of Witnesses).

Littell, Franklin Hamlin. *From State Church to Pluralism.* New York: Anchor Books, 1962, pp. 90-92.

_____. *The German Church: Struggle and the Holocaust.* Detroit, MI: Wayne State U. Press, 1974, 41 pp. (About a source of original documents on Witnesses and Nazi Germany).

Ljousert, Fryske Akademy *Bi jdrage tot de geschiedenis van de laat ste twee eeuwen, ũ nder redaksje fan J.J. Huizinga,* L.G. Jansma (en) C.H.A. Verhaar. Ljousert, Fryske Akademy, 1989, 264 pp. p. 195-231: Twa religieuze bewegings yn Harns (Mormonen en Tsjugen fan Jehovah) centuries, under authority of J.J. Huizinga, L.G. Jansma (and) C.H. A. Verhaar. pp. 195-231: Two religious movements in Harlingen (a Frisian town) (Mormons and Jehovah's Witnesses). (written in two languages, Dutch and Frissian, the official language in the Northern Province "Friesland").

Loughborough, John N. *The Great Second Advent Movement; Its Rise and Progress.* New York: Arno Press, 1972 (reprint). 480 pp.

Luchterhand, Elmer. "Social Behavior of Concentration Camp Prisoners: Continuities and Discontinuities with Pre-and Post-camp Life." Chapter 10 in *Survivors, Victims, and Perpetrators: Essays on the Nazi Holocaust,* ed. Joel E. Dimsdale. Washington, DC: The Hemisphere Pub. Corp., c. 1980. 259-281 pp. (A good study of the camp experience, including the importance of religious beliefs.)

MacGregor, Lorri. *Coping with the Cults.* Delta, B.C., Canada: MacGregor Ministries Outreach, 1985, Chapter 5, "How Jehovah's Witnesses Twist the Scriptures," pp. 48-56, 88 pp. Also much other material on JWs. (Covers the trinity, blood transfusion, the 144,000, and salvation).

Maeson, William, and Lawrence La Fave. "The Jehovah's Witnesses Today: A Study by Participant Observation" in *1960 Proceedings of the Southwestern Sociological Society,* Dallas, TX, 1960, pp. 102-104.

Magida, Arthur (Ed) *How to be a Perfect Stranger; A Guide to Etiquette in Other People's Religions Ceremonies.* Jewish Lights Pub. Woodstock, VT 1996 (p. 197-210 on Jehovah's Witnesses, Information supplied by Raymond Richardson of the Watchtower writing department. A guide on how non-Witnesses should behave at Witnesses meetings and functions.)

Malachy, Yona. "Jehovah's Witnesses and Their Attitude Toward Judaism and the Idea of the Return to Zion" in *Herzl Year Book,* Vol. 5, Raphael Patai, ed. New York: Herzl Press, 1963, pp. 175-208. (An extensive review of the history of Russell's and Rutherford's teaching as to Zionism and the Watchtower's modern radical turn around on this question).

Mann, Brenda J. "The Great Crowd: Ethnography of Jehovah's Witnesses" in *The Cultural Experience: Ethnography in Complex Society,* ed. James P. Spradley and David McCurdy. Chicago: Science Research Associates, 1972, pp. 157-168.

Mann, W.E. *Sect, Cult and Church in Canada.* Toronto, Canada: Univ. of Toronto Press, 1955.

Marnell, William H. *The First Amendment: The History of Religious Freedom in America.* Garden City, NY: Doubleday & Co., Inc., 1964, pp. 152, 173-183.

Martin, Paul. *Cult Proofing Your Kids.* Grand Rapids, MI.: Zondervan. (Covers the general problem of cults; Covers several Witness case histories)

Martin, Walter R. *The Christian and the Cults.* Grand Rapids, MI: Zondervan Publ. House, 1956, pp. 62-66.

_____. *The Kingdom of the Cults.* Minneapolis, MN: Bethany Fellowship, Inc., Publishers, 1965, revised 1968, Chapter 4 on Jehovah's Witnesses and the Watchtower, pp. 34-110, 325-332, 335. (A history and critique of doctrine from a fundamentalist's world view).

_____. *The Rise of the Cults.* Grand Rapids, MI: Zondervan Publ. House, 1955, revised and enlarged in 1957, 1977, and 1980, Chapter 2, "Jehovah's Witnesses and the Dawn Bible Students," pp. 19-33, and pp. 11-17, 73, 105-106. (Much history; also critiques doctrine).

Marty, Martin E. "The Jehovah's Witnesses" in *Our Faiths,* ed. Martin E. Marty. New York: Pillar Books, 1976, pp. 224-228.

Mason, Alpheus Thomas. *Harlan Fiske Stone: Pillar of the Law.* New York: Viking Press, 1956, pp. 525-535, 598-601.

_____, and William M. Beaney. *American Constitutional Law.* Englewood Cliffs, NJ: Prentice-Hall, Inc., 1954; 3rd ed., 1964, pp. 535-544.

Matheson, Peter (ed). *The Third Reich and the Christian Churches.* Grand Rapids, MI: Eerdmans Pub., Co., 1981. "Trial of Jehovah's Witnesses, 18 November 1944" pp. 101-102.

Mathis, J.J.W. *A Review of Russellism and Other Sects.* Arlington, TX: pub. by author, 1916, pp. 1-43.

Mathison, Richard R. *Faith, Cults and Sects of America.* Indianapolis, IN: Bobbs-Merrill, 1960; reprinted as *God Is a Millionaire* in 1962, pp. 44-49, 60-65, 278. Chapter 9 entitled "Jehovah's Witnesses," p. 61-64 briefly reviews the beliefs and history; little doctrine is covered. (Covers 53 small sects and cults, includes an excellent critique of the atheists).

Maxey, Chester C., and Robert Fluno. *The American Problem of Government.* New York: Appleton-Century-Crofts, Inc., 1934; 5th ed. 1949, pp. 491-492, 494.

Mayer, F.E. *The Religious Bodies of America.* St. Louis, MO: Concordia Publ. House, 1956, pp. 457-471.

McDowell, Josh, and Don Stewart. *Understanding the Cults.* San Bernardino, CA: Here's Life Pub. Co., 1983, Chapter 5, "Jehovah's Witnesses," pp. 55-82. (Primarily a critique of doctrine).

McGrath, John J., ed. *Church and State in American Law: Cases and Materials.* Milwaukee, WI: The Bruce Publ. Co., 1962, pp. 218-236, 274-314, hb.

McLean, W.T. *Isms, "Heresies" Exposed by the Word of God.* Grand Rapids, MI: Zondervan Pbl. House, 1951, Chapter 2, "Millennial Dawnism," pp. 12-15.

McLintock, A.H., ed. *An Encyclopaedia of New Zealand.* Wellington, New Zealand: R.E. Owen, Government Printer, 1966, Vol. 2, p. 460; Vol. 3, 64.

McLoughlin, William, ed. *Religion in America.* Boston: Houghton-Mifflin Co., 1968, pp. 45-46, 50, 57, 128, 345 (Winter 1967 *Daedalus*).

McPherson, Aimee Semple. *That Is That--Personal Experiences and Writings.* 791 pp. 1923, pp. 566-567.The Watchtower. (McPherson used this term to describe a intercession room.)

Mead, Frank S. *Handbook of Denominations in the United States.* Nashville, TN: Abingdon, 1980, 7th ed., pp. 145-148.

Melton, J. Gordon. *American Cult and Sect Leaders.* New York: Garland, 1986, pp. 180-182, 243-245, 354. (Biography of Russell and Rutherford).

_____ (ed). *The Encyclopedia of American Religions,* 5thd ed., "Jehovah's Witnesses" Detroit, MI: Gale Research, 1996, pp. 530-531.

Miller, Edith Starr. *Occult Theocracy*, Vol. 2, Hawthorne, CA: The Christian Book Club of America, 1933, pp. 539-540 (reprinted in 1968).

Miller, George W. *Amoral and Ethical Implications of Human Organ Transplants.* Springfield, IL: Charles C. Thomas, 1971, p. 5.

Miller, Merle. *Ike the Solder as They Knew Him.* New York: Putnam's Sons, 1987, pp. 77-83, 116, 506-507. (About Eisenhower's Witness background; much good material).

Miller, Stephen. *Mis Guiding Lights.* Kansas City, Missori: Beacon Hill Press, 1991. Chapter 3 on Jehovah's Witness: "The View from the Watchtower", p. 20-29 by Kurt Goedelman.

Minetree, Harry. *Cooley; The Career of a Great Heart Surgeon.* New York; Harpers Magazine Press 1973, 298 pp. (Recounts Colley's experiences with Witness patients) 67 pp.

Minority Rights Group. *Religious Minorities in the Soviet Union,* 1960-1970, Report No. 1, 1970.

Mitscherlich, Alexander, and Fred Mieke. *Doctors of Infamy: The Story of Nazi Medical Crimes.* Trans. Heinz Norden. New York: Henry Schuman, 1949.

Moberg, David O. *The Church as a Social Institution.* Englewood Cliffs, NJ: Prentice-Hall, Inc., 1962, pp. 79, 91-92, 403, 455, 458-459, 474.

Molland, Einar. *Christendom.* New York: Philosophical Library, 1959, "Jehovah's Witnesses," pp. 341-347.

Mollison, P.L. *Blood Transfusion in Clinical Medicine.* Oxford, England: Blackwell Scientific Publications, 1972, p. 140.

Moore, R. Laurence. *Religious Outsiders and the Making of Americans.* New York: Oxford University Press, 1986.

Moorehead, Caroline. *Troublesome People* ; *The Warriors of Pacifism.* Bethesda, MD: Adler &Adler 1987. (About war conscientious objectors).

Moorehead, William G. *Millennial Dawn; A Counterfeit of Christianity.* Chapter 9 in Vol.4 of *The Fundamentals.* pp. 109-130 Grand Rapids, MI: Baker Book House, 1993. (a reprint of the original four volume edition Los Angeles, 1917.) Ed. by R.A. Torrey.(A critique of Russell's teachings in this set of 4 volumes which gave rise to the term "fundamentalists ")

Morey, Robert. *Death and the Afterlife.* Minneapolis, MN: Bethany Pub. House, 1982, pp. 20-26, 75, 95-96, 118, 155, 202.

Morgan, Richard E. *The Politics of Religious Conflict.* New York: Pegasus, 1968, pp. 36, 78, 130.

_____. *The Supreme Court and Religion.* New York: The Free Press, 1972, pp. 58-74, 126, 146-147, 158.

Morris, R.B. *Encyclopedia of American History.* New York: Harper & Row, 1965, pp. 499, 586.

Mulder, H. *Tegenliggers. Enkele hedendaagsche bewegingen getoetst aan schrift en belijdenis.* Aalten, De Graafschap, 1941, 176 pp. (People coming from the wrong direction: Some modern movements put to test on Scripture and confession) (in Dutch).

Munders, Q.L. *Interne en externe rekrutering en kerkelijke gezindte. Sociologisch commentaar bij nog niet eerder gepubliceerde volkstellings-gegevens, met name m.b.t. enkele kleinere godsdienstige groepen in de stad Utrecht.* (Internal and external recruitment and church-inclination. Sociological comments not published befor the national population census was taken, special focus on some small religious groups in Utrecht). Utrecht, Sociologisch Institute der Rijksunivresiteit van Utrecht, 1970, 38 pp. (Modeldelingen van het Sociologisch Institute der Rijksuniversiteit van Utrecht, no. 64). (information of the Sociological College of the State University of Utrecht, number 64) (in Dutch).

Myers, Gustavus. *History of Bigotry in the United States.* New York: Random House, 1943, pp. 490-493. (A brief review of Witnesses and their persecution problems).

National Cyclopaedia of American Biography, Vol. XII, "Russell, Charles Taze." New York: James T. White & Co., 1904, pp. 317-318.

Neal, Steve. *The Eisenhower's.* Lawrence, KS: University Press of Kansas, 1984. (About Eisenhower's parents' religious views as Witnesses).

Neidhart, Ludwig. *Die Zeugen Jehovas.* (The Jehovah's Witnesses). Altenberge, Soest, CIS-Verlag, 1986, 200 pp. (in German).

Nelson, Wilton M., and Richard K. Smith. "Jehovah's Witness. Part I: The Background" (pp. 173-183) and Part II: Their Mission" (pp. 185-199). In *Dynamic Religious Movements: Case Studies of Rapidly Growing Religious Movements Around the World.* David J. Hesselgrave, ed. Grand Rapids: Baker Book House, 1978.

Nepveu, R.M. *Wat is dit voor geloof? Kennismaking met religies, stromingen en richtingen.* Ede, Bosch & Keuning, 1983, 208 pp. pp. 92-101: Jehovah's Getuigen: (Jehovah's Witnesses) (What is that belief? Acquaintanceship with religious bodies, trends and movements) (in Dutch).

Neve, J.L. *Churches and Sects of Christendom.* Burlington, IA: The Lutheran Literary Board, 1940, pp. 581-584; reprinted, Blair, NB: Lutheran Publ. House, 1952.

Newsweek Editors. *Religion in Action.* Silver Springs, MD: Dow Jones & Co., 1965, "Jehovah's Witnesses," pp. 108-111.

Niemoller, Wilhelm. "The Niemoller Archives" in *The German Church: Struggle and the Holocaust,* ed. Franklin H. Littell. Detroit, MI: Wayne State Univ. Press, 1974, p. 41.

Noonan Jr., John T. *The Believer and the Powers That Are.* (Cases, History, and Other Data Bearing on the Relation of Religion and Government). New York: Macmillan Publishing, 1987, 510 pp. (Numerous references to Witnesses, particularly in Part 3 "Contemporary Controversies").

Norman, E.R. *The Conscience of the State in North America.* Cambridge, MA: Cambridge Univ. Press, 1968, pp. 894.

O'Donnell, Thomas. *Medicine and Christian Morality.* New York: Alba House, 1975, pp. 45, 58-71.

Olmstead, Clifton. *History of Religion in the United States of America.* Englewood Cliffs, NJ: Prentice-Hall, 1960, pp. 522-523.

Oosthoek's Encyclopedie. Utrecht, Oosthoek's Uitgeverij. 4th vol. IX, 1950, p. 137: (6th ed. Vol. 8, pp. 72-73) Jehovah's Getuigen. (Jehovah's Witnesses).

Osborn, R.E. *The Spirit of American Christianity.* New York: Harper & Bros., 1958, p. 42.

Parkinson, James. *New Testament Manuscript and Translation Studies.* Los Angeles, CA: pub. by author, 1970, pp. 24.

Passantino, Robert, and Gretchen Passantino. *Answers to the Cultist at Your Door.* Eugene, OR: Harvest House Publishers, 1981, 200 pp. (Covers Witnesses, pp. 47-86; cults in general, pp. 3-46, 183-195; and The Way, Moonies, Mormons and Hare Krishna).

Pawelezynska, Anna. *Values and Violence in Auschwitz.* Berkeley: University of California Press, 1973. 86-89 pp. (About the Witnesses experience in Auschwitz.)

Penton, M. James. "The Eschatology of Jehovah's Witnesses in *The Coming Kingdom.* Barrytown, NY: International Religious Foundation, Inc., 1983, pp. 169-208.

_____. "Jehovah's Witnesses" in *Encyclopedia of Religion in the South.* Ed. Samuel S. Hill. Mercer University Press, 1984.

Persons, Stow. *American Minds: A History of Ideas.* New York: Holt, Rinehart, and Winston, 1958.

Peters, George N.H. *The Theocratic Kingdom.* Reprinted by Kregel Publications, Grand Rapids, MI, 1952, 3 Vols. (Does not discuss the Watchtower directly but extensive discussion of the Chiliastic, Adventists and Millennial movements, originally published in 1890).

Petrich, Hermann. *Unsere Sekten, Freikirchen und Weltanschauungsgemeinschaften.* (Our sects, free-church and worldview-movements). Berlin, Kranzverlag, 1928, 291 pp. (in German).

Pfeffer, Leo. *The Liberties of an American.* Boston, MA: Beacon Press, 1956, 2nd ed. 1963, pp. 50-55, 64, 79, 89, 107, 138-139, 246, 282-283.

_____ *Church, State and Freedom.* Boston, MA: Beacon Press, 1968, pp. 650-706.

_____. *The Religious Situation.* Boston, MA: Beacon Press, 1968, pp. 360-361.

_____. "The Legitimation of Marginal Religions in the United States." In *Religious Movement in Contemporary America*, pp. 9-26. I.I. Zaretsky and M. P. Leone, eds. Princeton, NJ: Princeton University Press, 1974, [Duke Div].

Pike, Royston. *Encyclopedia of Religion and Religions.* New York: Meridian Books, 1958, pp. 207-208.

Pingel, Falk. "Jehovah's Witnesses" In *Encyclopedia of the Holocaust.* Ed. by Israel Gutman. New York: Macmillan Pub. Co., 1990. pp. 742-743. (About the Witness' experience in the camps and Nazi Germany.)

Pinson, Roppel S. *Modern Germany: Its History and Civilization.* New York: Macmillan Co., 1966, p. 513. (On the treatment of Jehovah's Witnesses in Nazi Germany).

Pollock, J.C. *The Faith of the Russian Evangelicals.* New York: McGraw-Hill, 1964.

Poovey, William. *Your Neighbor's Faith.* Minneapolis, MN: Augsburg Publ. House, 1959, Ch. 14, pp. 107-113, pb. (student edition, pp. 112-118). (A sympathetic but critical treatment of the Witnesses, which shows where Lutherans have "fallen short in spreading the truth").

Potter, Charles F. *The Faiths Men Live By.* New York: Prentice-Hall 1955, pp. 308-310. 323 pp.

Powles, L.N. *The Faith and Practice of Heretical Sects.* 1962.

Prewitt, Kenneth, and Sidney Verba. *Principles of American Government.* 2nd ed. New York: Harper & Row, 1977, pp. 267-268.

Price, Ira M. *The Ancestry of Our English Bible.* New York: Harper & Row, 1956, p. 304.

Prosser, C.E. *Interesting Data on Biblical Subjects.* Los Gatos, CA: P.O. Box 989, n.d., 30 pp.

Qualben, Lars P. *A History of the Christian Church.* New York: Thomas Nelson & Sons, 1933, p. 465.

Rall, Harris Franklin. *Modern Premillennialism and the Christian Hope.* New York: Abingdon Press, 1920, pp. 16, 109-168. (A critique of Premillenialism of Millennial Dawnism and other Russellite and non-Russellite groups).

Rappoport, Roger. *The Super Doctors.* Chicago, IL: Playboy Press. 1975, 275 pp, 108-122 pp. on Denton Cooley, who is a major Jehovah Witness surgeon: hundreds of Jehovah's Witness flock to Cooley, one of the few surgeons willing to do most coronary procedures without blood) p. 115-116.

Reich, Warren T., ed. *Encyclopedia of Bioethics.* Vol. 1-4. New York: The Free Press, 1979, pp 133, 271, 1026, 1361, 1365, 1373, 1377, 1426, 1512, 1514, 1885.

Reiser, Stanley Joel et al. (Eds). *Ethics in Medicine.* Reprint of Norman Cantor, "A Patient's Decision to Decline Life-saving Medical Treatment," pp. 156-172, 199-200, Cambridge, MA: The MIT Press, 1977.

Renker, Z. *Unsere Brüder in den Sekten.* Limburg, Germany: Lahn-Verlag, 1964. (Our Brothers in the Sects.)

Reutter, E. Edmund. *Schools and the Law.* Reston, VA: National Association of Secondary School Principals, 1981, pp. 31, 40-41.

Rhodes, Arnold Black, ed. *The Church Faces the Isms.* New York: Abingdon Press, 1958, pp. 31, 69-71, 80-87, pb.

Rice, John R. *Some Serious, Popular False Doctrines Answered from the Scriptures.* Murfreesboro, TN: Sword of the Lord Publ., 1970, chapter on Jehovah's Witnesses by John Wimbush, pp. 293-316, hb. (A critique of Witness doctrines and a brief history).

Richards, Claud Henry. "Religion and the Draft: Jehovah's Witnesses Revisited" in *Law and Justice: Essays in Honor of Robert S. Rankin,* ed. Carl Beck. Durham, NC: Duke University Press, 1970, pp. 47-75.

Ridenour, Fritz. *So What's the Difference?* Glendale, CA: B/L Publications, 1967, Chapter 10 "Jehovah's Witnesses; There Is No Hell ... Hard Work Earns Heaven," pp. 130-143, pb. (Covers history, teachings, and doctrine from an evangelical world view).

Rinser, Luise. *A Women's Prison Journal; Germany, 1844.* New York: Schocken Books. 1987 pp. 16-27 (Covers the authors experience with Witnesses in the Nazi concentration camps)

Robertson, D.B. *Should Churches Be Taxed?* Philadelphia, PA: Westminster Press, 1968, pp. 36-37, 212-213, 223.

Robertson, Irving. *What the Cults Believe.* Chicago: Moody Press, 1966, Ch. 3 in on Jehovah's Witnesses, pp. 47-62, 120, 121, 125, 126, hb. (Covers mostly doctrine).

Robertson, Roland. *The Sociological Interpretation of Religion.* New York: Schocken Books, 1970, pp. 119, 134-135, 148, 166.

Robinson, Jacob, and Philip Friedman. *Guide to Jewish History under Nazi Impact.* Joint Documentary Projects Bibliographical Series No. 1. New York: KTAV Publishing House, 1973, p. 22.

Roche, John. *The Quest for the Dream.* New York: Macmillan, 1963, pp. 147, 200-202.

Rohr, John. *Prophets Without Honor: Public Policy and the Selective Conscientious Objector.* New York: Abingdon Press, 1971, pp. 30-32, 76-77.

Roll, William G. *The Poltergeist.* New York: New American Library, 1972, pp. 134-142 (Includes an experience of a Witness with dreams).

Roof, Wade Clark and William McKinney. *American Mainline Religion; Its Changing Shape and Future.* New Brunswick, NJ: Rutgers University Press. 1987. pp. 97-215. (An extensive survey covering many denominations including Witnesses).

Rosenberg, Alfred. "Die Ernsten Bibelforscher," in *Kampf um die Macht.* München: Published by author. 1937, pp. 328-332.

Rosten, Leo. *Religions in America.* New York: Simon & Schuster, 1952, revised 1963, pp. 96-102, 347-351, 356, 358, 361-362. (Chapter entitled "Who are Jehovah's Witnesses" by Melton G. Henschel, then a governing body member, now the Watchtower president; question and answer format).

Rotberg, Robert I. *The Rise of Nationalism in Central Africa: The Making of Malawi and Zambia 1873-1964.* Cambridge, MA: Harvard Univ. Press, 1965, pp. 66-71, 135-155, 162-169, 172-175.

_____, and Ali A. Mazrui. *Protest and Power in Black Africa.* New York: Oxford Univ. Press, 1970, p. 478-479, 486-489, 520-523, 530-531, 536-537, 544-549-558-559, 566-568, 996-997, 1002-1003.

Roueche', Berton. *The Man Who Grew Two Breasts.* New York; Truman Talley Books/ Dutton 1995. 197 pp. p. 67-86. (About a Witness who took canthaxanthin to "suntan," developed aplastic anemia, refused blood and died. In this case had she accepted a blood transfusion she would have lived).

Roy, Ralph, Lord. *Apostles of Discord.* 1953, pp. 20, 21. (About Witnesses reputation)

Rubin H. Ted. *Juvenile Justice: Policy, Practice, and Law.* New York: Random House, 1985, pp. 340-341, 347 (on the blood issue and the courts response).

Rubinsky, Yuri and Ian Wiseman. "Charles Russell and the Invisible Advent" in *A History of THE END of the World*, New York: Quill, 1982,   p. 118.

Rudolph, L.C. *Hooser Faiths; A History of Indiana's Churches and Religious Groups.* Bloomington, IN; Indiana Univ. Press 1995 688 pp. (Has a long chapter on Jehovah's Witnesses in Indiana, pp. 524-540).

Rule, Andrew K. "Jehovah's Witnesses" in *The Church Faces the Isms,* ed. Arnold B. Rhodes. Nashville, TN: Abingdon Press, 1958, pp. 80-87.

Rumble, Leslie, et al. *Radio Replies.* St. Paul, MN: 1939, Vol. I, pp. 312, 325-326;

1940, Vol. II, pp. 299, 327, 331-336; 1942, Vol. III, pp. 62, 84, 237.

Rusling, Geoffrey W. "Jehovah's Witnesses" in *Chamber's Encyclopedia*. London: International Learning Systems, Inc., Vol. 8, p. 70.

Sadlier, Steven. *The Spiritual Seekers Guide; The Complete Source for Religious and Spiritual Groups of the World*. Costa Mesa, CA: Allwon pub 1992. (Includes a section on Jehovah's Witnesses).

Salisbury, W. Seward. *Religion in American Culture: A Sociological Interpretation*. Homewood, IL: The Dorsey Press, 1964, pp. 10, 34, 97, 177, 195-202, 240-243, 313, 329-332, 335, 454.

Salvesen, Sylvia. *Forgive but do not forget*. London: Hutchinson 1958 p. 63-79, and 165-166, 186-187 Chapter 12 "Jehovah's Witnesses" pp. 83-91, 234 pp (One inmate and her experiences with Witnesses in the Nazi Camps).

Sanders, J. Oswald. *Cults and Isms, Ancient and Modern*. Grand Rapids, MI: Zondervan Publ. House (first ed. titled *Heresies, Ancient and Modern*, 1948; new revised and enlarged ed. 1962) (Ch. 7 on Jehovah's Witnesses, covers mostly doctrine, pp. 74-87, pb).

Scheurlen, P. *Die Sekten der Gegenwart*. (The modern sects). Stuttgart, Verlag der Evangelischen Gesellschaft, 1912, 192 pp. and 1923 revised ed. pp. 87-90: Die Russellianer (The Russellists). In revised edition: pp. 24-29: Internationale Vereinigung Ernster Bibelforscher (Millenniums-oder Russellites). (The International Association of Earnest Bible Students (Millennial Dawn People or Russellites)) (in German).

Schluckebier, F.W. *Gesunde Lehre und Irrlehren*. (Healthy teachings and false teachings). Wuppertal, Aussaat Verlag, 1964, 175 pp., (Bibl. Evangelical Lehr u. Sektenkunde) (in German).

Schwartz, Gary. *Sect Ideologies and Social Status*. Chicago: The University of Chicago Press, 1970, p. 20.

Schweizer. *Schweizer Lexicon in Sieben Bänden*. (Swiss lexicon in seven volumes). Zürich, Encyclois Verlag, 1945-1948, 1st volume, 1945, pp. 1230: Ernste Bibelforscher (Earnest Bible Students) (in German).

Scott, F.R. *Civil Liberties and Canadian Federalism*. Toronto, Canada: Univ. of Toronto Press, 1959.

Scott, Latayne C. *Why We Left a Cult*. Grand Rapids, MI: Baker Book House 1993. 207 pp. Has chapters by ex-Witness David Reed (p. 25-34) and Joan Cetnar (pp. 35-44) plus much on cults in general.

Sears, Clara Endicott. *Days of Delusion: A Strange Bit of History*. Boston: Houghton Mifflin Co., 1924, pp. 202-265. (A history of the Miller movement)

Seguy, Jean. *Les Sects Protestantes dans la France Contemporaine*. Paris: Beauchesne, 1956, (Protestant Sects in Contemporary France). (In French)

_____. "Témoins de Jéhoval," *Encyclopédia Universalis*, 1973, t. XV, p. 906-907. (Jehovah's Witnesses). (In French)

Seldes, George. *The Catholic Crisis*. New York: Julian Messner, Inc., 1939, pp. 116-117.

Semonche, John. *Religion and Constitutional Government in the United States*, pp. 44-

47, 57-58, 152-155, 190.

Shepperson, George, and Thomas Price. *Independent African.* Edinburgh, Scotland,
    1958, pp. 18-69, 92, 109-121, 147-161, 185, 210, 226, 323-355, 402, 411-417,
    431, 458-460, 498, 539.

Shuster, George N. *Religion Behind the Iron Curtain.* New York: Macmillan Co., 1954,
    pp. 38-39, 149. (A discussion of Witness persecution in Eastern Europe and the
    old USSR).

Sibley, Mulford Q., and Philip E. Jacob. *Conscription of Conscience: The American
    State and the Conscientious Objector, 1940-1947.* Ithaca, NY: Cornell Univ.
    Press, 1952.

Sire, James. *Scripture Twisting: 20 Ways Cults Misread the Bible.* Downers Grove, IL:
    Intervarsity Press, 1981.

Skilton, J.H. *The Translation of the New Testament into English 1881-1950.* 2 Vols.
    Ann Arbor, MI: University Microfilms, Inc., 1961, pp. xxxii, 125, 323-325, 327-
    329, 337, 343-345, 348, 350, 352.

Smart, Ninian. *The Religious Experience of Mankind.* New York: Charles Scribners
    Sons, 1969, pp. 22, 487, 488.

Smith, Chard Powers. *Yankees and God.* New York: Hermitage House. 1954. pp. 245,
    425. 528 pp. (Discusses the Witnesses in the Eastern USA)

Smith, Elwyn. *Religious Liberty in the United States.* Philadelphia, PA: Fortress Press,
    1972, pp. 251, 264-269, 286-287, 290-293, 302-303, 336-337.

Smith, H.S.; R.T. Handy; and L.A. Loetscher. *American Christianity.* New York:
    Scribners Sons, 1963, Vol. II, pp. 315, 332-336, 623.

Smith, Paul B. *Other Gospels.* London, England: Marshall, Morgan and Scott, 1970.

Smith, Wilber Morehead. *Egypt in Bible Prophecy: The Strange Cult of the Pyramidists.*
    Boston: W.A. Wilde Co., 1957, pp. 210, 213.

Sorauf, Frank J. "Jehovah's Witnesses." In *The Guide to American Law.* St. Paul, MN:
    West Publ. Co., 1984, pp. 336-337. (A review of Witness cases).

Spittler, Russell P. *Cults and Isms.* Grand Rapids, MI: Baker, 1962.

Staal, K.R. van *Tervg vit de Hel van Buchenwald.* Amsterdam, Nievwe wieken, 1945,
    48 pp. (Back from the Hell of Buchenwald) (Much on the Witnesses in
    Buchenwald).

Stanley, Manfred. *Jehovah in the City of Mammon: On the Sociology of Anti-thetical
    Worlds in Urbanism, Urbanization and Change,* ed. H. Mizruchi and P.
    Meadows. Boston: Addison-Wesley, 1969.

Starkes, M. Thomas. *Confronting Popular Cults.* Nashville, TN: Broadman Press,
    1972, Chapter 2, "Jehovah's Witnesses: Jesus Is Second Best," pp. 33-43, 118,
    pb. (A history and critique of beliefs and doctrine).

Starr, Isidore. *Human Rights in the United States.* New York: Oxford Book Co., 1964,
    pp. 25-26. (A short history of the general Witness human rights problems).

Stedman, Murray S. *Religion and Politics in America.* New York: Harcourt, Brace &
    World, Inc., 1964, pp. 5, 37, 74-77, 123.

St. John-Stevas, Norman. *Life, Death and the Law.* Bloomington: Indiana University Press, 1961, p. 47.

Strommen, Merton, ed. *Research on Religious Development: A Comprehensive Handbook.* New York: Hawthorne Books, Inc., p. 624.

Stroup, Herbert Hewitt. "The Attitude of the Jehovah's Witnesses Toward the Roman Catholic Church" in *Religion in the Making,* Vol. II, Jan. 1942, pp. 148-163.

_____. "Rutherford, Joseph Franklin" in *Dictionary of American Biography,* Supplement 3, 1941-1945. New York: Charles Scribners & Sons.

_____. "Jehovah's Witnesses." In *Encyclopedia of Religion.* Macmillan, 1987, p. 564-566.

Strout, Cushing. *The New Heavens and New Earth.* New York: Harper & Row, 1974, pp. 286-289, 311-312.

Struve, Nikita. *Christians in Contemporary Russia.* London, England: Harvill Press, 1967, Section on Jehovahs Witnesses (Yegovitsy) pp. 240-243 (also published by Charles Scribner & Sons in New York). (Covers the history, sociology, and problems such as the mass deportation of 1952 which 7,000 Soviet Witnesses were arrested and deported to Siberia).

Stuber, Stanley. *Denominations, How We Got Them.* New York: Association Press, 1958, pp. 110-111. (A factual summary of the Witnesses).

Swetnam, George. *Where Else But Pittsburgh?* Pittsburgh, PA: David & Warde, Inc., 1958, pp. 110-117, chapter VI, part 4 (About C.T. Russell).

Taraborrell, J. Randy. *Michael Jackson; The Magic and the Madness.* New York: Birch Lane Press, 1991. pp. 7-10, 16, 22, 54, 143, 172, 186-188, 199-200, 323-328, 358-359, 381, 391, 394, 437-438. (much on the harm the Watchtower caused to Jackson and the conflicts he had in being a Witness.)

Target, G.W. *Under the Christian Carpet: A Study of Minority Christian Sects.* London, England: Clifton Books, 1969. "Millions Now Living Will Never Die" pp. 139-148.

Tatum, Arlo, ed. *Handbook for Conscientious Objectors.* Philadelphia, PA: Larchwood Press, 1967, pp. 22, 36, 27, 19, 41. (On Witness cases and law related to Jehovah's Witness.)

Taylor, J.V. *Christianity and Politics in Africa.* London, England: Penguin, 1957.

_____, and Dorothea Lehmann. *Christians of the Copperbelt.* London, England: S.C.M., 1961. (About the growth of the churches in Northern Rhodesia. Numerous references including chapter 10 on the Jehovah's Witnesses).

Thomas, Frank W. *Kingdom of Darkness.* Plainfield, NJ: Logos International, 1973, pp. 35-39.

Thomas, Norman M. *The Conscientious Objector in America.* New York: Huebsch, Inc., 1923.

_____. *Is Conscience a Crime?* New York: Vanguard Press, 1927. Reprinted by Garland Publishing, Inc., 1972, pp. 33-34.

Thrupp, Sylvia, ed. *Millennial Dreams in Action.* New York: Schocken Books, 1970, pp. 32, 48-52, 148-155.

Toch, Hans. *The Social Psychology of Social Movements.* Indianapolis, IN: Bobbs-Merrill Co., 1965, pp. 132, 152, 220.

Todorov, Tzvetan. *Mikhail Bakhtin: The Dialogical Principle.* Theory and History of Literature, 13. Minneapolis MN: University of Minnesota Press, 1984.

Tomlinson, Lee Glen. *Churches of Today in the Light of Scripture.* Cincinnati, OH: Christ Leader Corp., 1927, "Russellism," pp. 97-109. Reprinted by Gospel Advocate, Nashville, TN, 1950, 1977.

Tompkins, Peter. *Secrets of the Great Pyramid.* New York: Harper & Row, 1978, pp. 113-116, 253.

Travis, Stephen. *The Jesus Hope.* Downers Grove, IL: Intervarsity Press, 1976, 128 pp. An extensive discussion of the second coming of Christ. The Witnesses are specifically discussed on pp. 86+ and other pages.

Tussman, Joseph, ed. *The Supreme Court on Church and State.* New York: Oxford Univ. Press, 1962, pp. 72-181, 205.

U.S. Government Printing Office. *Conscientious Objection: Special Monograph No. 11,* Vol. 1, 1950, pp. 9, 18-19, 26, 149-150, 153, 261-265, 269-272, 318, 320, 322-323, 326, 328, 338. (A detailed discussion of the conscientious objector and religion problem, the stand of various groups and shows how the Witnesses deceived the government; also shows Witnesses had the third highest percent of camp delinquents).

_____. *Enforcement of the Selective Service Law: Special Monograph No. 14,* 1950, pp. 80-81, 93-96, 98, 100, 110. (On the Witness draft experience).

_____. *Industrial Deferment: Special Monograph No. 6,* Vol. 1, 1947, pp. 269-270.

_____. *Legal Aspects of Selective Service,* revised Jan. 1, 1963, pp. 8-13, 19-23. (Jan. 1, 1969, ed. pp. 10-15. (On Witness' claim of ministerial and conscientious objector status).

_____. *Selective Service: 2nd Report,* 1943, p. 265.

_____. *Selective Service and Victory: 4th Report 1944-1945,* printed 1948, pp. 186, 265. (Gives the breakdown of convictions for professed religious objectors to war. The Witnesses were a major group in this category).

_____. *Selective Service as the Tide of War Turns: 3rd Report 1943-1944,* printed 1945, p. 178. (Shows conscientious objectors were never more than 0.04% of all registrants).

_____. *Selective Service Circular No. 3461, Supplement 9,* Sept. 28, 1943, pp. 1-4.

_____. *Selective Service in Peacetime Washington, U.S., 1942,* p. 197.

_____. *Trials of War Criminals Before the Nuremberg Military Tribunal, Vol. III* (a letter from Dr. Guertner dated 9-28-1939 about a Jehovah's Witness, August Dickmann, who was executed by the German government). Washington, D.C., 1951, pp. 331-332.

Vanacker, G. *De Religieuze sekten: religie, waanzin of bedrog?* Kapellen, De Nederlandse Boekhandel, 1986, 148 pp. (The religious sects; religion, madness or swindle?) (in Dutch).

Van Baalen, Jan Karel. *Our Birthright and the Mess of Meat: Isms of Today Analyzed and Compared with the Heidelberg Catechism.* Grand Rapids, MI: Wm. B.

Eerdmans Publ. Co., 1919 (one chapter on Jehovah's Witnesses).

_____. *The Gist of the Cults.* Grand Rapids, MI: Wm. B. Eerdmans Publishing Co., 1938 (revised 1951, 1962), Ch. 13 on Jehovah's Witnesses, pp. 257-276, hb. Trans. into Spanish as *El Caos de las Sectas,* Talleres Graficos; Barcelona, Spain, 1969, pp. 239-261, pb. Reprinted as *The Chaos of the Cults.* (Covers history and critiques doctrine from a fundamentalists world view).

Van Buren, James G. *Cults Challenge the Church.* Cincinnati, OH: Standard Pub. Co., 1965, Chapter 5, "Jehovah's Witnesses," p. 45-56.

Van Datmar. *Good in Nederland: een statistisch onderzoek naar godsdienst en kerkelijkheid in Nederland, ingesteld in opdracht van de Geillustreerde Pers N.D.* (God in the Netherlands: a statistical examination to religion and ecclesiastical attitude in The Netherlands, set up by and in charge of Geillustreerde Pers N.V.). (in Dutch) Amsterdam, Van Datmar, 1967. 201 +12 pp.

Van Sommers, Tess. *Religions in Australia.* Adelaide: Rigby Limited, 1966, "Jehovah's Witnesses," pp. 87-93.

Vasuden, Dr. *Uar bik nei pawite.* Aizawi, India: Synod Literature Committee, 1977, 88 pp. (On Witnesses, Seventh-day Adventists and Pentecostals).

Veldhuizen, H. *Sekten en stromingen.* Kampen, J.H. Kok, 1980, 157 pp. pp. 24-35, 155-157: Jehovah's Getuigen (Jehovah's Witnesses) (Sects and trends) (in Dutch).

Verrier, Henri. *The Face of the Cults.* LeQuenoy; Publ. by author, 1959, p. 17-29.

Visser, P. *Hedendaagse Secten: hun Wezen en Achtergrond.* Kampen, J.H. Kok, 1955, 132 pp. pp. 240-298: Jehovah's Getuigen (Jehovah's Witnesses) (Contemporary sects: their existence and background) (in Dutch).

Vlaisevich, Ivan Stepanovich. *Religious Sects.* Irkutsk: Irkutsk Book Publishing House, 1957, 37 pp. (in Russian).

Vogel, A. *Mijn leven en werk zoals verteld aan Klaas Mulder en Saskia van der Stoel.* Amsterdam, Sijthoff-Elburg, UGN, 1986, 192 pp. (in Dutch). (My life and work, as told to Klaas Mulder and Saskia van der Stoel; about a Swiss Witness doctor who has made world famous contributions to so called homeopathic medicine).

Vorspan, Albert, and Eugene J. Lipman. *Justice and Judaism.* New York: Union of American Hebrew Congregations, 1959, pp. 141-142.

Vries, W.G. de. *Het ene Woord en de vele sekten.* Holland: Goes, Oosterbaan & LeCointre, (The one Word and the many sects) 1984, 200 pp. (first printing: 1983).

Vugt, J.P.A. van. *Godsdienst en kerk in Nederland, 1945-1980. Een geannoteerde bibliografie van sociaal-wetenschappelijke en historische literatuur over de godsdienstige en kerkelijke ontwikkelingen in Nederland.* Nijmegen/Baarn, Katholiek Documentatie Centrum, 1981, 400 pp. Number 141, 367, 392, 525: Jehovah's Getuigen (Jehovah's Witnesses) (Religion and church in the Netherlands, 1945-1980. An annotated bibliography of social-scientific and historical literature about the religious and church-development in the Netherlands) (in Dutch).

_____. and B.M.L.M. van SON. *Nog eens: godsdienst en kerk in Nederland, 1945-1986. Een geannoteerde bibliografie van sociaal-wetenschappelijke en historische literatuur.* (Once again, religion and church in The Netherlands, 1945-1986). An

annotated bibliography of sociological-scientific and historical literature).
Hilversum, Gooi en Sticht, 1988, 452 p. pp.13, 29, 30, 46, 78, 147, 152.
Jehovah's Getuigen. (Jehovah's Witnesses) (in Dutch).

Walker, Allen. *Last-Day Delusions.* Nashville, TN: Southern Publishing Association,
1957, pp. 49-64, 108-128.

Walker, Eric Anderson. *A History of Southern Africa.* New York: Longmans, 1964.
973 pp. p. 667. (Discusses the Watchtower role in the violent copper belt strikes).

Walker, Luisa Jeter de. ¿ Cual Camino? Estudio de religiones y sectas. Miami, FL:
Editorial Vida, 1968 (2nd ed. 1972), Chapter 15, Los Testigos de Jehova, pp.
250-272, pb. (A study of religious sects). (Covers some history, but primarily
doctrine from an evangelical world view). (In Spanish)

Wallechinsky, David, and Irving and Amy Wallace. *The Book of Lists.* New York:
Bantam, 1978, p. 222. (Contains data on Watchtower book distribution)

Wallis, Roy. *Sectarianism: Analyses of Religious and Non-Religious Sects.* London:
Peter Owen Ltd., 1975, pp. 9-11, 39-40, 43, 70-86, 197, 211, hb.; New York:
John Wiley and Sons, 1975. (A sociological-historical study of select sects)

Ward, Larry. *Darkness versus Light.* Chicago, IL: Regular Baptist Press, 1953, 72 pp.
Lesson 12: Jehovah's Witnesses, pp. 63-67 (Covers doctrine and beliefs).

Warner, Charles W. *Quacks.* Jackson, MS: Charles Warner Publ., 1941, Witnesses
discussed on pp. 11, 13, 49, 55, 57-58, 189-190. (Covers the relationship
between medical quacks and religious sects and cults).

Washington, J.R., Jr. *Black Religion.* Boston, MA: Beacon Press, 1964, p. 117.

Watson, William. *Tribal Cohesion in a Money Economy: A Study of the Mambwe People
of Northern Rhodesia.* Manchester: Manchester University Press. 1958 246 pp.
pp. 84, 197-202.

Wellcome, Isaac C. *History of the Second Advent.* Boston, MA: Boston Advent
Christian Publ., 1874, 708 pp. (An important work in understanding the roots of
the movement that produced C.T. Russell).

Wells, G.A. *Religious Postures.* LaSalle, IL: Open Court, 1988, 269 pp, pb. p. 1-8, 21,
143, 228. (A powerful critique of the Witnesses as "extreme fundamentalists,"
which the author uses to illustrate what is wrong with religion in general).

Wentz, Frederick W. *Lutherans and other Denominations.* Philadelphia: Lutheran Church
Press, 1964, 117 pp., pb., Ch. 14, p. 96-102. (A brief critique of Witness beliefs
and practices).

Whalen, William Joseph. *Separated Brethren: A Survey of Non-Catholic Christian
Denominations.* Milwaukee, WI: The Bruce Pub. Co., 1958, Ch. 16 The
Jehovah's Witnesses, pp. 174-184, hb. (A sympathetic review of history and a
discussion of their faith and practice).

_____. *Faiths for the Few; A Study of Minority Religions.* Milwaukee, WI: The Bruce
Pub. Co. 1963. 201 pp., p. 20 and Chapter 11 "Jehovahs Witnesses" p. 77-85
and 178.

_____. *Minority Religions in America.* Staten Island, NY: Society of St. Paul, 1972,
Chapter on Jehovah's Witnesses pp. 85-95 and pp. 1, 3, 5, 9, 11, 37, 85-95, 99,
pb. Revised ed. 1981 pp. 63-71. 302 pp. (A review of history, teachings and
doctrine of the small sects, similar to Elmer Clark's *The Small Sects in America.*

A very fair review of these groups).

_____. "Jehovah's Witnesses" in *Encyclopedia Britannica*. Chicago, 1980, Vol. 10, pp. 131-132 (15th ed.).

Whitaker, Harry. "Jehovah's Witness" in *People We Meet*. Birmingham, England: The Christadelphians, 1976, pp. 10-11. (Critiques the Witness teaching of the spiritual resurrection).

Wilhite, J. Potter. *Modern Churches and the Church*. Tulsa, OK: Telegram Book Co., 1956.

Williams, George H. *The Radical Reformation*. Philadelphia: The Westminster Press, 1962. 1516 pp.

Williams, J.P. *What Americans Believe and How They Worship*. New York: Harper & Brothers, 1952 (2nd ed. 1962), pp. 439-441.

Williamson, A.E. "Millennial Dawn," in *The New Schaff-Herzog Encyclopedia of Religious Knowledge*, 1910 ed., Vol. 7, p. 374. Grand Rapids, MI: Baker Book House, 1954 reprint.

Wilson, Bryan. *Sects and Society*. Berkeley: Univ. of California Press, 1961, pp. 3, 91, 116-264, 294-295, 319, hb. (A study of Elim Tabernacle, Christian Science, and Christadelphians, the latter group which is very similar to Witnesses).

_____. *Religion in Secular Society: A Sociological Comment*. Baltimore, MD: Penguin Books, 1966. [personal copy] (also printed at London: C.A. Watts and Co., Ltd., 1966).

_____. *Religious Sects*. London: World University Library, 1970, pp. 10-17, 34, 98-99, 110-117, 170, 193, 194, 230, 237-239, pb. (A sociological review).

_____. "Jehovah's Witnesses" in *Man Myth and Society, Vol. 1*. New York: Marshall Cavendish Corp. 1970, pp. 1499-1500.

_____. *Religion in Sociological Perspective*. Oxford, England: Oxford Univ. Press, 1982, pp. 92, 109, 110, 111, 114, 132, 135, 143.

Wilson, John. *Introduction to Social Movements*. New York: Basic Books, 1973, pp. 118-119, 128-129, 171, 307, 318.

Winkler Prins Encyclopedie van de Tweede Wereldoorlog. (Winkler Prins Cyclopedia of the Second World War). Amsterdam. Vol. 1, 1980, p. 319. Jehovah's Getuigen (in Dutch).

Witt, Elder. *The Supreme Court and Individual Rights*, 2nd Ed. Washington, DC. *Congressional Quarterly*, 1988, pp. 34, 35, 38, 39, 41, 43, 49, 56, 57, 82, 88.

Words and Phrases, Vol. 1923. "Jehovah's Witnesses." St. Paul, MN: West Publishing Co., 1967, p. 9.

Wormser, Migot. *Le Systeme Concentrationnaire Nazi, 1933-1945*. Paris: Presses Universitaires de France. (The Nazi Concentration Camp System, 1933-1945.)

Wright, J. Stafford. "Jehovah's Witnesses" in *The New International Dictionary of the Christian Church*, ed. J.D. Douglas. Grand Rapids, MI: Zondervan Pub. House, 1974, pp. 527-528.

Wyrick, Herbert. *Seven Religious Isms*. Grand Rapids, MI: n.d., 99 pp. (one chapter on Jehovah's Witnesses.)

Yezzi, Ronald. "Blood Transfusions and the Right Of Religious Freedom." in *Medical Ethics*. New York: Holt, Rinehart, Winston, 1980, pp. 34-35.

Yinger, J. Milton. *Religion in the Struggle for Power: A Study in the Sociology of Religion*. Durham, NC: Duke Univ. Press, 1946, pp. 23, 209-210, 212.

_____. *Sociology Looks at Religion*. New York: Macmillan Co., 1961, 1963, pp. 46-48.

Zahn, Gordon C. *War, Conscience and Dissent*. New York: Hawthorne Books, Inc., 1967, p. 102. (Quotes Hess on Witness martyrs).

Zeigler, Harmon. *Interest Groups in American Society*. Englewood Cliffs, NH: Prentice-Hall, 1964, pp. 316, 326. (Discusses the Witnesses and social status, and the flag issue).

Zipfel, Friedrich. *Kirchenkampf in Deutschland, 1933-1945. Religionsverfolgung und Selbstbehauptung der Kirchen in der National-Sozialistischen Zeit*. Berlin, Walter de Gruyter and Co., 1965, p. 176-203. (Veröffentlichungen der historischen Kommission zu Berlin beim Friedrich-Meinecke-Institut der Freien Universität Berlin, Vol. 11). (Church struggles in Germany, 1933-1945. Religious persecution and the maintaining of the churches in the period of National Socialism) pp. 175-203: (with documentation in the a section in the back titled *Die Ernsten Bibelforscher*). (The Earnest Bible Students) (in German).

Zoeklicht Encyclopedie. Vraagbaak voor Noord-en Zuid Nederland. Arnhem, Van Loghum Slaterus. Supplement-deel, 1962, p. 195: Jehovah's Getuigen. (Searchlight Cyclopedia. Vade-mecum of North and South Netherlands) (in Dutch).

E. TRACTS

This section consists of short tracts, all published by religious houses, mostly of an evangelical or fundamentalist orientation. Almost all of them are about doctrine; most discuss the Witnesses' denial of the Trinity, immortality, hellfire, and similar issues. Unless the reader has a theological background or training, they are sometimes difficult to follow. Unfortunately, many are also inaccurate polemics that do not always reflect the Witness position, revealing more about the writer than the Witnesses. Some are printed by local print shops and are filled with mistakes and many are articles reprinted from religious magazines. Some consist of a personal history of someone who was at one time involved with the Watchtower Society. Many, however, are still very useful in a study of the Witnesses and their opposition.

Acts 17. *Jehovah's Witnesses vs. the Bible*. La Mesa, CA, n.d., 2 pp.

Adler, Kathie. *Biblical Christianity vs. the Cults*. Holbrook, NY: Narrow Way Ministries, n.d., 3 pp.

_____. *Jesus Answered, Watch Out That No One Deceives You. For Many Will Come in My Name, Claiming "I Am the Christ" and Will Deceive Many*. Holbrook, NY: Narrow Way Ministries, n.d., 2 pp.

_____. *Narrow Way Ministries*. Holbrook, NY: Narrow Way Ministries, n.d., 1 p.

Ahlen, A.C.M. *Sincerity Is Not Enough! Facts Worth Knowing About Jehovah's Witnesses*. Minneapolis, MN: Tract Mission, n.d., 6 pp.

Algermissen, Konrad. *Die Zeugen Jehovas*. Freiburg (im Breisgau), Seelsorge Verlag, 1949, 8 pp. (The Jehovah's Witnesses) (in German).

Alpha and Omega Ministries. *As Accurately as Possible.* c. 1985, 6 pp. (on the NWT).

_____. *Have You Been Made Righteous?* c. 1985, 6 pp. (On the basis of salvation).

_____. *What Is Alpha and Omega Ministries?* c. 1985, 7 pp.

_____. *Hiding the Divine Name.*

_____. *Mark 16:9-20; Scripture or Not? The Evidence.* c. 1985, 7 pp.

_____. *Granville Sharps Rule: Titus 2:13, 2 Peter 1:11.* c. 1985, 7 pp.

_____. *Prototokos: Its Meaning and Usage.* c. 1985, 7 pp.

_____. *The Common Traits of Cultism.* Holbrook, NY: Narrow Way Ministries, n.d., 8 pp.

_____. *Who Is Jesus That the Angels Worship Him?* Holbrook, NY: Narrow Way Ministries, n.d., 8 pp.

Allman, Brad. *The Double Jeopardy of Jehovah's Witnesses.* Gadsden, AL: J.W. Ministry, n d., ? pp. c. 1960 (on Christ's deity).

Apocalyptic Ministries. *Awake!* Wilmore, KY: c1994. (About salvation).

Armstrong, Arthur. *There Is a Worldwide Family! Are You a Member?* Detroit, MI: pub. by author, n.d., 4 pp. Revised and enlarged c. 1976, 6 pp. (How various sects compare with the Christadelphians).

_____. *Twelve Scriptural Reasons Why I Am Not a Jehovah's Witness!* Detroit, MI: pub. by author, n.d., 4 pp. Revised, retitled: *Are You Awake to the Personal Visible Return of Jesus Christ to Jerusalem in the Land of Israel?* 1981, 6 pp.

Barnes, Peter. *Jehovah's Witnesses at Your Door, What is Their Real Purpose in Calling?* San Diego, CA: Equippers, Inc., n.d., 8 pp. (About false prophesy of the Watchtower).

Becker, Norbert V. *Welcome to My Door If ...* St. Louis, MO: Concordia Tract Mission, n.d., 4 pp.

Betteley, Debrah and John Betteley. *Are You Awake to the Personal, Visible Return of Jesus Christ to Jerusalem in the Land of Israel.* Detroit, MI pub by author 6 pp., 1980 (Why Christianity is superior to the Watchtower).

Blizard, Paul. *They Wanted Our Baby to Die.* Brownwood, TX: Paul Blizard Ministries, 1984, 8 pp. (St. Louis, MO: Personal Freedom Outreach, n.d., 8 pp.)?

Boerwinkel, F. *Hoe de Jehovah's Getuigen tot het jaartal 1914 en de Adventisten tot het jaartal 1843 kwamen.* (Driebergen, Veritas, 1957), 4 pp. (How the Jehovah's Witnesses came to the year 1914 and the Adventists came to the year 1843).

Breda Centre. *Forty Reasons Why ...* Belfast, Ireland, n.d., 4 pp. (Covers the nature of God, man and the Gospel).

_____. *Watchtower Knots Untied.* Belfast, Ireland, 1985, 4 pp. (A critique of the Watchtower's view of a paradise Earth and two classes).

Brooks, Keith L., ed. *The Spirit of Truth and the Spirit of Error.* Chicago: Moody Press, 1969, 12 pp. (Compares cults with fundamentalism on major doctrines).

Brown, Dorothy M. *A Challenge to Jehovah's Witnesses.* Minneapolis, MN: Osterhus

Publ. House, n.d., 4 pp. Also published by Pilgrim Tract Society in Randleman, NC. (A dialogue with a Witness on Hell, resurrection and Jesus).

Cameron, Neil D. *The Analyst*. North Syracuse, NY: The Book Fellowship, n.d., 7 pp. (Gives Scriptural support for fundamentalism in contrast to cults).

_____. *The Curse of the Cults*. North Syracuse, NY: The Book Fellowship, n.d., 5 pp. (Shows cults deny basic doctrines of Christianity).

Cheshire, John. *Witnessing to Jehovah's Witnesses*. Toronto, Canada: Midnight Cry Crusade, n.d., 3 pp. Later revised and retitled *Witnessing to Jehovah's False Witnesses*. c. 1950. (on the bodily resurrection of Christ).

Christian Literature for Jehovah's Witnesses. *A Recorded Message for Jehovah's Witnesses--269-2882*. Scottsdale, AZ, c. 1976, 1 p.

Chretien, Leonard A. *I Am A Witness*. Garland, TX: American Tract Society, 6 pp, c. 1984.

_____. *Jehovah's Witnesses; Prophets, Promises, and Problems*. Garland, TX: American Tract Society, 16 pp., c. 1984. (Reviews prophecy failure and doctrine problems; well done).

A Christian Messenger. *Warning: Beware of Religious Doorknockers*. Western Australia: A Christian Messenger, 1983, 6 pp. (About blood).

Clausen, C.P. *Zeugen Jehovas vor der T**. B*defeld (Sauerland), Katholischer Schriftendienst, 1961, 4 pp. *(Jehovah's Witnesses at the door)* (in German).

Coleridge, W.J. *Whose Witnesses?* Los Angeles, CA: John Ferguson, n.d., 4 pp. (on the deity and resurrection of Christ).

Concordant Publisher's Concern. *Pastor Russell Writes*. Los Angeles, CA: c. 1925, 4 pp.

Cornelius, Heinrich. *Vereinigung gegen die Internationale Ernster Bibelforscher* (von Heinrich Cornelius). Bamberg, Christlichers Schriftenvertrieb J. Maar, 1925, 4 pp. (Association against the International Association of Ernest Bible Students by Heinrich Cornelius) (in German).

Coveney, Maurice. *...Are You Ready for Him?* Kelowna, B.C., Canada: Help Jesus Ministry, n.d., 3 pp. (How to Witness to a Witness).

_____. *Dear Jehovah's Witness: Can You Accept His Challenge?* Kelowna, B.C., Canada: Help Jesus Ministry, n.d., 4 pp.

_____. *Fact Sheet for Jehovah's Witnesses*. Kelowna, B.C., Canada: Help Jesus Ministry, n.d., 2 pp. (A date outline of the history of the Watchtower).

_____. *Help Jesus: World Crusade to Help Jehovah's Witnesses Meet Christ*. Kelowna, B.C., Canada: Help Jesus Ministry, n.d., 4 pp. (Tells about how and why Christians can witness to Jehovah's Witnesses).

_____. *Jehovah's Witnesses, Can You Accept the Challenge?* Kelowna, B.C., Canada: Help Jesus Ministry, n.d., 4 pp. (on the trinity).

_____. *Jesus Christ the Firstborn of All Creation*. Whittier, CA: n.d., 4 pp (reprinted from *Watch Out*, March 30, 1975). (Argues for the deity of Christ).

_____. *Mr. Jehovah's Witness ... Whom Can You Trust?* Kelowna, B.C., Canada: Help Jesus Ministry, c. 1976, 4 pp. (A take-off on a Watchtower article that claims the Watchtower can be trusted; shows that they have often been wrong).

_____. *Mr. J.W. ... Read This Reply to a W.T. Overseer, and "You Be the Judge!"* Kelowna, B.C., Canada: Help Jesus Ministry, c. 1979, 4 pp.

_____. *Some Definite and Indisputable Mistranslations Found in the Watchtower's Own "New World Translation" of the Bible.* Kelowna, B.C., Canada: Help Jesus Ministry, n.d., 4 pp. (Shows some problems with the NWT).

_____. *Some Helpful Hints.* Kelowna, B.C., Canada: Help Jesus Ministry, n.d., 2 pp. (Reveals some contradictions in the Watchtower Society).

_____. *The Balance of Life is in Christ.* Kelowna, B.C., Canada: Help Jesus Ministry, 1975.

_____. *The 144,000.* Kelowna, B.C., Canada: Help Jesus Ministry, 1975.

_____. *The Prophet Who Presumes to Speak in My Name...* Kelowna, B.C., Canada: Help Jesus Ministry, n.d., 4 pp. (Lists the record of prophetic failure of the Watchtower in general).

_____ *Warning!* Kelowna, B.C., Canada: Help Jesus Ministry, n.d., 4 pp. (On prophesy failure and the Watchtower).

_____. *Was He Around Recently? Beware of False Prophets at Your Door!* Kelowna, B.C., Canada: Help Jesus Ministry, n.d., 4 pp. (Background of the Watchtower).

_____. *The Watchtower or God ... Who Is Telling the Truth?* Kelowna, B.C., Canada: Help Jesus Ministry, n.d., 4 pp. (also entitled *The Watchtower or God...Who Is Lying?*). (Argues for the trinity).

_____. *The Way Out of the Fog...Christ!* Kelowna, B.C., Canada: Help Jesus Ministry, 1975.

_____. *Were You Told the Truth about 1975?* Kelowna, B.C., Canada: Help Jesus Ministry, n.d., 4 pp.

_____. *Why the name Jehovah's Witnesses?* Kelowna, B.C., Canada: Help Jesus Ministry, n.d., 4 pp. (Discusses why the Watchtower uses the term Jehovah).

_____. *Whatever Has Happened to One-Quarter of a Million Jehovah's Witnesses?* Kelowna, B.C., Canada: Help Jesus Ministry, c., 1979, 3 pp. (Discusses some of the Watchtower membership losses from the 1975 failure).

_____. *What Greek Scholars Really Think!* Kelowna, B.C., Canada: Help Jesus Ministry, n.d., 3 pp. (A set of quotes from Greek scholars who conclude that the NWT is a poor translation).

_____. *Who Is Jehovah? ... The Mystery of God.* Kelowna, B.C., Canada: Help Jesus Ministry, n.d., 4 pp. (Argues that Jehovah is part of the trinity).

_____. *The World's Most Dangerous Book!!* Kelowna, B.C., Canada: Help Jesus Ministry, n.d., 4 pp. (A critique of the New World Translation).

_____. *You Have Been Warned!* Kelowna, B.C., Canada: Help Jesus Ministry, n.d., 4 pp. (also revised issue entitled *Beware! You Have Been Warned!*). (Covers how persons become converted to Jehovah's Witnesses and how to avoid becoming ensnared).

_____. *"You Must Be Born Again."* Kelowna, B.C., Canada: Help Jesus Ministry, n.d., 4 pp.

Danger: Jehovah's Witnesses (Russellites). Oak Park, IL: Brotherhood of St. Mark of Ephesus, n.d., 6 pp.

Dawn Bible Students. *Are Blood Transfusions Forbidden by God?* East Rutherford, NJ: Dawn Publishers, c. 1952, 4 pp. (Written in response to the 1951 *Watchtower* article on this subject).

Druckerei des Johannes Bünder. *Augen Jehovas. Du sollst kein falsches Zeugnis geben!* Leutesdorf, 8 pp. (Witnesses of Jehovah. You shall not be a false Witness!) (in German)

E.J.T. *A Letter to a Millennial Dawnist.* London: pub. by author, c. 1928, 4 pp.

Emmanuel Gospel Center. *Questions for Readers.* Boston, MA: n.d., 7 pp.

Faith, Prayer & Tract League. *Jehovah's Witnesses Refuted.* Grand Rapids, MI: n.d., 2 pp.

Faith and Life Publications. *If Christ is Not God.* n.d., 4 pp. (Shows the Bible teaches that Christ is God).

Das Falsch Evangelium der Sich Selbst-ernennten Zeugen Jehovas. n.d., 4 pp.

Fisk, Rev. Samuel. *Judge Rutherford and Jehovah's Witnesses.* Manila, Philippine Islands, n.d., (c. 1950) 4 pp. (Lists Scriptures that contradict Watchtower teachings).

Fraser, Gordon. *Is the Jehovah's Witness Christian?*

Frye, Ronald. *The Kindly Yoke.* Medford, MN: Christian Respondent, 1986, 6 pp. (On the Watchtower teaching of sin).

_____. *The Faithful and Discreet Slave and Jehovah Witnesses.* 1987, 6 pp. (On Watchtower prophesy failure and the slave doctrine).

Gardner, Ron. *I Was A Jehovah's Witness.* Santa Clara, CA: CARIS. c1975.

Gigliotti, Carmen. *The* Watchtower ... *The Big Lie.* Santa Clara, CA: 1977, 4 pp. (Covers Watchtower prophecy failure and problems. The author was a Witness for forty-one years, a pioneer for seven, and a former member of the Bethel family. Includes the author's resignation letter;).

Goedelman, Martin Kurt. *Whom Can You Trust?* St. Louis, MO: Personal Freedom Outreach, 1980, 4 pp. (Shows you cannot trust the Watchtower; mostly on false prophecy).

_____. *Why the Name Jehovah's Witnesses?* St. Louis, MO: Personal Freedom Outreach, 1980, 4 pp. (A history of the name Jehovah; also shows Franz is not a Hebrew scholar as the Watchtower alleges).

_____. *Jehovah's Witnesses: The Christian View; A Christian Perspective of The Watchtower Bible and Tract Society.* St. Louis, MO: Personal Freedom Outreach, 1981, 4 pp.

_____. *The Deity of Jesus Christ According to the Scriptures.* St. Louis, MO: Personal Freedom Outreach, 1982, 4 pp. (A list of Scriptures showing Christ's deity).

_____. *Patterns in the Cults; An Examination of the Cults from a Christian Perspective to Aid the Believer in Facing One of the Greatest Dangers Confronting the Church Today.* St. Louis, MO: Personal Freedom Outreach, 1986, 4 pp. (A discussion of key doctrines and the teachings of major cults).

_____. *A Gospel Test for Jehovah's Witnesses.* St. Louis, MO: Personal Freedom Outreach, 1989, 4 pp. (Contrasts the Watchtower gospel and the N.T. gospel).

_____. *The Straw Men of the Watchtower Society.* St. Louis, MO, 1982, 1989, 4 pp. (Argues against the Scriptures the Society uses to disprove the trinity).

_____. *Questions for Jehovah's Witnesses.* St. Louis, MO: Personal Freedom Outreach, 1989, 6 pp. (Covers salvation, worship of Christ, the Resurrection, the NWT, and the prophetic failures).

_____ and Keith A. Morse. *A Faithful Witness Will Not Lie; But a False Witness Uttereth Lies.* St. Louis, MO: Personal Freedom Outreach, n.d., 8 pp. (Covers the Johnannes Greber affair, the translations that use "a god" for John 1:1, and the Society's misrepresentation).

_____. Are Blood Transfusions a Violation of God's Law? 4 pp., c. 1980. (Shows the Watchtower teaching on transfusions is not in violation of Old or New Testament law).

_____. *A True Christian Presentation To a Jehovah's Witness.* St. Louis, MO: Personal Freedom Outreach, n.d., 4 pp. (Lists scriptures that support the deity and bodily resurrection of Jesus Christ).

_____. *Destroying the Mediatorship of Christ.* St. Louis, MO: Personal Freedom Outreach, n.d., 4 pp. (Refutes the Society's argument that Christ is the mediator only to the 144,000).

_____. *He is Not Here...He is Risen, As He Said...; Jehovah's Witnesses and the Gospel of the Resurrection.* St. Louis, MO: Personal Freedom Outreach, n.d., 4 pp. (A critique of the Watchtower's doctrine of a spiritual resurrection of Christ).

_____. *Is the President of Jehovah's Witnesses "In the Truth?"* St. Louis, MO: Personal Freedom Outreach, n.d., 4 pp. (Shows Franz was not elected to be a Rhodes Scholar as the Society claims, and that the Society condones lying if it benefits them).

_____. *The Word; Who is He? According to Spiritism.* St. Louis, MO: Personal Freedom Outreach, n.d., 6 pp. (A critique of the Society's booklet of the same name).

_____ *The World's Most Dangerous Book!!: New World Translation of the Holy Scriptures.* St. Louis, MO: Personal Freedom Outreach, n.d., 4 pp. (A critique of the NWT; shows Franz is not a Hebrew scholar).

_____. *Who Changed Jehovah to Lord?* St. Louis, MO: Personal Freedom Outreach, n.d., 4 pp. (An excellent discussion of the use of Jehovah in the New Testament, specifically Howard's theory).

_____. *Why the Name Jehovah's Witnesses?* St. Louis, MO: Personal Freedom Outreach, n.d., 4 pp. (Discusses the problems with use of the term Jehovah).

_____. *Charles Taze Russell; Disfellowshipped.* St. Louis, MO: Personal Freedom Outreach. n.d., 6 pp. (Shows that Russell would be disfellowshipped if he were a Witness today).

_____. *Jehovah's Witnesses: The Christian View.* St. Louis, MO: Personal Freedom Outreach. 4 pp., 1981. (An outline of Watchtower history, publications, doctrines, false prophecies, and witnessing techniques).

Gospel, Jack. *The Bible and the Watchtower--Do They Agree?* Roseville, MI: pub. by author, c. 1975, n.d., 8 pp. (Shows the NWT contradicts Watchtower teachings).

Gospel Tract Distributors. *"Jehovah's Witnesses:" The True and the False.* Portland, OR: n.d., 14 pp. (On the deity of Christ).

Gruss, Edmond C. *Is the Watchtower Society God's Channel?* Brewerton, NY: n.d., 4 pp. (Later entitled *Who Is "the Channel" to God?* and published by Help Jesus Ministry of Kelowna, B.C., Canada). (A set of examples in which the Society reversed themselves on doctrine).

_____. *Delivered from the Jehovah's Witnesses.* Newhall, CA: Los Angeles Baptist College and Theological Seminary, 1972, 4 pp. (reprinted from *Challenge,* July 2, 1972). (Contains the author's testimony on why he left the Witnesses).

_____. *Jehovah's Witnesses: A Survey.* Newhall, CA: Los Angeles Baptist College and Theological Seminary, n.d., 2 pp. (Covers history and doctrine).

_____. *Why a Witness of Jesus Christ--Not a Jehovah's Witness?* Newhall, CA: Los Angeles Baptist College and Theological Seminary, n.d., 5 pp. (Covers the deity of Christ and salvation).

_____. *Jehovah's Witnesses: The Watchtower Society and Prophetic Speculation,* reprinted from *The Discerner,* Jan.-March 1972 issue, 3 pp.

Gudel, Joe. *Prophecy & the Watchtower.* Kent, OH: Bible & Tract Society, n.d., 4 pp. (Discusses several of the Watchtower prophecy failures).

_____. *Is Jesus Really Michael the Archangel?* Kent, OH: n.d., 4 pp. (A discussion of who Jesus is).

Guindon, Kenneth R. *New Birth Brings Freedom.* Van Nuys, CA: Van Nuys Baptist Church, 1974, 5 pp. (The author tells why he left the Witnesses).

_____. *How to Witness to Jehovah's Witnesses.* Gadsden, AL: J.W. Ministry, n.d., 1 p. (Gives points in converting a Witness).

Hadley, S. *Do "Jehovah's Witnesses" Follow Jehovah?* Danville, IL: Grace & Truth, Inc., n.d., 8 pp. (Argues for Christ's deity).

Hammond, Rev. T.C. *What Is Millennial Dawn Theory?* London, England: Charles J. Thynne, n.d., c. 1912.

Hatton, Max. *The New World Translation of the Bible.* Australia: pub. by author, c. 1967, 4 pp. (Hatton is an ex-Witness and now a Seventh-Day Adventist pastor).

_____. *Jesus Christ--The Firstborn of Creation.* Australia: pub. by author, n.d., 2 pp. (Argues for Christ's deity).

Heer, Johannes de. *Jehova's Getuigen en hun dwaalleer.* Driebergen, Het Zoeklicht, c. 1945, 8 pp. (Jehovah's Witnesses and their erroneous teachings). (A history and critique of doctrine).

Herleyn, Carl. *Eine Gegen-bestellung der Lehre der Zeugen Jehovas und der Lehre der Kirche Jesu Christi.* Emden, Bretzler, 1962., 8 pp. (An opposite thesis for the teachings of the Witnesses of Jehovah and the church of Jesus Christ) (in German).

Hickethier, C. Robert. *There Is a Way That Seemeth Right.* Darby, PA, n.d., 3 p. (Covers hell, the deity of Christ and the trinity).

Hill, William F. *Are "Jehovah's Witnesses" Really Witnessing for Jehovah?* Independence, IA: Calvary Evangelistic Center, 1974, 8 pp. (Covers the 144,000, hell, born again doctrine, and judgment).

Hirtenworte. *Die sogenannten "Ernsten Bibelforscher" sind Bibelfääscher.* Dulmen, A. Laumann, 1925, 4 pp. (The so-called "Earnest Bible Students" are Bible-falsifiers) (in German).

Hoe de Kerk denk over de Gentuigen van Jehova. Herderlijk schrijven van de Kerkeraad der Nederlands Hervormde Gemeente. Groningen, Kerkeraad, ca. 1945, 4 pp. (How the Church is thinking about the Jehovah's Witnesses. Pastoral letter from the Elders and Deacons of the Dutch Reformed Church of the city of Groningen).

Hutten, Kurt. *Sind die Zeugen Jehovas Ernste Bibelforscher?* Stuttgart, St. Quell Verlag, 1948, 1 p. (Are the Jehovah's Witnesses Earnest Bible Students?) (in German).

Jackson, J.L. *When Is the Firstborn Not the Firstborn?* New Hyde Park, NY: pub. by author, n.d., 3 pp. (Shows the term firstborn does not always mean first in order, but can mean first in priority and relates this to Watchtower teaching).

_____. *Is It Right to Worship Jesus?* New Hyde Park, NY: pub. by author, n.d., 7 pp. (Shows the scriptures teach worship of Jesus in contrast to the Watchtower teaching).

Jackson, Wayne N. *Are Jehovah's Witnesses True to the Bible?* Saltillo, MS: Barber Pub., 1978, 8 pp. (Covers the nature of humans, the kingdom and the Watchtower).

Jehovas Zeugen prophezeiten falsch. 4 pp. (Jehovah's Witnesses are false prophets).

Jolly, Raymond. *A Message for "Jehovah's Witnesses."* Chester Springs, PA: Laymen's Home Missionary Movement, n.d., 6 pp. (A critique of the Watchtower teaching on the ransom.)

Jung, Alois. *Zeugen Jehovas.* (Jehovah's Witnesses). Augsburg: Druck- und Verlagshaus, 1960, 8 pp. (in German).

Kaul, Arthur O. *Are Jehovah's Witnesses God's Witnesses?* St. Louis, MO: Concordia Tract Mission, n.d.

Kenner, Forrest L. *"Jehovah's Witnesses?" or Satan's Salesmen?* Lawton, OK: Bethel Baptist Church, n.d., 5 pp. (On the deity of Christ and the bodily resurrection of Christ).

Kleinknecht, Herm. *Zeugen Jehovas oder Zeugen Jesu Christi?* Neuendettelsau: Freimund Verlag, 1948, 2 pp. (Jehovah's, or Witnesses of Jesus Christ?) (in German).

Knoch, A.E. *Pastor Russell Writes Concerning the Universal Reconciliation* (Pastor Russell's letter printed with reply). Los Angeles, CA: n.d., 4 pp.

Koblenz, Marian. *Ernste Bibelforscher (Zeugen Jehovas).* Mannerkongregation, 1949, 8 pp. (Earnest Bible Students; Jehovah's Witnesses) (in German).

Kramer's Verlag, W. *Die Ernsten Bibelforscher.* (The Earnest Bible Students). Leipzig: Kramer's Verlag, 1922, 2 pp. (in German).

Linenmann, K. *Russellism.* St. Louis, MO: c. 1900, 2 pp.

MacGregor, Keith. *Beth-Sarim and the Watchtower Coverup.* Vancouver, B.C., Canada, n.d., 4 pp. (Shows the Watchtower is not honest today about Beth-Sarim; reprints the original deed).

MacGregor, Lorri. *Jehovah's Witnesses and the Blood Question.* Delta, B.C. Canada: Macgregor Ministries, 6 p. c. 1982. (A good brief review of the blood transfusion issue).

Magnani, Duane. *Dialogue on the Christian Cross.* Clayton, CA, n.d., 4 pp. (Argues Christ died on a cross, not a stake as Watchtower teaches).

_____. *Is Jesus Coming Again?* San Francisco, CA: Witness, Inc., 1976. (Covers their long history of prophecy failure).

_____. *Dear Jehovah's Witness, Please Consider These Things.* San Francisco, CA, n.d., 2 pp. (Reviews the Watchtower prophetic failures).

_____. *Discerning the Body.* Clayton, CA, n.d., 4 pp. (On the Watchtower doctrinal changes on body of last supper).

_____. *Do You Make Sure of All Things?* Clayton, CA, 1978, 8 pp. (Covers racism in the Watchtower, vaccination, 1925, forced unity, and Watchtower change of doctrine).

_____. *Eyes of Understanding: Examining Watchtower Armageddon Prophecies.* Clayton, CA, 1978, 2 pp. (Lists fifteen prophetic failures of the Watchtower, quoting the original prediction).

_____. *Introducing Witness, Inc.* Clayton, CA, n.d., 8 pp. (A background of this anti-Watchtower ministry founded by Duane Magnani, an ex-Witness).

_____. *Is Jesus Christ Worthy of Worship?* Clayton, CA, n.d., 4 pp. (Shows the Watchtower admits the Greek teaches that Stephen prayed to Jesus in contradiction to their official dogma).
_____. *Jesus, Spirit or Man?* Clayton, CA, n.d., 3 pp. (Argues for bodily resurrection of Christ).

_____. *Theocratic War Strategy or Lying to the Public.* Clayton, CA, n.d., 4 pp. (Documents that the Watchtower justifies lying if it is in the interest of their organization).

_____. *To Marry, or Not to Marry?* Clayton, CA, n.d., 4 pp. (Reviews the Watchtower's prohibition against marriage).

_____. *Watchtower Authority over Jehovah's Witnesses.* Clayton, CA, n.d., 4 pp. (shows Witness authority is not Bible but Watchtower).

_____. *What About 1975?* Clayton, CA, 1975, n.d., 4 pp. (Reviews this infamous prophetic failure).

_____. *What Happened in 1925?* Clayton, CA, n.d., 4 pp. (Reviews this past prophetic failure).

_____. *Keep Testing Whether You are in the Faith.* Clayton, CA: Witness, Inc., n.d., 4 pp. (Reviews some of the more well known Watchtower mistakes and doctrine changes).

Mantey, Julius Robert. *Grossly Misleading Translation.* Chicago, IL: pub. by author, n.d., 4 pp.

Martin, Walter R. *Jehovah's Witnesses and the Deity of Jesus Christ.* Oradell, NJ:

American Tract Society, n.d, 3 pp. (Critiques the Watchtower view of Christ).

_____. *Jehovah's Witnesses and the Resurrection of Jesus Christ.* Oradell, NJ: American Tract Society, n.d., 3 pp. (Argues for the bodily resurrection of Christ).

_____. *Jehovah's Witnesses and the Trinity.* Oradell, NJ: American Tract Society, n.d.

_____. *One Hundred Years of Divine Direction?* San Juan Capistrano, CA: Christian Research Institute, 1983, 6 pp.

Mason, Doug. *Anointed by the Spirit--How Is It Manifest?* Kilsyth, Victoria, Australia, n.d., 4 pp. (About salvation and how it can be achieved).

_____. *What the Watchtower Does Not Tell You.* Kilsyth, Victoria, Australia, n.d., 19 pp. (Shows the Watchtower is not always fully honest with their history).

Massalink, E.J. *So You Are a Jehovah's Witness?* Colton, CA: Colton Community Church, c. 1970, 4 pp.

Mavis, Jeanne M. *I Found the Truth When I Left the Watchtower.* Seattle, WA: pub. by author, c. 1980, 4 pp. (A personal testimony of a person who left the Watchtower; reasons include 1975 failure, doctrinal changes, and backbiting in the organization).

Maynard, R.W. *Are Jehovah's Witnesses in Error?* Minneapolis, MN: Osterhus Publ. House, n.d., 4 pp. (on soul sleep, and the work of Christ).

Midnight Cry Crusade. *Witnessing to Jehovah's False Witnesses.* Minneapolis, MN: Osterhus Publishing House, c. 1950, 4 pp. (A critique of Watchtower writings).

Mignard, Rev. Robert B. *Fifteen Reasons Why I Cannot Be a Jehovah's Witness.* Largo, FL: Evangelical Missionary Fellowship, c. 1965, 6 pp., reprinted by *Independent Fundamental Churches of America* in Westchester, IL: 1966, 4 pp. (On the trinity, and 144,000).

Miller, C. John. *Witnessing to Jehovah's Witnesses.* Philadelphia, PA: Westminster Theological Seminary, n.d., 4 pp. (The author is a professor of practical theology; he covers basic doctrine and how to witness to a Witness).

Montague, Havor. *The Watchtower Cult's Effect on the Human Mind.* 8 pp. (Discusses how the Watchtower adversely effects its members.)

Moorehead, William G. *Remarks on "Millennial Dawn."* New York: Loizeaux Brothers, c. 1891, 4 pp.

Murley, T.R. *Who in the Skies Can Be Compared to Jehovah?* Orangevale, CA, n.d., 8 pp. (Argues that Jehovah is Jesus Christ).

Nielsen, Rev. John R. *An Open Letter to the Jehovah's Witnesses.* St. Louis, MO: Concordia Tract Mission, n.d., 9 pp. (On the term Jehovah).

Nijmegen, Informatie-Centrum. *Een betrouwbaar getuige liegt niet, maar wie leugens uitblaast, is een vals getuige.* z.j., 2 pp. (A trustworthy witness does not lie, but one who blows out lies is a false witness).

_____. *Ein ernstige waarschuwing!* n.d., 4 pp. (A serious warning!). (A brief review of major doctrines).

Orr, William W. *Do You Know What These Religions Teach?* Minneapolis, MN: Religion Analysis Service.

Palmer, Rev. R.F. *What to Say to Jehovah's Witnesses at the Door.* Cambridge, MA: The Society of Saint John the Evangelist, n.d., 2 pp. (Hints to rebuke Witnesses at the door).

Pape, Günther. *Jehovas Zeugen an der Tü r: Wer sind sie? Informationen.* Rottweil, Verlag Aktuelle Texte, 1974, 6 pp. (Jehovah's Witnesses at the door: who are they? What is it that they want? information) (in German).

Parkerson, Nelson. *The Lies of the Serpent.* Ind. MO. Gospel Tract Society, 1982, 8 pp. (Argues that the Watchtower is a totalitarian system and discusses how this came about).

The Philippian Fellowship. *Jehovah's Witnesses on Trial: Is This a United Body of True Christians?* North Syracuse, NY: n.d., 4 pp. (Primarily quotes from the 1954 Scotland-Walsh trail showing that unity at all costs is Watchtower policy).

_____. *A Message to Friends of the "Watchtower."* North Syracuse, NY, n.d., 7 pp.

Pilgrim Tract Society. *Man Is a Soul: False Doctrines of Russellism and Seventh Day Adventism in the Light of God's Word.* Randleman, NC: n.d., 4 pp. (Critiques Russell's soul doctrine).

_____. *A Present-Day "Ism."* Randleman, NC, n.d., (c. 1950) 4 pp. (Covers doctrine and history of the Witnesses).

Pont, Charles E. *"Jehovah's Witnesses" Do Not Believe.* Minneapolis, MN: Religion Analysis Services, Inc., n.d., 6 pp. (Lists doctrines that Witnesses reject).

Price, E.B. *Jehovah's "Prophet?"* Pub. by author, n.d., 4 pp.

Quaisser, G.S. *Glaubst du alles, was und wie es in der Heiligen Schrift geschrieben steht?* Berlin, ca. 1961, 4 pp (Do you believe all what and who that is written in the Holy Scriptures?) (in German).

Questions for Jehovah's Witnesses. Gadsden, AL: J.W. Ministry, n.d., 2 pp.

Reed, David. *American Freedom Vs. Watchtower Power.* Stoughton, MA: Comments from the Friends, 1982, 6 pp. (Discusses the totalanarism in the Watchtower).

_____. *On Trial for Blood.* Stoughton, MA: Comments from the Friends, 1984, 8 pp. (Shows how irrational the Watchtower stand on blood is).

_____. *That's Not in My Bible.* Stoughton, MA: Comments from the Friends, 1985, 8 pp. (Covers the New World Translation decisions).

_____. *Caution, the Watchtower may Be Hazardous to Your Health.* 1985, Stoughton, MA: Comments from the Friends, 1983, 6 pp. (About Witness mental health).

_____. *The Watchtower Puts Jehovah's Witnesses on Trial For Blood.* Stoughton, MA: Comments from the Friends, 1984, 6 pp. (On the issue of blood transfusion. Very well done, using much history of the Society's position on this and similar issues).

Remmerswaal, J. *Spreekbeurt over de Getuigen van Jehova in Best.* Best, Actie-Radius, 1956, 8 pp. (Actie-Radius, 1956, no. 51). (Lecturing engagement about the Witnesses of Jehovah at Best, a village in the south of The Netherlands).

Richtsmeier, Melvin. *Jehovah's Witnesses: You Are Trying To Put Us In a Pinch!* St. Louis, MO: Personal Freedom Outreach, 6 pp.

Rockstad, Ernest B. *Questions for "Jehovah's Witnesses."* Andover, KS: Faith and Life Publications, n.d., 3 pp. Also published by Osterhus Publ. House of Minneapolis, MN, n.d., 4 pp. (On name Jehovah, soul, deity of Christ and resurrection and return of Christ).

Roundhill, Jack. *Jehovah's Witnesses.* London: Church Literature Ass. 1979, 4 pp.

Russellism or the International Bible Students' Association: The Teachings of Demons. Toronto, Canada, c. 1920, 2 pp. (A critique of Russell's major doctrine).

Salt Publications. *Jehovah's Witnesses/Do They Have the Truth?* Escondido, CA: n.d., 8 pp.

Schnell, William J. *Befreit. 30 Jahre ein Sklave der Wachtturms.* (Freedom. Thirty years a slave of the Watchtower Society). Frankfurt/ M., Elmer Klassen, 1957, 2 pp. (in German).

_____. *Witnessing to a Jehovah's Witness.* North Syracuse, NY: The Book Fellowship, n.d., 6 pp. (Tells how to convert Witnesses to Christ).

_____. *Who Are Jehovah's Witnesses?* Minneapolis, MN: Osterhus Publ. House, n.d., 8 pp. (Covers history and doctrine).

_____. *Witnessing for Christ to Jehovah's Witnesses.* Randleman, NC: Pilgrim Tract Society, n.d., 4 pp. (Tells how to convert Witnesses to fundamentalism).

Schulz, Chr. *Die Milleniumssekte (Bibelforscher) oder Lehrt die Bibel ewige Hellen qual?* Bamberg, Christlicher Schriftenvertrieb J. Marr, 1924, 4 pp. (The Millennium sect (Bible Students) or the Bible teaching of eternal hell/torture?). (in German).

Scott, Frank Earl. *Letter to Mr. Kaika.* Wallace, ID: pub. by author, 1973, 8 pp. (About prophecy, and the role of Jesus; Scott teaches that the Witnesses are a "people who made a complete separation from all parts of Christendom" a move which he approves of. Scott is a Dentist).

Smith, Jami. *Dear Brothers and Sisters.* CA: pub. by author, 1978, 2 pp.

_____. *Regarding That Year 1975.* CA: pub. by author, 1979, 2 pp.

Smith, Oswald J. *The Error of Jehovah's Witnesses.* Minneapolis, MN: Osterhus Publ. House, n.d., 4 pp. (Critiques deity of Christ, soul sleep, hell, and second chance).

Sowers, Ivan. *Asleep? How to Counteract Brainwashing by the Jehovah's Witnesses.* Youngstown, OH: Berean Baptist Church, n.d., 6 pp. (Covers hell, soul, cross, and Russell's life).

Stegenga-Stoove, A. *Het Wereldgericht!* Heemstede, Eigen uitgave, 1955, 2 pp. (The world's judgment) (by an ex-Witness).

St. Quell Verlag. *Zeugen Jehovas (Die "Ernsten Bibelforscher").* Stuttgart, 1933, 4 pp. Witnesses of Jehovah (Ernest Bible Students) (in German).

Storz, Peter. *Witnessing to the "Witnesses."* St. Louis, MO: Concordia Tract Mission, n.d., 5 pp. (Hints on how to Witness to Jehovah's Witnesses).

Stromberg, D.E. *If Christ Is Not God....* Minneapolis, MN: Osterhus Publ. House, n.d., 3 pp. (Argues for the deity of Christ).

Thomas, Fred W. *Are Jehovah's Witnesses Christians?* Vancouver, B.C., Canada: pub. by author, n.d., 8 pp. (Covers deity of Christ).

_____. *Are Jehovah's Witnesses Deceivers?* Vancouver, B.C., Canada: pub. by author, n.d., 8 pp. (revised ed. entitled *Who Are These Deceivers?;* also entitled *Are Jehovah's Witnesses Deceived?*). *(Covers soul, 144,000 and Christ).*

_____. *Beware of False Prophets.* Vancouver, B.C., Canada: pub. by author, n.d., 8 pp. (About Hell and Afterlife).

_____. *Beware of Their Deception.* Vancouver, B.C., Canada: pub. by author, n.d., 8 pp. (Covers blood transfusion, war and Watchtower dishonesty).

_____. *Christianity and Jehovah's Witnesses Contrasted.* Vancouver, B.C., Canada: pub. by author, n.d., 8 pp. (Covers Christ, salvation and the role of Christ in salvation).

_____. *Is It Wrong to Worship Christ as Jehovah's Witnesses Teach?* Minneapolis, MN: Osterhus Publ. House, n.d., 8 pp. (Argues it is scriptural to worship Christ).

_____. *Jehovah's Witnesses Deny Worship to Christ.* Vancouver, B.C., Canada: Faith Contenders Guild, n.d., 8 pp. (Shows it is scriptural to worship Christ).

_____. *Kingdom of Darkness.* Vancouver, B.C., Canada: pub. by author, n.d.

_____. *Masters of Deception.* Vancouver, B.C., Canada: pub. by author, n.d., 4 pp. (The author discusses his book and ministry).

_____. *Peddlers of Deception.* Vancouver, B.C., Canada: pub. by author, n.d., 8 pp. (Covers 1914 problem, bodily resurrection of Christ).

_____. *So You're Annoyed.* Vancouver, B.C., Canada: pub. by author, n.d., 2 pp. (The author's reasons for publishing tracts that are vitriolic--his words).

_____. *The Horrors of Hell.* Vancouver, B.C., Canada: pub. by author, n.d., 8 pp. (Argues for a fiery, everlasting hell).

_____. *Unmasking the Deceivers.* Vancouver, B.C., Canada: pub. by author, n.d., 8 pp. (Covers conversion process used by Jehovah's Witnesses, and hell).

_____. *Victims of Deception.* Vancouver, B.C., Canada: pub. by author, n.d., 8 pp. (About Watchtower hatred and the trinity).

Trombley, Charles. *Dear Jehovah's Witnesses, Please Consider These Things.* San Francisco, CA, n.d., 1 p.

_____. *Is Jesus Coming Again?* San Francisco, CA, c. 1976, 4 pp.

_____. *Jehovah's Witnesses and the Second Coming of Jesus.* Sarasota, FL, n.d., 4 pp.

_____. *Keep Testing Whether You Are in the Faith.* San Francisco, CA, c. 1976, 4 pp.

Twisslemann, Hans-Jurgen. *Bei Jehovas Zeugen--Nur draußen eine Klinke?* Itzehoe: Bruder-dienst, c. 1976, 4 pp. (In the Case of Jehovah's Witnesses ... Only a Door Knob on the Outside?)

_____. *Der Wachturm und der Staat.* Itzehoe: Bruder-dienst, c. 1976, 4 pp. (The Watchtower and the State).

_____. *Falsche Propheten unter uns.* Itzehoe: Bruder-dienst, c. 1976, 4 pp. (False Prophets Among Us).

_____. *Jehovas Zeugen und das Jahr 1975.* Itzehoe: Bruder-dienst, c. 1976, 4 pp. (Jehovah's Witnesses and the Year 1975).

_____. *Wer ist der kluge und treue Knecht von dem Jesus sprach?* Itzehoe: Bruder-dienst, c. 1976, 4 pp. (Who Is the Faithful and Discreet Servant of Whom Jesus Spoke?)

Wachtel, William. *The Parousia of Jesus.* Belle Plaine, IA: Abrahamic Faith Ministries, c. 1982, 6 pp. (Argues Parousia is not presence, nor secret as Witnesses teach).

Walhem, Charles William. *Jehovah's Witnesses.* N.p., n.d., 4 pp.

Watters, Randall, *Don't Read Your Bible!* Manhattan Beach, CA: pub. by author, 1981, 8 pp. (Shows the Watchtower teaches to replace the Bible with the Society).

_____. "The Good News of the Kingdom." Manhattan Beach, CA: pub. by author, 1981, 6 pp. (A general discussion about how to convert Witnesses).

_____. *What Happened at the World Headquarters of Jehovah's Witnesses in the Spring of 1980?* Manhattan Beach, CA: pub. by author, 1981, 8 pp. (An excellent review of the scism of 1980 by one that was involved).

_____. *The Watchtower Bible Tract Society--The Critical Years 1965-1985.* Manhattan Beach, CA: pub. by author, 1985, 8 pp.

_____. *Opening the Closed Mind.* Manhattan Beach, CA: Bethel Ministries, 1988. (How to reach Witnesses with the information against their world view).

Weathers, Paul. *The Torture Stake Theory Exposed; How Cults Have Staked Their Claim on Shaky Ground.* St. Louis, MO: Personal Freedom Outreach, c. 1985, 4 pp. (Argues against the Watchtower view that Christ did not die on a cross).

Westby, Wayne. *A Message for a Mess-Age.* Vancouver, B.C., Canada: pub. by author, n.d., 1p. (On salvation).

_____. *Christ's Witnesses.* Rose Valley, Saskatchewan, Canada: pub. by author, n.d., 8 pp. (A dialogue between an ex-Witness and an active Witness).

_____. *The Clocktower.* Vancouver, B.C., Canada: pub. by author, n.d., 2 pp. (On the gospel).

_____. *False Religion.* Vancouver, B.C., Canada: pub. by author, n.d., 2 pp. (Defines false religion).
_____. *Help the Blind.* N.d., 1 p. (Argues that some ideas blind one to Jesus, one is "Jehovah's Witness Cataracts").

_____. *Spirit Hijackers.* Vancouver, B.C., Canada: pub. by author, n.d., 2 pp. (on Christ's Deity).

_____. *Watchtower Watergate.* Vancouver, B.C., Canada: pub. by author, n.d., 2 pp. (On salvation).

_____. *Which Witness Is Right?* Vancouver, B.C., Canada: pub. by author, n.d., 2 pp. (On salvation).

Wheatley, H.A. *Jehovah's Witnesses vs. the Witness of Jehovah.* Camden, NJ: Grace Bible Institute, n.d., 6 pp. (Covers Christ's deity, hell, soul, and the resurrection of Christ).

Whitaker, Harry. *Why I Am Not a Jehovah's Witness.* Birmingham, England: Christadelphian Auxiliary Lecturing Society, c. 1980, 10 pp. (Covers doctrines that the Watchtower accepts that Christadelphians do not).

WtBTS--*Jehovah's Witnesses: Their Position*. London, England.

_____. *British Branch*. 37 Craven Terrce, London, England.

Yuille, Glenn. *Doctrines of Devils*. Pontiac, MI: pub. by author, n.d., 3 pp. (Covers several what he calls cults including Jehovah's Witnesses).

Zellner, Harold T. *Each Day for a Year*. Nazareth, PA: pub. by author, n.d., 4 pp.

Zions Tower of the Morning Tract Publications. *Food for Thinking Jehovah's Witnesses*. Detroit, MI: n.d., 4 pp.

Zuck, Roy B. *Letter to a Jehovah's Witness*. Chicago: Moody Bible Institute, 1974, 6 pp. (reprinted from March 1973 issue of *Moody Monthly*). (Argues for the deity of Christ against the Watchtower's view).

Zwolle, Informatie-Centrum *Jehovah's Getuigen nemen het niet zo nauw met de waarheid!* n.d., 4 pp. (Jehovah's Witnesses play fast and loose with the truth!) (in Dutch).

F.   Unpublished Manuscripts

The following are papers which were presented at professional conventions (such as Maesen, Aguirre, Rogerson) or were circulated among Witnesses. Manuscripts written specifically to protest various practices of the Watchtower Society are listed in that section.

Aguirre, Benigno E. "Social Upheaval, Organizational Change, and Religious Commitment: The Jehovah's Witnesses in Cuba 1938-1965." Presented at the 54th Meeting of the Southwestern Sociological Association.

Alston, Jon P., and David G. Johnson. "Cross-Culture Analyses of Missionary Success Among the Mormons, Jehovah's Witnesses, and Seventh-Day Adventists." Presented at Society for Scientific Study of Religion meeting, Oct. 1979, 33 pp.

Fields, Karen. "Witnessing for Jehovah in Colonial Zambia. An unquiet Mission." Paper presented at the Society for the Scientific Study of Religion Annual meeting, 1982?

Maesen, William August. "Cryptic Ambiguity and Belief-System Formulation: An Exploratory Study Viewing Watchtower Influence Upon Black Muslim Eschatology." Presented at the Michigan Sociological Association in Kalamazoo, MI, on Nov. 21, 1969, 15 pp. Mimeo.

_____, and Lawrence La Fave. "Conflict Resolution as Empirical Refutation of the Iron Law of Oligarchy." Presented at the annual meeting of the Southeastern Psychological Association, Louisville, KY, April 24, 1970, 9 pp. Mimeo.

Rogerson, Alan Thomas. "A Study of Educational Theory and Practice in the Sect of Jehovah's Witnesses Since 1945 with Special Reference to Education Beyond High School Age." Univ. of Cambridge, 1970.

G. Newsletters and Magazines on Jehovah's Witnesses

The following section includes newsletters and magazines which discuss primarily Jehovah's Witnesses; many of them are no longer in existence. The only one printed by Witnesses is the *Ham Association Newsletter*, which contains useful information about the Witnesses as a movement. Probably the most useful are William Schnell's (no longer published) and E.B. Price's papers (also no longer published), *Comments from the Friends* and *Bethel Ministries Newsletter*.

Association d' Infomration et d' Etude Sur les Témoins de Jéhovah tri-monthly (in French), Ap. 1990 (No. 1) to date most issues 24 pp.

Beisner, Jack (Ed.). *The Christian Research Institute Newsletter.* later Gretchen Passantino, then Howard Pepper. Vol. 1, No. 1, Winter 1979 to date, published quarterly, usually 8-12 pp. long. Discusses cults as a whole. The name was changed to *Forward* with vol. 2, No. 1 issue.

Frye, Ronald. *The Christian Respondent.* Vol. 1, May 1984, to Ap. 1991.

_____. *The Christian Challenge.* Vol. 1, July 1989 to date.

Guindon, Ken (Ed.). *Pros Aponolian.* Vol. 1, NO. 1, Sept.-Oct. 1974 to Vol. 3, No. 4, Oct-Dec. 1976, usually published bimonthly, each about 4-8 p. long.

Henke, David (Ed.). *Watchman Fellowship Newsletter.* Columbus, GA, May/June 1980 to date, 3 pp.

Jehovah's Witnesses HAM Association. A newsletter published monthly, each 2-4 pp. long; first issue about May 1969. Primarily contains information about HAM radio operation, but also discusses Witness activities and persons.

Lapin, Ron M.D. (Ed.). *The Journal of Bloodless Medicine and Surgery.* Vol. 1, No. 1, to date (quarterly) about 60 pages per issue. (Contains medical reports about bloodless surgery techniques, successes and failures).

_____. *Lifeline.* Vol. 1, No. 1. Winter Quarter 1981, 4 pp. 8.5 X 11 Quarterly. (Newsletter about the Bloodless Surgery institute of California).

Magnani, Duane. *New Light Gazette.* Volume 1, Number 1 (Spring 1997) 8 pp.

Morse, Keith (Ed.). *Personal Freedom Outreach.* St. Louis, MO, Vol. 1, No. 1 (April-June 1972) to date, 6 pp. each.

Müller, Willy (Ed.). *Christliche Verantwortung.* Founded 1959, 81 issues as of April 1976. Published bimonthly.

Pollina, Sergio and Achille, Aveta (Ed.) *COGIT Appunti Di Esegesi Biblica e Note Sui M.R.A* (An Italian newsmagazine about the Watchtower, covers a variety of material).

Price, E.B. (Ed.). *Witness.* Vol. 1, No. 1, March-April 1975 to date, published quarterly, usually 16-30 pp. in length. A magazine published by the Lay Activities Dept. of Victorian Conference of Seventh-Day Adventists of Victoria, Australia.

Raines, Ken (Ed). *J.W. Research Journal* Vol. 1 No. 1. Winter 1994 to date (published 4 issues a year mostly extensively footnoted and research articles).

Reed, David (Ed.). *Comments From the Friends.* Vol. 1, No. 1, 1981, quarterly, 16 pp. covers only Jehovah's Witnesses. (Much excellent news material).

Ross, Jonathan. *The Arian Conditionalist Newsletter.* Quarterly since 1984. 20-30 pp. (Much on Witnesses and Bible Students, mainly a scissors and paste production culled from various sources).

Schnell, William Jacob. (Ed.). *The Converted Jehovah's Witness Expositor.* Vol. 1, No. 1, 1958 to Vol. 8, No. 7 1969, usually published bimonthly; most issues about 12 pp. long. (Most all articles are by Schnell, much focus on doctrine; Schnell was in charge of the Watchtower Pioneer desk, supervising the American pioneer work, and also worked at the legal desk, and was a Zone Servant. He left the Society in April, 1952 after 30 years involvement and died on June 12, 1973 of Leiomysocarcomatoses).

Trombley, Charles (Ed.). *The Expositor.* Vol. 1, No. 1, First quarter 1963 to c. 1975, published quarterly, each about 24 pp. long. (Charles Trombley was an active Witness for 20 years until about 1964 when he left the movement).

_____. *Rhema: Sword of the Spirit.* Vol. 1, No. 1, Aug. 1976 to date, usually published monthly, some issues combined, usually 4 pp. long. (This newsletter deals less and less with the Witnesses, and later issues largely covers Trombley's charismatic ministry activities, especially in Africa).

Twisselman, Hans *Brucke Zum Menchen* Issued Quarterly. The 4th Issue of 1996 was number 128. 26 pp. Well done critiques of the Watchtower.

Van Buskirk, Mick (Ed.). *Christian Apologetics: Research and Information Service Newsletter.* Vol. 1, No. 1, Dec. 1976/Jan. 1977 to Vol. 3, No. 2, Third Quarter 1979, was published occasionally (About four times a year), each issue is about 8-12 pp. long.

Warner, Bill (Ed.). *Christian Apologetics Project News.* Vol. 1, No. 1, to Vol. 3, No. 1 (Jan. 1983), published quarterly, each issue is about 8-12 pp. long. Discusses cults in general.

Watters, Randall. *Bethel Ministries Newsletter.* Vol. 1, No. 1, Aug. 1982. Vol. 2, No. 5, Sept-Oct. 1983, called *Bethel Ministries, Inc.* as of Vol. 1, No. 4, 1992 and now called *Free Minds Journal,* 8.5 by 11 inch 12 page bimonthly (March-April 1992 issue is Vol. 11, No. 2). (Publishes many letters from readers and short research articles).

Wetter, Werner (Ed.) *Christen.* Wurtt, West Germany, Vol. 1, 1975 (?), to date. (Many articles critical of the Watchtower, but also include other material).

H. Reviews of the *New World Translation*

For minor reviews or comments, see the previous sections.

Barclay, W. "An Ancient Heresy in Modern Dress." *Expository Times,* Nov. 1953.

Beck, W.F. *A Dialogue About Jehovah's Witness' Bible, The New World Translation.* Concordia Publishing House, 1965, 14 pp.

Brown, A.C. *Translation of the English Bible.* 1970, p. 51.

Bruce, F.F. *The English Bible: A History of Translations.* London, England: Lutterworth Press, 1961, p. 184.

Byington, Steven T. "N.W.T." *The Christian Century,* 67 (Nov. 1, 1950), pp. 1295-1296.

_____. "How Bible Translators Work." *The Christian Century*, 68 (May 9, 1951), pp. 587-589.

_____. "Jehovah's Witnesses' Version of the O.T." *The Christian Century*, 70 (Oct. 7, 1953), pp. 1133-1134.

_____. "New World Old Testament." *The Christian Century*, 72 (Oct. 5, 1955), p. 1146

Countess, Robert H. "The Translation of THEOS in the New World Translation." *Bulletin of the Evangelical Theological Society*, 10 (Summer 1967), p. 160.

Dennett, H. *A Guide to Modern Versions of the New Testament*, Chicago: Moody Press, 1966, pp. 111-113.

Goodrich, R.D. *The New World Translation of 1950--An Unbiased Evaluation.* No. 232, 4 pp., 232A, 1 p.

Gruss, Edmond C. *Apostles of Denial.* Presbyterian and Reformed Publishing Co., 1970, pp. 196-214.

_____. "The New World Translation of the Holy Scriptures." *The Bible Collector*, 7 (July-Dec. 1975), pp. 3-8.

Guindon, K.R. *Why A New World Translation of the Holy Scriptures?* Unpublished manuscript 39 pp.

Haas, Samuel S. "The New World Translation of the Hebrew Scriptures." *Journal of Biblical Literature*, 74 (March 1955), pp. 282-283.

Hatton, Max. "The New World Translation of the Bible." *Australian Record*, Vol. 78, May 20, 1974, pp. 6-7.

Hatton, M. *The New World Translation of the Bible.* 4 pp.

Heydt, Henry J. "Jehovah's Witnesses: Their Translation." *American Board of Missions to the Jews.* N.d., pp. 1-19.

Hills, M.T. *The English Bible In America.* 1962, pp. 410, 416-7.

Kubo, Sakae and Walter Specht. *So Many Versions?* 1975, pp. 88-105.

Lewis, Jack P. "The New World Translation of the Holy Scriptures." *The Spiritual Sword*, 6 No. 1 (Oct. 1974), pp. 32-36.

Light, Dennis W. "Some Observations on the New World Translation." *The Bible Collector*, 7 (July-Dec. 1971), pp. 8-10.

Martin, Walter R., and Norman H. Klann. *Jehovah of the Watch Tower.* Grand Rapids, MI: Zondervan Publ. House, 1956, pp. 142-161.

Mattingly, J.F. "Jehovah's Witnesses Translated the New Testament." *Catholic Biblical Quarterly,* 13, (Oct. 1951), pp. 439-443.

_____. *A Grossly Misleading Translation.* 3 pp.

McCoy, R.M. "Jehovah's Witnesses and Their New Testament." *Andover Newton Quarterly,* 3 (Jan. 1963), pp. 15-31.

Metzger, Bruce M. "Jehovah's Witnesses and Jesus Christ." *Theology Today,* 10 (April 1953), pp. 65-85.

_____. "Review of the *New World Translation of the Christian Greek Scriptures*." *Princeton Seminary Bulletin*, Vol. 44, No. 4, Spring 1951.

_____. "Review of the *New World Translation of the Christian Greek Scriptures*." *The Bible Translator*, 15 (July 1964), pp. 150-152.

Parkinson, James. *New Testament Manuscript and Translation Studies.* Published by author 1970, p. 28.

Reumann, John. *Four Centuries of the English Bible.* Philadelphia: Mullenberg Press 1961, p. 53.

Rotherham, Joseph.B. Review of Russell, Charles T. *The Divine Plan of the Ages* . Reviewed in *The Rainbow* Dec. 1886, pp. 507-517.

Rowley, H.H. "How Not to Translate the Bible.' *Expository Times*, 65 (Nov. 1953), pp. 41-42.

_____. "Jehovah's Witnesses' Translation of the Bible." 1881-1950 *Expository Times*, Vol. 67 (Jan. 1956), pp. 107-108.

Skilton, J.H. *The Translation of the New Testament Into English.* 1971, p. 125, 323-5, 337, 343-5, 348, 350, 352, xxxii (Ph.D. Dissertation).

Stedman, Ray C. "The New World Translation of the Christian Greek Scriptures." *Our Hope*, 60 (July 1953), pp. 29-39.

Stuermann, Walter E. "The Bible and Modern Religions: III. Jehovah's Witnesses." *Interpretation,* 10 (July 1956), pp. 339-346.

Sturz, Harry A. "Observations on the New World Translation." *The Bible Collector*, 7 (July-Dec. 1971), pp. 11-16.

Thomson, Alexander. "An Interesting New Version." *The Differentiator*, 14 (April 1952), pp. 52-57.

_____. "An Interesting New Version." *The Differentiator*, 16 (June 1954), pp. 131-136.

_____. "An Interesting New Version." *The Differentiator*, 17 (Dec. 1955), pp. 257-262.

_____. "Jehovah's Theocratic Organization." *The Differentiator*, 21 (June 1959), pp. 98-104.

Whittington, John. "A Review of the *New World 'Translation' of the Bible.*" *Thrust.* Vol. 1, No. 2, 1980, pp. 42-47.

Winter, Thomas N. "Review of the Kingdom Interlinear Translation" in *The Classical Journal*, Vol. 69, No. 4, April-May, 1974, pp. 375-376.

Wright, G.W. *Perversions and Prejudices of the New World Translation.* Star Bible & Tract Co., 80 pp.

I.   Court Cases Involving Jehovah's Witnesses

Witnesses have been taken before the courts thousands of times in the United States, Canada, and many other countries of the world. Thus, the cases listed here are all Supreme Court and the more important State court cases. It would be impossible to locate all court cases Witnesses have fought because most were in local courts.

Supreme Court Cases
From *The Supreme Court Reporter* listed according to topics.

1. SOLICITATION AND STATE ORDINANCE CASES

Lovell v. City of Griffin, 303 U.S. 444 (1938), pp. 444-453.
Schneider v. Irvinton, N.J., 308 U.S. 147 (1939), pp. 147-165.
Largent v. Texas, 318 U.S. 418 (1943), pp. 418-422.
Jamison v. Texas, 318 U.S. 413 (1943), pp. 413-417.
Martin v. City of Struther, (Ohio), 319 U.S. 141 (1943), pp. 141-157.
Prince v. Massachusetts, 321 U.S. 158 (1944), pp. 158-178. (In *Prince,* the court upheld a statute which prohibited children from distributing religious literature violation of child labor laws, as necessary to protect the states interest in child safety. The case involved a guardian who allowed her nine year-old ward to sell Witnesses' literature on city streets in accordance with both the guardian's and ward's religious beliefs. The guardian, Mrs. Prince, argued that the statute infringed on both her parental rights guaranteed under the due process clause and her freedom of religion under the first amendment. The court acknowledged that parents have the right to give children religious training. However, the the family unit is not above government regulation even against a claim of religious liberty, and that neither parental rights or freedom of religion is beyond limitation. The state has the right and obligation to protect children if their safety is endangered. As long as Massachusetts' labor statutes are necessary to protect children, the statues are constitutionally valid.)

2. PERMIT, PARK, AND PARADE CASES

Cox v. New Hampshire, 312 U.S. 569 (1941), pp. 569-178.
Niemtko v. Maryland, 340 U.S. 268 (1951), pp. 268-289.
Fowler v. Rhode Island, 345 U.S. 67 (1953), pp. 67-70.
Poulos v. New Hampshire, 345 U.S. 395 (1953), pp. 395-426.

3. SOUND DEVICES AND "FIGHTING WORDS" CASES

Cantwell et al. v. Connecticut, 310 U.s. 296 (1940), pp. 296-311.
Chaplinsky v. New Hampshire, 315 U.S. 568 (1942), p. 568-574.
Saia v. New York, 334 U.S. 588 (1948), pp. 558-572.

4. LIFE, LIBERTY, AND LICENSE TAXES CASES

Jones v. Opelika, 316 U.S. 584 (1942), pp. 584-624.
Murdock v. Jeannette, Pennsylvania, 319 U.S. 105 (1943), pp. 105-140.
Douglas v. City of Jeannette, 319 U.S. 157 (1943), pp. 157-181.
Busey et al v. District of Columbia, 319 U.S. 579 (1943), pp. 579-583.
Follett v. Town of McCormick, 321 U.S. 573 (1944), pp. 573-581.
Janice Paul v. Watchtower Bible and Tract Society of New York et al.

5. FLAG SALUTE CASES (Students).

Minersville School District v. Gobitis, 310 U.S. 586 (1940), pp. 586-607.
Taylor v. Mississippi, 319 U.S. 583 (1943), pp. 583-590.
West Virginia State Board of Education v. Barnette, 319 U.S. 624 (1943), pp. 624-671.
Mathews v. Hamilton, 320 U.S. 707 (1943).

6. PEDDLING AND PRIVATE PROPERTY CASES

Marsh v. Alabama, 326 U.S. 501 (1946), pp. 501-517.
Tucker v. Texas, 326 U.S. 517 (1946), p. 517-521.

7. CONSCRIPTION AND CONSCIENCE (C.O.) CASES

Falbo v. United States, 320 U.S. 549 (1944), pp. 549-561. (The Supreme Court in 1944
    considered the case of a Jehovah's Witness who had refused to report to Civilian
    Public Service. Falbo Claimed the order was illegal and that he should have been
    exempted in class IV-D, but the lower courts denied this difference. The Supreme
    Court denied judicial review because, by refusing to report, Falbo had not taken all
    the steps in the Selective Service process. The court reasoned that, had he reported
    as ordered, he might still rejected at the induction center.)

Estep v. United States, Smith v. United States, 327 U.S. 114 (1946), pp. 114-146. (This
    was a split decision, and of the original majority of 5, only 2 Justices remain on
    the court (Douglas and Black). Subsequent cases affirmed the right of judicial
    review after the administrative process has been exhausted.)

Gibson v. United States, Dodez v. United States, 329 U.S. 338 (1946), pp. 338-361.
    (Two Jehovah's Witnesses, who claimed they were ministers but were still
    ordered to Civilian Public Service, won a right to judicial review.)

Sunal v. Large, Alexander, Warden v. United States ex. rel. Kulick, 332 U.S. 174
    (1947), pp. 174-193.

Cox v. United States, 332 U.S. 442 (1947), pp. 442-459. (A 5-4 Supreme Court vote
    upheld a local broad's denial of IV-D to a Jehovah's Witness, despite the fact that
    Cox had been devoting all his time to his ministry and had no other employment.
    The court held that the denial of IV-D was final unless there was "no basis in fact"
    for the local board's action, and the narrow scope of judicial review was held to be
    similar to that available to registrants who claimed to have been improperly
    inducted and who sought habeas corpus. The court also declared that in criminal
    trials, a court's review of a local board's classification of a registrant was properly
    limited to the evidence which was before the local board.)
Dickinson v. United States, 346 U.S. 389 (1953), pp. 389-401.
Gonzales v. United States, 348 U.S. 407 (1955).
Witmer v. United States, 348 U.S. 375 (1955), pp. 375-384.
Sicurella v. United States, 348 U.S. 385 (1955), pp. 385-396.
Simmons v. United States, 348 U.S. 397 (1955), pp. 397-406.
Bates v. United States, 348 U.S. 966 (1955).
Simon v. United States, 348 U.S. 967 (1955).
DeMoss v. United States, 349 U.S. 918 (1955).
Patteson v. United States, 351 U.S. 215 (1956).
Johnston v. United States, 351 U.S. 315 (1956), pp. 215-224.
Gonzales v. United States, 364 U.S. 59 (1960), pp. 59-75.
Yenus v. United States, (1961).

Cases in *The Supreme Court Reporter* involving Jehovah's Witnesses.

1. *CONSCRIPTION AND CONSCIENCE (C.O.) CASES*

United States v. Grieme, Same v. Sadlock, 128 F. 2d 811 (1942), pp. 811-815.
Base v. United States, 129 F. 2d 204 (1942), pp. 204-210.
Goff v. United States, 135 F. 2d 610 (1943), pp. 610-613.
United States ex. rel. Hull v. Stalter, 151 F. 2d 633 (1945), pp. 633-639.
United States ex. rel. Arpaia v. Alexander, 68 F. Suppl. 820 (1946), pp. 820-823.
Knox v. United States, 74 S. Ct. 152 (1953), pp. 152-160.
Jewell v. United States, Thomas v. United States, 208 F. 2d 770 (1953), pp. 770-772.
United States v. Lowman, 117 F. Suppl. 595 (1954), pp. 595-598.
United States v. Edminston, 118 F. Supp. 238 (1954), pp. 238-240.
White v. United States, 215 F. 2d 782 (1954), pp. 782-791.
Tomlinson v. United States, 216 F. 2d 12 (1954), pp. 12-18.
Hacker v. United States, 215 F 2d 575 (1954), pp. 575-576.
Brown v. United States, 216 F. 2d 258 (1954), pp. 258-260.
Campbell v. United States, 221 F. 2d 454 (1955), pp. 454-460.
Witmer v. United States, 75 S. Ct. 392 (1955), pp. 392-397.
Sicurella v. United States, 75 S. Ct. 403 (1955), pp. 403-409.
Gonzales v. United States, 75 S Ct. 409 (1955), pp. 409-415.
Simmons v. United States, 75 S. Ct. 397 (1955), pp. 397-402.
United States v. Diercks, 223 F. 2d 12 (1955), pp. 12-15.
United States v. Ransom, 223, F. 2d 15 (1955), pp. 15-19.
Olvera v. United States, 223 F. 2d 880 (1955), pp. 880-884.
Rowton v. United States, 229 F. 2d 421 (1956), pp. 421-422.
United States v. Kahl, 161 (1956), pp. 161-166.
United States v. Capehart, 141 F. Supp. 708 (1956), pp. 708-719.
Capehart v. United States, 237 F. 2d 388 (1956), pp. 388-390.
Pate v. United States, 243 F. 2d 99 (1957), pp. 99-108.
United States v. Cheeks, 159 F. Supp. 328 (1958), pp. 328-330.
Manke v. United States, 259 F. 2d 518 (1958), pp. 518-524.
Wiggins v. Unites States, 261 F. 2d 113 (1958), pp. 113-119.
Rogers v. United States, 263 F. 2d 283 (1959), pp. 283-287.
United States v. Tettenburn, 186 F. Supp. 203 (1960), pp. 203-212.

2. *OTHER CONSCRIPTION CASES*

Amecus Brief of Watchtower 50 pp., Amis Curie of Christian Information Service, Inc.,
        26 pp. and response by Kelner and Kelner, 19 pp.
United States v. Peter Machin Fry. U.S. Court of Appeals, Second Court, Oct. Term
        1952. Appellant's Brief by Hayden C. Covington is 75 pp.

3. *BLOOD TRANSFUSION CASES*

People v. Labrenz, 104 North Eastern Reporter (2d) (Illinois, 1952), pp. 769-774.
Powell v. Columbia Presbyterian Medical Center, 49 misc. 2d 215, 216, 267 N.Y.S. 2d
        450, 451 (Sup. Ct. 1965).
United States v. George, 239 F. Supp. 752 (1965), pp. 752+.
Jehovah's Witnesses v. Kings County Hospital, 278 F. Supp. 488 (W.D. Wash. 1967),
        pp. 488-502. Affirmed 278 N.E. 2d 919 (N.Y. 1972).
John F. Kennedy Memorial Hospital v. Heston, 47 Notre Dame Law 571 (1972).
Sampson, 317 N.Y.S. 2d 641 (Fam. Ct. Ulster Cy. 1970); affirmed, 323 N.Y.S. 2d 253
        (A.D. 2d 1971); affirmed 278 N.E. 2d 919 (N.Y. 1972).
Green, 286 A. 2d 681 (Pa Super. 1971); 293 A. 2d 387 (Pa. 1972); 307 A. 2d 279 Pa.
        1973).
Foxmire v. Nicoleau 75 N.Y. 2d 218, 222, 551 N.Y.S. 2d 876, 877.
The Public Health Trust of Dade County Florida v. Norma Wons. Case 86-985, 22 pp.
        (1990).

4. *EMPLOYMENT CASES* (loss of job because of Witness faith or practice).

Lincoln vs. True, U.S. District Court, Kentucky, June 3, 1975, No. C74-483 L(A),
   reprinted in *Fair Employment Practice Cases,* Washington, DC, The Bureau of
   National Affairs, Inc., Vol. 13, 1977, pp. 199-200.

Redmond vs. GAF Inc., U.S. Court of Appeals, Seventh Circuit (Chicago), April 10,
   1978, No. 76-1839, reprinted in *Fair Employment Practice Cases,* Washington, DC,
   the Bureau of National Affairs, Inc., Vol. 17, 1978, pp. 208-213.

Gavin, Charles R. vs. Peoples Natural Gas Co. In *Employment Practice Decision,*
   Chicago, Commerce Clearing House, Inc., 1979, Vol. 19, pp. 6431-6440, Para.
   9033.

Thomas vs. Review Board of the Indiana Employment Security Division, 79-952 (April
   6, 1981), 21 pp.; Supreme Court of Indiana 391 N.E. 2nd 1127 (1979) also 450 U.S.
   707 (1981).

EEOC Decision ¶6645, No. 76-60, Nov. 20, 1975, in *Employment Practice Decisions,*
   Chicago, Commerce Clearing House, 1980, Vol. 20.

Palmer v. Board of Ed. of City of Chicago, 466 F. Supp. 600 (1979), pp. 600-605. An
   elementary teacher who was fired for not saluting was upheld. Brief submitted to
   Supreme Court Oct. Term, 1979, printed in booklet form, typeset, No. 79-738. The
   Supreme Court refused to hear the case, thus letting the lower court decision stand.
   For EEOC decision, see Vol. 22, *Employment Practices Decisions,* ¶30, 692-30, 694,
   pp. 14, 638-14, 644.

Miscellaneous American Cases

Nicholson v. Merstetter, 68 Missouri Appeal Reports, Oct. Term 1897, Vol. 68, pp. 441-
   447. (In this case J.F. Rutherford was accused of illegally taking possession of a cash
   register).

Moyle v. Rutherford, 261 App. Div. 9698, 26 N.Y.S. 2d 860. Kings County Clerk
   Index, 1992, 15845 (1940).

Moyle v. Franz et al. (Appeal of above case) 267 Ap. Div. 423, 46 N.Y.S. (2d) 667,
   aff'd, pp. 666-677, 293 N.Y. 842, 59 N.E. (wd) 437 (1944). The printed transcript
   is 3 volumes of pages. Moyle was an attorney for the Society but left because of what
   he perceived as un-Christian practices at Bethel. The Society twice printed an
   announcement regarding his leaving and Moyle sued for slander and won. (*60 Sup.
   Ct. Reporter 1010, Vol. 60, No. 15, June 15, 1940*). The original transcript was
   reprinted by Wm. Centnar, Photo reproduction in one Vol.

Rutherford v. United States, U.S. District Ct., Eastern District of New York, June Term
   of 1918 (June 20, 1918; District Judge Harland S. Howe). Rutherford and six board
   members were convicted of sedition. The court record, all 1,493 pages, was
   reprinted by Witness, Inc., in 1984 (2 Vol., paper).

Rutherford et al. v. United States, 258 Fed. Rep. 855 (1919), pp. 855-867. An appeal to
   reverse the decision of the District Court of United States for the Eastern District of
   New York. Rutherford won the appeal, 2 to 3. The case was later dismissed and the
   charges dropped. Many lesser members, however, went to jail and served full terms
   for their part in distributing the offending materials. See Shaffer v. United States, 255
   Fed. 886 (9th Cir. 1919); Stephens v. United States, 261 Fed. 590 (9th Cir. 1919);
   Hamm v. United States, 261 Fed. 907 (9th Cir. 1920); Sonnenberg v. United States,
   264 Fed. 327 (9th Cir., 1920).

John v. Arizona, 319 U.S. 103 (1943).

Local Freedom of Religion Cases

Watchtower Bible & Tract Soc. v. Metropolitan Life I. Co., 69 N.Y.S. 2d 385 (1947), pp. 385-394. This is a "right to proselytize" court case.

People v. Mastin, 80 N.Y.S. 2d 323 (1948), pp. 323-329. The Watchtower Society in this case tried to gain tax-exempt status partly because a large amount of products of the farms were sold to the public.

People ex. rel. Watchtower Bible and Tract Society v. Haring, 8 N.Y. 2d, pp. 350-358, Nov. 17, 1960; also in 207 *New York Supplement 2nd Series*, pp. 673-679.

State ex rel. Wilson & Shadman v. Russell, Police Chief, City of Clearwater (unanimous opinion of Florida Supreme Court April 8, 1941).

Hibshman v. Kentucky (Pike Circuit Court opinion March 17, 1941).

Rosco Jones v. City of Opelika (Alabama Court of Appeals opinion March 19, 1941).

People v. Kieran, 26 NYS 2d 291.

People v. Kudovici, 13 NYS 2d 88.

People v. Guthrie, 26 NYS 2d 289.

Tucker v. Randall, 15 A 2d 324 (New Jersey).

Commonwealth v. Anderson, 32 NE 2d 684.

Roland Lefebvre (unanimous opinion N.H. Supreme Court May 6, 1941). (The lower court committed the Lefebvre children who had been expelled from school for refusal to salute the flag to reform school. In May, 1941, the State of New Hampshire Supreme Court held that Jehovah's Witnesses were not acting contrary to the law when they refused to salute the flag and that expulsion from school for such refusal did not constitute juvenile delinquency or a violation of the law, and therefore released the children.)

California v. Northum, 108 Cal. Supp. 295.

South Holland (Illinois) *v. Stein*, 26 NE 2d 868.

Thomas v. Atlanta (Georgia), 1 S F. 2d 592.

Cincinnati v. Mosier, 61 Ohio App. 81.

Semansky v. Stark, Sheriff (Louisiana), 199 So 129.

People v. Sandstrom, 279 N Y 523.

City of Portsmouth (Ohio) *v. Stockwell* (opinion Court of Appeals Fourth District of Ohio, November 1940).

In re Jones, N Y S 2d 10.

De Berry v. City of La Grange (Georgia), 8 S E 2d 146.

City of Gaffney (S.C.) *v. Putnam* (opinion by South Carolina Supreme Court June 2, 1941).

Zimmerman v. Village of London (opinion by U.S. District Court Southern District of Ohio, April 25, 1941.

Reid v. Brookville et al. (Opinion by U.S. District Court for the Western District of Pennsylvania, May 2, 1941.

Douglas v. Jeanette (Opinion by U.S. District Court for the Western District of Pennsylvania, May 2, 1941.

Kennedy v. City of Moscow (opinion by U.S. District Court of Idaho, May 14, 1941).

State ex rel. Hough v. Woodruff, Police Chief (opinion by Florida Supreme Court, May 27, 1941.

Swaggert Ministries vs. Board of Equalization of California. Supreme Court of the United States No 88-1374 (Brief filed by the Watchtower argued in favor of Swaggart as to taxing religious literature) Submitted by James M. McCabe and Donald T. Ridley, both Watchtower attorneys.

Custody Cases

John McRay Mollish v. Doris Ann Mollish, 494 S.W. 2d 145-153.

Salvagio v. Barnett, TX Civ. App 248, S.W. 2d 244, 247.

Prince v. Mass. 321 U.S. 158 (1944).

Pogue v. Pogue, 89 Pa D. & C. 588 (1954)

Robertson v. Robertson, 19 Wash App 425, 575 p. 2d 1092 (1978).

Morris v. Morris, 271 Pa Super. 19, 412 A. 2d 139 (1979)
Felton v. Felton, 383 Mass. 232, 418 N.E. 2d 606 (1981).
Bentley v. Bentley, 86 A.D. 2d 926, 448 N.Y.S. 2d 559 (1982).
LeDoux v. LeDoux, 234 Neb. 479, 452 N.W. 2d (1990).

Court Cases Involving C. T. Russell

Marie F. Russell v. Charles T. Russell. No. 202 April Term, 1908. Appeal C.P. No. 1 Allegheny Co., filed Oct. 19, 1908, 8 pp.

Marie F. Russell v. Charles T. Russell. No. 459 June Term, 1903. Court of Common Pleas No. 1, Allegheny Co. Summary filed Sept. 1908, 4 pp. This is the famous Russell divorce case.

Marie F. Russell v. Charles T. Russell. No. 459 June Term, 1903. Application for trial by jury filed Dec. 7, 1903. Response (on the above case) by C.T. Russell, 3 pp.; opinion (on the above case against Russell) by J. Macfarlane, 5 pp.; response by C.T. Russell, 3 pp.; F.I. F.A. Nov. 30, 1908, 3 pp.; answer to sheriff's interpleader, 1 p.

Charles T. Russell v. Brooklyn Eagle (Defendant) No. 12, 462, Sup Ct., App. Div. 2d, 1911, p. 236.

Russell v. Russell, 37 Pa. Superior Ct. 348 (1908), pp. 348-354. Mrs. Russell went back to court to insure Russell's payment of her alimony.

Marie F. Russell v. Charles T. Russell. No. 202 April Term, 1908. Appeal C.P. No. 1 Allegheny Co. filed Oct. 19, 1908, 8 pp.

Canadian Cases

Rex v. Kinler et al., St. Fracais, 1925, Sept. 10. From *Quebec Official Law Reports (Superior Court)*, Vol. 63, 1925 (p. 483), 2 pp.

Robert Donald v. Board of Education for the City of Hamilton, A.S. Morris and C.B. Hoyce, Trial at Hamilton, delivered Sept. 12, 1944, 9 pp.

Robert Donald v. Board of Education for the City of Hamilton, et al. Court of Appeal, delivered June 6, 1945, 9 pp.

Robert Donald v. Board of Education for the City of Hamilton, A.W. Morris, and C.B. Hoyce, The Supreme Court of Ontario, June 6, 1945. O.R., 3O.L.R. 424 O.W.N. 526 Reversing O.R. 475 4 D.L.R. 227 O.W.N. 559 (1944).

Walter Lloyd Evans v. The King, the County Court of the County of Simcoe, Nov. 8, 1945, 4 pp.

Greenless v. Attorney General for Canada, Court of Appeal, delivered Dec. 26, 1945, 7 pp.

Eustice W. Kite v. Rex, The County Court of Manaimo, Holden at Manaimo, June 7, 1949, 8 pp. 2. W.W.R. 195, 8 C.R. 278 95 C.C.C. 67.

Boucher v. The King, 1949.

His majesty the King on the Information of Joseph Mackie v. George Naish, Police Magistrate's Court, Saskatoon, Sask., Feb. 18, 1950, 13 pp. 1 W.W.R. 987.

Esymier v. Edmond Roamin, Province of Quebec, District of Pontiac, No. 5201, Superior Court, Campbell's Bay, June 10, 1952, 7 pp.

Saumer v. City of Quebec, 1953, 1952?

Esymier Chaput v. Edmond Roain et al., Providence of Quebec, District of Montreal, No. 4873, Court of Queen's Bench (in Appeal), 6 pp. Appeal side, 1 p., July 1954.

Chabot v. Roman, 1955.

Chabot v. School Commissioners of Lamorandiere Q.B. 707, 12 D.L.R. (2nd) 796 (C.A.). 1957.

Cajeten Chabot v. Les Comissaires d'Ecoles de la morandiens and The Honourable Attorney General for the Province of Quebec, Province of Quebec, District of Quebec, No. 5156, Court of Queen's Bench (Appeal Side), n.d., 11 pp.

Frank Grundy v. The King, 12 pp. (Appendix "A." 10 pp).

Mario Furland v. La Cité de Montréal, Provine de Quebec, District de Montréal, No. 164 (m), (Cour du Banc du Roi Jurisdiction d'Appel), 5 pp.

J.B. Duval et al. v. His Majesty the King, Province of Quebec, District of Montreal, No. 232, Court of King's Bench (Appeal Side), 12 pp.

Forsyth v. Children's Aid Society of Kingston O.R. 49, 35 D.L.R. (2nd) 690, 1963.

Australian Case

Adelaid Company of Jehovah's Witnesses, Inc., v. The Commonwealth (1943) 67 C.L.R.

Scottish Case

Douglas Walsh vs the Right Honorable James Latham Clyde, M.P., P. C., Scotland, 1954, 762 pp. (contains testimony of Covington, Franz, Suiter, Hughes, Chitty and Hopley. The entire transcript has been reprinted by Witnesses Inc., Clayton, CA.).

MAGAZINE AND JOURNAL ARTICLES

This section is divided into the following topics: (1) the blood issue, (2) court cases, legal problems, and persecution (3) the flag salute issue, (4) sociological and psychological studies (5) history and (6) theology and doctrine. Many articles fall into the news category, i.e., reporting of a specific court trial or a discussion of some blood transfusion cases. Those in professional journals, such as the *American Political Science Review* and the *American Journal of Sociology*, tend to be the most accurate, and those in popular magazines such as the *Saturday Evening Post* tend to be the least, and are sometimes blatantly incorrect. Articles in popular religious magazines discuss primarily theological matters, and, unfortunately, many of the writers have a poor understanding of the religious beliefs, doctrines, faith, and practice of the Witnesses.

Magazine and journal articles are extremely useful because they report events as they happen, and thus strongly reflect the current *zeitgeist*. One can glean the flavor of how the Witnesses were received historically by the public, and especially the press, by reviewing articles printed in the 1930s and 1940s in *Newsweek, Time, Saturday Evening Post,* etc. While the Witnesses are not always treated much more courteously in the public press today, in the 1930s and 1940s they were often seen as dangerous, or at least on the lunatic fringe, attracting mostly misfits and oddballs. The Witnesses are slowly becoming much more respectable, more middle class, better organized, wealthier, and a permanent part of the American religious scene. Authors who are unknown (this is often the case in short, one-page news articles) are listed under the article title.

A. The Blood Issue (both medical and legal aspects)

Ackerman, Terrance. "The Limits of Beneficence: Jehovah's Witnesses and Childhood Cancer." *The Hastings Center Report,* 10 (4) Aug. 1980.

"Adult Jehovah's Witnesses and Blood Transfusion." *Journal of the American Medical Association*, 219 (11) 273-274 1972.

"Adult patient Compelled to Take Blood Transfusion Contrary to Religious Belief." *Catholic Lawyer*, 10: 260-263 Summer 1964.

Aguilera, P. "Transfusiones de sangre en Testigos de Jehova." *Revista Medica de Chile*, 121 (4): 447-51 April, 1993. (Blood transfusions in Jehovah's Witnesses.) (concludes physicians should respect the rights of adults to refuse transfusions but disregard the parents rejection).

Akingbola, O.A., J.R. Custer, T.E. Bunchman, A.B. Sedman. "Management of Severe Anemia Without Transfusion in a Pediatric Jehovah's Witness Patient." *Critical Care Medicine*, 22 (3) 524-8 Mar., 1994.

Aldea, G.S. et al. "Effective Use of Heparin-Bound Circuits and Lower Anticoagulation for Coronary Artery Bypass Grafting in Jehovah's Witnesses." *Journal of Cardiac Surgery*, 11(1): 12-27, 1996.

"The All Writs Statute and the Injunctive Powers of a Single Appellate Judge." *Michigan Law Review*, 64: 324-365.

Alvik, A. "Jehovas Vitner. Blodoverfocing mot Pasientens Vilje." *Tidsskrift for Den Norske Laegeforening,* 116 (18): 2216, 1996 Aug 10. (Jehovah's Witnesses. Blood Transfusion against the Patient's Will) [Norwegian]

Amonic, Robert, et. al. "Hyperbaric Oxygen Therapy in Chronic Hemorrhagic Shock." *Journal of the American Medical Association*, 208 (11) 2051-2054 June 16, 1969.

Amor, Alegre A., et al. "Emergency transfusion in an under age patient in a Jehovah's Witness family. What does the current law indicate?" *Medical Clinics (Barcinola)*, 1988, Sept, 10; 91(7):275. (Spanish).

Anderson, Cerisse. "Hospital to Appeal Blood Transfusion Case." (New York) 201 *New York Law Journal*, Jan. 10, 1989.

_____. "Jehovah's Witness Loses Blood-Sample Defense." (New York), Vol. 201 *New York Law Journal,* Feb. 23, 1990.

_____. "Legislation Urged on Issue of Treatment: Minors' doctrine suggested in ruling on transfusion." (New York) Vol. 203 *New York Law Journal*, May 23, 1990.

Anderson Gary R. "Medicine vs. Religion: The Case of Jehovah's Witnesses." *Health & Social Work*, 8(1) 31-38, Winter 1983.

Andreassen, M. "Transfusion and Jehovah's Witnesses." *Ugeskr Laeger*, 138 (30) 1847-1848 July 19, 1976 (Danish).

Annexton, May. "Autotransfusion for Surgery: A Comeback." *Journal of the American Medical Association*, 240 (25) 2710-2711, Dec. 15, 1978.

Aradine, C.R. "A Faculty Nurse Responds: Identify the Issues." *Journal of Christian Nursing*, 4 (2) 14-15 Spring, 1987 (A review of the problem of patient rejection of transfusions from a nurses view).

_____. "Conflict: Religious Belief v. Emergency Care...Patients Who Have Refused to Consent to Life-Saving Blood Transfusions." *Emergency Nurse Legal Bulletin*, 8 (4) 2-9. Fall, 1982.

"Are Jehovah's Witnesses Right?" *Ugeskr Laeger,* 150 (39): 2356-2357. Sept. 26, 1988 (Danish).

Asbill, M.C., et al. "A Jehovah's Witness with thrombocytopenia." *Hospital Practitioner*, Sept. 19(9):82CC, 82GG, 82KK. Sept. 1984.

Asser, Seth M. and Rita Swan. "Child Fatalities From Religion-motivated Medical Neglect." *Pediatrics.* 101(4):625-629. April, 4 1998.

Atabek, U.; R. Alvarez; M J. Pello; J.B. Alexander; R.C.Camishion; C. Curry; and R.K. Spence. "Erythropoitin accelerates Hematocrit Recovery in Post-Surgical Anemia." *American Surgeon* 61 (1): 74-77, 1995 Jan.

"Authorization of Involuntary blood Transfusion for Adult Jehovah's Witness Held Unconstitutional." *Michigan Law Review,* Jan. 1966, 64: 554-561.

"Autotransfusion and Jehovah's Witnesses: Abstract." *Linacre Quarterly, Nov.* 1964, 31: 222.

Azuno, Y. and K.Kaku, "Percutaneous Nephrolithotripsy Supported by Recombinant Factor VIII in a Patient With Hemophilia A, a Jehovah's Witness" *Rinsho Ketsueki-- Japanese Journal of Clinical Hematology.* 36 (12): 1337-1341, 1995 Dec. [Japanese]

"Baby Dies as Parents Rule Out Transfusions." *Cleveland News.* Jan. 15, 1954.

Back, B., G. Place, J. Benichou, P. Testas and Y. Noviant, "Surgery of the Esophagus under Hemodilution and Autotransfusion in a Jehovah's Witness." *Anesthesie Analgesie Reanimotologiya,* Jan.-Feb. 1976,33 (1): 135-145.[French]

Bailey, Charles. "Management of the Major Surgical Blood Loss Without Transfusion." *Journal of the American Medical Association,* Dec. 12, 1966, 198 (11): 1171-1174.

_____. "Open Heart Surgery Without Blood Transfusion." *Vascular Diseases,* Dec. 1968, 5 (4): 179-187.

_____. "Electrolyte Solution in Surgical Patients Refusing Transfusion." *Journal of the American Medical Association,* March 29, 1971,215 (13): 2077-2083.

Bamberger, David H. "Mercy Hospital, Inc. v. Jackson: A Recurring Dilemma for Health Care Providers in the Treatment of Jehovah's Witnesses." *Maryland Law Review,* Spring 1987,46: 514-532.

Barker, Jason. "Bulgaria and Blood." *Watchman Expositor.* 15(3):18-20 1998. (About the Watchtower now allowing Witnesses in Bulgaria to take transfusions)

Barnard, Jim. "Artificial Blood: Medical Breakthrough That Will Save Thousands-- Doctors Claim Miracle Blood Has No Type--Anyone Can Use It." *National Examiner,* Jan. 8, 1980, p. 3.

Barnikel, W. "Blood Transfusion and Patient's Consent." *Deutsche Medizinische Wachen-Schrift,* March 26, 1979, 104 (13): 330-331. [German]

Barton, Frank. "The Battle Over Blood." *Today's Health,* Feb. 1966, pp. 44, 46, 79, 80.

Bausch, L.C. "Blood Transfusions and the Jehovah's Witness--Neonatal Perspectives." *Nebraska Medical Journal,* Aug., 1991, 76 (8): 283-4.

Beall, Arthur C., et al. "Physiological Studies during Cardiopulmonary Bypass Eliminating Hepernized Blood." *Diseases of the Chest,* Jan. 1965,47 (1): 7-16.

_____. "Open Heart Surgery Without Blood Transfusion." *Archives of Surgery,* April 1967, 94: 567-570.

Bearb, M.E., et al. "Epidural blood patch in a Jehovah's Witness" *Anesthesiology Analg,* Oct, 1987, 66 (10): 052.

Begley, Grant F. "Religion Affects Practice of Medicine." *Texas Medicine,* Dec. 1970, 66: 25, 26.

Benfield, D.G. "Giving Blood to the Critically Ill Newborn of Jehovah's Witness Parents: The Human Side of the Issue." *Legal Aspects of Medical Practice,* June 1978,6 (6): 33-36.

Benson, K.T. "The Jehovah's Witness patient: considerations for the anesthesiologist."

Anesthelogy Analogues. Nov. 1989, 69 (5): 647-656. Reprinted in *Current Review for Nurse Anesthetists*, Oct. 18, 1990,13 (10): 75-80.

Berger, M.R. "Jehovah's Witnesses and the Problem With Blood." *Orthopedics*, Oct. 1990, 13 (10): 75-80.

Bergman, Jerry. "Thousands Go To Their Deaths Each Year." *Free Minds Journal*, 13 (5): 9-10, 1994.

_____. "The Watchtower, Quack Science and Homicide." *JW Research*, Winter, 2 (1): 3-6, 1995.

_____. "Aluminum: Satan's Metal and Killer of Millions? The Watchtowers Incredible Crusade Against Aluminum." *JW Research Journal* Fall 1996 3 (4): 9-25.

Bernstein, Sid. "Religion and Disease Debate." (ConSIDerations) (Column) *Advertising Age*, May 28, 1990, 61 (22): 24.

"Birthright." *Church and State*, Sept. 1964,17 (8): 9. (About transfusions and unborn).

Blajchman, M.A. "Transfusion-Related Issues in Jehovah's Witness Patients." *Transfusion Medicine Reviews*, Oct., 1991, 5 (4): 243-6.

Blogg, C.E., et al. "Surgery in Jehovah's Witnesses" (letter comment). *Canadian Journal of Anesthesiology*, Apr. 1990, 37 (3): 91-2.

Blomdahl, Rune. "Swedish Conscientious Objectors Win Bloodless Battle." *Liberty*, Nov.-Dec. 1978, 67: 18, 19.

"Blood for a Baby." *Newsweek*, April 30, 1951, p. 25.

"Blood Transfusion and Jehovah's Witnesses." *Nouvelle Presse Medicale*, May 1975, 4 (20): 513-1518.

"Blood Transfusion Court Case." *Church and State*, Jan. 1963, 16 (1): 13.

"Blood Transfusion Does Not Violate Bible Teachings." *Herald of the Coming Age*, June 1974, 24 (5): 16.

"Blood Transfusion--Jehovah's Witnesses." *Journal of the American Medical Association*, Feb. 23, 1957, pp. 660-661.

"Blood Transfusion Refused on Religious Grounds." *Anesthesia and Analgesia*, July-Aug. 1973, 52: 529-530.

"Blood Transfusions--Jehovah's Witnesses." *Medicine and the Law*, Feb. 23, 1975, 163 (8): 660, 661.

Bloodwell, D.R., et al. "Aortic Valve Replacement and Correction of Fetology of Fallot's tetralogy with Double Outlet Right Ventricle in a Jehovah's Witness: Case Report." Submitted for publication.

Blvhm, Reneta et al. "Aplastic Anemia Associated with Canthaxanthin Ingested for Tanning Purposes." *JAMA* 264 (9): 1141-1142. Sept. 5, 1990 (About a Witness who died due to refusing blood).

Boba, Antonio. "Support of Blood Volume During Operation Without Blood Transfusion." *Surgical Forum*, Oct. 1966, 17: 61-63.

Bock, R.W. "Juristischer Kommentar zur Ablehnung von Bluttransfusionen." *Anasthesiologie, Intensivmedizin, Notfallmedizin, Schmernztherapie*, 31 (8): 506-

507, 1996. (Legal Comment on Refusal of Blood Transfusions) [German]

Boggs, D.R. "Jehovah's Witnesses with Leukemia." *Hospital Practitioner*, Mar. 15, 1985, 20 (13): 92, 94-5, 98 .

Bolooki, H. "Treatment of Jehovah's Witnesses: Example of Good Care." *Miami Medicine*, 1981, 51: 25-26.

Bonakdar, Mostafa I., et al. "Major Gynecologic and Obstetric Surgery in Jehovah's Witnesses." *Obstetrics and Gynecology*, Nov. 1972, 60 (5): 87-590.

Bonnett, C.A., et al. "Total hip replacement in Jehovah's Witnesses under spinal anesthesia without transfusion." *Canadian Journal of Anesthesia*, Apr. 1990 37 (3):391-392. (Comment on *Canadian Journal of Anesthesia*, 1989, 36 (5): 578-585. .

_____. "Total hip replacement in Jehovah's Witnesses under spinal anesthesia without transfusion." *Orthopedic Review*, Jan. 1987,16 (1): 43-7.

Bortolotti, V., et al. "Open Heart Surgery in Jehovah's Witnesses." *Geornale Italiano de Cardiologia*, Bosomworth, Peter. 1979, 9 (9): 996-1000.

Bosomworth, Peter. "Replacement of Operative Blood Loss of More Than 1 Liter with Hartmann's Solution." *Journal of the American Medical Association*, Feb. 5, 1968,203 (6): 399-402.

Botero, C.; Smith, C.E. and Morscher, A.H. "Anemia and Perioperative Myocardial Ischemia in a Jehovah's Witness Patient." *Journal of Clinical Anesthesia*, 8 (5): 386-391, 1996 Aug.

Bowen, J.R., et al. "Posterior spinal fusion without blood replacement in Jehovah's Witnesses." *Clinical Orthopedist*, Sept. 1985, pp. 284-288.

Boyd, Marke E. "The Obstetrician and Gynaecologist and the Jehovah's Witness." *Journal of the Society of Obstetricians and Gynaecologists of Canada*, July/ August 1992, Guest Editorial, pp. 7-9.

Brace, J.W. "Treating Jehovah's Witnesses." *British Medical Journal*, Sep. 5, 1992, 305 (6583): 588-9. (Brace is a Watchtower official; in this letter, he tried to defend the Watchtower stand on blood transfusion.)

Brace, J.W. "Managing Patients Who Refuse Blood Transfusions. Register of Willing Consultants Exists [letter; comment]. *British Medical Journal* 309 (6952): 475, 1994.

Brahams, Diana. "Right to Refuse Treatment." *Lancet*, Aug., 1992, pp. 297-299.

_____. Jehovah's Witnesses Transfused Without Consent: A Canadian Case. *The Lancet*. 2(8676):1407-8 1989

Bratton, Robert. "The Right to Die: A Constitutional One?" *The Jurist*, Winter 1981, pp. 155-175.

Breig, J. "Tough to Be a Justice: Refusal of Blood Transfusions." *Ave Maria*, 98 (15) Nov. 2, 1963.

Bricker, D.L., et al. "Repair of Acute Dissection of the Ascending Aorta, Associated with Coagulation of the Thoracic Aorta in a Jehovah's Witness." *Journal of Cardiovascular Surgery*, May-June 1980, 21 (3): 374-378.

Brimacombe, J.; G. Clarke, and L. Craig. "Epidural Blood Patch in the Jehovah's Witness [letter]. *Anesthesia & Intensive Care*. 22 (3): 319, 1994 Jun.

Broccia, G. "Long-term Continuous Complete Remission of Acute Myeloid Leukemia in a Jehovah's Witness Treated Without Blood Support." *Haematologica*, Mar-Apr., 1994, 79 (2): 180-1.

Brodsky, J.W. et al. "Hypotensive anesthesia for scoliosis surgery in Jehovah's Witnesses" *Spine*, March, 1991, 16 (3): 304-306.

Brown, A.S., et al. "Fluosol-DA, a perfluorochemical oxygen-transport fluid for the management of a trochanteric pressure sore in a Jehovah's Witness" *Annals of Plastic Surgeon*, May, 1984,12 (5): 449-453.

Brown, Howard G. "Opinions of Trial Judges: Parental Right to Refuse Medical Treatment." *Crime and Delinquency*, 1965, pp. 377-385.

Brown, Tom. "The Courageous Last Days of Wife Who Sacrificed Her Life to Save Our Unborn Child." *National Inquirer*, July 15, 1980, p. 3.

Buie, Jim. "A Blood Feud; Jehovah's Witnesses and Judge Joust Over Group's Opposition to Blood Transfusions," *Church State*, Oct. 1983, pp. 8-9.

Bunte, H. "Ihr Patient ist Zeuge Jehovas." *Zentralblatt fur Gynakologie*, 117 (2): 113, 1995. (Your patient is a Jehovah's Witness) [German]

Bureau of Legal Medicine & Legislation. *Blood Transfusion: Court's Right to Order, People v. Labrenz.* 104 N.E. (2nd) 769 (Illinois, 1952).

Buresta, C., F. Mungo, and C. Cascio. "Alternative Methods to Blood Transfusion in General Surgery." *The Institute of Bloodless Medicine and Surgery*, Spring, 1983,1 (2): 37-38.

Burnett, C.M., et al. "Heart transplantation in Jehovah's Witnesses. An initial experience and follow-up." *Archives of Surgery*, Nov. 1990, 125 (11): 1430-1433.

Burrows, R., F. Fabian and E.M. Barker. "Emergency treatment of Jehovah's Witnesses." *South African Medical Journal*, Sept. 7, 1991, 80 (5): 218.

Busse, J. and Wesseling, C. "Tolerierung eines extremen intraoperativen Blutverlustes bei einer Zeugin Jehovas." *Anesthesiologie, Intensivmedizin, Notfallmedizin, Schmerztherapie*, 31 (8): 498-501, 1996 Oct. (Tolerating extreme intraoperative blood loss by a Jehovah's Witness patient). [German]

Busuttil, D. and Copplestone, A. "Management of Blood Loss in Jehovah's Witnesses [editorial]" *British Medical Journal* 311 (7013): 1115-1116, 1995 Oct 28.

Byrne, M.P. "Abdominal Aortic Aneurysm Surgery in the Jehovah's Witnesses." *Illinois Medical Journal*, July 1976, 150 (1): 87-90.

Cagne, C. "Connaitre et comprendre le temoin de Jehovah. 2e partie". *Revue de l Infirmiere*, 19: 60-64 and (1): 57-62, Jan 1995. (Knowing and Understanding a Jehovah Witness Patient) [French]

Calthorpe, D.A. "The Use of A Cell Saver in a Jehovah's Witness Undergoing major Cardiac Surgery." *Medical Journal*, Nov. 1983, 76 (11): 460-461.

Cantor, Norman L. "A Patient's Decision to Decline Life-saving Medical Treatment: Bodily Integrity vs. the Preservation of Life." *Rutgers Law Review*, 1973, 26: 228-264. Reprinted in Reiser (Ed) "Ethics in Medicine," Cambridge, MA: The MIT Press, 1977.

Carrizosa, Philip. "New Transfusion Trial Awaits; Jehovah's Witness Parents' Award Properly Voided, Appeal Court Rules" (California) *Los Angeles Daily Journal*, July

29, 1992, p. 3.

Carroll, P.A. "When A Jehovah's Witness Refuses A Transfusion" *Nursing*, 1995 Aug.25 (8): 60-61.

Carson, Jeffrey. "Severity of Anemia and Operative Mortality and Morbidity." *The Lancet*. April 7, 1988. pp. 727-729.

_____. "Morbidity Risk Assessment in the Surgically Anemic Patient." *The American Journal of Surgery* 170(6a): 328S-36S Dec. 1995

Celenza, Marlo. "Blood Transfusion and Jehovah's Witnesses and the Bible." *The New Creation*, 35(10): 10-15. Oct. 1975

Chaney, M.A. and M.K. Aasen. "Severe Acute Normovolemic Hemodilution and Survival." *Anesthesia & Analgesia*, Jun., 1993, 876 (6): 1371-2. (A letter and comment.).

Chikada, M.; A. Furuse; Y. Kotsuka and K. Yagyu. "Open-heart Surgery in Jehovah's Witness Patients." *Cardiovascular Surgery*. Jun 1966 4 (3): 311-314.

Clancy, Leo. "Inquirer Story of Bloodless Operation Helped Crippled Reader 'Walk Tall' Again." *National Inquirer*, Jan. 20, 1974, p. 6.

Clapp, Rodney. "The Jehovah's Witnesses Are a 'Killer Cult' Says a Defector." *Christianity Today*, Nov. 20, 1981,25 (20): 70, 72.

Claridge, Thomas. " MD's Transfusion may have saved life, but Jehovah's Witness wins $20,000." *The Globe and Mail,* December 24, 1987.

Clarke, J.F.M. "Surgery in Jehovah's Witnesses." *British Journal of Hospital Medicine*, 1982, 27: 497-500.

Cleveland, S.E. "Jehovah's Witnesses and Human Tissue Donation." *Journal of Clinical Psychology*, April 1976, 32 (2): 453-458.

Cockett, Abraham, et al. "Hyperbaric Oxygen Therapy in Chronic Hemorrhagic Shock." *Journal of the American Medical Association*, June 16, 1969, 208 (11): 2051-2054.

Cole, Bill. "Blood Specialist Claims ... Half of All Blood Transfusions in America Are Unnecessary." *National Inquirer*, March 6, 1975.

Coll, C.E. "Care of Jehovah's Witnesses." *Anesthesia*, May 1984, 39 (5): 497-498.

Collins, S.L. and G.A. Timberlake. "Severe Anemia in the Jehovah's Witness: Case Report and Discussion." *American Journal of Critical Care*, May, 1993, 2 (3): 256-9. (About the management of a Witness seriously injured in an airplane crash and who lost much blood.)

"Compulsory Medical Treatment and a Patient's Free Exercise of Religion." *Medical Legal Bulletin*, March 1975, 24 (3): 1-10.

Connolly, J.R., et al. "Total Hip Replacement in a Jehovah's Witness Using Hypotensive Anesthesia." *Nebraska Medical Journal,* Aug. 1977, 62 (8): 287-290.

Cooley, Denton, et al. "Open Heart Surgery in Jehovah's Witnesses." *The American Journal of Cardiology,* June 1964, 13 (6): 779-781

_____. "Physiologic Studies during Cardiopulmonary Bypass Eliminating Heparinized Blood." *Diseases of the Chest*, Jan. 1965, 47 (1): 7-16.

_____. "Cardiac Valve Replacement Without Blood Transfusion." *American Journal of Surgery*, Nov. 1966, 112: 734-751.

_____. "The Anesthesiologist and the Cardiac Surgeon." *Anesthesiology*, Aug. 1970, 33 (2): 126-127.

_____. "Vascular Surgery in Jehovah's Witnesses." *Journal of the American Medical Association* Aug. 10, 1970, 213 (6): 1032-1034.

_____. "Conservation of Blood During Cardiovascular Surgery." *American Journal of Surgery*, Dec.1995. 170 (6A Suppl): 53S-59S.

Cooper, J.R. "Perioperatie considerations in Jehovah's Witnesses." *International Anesthesiology Clinic*, Fall 1990, 28 (4): 210-215.

Cooper, P.D. "Managing Patients Who Refuse Blood Transfusions. Will Consent if Confidentiality Is Maintained. *British Medical Journal*, 309 (6952): 475, 1994 Aug. 13.

Cooper, R. and N. Quincy "Elective Surgery in an Anaemic Jehovah's Witness. *British Journal of Hospital Medicine*, 56 (2-3): 107-108, 1996.

Corno, A.F., et al. "Heart transplantation in a Jehovah's Witness." *Journal of Heart Transplantation*, Mar.-Apr. 1986, 5 (2): 175-177.

Coselli, J.S. Buket, S. and Van Cleve, G.D. "Successful Reoperation for Ascending Aorta and Arch Aneurysm in a Jehovah's Witness." *Annals of Thoracic Surgery*, 58 (3): 871-873, 1994 Sep.

"Court Orders Blood Transfusions for Twins over Mother's Objection." *Liberty*, Jan.-Feb. 1979, 67: 30.

"Court Orders Transfusion." *Church and State*, March 1966, 19 (3): 9.

"Court Refuses Ruling in Transfusion Dispute." *Hospital Progress*, Aug. 1974, 45: 12.

Cowart, Virginia Snodgrass. "Can 'Artificial Blood' Live Up to Public Billings?" *The Journal of the American Medical Association*, Feb. 26, 1982, 247 (8): 1104-1105.

Cox, M. and Lumley, J. "No Blood or Blood Products. [editorial]" *Anesthesia*, 50 (7): 583-585, 1995 July.

Craig, Douglas B. "Jehovah's Witness." *Canadian Journal of Anesthesia*, Sep., 1991, 38 (6): 801-2. (A letter about the problem of objections to blood transfusion; points out that a major problem is "informed refusal.")

Cullis, J.O., et al. "Jehovah's Witnesses with leukemia" (letter; comment). *Lancet*, Oct. 1990, 336 (8722): 1075-1076. Comment on: *Lancet* Vol. 336, No. 8714, Sept. 1990, pp. 563-564.

Cundy, J.M. "Jehovah's Witnesses and Hemorrhage." *Anesthesia*, 1980, 35: 1013-1014.

Curry, J. "Bloodless Surgery Meets Patients Needs for Alternatives." *O R Manager*, Jan. 1993, 9 (1):12-13.

Dalenius, E. "Blood Transfusion and Jehovah's Witnesses." *Lakartidningen* (Stockholm) Jan. 14, 1970, 67: 206-207.

Deitch, E.A.; Guillory, D. and Cruz, N. "Successful Use of Recombinant Human Erythropoitin in a Jehovah's Witness with a Thermal Injury." *Journal of Burn Care &*

Rehabilitation, 15 (1): 42-45, 1994 Jan-Feb.

Dean, Paul. "Nurse Refuses Transfusion, Dies." *Arizona Republic,* March 9, 1968.

DeTouzalin, H. "Refusal to Consent to a Treatment by the Parents of a Minor Child in Danger of Dying." *Nouvelle Presse Medicale*, May 17, 1975, 4 (20): 1515-1517.

Dixon, J.L. "Jehovah's Witnesses and Blood Transfusion." *Connecticut Medicine*, July 1975, 39 (7): 433-437.

Dixon, Lowell. "The Reason Why." *Ethicon*, Jan. 1973, 10 (7): 14, 15.

_____, and Gene Smalley. "Jehovah's Witnesses: The Surgical/Ethical Challenge." *The Journal of the American Medical Association*, Nov. 27, 1981, pp. 2471-2472. Reprinted in *Awake!*, June 22, 1982, pp. 25-27.

Doll, P.J. "Refusal of a Life-saving Transfusion: To What Extent May This Refusal by a Traffic Accident Victim Influence the Increase in Damages and Benefits Solicited by Those with a Right to Them?" *Nouvelle Presse Medicale*, May 17, 1975, 4 26): 1517-1518.

Donner, B.; M. Tryba; K. Kurz-Muller; P. Vogt; U. Steinau; M. Zenz, and U. Pern. "Anasthesiologisches and Intensivmedizinisches management bei Schwer Brandverletzten Kindern der Zugen Jehovas." *Anaesthesist*, 45(2): 171-175, 1996 Feb. (Anesthesia and Intensive Care Management of Severely Burned Children of Jehovah's Witnesses) [German]

Dor, V., et al. "Value of Extra-corporeal Circulation in Autoperfusion. Technical and Laboratory Problems in More Than 800 Cases Including 52 Jehovah's Witnesses." *Annales de Chirurgie-Thoracique et Cardiovasculaire* , Oct. 1977, 16 (4): 276-284.

Dor, V., Mermet B. Kreitmann P, et al. "Chirugie Cardiaque Chez les témoins de Jéhovah. A propose de 47 observations." *Archives Des Maladies Du Coeur et Vaisseurx* 70 (5): 549-59, May 1977 [French].

_____, et al. "Value of Extra-corporeal Circulation in Autotransfusion. Technical and Laboratory Problems in More Than 800 Cases Including 52 Jehovah's Witnesses." *Annales de Chirugie-Thoracique et Cardiovasculare* , Oct. 1977, 16 (4): 276-284. [French]

Dornette, W.H.L. "Jehovah's Witnesses and Blood Transfusion: The Horns of a Dilemma." *Anesthesiology Analogues*, 1973, 542: 272+.

Drew, N.C. "The Pregnant Jehovah's Witness." *Journal of Medical Ethics*, Sept. 1981, 7 (3): 137-139.

Drummond, Pauline. "Organizing a Bloodless Coup." News Focus Section of *The Health Service Journal*, 27 June 1991.

Duh, S.V. "Physician reaction to refusal of blood transfusions by Jehovah's Witnesses". *Journal of the National Medical Association*. May 79 (5): 467, 471, 1987.

Dumitru, A.P. "The Anesthesiologist and the Jehovah's Witnesses." *Anesthesia and Analgesia*, March-April 1965, 44: 197-198.

Dunphy, J.E. "Ethics in Surgery: Going Beyond Good Science." *Bulletin of the American College of Surgeons*, 63 (6): 12. 1978

Elton, A.; P. Honig; A Bentovim and J. Simons. "Withholding Consent to Lifesaving Treatment: Three Cases." *British Medical Journal*, 310 (6976): 373-377, 1995 Feb 11.

"Emergency Treatment of Jehovah's Witnesses." *South African Medical Journal*, Dec., 1991, 80 11-12): 626-8.

"Faith and Blood." *Time*, May 12, 1952, 59: 55.

Fatteh, M.M. "Jehovah's Witnesses, How Can We Help Them?" *Journal of the Medical Association of Georgia*, Dec. 1980, 69 (12): 977-979.

Fell, S.J. "Alternatives to Blood Transfusions for Jehovah's Witnesses and Others: Respecting a Patient's Right to Refuse Medical Treatment." *Medical Assistant*, Jan-Feb. 1993, 26 (1): 24-27.

Ferdinand, R. "Jehovah's Witnesses and Advance Directives." *American Journal of Nursing*, 96 (3): 64, 1996 Mar.

Fernstrom, V. "Blood Transfusion: Religious Faith Versus Medical Ethic." *Lakartidningen* (Stockholm), 1969,66 (19): 4834-4835.

Findley, Larry and Paul Redstone. "Blood Transfusion in Adult Jehovah's Witnesses: A Case Study of One Congregation." *Archives of Internal Medicine*, 1972, 142:606-607.

Findley, Larry, et al. "Jehovah's Witnesses and the right to refuse blood." *New York State Journal of Medicine*, Sept. 1988, 88 (9): 464-465.

Fishbein, Morris, ed. "What Does a New Heart Do to the Mind?' *Medical World News*, May 23, 1969, 10 (21): 17-18.

Fitts, William, et al. "Blood Transfusion and Jehovah's Witnesses." *Journal of Surgery, Gynecology and Obstetrics*, 959, 108 (3): 502-507.

Fletcher, J.L. Jr., J.C. Perez, and D.H. Jones. "Successful Use of Subcutaneous Recombinant Human Erythropoitin Before Cholecystectomy in an Anemic Patient with Religious Objections to Transfusion Therapy." *American Surgeon*, Nov., 1991, 57 (11): 697-700. (Use of recombinant made human erythropoitin in a Witness with end-stage renal disease.)

Flowers, Ronald B. "Freedom of Religion Versus Civil Authority in Matters of Health: On Matters of Blood." *Annals of The American Academy of Political and Social Science.* Nov. 1979, 446: 156-159.

Foley, W.J. et al. "Jehovah's Witnesses and the Question of Blood Transfusion." *Postgrad Medicine*, 1973, 53: 109+.

Folk, F.S., et al. "Open Heart Surgery Without Blood Transfusion." *Journal of the National Medical Association*, 1969, 61: 213-218.

Fontanarosa, P.B., G.T. Giorgio. "Managing Jehovah's Witnesses: Medical, Legal, and Ethical Challenges." *Annals of Emergency Medicine*, Oct., 1991, 20 (10): 1148-9.

Fontanarosa, P.B., et al. "The role of the emergency physician in the management of Jehovah's Witnesses." *Annals of Emergency Medicine*, Oct. 1989, 18 (10): 1089-1995.

Fontein, B.T. "Jehovah's Witnesses and blood transfusion." *Ned Tijdschr Geneeskd*, Apr. 1991, 135 (13): 618-622. (Dutch).

Ford, J.C. "Refusal of Blood Transfusions by Jehovah's Witnesses." *Linacre Quarterly*, Vol. 22, Pt. I, Feb. 1955, pp. 3-10; Pt. II, May 1955, pp. 41-50. Reprinted in *Catholic Lawyer*, Vol. 10, Summer 1964, pp. 212-226.

Fox, A.W. "Managing Patients Who Refuse Blood Transfusions Puts Additional Burdens on the Rest of Society." *British Medical Journal*, Jul. 9, 1994, 309 (6947): 124-5.

Fox, J. "Caught Between Religion and Medicine." *Association of Operating Room Nurses Journal*, July, 1990, 5 (4): 131, 132, 134, 136+.

Fox, Martin. "Doctor Cleared of Malpractice in Death of Jehovah's Witness." (New York State) *New York Law Journal*, May 13, 1986, p1, col. 3.

Frackiewicz, E.J. and R. Lee. "Use of a Blood Substitute in a Patient Who Refuses to Accept a Transfusion." *American Journal of Hospital Pharmacy*, 48 (10): 2176; discussion 2176-80, Oct. 1991.

Frankel, L.A. "Childhood Cancer and the Jehovah's Witness Faith." *Pediatrics*, 1977, 60 (6): 916-921.

Freitag, P. "Management of a Multiply Injured Jehovah's Witness With Severe Acute Anemia." *Orthopedic Review*, May, 1994, 23 (5): 375.

Frey, R. "Refusal of Blood Transfusion for Religious Reasons." *Anesthesiologist*, July 1972, 21: 316.

Ganiats, T.G., et al. "Intrauterine transfusion: ethical issues involving a Jehovah's Witness mother [clinical conference] [published erratum appears in (*Journal of Family Practice*, Vol. 25, No. 2, Aug. 1987, pp. 112] *Journal of Family Practice*, May 1987, 24 (5): 467-472.

Garcia, Fred, Ron Lapin and Guenter Corssen." "General Anesthesia for the Anemic Patient Without Blood Therapy." *Institute of Bloodless Medicine and Surgery*, 1 (2): 20-22.

Gardner, Bernard, John Vivona, Antonio Alfonso, and Horrace Herbsman. "Major Surgery in Jehovah's Witnesses." *New York State Journal of Medicine*, May 1976, 76: 765-767.

Garner, Carl B., et al. "The Jehovah's Witnesses and Blood Transfusion." *Thrust*, 1980, 1 (2): 89, 90.

Garvey, John H. "Freedom and Equality in the Religion Clauses." *Supreme Court Review Annuals*, 1981, pp. 193-221.

Genden, E M and B. H. Haughey. "Head and Neck Surgery in the Jehovah's Witness Patient." *Otolaryngology--Head & Neck Surgery*, 114 (4): 669-672, 1996 Apr.

Gest. Ted. "When Lawyers Second-Guess Doctors." *U.S. News and World Report*, Feb. 13, 1984, pp. 45-47.

Gibbs, Richard F. "Jehovah's Witnesses and the question of blood." *Legal Aspects of Medical Practice*, June 1987, 15: 4-6.

Gill, G. "Adenotonsillectomy in a Jehovah's Witness with Blood Dyscrasia." *Archives of Otolaryngology*, June 1975, 101 (6): 392-394.

Gise, L.H., et. al. "Medical psychiatric rounds on a gynecologic oncology service: end-stage cervical carcinoma in a Jehovah's Witness refusing treatment [clinical conference]." *General Hospital Psychiatry*, Sept. 1989, 11 (5): 372-376.

Goetsch, C. "Aspects of Refusal of Blood Transfusion." *American Journal of Obstetrics and Gynecology*, June 1, 1968, 101: 390-396.

Goldberg, S.L. "Should Jehovah's Witnesses be denied intensive chemotherapy for acute leukemia?" [letter]. *New England Journal of Medicine*, Mar. 1990, 232 (11): 777-778.

Goldman, E.B. and H.A. Oberman. "Legal Aspects of Transfusion of Jehovah's Witnesses." *Transfusion Medicine Reviews*, Oct., 1991, 5(4): 263-70.

Gollub, Seymour, et al. "Electrolyte Solution in Surgical Patients Refusing Transfusion." *Journal of the American Medical Association*, March 29, 1971, 215 (13): 2077-2083.

_____. "Management of Major Surgical Blood Loss Without Transfusion." *Journal of the American Medical Association*, Dec. 12, 1966, 198 (11): 1171-1174.

Gomboltz, H. et al. "Open heart surgery in Jehovah's Witnesses." *Wien Klin Wochenschr*, June 7, 1985, 97 (12): 25-30 (English. Abstract) [German].

_____. "10 years' experience with heart surgery in Jehovah's Witnesses." *Anesthesiologist*, Aug. 1989, 38 (8): 385-290 (English. Abstract) [German].

Gomez-Almaguer D., G. Ruiz-Arguelles, A. Lozano de la Vega dn B.J. Garcia-Guajardo. "Leucemia aguda en Testigos de Jehova: dificultades en su manejo". *Revista de Investigacion Clinia*, Oct-Dec., 1990, 42 (4): 317-320. "Acute leukemia in Jehovah's Witnesses" difficulties in its management."(About six patients with acute lymphoblastic leukemia; four of the children were transfused without resorting to legal pressure.) [Spanish]

Gonzalez, Elizabeth Rasche. "The Saga of 'Artificial Blood'" Fluosol a Special Boon to Jehovah's Witnesses." *The Journal of the American Medical Association*, Feb. 22, 29, 1980, 243 (8): 719-720, 724.

Gordon, M.E., et al. "Peptic Ulcer Hemorrhage: Vasopressin for a Jehovah's Witness." *Annals of Internal Medicine*, Sept. 1973, 79: 451-452.

Gould, Sreven N. et al. "Fluosol-DA as a Red Cell Substitute in Acute Anemia." *The New England Journal of Medicine.* June 26, 1986, 314 (26): 1653, 1656.

Granger, C. "Managing a Jehovah's Witness Who Agrees To Blood Transfusion." *British Medical Journal*, Sept. 3, 1994, 309 (6954): 612.

Grant, A.B. "Exploring an Ethical Dilemma." *Nursing*, Dec., 1992, 22 (12): 52-4.

Grebenik, C.R., M. E. Sinclair and S. Westaby. "High Risk Cardiac Surgery in Jehovah's Witnesses." *Journal of Cardiovascular Surgery*, 37 (5): 511-515, 1996 Oct. (Concludes routine cardiovascular surgery can often be performed without blood transfusion. Complex cardiac surgical procedures, however, especially reoperations, are often associated with heavy blood loss and large transfusion requirements. Anesthetists and surgeons caring for Witnesses are often unwilling to offer such high risk surgery without recourse to blood transfusion).

Green, D., et al. "Erythropoitin for anemia in Jehovah's Witnesses" [letter]. *Annals of Internal Medicine*, Nov. 1, 1990, 113 (9): 720-721.

Green, Jennifer. "Death with Dignity." Nursing Times. 88(5):36 -37 Jan. 29, 1992 (Part of a series explaining how nurses should deal with different faiths at the time of death.)

Griffin, Jerry (Ed). "Third Jehovah's Witness Receives Synthetic Transfusion." *Bible Advocate*, May 1982, 116 (5): 21.

_____. "Jehovah's Witness Charges 'Spiritual Rape' in Blood Dispute." *Bible Advocate*, Sept 1984, 118 (9): 22.

"Guides to the Judge in Medical Orders Affecting Children." *Crime and Delinquency*, April 1968, 14 (2): 107-120.

Gyles, Harold. "Report on the Inquest Into the Death of Daniel Kennett." (Manitoba). *Health Law in Canada*, Fall 1986, 7: 52(8).

Habibi, B. "Transfusion et Temoins de Jehovah." *Revue Francaise de Transfusion et de Hemobiologie*. Jan., 1992, 35 (1): 13-23. (Transfusion and Jehovah's Witnesses (published erratum appears in *Revue Francaise de Transfusion et d Hemobiologie*, 1992, Mar. 35(2) Review) [French].

Haeische, G. "Transfusion Refusal for Religious Reasons." *Deutsche Medizinische Wochenschrift*, Dec. 19, 1975, 100 (51): 2622.

Hall, George. "Blood Transfusions and Jehovah's Witnesses." *The New Physician*, May 1964, 13: A-81, A-83.

Hallman, Grady. "Vascular Surgery in Jehovah's Witnesses." *Journal of the American Medical Association*, Aug. 10, 1970, 213 (6): 1032-1034.

Halloway, J.S., Jr. "Blood Transfusion--Jehovah's Witnesses." *Journal of the American Medical Association*, Feb. 23, 1957, 163: 660.

Handel, K. "Correction of Double-Outlet, Right Ventricle with Pulmonary Stenosis and Aortic Insufficiency in a Jehovah's Witness." *The Annals of Thoracic Surgery*, May 1971, 11 (5): 472-478.

_____. "Court Decision on the Refusal to Permit a Blood Transfusion." *Oeffentliche Gesundheits-Weson*, Dec. 1966, 28: 536-538.

Hargest, Robert F. "Lifesaving Treatment for Unwilling Patients." *For Biblical Faith*, May 1968, 36: 695-706.

Hargis, J.B., et al. "Induction chemotherapy in Jehovah's Witnesses with leukemia" [letter]. *Lancet*, Sept. 1, 1990.

Harris, S.L. "Postoperative Orthopedic Blood Salvage and Reinfusion." *Orthopedic Nursing*, Sep-Oct., 1992, 11 (5): 8.

Harris, T.J., et al. "Exsanguination in a Jehovah's Witness." *Anesthesiology*, Oct. 1983, 38 (10): 989-992.

Hartman, George "Jehovah's Witnesses." *U.S. News and World Report*, March 19, 1984, p. 8.

Harvey, J.P. "A Question of Craftsmanship." *Contemporary Orthopedics*. 1980, 2: 629.

Hasibeder W., et al. "Anemia and Jehovah's Witness". *Anesthesia*. Mar. 1988, 43 (3): 255-256.

Healey, J.M. "Treating a Jehovah's Witness adult: beneficence or respect for autonomy?" *Connecticut Medicine*, May 1990, 54 (5): 293.

_____. "The Jehovah's Witness parent's right to refuse treatment." *Connecticut Medicine*, June 1990, 54 (6): 357.

"Health Matters: Refusing Transfusing." *Today's Health*, Feb. 1979.

"Heart Surgery Without Transfusion." *Reader's Digest*, Jan. 1978, p. 152.

Heaton, P.B. "When passion displaces logic" *Canadian Medical Association Journal*,

Jan. 1990, 14 (1): 12. Comment on: *Canadian Medical Association Journal*. Oct. 1989, 13 (7): 707.

Hecker, W.C. "Jehovah's Witnesses: The Free to Die." *M.M.W. Muenchener Medizinische Wachenschrift*, March 2, 1979,120 (9): 257. [German].

Heimbecker, R.O. "Blood Recycling Eliminates Need for Blood" *Canadian Medical Association Journal*. 155 (3): 275-276, 1996 Aug 1.

Henderson, A.M., et al. "Cardiac surgery in Jehovah's Witnesses. A review of 36 cases." *Anesthesia*, Jul. 1986, 41 (7): 748-753.

Henling, C.E., et al. Cardiac operation for congenital heart disease in children of Jehovah's Witnesses." *Journal of Thoracic Cardiovascular Surgery*, 1985, 89 (6): 914-920.

Herbsman, H. "Treating the Jehovah's Witness." *Emergency Medicine*, 1980, 12: 73-76.

Hetreed, Michael. "Large Volume Bloodless Replaced with Plasma Expanders." *Anesthesia*, 1980, 35: 76-77.

Hirose, Tervo. "Electrolyte Solution in Surgical Patients Refusing Transfusion." *Journal of the American Medical Association*, March 29, 1971, 215 (13): 2077-2083.

Hirsh, Harold L. "Asteric Management of Jehovah's Witness Patients. *Legal Aspects of Medical Practice*, Oct. 1988, 16: 3-4, 11-12.

Hoaken, Paul. "Treatment of Jehovah's Witnesses." *Canadian Medical Association Journal*, Oct. 1, 1983, 129 (7): 678.

Holloway, J.S., Jr. "Blood Transfusion--Jehovah's Witnesses." *Journal of the American Medical Association*, Feb. 23, 1957, 63: 660.

Honig, J.F., H. Lilie, H.A. Merten and U. Braun. "Die Weigerung in die Einwilligung zur Bluttransfusion. Rechtliche und medizinische Aspekte am Beispiel der Zeugen Jehovas." *Anesthesiologist*, Jul., 1992, 41 (7): 396-8. (The refusal to consent to blood transfusion. Legal and medical aspects of using Jehovah's Witnesses as an example.) [German].

Horty, J.F. "Liability Nightmares, Patient Refuses Transfusion." *Modern Hospital*, Oct. 1971, 117: 78-80.

Hovland, N. "Blodforbudet for Jehovas Vitner." *Tidsskrift for Den Norske Laegeforening."* Jan., 1993, 113 (1): 77-8.

How, W. Glen. "Blood Transfusion." *Canadian Doctor*, Dec. 1960, pp. 37-58. Reprinted in *Canadian Law Journal*, Fall 1960, as "Religion, Medicine and Law," pp. 365-421.

_____. "Treatment of Jehovah's Witnesses" [letter]. *Canadian Medical Association Journal*, Feb. 1984, 130 (3): 253, 256

Howell, P. J., et al. "Severe acute anemia in a Jehovah's Witness. Survival without blood transfusion." *Anesthesia*, Jan. 1987, 42 (1): 44-48.

Howie, R.N. "Jehovah's Witnesses and Blood Transfusion of Infants." *New Zealand Medical Journal*, Aug., 1992, 105 (939): 307-8.

Husebekk, A. "Jehovas vitnen og fremskritt innenfor." *Tidsskrift for Den Norske Laegeforening*, Apr., 1993, 113 (10); 1258. (Jehovah's Witnesses and progress within transfusion medicine.) [Norwegian].

Huisman, J. "What can be done for mother and child in the case of irregular antibodies in pregnant Jehovah's Witnesses?" [letter]. *N. Ned Tijdschr Geneeskd*, Aug. 29, 1987, 131 (35): 1535. [Dutch].

Jacob, Harry, et al. "The Scientific Mind at Work (and Play)." *Journal of the American Medical Association*, July 3, 1981, 246 (1): 25-29.

Jacobson, L. "Jehovas vittnen och blodtransfusion." *Lakartidningen*, 93 (38): 3227, 1996 Sep 18. (Jehovah's Witnesses and Blood Transfusion) [Swedish].

"Jehovah's Witness Dies for Faith." *Insight*, Feb. 11 p. 23, and Oct. 28, 1975, 6: 17.

"Jehovah's Witnesses and the Refusal of Blood Transfusions: A Balance of Interests." *The Catholic Lawyer*. v. 33(1): 361-81.

Jehovah's Witnesses and the Transfusion Debate: 'We are not Asking For the Right To Die.'" *Canadian Medical Association Journal*, Jun., 1991, 144 (11): 1380, 1382.

_____. "Jehovah's Witnesses and Transfusions in Minors." (Editorial) *Trauma*, Feb. 1991, 32: 1-4.

"Jehovah's Witnesses and Transfusions" (Congress of U S --Dear Readers), *Spinal Column*, June 5, 1967, p. 1.

"Jehovah's Witnesses Sue in Federal Court in State of Washington to Restrain Forced Transfusion." *Journal of the Indiana State Medical Association*, 1966, 59 (8): 958.

"Jehovah's Witnesses Test Religious Liberty." May 6, 1965.

Jim, R.I. "Use of erythropoitin in Jehovah's Witness patients." *Hawaii Medical Journal*, June 1990, 49 (6): 209.

Johnson, P.W., et al. "The use of erythropoitin in a Jehovah's Witness undergoing major surgery and chemotherapy" [letter]. *British Journal of Cancer*, Mar. 1991, 63 (3): 476.

Jonsen, Albert R. "Blood Transfusions and Jehovah's Witnesses. The Impact of the Patient's Unusual Beliefs in Critical Care." *Critical Care Clinician*, Jan., 1986, 2 (1): 91-100.

_____. "Involuntary Treatment in Medicine." *Annual Review in Medicine*. 37: 41-48 1986.

Josefsson, G. "Primar Hoftledsplastik hos 14 Jehovas Vittnen." Inga Blodningsrelaterade Komplikationer Noterades." *Lakartidningen*, 93 (38): 3237-3238, 1996 Sep 18 (Primary hip arthroplasty in 14 Jehovah's Witnesses. No complications related to bleeding were reported) [Swedish]

Juliusson, G. "Immediate or Delayed Therapy with 2-CdA for Hair Cell Leukemia in Jehovah's Witness? [letter]" *American Journal of Hematology*, 53 (1): 49, 1996 Sep.

Kahle, R. and R. Dietrich. "Argumente der Zeugen Jehovas fur die Ablehnung von Bluttransfusionen." *Anasthesiologie, Intensivmedizin, Notfallmedizin, Schmerztnerapie*, 31 (8): 490-491, 1996 Oct. (Arguments of Jehovah's Witness for Refusing Blood Transfusions) [German]

Kamat, P.V., C. B. Baker and J.K. Wilson. "Open Heart Surgery in Jehovah's Witnesses: Experience in a Canadian Hospital." *Annals of Thoracic Surgery*, 1977, 23 (4): 367+.

Kambouris, A.A. "Major abdominal operations on Jehovah's Witnesses." *American*

Surgeon, June 1991, 53 (6): 350-356.

Kanumilli, V.; R. Kaza; C. Johnson and C. Nowacki, C. "Epidural Blood Patch for Jehovah's Witness Patient." *Anesthesia and Analgesia*, 77 (4): 872-873, 1993 Oct.

Kaplan, R.F., et al. "Transfusions for Jehovah's Witnesses." *Anesthesia and Analgesia*, 1983, 62 (1): 122.

Kaufman, D.B., et al. "A single-center experience of renal transplantation in thirteen Jehovah's Witnesses" *Transplantation*, June 1988, 45(1): 1045-1049.

Kearney, D.J. "Leukemia in Children of Jehovah's Witnesses--Issue and Priorities in a Conflict of Care." *Journal of Medical Ethics*, 1978, 4 (1); 32-35.

Kelly, A.D. "Aequanimitas (Two Mistakes)." *Canadian Medical Association Journal*, Feb. 18, 1967, 96: 432. (About the refusal of a Detroit hospital to treat a Jehovah's Witness.)

Kelly, J.L., T.W. Burke, B. Lichtiger, J.F. Dupuis. "Extracorporeal Circulation as a Blood Conservation Technique for Extensive Pelvic Operations." *Journal of the American College of Surgeons*, Apr., 1994, 178 (4): 397-400. (Discusses a form of homologous blood source that the Watchtower accepts.)

Kevorkian, Jack. "Our Unforgivable Trespass." *Clinical Pediatrics*, Dec. 1966, 5 (12): 40A, 41A.

Kim, D., H. Slater, I.W. Goldfarb, E.J. Hammell. "Experience With Patients With Burns Who Refuse Blood Transfusion for Religious Reasons." *Journal of Burn Care & Rehabilitation*, Sep-Oct., 1993, 14 (5): 541-3.

Kinast, B. "Witness to Success" *Nursing*. 26 (1): 6, 1996 Jan.

Kirchgesser, G. and H. Dittmer. "Zum Behandlungsproblem Polytrauma bei Zeugen Jehovas." *Chirurg*, Jun., 1992, 63 (6): 523-5. (The problem of multi-trauma treatment in Jehovah's Witnesses.) [German]

Kitchens, Craig S. "Are Transfusions Overrated? Surgical Outcome of Jehovah's Witnesses." (Editorial) *American Journal of Medicine*, Feb. 1993, 94: 117-120. (Reviews 16 studies of bloodless surgery, concluding that .5 to 1.5% of all operations in the studies reviewed were complicated by anemia resulting in death, which could translate into a large number of deaths annually.)

Klein, Woody. "Faith Stronger Than Blood." *New York Telegram*, July 31, 1958.

Kleinman, I. "Written Advance Directives Refusing Blood Transfusion: Ethical and Legal Considerations." *American Journal of Medicine*, Jun., 1994, 96 (6): 563-7. (Examines two cases of Witnesses who signed cards refusing blood and were subsequently transfused. In the Canadian case, the physician was found liable for battery. In the American case a guardian was appointed who authorized the transfusion.)

Koenig, H.M.; E. A. Levine; D. J. Resnick and W. J. Meyer. "Use of Recombinant Human Erythropoitin in a Jehovah's Witness. *Journal of Clinical Anesthesia*, 5 (3): 244-247, 1993 May-Jun.

Kolflaath, J. "Jehovas vitner. Nye rundskriv loser ikke gamle problemer." *Tidsskrift for Den Norske Laegeforening*, 116 (18): 2216. (Jehovah's Witnesses. New Circulars Do Not Solve Old Problems) [Norwegian]

Koller, Elizabeth R. "Religious Convictions May Bring Felony Convictions. (California) (Case Note) *Pacific Law Journal*, July 1990, pp. 1069-1105.

Kron, T.K., et al. "A Jehovah's Witness and homograft oscular implantation" [letter]. *Archives of Otolaryngology*, Jul. 1984, 110 (7): 485.

Kunz, J. and R. Mahr. "Management of Severe Blood Loss After Tumor Resection in a Jehovah's Witness." *Gynakologisch-Geburtshilfliche Rundschau.* 35 (1): 34-37, 1995.

Kyger, E.R. 3d, et al. "Management of Jehovah's Witness patients" [letter]. *Annals of Thoracic Surgery*, July 1990, 50 (1): 167.

_____. Synthetic erythropoitin and Jehovah's Witnesses" [letter]. *Journal of Thoracic Cardiovascular Surgery*, Feb. 1991, 101(2): 369.

Lam, S.Y.S. "Malette v. Shulman." *Professional Negligence*, July-Aug, 1989, pp. 118-120.

Lang, M., et al. "Sequential Triple-valve Replacement in a Jehovah's Witness." *Canadian Medical Association Journal*, Feb. 23, 122 (4): 433-435.

_____. "Major Abdominal Surgery in the Jehovah's Witness Patient." *Journal of Abdominal Surgery*, 21 (5): 92-94, 1979.

Langone, John. Bloodless Surgery. *Time* 150(19):74-76 Fall 1997.

Langslow, A. "Nursing and the Law. Witness to Battery?" *Australian Nursing Journal*, Aug., 1993, 1 (2): 35-7.

Lapin, Ron. "Major Surgery in Jehovah's Witnesses." *Contemporary Orthopedics*, 1980, 2: 647-654.

_____. "The Strength of Our Convictions." *The Journal of Neurological and Orthopedic Surgery*, July 1982, 3(2): xvi.

Larson, B. and N. Clyne. "Fallbeskrivning. Erytropoetin ersatte blodtransfusion." *Lakartidningen*, Apr., 28, 1993, 90 (17): 1662. (A case report. Erythropoitin replaced blood transfusion.) [Swedish].

Larson, S. J. "Blood Transfusion, Religious Beliefs and Medical Ethics." *Ugeskr Laeger*, July 19, 1976, 138 (30): 1844-1847.

Laurent C. "Blood Rights." *Nursing Times*, Jul. 17-23, 1991, 87 (29): 20.

Law, E.J., et al. "The use of erythropoitin in two burned patients who are Jehovah's Witnesses." *Burns*, Feb. 1991, 17 (1): 75-77.

"The Law and the Life." *Time*, April 30, 1951, 57: 84, 85.

Lawry, K.; J. Slomka and J. Goldfarb. "What Went Wrong: Multiple Perspectives on an Adolescent's Decision to Refuse Blood Transfusions." *Clinical Pediatrics*, 35 (6): 317-321, 1996 Jun.

Layon, A.J., et al. "And the patient chose: medical ethics and the case of the Jehovah's Witness." *Anesthesiology*, Dec. 1990, 73 (6): 1258-1262.

Leatherwood, J. "Impact of Religious Beliefs on Medical Care...Jehovah's Witnesses...Renal Transplants." *American Nephrology Nurses Association Journal*, Dec., 1986, 13 (6): 336-337.

Lebeaupin, B. "Blood Transfusion and Jehovah's Witnesses." *Anesthésie Analgésie Réanimation* (Paris), April-June 1961, 18: 371-381.

Levine, Carol. "A Verdict Against Doctors in a Jehovah's Witness Case." *Hastings Center Report*, June 1984, 14: 2-3.

Levine, M. "Religious Objection to Transfusion." *Military Medicine*, Oct. 1965, 130: 1023-1024.

Levinsky, L., et al. "Intracardiac Surgery in Children of Jehovah's Witnesses." *Johns Hopkins Medical Journal*, May 1981, 148 (5): 196-198.

Lewis, C.T., et al. "Risk factors for cardiac operations in adult Jehovah's Witnesses." *Annals of Thoracic Surgery*, Mar. 1991, 151 (3): 448-450.

Liang, B.A. and G. W. Ostheimer. "Legal Issues in Transfusing a Jehovah's Witness Patient Following Cesarean Section.' *Journal of Clinical Anesthesia*, 7 (6): 522-524, 1995 Sep.

Lichtiger, B. "Hemotherapy During Surgery for Jehovah's Witnesses: A New Method." *Anesthesia and Analgesia*, July 1982, 61 (7): 618-619.

Lilletvedt, H.J. "Jehovas vitner og blodtransfusjon--rettslige forhold." *Tidsskrift for Den Norske Laegeforening*, 114 (2): 190-2. Jan. 20, 1994 (Jehovah's Witnesses and blood transfusion--legal aspects.) (Covers the Norwegian penal code which causes "unnecessary trouble for Jehovah's Witnesses.") [Norwegian]

Lin, C.P.; M. J. Huang; H.J. Liu; I. Y. Chang and C. H. Tsai. "Successful Treatment of Acute Promyelocytic Leukemia in a Pregnant Jehovah's Wintess with All-Trans Retinoic Acid, rhG-CSF, and Erythropoitin [letter]" *American Journal of Hematology*. 51 (3): 251-252, 1996 Mar.

Little, V. "Nurses and Their Religions. Bearing Witness...Jehovah's Witnesses." *Nursing Times*, Feb., 1984, 80 (6): 47-48.

Litvan, H.; E. Santacana; J. I. Casas; A. Aris; J. M. Villar Landeria. "Aprotinin Therapy to Reduce Blood Loss in Jehovah's Witnesses." *Canadian Journal of Anesthesia*. 41(1): 77-78, 1994 Jan.

Lockwood, D.N., et al. "A severe coagulopathy following volume replacement with hydroxyethyl starch in a Jehovah's Witness." *Anesthesia*, May 1988, 43 (5): 391-393.

Loos, W.; W. Kuhn; A. Prechtl; B. Schmalfeldt; R. Hipp and J. Kycia. "Blutbedarf in der operativen Gynakologie. Strategien zur Vermeidung von Frembludt." *Fortschritte der Medizin*, 112 (29): 405-409, 1994 Oct 20. (Blood Transfusion in Surgical Gynecology. Strategies for Preventing Homologous Blood Transfusion) [German]

Lorhan, P.H. et al. "Anesthesia for a Jehovah's Witness with a Low Hematocrit." *Anesthesiology*, July-Aug. 1968, 29 (4): 847-848.

_____, et al. "Hyperbaric Oxygen Therapy in Chronic Hemorrhagic Shock." *Journal of the American Medical Association*, June 16, 1969, 208 (11): 2051-2054.

Lowman, Ron. "As Doctor He's For, As Witness He's Against." *Toronto Daily Star*, Thursday, July 3, 1957.

Luban, N.L. and S.L. Leikin. "Jehovah's Witnesses and Transfusion: The Pediatric Perspective." *Transfusion Medicine Reviews*, Oct. 1991, 5 (4): 253-8.

McDermott, P.J. "Jehovah's Witness: A Management Dilemma in Severe Maxillofacial Trauma." *British Journal of Oral & Maxillofacial Surgery*, Oct., 1992, 30 (5): 331-4. (The case of a 24 year old male who "died from maxillofacial injuries because transfusion was denied.")

McDonald, R.T., et al. "Blood, the Jehovah's Witness and the Physician." *Arizona Medicine*, Oct. 1967, 24: 969-973.

McGraw, J.P. "Use of recombinant human erythropoitin in a Jehovah's Witness" [letter]. *Journal of Trauma*, Jul. 1991, 3 (7): 1017-1018.

McTaggart, Lynne. "Blood medicine." *What Doctors Don't Tell You*, 3(2): 1-3 c. 1993. (Special report in a monthly medical pressure-group newsletter on the Witnesses and the various risks from blood transfusions. McTaggart is not a witness, but was supplied medical articles by the Watchtower).

Macklin, Ruth. "Consent, Coercion, and Conflicts of Rights." *Perspectives in Biology and Medicine*, Spring, 1977, 20 (3): 360-371.

_____. "The inner workings of an ethics committee: latest battle over Jehovah's Witnesses." *Hastings Center Report*, Feb. Mar, 1988, 18 (1): 15-20. (Blood transfusions to pregnant women; the legal and moral issues surrounding the blood-Witness conflicts).

MacLean, D. "Jehovah's Witnesses." *Australian Family Physician*, June 1986, 15 (6): 772-774.

Maddox, Robert. "Jehovah's Witness--Mother should have been allowed to refuse blood transfusion, says court." *Church and State*, March 1987, 40 (3): 3, 18.

Madura, J.A. "Use of Erythropoitin and Parenteral Iron Dextran in a Severely Anemic Jehovah's Witness With Colon Cancer." *Archives of Surgery*, 128 (10): 1168-1170, 1993 Oct.

Mann, Marianne Culkin, J. Votto, J. Kambe and M.J. McNamee. "Management of the Severely Anemic Patient Who Refuses Transfusion: Lessons Learned During the Care of a Jehovah's Witness." *Annals of Internal Medicine*, Dec. 15, 1992, 117(12): 1042-1049. (Covers options available to physicians.)

Marelli, T.R. "Use of Hemoglobin Substitute in the Anemic Jehovah's Witness Patient." *Critical Care Nurse*, 14 (1): 31-38, 1994 Feb.

Martens, P.R. "Desmopressin and Jehovah's Witness." *Lancet*, June 10, 1989, 1 (8650): 1322.

Martin, J.B. "A Home Health Nurse Responds. Seek Understanding." *Journal of Christian Nursing*, Spring, 1987, 4 (2): 12-13.

Masulis, Karen. "When Parents Refuse Treatment for Their Children." *Journal of Christian Nursing*, Spring, 1987 (About Witnesses why try to prevent their children from receiving a blood transfusion; also reviews a case history). 4(2): 9-11.

"Medical Alert' for Witnesses." *Journal of the American Medical Association*, 1953,151: 1435.

"Medical Alert' for Witnesses." *Journal of the American Medical Association*, July 3, 1981, 246 (1): 19.

"Medicolegal Aspects of Blood Transfusion." *Journal of the American Medical Association*, 1953, 151: 1435.

Meidell, N.K. and U. Kongsgaard. "Blodoverforing og Jehovas vitner--problemstillinger ved livstruende tilstander. En spoorreundersokelse blant norske anestesiologer." *Tidsskrift for Den Norske Laegeforening*, 116 (23): 2798-2798, 1996 Sep 30. (Blood Transfusion and Jehovah's Witnesses--problems in Life-threatening conditions. A questionnaire among Norwegian Anesthesiologists) (A study of Norwegian doctors found that up to 79% of the responding physicians would transfuse their Witness patients against their will). [Norwegian]

Milhollin, G. "The Refused Blood Transfusion: An Ultimate Challenge for Law and Morals." *National Law Review*, 1965, 10: 202-214.

Miller, Nicholas. "The Prince of Faith." *Liberty* 92 (4): 26-27. July-Aug 1997. (About a Witness who refused blood, and as a result became bedridden, and sued the insurance company to pay for her choice which cost her her health and the insurance company a lot of money).

Minuck, Max, et al. "Anesthesia and Surgery for Jehovah's Witnesses." *Canadian Medical Association Journal*, May 27, 1961, 84: 1187-1191.

Miyaji, K.; A. Furuse; M. Takeda; M. Chikada; M. Ono and M. Kawauchi. "Successful Conduit Repair Using Aortic Homograft in a Jehovah's Witness Child." *Annals of Thoracic Surgery*, 62 (2): 590-591, 1996 Aug.

Moghtader, J.C.; R. F. Edlich; P. D. Mintz; G. C. Zachmann and H. N. Himel. "The Use of Recombinant Human Erythropoitetin and Cultured Epithelial Autografts in a Jehovah's Witness with a Major Thermal Injury." *Burns* 20 (2): 176-177, 1994 Apr.

Moore, J.L. "Religion and Blood Transfusion." *Journal of the Medical Association of Georgia*, Sept. 1964, 53: 304.

More, Thomas J. "Court Orders Blood Transfusion After Mother To Be Refuses." *Chicago Sun-Times*, May 6, 1981, pp. 12.

Morecroft, J.A.; R. A.Wheeler; D.P. Drake and V. M. Wright. "Management of Blood Loss in Children of Jehovah's Witnesses *British Medical Journal* ,312 (7027): 380-381, 1996 Feb 10.

Morgan, Paul. "New Jersey Supreme Court Orders Pregnant Jehovah Witness to Consent to Blood Transfusion to Save Unborn Child" (Case: *Memorial Hospital v. Anderson*). *For Biblical Faith*, Oct. 1964, 23: 80-86.

Morikawa, S. "Refusal of Blood Transfusion and the Jehovah's Witness." *Japanese Journal of Anesthesiology*, Oct. 1974, 23 (11): 1130-1132.

Mulder, P.A. "Antibodies in pregnant Jehovah's Witnesses." (letter) *Ned Tijdschr Geneeskd*, Dec. 26, 1987, 131 (52): 2439-2440. [Dutch].

Murphy, E.K. "Court actions regarding refusal of blood products." *AORN Journal* Mar. 1989, 49 (3): 874, 876, 878-879.

Najand, A. "Anesthesiste-reanimateur et temoins de Jehovah." *Annales Francaises d Anesthesie et de Reanimation*, 1992, 11 (2): 237-40. (Anesthesiologists and Jehovah's Witnesses.) [French]

Nearman, H.S. "Postoperative Management of a Severely Anemic Jehovah's Witness." *Critical Care Medicine*, Feb. 1983, 11 (2): 142-143.

Nelson, B.S.; L.E. Heiskell; S. Cemaj; T.A. O'Callaghan and C.E. Koller. "Traumatically Injured Jehovah's Witnesses: A Sixteen-Year Experience of Treatment and Transfusion Dilemmas at a Level I Trauma Center." *Journal of Trauma*, 39 (4): 681-685, 1995 Oct.

Nelson, C.L., et al. "Total Hip Replacement Without Transfusion." *Contemporary Orthopedics*, 1980, 2: 655-658.

_____, et al. Total hip arthroplasty in Jehovah's Witnesses without blood transfusion."

Journal of Bone Joint Surgery 1986, 68 (3): 350-353.

Nelson, C.L and Fontenot, H.J. "Ten Strategies to Reduce Blood Loss in Orthopedic Surgery." *American Journal of Surgery*, 170 (6A Suppl): 64S-68S, 1995 Dec.

Neptune, W.B., et al. "Clinical Use of a Pump-Oxygenator Without Donor Blood for Priming or Support During Extracorporeal Perfusion." *Circulation*, 1960, 20: 745.

Nielsen, William. "The Biblical Laws Against Transfusions Reexamined--A Christian Physician's Viewpoint." *Transfusion Medicine Reviews*, Oct., 1991, 5 (4); 271-3.

Nixon, Robert W. "Beliefs Cost Mother Her Children." *Liberty*, May-Je 1972, 67: 6, 7.

Noble, William H. "CMPA and Jehovah's Witness." *Canadian Journal of Anesthesia*, Mar. 1991, 38 (2); 262-263. (Concerns the problem of how to deal with patients who reject blood transfusions.)

"The Nurse Responds: Pondering Parent's Rights." *Journal of Christian Nursing*, Spring, 1987, 4 (2): 15-16 (Reviews a case history of a Witness infant who needed a transfusion which was ordered by the court).

Nussbaum, W.; N. deCastro and F W Campbell "Perioperative Challenges in the Care of the Jehovah's Witness: A Case Report." *AANA Journal*, 62 (2): 160-164, 1994 Apr.

O'Donnell, T. "Jehovah's Witness and the Problem of Blood Transfusion." *Linacre*, may 1965, 32: 169-172.

Ohyanagi, H. et al. "Surgical use of flurosol-DA in Jehovah's Witness patients." *Artificial Organs*, Feb. 1984, 8 (1): 10-18.

Oian, P. "Jehovas vitner--blodoverforing eller ikke? Blir legen alltid taperen?" *Tidsskrift for Den Norske Laegeforening*. 116 (5): 646-647, 1996 Feb 20. (Jehovah's Witnesses--Blood Transfusion or Not? Are Physicians all-time Losers?) [Norwegian]

Oliveria, S.A.; R. M. Bucno; J. M. Souza; D.F. Senra and M. Rocha-e-Silva. "Effects of Hypertonic Saline Dextran on the Postoperative Evolution of Jehovah's Witnesses Patients Submitted to Cardiac Surgery With Cardiopulmonary Bypass." *Shock*, 3 (6): 391-394, 1995 Jun.

Olsen, J.B. "Open-heart surgery in Jehovah's Witnesses" *Scandinavian Journal of Thoracic Surgery*, 1990, 24 (3): 165-169.

Oneson, R., et al. "Jehovah's Witnesses and autologous transfusion" (letter). *Transfusion*, Mar-Apr. 1985, 25 (2): 179.

"On the Side of Life." *Time*, Feb. 21, 1964, pp. 76, 78.

Orloff, Marshall. "Blood Transfusion and Jehovah's Witnesses." *Journal of Surgery, Gynecology and Obstetrics*, 108, 159: 502-507.

Ott, David, A. and Denton Cooley. "Cardiovascular Surgery in Jehovah's Witnesses." *Journal of the American Medical Association*, Sept. 19, 1977, 238 (12): 1256-1258.

Panchal, H.I., et al. "Severe coagulopathy in Jehovah's Witness" (letter). *Anesthesia*, Jan. 1989, 44 (1): 71-72.

Paris, J. "Forced Medications" By Whose Right?" *America*, 1975, 133 (15): 323-325.

_____. "Compulsory Medical Treatment and Religious Freedom: Whose Law Shall Prevail?" *University of San Francisco Law Review*, Vol. 10, 1975, pp. 1035.

Parker, R.I. "Aggressive Non-Blood Product Support of Jehovah's Witnesses." *Critical Care Medicine*, Mar., 1994, 22 (3): 381-2.

Pearlman, E.S. and S.K. Ballas. "When to Transfuse Blood in Sickle Cell Disease? Lessons from Jehovah's Witnesses." *Annals of Clinical & Laboratory Science*, 24 (5): 396-400, 1994 Sep-Oct.

Perry, C. "Jehovah's Witnesses and the Quality of Life." *Westminster Institute Review*, Sum., 1983, 2 (4): 8-10.

Pertek, J.P. and G. Decroix. "A propos du refus de transfusion sanguine par le patient." *Annales Francaises d Anesthesie et de Reanimation*, 1992, 11 (2): 236-7. (Apropos of patient's refusal for blood transfusion.) [French]

"Physical Welfare vs. Religious Liberty." *Church and State*, June 1968, 21 (6): 14.

Pierre-Louis, C. "The Refusal of Transfusion for Religious Reasons." *Bulletin of the Association of Medicine in Haiti*, Oct. 1972, 12: 78-82.

Pogrel, M.A. and A. McDonald. "The Use of Erythropoitin in a Patient Having Major Oral and Maxillofacial Surgery and Refusing Blood Transfusion." *Journal of Oral & Maxillofacial Surgery*, 53 (8): 943-945, 1995 Aug.

Polley, J.W. R.A. Berkowitz, T.B. McDonald, M. Cohen, A. Figueroa, D.W. Penney. "Craniomaxillofacial Surgery in the Jehovah's Witness Patient." *Plastic & Reconstructive Surgery*, May, 1994, 93 (6): 1258-63.

Popovsky, M.A., and S.B. Moore. "Autologous transfusion in Jehovah's Witnesses" (letter). *Transfusion*, Sep-Oct. 1985, 25 (5): 444.

Poronovich, Walter. "Child Dies After Refusing Blood Transfusion." *Religious Freedom Alert*, March, 1986, 1 (2): 10.

Porter, E.; S. Ahn; P. Cunningham and J. Lazerson. "Anemia in a Premature Infant of a Jehovah's Witness." *Hospital Practice (Office Edition)*, 29 (5): 99-100, 1994 May 15.

Posnikoff, Jack. "Cure of Intracranial Aneurysm Without Use of Blood Transfusion." *California Medicine*, Feb. 1967, pp. 124-127.

Pousda, L., et al. "Erythropoitin and anemia of gastrointestinal bleeding in a Jehovah's Witness." *Annals of Internal Medicine*, Apr 1990, 112 (7): 552.

Quenu, L., et al. "Is it Possible to Consider a Refusal of Blood Transfusion Because of Religious Convictions?" *Nouvelle Presse Medicale*, Nov. 14-Dec. 1974, 3 (41-43): 2575-2576.

Quintero, C. "Blood Administration in Pediatric Jehovah's Witnesses." *Pediatric Nursing*, Jan-Feb., 1993, 19 (1): 46-48.

Raleigh, Fitkin. "New Jersey Supreme Court Orders Pregnant Jehovah Witness to Consent to Blood Transfusion to Save Unborn Child" (Case: *Memorial Hospital vs. Anderson*). *For Biblical Faith*, Oct. 1964, 33: 80-86.

Ramos, H.C.; S. Todo; Y. Kang; E. Felekouras; H.R. Doyle and T.E. Starzl. "Liver Transplantation Without the Use of Blood Products." *Archives of Surgery*, 129 (5): 528-532; discussion 532-533, May 1994.

Rector, Milton. "Guides to the Judge in Medical Orders Affecting Children." *Crime and Delinquency*, April 1968, 14 (2): 107-120.

"Recycling Blood." *Time*, March 16, 1981 117 (11).

"Refusal of Blood Transfusions by Jehovah's Witnesses." *Catholic Lawyer* Nov.10, Summer 1964, pp. 212-226.

"Refusal of Parental Consent to Blood Transfusion." *British Medical Journal*, Dec. 1965,2 (5476): 1494.

Reid, M.F., et al. "Eclampsia and hemorrhage in a Jehovah's Witness" (letter). *Anesthesiology*, Mar 1986, 41 (3): 324-325.

Richards, F. "What They Believe and Why: Roman Catholics, Jehovah's Witnesses, Christian Scientists, *Nursing Mirror*, Apr., 14, 1977, 144: 65-66.

Ridley, Donald T. "Accommodating Jehovah's Witnesses Choice of Nonblood Management." *Perspectives of Healthcare Risk Management,* Winter 1990, pp. 1-6.

Rieger, H.J. "Refusal of Blood for Religious Reasons." *Deutsche Medizinische Wachenschrift*, March 12, 1975, 100 (12): 172-173.

Rigor, Benjamin. "Replacement of Operative Blood Loss of More Than 1 Liter with Hartmann's Solution." *Journal of the American Medical Association*, Feb. 5, 1968, 203 (6): 399-402.

Robb, N. "Ruling of Jehovah's Witness Teen in New Brunswick May Have 'Settled the law' for MDs" *Canadian Medical Association Journal*, 151 (5): 625-628, 1994 Sep 1.

_____. "Jehovah's Witnesses Leading Education Drive as Hospitals Adjust to No Blood Requests." *Canadian Medical Association Journal*, 154 (4): 557-560, 1996 Feb 15.

Roberts, J. "Religion Should Not Put a Child's Health At Risk." *British Medical Journal*, 312 (7026): 268-269, 1996 Feb 3.

Roen, P.R., and F. Velcek. "Extensive Urologic Surgery without Blood Transfusion." *New York State Journal of Medicine*, 1972, 72: 2524-2527.

Rogers, R. "No Blood or Blood Products" *Anesthesia*, 50 (11): 1013, 1995 Nov.

Rooney, John Flynn. "Jehovah's Witness' Malpractice Suit Reinstated." (Illinois) *Chicago Daily Law Bulletin*, Oct. 3, 1990, p. 1, col. 5.

Rosam, E.D. "Patients' Rights and the Role of the Emergency Physician in the Management of Jehovah's Witnesses." *Annals of Emergency Medicine*, Oct., 1991, 20 (10): 1150-2.

Rosen, P. "Religious Freedom and Forced Transfusion of Jehovah's Witness Children." *Journal of Emergency Medicine*, 14 (2): 241-242, 1996 Mar-Apr.

Rosengart, T.K., R.E. Helm, J.Klemperer, K.H. Krieger, O.W. Isom. "Combined Aprotinin and Erythropoitin Use For Blood Conservation: Results With Jehovah's Witnesses." *Annals of Thoracic Surgery*, Nov., 1994, 58 (5): 1397-403.

Rosengart, T.K., R.E. Helm, W.J. DeBois N. Garcia, N. Krieger and O.W. Isom. "Open Heart Operations Without Transfusions Using a Multimodality Blood Conversion Strategy Technique." *Journal of the American College of Surgeons*. 184(6):618-629 1997.

Rosenthal, Elizabeth. "Blinded by the Light." *Discover*, Aug. 1988, 9 (8): 28-31. (A physician discusses her futile attempt to save the life of a Jehovah's Witness who refused blood).

Roth, A.B., et al. "When the Patient Refuses Treatment: Some Observations and Proposals for Handling the Difficult Case." *St. Louis Law Review*, 1979, 23: 429+.

Rothstein, P. et al. "Preoperative use of erythropoitin in an adolescent Jehovah's Witness." *Anesthesiology*, Sep. 1990, 73 (3): 568-570.

Rottlander, W. "Refusal of Blood Transfusion on Religious Grounds." *Medizinische Klinik*, June 30, 1966, 61: 1049-1051.

Roy-Bornstein, C.; L.D.Sogor and K. B. Roberts. "Treatment of a Jehovah's Witness with Immune Globulin: Case of a Child with Kawasaki Syndrome." *Pediatrics*, 94(1): 112-113, 1994 Jul.

Rozovsky, Lorne. "Jehovah's Witnesses and the Law." *Canadian Hospital*, March 1971, 48: 41-42.

_____, and F.A. Rozovsky. "Treating the Jehovah's Witness Patient." *Canadian Doctor*, 1982, 48 (2): 81-84.

Runner, Brenda J. "Constitutional law--seventeen year old Jehovah's Witness, diagnosed with acute leukemia, made an independent and mature decision to follow her religious beliefs in refusing blood transfusions and could not be prevented from exercising her constitutional right to free exercise of religion solely because of her minority status." *Journal of Family Law*, Feb. 1989, 27: 524-528.

Rush, Benjamin. "Replacement of Operative Blood Loss of More Than 1 Liter with Hartmann's Solution." *Journal of the American Medical Association*, Feb. 5, 1968, 203 (6): 399-402.

Russell, Geraldine and Donald Wallace. "Jehovah's Witnesses and the refusal of blood transfusions: a balance of interests." *Catholic Lawyer*, Fall, 1990, 33 (4): 361-381.

Sacks, D.A., et al. "Blood transfusion and Jehovah's Witnesses: Medical and legal issues in obstetrics and gynecology." *American Journal of Obstetrics and Gynecology*, Mar. 1986, 154 (3): 483-486.

_____ and Richard H. Koppes. "Caring for the Female Jehovah's Witness: Balancing Medicine, Ethics, and the First Amendment." *American Journal of Obstetrics & Gynecology*, Feb., 1994, 170 (2): 452-5 (Notes that in his experience some Witnesses will accept blood transfusions).

Saha, A., M. Elstein. "Managing Patients Who Refuse Blood Transfusions. Register of Willing Consultants Is Needed." *British Medical Journal*, July 9, 1994, 309 (6947): 125.

Salyer, David R. "Fosmire v. Nicoleu." (Refusal of medical treatment by a pregnant Witness). (New York). *Issues in Law & Medicine*, Winter, 1990, 6 (3): 305-308.

Sandiford, F.M., et al. "Aorto-coronary Bypass in Jehovah's Witnesses: Report of 36 Patients." *Journal of Thoracic/Cardiovascular Surgery*, 1984, 68: 1-7.

_____. "Aortocoronary Bypass in Jehovah's Witnesses: Review of 46 Patients." *American Surgeon*, Jan. 1976, 42 (1): 17-22.

Schaefer, Clara. "Electrolyte Solution in Surgical Patients Refusing Transfusion." *Journal of the American Medical Association*, March 29, 1971, 215 (13): 2077-2083.

Schechter, D.C. "Problems Relevant to Major Surgical Operations in Jehovah's Witnesses." *American Journal of Surgery*, 1968, 116: 73-80.

Schemonsky, Natalie Kaplin. "Informed Refusal." (Washington). *Legal Aspects of*

Medical Practice, Nov. 1985, pp. 5-6.

Schiff, S.J. and S.L. Weinstein. "Use of Recombinant Human Erythropoitin to Avoid
Blood Transfusion in a Jehovah's Witness Requiring Hemispherectomy." *Journal of
Neurosurgery*, Oct., 1993, 79 (4): 600-2. (Use of erythropoitin in a two-stage
hemispherectomy without blood transfusion.)

Schumacher, H. "Fremdblutkonserven bei schwerbrandverletzten Zeugen Jehovas."
Chirurg, 65 (12): 1155, 1994 Dec. (Homologous Blood Transfusion in Severely
Burned Jehovah's Witnesses) [German]

Schutte, James E. "Will a patient's religion hobble your medical decisions?" (Jehovah's
Witnesses). *Medical Economics*, April 17, 1989, p. 143(5).

Schweitzer, M.and P.M. Osswald "Letaler hamorrhagischer shock bei einem Zeugen
Jehovas." *Anesthesiologie, Intensivmedizin, Notfallmedizin, Schmerztherapie*, 31
(8): 504-506, 1996 Oct. (Fatal hemorrhagic shock in a Jehovah's Witness.) [German]

Seifert, P.E., et al. "Myocardial revascularization in Jehovah Witnesses." *Wisconsin
Medical Journal*, Apr. 1989, 88 (4): 19-20.

Selby, I.R. and J. Lerman. "Anesthesia for Jehovah's Witnesses" *Anesthesia*, 51 (1):
95-96, 1996 Jan.

Seu, P.; G. Neelankanta; M. Csete; K. M. Olthoff; S. Rudich; M. Kinkhabwala; D. K.
Imagawa; L. I. Goldstein; P. Martin; C.R. Shackleton and R. W. Busuttil. "Liver
Transplantation for Fulminant Hepatic Failure in a Jehovah's Witness." *Clinical
Transplantation*, 10 (5): 404-407, 1996 Oct.

Sharpe, David. "Lifesaving Treatment for Unwilling Patients." *Fordham Law Review*,
May 1968, 36 (4): 695-706.

Sheldon, M. "Ethical Issues in the Forced Transfusion of Jehovah's Witness Children."
Journal of Emergency Medicine, 14 (2): 251-257, 1996 Mar-Apr.

Siebrasse, Norman. "The requirement of consent in medical emergencies." (Ontario)
(case note). *Law Journal*, Dec. 1989, 34: 1080-1098.

Simmons, Wilton, et al. "Vascular Surgery in Jehovah's Witnesses." *Journal of the
American Medical Association*, Aug. 10, 1970, 213 (6): 1032-1034.

Singelenberg, Richard. "The blood transfusion taboo of Jehovah's Witnesses: origin,
development and function of a controversial doctrine." *Social Science of Medicine*,
1990, 31 (4): 515-523. (On some of the reasons the taboo is maintained).

_____. "Jehovah's Witness." *British Journal of Oral and Maxillofacial Surgery*, June,
1993, 31 (3): 195. (Letter.)

Sire, J.W. "A Cult Expert Responds; Resist False Teaching. *Journal of Christian
Nursing*, Spring, 1987, 4 (2): 13-14. (Argues the Watchtower has a distorted grasp
of Hebrew dietary laws and God's laws).

Smith, A.G. "Managing Patients Who Refuse Blood Transfusion. Chemotherapy for
Haematological Malignancies can be Fatal." *British Medical Journal*, 309 (6947): 125,
1994 Jul 9.

Smith, Earl Belle. "General Surgery in Jehovah's Witnesses; Personal Experience: A 22
Year Analysis." *Journal of the National Medical Association*, July 1980, 22: 657-660.

_____. "Surgery in Jehovah's Witnesses." *Journal of the National Medical Association*,
Jul. 1986, 78 (7): 669-669, 673.

Sneierson, H. "Autotransfusion for Massive Hemorrhage Due to Ruptured Spleen in
Jehovah's Witness." *New York Journal of Medicine*, June 15, 1967, 37: 1769-1771.

Snook, N.J.; H.A. O'Beirne; S. Enright; Y. Young; M. C. Bellamy. "Use of
Recombinant Human Erythropoitin to Facilitate Liver Transplantation in a Jehovah's
Witness." *British Journal of Anesthesia*, 76 (5): 740-743, 1996 May.

Soutoul, J.H., et al. "Refusal of blood because of being Jehovah's Witnesses or for fear
of AIDS. Deontologic and legal aspects." *Journal of Gynecology, Obstetrics, and
Biological Reproduction* (Paris), 1988, 17 (8): 965-980. (English. Abstract. article in
French).

Sowade, O.; H. Warnke and P. Scigalla. "Operationen mit der Herz-Lungen-Maschine
bei erwachsenen Patienten der Glaubensgemeinschaft. 'Zeugen Jehovah's.'"
Anaesthesist, 44(4): 257-264, 1995 Apr. (Operations with a heart-lung machine in
adult members of Jehovah's Witnesses.) [German]

Sparling, E.A.; C.L. Nelson; R. Lavender and J. Smith. "The Use of Erythropoitin in the
Management of Jehovah's Witnesses Who Have Revision Total Hip Arthroplasty."
Journal of Bone & Joint Surgery--American Volume 78 (10): 1548-1552, 1996 Oct.

Spence, Richard K., James B. Alexander, Anthony J. Del Rossi and Aurel D. Carnaianu
et al. "Transfusion Guidelines for Cardiovascular Surgery: Lessons Learned From
Operations in Jehovah's Witnesses." *Journal of Vascular Surgery*, 1992, 16:825-
831). Reprinted in *The Journal of the American Medical Association*, Feb. 17, 1993,
p. 857 (Covers alternatives to homologous blood transfusion, autologous predonation
and intraoperative autotransfusion of the 59 patients, one died of operative bleeding
complications).

_____. "The Jehovah's Witness Patient and Mediocolegal Aspects of Transfusion
Medicine." *Seminars in Vascular Surgery*, Jun., 1994, 7 (2): 121-6 (Covers the many
problems in dealing with Witness patients).

Spence, R.K. "Surgical Red Blood Cell Transfusion Practice Policies. Blood
Management Practice Guidelines Conference." *American Journal of Surgery*, 170 (6A
Suppl): 3S-15S, 1995 Dec.

Spence, R.K. "Management of Severe Anemia in a Pediatric Jehovah's Witness Patient."
Critical Care Medicine, 23 (2): 416-417, 1995 Feb.

Spencer, Gary. "Blood transfusions held improper: appeals court finds hospital violated
rights of Jehovah's Witness." (New York). *New York Law Journal*, Jan. 19, 1990,
203: 1, col. 3.

Spencer, J.D. "The Witnesses Could Win." *Legal Aspects of Medical Practice*, 1978, 6
(6): 45-49.

Spinal, C. "For Religious Rights." (Letter to Editor), *Fordham Law Review*. "State Can
Save Child's Life Despite Jehovah's Witnesses Parents." *Catholic Layman*. Oct.,
1963, 77: 61.

"St. Thomas, Ontario: Blood Transfusions." *Church and State*, March 1959, 12 (3): 5.

"Surgery Without Blood Transfusions." *Journal of the Iowa Medical Society*, Jan. 1978,
68 (1); 19-20.

Stein, J.I., et al. "Open heart surgery in children of Jehovah's Witnesses: extreme
hemodilution on cardiopulmonary bypass." *Pediatric Cardiology*, Jul. 1991, 12 (3):
170-174.

Stone, D.J., et al. "DDAVP to reduce blood loss in Jehovah's Witnesses" (letter).

Anesthesiology, Dec. 1988, 69 (6): 1028.

Studdard, P.A., et al. "Jehovah's Witnesses and blood transfusion. Toward the resolution of a conflict of conscience." *Alabama Journal of Medical Science*, Oct. 1968, 23 (4): 454-459.

Sugarman, Jeremy, et al. "Medical, Ethical and Legal Issues Regarding Thrombolytic Therapy in the Jehovah's Witness." *American Journal of Cardiology*, Dec. 1, 1991, 68: 1525-1530.

Sureau, C. "Can a Refusal of Blood Transfusion for Religious Convictions Be Accepted?" *Nouvelle Presse Medicale* (Paris), Oct. 12, 1974, 3 (34): 2188-2190.

Svigals, Robert. "Electrolyte Solution in Surgical Patients Refusing Transfusion." *Journal of the American Medical Association*, March 29, 1971, 215 (13): 2077-2083. "Terry and the Parents." *Newsweek*, Jan. 18, 1971, 77: 43.

Swan, Rita. " Children, Medicine, and the Law" *Advances in Pediatrics*. 1997 44:491-543 (An excellent discussion about 18 sects that oppose orthodox medical care and require their members to rely on faith healing or similar: Much on the Watchtower antiblood stance and children).

Tessmann, R. and U. vonLupke. "Uberleben einer schwersten Blutungsanamie bei einer Zeugin Jehovas." *Anasthesiologie, Intensivmedizin, Notfallmedizin, Schmerztherapie*, 31 (8) 501-504, 1996 Oct. (Survival of very severe hemorrhage-induced anemia in a Jehovah's Witness) (in German)

Testas, P. "Acute Hemodilution in Normouplemia. Possibilities of Major Surgical Operations Without Transfusion: Apropos of an Esogastrectomy in a Jehovah's Witness." *Chirugie*, March 12-19, 1975, 161 (4): 266-271.

"Their Life is in the Blood: Jehovah's Witnesses, Blood Transfusions and the Courts." Vol. v 10 *Northern Kentucky Law Review*, Spring. 1983, pp. 281-304.

Thomas, George, et al. "Some Issues Involved with Major Surgery on Jehovah's Witnesses." *The American Surgeon*, July 1968, 34 (7): 538-543.

Thomas, J.E. "Ethical Reflections on Patient Refusals of Life-Saving Treatment." *Transfusion Medicine Reviews*, Oct., 1991, 5 (4): 259-62.

Thomas, J.M. "Meeting the Surgical Ethical Challenge Presented by Jehovah's Witnesses." *Canadian Medical Association Journal*, May 15, 1983, 128: 1153-1154.

Thompson, Anthony. "She May Die If She Chooses." *Liberty*, Jan.-Feb. 1977, 67: 25.

Thompson, James. "Hyperbaric Oxygen Therapy in Chronic Hemorrhagic Shock." *Journal of the American Medical Association*, June 16, 1969, 208 (11): 2051-204.

Thompson, H.A. "Blood transfusions and Jehovah's Witnesses" *Texas Medicine*, Apr. 1989, 85 (4): 57-59.

Thompson, Larry. "Five receive transplants without blood transfusions." (Texas Heart Institute performs heart transplants on Jehovah's Witnesses). *The Washington Post*, Nov. 27, 1990, 113: WH5, col. 1.

Thurkauf, G.E. "Understanding the Beliefs of Jehovah's Witnesses." *Focus On Critical Care*, June, 1989, 16 (3): 199-204.

Tierney, W.M., et al. "Jehovah's Witnesses and blood transfusion: physicians' attitudes and legal precedents." *Southern Medical Journal*, Apr. 1984, 77 (4): 473-478.

"Transfusion for Minor Patient Despite Parents' Religious Objections." *Anesthesia and Analgesia*, May-June 1973, 52: 462-463.

"Transfusion Case to be Fought by Witnesses." *Christian Century Magazine*. June 13,1951, p.701.

"Transfusion Friction." *Church and State*, Nov. 1981, 34 (10); 22.

"Transfusion to Unwilling Witness Ruled Illegal." *Pentecostal Evangelical*, Jan. 16, 1966.

Trent, B. "Jehovah's Witnesses and the transfusion debate: "We are not asking for the right to die." *Canadian Medical Association Journal*, Mar. 15, 1991, 144 (6): 770-776. Comment, Vol. 144, No. 11, Jun. 2, 1991, pp. 1380, 1382.

Trouwborst, A., et al. "Hypervolaemic haemodilution in an anemic Jehovah's Witness." *British Journal of Anesthesia*, May 1990, 64 (5): 646-648.

Tsang, V.T.; R.J. Mullaly; P. G. Ragg; T.R. Karl; R. B. Mee. "Bloodless Open-Heart Surgery in Infants and Children." *Perfusion* 9 (4): 257-263, 1994.

Tsubokawa, K.; M. Narita; E. Mase; I. Murakami; T. Otagiri; N. Kurokochi and K. Mori. "[Anesthetic management of ten Jehovah's Witness patients]" *Masui-Japanese Journal of Anesthesiology*, 45 (1): 111-114, 1996, Jan. [Japanese].

"Tvungen blodoverforing." *Tidsskrift for Den Norske Laegeforening*. 116 (1): 109, 1996 Jan 10. (Compulsory Blood Transfusion.) [Norwegian]

Ulsenheimer, K. "Verweigerung der Bluttransfusion aus religiösen Gründen." *Geburtshilfe und Frauenheilkunde*, Jun., 1994, 54 (6): M83-6. (Refusal of Blood Transfusion for Religious Reasons) [German].

"Unscientific Christian Creeds Doom Millions to Needless Death." *Mohammed Speaks*, Sept., 1966, pp. 7, 8. (About the many deaths caused by the Watchtower blood doctrine.)

Ushijima, A. et al. "Administration of recombinant erythropoitin to a patient with malignant lymphoma who refused blood transfusion." *Rinsho Ketsueki*, Oct. 1990, 31 (10): 1698-700 [English. Abstract, article in Japanese]

van Leusen, R.; H.E. Deenik and F. G. Buskens. "Successful Renal Autotransplantation for Renal Failure with Prolonged Oliguria in a Jehovah's Witness with Fibromuscular Dysplasia of the Renal Arteries." *Netherlands Journal of Medicine*, 45 (5): 221-224, 1994 Nov.

Vanelli P., P. Castelli, A.M. Condemi, and C. Santoli. "Blood Saving in Jehovah's Witnesses." *Annals of Thoracic Surgery*, Oct., 1991, 52 (4): 899-900.

Velin, P.; D. Dupont; C. Puig and A. Golkar. "Erythropoietine humaine recombinante et anemie due premature de parents Temoins de Jehovah." (Human recombinant erythroprotein and anemia in premature infants of parents who are Jehovah's Witnesses) [French]

Vercillo, Authur P., and Susan Duprey. "Jehovah's Witnesses and the transfusion of Blood Products." *New York State Journal of Medicine*, Sep. 1988, 88 (9): 493-494.

Victorino, G. and D.H. Wiser. Jehovah's Witnesses: Unique Problems in a Unique Trauma Population" *Journal of the American College of Surgeons*. 184(5):458-468 1997.

Vincent, J.L. "Transfusion in the exsanguinating Jehovah's Witness patient--the attitude of intensive-care doctors." *European Journal of Anesthesiology*, Jul. 1991, 8 (4): 297-300.

Vogt, P.M., K. Kurz-Muller, F.W. Peter, R. Buttemeyer, M. Tryba, and H.U. Steinau. "Einsparung von Fremdblutgaben bei schwerbrandverletzten Zeugen Jehovas." *Chirurg*, Nov., 1994, 65 (11): 1066-8. (Preventing blood transfusion in a severely burned Jehovah's Witness) [German]

Watters, Randall. "Is Blood Forbidden Among Jehovah's Witnesses?" *Free Minds Journal* 11(5):2, 12, Sept.-Oct., 1992.

Watts, G.T. "NHS Trusts and Jehovah's Witnesses." *Lancet*, Vol. 339, No. 8808, Jun., 1992, p. 1545.

Weinberger, Morris; William M. Tierney; James Y. Green; and Albert P. Studdard. "The Development of Physician Norms in the United States; The Treatment of Jehovah's Witness Patients." *Social Science & Medicine*, 1982, 16(19): 1719-1723.

"When Patients Refuse Blood...Jehovah's Witnesses." *Emergency Medicine*, Oct. 30, 1984, 16 (18): 65, 69.

Williamson, Willie P. "Life or Death--Whose Decision?" *Journal of the American Medical Association*, Sept. 5, 1966, 197 (10): 139-141.

Winter, R.B., et al. "Jehovah's Witnesses and Consent." *Journal of Legal Medicine*, 1974, 2 (9): 9.

"Without Transfusion." *Inside Baylor Medicine*, 1968, 2: 2-4.

Wittman, P.H. and F.W. Wittmann. "Total Hip Replacement Surgery Without Blood Transfusion in Jehovah's Witnesses." *British Journal of Anesthesia*, Mar., 1992, 68 (3): 306-7. (12 cases are described and compared to a control group, each which received 3 units of blood.)

Wittmann, F.W. and P.H. Wittmann. "Revision of Total Hip Replacement in Jehovah's Witnesses" *British Journal of Anesthesia*, 72 (2): 252, 1994.

"Witnesses' Campaign Will Stress Position on Blood Transfusions." *Liberty*, Nov.-Dec. 1977, 67: 30.

Woloski, Rosalie. "As God Was Their Witness." *Maclean's*, Sept. 21, 1981, pp. 24-26.

_____. "Blood, Toil, Tears and Death." *Maclean's*, April 20, 1981, 94: 33.

Wong, D.H., et al. "Surgery in Jehovah's Witnesses." *Canadian Journal of Anesthetics*, Sep. 1989, 36 (5): 578-585. Comment, Vol. 37, No. 3, Apr. 1990, pp. 391-392.

Wong, K.C. "Hemodilution and Induced Hypotension for Insertion of a Harrington Rod in a Jehovah's Witness." *Clinical Orthopedics and Related Research*, Oct. 1980, 152: 237-240.

Wood, Kenneth H. "Blood Transfusions." *Review and Herald*, Dec. 3, 1959, 136: 4-5.

Zander, R. and B. von Bormann. "Life Without Hemoglobin" *Anasthesiologie, Intensivmedizin, Notfallmedizin, Schmerztherapie*, 31 (8): 488-490, 1996 Oct.

Zaorski, J.R., et al. "Open Heart Surgery for Acquired Heart Disease in Jehovah's Witnesses: A Report of 42 Operations." *American Journal of Cardiology*, 1972, 29: 186-189.

Zaremski, M.J. "Blood Transfusions and Elective Surgery: A Custodial Functional of Ohio Juvenile Court." *Cleveland State Law Review*, 23 (2): 231-244.

Zieg, P.M.; S.M. Cohn and D.S.Beardsley, "Nonoperative Management of a Splenic Tear in a Jehovah's Witness with Hemophilia." *Journal of Trauma* 40 (2): 299-301, 1996 Feb.

B. Court Cases, Legal Problems, and Persecution   (see also Flag Cases)

"ADL Objects to Greek Court's Comparison of Jews with Witnesses." *The Christian New*, Jan. 28, 1985, p. 13.

Alexander, David. "Fun with Missionaries." *The Humanist*, Sept./Oct., 1990, 150 (5): 45-46. (A critical, often mocking critique of the Witnesses).

Balter, Harry G. "Freedom of Religion Interpreted in Two Supreme Court Decisions." *The State Bar Journal of the State Bar of California*, June 1940, 15 (6): 160-165."

"Bearing Witness." *Time*, April 20, 1981, 117 (11): 51. (About a Witness who quit his job after he was transferred to a defense plant.)

Beers, Gilbert V. "A Tanzanian Government Official Has Ordered the Demolition of All Jehovah's Witness Kingdom Halls." *Christianity Today*, May 18, 1984, p. 88. (About the persecution in socialist Tanzania).

Bergman, Jerry. "Theocratic War Strategy; Why Witnesses Lie in Court." *Free Minds Journal*, Mar/Ap, 1994, 13 (2): 1-5.

_____. "Do Witness Psychologists Turn In Their Patients?" *Free Minds Journal*, 13 (4): 10-11, 1994.

_____. "Watchtower Threatens." *Free Minds Journal* 14 (5) Nov./Dec. 1995 p. 8-11.

_____. "Jehovah's Witnesses: A Brief History of a Century of Religious-State Conflicts." *JW Research Journal* 3 (1): 18-28, 1996.

_____. "Why Jehovah's Witness Leave the Watchtower." *JW Research Journal* 3 (1): 29-32, 1996.

_____. "Dealing with Jehovah's Witness Custody Cases." *Creighton Law Review*." 1996 29 (4) 1483-1516. (A review of the literature on custody)

_____. "The Jehovah's Witnesses' Experience in the Nazi Concentration Camps; A History of Their Conflicts with the Nazi State." *Journal of Church and State* Winter 1996 38 (1): 87-113.

"Bible Teaching Banned in Liberia." *Church and State*, June 1969, 22 (6): 10.

Blodgett, Nancy. "Confidentiality vs. Doctrine; Jehovah's witness lawyers, workers face dilemma." *ABA Journal*, Feb. 1, 1988, 74: 16. (Discusses the new Watchtower doctrine requiring Witnesses to ignore their professions' rules of ethical conduct and break confidentiality rules and turn in Witnesses who violate Watchtower policy such as those who accept a blood transfusion).

Bolmdahl, Rune. "Swedish Conscientious Objectors Win Bloodless Battle." *Liberty*, Nov.-Dec. 1978, pp. 18-19.

Bourdin, Louis B. "Freedom of Thought and Religious Liberty under the Constitution." *Lawyers Guild Review*, June 7, 1944, 4 (3): 9-24.

Burns, David. "The Zebroskis' 12-year Marathon; The Latest Episode in a Bitter Battle Against the Witnesses." *Alberta Report*, June 27, 1988, p. 30. (About Zebroski's law-suit against the Watchtower for being disfellowshipped. They later lost).

Butler, W.J. "Right of Free Listening." *Catholic World*, Dec. 1948, 168: 200-201.

Campbell, Courtney S. "The Pure Church and the Problem of Confidentiality." *The Hasting's Center Report*, Feb-Mar., 1988, 18 (1): 2.

Carrizosa, Philip. "Church 'shunning' held protected, not tort matter." *The Los Angeles Daily Journal*, June 11, 1987, 100: 1, col. 4.

"Civil Rights vs. Property." *The New Republic*, Jan. 21, 1946, 114: 69.

Cohen, Lori. "Another Crooked Lawyer." *Alberta Law Report*. Sept 23, 1985 p. 232. (About Jehovah Witness lawyer Water Shandro who was jailed for "stealing more than $200,000 from his clients . . . more than half of it was from fellow Jehovah's Witnesses").

"Constitutional Law--Due Process Under the Fourteenth Amendment--Freedom of Religion, Speech and Assembly." *Minnesota Law Review*, April 1948, 32 (5): 498-502.

Dilliard, Irving. "About-Face to Freedom." *The New Republic*, May 24, 1943, 108: 693-695. (Discusses Supreme Court reversal of a Witnesses flag case).

Dimmler, Eleni. "Pope Calls Mormons and Jehovah's Witnesses Anti-Ecumenical." *Christian News*, Feb. 18, 1985, p. 2.

Doyle, Denise J. "Religious Freedom In Canada." *Journal of Church and State*, Autumn 1984, 26 (3): 413-435 (p. 420-427 covers Candian Witnesses cases and Canada).

Eliff, Nathan. "Jehovah's Witnesses and the Selective Service." *Virginia Law Review*, 1945, 31: 811-834.

Engardio, Joel P. "Jehovah's Witnesses' Untold Story of Resistance to Nazis." *The Christian Science Monitor*, International Edition, Boston. November 8-14, 1996, page 1 and 13. (Reviews the Society's video *Stand Firm* premiered at the Ravensbruck concentration camp on November 6, 1996).

Florka, Robert R. "Constitutional law--freedom of religion--state's denial of unemployment benefits to Jehovah's Witness who quit armaments production job for religious reasons violates first amendment's free exercise clause." (Case note). *University of Detroit Journal of Urban Law*, Winter 1982, 59: 217-229.

Fraser, R.B. "How Will Supreme Court Weigh Duplessis' Power?" *Macleans, Canada's National Magazine*, July 7, 1958, 71: 2.

"Freedom to Proselyte." *Newsweek*, March 12, 1945, 25: 88.

Green, J.R. "Liberty Under the Fourteenth Amendment." *Washington University Law Quarterly*, Summer 1942, 27: 497-562.

"Homecoming." *Time*, Dec. 1, 1975, p. 60. (On the persecution in Malawi).

Howerton, Huey B. "Jehovah's Witnesses and the Federal Constitution." *Mississippi Law Journal*, March-May 1946, 17 (1); 347-371.

Hunter, Ian A. "Would This Couple Make Good Citizens of Canada?" *United Church Observer*, Nov. 1976, pp. 27, 18.

"In Re Jehovah's Witnesses." *The Fortnightly Law Journal*, Feb. 15, 1947, 16: 221, 222.

"Jehovah's Witnesses and the Supreme Court." *The Sign*, June 1943, 22: 645.

"Jehovah's Witnesses and the Supreme Court." *Social Service Review*, June 1943, 17: 226.

"Jehovah's Witnesses Meeting Halls Order Raced in Tasmania." *Religious News Service*, March 20, 1984 (printed in *Christian News*, April 2, 1984, p. 12.

"Jehovah's Witnesses: Persecution, Past and Present." *The Wiener Library Bulletin*, 1951, 5: 8.

"Jehovah's Witnesses 'Shunning' Passes Court Scrutiny." *Church and State*, July, Aug. 1987, 40 (7): 21.

Kaplan, William. "The Supreme Court of Canada and the protection of minority dissent: the case of the Jehovah's Witnesses." (1989 Viscount Bennett Seminar) *University of New Brunswick Law Journal Annual*, 1990, 39: 65-77.

Kent, Peter. "Seminar Discussion: Kaplan." (Viscount Bennett Seminar) Vol. 39, University of New Brunswick Law Journal Annual, 1990 pp. 78-84.

"Kenya Has Banned Missionaries." *Christianity Today*, Sept. 28, 1973, 17 (9): 57.

King, Christina E. "Strategies for Survival: An Examination of the History of Five Christian Sects in Germany 1933-1945." *Journal of Contemporary History*, April 1979, 14 (2): 211-234. (About the Witnesses and similar groups in Nazi Germany who were persecuted and their response).

_____. "Pacifists, Neutrals or Resisters? Jehovah's Witnesses and the Experience of National Socialism." *Bulletin of the John Rylands University Library*, Autumn, 1988, 70: 149-156. (A well done study of Witnesses in Nazi Germany and the basis of their objection to war).

King, Kathleen Piker and Dennis E. Clayson. Perceptions of Jews, Jehovah's Witnesses, and Homosexuals. *California Sociologists*, Winter 1987, pp. 49-67.

King, R.C.C. "Constitutional Legacy of the Jehovah's Witnesses." *Social Science Quarterly*, Sept. 1964, 45: 125-134.

"Konzentrations Lager." *Sunday Mirror* (Magazine Section), Feb. 9, 1941, pp. 2, 12. (Concentration Camp.)

Lautmann, Rüdiger. "Categorization in Concentration Camps as a Collective Fate: A Comparison of Homosexuals, Jehovah's Witnesses and Political Prisoners." *Journal of Homosexuality*, 1990, 19 (1): 67-88.

Luchterhand, Elmer. "Prisoner behavior and social system in the Nazi concentration camps." *International Journal of Social Psychiatry*, 1967, 13 (4): 245-267. (Discusses the camps in general, and covers the Witnesses).

Lunny, Rev. W.J., and Ethel Douglas. Letters (in response to the Nov. 1976 article "Would This Couple Make Good Citizens of Canada?"). *United Church Observer*, Jan. 1977, p. 2.

MacGowan, Gault. "Jehovah's Witnesses." *Catholic Digest*, Vol. 3, Jan. 1938, pp. 71-76.

Maddox, Robert L. "Beware of Pompey." *Church and State*, Feb. 1985, p. 23. (About disfellowshipping and issues raised by Jim Penton).

_____. "Jehovah's Witnesses Lose Indian Anthem Appeal." *Church and State*, Feb. 1986, 39 (2): 22.

_____. "Reflections on Surviving Morton Downey." *Church and State*, Dec. 1988, 41 (12): 21. (On the efforts to enforce by law flag saluting).

Mair, Tracy. "I Literally Went Through the Roof." *New Idea*, Nov. 9, 1985, p. 22. (About a Kingdom Hall bombing; one was killed, 55 injured).

Martens, Doreen. "Jehovah's Witnesses Exhorted to Breach Client Confidentiality." *Winnipeg Free Press*, September 5, 1987.

McAninch, William Shepard. "A catalyst for the evolution of constitutional law: Jehovah's Witnesses and the Supreme Court." *University of Cincinnati Law Review*, Spring, 1987, 55: 997-1077.

Mendez, Albert. "A House Divided." *Church and State*, April 1985.

Mentaxoo, John C. "Spreading the liability." *The National Law Journal*, Oct. 7, 1985, 8: 47, col. 2. (Whether Jehovah's Witnesses are liable for traffic accident suffered by members while proselytizing for the Watchtower).

Moss, Debra Cassens. "Religion vs. Custody." *ABA Journal*, Nov. 1, 1988, pp. 32-33. (A brief review of the Witness custody case problems).

Munters, Quirinus J. "Recruitment as a Vocation: The Case of Jehovah's Witnesses." *Sociologia Neerlandica*, 1971, 7 (12): 88-100.

Naso, James V. "How far is the Supreme Court willing to go?" (case note). *Ohio Northern University Law Review*, Winter, 1983, 10: 193-201.

Nightingale, L. "Why banned in Australia?" *Investigator Magazine*, Jan., 1989, No. 4, p. 23. (Discusses why Witnesses were banned in Australia).

O'Brien, Kenneth R., and Daniel O'Brien. "Freedom of Religion in Restatement of Inter-Church-and-State Common Law." *The Jurist*, Oct. 1946, 6: 503-523.

"Opinions of the Supreme Judicial Court: Commonwealth vs. William Johnson, Jr and Others." *Advance Sheets*, pp. 1351-1360.

Owen, Ralph Dornfield. "Jehovah's Witnesses and Their Four Freedoms." *University of Detroit Law Journal*, March 1951, 14 (3): 111-113.

"Parents' Rights." *Newsweek*, Feb. 14, 1944, p. 86. (About the Mrs. Sarah Prince Case, a Witness who argued that children and parents are not required to obey child labor laws when involved in street preaching and sales of religious literature).

Pound, Roscoe. "Constitutional Law--Jehovah's Witnesses." *Notre Dame Lawyer*, Nov. 1946, 22: 82-94.

"Recent Jehovah's Witnesses Cases." *International Judicial Association Bulletin*, July 1941, 10: 5-7.

"Religious Freedom and the Jehovah's Witnesses." *Virginia Law Review*, Jan. 1948, 34: 77-83.

"Religious Liberty under the Constitution of the United States." *Michigan Law Review*, Nov. 1940, 39: 149-152.

"Religious Liberty Under the Constitution of the United States." *Southern California Law Review*, Nov. 1940, 14: 57-58, 73-76. (Not the same as below).

"Religious Liberty under the Constitution of the United States." *University of Detroit Law Journal*, Nov. 1940, 4: 38-41. Not the same as above.

"Religious objection to alcohol test fails" *New York Law Journal*, Mar 17, 1989, 201; 1,

Richardson, James T. "Minority Religions, Religious Freedom, and the New Pan-European Political Institutions." *Journal of Church and State*. Winter 1995, 137 (1): 39-60. (Covers several Jehovah's Witness human rights cases in Europe, both child custody and pacifism.)

Schur, Morris J. "The Theology of the Jehovah's Witnesses and Its Conflict with Earthly Governments." *Western Political Quarterly*, 1967, 17: 101.

Semprum, Jorge. "A day in Buchenwald." *Dissent*, Fall, 1982, pp. 425-430. (An account of Witnesses in Buchenwald).

Singelenberg, Richard "Religieuze Stigmatisering? Toewijzing-Sperikelen Rondom het Jehovah's Getuige-ouderschap" *Tyschrift voor Familie and Jeudecht*. 1992 14 (8): 180-183 (Religious Stigmatization? Vissitudes of Custody around Jehovah's Witness Parenthood" in *Journal of Family and Juvenile Law*) (Discusses a case in which the Witness father is given custody. Concludes that the courts are biased against the Witnesses)

Stephenson, Wendy. "Penton Target of Witness 'Witchhunt'" *The Lethbridge Herald*, October 11, 1980.

"Suing Jehovah's Witnesses." *Alberta Report*, Nov. 21, 1980, 7 (51): 24-25.

"Supreme Court Comes to Order." *Collier's Magazine*, June 12, 1943, p. 78.

"Supreme Court Decision Allows Local Limitation of Free Press." *Publishers Weekly*, June 20, 1942, 141: 2266.

"Supreme Court Reverses Convictions of Jehovah's Witnesses." *Publishers Weekly*, Feb. 16, 1946, 149: 1137.

"Supreme Court Reverses Decision in Jehovah's Witnesses Case." *Publishers Weekly*, May 8, 1943, 143: 1820.

"Supreme Court Reverses Stand on Anti-Peddling Ordinances." *Public Management*, June 1943, 25: 179.

"The All Writs Salute and the Injunctive Power of a Single Appellate Judge." *Michigan Law Review*, Dec. 1965, 64: 324-352 (On the Judge Wright Jehovah's Witness blood case decision).

"The Sources and Limits of Religious Freedom." *Illinois Law Review*, May-June 1946, 41 (1); 53-80.

Taylor Jr., Stuart. "Jehovah's Witness awaits court word; constitutional conflicts are focus of the justices' deliberations." *The New York Times*, Dec. 15, 1980, p. 1, 15, col. 3.

Tietz, J.B. "Jehovah's Witnesses: Conscientious Objectors." *Southern California Law Review*, Feb. 1955, 28: 123-137.

"Two Liberal Opinions from the Federal Courts." *Social Service Review*, Dec. 1942, 16: 672.

"Victory without Peace." *Extension*, Aug. 1943, 38: 19.

Votaw, Herbert H. "Jehovah's Witnesses and Freedom of Speech." *Liberty*, 4th Quarter 1948, 43: 16-20.

Walosin, Frank. "Terror in Malawi." *Bachelor News*, Mar. 2, 1968, p. 3. (About the persecution in Malawi; very favorable to Witnesses).

Wise, Stuart M. "'Holy' courtship and divorce." *The National Law Journal*, June 14, 1982, p. 47. (About a Jehovah's Witnesses sued for alienation of affection).

"Witness on Trial: Judicial Intrusion Upon the Practices of Jehovah's Witness Parents." *Florida State University Law Review*. (Summer '93) 21: 205-22. (About the Mendez child custody case).

"The Witnesses (Outlawed in Poland)." *Time*, July 17, 1950, p. 71.

"Witnesses Spartan Trials. *Time*, Sept. 9, 1966, pp. 58-59. (About Witness persecution in Greece, mostly because of their refusal to be inducted into the military).

"Witnesses Upheld by Court." *Religious Freedom Alert*, Sept-Oct. 1985, 1 (12): 19.

"Witnesses Win." *Church and State*, Sept. 1974, 27(9): 22. (About a tax case in Brooklyn, NY).

Wright, H. "Religious Liberty under the Constitution of the United States." *Virginia Law Review*, Nov. 1940, 27: 75-87.

Young, Phyllis A. "Jehovah's Witnesses." *Department of State Bulletin*, Nov. 1986, 86 (2116): 80. (On Witness persecution in Russia).

C. The Flag Salute Issue (see also Court Cases)

A., J.S. "Religious Freedom, Flag Salute in Public Schools." *Washington Law Review*, Nov. 1940, 15: 265, 266.

Anderson, P.H. "Religious Freedom, Flag Salute in Public Schools." *Georgia Bar Journal*, May 1940, 2: 74-76.

B., W.C. "The Supreme Court Hands Down an Educationally Significant Decision." *School and Society*, June 26, 1943, 57 (1487): 696, 697.

Baldus, S.A. "Saluting the Flag." *Extension*, Dec. 1940, 35: 8, 19.

Bergman, Jerry. "Religious Objections to the Flag Salute." *The Flag Bulletin*. 6(3):1-4 May-June 1997.

_____. "Modern religious objections to the mandatory flag salute and Pledge of Allegiance in the United States." *Christian Quest*, Summer 1989, 2 (1): 19-44). (A review of the flag salute controversy in the United States concluding that the children were caught between two inhumane institutions, the state and the Watchtower).

_____. The Modern Religious Objection to Mandatory Flag Salute in America." *Journal of Church and State*. Spring 1997 39(2):501-522.(A summary of the flag salute controversy in America).

Blakely, P.L. "Omnipotent Schoolboards: Enforced Flag Salute." *America*, June 22, 1940, 63: 286-287. Correspondence about July 6, 1940, pp. 353-354.

_____. "Flag Salute vs. Oregon Case." *America*, June 15, 1940, 63: 259-260.

"Breeding Peace Martyrs in Cradle: Children of Jehovah's Witnesses Refuse to Salute the Flag." *Literary Digest*, May 2, 1936, 21: 18.

Chambers, M.M. "Flag Salute Before the Bench." *Nations Schools*, June 1939, 23: 62.

_____. "You Can't Come to School." *Nations Schools*, Dec. 1937, 20: 33, 34.

"Chief Justice Hughes Interrupts." *Ave Maria*, April 20, 1940, 54: 483.

"Children Must Salute the Flag." *The New Republic*, June 17, 1940, p. 810.

"Compulsory Flag Salute." *Journal of Education*, Dec. 1937, 120: 195.

"Constitutional Law--Due Process Under the Fourteenth Amendment--Freedom of Religion, Speech, and Assembly." *Minnesota Law Review*, 1948, 32: 498-502.

"Constitutional Law--Freedom of Religion--Public Schools--Compulsory Flag Salute." *Minnesota Law Review*, April 1943, 27 (5): 471, 472.

"Constitutional Law--Freedom of Worship--Salute to the Flag." *St. John's Law Review*, Nov. 1938, 13: 144-147.

"Court and the Flag." *Newsweek*, June 21, 1943.

Coutts, Mary T. "How the Flag Pledge Originated." *Journal of Education*, Oct. 1942, 125 (7): 225, 226.

Cunningham, Juanita. "Our American Flag." *The Grade Teacher*, Feb. 1937, 54: 64, 65.

Cupples, H.L. "Protection of Personal Liberties Under the Fourteenth Amendment: The Flag Salute." *George Washington Law Review*, May 1940, 8: 1094-1097.

Dilliard, Irving. "Salute to the Court: Jehovah's Witnesses Cases." *The New Republic*, March 1, 1943, 108: 276, 277.

"Education: 'Devil's Emblem.'" *Time*, Nov. 18, 1935, p. 59. (About Jehovah's Witnesses who refuse to salute the flag).

F., J.F. "Religious Freedom. Flag Salute in Public Schools." *New York University Law Quarterly Review*, Nov. 1940, 18: 124-127.

Fennell, W.G. "The Reconstructed Court and Religious Freedom; the Gobitis Case in Retrospect." *New York University Law Quarterly Review*, Nov. 1941, 19: 31-48.

"The Flag Ritual." *Journal of Education*, Jan 1941, 124: 25.

"The Flag Salute." *Journal of the National Education Association*, Dec. 1943, 32 (9): 265, 266.

"Flag Salutes and Food." *Social Service Review*, Sept. 1940, 14: 574, 575.

"Flag Saluting Case." *Extension*, Vol. 37, Aug. 1942, pp. 19, 20.

Frankfurter, F. "Religious Freedom." *The New Republic*, Vol. 102, June 24, 1940, pp. 843, 852-855. Contains the complete text of dissent with editorial comment on the flag salute case.

"Freedom of Religion--Compulsory Flag Salute." *Michigan Law Review*, Aug./Oct.

1943, 42: 186, 187, 319-321.

"Freedom of Religion--Compulsory Flag Salute." *Minnesota Law Review*, Jan. 1944, 28: 133.

"Freedom of Religion--Flag Salute--Duty of Lower Federal Court to Follow Unreversed Decisions of Supreme Court." *Columbia Law Review*, Jan. 1943, 43: 134, 135.

"Freedom of Religion--Flag Salute--Duty of Lower Federal Court to Follow Unreversed Decisions of Supreme Court." *George Washington Law Review*, Dec. 1942, 11: 112-114.

Fuller, Helen. Section 52 Is News." *The New Republic*, Feb. 15, 1943, p. 204.

Glasser, Ira. "Not pledging allegiance: it can be patriotic." *Religion in Public Education*. Summer 1988, 15: 235.

Glenn, Patricia. "Junk Food Religion." *Liberty*, Sept.-Oct., 1983, p. 3.

"God's in His Heaven...." *Newsweek*, July 5, 1943, pp. 81, 82. (About the Gobitis flag salute case; a well done story).

H., W.T. "Freedom of Religion--Compulsory Flag Salute." *Temple University Law Quarterly*, Aug. 1943, 17: 465-466.

H., W.W. "Religious Freedom. Flag Salute in Public Schools." *Temple University Law Quarterly*, July 1940, 14: 545-547.

Hodgdon, Daniel R. "Flag-Salute Issue Settled." *Clearing House*, Nov. 1944, 19: 192, 193.

_____. "No More Compulsory Salutes Allowed." *Clearing House*, April 1947, 21: 499, 500.

Howard, F.L. "Civil Liberties, Freedom of Religion, Compulsory Flag Salute." *Montana Law Review*, Jan. 1941, 6: 106-111.

"I Pledge a Legion." *Journal of Education*, March 1, 1937, 120: 122, 123. (Not the same as the article by Moser below).

"Jehovah Reversal." *Newsweek*, May 10, 1943, pp. 40, 42.

"Jehovah's Witnesses and Supreme Court." *Sign*, June 1943, 22: 645.

"Jehovah's Witnesses Convicted." *Ave Maria*, Feb. 22, 1941, 53: 227.

"Jehovah's Witnesses lose Indian Anthem appeal." *Church and State*, Feb. 1966, p. 22. (The court ruled that chanting the National Anthem is a secular act, thus Witness children can be expelled for not chanting).

"Jehovah's Witnesses. The American Flag and the Courts." *Social Service Review*, Sept. 1940, 14: 574, 575.

"Judiciary 4 to 5; 5 to 4." *Time*, May 17, 1943, p. 21.

Kearney, J.J. "Supreme Court Abdicates as nation's School Board." *Catholic Educational Review*, Oct. 1940, 38: 357-360.

Kim, Richard C.C. "The Constitution, the Supreme Court, and Religious Liberty." *Journal of Church and State*, 1964, 6: 333-343.

Lang, Daniel. "A Reporter At Large, Love of Country." *The New Yorker*, July 30, 1973, 49 (23): 35-48.

Levene, L. "Religious Freedom, Flag Salute in Public Schools." *Cornell Law Quarterly*, Dec. 1940, 26: 127-130.

"Lynn, Mass. Schoolboy Refuses to Salute the Flag." *America*, Oct. 5, 1935, 53: 615.

Maddox, Robert L. "With liberty and justice for all?" *Church and State*, 1988, 41: 215. (1940 persecution of Jehovah's Witness, regarding pledge of allegiance).

Mayer, Jean Francois. "Les Témoins de Jéhovah, un siécle déja, L'ére des fondateurs, *Notre Histoire*, No. 5, Oct., 1984, pp. 34-38.(The Jehovah's Witnesses, A Century Already. The Year of Our Foundation) [French]

Moreau, A. Scott. "Jehovah's Witnesses." *East African Journal of Evangelical Theology.* 17 (1): 10-27, 1988.

Moser, A.C., and Bert David. "I Pledge a Legion." *Journal of Educational Sociology*, March 1936, 9: 436-440.

Nesbitt, J.S. "Civil Liberties, Freedom of Religion, Compulsory Flag Salute." *Georgia Bar Journal*, Nov. 1940, 3: 66, 67.

Olander, Herbert T. "Children's Knowledge of the Flag Salute." *Journal of Educational Research*, Dec. 1941, 35 (4): 300-305.

"Our Pledge of Allegiance--A Task for Tomorrow." *Ohio Schools*, Oct. 1942, 21: 306, 307, 327.

Punke, Harold H. "The Flag and the Courts in Free Public Education." *Journal of Religion*, April 1944, 24: 119-130.

"The Pure Church and the Problem of Confidentiality [Jehovah's Witnesses]." *Hastings Center Report*, Feb.-Mar. 1988, 18: 2.

"Religious Freedom and the Jehovah's Witnesses." *Virginia Law Review*, Jan. 1948, 34: 77-83.

"Religious Freedom, Flag Salute in Public Schools." *St. John's Law Review*, November 1940, 15: 95-97.

"Religious Freedom, Flag Salute in Public Schools." *International Juridical Association Bulletin*, July 1940, 9 (1): 10-12.

Remmlein, M.K. "Freedom of Religion--Compulsory Flag Salute." *George Washington Law Review*, Dec. 1943, 12: 70-80.

"A Reporter at Large: Love of Country." *The New Yorker*, July 13, 1973, pp. 35-46. (An important article which discusses a case history of a teacher who refused to salute the flag for personal reasons. The teacher was not a Jehovah's Witness).

Ruediger, W.C. "Saluting the Flag." *School and Society*, June 26, 1943, 21: 696, 697.

Scott, Moreau, A. "Jehovah's Witnesses." *East African Journal of Evangelical Theology*, 7 (1): 10-27, 1988.

S., D.E. "Religious Freedom, Flag Salute in Public Schools." *University of Cincinnati Law Review*, May-Nov. 1940, 14: 444-447.

Shenk, Phil M., ed. "Fire Unpatriotic School Teacher." *Sojourners*, March 1980, p. 6.

Slade, T.B. "Freedom of Religion--Compulsory Flag Salute." *Georgia Bar Journal*,
    Feb. 1944, 6: 249, 250.

Stoltzfus, Grant M. "When the flag goes by." *Christian Living*, Oct. 1971, 18: 2-9.

Stone, H.F. "Religious Freedom." *The New Republic*, June 24, 1940, 102: 843, 852-
    855. (Flag salute case: complete text of majority opinion and of dissent with
    editorial comment).

"Supreme Court Reversal." *Ave Maria*, May 22, 1943, 57: 644.

Waite, Edward F. "The Debt of Constitutional Law to Jehovah's Witnesses." *Minnesota
    Law Review*, March 1944, 28 (4): 209-246.

Ward, Pamela. "Rita's choice: The Florida courts forced a Miami mother to decide: Your
    religion or your child." *Church and State*, May 1988, 41: 104-107.

"Weight of Witnessing." *America*, Aug. 19, 1950, 83: 507.

Wiltbye, John. "Counsel for Saivey and the Chief Justice..."

Wilthy, J. "Jehovah's Witnesses Before the Supreme Court." *America*, April 20, 1940,
    63: 35-36.

Wingerd, S. "Civil Liberties, Freedom of Religion, Compulsory Flag Salute." *Journal of
    the Bar Association of Kansas*, 1941, 9: 276-280.

"With Script and Staff (Schoolboy refuses to salute flag)." *America*, Oct. 5, 1935, 53:
    614.

"Witnesses of Jehovah." *Sign*, Dec. 1945, 25: 27-28.

"Zoning Hits Minority Church." *Church and State*, March 1982, 35 (3): 17.

D. Sociological and Psychological Studies

Abrahams, Edward. "The Pain of the Millennium: Charles Taze Russell and the
    Jehovah's Witnesses, 1879-1916." *American Studies*, 1977, 18: 57-70.

Aguirre, Benigno. "Organizational Change and Religious Commitment of Jehovah's
    Witnesses and Seventh-Day Adventists in Cuba, 1938-1965." *Pacific Sociological
    Review*, April 1980, 23 (2): 171-179.

Aiken, James M. "I Was Brainwashed by the Jehovah's Witnesses." *Power For Living*,
    Oct. 18, 1964.

Allison, Anette. "Debbie's Perfect." *Womans Day*. Aug. 6, 1991, p. 12. (About former
    television star Debbie Newsome who quit her acting career to become a Jehovah's
    Witness).

Alston, John P. and B.F. Aguirre. "Congregational Size and the Decline of Sectarian
    Commitment: The Case of the Jehovah's Witnesses in South and North America."
    Sociological Analysis, Spring 1979, 40 (1): 63-70.

Alston, John P. "Organizational Change and Religious Commitment of Jehovah's
    Witnesses and Seventh-Day Adventists in Cuba, 1938-1965." *Pacific Sociological
    Review*, April 1980, 23 (2): 171-179.

Andre, J. "Religious Group Value Patterns and Motive Orientations." *Journal of

Psychology and Theology, 1980, 8 (2): 129-139.

Arsenault, Joseph A. "Jehovah's Witnesses." *Free Inquiry*, Summer, 1985, 5 (2): 55, 58.

Assimeng, John Maxwell. "Jehovah's Witnesses: A Study in Cognitive Dissonance." *Universitas* (Pub. by the University of Ghana), Sept. 1973, 92: 103-105.

Beckford, James A. "The Embryonic Stage of Religious Sect's Development: The Jehovah's Witnesses." *Sociological Yearbook of Religion in Britain*, 1972, 5: 11-32.

_____. "Organization, Ideology and Recruitment: The Structure of the Watchtower Movement." *The Sociological Review*, No.v 1975, 23 (4): 893-909.

_____. "New Wine in New Bottles: A Departure from Church-Sect Conceptual Tradition." *Social Compass*, 1976, 23: 71-85.

_____. "Sociological Stereotypes of the Religious Sect." *The Sociological Review*, Feb. 1978, 26 (1): 109-123.

_____. "Structural Dependence in Religious Organizations: From 'Skid-Row' to Watchtower." *Journal for the Scientific Study of Religion*, 1976, 15 (2): 169-175.

_____. "The Watchtower Movement World-Wide." *Social Compass*, 1977, 24: 5-31.

_____. "Accounting for Conversion." *British Journal of Sociology*, 1978, 29: 249-262.

_____. "Sociological Stereotypes of the Religious Sect." *Sociological Review*, 1978, 26: 109-123.

Bergman, Jerry. "The Pessimistic Sect's Influence on the Mental Health of its Members." *Social Compass*, 1977. 24 (1): 135-147.

_____. "Jehovah's Witnesses and Mental Illnesses." *Christian Apologetics: Research and Information Service Newsletter* (CARIS), Feb./Mar. 1977. 3 (2): 2-5.

_____. "The Life of One Raised as One of Jehovah's Witnesses." *Christian Apologetics: Research and Information Service Newsletter* (CARIS), 1979. 3 (1): 8-9.

_____. "Jehovah's Witnesses and Blood Transfusion." *The Journal of Pastoral Practice*, 1980. 4 (2): 67-85.

_____. "What is Bethel?" *The Bible Examiner*, October 1981. 1 (4): 12-13.

_____. "Watchtower: Past and Present." *Comments from the Friends*, Spring 1984. 3 (2): 2.

_____. "Recent Turmoil of the Watchtower Society in Russia." *The Discerner*, April-June 1985. 11 (10): 13-15.

_____. Les Conséquences de l' éducation "Témain de Jéhovah," *Informez Vous*, Juillet, 1991, pp. 3-19.

_____. "Die Psyche der Zeugen Jehovas." *Psychologie Heute*, Feb. 1992, pp. 12-13 (taken from Bergman's writings by the editor).

_____. "De geestelijke gezondheid van Jehova-getuigen." *Psychologie*, April 1992, p. 6 (taken from Bergman's writings by the editor).

_____. "Reading Bumps and Faces: Phrenology and Physiognomy; A History of the Watchtower's Experience." *JW Research Journal* 3 (2) Spring 1996 p. 26-28.

_____. "Why Jehovah's Witnesses have a High Mental Illness Level." *Christian Research Journal.* Summer 1996 19 (1): 36-41.

_____. "Why Jehovah's Witnesses Have Mental Problems." *JW Research Journal* 3 (3): 6-17 Sum. 1996.

Biebuych, Daniel. "La Société Kumu Face au Kitawala." *Zaire*, Vol. 11, No. 1, Jan. 1957, pp. 7-40. (Kuma Society in Relation to Jehovah's Witnesses) (in French).

Blackwell, Brian and Suzanne Monks. "The Cult Busters." *New Idea*, March 3, 1986, pp. 6-9. (About Australian leading cult deprogrammers, one is an ex-Witness, Jan Groenveld; also discusses a blood transfusion case).

Bram, Joseph. "Jehovah's Witnesses and the Value of American Culture." *Transactions of the New York Academy of Sciences*, 1956,19: 47-53.

Brausch, G. "Intégration des institutions coutumieves dans l'action sociale en Afrique centrale." *Problémes d'Afrique Centrale* (Problems of Central Africa), No. 33, 1956, p 4 (in French). (Integration of the Customs Institutions in the Social Action in Central Africa).

Campbell, Roger F. (Told by Shirley Lyon). "Jehovah's Witnesses Built a Wall Between My Husband and Me." *Voice*, Feb. 1971, pp. 4, 5.

Cohn, Werner. "Jehovah's Witnesses as a Proletarian Movement." *The American Scholar*, 1955, 24: 281-98.

_____. "Jehovah's Witnesses and Racial Prejudice." *The Crisis*, Jan. 1956, 63: 5-9.
Coleman, James S. "Social Cleavage and Religious Conflict." *Journal of Social Issues*, 1956, 12 (3): 44-56.

Dericquebourg, Régis. "Les Témoins de Jehovah dans le nord de la France: implantation et expansion" (intro. in English and article in French). *Social Compass*, 1977, 24 (1): 71-82. (Jehovah's Witnesses in Northern France--Establishment and Expansion.)

_____. "Attitudes des Témoins de Jéhovah et des baptistes face a l'occupant dans le Nord de la France pendant la deuxiéme guerre modiale," *Review du Nord*, Avril-Juin 1978, pp. 439-444. (*Review of the North*, April-June, (Attitudes of the JW's and the Baptists Towards The Occupation in Northern France During the Second World War).

_____. "Naissance d'un prophétisme en société industrielle. Rationalité et économie du charisme. A propos de Charles Taze Russell." *Mélanges de Science Religieuse*, XXXVI, No 3, Sept. 1979, pp. 175-190. (Birth of a Prophesy in the Industrial Society. Rationality and economy of Charisma, as proposed by Charles T. Russell).

_____. "Le Bethel, ordre religieux jehoviste?" *Archives de sciences sociales des religions*, 1980, 25: 77-88. (Is Bethel A Religious Order?).

_____. "La place des Témoins de Jéhovah dans les groupes sectaires d'aprés officiels." *Mélanges de sciences religieuse*, XXXVIII, 1981, No 2. (The Place of J.W.s in the Group Sects From Official Survey).

_____. "Vocabulaire Jéhoviste." *Mouvements religieux*, Avril, 1984. (*Religious Movements*, April 1984, "Jehovah's Vocabulary").

_____. "Le Jéhovisme; Une conception Comportementaliste de la Vie Religieuse." *Archives de sciences sociales des religions*, 1986, July-Sept. 1986, 62 (1): 161-176. (The Jehovahism, A Behavioral Conception of the Religious Life).

_____. Le Jéhovisme: contre-emprise a la modernite (English. abst). *Archives de sciences sociales des religions*, July-Sept., 1989, 34: 93-112. (The Jehovah's Witnesses An Enterprise Against Modernity).

_____. "Religion et Thérapie" in Extrait des *Archieves de Sciences Sociales des Religions*, No. 55/2, 1983. (Religion and Therapy).

_____. "Note de sociologie religieuse: La place des Témoins de Jéhovah dans les groupes sectaires d'aprés leurs écrits officiels" in *Mélanges de Science Religieuse*, No 3, Spetembre, 1981, pp. 127-132. ("Note From Religous Sociology. The Place of the JW's in the Bigoted Groups According to Their official writings").

_____. "Les Sectes Religieuses" in *Savoir Pour Comprendre et Conseiller*, No. 309, Mars, 1978. (The Religious Sects in *To Know For Comprehension and Council*).

Dewing, Kathleen. "Some Characteristics of the Parents of Creative Twelve-Year-Olds." *Journal of Personality*, March 1973, 41 (1): 71-85. Found children of Jehovah's Witnesses were rated "highly creative" more often than non-Witness children.

"Did Yahshua Die to Save the House of Kyrious?" *World Today Analyzed in Prophecy's Spotlight*, April 1976, pp. 10, 11.

Dobbelaere, K., B.R. Wilson. "Les TéMoins de Jéhovah dans un pays catholique" in *Sommaire*, 25° Année, Juillet-Septembre, 1980, pp. 89-110. (Jehovah's Witnesses in a Catholic Country).

Drake, Betty. Letter from Mrs. L. Robinson, Baltimore, MD., in section titled "Speak Out America." *National Examiner*, Jan. 15, 1980.

Gilbert, Jennifer. "Why Debbie Newsome Is Praying To God." *Women's Day*, June 26, 1990, pp. 6-7. (About a former television star who became a Jehovah's Witness; Her husband is now in jail on drug charges).

"Hare Krishnas in the Dock." *Newsweek*, Sept. 29, 1980, p. 83.

Harris, Richard. "A Reporter at Large; I'd Like to Talk to You for a Minute." *The New Yorker*, June 16, 1956, 32: 72-80.

Harrison, Barbara Grizzuti. "Life with Jehovah." *Ms.*, Dec. 1975, 4 (6): 56-59, 89-92. (Harrison had a prominent position at the Watchtower headquarters and discusses her experiences; unfortunately her language offended many readers. Otherwise an excellent, insightful article)

Letters in response to the above article. *Ms.*, April 1976, pp. 4, 6.

_____. "The Way We Live Now: Papa Mia." *Ms.*, June 1977, 5 (12): 30-32.

_____. "Estranged from Joy." *McCall's Magazine*, Dec. 1977, pp. 111, 188, 190, 191.

"How God Changed Teresa Graves' Life!" *Movie Mirror*, Nov. 1974, 19(1): 28, 60.

Hyman, Bronwen. "Persistent allegiance to a religious group (Jehovah's Witnesses as ethnogenic case study)." *Sociological Review*, 1989, 18 (3): 273-282.

Iannaccone, Laurence R. "A Formal Model of Church and Sect." *American Journal of Sociology*. 94:S241-S268. 1988. (An excellent discussion of Sects and how they can be defined).

_____. "Why Strict Churches are Strong." *American Journal of Sociology.* 99(5):1180-1211. 1994. (An excellent discussion of why churches that stress high moral standards and commitment such as the Witnesses are growing).

Jadot, F.; J. Paquay and M. Timsit " Attitudes Concerning Military Duty and Personality Structures: Clinical Psychometric and Projective Study of Jehovah's Witnesses and Conscientious Objectors" *Acta Psychiatrica Belgica* 79(3): 254-273 May-Je 1979.(in French) (A study of the pathology of Witnesses, found to be greater than a control group)

Janner, Von J. "Die Forensisch-Psychiatrische und Sanitätsdienstliche Beurteilung von Dienstverweigerern." *Schweizerische Medizinische Wochenschrift*, 1963, 93 (23): 819-826.

Jefferson, Marge. "Touch of the Poet." *Newsweek*, Oct. 29, 1975, p. 51. (About Patti Smith, an ex-Witness).

"Jehovah's Vittnen på Frammarsch." *Religions Sociologiska Institute*, No. 133, Oct. 1976, 25 pp. (Jehovah's Witnesses on the Move.).

Jubber, Ken. "The Persecution of Jehovah's Witnesses in Southern Africa" (intro. in French and article in English). *Social Compass*, 1977, 24 (1): 121-134.

Kater, Michael K. "Die Ernsten Bibelforscher im Dritten Reich." *Vierteljahrhefte für Zeitgeschichte*, 17 Jahrgang, Heft 1/Jan. 1979, pp. 181-218. (The Jehovah's Witnesses in the 3rd Reich).

Knoch, Adolph Ernst. "An Appeal to the I.B.S.A." *Unsearchable Riches*, Vol. 23, 1932, pp. 327-330.

_____. "Brother Bundy's Journey." *Unsearchable Riches.* Vol. 30, 1939, p. 263.

_____. *Unsearchable Riches*, 56 (3): 13.

La Farge, Christopher. "Mickey Spillane and His Bloody Hammer." *Saturday Review*, 1954, 37 (6): 11, 12. (Spillane was a Witness for many years).

Lamping, Severin. "Mister Rutherford." *Sodalist*, Feb. 1938. Condensed in *Catholic Digest*, April 1938, 2: 5-7.

Larson, Charles R. "Invitation to a Wedding." *McCall's Magazine*, Aug. 1977, pp. 128, 191-193.

"Les Cuites Syncretiques Ont Fait l'Objet de Plusieurs Publications il Est Fait Occasionnelment Allusion au Kitawala ou á des Mouvements Analogues dans Certaines d'Entre Elles--Paris." *Sociologie Actuelle de l'Afrique Noire*, 1954. ("The "Cuites Syncretiques" were the object of several publications. This work occasionally alluded to the Kitawala or to certain analogous movements).

Lockwood, Robert. "How Jehovah's Witnesses Attack Catholicism." *Sunday Visitor*, Dec. 2, 1973, pp. 1, 12, 13.

"The Lost Word of Jehovah's Witnesses." *Power for Living*, Dec. 24, 1972.

"Lying Lips Abomination to the Lord." *Zion's Herald*, May 1976, p. 234.

Lyon, Shirley. "Jehovah's Witnesses Built a Wall Between My Husband and Me." *Voice*, Feb. 1971, pp. 4-5.

Maesen, William A. "Abstract of 'An Empirical Refutation of the Iron Law of Oligarche':
    United States Supreme Court Decisions Re the Jehovah's Witnesses."
    Sociological Abstracts, 17 (5): 103. Abstract number 09041.

_____. "Watchtower Influence on Black Muslim Eschatology." *Journal for the
    Scientific Study of Religion*, Winter 1970, 9 (4): 321-325.

_____. "The Jehovah's Witnesses Today: A Study by Participant Observation."
    Proceedings of the Southwestern Sociological Society, 1960, 9: 102-4.

Marinelli, Giovanni. "I testimoni de Geova in Italia." *Il Regno Documenti*, Anno XXXI,
    n. 542, 1 gennaio, 1986, pp. 56-63.

Mason, Joni. Letter in Response to "Invitation to a Wedding" (Aug. 1977). *McCall's
    Magazine*, Nov. 1977, p. 10.

Mellor, Steven. "Religious Group Value Patterns and Motive Orientations." *Journal of
    Psychology and Theology*, 1980, 8 (2): 129-139.

Montague, Havor. "The Pessimistic Sect's Influence on the Mental Health of Its
    Members: The Case of Jehovah's Witnesses" (intro. in French and article in
    English). *Social Compass*, 1977, 24 (1): 135-147. (A review of the research on
    the mental illness concerns of the Witnesses).

"Mother Denied Custody after Change in Religion." *Liberty*, Jan-Feb. 1982, 77 (1): 27.

Munters, Quirinus J. "Recruitment as a Vocation: The Case of Jehovah's Witnesses."
    Sociologica Neerlandica 7, 1971, pp. 88-100.

_____. "Abstract of 'Recruitment as a Vocation: The Case of Jehovah's Witnesses.'"
    Sociological Abstracts, 1973, p. 1178.

_____. "Recruitment et candidats en puissance" (intro. in English and article in French).
    Social Compass, 1977, 24 (1): 59-69. (Recruitment of Jehovah's Witnesses and
    Potential Candidates).

Nichol, Francis D. "The Editor's Mailbag." *Review and Herald*, Volume 141 April 9,
    1964.

Niklaus, Robert. "Ex-Jehovah's Witnesses Protest the Group's Practiced Shunning
    Former Members." *Christianity Today*,. Nov. 9, 1984, 28 (16): 63-66.

"Nudie Housing Idea Takes Off." *Moneyworth*, Feb. 28, 1977, p. 1. (About a former
    Witness).

Odebiyi, A. I. "Cultural Influences and Patient Behavior: Some Experiences in the
    Pediatric Ward of a Nigerian Hospital." *Child Care, Health and Development.*
    10(1): 49-59 Jan-Feb 1984. (Discusses Blood Issue and Witnesses).

Palmer, Phillip G. "Reply--Witnesses." *New Society*, July 26, 1973, p. 231.

Phillips, Wayne. "What Impels Jehovah's Witnesses." *New York Times Magazine*,
    Aug. 10, 1958, pp. 15, 48, 49.

"Photos." *Oui*, Oct. 1974, p. 14. (Discusses *Watchtower* magazine).

Potter, Bob. "The Psychology of Fundamentalism." *The Free Thinker*, 1984, 104: 60-
    61. (Covers Witnesses and other sects).

Ramos, Frank. "Jehovah's Witnesses." (*New York Times Magazine*, a reply to Phillips
    above). 1958.

Redekop, Calvin. "Decision Making in a Sect." *Review of Religious Research*, Fall 1960, 2 (2): 79-86.

_____ "The Sect Cycle in Perspective." *Mennonite Quarterly Review*, April 1962, 36 (2): 155-161.

_____. "The Sect from a New Perspective." *Mennonite Quarterly Review*, July 1965, pp. 204-217.

Regehr, Ernie. "Jehovah's Witnesses in Africa." *Christian Century*, Jan. 7, 1976, 93: 17, 18.

Religion och Kulture, 1976, 47 (4): 1-20. (Complete issue on the Witnesses) (in Swedish).

Russell, Gordon, Arthur Goddard and M. James Penton. "The Perception of Judeo-Christian Religion." *Canadian Journal of Behavioral Science*, 1979, 11 (2): 140-152.

Rylander, Gosta. "En Medicinsk-psykiatrisk-socialogisk under-sokning av Jehovah's Vittnen." *Nordisk Medicin*, Jan.-March 1946, 29 (1): 526-533. (A Psychological and Sociological Study of Jehovah's Witnesses).

Salholtz, Eloise. "Are They False Witnesses?" *Newsweek*, July 20, 1981, p. 75.

Seguy, Jean. "Messianisme et échec Social" Les Témoins de Jéhovah." *Archives de Sociologie des Religions*, No. 21, Janvier Juin 1966, pp. 89-99. (Millenarianism and social failures: Jehovah's Witnesses). (In French)

"Short Takes." *Time*, Feb. 28, 1972, p. 46. Playmate studying to be a Jehovah's Witness. Se also *Playboy Magazine*, Nov. 1971, cover and p. 94.

Singelenberg, Richard. "It Separated the Wheat from the Chaff: The '1975' Prophecy and Its Impact among Dutch Jehovah's Witnesses." *Sociological Analysis* Spring, 1989, 50: 23-40.

Smith, Patti. "Penthouse Interview." *Penthouse*, April 1976, 7 (8): 124-126, 150. (Smith was raised a Witness).

Sprague, Theodore W. "Some Notable Features in the Authority Structure of a Sect." *Social Forces*, March 1943, 21: 344-350. (A summary of his Ph.D. thesis at Harvard).

Stark, Rodney and Laurence Iannaccone. "Why the Jehovah's Witnesses Grow so Rapidly: A Theoretical Application." *Journal of Contemporary Religion*. 22(2);133-157. 1997. (An excellent study on church growth).

Stevenson, W.C. "Big Brother Knorr: Review of Year of Doom 1975." *Times Literary Supplement*, March 7, 1968, p. 234.

Ström, Ake. "Jehovah's Witnesses' Three Periods." In *New Religions: Based on Papers Read at the Symposium on New Religions Held at Abo on the 1st-3rd of Sept. 1974*, 141-53. Ed. Haralds Biezais. Stockholm: Almqvist & Wiksell International, 1974.

Stroup, Herbert. "The Attitude of Jehovah's Witnesses Toward the Roman Catholic Church." *Religion in the Making*, Jan. 1942, 2 (2): 148-163.

_____. "Class Theories of the Jehovah's Witnesses." *Social Science*, April 1944, 19 (2): 94-97. (Discusses the heaven and earth class teaching).

Student Action Committee. "Sister Dies as a Result of Rape" in *Obsidian*, Oct. 30, 1978, p 3.

Vermander, Jean Marie. "Etat présent des études sur les Témoins de J'hovah." *Mélanges de Science Religieuse*, XXXIV'me année, N° 3, 1977 p. 181 (many references).

Wah, Carolyn R. "Mental Health and Minority Religions: The Latest Battle in Custody Battles." *International Journal of Law and Psychiatry*. 1994 17 (3): 331-345. (An article written by a Watchtower attorney to defend and explain the Watchtower's position in these cases).

_____. "Religion in Child Custody and Visitation Cases: Presenting the Advantage of Religious Participation." *Family Law Quarterly* Sum 1994 38 (2): 269-288. (Tries to make the case for Witnesses rights in court; notes that Jehovah's Witnesses only object to the use of heterologous blood transfusions (p. 276) in contrast to Watchtower teaching).

Weishaupt, Kaynor J. and Michael Stensland. Wifely Subjection: Mental Health Issues in Jehovah's Witness Women." *Cultic Studies Journal* 14 (1): 106-144 1997 (They found mental illness among Witness women was above average).

Whitbread, Jane. "Poor Boy's Rich Life." *Look*, Vol. 17, Sept. 6, pp. m8-m10+.

Wilson, Bryan. "Aspects of Kinship and the Rise of Jehovah's Witnesses in Japan" (intro. in French and article in English). *Social Compass*, 1977, 24 (1): 121-134.

_____. "The Debate over Secularization: Religion, Society and Faith." *Encounter*, Oct. 1975, 45: 77-83.

_____. Jehovah's Witnesses in Africa." *New Society*, July 17, 1973, 25 (562): 73-75.

_____. "Jehovah's Witnesses in Kenya." *Journal of Religion in Africa*. 1974, 5:128-149.

_____. "When Prophecy Failed." *New Society*, Jan. 26, 1978, 26: 183, 184.

"Wise Up! Is God a 'Dope'?" *National Lampoon*, Dec. 1974, pp. 57-59.

Woefkin, C. "The Religious Appeal of Premillenarianism." *Journal of Religion*, Vol. 1, pp. 255-260.

"You Can Win a Soul for Christ." *Our Sunday Visitor*, Oct. 2, 1955.

Younghusband, Peter. "Persecution in Malawi." *Newsweek*, May 10, 1976, pp. 106-107. (About Malawi's ban on the Watchtower).

Zymunt, Joseph F. "Prophetic Failure and Chiliastic Identity: The Case of the Jehovah's Witnesses." *American Journal of Sociology*, 1970, 75: 926-948.

_____. "When Prophecies Fail; A Theoretical Perspective on the Comparative Evidence." *American Behavioral Scientist*. 16 (2): 245-268. Nov-Dec 1972 (A general discussion of how churches deal with prophecy failure).

_____. "Movements and Motives: Some unresolved issues in the Psychology of Social Movements." *Human Relations* 25 (5): 449-469. (Covers why people join social movements and cults, including reasons as alienation, attraction and control concerns.)

E. History of the Watchtower Society and Jehovah's Witnesses

Adams, Phillip. "Jehovah's Blinkered, Bigoted Witnesses." *The Bulletin*, March 5, 1985, pp. 70-71. (A critical review of the Watchtower history; discusses their mental health problems).

Alexander, Tomsk´y. "Jehovah's Witnesses in Czechoslovakia." *Religion in Communist Lands*, Spring, 1986, 14 (9): 102-103.

Alnor, William. "Jehovah's Witness Growth Slows." *Moody Monthly*, Jan. 1987, p. 37. (About the Watchtower problems, especially with dissidents).

_____. "Ex-JWs Organize Outreach." *Eternity Magazine*, Jan. 1987, 38: 27-28.

Amidon, Beulah. "Can We Afford Martyrs?" *Survey Graphic*, Sept. 1940, 29: 457.

"Anthem or Prayer [news; India; Jehovah's Witnesses]." *Christianity Today*, 30 (3): 52, Feb. 21, 1986.

"Anti-Zionist 'Watchtower' Movement Betrayed 'Founder's' Prophetic Call." *United Israel Bulletin*, 34 (2): Summer 1977, pp. 1, 4.

"Argentinia's Military Government Has Abolished a Decree That Banned Jehovah's Witnesses." *Christianity Today*, Feb. 20, 1981, 25 (4): 49, 50.

Armstrong, Herbert W. "No! I Never Was a Jehovah's Witness or a Seventh-Day Adventist!" *Plain Truth*, Nov. 1970, pp. 106, 107. Revised and reprinted in May 1985, pp. 1, 43.

Assimeng, John Maxwell. "Sectarian Allegiance and Political Authority: The Watchtower Society in Zambia 1907-35." *Journal of Modern African Studies*, No. 1, 1970, 8: 97-112.

Baccaccio, Gaetano. "The Watchtower in Trouble." *The New Creation*, Jan-Feb. 1985, 46 (1-2): 17-22.

Beatty, Jerome. "Peddlers of Paradise." *Reader's Digest*, Jan. 1941, pp. 78-81.

Beckford, James A. "Les Témoins de Jehovah á travers le mond" (in French, intro. in English). *Social Compass*, 1977, 24 (1): 5-31. (Jehovah's Witnesses Worldwide).

Bergman, Jerry. "Witnesses to a New Area of Book Collecting." *Book Collector's Market* Vol. 4, May-June, 1979, pp. 1-9.

"Besynnerliga men anda beundransvarda." *En Ny Varld*, May 1946, 5: 17. (Strange, But Also Wonderful) (in Swedish).

"Big Week for Witnesses" (Annual Convention, St. Louis, MO). *Newsweek*, Aug. 18, 1941, p. 50.

Bills, V. Alex. "Wilson's Emphatic Diaglott." *The Bible Collector*, No. 2, Apr.-June 1965, pp. 1, 3-5.

Binsse, Harry L. "Religion and a Liquor License." *Commonweal*, Jan. 10, 1947, pp. 317, 318.

Blackwell, Brian and Suzanne Monks. "The Cult Busters." *New Idea*, March 15, 1986, pp. 6-9. (About self-help groups for ex-Witnesses).

Blandre, Bernard. "Russell et les Etudiants de la Bible 1870-1916." *Revue de l'Histoire des Religions*, 1975, 187: 181-199. (in French). (Russell and the Students of the Bible).

_____. "Le Christ de retour en 1873" in *Revue de L'Histoire Des Religions*, 1880. (Did Christ Return in 1873.)

_____. "La Premiere Brochure de Russell." *Review Historical Religions*, Oct.-Dec. 1982, pp. 405-415. (The first booklet of C.T. Russell) (In French) (A history of the early work of Russell).

_____. "une expansion planétaire." *Notre histoire*, No. 5, Octobre, 1984, pp. 38-42. (A Planetary Expansion) (Adventists to Russell).

_____. "Aux origines des Témoins de Jéhovah, des adventistes á Russell (1843-1882)." numéro spécial de *Mouvements Religieux*, No. 59, avril-mai, 1985.

_____. "Russell et le bie miraculeux." *Revue de l'Histore des Religions*, Vol. 205, Ap-Je, 1988, pp. 181-193. [conflict between *Brooklyn Daily Eagle* and Charles Taze Russell, 1908] (in French).

_____. L'Organisation des Témoins de Jehovah" PJR, 1989, 6: 50-60. (The Organization of Jehovah's Witnesses). (In French)

Blessing, William L. "Jehovah's Witnesses. *Showers of Blessing*, June 1978, 690: 14, 15. Reprinted in *Blessing Letter*, June 1978, pp. 1-4.

Bradley, Bob. "Observations from the Watchtower." *Printing Today*, September 1981, pp. 36-38.

_____. "Printing Power for the Promotion of Religion." *Lithoprinter Week*, 22 September 1982, pp. 12-14 and cover photograph.

Bradley, R.O. "Watchtower Bible and Tract Society Employs Offset Letterpress Mix for Multimillion Runs in Brooklyn." *Graphic Arts Monthly and the Printing Industry*, March 1982, p. 140-4(?).

Branch, Craig. "The Culting of Christianity." *New Man* Oct 1996 3 (7): 40-45.

Branden, Ruth. "Jehovah 1975." *New Society*, Aug. 7, 1969, pp. 201-202. (A good review of the Witness practice and lifestyle teachings. Branden notes the Witnesses clearly teach that "Armageddon will happen in 1975 if not earlier" p.202).

Brozan, Nadine. "Case of Self-Sufficiency." *Harper's Magazine*, Vol. 246, March 1973, p. 7. (About the Bethel complex and how they make their own ink, repair their own shoes, build their own furniture, etc.).

Bryant, Delmar H. "When Futurism Failed." *Christ Is the Answer*, March 1973, pp. 16-18.

Butt, Julia. "Jehovah's Hard Hats." *The Telegraph Magazine* (London), July 21, 1990, pages 46-50. (On the quick-build Kingdom Hall project and the people involved).

"California Cults." *Time*, March 31, 1930, 15 (13): 60-61.

Calzon, Frank. "Report: Jehovah's Witnesses in Cuba." *World view*, Dec. 1976, 19 (12): 13, 14.

Cameron, Gail. "Mickey Spillane Is at It Again--The Soft Side of a Hard Egg." *Life*, Sept. 8, 1961, 51 (10): 127-129. Spillane was a Witness for many years.

Campiche, Roland J. "Sectas y nuevos movimientos religiosos (NMR), divergencias y convergencias. *Cristianismo Soc* 1987, 25 (3): 9-1.

"Canada: Le Chef Is Dead." *Time*, Sept. 14, 1959, 74: 38, 41. (About Duplessis, a government antagonist of the Witnesses).

Carr, A.M. "Witnesses of What?" *Columbia*, Nov. 1958, 38: 4+.

"Cartoon about Jehovah's Witnesses." *Crucible*, July 1979, p. 4.

Chamberlin, William J. "A Rare Translation-George N. LeFevre's New Testament." *The Bible Collector*, No. 35, Jl-Sept, 1973, pp. 1-5.

_____. "More on Wilson's Emphatic Diaglott." *The Bible Collector*, No. 33, Jan-Mar, 1973, pp. 2, 7, 8.

"Changing the Guard at the Watchtower." *Alternative*, Feb., 1981, About the new president of the *Watchtower*, Fred Franz.

Clapp, Rodney. "The Watchtower Cracks Again." *Christianity Today*, Feb. 19, 1982, 26 (4): 27, 32. (About the Raymond Franz and other 1980 defections).

"Cloud of Witnesses." *Time*, July 27, 1953, p. 72.

Cohen, Lori. "Another Crooked Lawyer." *Alberta Law Report*, Sept. 23, 1985, p. 14. (About a Witness lawyer, Walter Shandro, 53 then, who stole over $200,000 from his mostly Witness clients).

Cole, Marley. "Jehovah's Witnesses: God's Army on the March." *Color*, Aug. 1953, pp. 24-28.

_____. "Jehovah's Witnesses--Religion of Racial Integration." *Crisis*, Vol. 60, April 1953, pp. 205-211.

_____. "Mob Rule in Crossville." *Nation*, June 9, 1951, 172: 539-541.

_____. "Speaking of Trailerists: They're Rolling Toward Heaven." *Trailer Life*, may 1953.

_____. "Theocratic Trailer City." *Trailer Topics*, April 1953, pp. 19, 70, 72, 74, 77.

_____. "Training Africans for Better Life" as told by George Brumley. (*Color*, April 1953, pp. 18-21.

_____. "World's Fastest Growing Religion." *Color*, Dec. 1952, pp. 30-35.

Collision, James W. "By Leaps and Bounds--A Report on Jehovah's Witnesses." *Voice of St. Jude*, July 1959, 25: 24-28.

"Conscientious Objectors and Jehovah's Witnesses." *DePaul Law Review*, Spring-Summer 1955, 24: 296-306.

"Convert's Husband Loses Damage Suit." *Moody's Monthly*, Nov. 1982, 83 (3): 134.

"The Crime of Airman Cupp." *Commonweal*, Dec. 21, 1956, pp. 301, 302.

Cross, Sholto. "Social History and Millennial Movements: The Watchtower in South Central Africa" (introduction in French, article in English). *Social Compass*, 1977, 24 (1): 83-95.

Cunnisen, Ian. "A Watchtower Assembly in Central Africa." *International Review of Missions*, Oct. 1951, 40: 456-569.

_____. "Jehovah's Witnesses at Work: Expansion in Central Africa." *The British Colonies Review*, 1st Quarter 1958, 29: 13.

Dahlin, John E. "An Exodus from the Jehovah's Witnesses." *The Discerner*, Jan. 2, 1983, 11 (1): 10.

Dailey, K. "Jehovah's Witnesses." *Information*, Dec. 1955, 69: 25-30.

Dart, John. "Singer Michael Jackson Drops Out of Jehovah's Witnesses Sect." *Los Angeles Times*, June 7, 1987, Sec. II, p. 1, Col. 4.

Davidson, Bill. "Jehovah's Traveling Salesmen." *Collier's Magazine*, Nov. 2, 1946, 118 (18): 12, 13, 72-77. Reprinted in *Reader's Digest*, Jan. 1947, pp. 77-80.

Davis, Larry L. "Larry L. Davis Reports on 1971 Colorado Bible Students Convention at Fort Colins." *United Israel Bulletin*, Nov. 1971, 28 (3): 1, 3.

"Departing Leaders Reveal Cracks in the Watchtower." *Christianity Today*, Dec. 12, 1980, 24 (21): 68-71.

Doherty, J.E. "Jehovah's Witnesses." *Liquorian*, March 1953, 41: 151-157.

"Efforts to Curb Jehovah's Witnesses." *Church and State*, May 1974, 27 (5): 16.

"800 Baptisms an Hour." *Newsweek*, Aug. 19, 1946, p. 78. (About the Cleveland Assembly mass baptism on Aug. 9, 1946).

Ehlert, Arnold D. "The Byington Bible." *The Bible Collector*, No. 35, July-Sept, 1973, pp. 2, 5, 7.

"Eine schleichende Haresie." *Zentral-Blatt*, June 1937, 30: 106. (A Creeping Heresy) (in German).

"The End Is Near (cont'd)." *Time*, July 11, 1977, 110: 64, 69.

"End of All Kingdoms in 1914 'Millenial Dawners' 25 year prophecy." *The World Magazine*, August 30, 1914. (often quoted in current witness literature).

E., J. H. "Among the Elect--An Evening with the Russellites." *The Christian World*. August 14, 1919. (Writer attended and reviewed a Bible Student meeting, where the seventh volume is a topic of conversation).

Epstein, Arnold Leonard. "The Millennium and the Self: Jehovah's Witnesses on the Copperbelt in the '50s." *Anthropos: International Review of Ethnology and Linguistics*, 1986, 81 (4-6): 529-554.

Eutychus and His Kin: A Case of Conversion from the Jehovah's Witnesses." *Christianity Today*, 1964, 9: 305.

"Ex-Jehovah's Witnesses Gathered." *Christianity Today*, Dec 7, 1979, 24: 52.

Faber, Harold. "Jehovah's Witnesses Building Education Center on New York Farm." *The New York Times*, April 7, 1991, p. Y20.

Fecher, R.J. "Made in U.S.A." *Nuntius Aulae*, 1961, 43: 169-177.

Felix, R. "Fight Fire with Fire." *Catholic Mind*, Aug. 8, 1939, 37: 788.

"Fighting Fire with Fire." *America*, Aug. 12, 1939, 61: 424 (Activities of Judge Rutherford).

Furlong, Monica. "Nuts in April." *The Spectator*, April 29, 1960, 204: 609. (An incisive critique of both the Watchtower and moral re-armament and their beliefs).

Gdovia, G. "Jehovah's Witnesses: Hard Sell Converting." *Information*, Aug. 1959, 73: 3-11.

Gledhill, Ruth. Waiting for Armageddon. *Sunday Times* (London), December 11, 1993. (Religious reporter's weekley column where she attends religious meetings of various faiths and gives them stars for various criteria. This week she attended a Kingdom Hall in Bristol, UK).

"God's New World: Jehovah's Witnesses Surprise the World with Their Unusual Beliefs and Steadfast Courage." *Our World*, Nov. 1953,8 (11): 17-24.

"Greeks Arrested for Proselytizing." *Church and State*, Nov. 1959, 12 (10): 3.

"Greeks Execute Objector; Britain Releases Green." *News Notes of the Central Committee for Conscientious Objectors*, Feb. 1949, 1 (2): 1.

Greenberg, Keith Elliot. "The View From the Watchtower." *Brooklyn Bridge.* March 1997. 2 (7): 32-39 (About Bethel factories and the Watchtower headquarters).

Griffin, Jerry (Ed). "Michael Jackson called Returned Christ by Fringe Jehovah's Witness Group." *Bible Advocate*, Feb. 1985, 119 (2): 21.

"Growth Arrested." *Time*, Feb. 13, 1978.

Gruss, Edmond and Leonard Chretien 'Beth-Sarim', "A False Prophet and False Prophecy" *Christian Research Journal.* 20 (1): 22-29 Sum 1997 (About the Watchtower house built for the heavenly princes of the old Testament and the failure of the WT predictions).

_____. "Beth-Shan and the Return of the 'Princes': The Untold Story" *Christian Research Journal*, 20 (2): 35-41. Nov./Dec. 1997. (About the Watchtower house built for the heavenly princes and the failure of the WT predictions and their cover up).

"He Was Present at Historic Hippodrome Meeting in 1910." *United Israel Bulletin*, Nov. 1971,28 (3): 3.

Henderson, R.E. "Pastor Russell." *Overland Monthly*, Jan. 1917, 69: 56. A Poem.

"Heresy Trial in Lethbridge." *Alberta Report*, Feb. 27, 1981, 18: 24-26.

Higgins, J. "Jehovah's Witnesses at Your Door." *Liquorian*, Oct. 1972, 60: 16-19.

High, Stanley S. "Armageddon, Inc." *Saturday Evening Post*, Sept. 14, 1940, 213: 18, 19, 50, 54, 58.

Hodiak, Rohdan. "Witnesses 'Coming Home' For Centennial Celebration." *Christian News*, Oct. 1, 1984, 22 (36): 1, 19.

Hoefle, John. "Bible Scholar John J. Hoefle Analyzes Joel's Prophecies Relating to the Latter Days." *United Israel Bulletin*, Winter 1983-84, 40:1, 4.

_____. "Biography of John J. Hoefle." *Epiphany Bible Students Association*, July/Aug., 1984, No. 349, pp. 5-10. (Special Issue on the life work of John Hoefle, an early Bible Student and founder of Epiphany Bible Students Association--see Section F.1).

Holas, B. "Bref Apercu Surles Principaux Cultes Syncrétiques de la Basse Cote

D'Ivoire." *Africa*, 24 (1): Janvier, 1954. (in French). (Brief Survey of the Principle Cults From the Ivory Coast).

Holt, R. "What on Earth Is Jesus Waiting For?" *These Times: Special Issue*, July 1, 1975, p. 7.

Hooker, J.R. "Witnesses and Watchtower in the Rhodesias and Nyasaland." *Journal of African History*, Jan. 1965,6 (1): 91-106.

Hopkins, Joseph M. "Religious Freedom for All--Except Jehovah's Witnesses." *Columbia Law Review*, Feb. 20, 1981, 25 (4): 46-48.

Horowitz, David. "Founder of Anti-Zionist J.--Witnesses Hailed Zionism as Being Biblically Prophetic." *United Israel Bulletin*, March 1971, 28 (1): 1, 4.

_____. "Pastor Rusell's 'The Restoration of Israel.'" *United Israel Bulletin*, March 1971, 28 (1): 4.

_____. "Pastor Charles Taze Russell Evokes National Interest." *United Israel Bulletin*, July 1971, 28 (2): 4.

_____. "Pastor Charles T. Russell Article Evokes National Interest; Noted Bible Scholars React Favorably; Events Vindicate Founder." *United Israel Bulletin*, July 1971, 28 (2): 1.

_____. "Pastor Russell, in 1897, Spoke of Herzl's 'Jewish State.'" *United Israel Bulletin*, Nov. 1971, 28 (3): 1, 3.

_____. "What Happened to Pastor Russell's Original Will?" *United Israel Bulletin*, Nov. 1971, 28 (3): 4.

_____. "Pastor Russell Cheered by Audience of Hebrews." *United Israel Bulletin*, 1971.

_____. "Pastor Russell Cited at UI's Founders' Meeting in 1944." *United Israel Bulletin*, Dec. 1972, 29 (3): 1, 2.

_____. "Anti-Zionist 'Watchtower' Movement Betrayed 'Founder's' Prophetic Call." *United Israel Bulletin*, Summer 1977, 34 (2): 1, 4.

_____. "Raymond Jolly, Associate of the Late Pastor Russell, Recalls His Years Working with Noted Bible Scholar." *United Israel Bulletin*, Winter 1977, 34 (3): 4.

_____. "Pastor Charles T. Russell's Famous Pro-Zionist 1910 Hippodrome Speech Recalled." *United Israel Bulletin*, Summer 1980, 37 (2): 1, 4.

_____. "Historical Pastor Charles Taze Russell Volume Published." *United Israel Bulletin*, Winter 85-86, 42 (2): 1, 3.

_____. "History Professor Charges Rutherford and Co-Betrayors of Pastor Russell Sought Favor With the Nazis in 1933." *United Israel Bulletin*, Winter 1986-1987, pp. 1, 3.

How, Glen. "A Portrait." *MacLean's; Canada's National Magazine*, Jan. 4, 1964, 77: 12.

Hubbard, J. Glen. "I Examine a Book Published by Jehovah's Witnesses." *Two Worlds*, March 1969, pp. 80-84.

Hutchinson, Paul. "The President's Religious Faith." *Christian Century*, March 24,

1954, pp. 362-369. Published simultaneously in *Life*, March 22, 1954, 36: 151-170. (About Eisenhower, who was raised by a Witness mother but later rejected this faith).

"In Memoriam:" Fredrick Homer Robinson." *Unsearchable Riches*, 1932, 23: 292-297.

"Italian Military Court." *Christianity Today*, April 27, 1973, 18: 48.

Jeavons, Art. "Letter to the Editor." *The Plain Truth*, April 19, 1975, p. 13.

"Jehovah's Witness Sues Disney World." *Church and State*, Dec. 1982, 35 (11): 19.

"Jehovah's Witnesses." *Time*, June 10, 1935, 25 (23): 34-36.

"Jehovah's Witnesses." (Editorial). *Liberation*, Summer 1958, 3: 3.

"Jehovah's Witnesses." *Weekend*, Aug. 6, 1960, pp. 24-25. (A review of the Witnesses in Australia).

"Jehovah's Witnesses, The." *Pix*, July 18, 1964, pp. 42-44. (About the Jehovah's Witnesses in Australia).

"Jehovah's Witnesses Arrested in Spain." *Church and State*, Oct. 1969, 22 (9): 10.

"Jehovah's Witnesses: CIA Cover?" *Muhammad Speaks*, June 12, 1970, p. 12.

"Jehovah's Witnesses Convicted of Proselytizing." *Church and State*, Jan. 1974, 27 (1): 19.

"Jehovah's Witnesses: Hard Sell Converting." *Information*, Aug. 1959, 73: 3-11.

"Jehovah's Witnesses: Holding Doomsday at Hand, Sect Steps up Propaganda." *Newsweek*, June 26, 1939, 13: 29.

"Jehovah's Witnesses Prosecuted by Orthodox Church." *Church and State*, Feb. 1959, 12 (2): .

"Jehovah's Witnesses Push 'Creationism' in Schools." *Church and State*, May 1982, 35 (5): 17.

"Jehovah's Witnesses Sentenced to Death in Greece." *Church and State*, March 1966, 19 (3): 10.

"Jehovah's Witnesses Sentenced to Death in Greece." *Church and State*, Oct. 1966, 19 (9): 10.

"Jehovah's Witnesses Threatened with Expulsion." *Church and State*, Jan. 1973, 26 (1): 21.

"Jehovah's Witnesses: U.S.--Born Religious Society Attracts Increasing Number of Negro Converts." *Ebony*, Oct. 1951, 6: 98-104.

"Jehovah's Witnesses Who Refuse to Salute U.S. Flag, Hold Their National Convention." *Life*, Aug. 12, 1940, 9: 20, 21.

"Jehovah's Vitten i Finland retireade inte." *En Ny Varld*, March 1946, 5: 17. (Jehovah's Witnesses in Finland Don't Give Up.) (in Finnish).

Jenkins, Clare. "Knocking on Heaven's Door." *Times Educational Supplement*, Dec. 21, 1990, No. 3886, p. 17.

Johnston, Richard W. "Death's Fair-Haired Boy: Sex and Fury Sell 13 Million Gory Books for Mickey Spillane." *Look*, Aug. 28, 1953, 17: 79-95. Spillane was a Witness.

Johnstone, Kenneth. "Who Exactly are these Jehovah's Witnesses?" *Montreal Standard*, Jan. 4, 1947, pp. 12-15. (A general history, much on their legal problems).

"Judge Declined Jehovah's Witnesses' Citizenship." *Church and State*, May 1969, 22 (5): 11.

Kelsey, Laura. "Laura Kelsey Cites Pastor Charles T. Russell's Vision For a Resurrected Israel."

Kennedy, J.S. "I Admire the Jehovah's Witnesses." *Columbia*, Jan. 1943, 22: 7+. Reprinted in *Catholic Mind*, Vol. 41, May 1943, pp. 39-45.

Lage, Laura. "The Watchtower. The Truth That Hurts." *Free Inquiry*, Winter, 1984-85, 5 (1): 25-31.

Lawson, W. "How Do You Explain the Rapid Growth of Jehovah's Witnesses?" *Church Order*, Nov. 1964, 5: 690.

Leman, Johan. "Jehovah's Witness and Immigration in Continental Western Europe." *Social Compass 26*, 1979, pp. 41-72.

Lewis, Richard Warren. "Then Time Out for Bible Study." *TV Guide*, 22 (48): Nov. 30, 1974; 22 (49): Dec. 6, 1974, pp. 20-23, cover.

Lobsenz, Norman M. "The Embattled Witnesses." *Coronet*, Jan. 1956, pp. 129-133.

Lockwood, Robert. "How Jehovah's Witnesses Attack Catholicism." *Our Sunday Visitor*, Dec. 2, 1973, 62: 1, 2.

_____. "Latin Catholics Target for Jehovah's Witnesses." *Our Sunday Visitor*, Nov. 25, 1973, 62: 1, 6.

MacGowan, Gault. "Jehovah's witnesses (They Sell Books)." *Catholic Digest*, Nov. 1938, 3: 71-76.

Maddox, Robert (Ed.). "Jehovah's Witness Shunning Passes Court Test." *Church and State*, Sept. 1985, 38 (8): 22.

"Malawi Expels Witnesses." *Church and State*, Jan. 1966, 22 (1): 10.

"Marching to Armageddon." *Time*, Aug. 11, 1958, pp. 35-36. (A brief history of the Watchtower focusing on the 1958 International Convention).

Marriages Performed by Jehovah's Witnesses Not Valid." *Church and State*, Feb. 1971, 24 (2): 19.

Martin, Pete. "Pete Martin Visits a Family of Jehovah's Witnesses." *Christian Herald*, April, 1966, 89: 23-25, 42-49, 76-79.

Martin, Walter R. "Herbert W. Armstrong the All-American Cultist." *Youth Illustrated*, Oct. Nov., Dec. 1970, pp. 34-39.

"Massing of the 'Witnesses.'" *Newsweek*, Aug. 4, 1958, p. 49.

Mather, George and Elliot Miller. "Back to One Overseer--The Watchtower Credibility Gap Widens." *Forward*, 1980, 7 (1): 5, 19.

Mattison, Mark M. "The Provenance of Russellism" *The Church of God General Conference History Newsletter.* (Newsletter of Church of God Abrahamic Faith). Mattison records the contacts Russell had with the Church of God, including as a guest speaker at a 1895 conference. By 1909 their magazine *Restitution Herald* was attacking Russell's theology in no uncertain terms.)

Maust, John. "Departing Leaders Reveal Cracks in the Watchtower." *Christianity Today,* Dec. 12, 1980, 24: 68-69, 71. (About the 1980 defections, primarily Franz and Dunlop).

McClure, Charles. "Predictions by the Watchtower that all failed." *The New Creation,* VJan-Feb. 1987, 48 (1 and 2): 21 -22 (About Watchtower prophesy failed).

McGinnis, H.C. "Russell, Then Rutherford Spawn Jehovah's Witnesses." *America,* Feb. 8, 1941, 64: 481-482.

_____. "Rutherford and His Witnesses Find Your Catholics a Bad Lot." *America,* Feb. 15, 1941, 64: 512-513.

_____. "Rutherford in a Palace, His Witnesses in the Slums." *America,* March 1, 1941, 64: 569-570.

_____. "Rutherford Warns His Dupes on Religion and Government." *America,* Feb. 22, 1941, 64: 542-543.

McKay, Bob. "Door-to-Door to the End of the World." *Ohio Magazine,* May, 1986, 9 (2): 48-56, 115-116. (A story of John Benz, an active Witness, and his Witness work and life background and the frustrations of the Witness work).

McLoughlin, William G. "Is There a Third Force in Christendom?" *Daedalus,* Winter, 1967, 96 (1): 43-68.

Meisler, Stanley. "Jehovah's Witnesses in Africa--The Martyrdom Safari!" *Nation,* July 16, 1973, 217: 51, 52. (A good brief review of the Watchtower activities in Zambia, Kenya, Malawi and Africa in general).

Melrose, K.M.C. "Reply." *Spectator,* Aug. 12, 1955,195: 221.

Meyer, Jacob O. "Letter to Frederick Franz, President, WTB and T Society of NY." The Sacred Name Broadcaster. Nov 1983 pp. 4-5. (Meyer wrote he had never been a Witnesses and that the Assemblies of Yahweh of Bethel, PA. was not a Watchtower splinter group.)

"Michael Jackson the Messiah?" *Christian Inquirer,* Jan. 1985, p. 11.

Mitchell, R.J. "Jehovah's Witnesses in Cuba." *Worldview,* 1977, 20 (4): 2. (Reply to a previous article).

"Modern Crusaders." *Ave Maria,* Sept. 24, 1938, 48: 407.

Moley, Raymond. "The Boot Is on the Other Leg." *Newsweek,* June 29, 1942, p. 68.

Montgomery-Fate, Carol, and Tom Montgomery-Fate. "Guatemala: indigenous lives [report, Two stories from the uplands]." *Christianity and Crisis,* Nov. 23, 1987, 47: 413-416.

Morgan, Brian. "Jehovah's Real Witnesses. *Glad Tidings,* Apr. 1992, pp. 6-7. (Argues that the Israelites are Jehovah's Witnesses, not the Watchtower Society followers).

Moyle, Peter-Simon Olin. "The Legal Case Against the Watchtower Exposed by a Former 'Insider.'" *United Israel Bulletin,* Feb. 1972, 29 (1): 1, 2.

_____. "More Light on the Watchtower's Deviation." *United Israel Bulletin*, Dec. 1972, 29 (3): 1.

Muhlen, Norman. "The World's Worst Woman." *Saturday Evening Post*, July 2, 1955, pp. 24, 74-77. (About an East German persecutor of Jehovah's Witnesses, Hilde Benjamin, called Red Hilde. She was the East German minister of justice for many years).

Muller, Albert. "These Jehovah's Witnesses." *America*, June 2, 1961, 105: 464-465.

"Needless New Religions." *Literary Digest*, March 23, 1912, p. 596.

Nelkin, Dorothy. "The Science-Textbook Controversies." *Scientific American*, April 1976, 234 (4): 33-39.

"New York Court Tax-Exempt." *Christianity Today*, Sept. 13, 1974, 19: 88.

"New York Witnesses the Witnesses." *America*, Sept. 9, 1958, 99: 483.

Nichols, Beverly. "Wimbley Assembly." *Sunday Chronicle*, Dec. 16, 1951.

Nicklin, Lenore. "The Irwin Babies; Australia's Newest Quads.' *The Australian Women's Weekly*, march 17, 1982, pp. 2-3. (About a Witness family that had quadruplets).

Niklaus, Robert L. "Ex-Jehovah's Witnesses Protest Group's Practice of Shunning Former Members." *Christianity Today*, Nov. 9, 1984, 28: 63, 64-66.

"Nigeria." *Journal of Church and State*, Autumn 1973,15 (3): 491.

"No Fiery Hell." *Newsweek*, Aug. 4, 1958, p. 49.

"Non-Jewish Reader Says the 'Jews Are God's Time-Clock.'" *United Israel Bulletin*, Spring 1975.

O'Brien, John A. "Jehovah's Witnesses--A Visit to Headquarters." *Catholic Digest*, Dec. 1962, 27: 61-63.

_____. "A Visit to Jehovah's Witnesses." *Pastoral Life*, Nov. 1963, 2: 20-24.

"On From Yankee Stadium." *Time*, Aug. 2, 1963, p. 40.

Ostling, Richard N. "Witness Under Prosecution." *Time*, Feb. 22, 1982, 119: 66. (A good summary of the Raymond Franz case and Watchtower problems).

Paulus, Jean Pierre. "Le Kitawala au Congo Belge." *Review de l'Institute de Sociologie*, Nos. 2-3, 1956, pp. 257-270. (The Watchtower in the Belgian Congo.)

Payton, G.H. "Witnesses of the Millennium." *New Statesman and Nation*, No. 1074, Oct. 6, 1951, pp. 362-362. (About the 1951 International Assembly in New York; a good discussion on the Watchtower end times-last days teaching. Shows that the Watchtower confidently looked forward to 1975 as the end, even in 1951).

"A Peculiar Investigation of Missions." *The Missionary Review of the World*, July 1912, 25: 538.

Pelletier, Pam. "Scaling the Jehovah's Witnesses Watchtower." Reprinted from *Moody Monthly*, Aug. 1977. *The Lookout*, Feb. 26, 1978, 40 (9); 6, 7.

Penton, M. James. "Jehovah's Witnesses and the Secular State: A Historical Analysis of Doctrine." *Journal of Church and State*, Winter 1979, 21 (1): 55-72.

"Persecution in Malawi." *Church and State*, Feb. 1968, 21 (2): 10.

Porter, Thomas. "Star of 'Get Christie Love' Now Preaching Door-to-Door." *National Enquirer*, April 27, 1976, p. 8.

Pottersman, Arthur. "The Terrible Mr. Spillane, and the Girl He Married Right off a Book Jacket." *Detroit Free Press--Sunday Magazine*, June 11, 1976, pp. 45, 46. Spillane was a Witness.

Quick, Griffith. "Some Aspects of the African Watchtower Movement in Northern Rhodesia." *International Review of Missions*, Vol. 29, April 1940, pp. 216-226.

Randle, Lois. "The Apocalypticism of the Jehovah's Witnesses." *Free Inquiry*, Winter 1984-1985, 5 (1): 18-24.

"Record of Witnesses." *Life*, Aug. 11, 1958, 45: 117, 118. Rally.

"Record Record." *Newsweek*, Oct. 29, 1951, p. 78.

Regehr, Ernie. "Jehovah's Witnesses in Africa." *The Christian Century*, January 7-14, 1976, pp. 17-8.

"Reign of Terror in Malawi." *Church and State*, Feb. 1973, 26 (2): 53.

Rogerson, Alan Thomas. "Témoins de Jéhovah et Etudiants de la Bible. Qui Est Schismatique?" (intro. in English and article in French) (English translation mimeographed, 7 pp.). *Social Compass*, 1977, 24 (1): 33-43. (Jehovah's Witnesses and Bible Students--Who is Schismatic?)

Roll, William G. "Prankish Ghost Puts on Eerie Display for Investigators." *National Enquirer*, Feb. 25, 1975, p. 6. About a Witness family.

Ross, J.J. "Editorial: Being 'Labeled.'" *The Gospel Witness*, July 14, 1927, pp. 8-13.

Rubinger, David. "Religious zeal, Sam Zell and a local success story." *Atlanta Business Chronicle*, Oct. 28, 1991, p. 1(2). (Jehovah's Witnesses based Mighty Distributing System of America, Inc., acquired by Sam Zell of North Riverside Holdings, Inc., company profile).

"Russellism Admitting Its Mistakes." *The Watchman*, Dec. 1916, 25: 11-15.

"Russellism--or the Coming of a False 'Christ.'" *The Watchman*, Vol. 24, April, June, Aug., Sept., Oct. 1915, pp. 162-166, 267-272, 363-367, 406-410, 454-458.

Rutherford, J.F. "The Late Pastor Russell: Biographical Sketch by His Successor." *Overland Monthly*, April 1917, 69: 296-302.

"Rutherford's Flock." *Newsweek*, Aug. 5, 1940, p. 42.

Salter, Walter. "Letter from Walter Salter." *Unsearchable Riches*, 1939, 30; 198.

"Salvation at the Door Step." *Detroit Free Press--Sunday Magazine*, April 18, 1976, pp. 6-10.

"Say Yeah!" *Time*, Jan. 5, 1976, pp. 76, 77. (About ex-Witness Patti Smith).

Schnell, William J. "When They Come to Your Door." *Lutheran Standard*, Aug. 18, 1970, pp. 6+.

"School Board Reverses Ban." *Church and State*, Nov. 1959, 12 (10): 8.

Schórr, Jose. "You Be the Judge." *Saturday Evening Post.*

Semprun, Jorge. "A Day in Buchenwald." *Dissent*, Fall 1982, pp. 425-430.

Sheehey, Thomas. Jehovah's Witnesses and the Military." *The Discerner.* Jan-Feb 1997
    17 (1): 3-7.

Sheler, Jeffery L. Graying the Prophets; Religion Confronts Aging Patriarchies." *U.S.
    News and World Report*, Je 13, 1994. pp. 75-76. (About failed prophecy and the
    Watchtower and other groups; the section on the Watchtower focuses on the 1914
    date and the failure of the end to come within the generation that saw 1914.)

"Short History of Jehovah's Witnesses." *Sign*, Vol. 38, Sept. 1958, p. 50.

"Singapore De-Registered Jehovah's Witnesses." *Church and State*, Vol. 25, No. 3, p.
    20.

Smith, Theodore A. "Regarding Founder of Jehovah's Witnesses." *United Bulletin*, Vol.
    28, No. 2, Dec. 1972, pp. 1, 2.

"Smoking." *Christianity Today*, Vol. 19, Jan. 18, 1974, p. 52. (Discusses the new
    expulsion rule for Jehovah's Witnesses who smoke).

Southerworth, H.R. "Jehovah's 50,000 Witnesses." *Nation*, Vol. 151, Aug. 10, 1940,
    pp. 110-112.

Swetnam, George. "A Man and His Monument." *The Pittsburgh Press*, June 25, 1967,
    page 7. (Story of Pyramid monument by Russell's grave and its history. Swetnam
    also wrote the book *Where Else But Pittsburgh* which discussed Russell's work in
    Pittsburgh).

Tedo, James. "This We Believe." *Color*, c. 1951, pp. 128, 129.

Tennant, Hal. "Jehovah's Witnesses: The New Look of a Turbulent Sect." *MacLean's
    (Canada's National Magazine)*, Aug. 25, 1962, 75: 40, 41.

"A 'Terrible Upheaval.'" *Newsweek*, July 4, 1955, p. 58.

Testa, Bart. "Bearing Witness to a Mass Exodus." *Maclean's (Canada's National
    Magazine)*, March 16, 1981, pp. 47-9.

"Testimony by Mr. Overman and Others Relative to the Charges of Sedition Against
    Rutherford and Others." *Congressional Record of the United States*, May 4,
    1918, pp. 6050-6053.

"Theocracy Girded for the End." *Alberta Report*, June 4, 1984, 25: 34-38. (About
    current Witness internal upheaval; also discusses the Botting book (1984).

Thurston, H. "Rutherford and the Witnesses of Jehovah: Are They Apostles of
    Anarchy?" *Catholic Mind*, Aug. 8, 1939, 37: 769-787.

Thurston, Robert. Judge Rutherford and the Witnesses of Jehovah." *America*, Vol. 61
    Aug. 8, 1939.

Townsend, R and W.M. Alnor. "When Christians Meet Jehovah's Witnesses: Mars hill
    Collection Series." *Christian Herald*, April 1988, 111: 36-9.

Tucker, Ruth A. "Nonorthodox sects report global membership gains: church leaders say
    some Third World Christians are being misled by the groups [news]." *Christianity
    Today*, June 13, 1986, 30 (9): 48, 50, 51.

"20 Jehovah's Witnesses Sentenced to Long Prison Terms." *Church and State*, Nov. 1974, 27 (11): 13.

"Upholds Right to Attack Religions" (in Mineola, NY)." *Church Management*, May 1940.

Vandenberg, Albert V. "Charles Taze Russell: Pittsburgh Prophet, 1879-1909." *Western Pennsylvania Historical Magazine*, 1986, 69: 3-20.

van Fossen, Anthony B. "How Do Movements Survive Failures of Prophecy?" *Research in Social Movements, Conflicts and Change*, 1988, 10: 193-212.

"Waiting for Armageddon." *Time*, Aug. 14, 1950, pp. 68, 69. (About the 1950 Yankee Assembly and the Watchtower teachings).

Walker, Charles R. "Fifth Column Jitters." *McCall's Magazine*, Jan. 1940, pp. 9, 10, 116.

Washington, George. "Irish Jehovah's Witnesses Defect." *Christian Inquirer*, March 1964, p. 18.

Watt, David. "Two Cheers for Theocracy." *Spectator*, Aug. 5, 1955, 195: 190.

Weatherbe, Stephen. "Witness Jackson" *Alberta Report*, June 4, 1984, 1 (25): 35. (About superstar Michael Jackson, then an active Jehovah's Witness, now disfellowshipped).

Whalen, William J. "All About Jehovah's Witnesses." *U.S. Catholic*, April 1979, 73: 93-99.

_____. "Jehovah's Witnesses: Gonna Take a Fundamental Journey." *U.S. Catholic*, Jan 1979, pp. 28-34.

_____. "Jehovah's Witnesses' New Look." *Lamp*, Oct. 1961, 59: 8, 9, 29, 30.

_____. "Jehovah's Witnesses: They Expect the Battle of Armageddon to Start Any Day." *Our Sunday Visitor*, Vol. 65, April 3, 1977.

_____. "What I Like About Jehovah's Witnesses." *U.S. Catholic*, July 1964, 30: 17-19.

_____. When Jehovah's Witnesses Call." *Marriage*, March 1963, 45: 42.

_____. "Who Are Jehovah's Witnesses?" *Sign*, April 1960, 39: 29-31.

"What Price Cynicism?" *Time*, May 6, 1957, p. 89.

Whitby, Alan R. "The Watchtower (ISBA) Records." *The Historical Record and A.V. Collector*, Issue 27, 1993, pp. 20-26. (An excellent review of the Watchtower history of phonograph recordings starting with the photodrama of creation. (1914) has a list of all Angelophone and Rutherford records plus Watchtower voice quartet recordings (c. 1936) and other records.

_____. "The Mystery of Herman Heinfetter." *Bible Collectors' World,* Volume 12, No. 1 (Jan-March 1996). (Cited as 'J' authority, a translation that also used Jehovah in the NT; in the 1984 Students' Edition New World Translation, Heinfetter's work in Britain in the 1850s and 1860s which extensively used 'Jehovah' in the New Testament, and the controversial 'a god' in John 1: 1 as did Benjamin Wilson's Diaglott).

"Whither the Witnesses?" *Newsweek*, July 19, 1950, p. 46.

"Will the Real Teresa Graves Please Stand Up?" *Ebony*, Dec. 1974, pp. 68, 70.
     Subtitled "Star of 'Get Christie Love' series is devout Bible student."

Wilson, Robert Anton. "The fastest-growing Religion in the World." *Fact*, Vol. 1, No.
     6, Nov.-Dec. 1964, pp. 42-49. (A review of Witness life, headquarters, their
     positive and negative aspects, what attracts people to them, witnesses as people; an
     interesting well written piece which is marred by many inaccuracies).

"Witness Angle." *Newsweek*, March 22, 1943,21: 68.

"The Witnesses Begin to Question." *Alberta Report*, Aug. 15, 1980, 7 (47): 36.

"Witnesses Examined." *Time*, July 29, 1940, pp. 40, 41.

"Witnesses in Detroit." *Time*, Aug. 5, 1940, p. 39.

"Witnesses in Trouble." *Time*, June 24, 1940, p. 54.

"Witnesses Expelled." *The Christian Century*, April 7, 1982, p. 402.

"A Witness Explanation." *Christianity Today*, Feb. 6, 1981, 24: 8, 9.

"The Witnesses." *Time*, June 30, 1961, p. 47. (On the 1961 Yankee Stadium Assembly;
     quotes Knorr who claimed blood transfusions were "forbidden in the Bible" and
     "unhealthful as well" citing "moral insanity, sexual perversions, repression,
     inferiority complexes, petty crimes" as some of the evil consequences of taking
     blood).

"The Witnesses Hear the Word." *Life*, Aug. 14, 1950, 29: 32, 33.

"Witnesses, Jehovah's." *America*, Dec. 7, 1935, 54: 196.

"Witnesses of Jehovah." *The Sign*, Dec. 1945, 25: 645.

"Witnesses Want Windham to Teach Creationism." *Newsletter on Intellectual Freedom*,
     31 (1): p. 5.

"Witnesses Win." *Church and State*, Sept. 1974, 27 (9): 22.

"Witnessing for Jehovah." *Newsweek*, Aug. 3, 1953, pp. 44, 45.

"Witnesses of Jehovah." *The Social Bulletin*, Dec. 1945, No. 13, p. Montreal Ecole
     Sociale Populaire. (A critique of the Witness movement in Canada; says they
     spread "irreligion and hatred").

"Witnessing the End." *Time*, July 18, 1969, pp. 62, 63. (Covers Watchtower last days
     teaching--notes they date the end of the world in Autumn, 1975).

Woodard, Mary. "Cults, Movements, and World Religions--Sorting It all Out." *Lay
     Witness* May 1997 18 (4): 26-27. (Woodard, now a Catholic, was a 3rd
     generation Witness).

Woodward, E.P. "Another Gospel: An Exposure of the System Known as Russellism."
     The Safeguard and Armory, 1914, 19: 1-123.

Woodward, Kenneth. "Are They False Witnesses?" *Newsweek*, July 20, 1981, p. 75.
     (About the internal Watchtower problems and prophesy failure).

_____. "Witness for the Millennium." *Newsweek*, Oct. 15, 1984, p. 120. (Focuses on
     their prophesy failures and internal problems).

"World Scene." *Christianity Today*, March 3, 1972, 17: 48.

Worrell, Denise. "Michael Jackson, Why He's a Thriller." *Time*, March 19, 1984, pp. 54-63. (Jackson was then an active Jehovah's Witness).

"The Word and the Way According to Victor Wierville." *Christianity Today*, Sept. 26, 1975, 20: 40, 42.

"Wrath." *Newsweek*, Nov. 8, 1943, p. 70. (About Witness conscientious objectors in prison).

Yamamoto, J. Isamu. "Sects Target new Areas, Make Subtle Changes." *Christianity Today*, Oct. 22, 1990, 34 (15): 52.

Yglesias, Linda. "All Along the Watchtower. The Jehovah's Witnesses siege of Brooklyn Heights." 3 pp.

Young, Scott. "Jehovah's Secret Agents." *MacLean's Magazine*, March 1, 1947, pp. 9, 62-64. (About the Witnesses in Canada, beliefs, history, the people involved).

"Zambia and Malawi: Whose Witnesses?" *The Economist*, Vol. 245, No. 6747, Dec. 16, 1972, pp. 10 11.

"Zygmunt, Joseph F. "Jehovah's Witnesses in the U.S.A.--1942-1976" (intro. in French and article in English). *Social Compass*, 1977, 24 (1): 45-47.

F. Theology and Doctrine

"An open letter to Jehovah's Witnesses." *The New Zealand Lutheran*, Vol. 10, No. 6, Aug. 1965, pp. 2-6. (Discusses the Divinity of Christ).

"Armageddon--Canceled until Further Notice?" *Eternity*, May 1975, 26: 6.

Armstrong, Arthur. "Antichrist Answered." *Logos*, 1978, pp. 240, 241.

_____. "The Truth vs. Jehovah's Witnesses." *Logos*, June 1977, 43 (9): 272.

"Attend Bible Classes of The Jehovah's Witnesses." *Extension*, June 1956, 53: 37.

"The Authority of the Scriptures." *The Discerner*, Oct.-Dec. 1955, 2 (2): 5-7.

Baker, Oscar M. "Jehovah's Witnesses." *Truth for Today*, Feb. 1961, p. 28.

Baldus, S.A. "Witnesses of Jehovah." *Extension*, Nov. 1940, 35: 19.

Bales, James D. "The Godhead." *The Spiritual Sword*, Oct. 1974, 6 (1): 1-3.

Barclay, William. "An Ancient Heresy in Modern Dress." *The Expository Times*, Nov. 1953, 65 (2): 31, 32.

Bechtle, John D. "And the Word Was What?" *The Discerner*, Oct.-Dec. 1975,8 (8): 7-10.

Beenken, Gilbert. "Misinterpretations of the Biblical Subject of Eternity." *The Discerner*, Oct.-Dec. 1965, 5 (4): 6-11.

Bevins, John. "A Loyal Witness, but a Stranger to Grace ... In the Organization, but Outside the Pale." *Evangelical Times, special issue, Christ and the Watchtower*, 974, 1: 6.

"Bible (in) Version." *Eternity*, Nov. 1981, p. 14.

Binsse, H.L. "Religion and a Liquor License." *Commonweal*, Jan. 10, 1947, 45: 317-318.

Bjorklund, Andy. "Who Speaks for Jehovah?" *Advent Christian Witness Missions*, June, 1980, pp. 4-6.

Blackford, Dick. "Jehovah's Witnesses." *Preceptor*, 23 (8): 1974.

"Boom in Doom." *Logos*, Feb. 1977, 43 (5): 158, 159.

Braden, Ruth. "Jehovah 1975." *New Society*, 1969, 14: 201, 202.

Burnside, G. "An Open Letter to Jehovah's Witnesses." *Australian Record*, vol. 73 Sept. 29, 1969.

Button, L.C. "No Longer a Mormon." *The Discerner*, Oct.-Dec. 1966, 5 (8): 7. (Discusses the author's experience with the Witnesses).

Canedy, Herbert V. "The Hazards of Date-Setting." *The Discerner*, July-Sept. 1976, 2 (11): 8, 10-12.

_____. "Quintuplet Cults, or Brothers Under the Skin." *The Discerner*, July-Aug. 1947, 1 (2); 5.

_____. "Satan's Strategy in His War of Worlds." *The Discerner*, July-Sept. 1958, 2 (11): 13, 14.

Carter, Cecil J. "The New American Standard Version and the Deity of Christ." *Plains Baptist Challenger*, Feb. 1977, 36 (1): 1, 3.

Cetnar, William. "Why I Was Kicked Out of the Watchtower." *Eternity*, Oct. 1980, 31 (9): 40-42.

Clevenger, Eugene W. "Sin and Salvation." *The Spiritual Sword*, Oct. 1974, 6 (1): 18-20.

Cohen, D. "Let's Hear It for Doomsday." *The Humanist*, July-Aug. 1976, pp. 22-26.

Cotton, Richard E. "In the Watchtower Movement for 18 Years, When God Rode Out to Conquer My Heart." *Evangelical Times, (special issue, Christ and the Watchtower)* Vol. 1, 1974, pp. 4, 5.

_____. "Will the World End This Year?" *Evangelical Times*, Jan. 1975, 9 (1): 1, 2.

Countess, R.H. "Translation of 'Theos' in the New World Translation." *Journal of the Evangelical Theological Society*, Summer 1967, 10: 153-160.

Dahlin, John E. "I Saw Jehovah's Witnesses at Work in Europe." *The Discerner*, Oct.-Dec. 1955, 2 (8): 12, 13.

_____. "Unscriptural Cults of Our Time--a Review." *The Discerner*, Oct.-Dec. 1957, 2 (8): 2-6.

_____. "Common Characteristics of Cults." *The Discerner*, July-Sept. 1958,2 (11): 2-4.

_____. "Cultists Are past Masters in Distorting the Scriptures." *The Discerner*, April-June 1959, 2 (2): 12-14.

_____. "The Tragic Errors of Present-Day Cultists." *The Discerner*, Oct.-Dec. 1963, 4 (8): 2-5.

_____. "The Jehovah's Witnesses as Dangerous Innovators." *The Discerner*, July-Sept., 1964, 4 (11): 2-5.

_____"The Great Success of Cults in Our Time." *The Discerner*, April-June 1967, 5 (10): 2-5

_____. "The Jehovah's Witnesses." *The Discerner*, Jan.-March 1970, 6 (9): 3, 4.

_____. "Some Guidelines in Dealing with Cultists." *The Discerner*, Oct.-Dec. 1970, 6 (12): 2-5.

Dalyik. "Jehovah's Witnesses." *Information*, Dec. 1955, 69: 25-30.

d'Anjou, M.J. "Actualité Religieuse." *Relations*, Nov. 1960, 20: 300, 301. (Religious News.)

Darby, George. "Cultist Activity in the Last Days." *The Discerner*, April-June 1963, 4 (6): 5-8.

"Darkness vs. Light." *Regular Baptist Press*, April 1953, pp. 63-67.

Davies, Horton. "Centrifugal Christian Sects." *Religion in Life*, Summer 1956, 25: 328, 329.

Deaver, Roy. "Christ--His Person." *The Spiritual Sword*, Oct. 1974, 6 (1): 4-11.

_____. "The Witnesses and 1 Peter 3:18." *The Spiritual Sword*, Oct. 1974, 6 (1): 14-16.

"A Defense of the True Bible Chronology." *The Present Truth and Herald of Christ's Epiphany*, March-April 1970, pp. 23-28.

"The Deity of Our Lord." *The Discerner*, Oct.-Dec. 1960, 3 (8): 9-13.

Dencher, Ted. "Do Not Slam Your Door to a Jehovah's Witness." *Herald of His Coming*, (449), May 1979, 38 (5): 7-8.

_____. "From Watchtower to Christ." *The Evangelical Christian*, Feb. 1962, pp. 18-20.

_____. "The Seven Errors of Russellism." *The Alliance Witness*, March 20, 1963, pp. 7-8.

_____. "The Watchtower vs. the Bible." *The Alliance Witness*, Aug. 21, 1966, pp. 5-6.

_____. "How Can We Help Jehovah's Witnesses?" *Church Herald*, July 26, 1974, pp. 14ff.

"Devils That Tempt." *Megiddo Messenger*, Feb. 1975, 62 (2): 9-11.

Dixon, A.C. "Russellism under the Searchlight." *The Life of Faith*, May 5, 1915, pp. 519-520.

Doherty, J.E. "Jehovah's Witnesses." *Liquorian*, March 1953, 41: 151-157.

Dugre, Alexandre. "Sur le Front de l'Heresie." *Ma Paroisse*, Feb. 1954, pp. 8, 9. (At the Front of Heresy.)

_____. "Faux témoins d'un Faux Jehovah." *Relations*, Feb. 1954, 14: 34-37. (False Witnesses of a False Jehovah.) (In French).

_____. "Sur le Front Jehovah." *Relations*, March 1954, 14: 80-83. (On the Jehovah's Witness Front.)

Dujardin, Richard. "Jehovah's Witnesses Debate Doomsday in the Year 1984, While Leaders Downplay Deadline Set by Sect." *Religious News Service*, July 1, 1984.

Duncan, Homer. "Jesus Christ Is Not God." *The Discerner*, July-Sept. 1977,9 (3): 11-13.

Eddy, G. Norman. "The Jehovah's Witnesses: An Interpretation." *Journal of Bible and Religion*, 1958,(26): 115-121.

"80,000,000 Books." *Logos*, March 1978, 144 (6): 176, 177.

Emch, William N. "What Do Jehovah's Witnesses Teach?" *Lutheran Standard*, Sept. 17, 1955, 112(48): 3.

_____. "Who Are Jehovah's Witnesses?" *Lutheran Standard*, May 23, 1959, 117: 13, 14.

Estes, T. "Jehovah's Witnesses Won't Tell Who Translated Their Bible." *Gospel Defender*, 1962, 3 (7): 4.

Feyles, G. "Los Testigos de Jehova." *Didascalia*, July 1964, 18: 297-305. (The Jehovah's Witness.)

Finnerty, Robert. "Faith of Our Fathers Part I; Were The Early Christians Jehovah's Witnesses?" *Christian Research Journal* Winter 1996 18 (3): 28-35 (Concludes that the Watchtowers claim that they teach restored early Christianity is false).

Fisher, Ronald. "Why and How of Reaching Jehovah's Witnesses." *Evangelical Missions Quarterly*, Oct. 1976, 12 (4): 227-238.

Fisk, Samuel. "Meeting a Jehovah's Witness at the Door." *The Discerner*, July-Sept. 1971, 7 (3): 9-13.

Fletcher, Austen G. "The Only Begotten: How Does This Term Apply to Christ?" *Ministry*, April 1977, 50: 40-42.

Gager, Leroy. "Who Are Jehovah's Witnesses?" *the Discerner*, Oct.-Dec. 1955, 2 (2): 3, 4.

Garner, Carl B. "What Is Man According to the Witnesses?" *Thrust*, 1980, 1 (1): 23-29.

Gehring, Luke. "False Witness: A Dialogue with Jehovah's Witnesses." *Orthodoxy* Nov.-Dec. 1988, 10: 22-27.

Gilbert, Richard R. "Waiting for Armageddon: Jehovah's Witnesses." *Presbyterian Life*, Aug. 15, 1962, 15: 5, 6, 31-34.

Godwin, Dewey. "Jehovah's Witnesses Heresy." *Sword of the Lord*, Feb. 10, 1984, 50 (3): 1, 18-20.

Goedelman, Kurt. "Jehovah's Witnesses and the Gospel of the Resurrection." *The Journal of Pastoral Practice*, 1979, 3 (2): 128-130.

Gruss, Edmond E. "Is the Watchtower Society God's Channel?" *The Discerner*, July-Sept. 1973, 7: 11-14.

_____. "Jehovah's Witnesses." *Moody Monthly*, 1971.

_____. "Now a Witness for Jesus Christ, Not a Jehovah's Witness." *The Discerner*, Jan.-March 1970, 6 (9): 8-11.

_____. "The Watchtower Society and Prophetic Speculation." *The Discerner*, Jan.-March 1972, 7 (5): 13-15.

Harris, Chester Radger "Seduction to Conversation." *Bible Advocate*, July-Aug. 1994, 128 (7): 4-5, 16.

_____. "Truth and Consequences." *Bible Advocate*, Sept. 1994 128 (8): 8-11. (The author's journey from the Watchtower.)

_____. "Inaccurate Knowledge." *Bible Advocate*, Oct. 1994, 128 (9): 14-16. (About Witness mistakes, prophesy failure etc.)

_____. "Sand Castle Doctrine." *Bible Advocate*, May 1996, 130 (4): 10-12. (Discusses the newest major change in the Watchtower's 1914 doctrine, a key doctrine).

Hassell, J.W. "The Truth About Jehovah's Witnesses." *Southern Presbyterian Journal*, May 2, 1951, 12: 6, 7

Hawk, Ray. "Salvation and the Witnesses." *Thrust*, 1980, 1 (2): 48-51.

Haynes, Carlyle B. "Russellism Admitting Its Mistakes." *The Watchman*, Dec. 1916, 25: 11-15. (An SDA publication)

_____ "Russellism--or the Coming of a False Christ." *The Watchman*, Apr. 1915, 24: 162-166.

_____. "Russellism--or the Coming of a False Christ." *The Watchman*, June 1915, 24: 267-272.

_____. "Russellism--or the Coming of a False Christ." *The Watchman*, Aug. 1915, 24: 363-367.

_____. "Russellism--or the Coming of a False Christ." *The Watchman*, Sept. 1915, 24: 406-410.

_____. "Russellism--or the Coming of a False Christ." *The Watchman*, Oct. 1915, 24: 454-458.

Hedegord, David (Ed.). "Dring Jehovas Vitten." *For Biblical Faith*, No. 3, 1958, pp. 107-116. (About Jehovah's Witnesses)

Henschel, Milton G. "Who Are Jehovah's Witnesses?" *Look*, July 28, 1953, 17: 76, 77. (Henschel was then a Watchtower Headquarters member. He is now President).

The Herald of the Epiphany, Special Edition, Feb. 15, 1959, 4 pp.

Herbert, Gerard. "Les Témoins de Jehovah." *Relations*, Oct. 1960, 20: 259-262. (The Jehovah's Witnesses)

_____. "Ou en sont les Témoins de Jehovah." *Relations*, Sept. 1963, 23: 63-266. (The Present State of Jehovah's Witnesses)

Herrgott, Jean. "French Evangelist Endures Sanatorium, Millennial Dawnists to Serve His Savior." *Greater Europe Report*, March-April 1974, 4 (2): 3, 6.

Higgens, J. "Jehovah's Witnesses at Your Door." *Liquorian*, Oct. 1972, 60: 16-19.

Hill, Robert. Why I am not a Bible Student. *The Discerner.* Pt I July-Sept. 1997 17(3):7-11; Pt II Oct.-Dec. 1997 17(4):6-12; Pt III Jan.-Mar. 1998 18(1):9-16. (Critiques mostly doctrine).

Hill, William F. "Are Jehovah's Witnesses Really Witnessing for Jehovah?" *The Discerner*, April-June 1975, 8 (6): 12-14.

Hobbs, A.G. "A General Look at Jehovah's Witnesses." *The Spiritual Sword.* Oct. 1974, 6 (1): 41-46.

Hoekema, Anthony. "Assessing Jehovah's Witnesses." *Christianity Today*, July 21, 1967, 11: 14-17.

Hoffman, J. Reynolds. "Is Jehovah God?" *Ministry*, June 1982, 55: 22-24.

Holmes, John Haynes. "The Case of Jehovah's Witnesses." *Christian Century*, July 17, 1940, 57: 896-898, *Response*, July 31, 1940, p. 953.

Homan, Roger. "Teaching the Children of Jehovah's Witnesses." *British Journal of Religious Education*, Sum. 1988, 10: 154-159.

Hope, S. "Be Prepared for Jehovah's Witnesses." *Presbyterian Journal*, May 7, 1975, p. 13.

"How to Spot a Cult." *Moody Monthly*, Aug. 1977, p. 32.

"Is Armageddon Imminent?" *Insight*, Oct. 28, 1975, 6: 17.

"Is It a Sin to Change Religions?" *Evangelical Times, Special Issue, Christ and the Watchtower*, 1974, 1: 2.

"Is It Wrong to Refuse to Argue with Jehovah's Witnesses?" *Messenger of the Sacred Heart*, Feb. 1956, 91: 50, 51.

"Is Something Happening in the Watchtower Movement?" *Evangelical Times, special issue, Christ and the Watchtower*, 1974, 1: 1.

Jackson, Wayne. "The Church (The Kingdom)." *The Spiritual Sword*, Oct. 1974, 6 (1): 22-24.

_____. "The Lord's Return." *The Spiritual Sword*, Oct. 1974, 6 (1): 25-27.

_____. "Answering False Doctrines Relating to Revelation." *Christian News*, June 3, 1985, pp. 13-14.

_____. "When the Watchtower Witnesses Come Calling." *Christian Courier*, Sept. 1985, 21 (5): 17-18.

"Jehovah's Witnesses Issue." *Ministry*, Oct. 1940, 13: 9.

"Jehovah's Witnesses." *Catholic Mind*, July 1945, 43: 421.

"Jehovah's Witnesses Do Not Believe." *The Discerner*, July-Sept. 1964, 4 (11): 14, 15.

"Jehovah's Witnesses Refuted by the Bible." *Herald of the Coming Age*, Oct. 1969, 20 (3): 48.

"Jehovah's Witnesses: The Christian View--Personal Freedom Outreach of St. Louis, Missouri." *The Journal of Pastoral Practice*, 1979, 3(1): 95-113.

"Jehovah's Witnesses vs. Scripture." *Megiddo Messenger*, Oct. 1966, 53 (10): 14-16.

"Jehovah's Witnesses: Watchtower Woes." *Eternity*, March, 1981,32: 12.

Johnson, Andrew E. "Laymen's Home Missionary Movement." *The Discerner*, Jan.-March 1968, 6 (1): 6, 7, 15. (About this offshoot of the Jehovah's Witnesses.)

_____. "Witness with False Evidence." *Good News Broadcaster*, Jan. 1973, pp. 10ff.

_____. "Witnesses with False Evidence." *The Discerner*, Jan.-March 1973, 7 (9): 9-12.

Johnson, Ralph A. "What Next for Jehovah's Witnesses?" *Sound Witness* June-July, 1993. (About the future of the Watchtower.)

Jones, Jerry. "Baptism." *The Spiritual Sword*, Oct. 1974, 6 (1): 20-22.

Kelcy, Raymond C. "Punishment of the Wicked." *The Spiritual Sword*, Oct. 1974, 6 (1): 38-40.

King, Chad J. "Jehovah's Witnesses." *The Discerner* Vol. 16 No. 1 Jan.-March 1996 p. 3-7. (About the continuing revelation and other problematic doctrines).

Knuteson, Roy E. "The God of the Jehovah's Witnesses." *The Discerner*, July-Sept. 1963, 4 (7): 6-9

_____. "The Kingdom Concept of the Jehovah's Witnesses." *The Discerner*, July-Sept. 1964, 4 (11); 10-14.

_____. "An Open Letter to a Jehovah's Witness." *The Discerner* July-Sept 1997 17 (3): 4-6. (On the Deity of Christ)

"La Cour Supréme et les Témoins de Jehovah." *Relations*, Nov. 1953, 13: 286. (The Supreme Court and Jehovah's Witnesses)

"La Divinidad de Jesus Frenta a los 'Testigos de Jehova." *Didascalia*, 1967, 21 (2): 97-102. (The Divinity of Jesus Face to Face with the Jehovah's Witnesses)

Lagoon, Steve. "Myths Involving the Jehovah's Witnesses." *The Discerner* Oct-Dec 1993. 14 (8): 2-6. (Discusses common misconceptions about Watchtower doctrine.)

Larsen, David L. "Cultic Distortion of the Holy Scriptures." *The Discerner*, Oct.-Dec. 1970, 6 (12): 5-9.

Larsen, Robert L. "Where Is Elijah?" *Ministry*, Nov. 1971, 44: 32, 33.

Laursen, Gerald A. "How to Witness to Jehovah's Witnesses." *Evangelical Beacon*, Aug. 10, 1971, pp. 10, 11.

Ledit, J.H. "Les Témoins de Jehovah." *Relations*, Feb. 1947, 6: 43-46. (The Jehovah's Witnesses)

_____. "Les Témoins se reorganisent." *Relations*, Aug. 1943, 3: 212-214. (The Witnesses Reorganize)

Lusk, Maurice, III. "Christ--His Resurrection." *The Spiritual Sword*, Oct. 1974, 6 (1): 14-16.

Martin, Walter R. "Jehovah's Witnesses and the Gospel of Confusion." *Eternity*, Sept. 1957, 8: 22, 23, 36, 37.

McCluskey, N.G. "Who Are Jehovah's Witnesses?" *America*, Nov. 19, 1955, 94: 204-208. Reprinted in *Catholic Digest*, Vol. 20, March 1956, pp. 56-61.

McCord, Hugo. "Man--His Nature and Death." *The Spiritual Sword*, Oct. 1974, 6 (1): 16-18.

McGinnis, H.C. "Who Are the Holy Crusaders Joining Jehovah's Witnesses?" *America*, Vol. 64, March 22, 1941, pp. 651-652. Reprinted as "Witness Jehovah's Witnesses." *Catholic Digest*, July 1941, 51: 53-59.

McInerney, T.J. "Watchtower Zealots." *Sign*, Vol. 26, Dec. 1946, pp. 39-41. Abridged in *Catholic Digest*, Feb. 1947, 11: 102-103.

"Message of the Revelation in 1942, The." *Lutheran Church Quarterly*, 1942, 15: 296-299.

Metzger, Bruce M. "The Jehovah's Witnesses and Jesus Christ: A Biblical and Theological Appraisal." *Theology Today*, April 1953, 10 (1): 65-85.

Mignard, Robert B. "Fifteen Reasons Why I Cannot Be a Jehovah's Witness" (reprint of tract with same title). *The Discerner*, April-June 1966, 5 (6):12-15. Reprinted in Oct.-Dec. 1976, 8 (12): 13-16. Also reprinted in *The Voice*, June 1966.

Miller, Ed L. "The Logos Was God." *Evangelical Quarterly*, April-June, 1981, 53: 65-77.

Moffitt, Jerry. "Everlasting Punishment." *Thrust*, 1980, 1 (2): 58-66.

Morey, Robert. "A Jehovah's Witness? Next Time Open the Door." *Christianity Today*, Sept. 3, 1982, 26 (14): 37-39.

Muller, Albert. "Jehovah's Witnesses Call." *Homiletic and Pastoral Review*, May 1963, 63: 676-683.

"Name of God, The." *Herald of Holiness*, June 18, 1969, p. 10. A critical analysis of Witnesses' use of the name Jehovah.

"New Notes." *The Journal of Pastoral Practice*, 1979, 3 (2): 131, 132.

O'Brien, John A. "Challenge of the Witnesses." *American Ecclesiastical Review*, Oct. 1947, 117: 284-290.

_____. "Light on Jehovah's Witnesses." *Our Sunday Visitor*, p. 29.

"Ominous Decision." *Time*, June 22, 1942, p. 55. Jehovah's Witnesses can be forced to pay peddler's tax.

"Ontario: Jehovah's Witnesses." *Time*, Sept. 25, 1944, p. 17.

"Organizations: Glad Assembly." *Time*, Aug. 19, 1946, p. 24.

Oswald, M. Donovan. "The Jehovah's Witnesses." *Ministry*, Vol. 22, June 1949, pp. 17-19.

Patania, Connie. "From Jehovah's Witnesses to Life in Jesus Christ!" *Deeper Life*, Sept. 1979, p. 5.

Paul, J.M. "Russellism Refuted." *The Christadelphian Advocate*, No. 1915, pp. 327-330.

Pellitier, Pam. "Scaling the Jehovah's Witnesses Watchtower." *Moody Monthly*, Aug. 1977, pp. 33-35.

"People." *Moody Monthly*, Dec. 1977, pp. 20-22. (About Inga Markmiller, a Jehovah's

Witness opera singer).

Perry, Victor. "Jehovah's Witnesses and the Deity of Christ." *Evangelical Quarterly*, Jan.-March 1963, 35: 15-22.

Pickering, Ernest. "Jehovah's Witnesses--The Doctrine of the Church." *The Discerner*, Jan.-March 1961, 3 (9); 11-15.

Plante, A. "L'Incident de Shawinigan." *Relations*, June 1950, 10: 155-157. (The Incident at Shawinigan [a city in South Quebec].)

Prescott, William W. "Jehovah--Jesus." *Review and Herald*, April 28, 1921, 98: 3-5.

Price, E.B. "How to Work for Jehovah's Witnesses." *Ministry*, April 19, 1962, 35: 34-36.

_____. "How to Win Jehovah's Witnesses." *Australian Record*, Vol. 66 Feb. 12, 1962.

"Pseudo-Science and Pseudo-Theology (A) Cult and Occult." *Journal of the American Scientific Affiliation*, March 1977, pp. 24, 25.

Putnam, C.E. "Are Russell and Rutherford God's Prophets?" *Moody Monthly*, April 1939, 39: 434-436.

"Quebec: The Witnesses." *Time*, Oct. 1, 1945, p. 42.

"Questions and Answers." *Migiddo*, May 26, 1962, 49 (11); 11.

"Questions and Answers." *Megiddo Messenger*, July 7, 1962, 49 (14): 11.

"Questions and Answers." *Megiddo Messenger*, Dec. 1967, 54 (12); 23.

"Questions and Answers." *Megiddo Messenger*, May 1968, 55 (5): 15.

"Questions and Answers." *Megiddo Messenger*, July 1968, 55 (7): 23.

"Questions from Readers." *Epiphany Bible Students Association*, 251: 6-8.

Read, W.E. "The Name of God (Part I)." *Ministry*, Feb. 1969, 42: 29-32.

_____. "The Name of God (Part II): Jesus as 'The Lord Thy God.'" *Ministry*, March 1969, 42: 36-39.

Rhodes, Oran. "The Holy Spirit and the Witnesses." *Thrust*, 1980, 1 (1); 18-22.

_____. "The Kingdom and 1914." *Thrust*, 1980, 1 (2): 70-75.

Ritchie, C.J. "Jesus and Jehovah." *Signs of the Times*, Vol. 96, March 1963, pp. 21-23, 31.

Rogerson, G. "1914 in Bible Prophecy, Part I." *Signs of the Times* (Australia), Aug. 1, 1974, 88:2-4.

_____. "1914 in Bible Prophecy, Part II: The Law of Probabilities and 1914." *Signs of the Times*, Sept. 1, 1974,88: 10-13.

_____. "1914 in Bible Prophecy, Part III: Chronology of the Seventy Years as It Affects 1914." *Signs of the Times*, Oct. 1, 1974, 88: 10-12.

_____. "1914 in Bible Prophecy, Part V: Do the Signs Indicate 1914?" *Signs of the*

Times, Dec. 1, 1974, 88:18-20.

Roggio, Sal. "Witnesses" True or False." *Christian Citizen Magazine*, Aug. 1981, 1 (6): 33-34. (Reviews the Trinity, and person of Christ doctrines of the Witnesses).

Rosen, Moishe. "Titles." *Jews for Jesus Newsletter*, 1977, 10: 1.

Rumble, L. "Witnesses of Jehovah." *Homiletic and Pastoral Review*, July 1954, 54: 873-884.

S.S. "After Thirty Years." *Logos*, 1980?, pp. 176-177.

Sage, Wayne. "The War on the Cults." *Human Behavior*, Oct. 1976, pp. 40-49.

Sanders, Evelyn. "When You Meet Jehovah's Witnesses." *Evangelical Beacon*, Oct. 31, 1972, 46 (3): 8, 9.

_____. "When You Meet Jehovah's Witnesses." *Presbyterian Journal*, May 15, 1974, pp. 9ff.

_____. "When You Meet Jehovah's Witnesses." *Princeton Seminary Bulletin 44*, 1974, 30 (3):9, 10.

Schmuck, Terry. "Set Free by the Truth." *The Discerner*, Oct.-Dec. 1977, 9 (4): 10, 12.

Schnell, William. "Open Letter to Jehovah's Witnesses" (6th letter). *The Discerner*, July-Sept. 1968, 6 (3):14, 15.

_____. "Witnessing for Christ to Jehovah's Witnesses." *United Evangelical Action*, Vol. 19, July 1960, pp. 163+. Also printed in *Action*, July 1960, pp. 7, 8.

"Second Advent of Christ, The." *Megiddo Messenger*, Feb. 17, 1962, pp. 13-16.

"Second Coming--Visible or Invisible, The." *Megiddo Messenger*, Feb. 17, 1962, pp. 7-9.

Shahan, R. "I Was a Jehovah's Witness." *Lutheran Standard*, Feb. 5, 1977, pp. 8ff.

Simmel, O. "Sind die Ernsten Bibel Forscher Ernst Zu Nehaman?" *Stimmen*, Vol. 146, Sept. 1950, pp. 466-469. Should We Take the Bible Students [J.W.'s] Seriously?

Smith, Wilbur N. "Jehovah's Witnesses." *Christianity Today*, Vol. 5, Dec. 19, 1960, pp. 16-18.

"Smoking." *Church Management*, 50(2) , April 1974.

Spivey, Arnold. "A Look at Jehovah's Witnesses." *Sabbath Recorder*, 200(3) March 1978, pp. 7, 28.

Sprague, Theodore W. "The 'World' Concept Among Jehovah's Witnesses." *Harvard Theological Review*, Vol. 39, April 1946, pp. 109-140.

Springstead, William A. "Hermeneutics of Jehovah's Witnesses." *The Discerner*, 3(6):8-10 April-June 1960.

_____. "Jehovah's Witnesses' Amazing Switch in Doctrine." *The Discerner*, 2(2):9-11, 15 April-June 1959.

Starkes, M. Thomas. "Armageddon's Army: The Jehovah's Witnesses." *Home Missions*, March 1975.

Starling, Norman W. "The Name 'Jehovah's Witnesses.'" *Thrust*, 1(2):67-69 1980.

Stedman, Ray C. "The New World Translation of the Christian Greek Scriptures." *Our Hope*, Vol. 60, July 1953, pp. 29-39.

Stevens, Josephine. "Witnesses." *New Society*, Aug. 23, 1973, p. 474.

Strelkov, M.S. "Outwitting the Witnesses." *St. Anthony's Messenger*, Vol. 66, Sept. 1958, pp. 37-41.

Stuermann, Walter. "The Bible and Modern Religions III." *Interpretation:" A Journal of Bible and Theology*, 10(3): 323-346 July 1956.

Swanson, Collene. A Letter On Jehovah's Witnesses. *Moody Monthly*, Dec. 1977, p. 9.

Swetmon, Bill. "Jehovah's Witnesses Translations of I Peter 3:15." *The Spiritual Sword*, 6(1): 36, 37 Oct. 1975.

Tarbet, Don. "Jehovah's Witnesses Doctrine About Christ." *Thrust*, 1(1):10-17 1980 .

_____. "The 'Trinity.'" *Thrust*, 1(2):52-57 1980.

Terry, George. "Jehovah's Witness Presiding Elder Exclaims, 'I've Been Born Again!'" *Evangelical Times, Special Issue Christ and the Watchtower*, Vol. 1, 1974, pp. 2, 3.

_____. "A Problem Verse for Christians?" *Evangelical Times, Special Issue Christ and the Watchtower*, Vol. 1, 1974, p. 3.

Thiele, Edwin R. "Jehovah's Witnesses and the Dates of the Babylonian Captivity." *Ministry*, 49(2):17-19 Feb. 1976.

"Thirty Years a Watchtower Slave." *Power*, Vol. 16, No. 1, Jan.-March 1958, 8 pp. Reprinted in *The Discerner*, 2(11):8, 9-12, July-Sept. 1958.

Thompson, Robert F. "My Lord and My God. Part 1: Why Jehovah's Witnesses Are Wrong About the Deity of Christ." *Ministry*, 49(9): 20-23 Sept. 1976.

_____. "My Lord and My God. Part 2." *Ministry*, 49(11):22-24 Nov. 1976.

Thomson, Alexander. "Jehovah's Theocratic Organization." *The Differentiator*, 21(3) June 1959, pp. 98-104.

"To 'Christie Love,' Star Teresa Graves, Religion More Important Than Show Business." *Midnight*. 22(2):4 July 14, 1975. (About movie star Teresa Graves' conversion to the Witnesses).

Trombley, Charles. "A Wedge in My Foundation." *Voice*, March 1963.

"Twenty Questions on a Witness' Mind." *Evangelical Times, special issue, Christ and the Watchtower*, Vol. 1, 1974, pp. 1-8.

Van der Goes, Catherine. "Why I Quit the Jehovah's Witnesses." *The Discerner*. 7(9):13, 14 Jan.-March 1973. Reprinted from *Power for Living*, 1972.

"Victory Without Peace." *Extension*, Aug. 1943, p. 19.

Warren, Thomas B. "Editorial: Jehovah's Witnesses: A System of Infidelity." *The Spiritual Sword*. 6(1):3, 4 Oct. 1974. Also see inside cover.

Whalen, William. "What Can the Jehovah's Witnesses Teach Us?" *Ave Maria*, Vol. 95,

Feb. 24, 1962, pp. 26-29; also Vol. 94, July 8, 1961, p. 17.

_____. "We Can Learn Something from Jehovah's Witnesses." *St. Anthony Messenger*, Vol. 80, May 1973, pp. 18-21.

Wharton, Gary. "I Came Back." *The Evangelical Christian*, July 1967, pp. 19-22. (The story of Stan Thomas.)

Whittington, John. "History of Jehovah's Witnesses." *Thrust*, Vol. 1, 1980, pp. 10-17.

"Who Are God's True Witnesses?" *Herald of the Coming Age*, p. 20.

Williams, James Erie. "A Letter to a J. Witnesses." *The New Creation*. 55(9+10):31-33 Sept.-Oct., 1994. (On Watchtower teaching about Jesus.)

Wimbish, John S. "What Is a Jehovah's Witness?" *The Sword of the Lord*. 47(47):1, 8-14, Nov. 20, 1981.

"Witnesses Deny Christian Tie." *Presbyterian Life*, Sept. 1, 1969.

Woods, Guy N. "New Heavens--New Earth." *The Spiritual Sword*. 6(1):27-29, Oct. 1974.

"Working with Jehovah's Witnesses." *Ministry*. Vol 42, Aug. 1943, pp. 46, 47.

Workman, Gary. "The Watchtower Doctrine of the Last Things." *Thrust*. 1(1): 30-40 1980.

_____. "The Watchtower Doctrine of the Last Things (Part 2)." *Thrust*. 1(2):76-88 1980.

Zuck, Roy. "Letter to a Jehovah's Witness." *Moody Monthly*, Vol. 73, March 1973, pp. 30-33, 90, 91.

Zygmunt, Joseph. "Jehovah's Witness in the USA 1942-1976." *Social Compass*. 24 (1): 45-57, 1977.

G. Reviews of Books on the Watchtower

Alfs, Matthew. *Evocative Religion of Jehovah's Witnesses*. Review in the *Christian Century* 108(22): 730 July 24, 1991: and by John P. Alston in *Journal of Church and State* 34(4): 883. Autumn, 1992: by Richard Singlenberg in *Journal for the Scientific Study of Religion*. 31(2): 234-235 June 1992; and by Erling Jorstad in *Church History* 62(3): 440 Sept. 1993.

Beckford, James A. *The Trumpet of Prophecy: A Sociological Study of Jehovah's Witnesses*. Reviews in: *Contemporary Sociology--A Journal of Reviews* by M.G. Taylor, 5(6):804,1976. *Encounter* by Bryan Wilson, Vol. 45, Oct. 1975, p. 77. *International Review of Modern Sociology* by K.M. Wulff, 6(2):418-420 1976. *Journal for the Scientific Study of Religion* by William Kaeson, 16(1):106-109 March 1977. *New Statesman and Nation* "On the Doorstep" by Bryan Wilson, Vol. 90, Sept. 19, 1975, p. 340. (Very positive about Beckford's work). *Social Forces* by J.P. Alston, 55(1):211 1976. *Social Forces* by Val Clear, 55(1):211 1976. *Times Literary Supplement* by John Whitworth, June 4, 1976, p. 679. *Sociological Analysis* by J.F. Zygmunt, 37(4):353-354, 1976.

Bergman, Jerry. *Jehovah's Witnesses and Kindred Groups: A Historical Compendium and Bibliography*. Reviewed in *ADRIS Newsletter*, 13(4):89 July-Sept. 1984 Also reviews in: *American Reference Book Annual* by James H. Sweetland, 1985, p. 476. *Choice* by H.T. Hutchinson, Jan. 1985, p. 658. *Cornerstone* by

Eric Pement, Vol 15, No. 79, n.d. *International Social Science Review* by Plano
D. Bardis, n.d. *Religious Studies Review* by Bruce David Forbes, 11(4):419 Oct.
1985. *Theology Digest* by Charles W. Heiser, 32(1):61 Spring 1985.

_____. *Jehovah's Witnesses and the Problem of Mental Illness.* Reviewed by Kaynor
J. Weishaupt in *Free Minds Journal.* 12(6):12 Nov.-Dec. 1993. Also reviewed
by David A. Cook in the *Discerner.* 15(1):16-17 1995.

Botting, Heather and Gary. *The Orwellian World of Jehovah's Witnesses. The American
Rationalist.* Review by Gordon Stein in Sept.-Oct. 24(3):47 1984.
Canadian Journal of History. Review by M. James Penton. Feb. 1987, 138-141.

Cole, Marley. *Jehovah's Witnesses, The New World Society."* Review in *Nation,* Vol.
181, Oct. 1, 1955, p. 290. Reviews in:*The Discerner.* 2(2):14 Oct.-Dec. 1955.
Herald Tribune Book Review, July 31, 1955, p. 290.

_____. *Living Destiny, The Man from Mathew, Mark, Luke, John.* Review in *The
Bible Collector* by Arnold Ehlert, July-Sept. 1984, No. 79, pp. 2, 6.

Dencher, Ted. *The Watchtower Heresy Versus the Bible.* Review in *The Discerner* by
John Dahlin, 4(7):14-15 July-Sept. 1963.

DeVore, Steve and Steve Lagoon. "Blood, Medicine and the Jehovah's Witnesses."
Reviewed by David A. Cook in *The Discerner.* 15(3): 20-21 July-Sept. 1995.

Fields, Karen E. *Revival and Rebellion in Colonial Central Africa.* Reviewed in *Choice*
Vol. 23 June 1986 p. 1586 by T. F. Taylor; *Times Literary Supplement* July 4,
1986 p. 726 by Richard Gray; *Contemporary Sociology* Vol. 15 Sept 1986 p. 722
by Susan Geiger, and in *American Journal of Sociology* Vol. 92 March 1987 p.
1240 by Bryan R. Wilson.

Franz, Raymond. *Crisis of Conscience.* Reviews in: *Canadian Journal of History.*
Review by M. James Penton, Feb. 1987, pp. 138-141. *Christianity Today* by
James Penton, March 2, 1984, pp. 64-67. *The Discerner* by Jerry Bergman,
11(8):4-7 Oct.-Dec. 1984.

_____. *In Search of Christian Freedom.* Reviewed by P. W. Williams in *Choice* 29(10):
1562 June 1992.

Gruss, Edmond. *Jehovah's Witnesses: Apostles of Denial."* *Moody Monthly,* Jan. 1971,
pp. 40-41. Review reprinted in *The Discerner* 7(10):12 Jan.-March 1971.

Harrison, Barbara Grizzuti. *Visions of Glory: A History and a Memory of Jehovah's
Witnesses.* Reviews in: *Commonweal* by Jack Miles, Vol. 105, Dec. 22, p. 818.
Library Journal by Elise C. Dennis, Vol. 103, Aug. 1978, p. 1501. (She stresses
the book's writing quality and catharsis value for the author). *Ms.* by Catharine R.
Stimpson, Oct. 1978, pp. 43-45. *The Nation,* "How I Got Over" by Lisa
Gubernick, Vol. 228, Jan. 1979, pp. 22-25. (A very favorable review.) *New
York Times Book Review* by Vivian Gornick, Nov. 19, 1978, p. 9. *New York
Review of Books,* Vol. 25, Oct. 26, 1978, p. 53. *Saturday Review,* Vol. 5, Sept.
16, 1978, p. 47. *The Worldview.* 21(10): 21 Oct. 1978.

Hoekema, Anthony. *The Four Major Cults.* Review in *The Discerner* by David Larson,
5(2):14, 15 April-June 1965.

Jasmin, Damien. *Les Témoins de J'hovah.* Reviews in *Les dossiers de l'histoire,* no. 16,
Nov. Dec. 1978, pp. 98-102. Reviews in the *Bulletin* by Pierre Le Cabellec,
interparoissial de Lorient, Janvier, 1976. *Historia* by Maurice Colinon, special
sectes, No. 382 bis, 1978, pp. 26-34. *Historama* by Christian Meget, no. hors
série, No. 36, Oct. Nov., 1978, pp. 47-52.

Jonsson, Carl Olof. *The Gentile Times Reconsidered.* Review in *The Bible Examiner and Christian Review* by Alan Thomas Rogerson, Dec. 1983, p. 14.

Kaplan, William. *Jehovah's Witnesses and Their Fight for Civil Rights.* Reviewed by Karim Benyekhlef in *Juridique Themis* , Vol. 24, Summer 1990, pp. 403-406 and by Jerry Bergman in both *Journal of Church and State.* 32(2):424-425 Spring 1990 and *The Christian Quest* Vol. 3, No. 1, Spring 1990. pp. 101-110. Also reviewed by Aubery Golden in *The Canadian Forum* 69(794): 55-56 Nov. 1990, by T. D. Regehr in *Canadian Historical Review* (2)72: 256 June 1991, and F. L. Morton in *Canadian Journal of Political Science* 24(2): 398-399 June 1991.

King, Christine E. *The Nazi State and the New Religion.* Review by Richard Besset in *History Today*, June 1985, Vol. 35, and by Ian Kershaw in *History* Vol. 69 June 1984 p. 360.

Le phénoméne sectaire comme révélateur social. (The Sectarian Phenomenon like socially revealing). Reviewed in *Autrement* by Jean S'Guy 12/78, p. 71.

Manwaring, David. *Render Unto Caesar: The Flag-Salute Controversy.* Reviews in: *Library Journal* by Joseph Andrews, Vol. 87, June 15, 1962, p. 2387. *Political Science Quarterly* by Harold Stahmer, Vol. 78, March 1963, pp. 159, 160.

Martin, Walter. *Jehovah of the Watchtower.* Reviewed by Douglord Young in *The Discerner*, 2(2):15 Oct.-Dec. 1955 and by G.D. Young and J.F. Mattingly in *Northwestern Pilot*, May 1954.

McKinnley, George D. *Theology of Jehovah's Witnesses.* Review by Frank B. Price in *International Review of Missions*, Vol. 52, Oct. 1963, pp. 467-470.

Newton, Merlin Owen. *Armed With the Constitution* Reviewed by J. R. Vile in Choice 32(11-12): 1801 July, 1995; Virginia Van der Veer Hamilton in *The Journal of American History* 82(3): 1284-1285 Dec. 1995; Samuel C. Shepherd in *Journal of Southern History* 62(2): 409-410 May, 1996; and by John Braeman in *The American Historical Review* 101(5)1642 Dec. 1996.

Oakley, Debbie and Helen Ortega. *Mom and Me* reviewed by Jerry Bergman in *The Discerner*, 9(12):9-11 1979.

Penton, James M. *Jehovah's Witnesses in Canada.* Reviews in: *Church and History* by John W. Netter, 47(1):98, 99 March 1978. *Journal of Church and State* by J.K. Zeman, 20(2):341-343 Spring 1978.*Quill and Quire* by J.L. Granatstein, Nov. 1976, p. 36.*Revve de Nord* by Régis Dericquebourg, Sept. 1978.*Times Literary Supplement* by Bryan Wilson, April 1, 1977 (An excellent, very positive review).

_____. *Apocalypse Delayed; The Story of Jehovah's Witnesses* by James Penton Reviewed by Jerry Bergman in *The Discerner*, 12(1):9-12 Jan-Mar 1986. Also reviewed in *The Christian Century*. Vol. 103 Feb. 19, 1986 by Robert Handy and in *Choice* Jan. 1986 p. 754 by W.L. Pitts in *Christianity Today* Vol. 29 Nov. 22, 1985 p. 43 by the editor, and in *The American Historical Review* Vol. 91 Dec. 1986 p. 1279 by Timothy P. Weber.

Reed, David. *Behind the Watchtower Curtain: The Secret Society of Jehovah's Witnesses* reviewed by Hero M. Lucas *Cultic Studies Journal.* 8(1):80-81 1990.

_____. "The Tragic Consequences of Faith." Review of *Blood on the Alter.* Reviewed by Dave Mackmiller in *Free Inquiry,* Summer 1997 17 (3): 61-62. Also reviewed by Jerry Bergman in *The American Rationalists.* May-June 1997 42 (1): 19 and in the *JAMA* Feb. 5, 1997 227(5)425 by Marianne Mann, M.D.

Schnell, William J. *Thirty Years a Watchtower Slave.* Review by Stanley Roland Jr. in

The Nation by Vol. 182, Nov. 24, 1956, p. 464. (A good brief summary of Schnell's classic historical book).

_____. *Trente Ans Esclave des Témoins de J´éhovah*. Review in *M´longes de Science Religieuse* by R. Dericquebourg 34(3) Sept. 1972.

Ségaud, Evelyne. *Confessions d'un Ancien Témoin de Jéhovah*. Review in *Comptes Rendus* by R. Dericquebourg, 1977, p. 190. (Confessions of a former J.W.).

Sterling, Chandler W. *The Witnesses: One God, One Victory*. Review in *Library Journal* by D.W. Dayton, Vol. 110, May 1, 1975, p 863.

Stevenson, W.C. *The Inside Story of Jehovah's Witnesses*. Reviews in*Library Journal* by Edith French, Vol. 93, Oct. 1, 1968, p. 3566. *New Statesman and Nation* by Peter Sedgwick, Vol. 75, Jan. 12, 1968, p. 48.

Stroup, Herbert. *The Jehovah's Witnesses*. Reviews in: *American Political Science Review*, by Ethan P. Allen, 41(1):167 Feb. 1947. *The Social Service Review* by S.P. Breckinridge, Vol. 20, 1946, p. 123. *The American Sociological Review* by Stanley Chapman, 11(1) Feb. 1946. *Social Science*, by Edna Cooper, 24(2):365-366 March 1946. *The American Catholic Sociological Review* by Joseph H. Fichter, Vol. 7, 1946, p 209. *Social Research* by Martin H. Neumeyer, Vol. 30, Sept.-Oct. 1945, pp. 74. *The Journal of Educational Sociology* by George E. Payne, 19(4). Dec. 1945, p. 269. *New Statesman and Nation* by V. S. Pritchett, "The Religion of Hate," Vol. 30, Oct. 13, 1945, p. 248-249. *Social Science*, 21(2):140-141 April 1946. *Spectator* by S.K. Ratcliffe, Vol. 175, Oct. 5, 1945, p. 316. *Lutheran Church Quarterly* by Theodore Tappert, 19(2):219-220 April 1946. *Rural Sociology* by Thomas Alfred Tripp, 10(1-4):344-345 1945.

_____, and Damien Jasmin *Les Temoins de Jehovah*. Review in *The Canadian Historical Review* by R.A. Preston, 29(1):70-74 March 1948.

Thomas, Stan. *Jehovah's Witnesses and What They Believe*. Review in *The Evangelical Christian* by Gary Wharton, July 1967, p. 22.

Whalen, William J. *Armageddon Around the Corner*. Reviews in:*Journal for the Scientific Study of Religion* by Theodore W. Sprague, 3(1):137-138 Fall 1963. *Review of Religious Research* by Charles C. Braden, 5(2):120, 121 Winter 1964.

White, Timothy. Review of: *A People for His Name: A History of Jehovah's Witnesses and an Evaluation*. Book Notes *Church History*, 38(1):128 March 1969.

AMERICAN OFFSHOOTS OF THE WATCHTOWER SOCIETY

Since its inception, the Watchtower Bible & Tract Society has experienced scores of schisms, some fairly major. The largest or more important of these offshoots are discussed below. In the case of some early offshoots, such as the Pastoral Bible Institute, even though the leaders were expelled from Bethel, some were still democratically elected elders in the local Watchtower ecclesia and retained that position. On the other hand, Rutherford could, and often did, forbid dissidents to be official pilgrims.

The 1917-1919 divisions became increasingly great until in the United States four major movements arose--the Watchtower Bible & Tract Society, the Pastoral Bible Institute, the Layman's Home Missionary Movement, and the Standfast Bible Students. In Britain, several other major splits occurred at this juncture in Watchtower history. The Watchtower increasingly tried to differentiate itself from the offshoots, but it was not until 1931, when Rutherford introduced the name "Jehovah's Witnesses," that a clear distinction between various Bible Student groups and the Watchtower existed.

Actually, the Jehovah's Witnesses are as much an offshoot of Russell's movement as are the Standfasters or Layman's Home Missionary Movement; Allan Rogerson noted, "from 1919 to 1932 [Rutherford] systematically changed all aspects of the sect: [its] norms and values, ideology, patterns of evangelization and worship, internal structure, group commitments and perhaps inevitably its members."

Even before Russell's death, several prominent Watchtower leaders disagreed with some of Russell's teachings and led some members to separate from the Watchtower. In 1908-1909 E.C. Henninges, head of the Australian branch of the Watchtower Society, and M.L. McPhail, of the Chicago class (a term which means church), united against certain of Russell's ideas concerning the Covenant and Christ's ransom. The resultant schism cost Russell most of his Australian following and much of his U.S. following. The U.S. group that divided at this time became the Christian Believers Assembly.

When Russell died, the current directors of the Watch Tower Bible and Tract Society were Vice President A.I. Ritchie; Secretary-Treasurer William E. Van Amburgh, and James D. Wright, Isaac F. Hoskins, Henry Clay Rockwell (replaced on March 29, 1917, by Robert H. Hirsh), and Joseph F. Rutherford. All of these men had been personally appointed by Russell. Two days after Russell died, Andrew N. Pierson was elected by the committee to fill the vacancy left by Russell. The Executive Board included A.I. Ritchie, William E. Van Amburgh, and Joseph F. Rutherford. The Editorial Committee (which supervised all publications) was William E. Van Amburgh, Joseph F. Rutherford, Fred H. Robinson, H.C. Rockwell, and Robert H. Hirsh. The pastoral work (primarily an organized way of following up interest expressed by potential converts continued under the direction of Menta Sturgeon, and A.H. MacMillan was in charge of the office staff.

The first election of the Society's officers after Russell unexpectedly died occurred on Saturday, January 6, 1917, during the two-day Pittsburgh convention. Joseph Franklin Rutherford was elected President A.N. Pierson, Vice President (over A.I. Ritchie), and W.E. Van Amburgh was reelected Secretary-Treasurer. The Executive Committee was also at this time dissolved. The validity of this election has been the subject of endless debate ever since.

A major factor which caused the first major division after Russell died was the publication of *The Finished Mystery* (the seventh volume of *The Studies of the Scriptures*, often referred to as *The Seventh Volume*). In November of 1916, at Rutherford's urging, the Executive Committee requested Clayton J. Woodworth and George H. Fisher of Scranton, Pennsylvania, to compile a volume on Ezekiel and Revelation (and also the Canticles) from Russell's notes to be published as the "posthumous work of Pastor Russell." After they read it, four members of the Watch Tower Board of Directors, R.H. Hirsh, I.F. Hoskins, A.I. Ritchie, and J.D. Wright, objected to the publication of this work and to several other aspects of Rutherford's administration.

On July 17, 1917, Rutherford claimed that since the Society's charter required the election of directors, only the three officers who had been elected in January were "legal" board members. He then appointed   A.H. MacMillan, G.H. Fisher, J.A. Bohnet, and W.E. Spill to the board to replace Ritchie, Hirsh, Wright, and Hoskins. The controversial *Seventh Volume* was published the same week.

Hirsh and the other ousted board members then published a protest pamphlet during the summer called *Light After Darkness.* In October Rutherford tried to answer this pamphlet with a special *Harvest Siftings No. 2.* Within a month, P.S.L. Johnson published his version (which is probably the most accurate), *Harvest Siftings Reviewed.* A straw poll of classes in December indicated that 95% of the Bible Students backed Rutherford in the dispute (although most Bible Students did not know much about it and few had any first-hand knowledge). The annual election of Society officers and the first election of the Board of Directors since Russell's death was held January 5, 1918, during the January 2-6 Pittsburgh convention. R.H. Barber was nominated director; and the other nominees were J.F. Rutherford, William E. Van Amburgh, A.H. MacMillan, A.N. Pierson, W.E. Spill, J.A. Bohnet, and G.H. Fisher. Also F.H. McGee of the Trenton, New Jersey class nominated the following: Menta Sturgeon, H.C. Rockwell, A.I. Ritchie, R.H. Hirsh, I.F. Hoskins, J.D. Wright, and Paul S.L. Johnson (Johnson later withdrew). Rutherford, MacMillan, Van Amburgh, Spill, Bohnet, Anderson (not nominated), and Fisher were elected. In addition, McGee and W.J. Holister (who was also not nominated) received about 13% of the total votes. Rutherford was reelected President; Anderson was elected vice President and Van Amburgh was reelected Secretary-Treasurer. The convention also voted to request R.H. Hirsh to resign from the Editorial Committee.

Among those who parted with the Society about 1918 included McGee and his nominees, R.E. Streeter, I.I. Margeson, H.A. Fireses, P.L. Read, and P.E. Thomson. A.E. Burgess wavered for a year before finally leaving, and soon Raymond G. Jolly sided with Paul S.L. Johnson who left earlier.Those avowing loyalty to the Society at that time (although most later left) include O.L. Sullivan, F.T. Horth, M..L. Herr, E.J. Coward, E.H. Thomson, W.E. Page, J.F. Stephenson, E.D. Sexton, H.H. Riemer, W.A. Baker, R.E. Nash, C.P. Bridges, W.J. Thorn, G.S. Kendall, B.M. Rice, J. Hutchinson, E.A. McCosh, Jesse Hemery (the British branch manager for half a century, and who left the Society in the early 1950s), E.G. Wylam, H.J. Hoeveler, F.P. Sherman, and J.R. Muzikant. Dr. L.W. Jones was not then in opposition, but later left. Also about this time Edwin Bundy, who had dissented from the Society from 1912 to 1917, returned to its fellowship, but he later again left.

Many viewpoints in the movement at this time existed about Russell's work. Some concluded that Pastor Russell's teachings should be strictly adhered to; others believed they know the date when the Church will be completed (or concluded that a great witness work is now due the Jews). Still others believed the Church does not at this time have any special work or "harvest" message. Some Bible Students even felt they have received or are receiving direct revelations from God or Christ. These beliefs frequently generated publications.

In time, most every well-known early Bible Student left the Watchtower Society. Even Dr. Leslie W. Jones of Chicago, who from about 1904 to 1916 published the Souvenir Convention Reports and the first Pittsburgh Reunion Convention souvenir reports, left in the 1920s. Currently the total number of Bible Students outside the Society who profess consecration and partake of the Memorial, the Lord's Supper, the only sacrament that the Watchtower and its offshoots practice, is over 10,000, over half of whom are overseas. About one-hundred or more immersions of those who profess the "high calling" (life in heaven) occur annually.

Bibliographically, the most frustrating characteristic of this literature is its anonymity. Much of it lists no author or publisher, place of publication, or date. There are several reasons for this anonymity. It was Pastor Russell's practice; his name often did not appear anywhere on his own works. It also allows publications to freely move from one group to another without reference to the group or the author. Many feel a work should be judged on its own merits and not rejected solely because the writer may belong to a dissident ecclesia or a group which is not held in favor by mainline Bible Students. Many also wish to encourage the utilization of their work by a variety of Bible Student groups. They may for this reason leave a blank area on the back so that the local ecclesia or group can rubber-stamp its imprint if that ecclesia finds the tract or booklet useful for distribution.

Much of this literature is also extremely rare and often only photocopies or references in other bibliographies are available. Often publications bear only an insignia such as Published by Cincinnati Bible Students," or "published by Berean Bible Students" (Berean is a popular name for various Bible Student groups). In many cases this information can be supplied only by a chance acquaintance with the author or someone who knows him or her. These various movements are usually organized around a periodical, a personality, or both. The periodical serves as a means of communication and group cohesiveness and is often the major polemical organ. Most groups also published books, booklets and pamphlets, and a veritable flood of ephemera. Many consider themselves independent Bible students, and while they adhere to their doctrinal particularities, they often do not let this adherence interfere with their widespread intermingling and swapping of speakers and literature.

A. The Christian Millennial Church

The New Creation Bible Students (at one time called *Associated Bible Students of L'Aurora Millenniale* and later *Millennial Bible Students Church*) are related to one of the earliest offshoots of Russell's movement, the M.L. McPhail Schism. They are theologically similar to most other Bible Student groups, although somewhat more liberal. The headquarters is in Hartford, Connecticut, and the group is associated with the Western Bible Students. They circulate a national magazine, *The New Creation*, which was begun in 1940 by its current editor, Italian-American Gaetano Boccaccio who left the Society in 1928. Many books and booklets are published in several languages. The branch in Italy is called *Mensile della chiesa Cristianna Millenarista*. They are theologically similar, but administratively separate from the Western Bible Students. Since 1980 they have advocated the unity of all Bible Student groups.

The work in Italy actually began in Hartford, Connecticut, in 1939 when the Elders of the Italian Bible Students classes in Connecticut and Massachusetts voted to expand the work to Italy through a new magazine published in Italian and printed in America called *L'Aurora Millenniale (Millennial Dawn)*. Unfortunately, World War II intervened, and communications to Italy could not be resumed until after the war ended.

At that time the Italian group contracted with a Baptist publishing house in Italy (*Verita Evangelica*) to print a series of advertisements offering a free copy of their magazine to any one who requested it. A general description of the subjects dealt with was also included. Through the magazine and the correspondence that followed, Mr. and Mrs. Mario Celenza were converted, and because of their zeal, they were sent names and addresses of other readers to visit or contact by mail. Then in 1948, Umberto Spadaccina of Erie, Pennsylvania, was sent as a pilgrim who, with the Celenzas, visited readers in various cities and towns in south Italy and Sicily.

The fervor of the new converts, especially their denunciations of the immortality of the soul, hellfire, and trinity doctrines, provoked some attacks from the Protestant churches in Italy. In 1962 it was voted to transfer the publication of *L'Aurora Millenniale* from Hartford to Pescara, and Gaetano Boccaccio turned over the editorship of the magazine to Mario Celenza. A few years later, the name of the magazine was changed to *La Nuova Creazione* after the American magazine *The New Creation*.

In 1970, Mr. and Mrs. De Palma, after a trip to Italy to visit the brethren there, concluded an Italian headquarters was needed. An appeal was made for funds, and on July 26, 1971, the brethren bought a five-room condominium in which to hold meetings and other activities. After their last trip to Italy, De Palma and Celenza started a campaign to achieve the unity of Bible Student groups which resulted in the formation of the "federation of Bible student Churches and Bible classes" which had a common constitution, interests, and initiatives, and a true unity of the spirit but allowed each group to remain fully independent.

Gaetano Boccaccio had this goal in mind for years. He also changed the name *Associated Bible Students of L'Aurora Millenniale* to *Millennial Bible Students Church* and later to *Christian Millennial Church*, because of the possibility of the work becoming connected in the minds of the people with the Jehovah's Witnesses (whose governing body, the Watchtower Society, a few years ago again started publishing in Italy under their old name, The International Bible Students Association). *The New Creation* magazine then became the official publication of the Christian Millennial Church. During the past five years, it has expanded and now stresses the unity of all Bible Student groups in America.

In Italy fellowships now exist from Milan in north Italy to the toe of the peninsula. From time to time, Mario Celenza visits these various groups, leading Bible studies and proselytizing to outsiders. Since 1939 the Italian-American brethren in America have supplied much of the needed funds since Italy has never been a very wealthy nation. However, over the years gradually many of the major American supporters have died, and of the few still living, most are retired.The Christian Millennial Church, also called *The Congregation of Bible Students* (Hartford, CT) for the first thirty years used the name *Associated Bible Students*. Gaetano Boccaccio has directed this group from the 1930s to 1996 when he died.

Magazines

The New Creation. Vol. 1, No. 1, Jan. 1939 to date monthly, lately bimonthly. The Italian *New Creation* entitled *La Neuva Creazione*, is published in Italy and is similar in content to the English language edition. Published monthly, the English-language edition averages about 30 pp. and the Italian 22 pp. The Italian edition was published in Hartford, CT, until 1962 and was named *L'Aurora Millenniale* until about 1965 when the name was changed to the present title.

Newsletter for Christian Millennial Church Members. Published semi-monthly (first issue April 1980, Vol. 1), 5 pp.

Booklets

Anonymous. *The ABC of Salvation and Eternal Life.* Hartford, CT, n.d., 24 pp.
_____. *All Things New; The End of Evil.* 1984, 8 pp.
_____. *Do You Have an Immortal Soul?* n.d.,16 pp.
_____. *God's Plan for Humanity.* 20 pp.
_____. *God's Plan of the Ages.* Hartford, CT, n.d., 28 pp.
_____. *Has the Church a Share in the Sin Offering?* Hartford, CT, n.d., 14 pp.
_____. *Justification to Life: When & How?*
_____. *Knowledge...Understanding and Wisdom.* Hartford, CT, n.d., 16 pp.
_____. *The Most Important Three R's.*
_____. *1000 Years of Peace.* Hartford, CT, n.d., 24 pp.
_____. *One World Government.* 1981, 8 pp.
_____. *The Rich Man and Lazarus.* Hartford, CT, n.d., 20 pp.
_____. *"We Believe."* Hartford, CT, 1980, 19 pp.
_____. *What Is the Resurrection of the Dead?*
_____. *When Will Wars, Sickness, Pain and Death Cease?*
_____. *Truth or Tradition; Did Our Lord Die on Good Friday?* Hartford, CT, n.d., 12 pp. (concludes that He did not).
Boccaccio, Gaetano. *Truth or Tradition?* Hartford, CT, 1982, 12 pp.
DiMarco, Sabby. *This One Thing I Do.* Hartford, CT, n.d., 12 pp.
Kemp, Roy. *A Treatise on Love.* Hartford, CT, n.d., 8 pp.
Sadlack, Emil. *Our Lord's Return.* Hartford, CT, n.d., 14 pp. (translated from the German).

B. The Christian Believers Conference

M.L. McPhail and A.E. Williamson led the "New Covenant" people in the United States. His major work was *The Covenants*, published privately in 1909. Out of his leadership grew the *New Covenant Believers*, later called the *Christian Believers Conference*. They have relied heavily on Henninges' literature; their own publications are scarce. The Cicero, IL, class has been publishing recently under the imprint of the *Berean Bible Students Church*.

The most active group left from the above split is the Berean Bible Students Church in Cicero, IL. Since Charles T. Russell defined the atonement in a most "unorthodox" way, not unexpectedly dissent from his perspective soon surfaced. J.H. Paton, the first to break with Russell, soon promulgated his own speculations in both a book and his own magazine. Then in 1909 a significant challenge to Russell arose from three prominent leaders (pilgrims) within his movement--Henninges, M.L. McPhail, and A.E. Williamson. They rejected Russell's view of the ransom atonement because it elevated the church to the place of Christ as the redeemer and mediator for humanity. They interpreted Russell's theology as teaching Christ was only a part of the sin-offering presented to God. They also rejected the identification of Russell with "that servant" of Matthew 25:45-47.

In the midst of the two-year long controversy, Henninges led many of Australians out of Russell's group, and McPhail and Williamson started their own groups in New York and Chicago. In America the groups first used the name *Christian Believers Conference*. Continuing polemics by the descendants of Henninges and McPhail also caused them to conclude that the idea of the elect being limited to 144,000 was "mere assumption." They also now teach that the Lord did not come invisibly in 1914 (or 1925), but has always been present (Matthew 18:20).

The Christian Believers Conference is organized very loosely, being held together primarily by the Publications Committee that published *The Kingdom Scribe*, a journal discontinued in 1975. The most active ecclesia as of the 1980s was the *Berean Bible Students Church* in Cicero, Illinois, which publishes the main periodical serving the group nationally. Since 1910, an annual conference, in recent years in Grove City, Pennsylvania, has been held. It meets for mutual edification and Bible instruction but has no legislative authority.

Booklets

Berean Bible Study Guide. N.d., 19 pp.
God's Plan for Humanity. 20 pp.
Constas, Constantine J. *Do the Scriptures Teach Universal Salvation?* 1965, 39 pp. A reprint of a work by C.J. Constas of the *Free Christian Church* in Athens against the *Concordant Version of the Holy Scripture.*
Polychronis, Andrew, and Larry and Wayne Urbaniak. *God and Man.* N.d., 48 pp.

Magazines

The Kingdom Scribe, ed. Charles Loucky. Vol. 1, 1908 to Vol. 53, 1975 (last issue).
Berean News. Vol., No. 1, Feb. 1956 to Vol. 19, No. 11, Dec. 1975, published monthly, each about 9 pp. long.

Convention Reports

Souvenir Notes from the Reunion Convention of Christian Bible Students. Pittsburgh, PA, No. 1, 2, 3, 1929, No. 5, 1936, was at Hamilton, Ontario 135 pp.
Kuehn, Hugo, ed. *Convention Report, Sharon, Pennsylvania, 1937 and Other Helpful Discourses* (No. 6). New York: Pub. by Ed., No. 6. 1937, 120 pp.

A related group, the *Christian Believers Fellowship* of Staten Island, NY, has published several tracts, which are distributed by the New Creation Bible Students as is all Christian Believers literature. The most important of these is *God's Plan for Humanity.*

N.d., 20 pp. OTHER GROUPS related to this offshoot include the Milwaukee Ecclesia of Free Bible Students led by Wesley J. Ladwig. Its perspective was closest to the Berean Christian Conference except he was evidently a universalists. Periodicals by this general group of Bible Students, all of uncertain date of origin, place of publication, and/or present status, include a 32 pp Journal called *The Round Table of Scripture* (c 1942 until Ladwig's death in 1952).

The Candlestick. St. John's, Newfoundland, Canada. 1946-?? Edited by J.L. Butler.
Studies in the New Creature. St. Joseph, MO. Published by M.E. Rumer in the 1930s.
Open Letter: A Word to the Watchers. Irregular; edited by T. Contopulos, Bellaire, NY, in the 1960s. issues are 60-72 pp. At least 11 issues printed.

C. The Pastoral Bible Institute

The 1917 problems in the Watchtower resulted in the expulsion of four board members and others, including R.H. Hirsh, I.F. Hoskins, A.I. Ritchie, and J.D. Wright. Part of this schism was caused by a power struggle and part by their opposition to Volume VII of the *Studies in the Scriptures*. This was supposedly the posthumous work of Charles T. Russell, but it was actually written by Clayton J. Woodworth and George H. Fisher. The seventh volume expounded a number of new theological ideas which many considered unscriptural; thus, opposition to this work developed. This group opposed Rutherford's attempt to control the Society until the decisive elections at the 1918 Convention convinced them that opposition was now futile.

After Rutherford's conclusive victory, several prominent brethren withdrew and with about fifty colleagues and supporters, began the Pastoral Bible Institute (PBI). The first convention after Russell died that was held independent of the Watchtower took place July 26-29, 1918, in Asbury Park, NJ. In November of 1918 two to three-hundred persons attended the second convention at Providence, RI. At this meeting the Pastoral Bible Institute was formed in order to resume orthodox Russell work independently of the Watchtower. In 1918 their new periodical *The Herald of Christ's Kingdom* was established, edited by R.E. Streeter until his death in December 1924.

Ingrahm I. Margeson, Harvey A. Friese, and of course Wright, Hoskins, Ritchie, and Hirsh were in the forefront of the PBI work. The PBI later published Streeter's books on Revelation (1925) and (posthumously) Daniel in 1928. The PBI offices were in Brooklyn on 177 Prospect Place until the 1960s. The work was then split between St. Louis and Batavia, IL, and the Brooklyn property was sold. An annual convention at Atlantic City, NJ is closely associated with the PBI. The classes at the local churches are largely independent of the "corporation" (or headquarters) although the doctrine is still largely that developed by Russell, and his major works are kept in print. Certain dates and other changes were introduced, but in contrast to some Bible Student groups such as the Dawn Bible Students, the group is not active in proselytizing.

The PBI, since it does not stress proselytizing, and has experienced several major setbacks (they had expected the year 1934 to see "the glorification of the saints," for example) has steadily declined since its founding in 1918. One reason is because not much stress was on indoctrinating children because their primary goal was "perfecting the saints," and only adults can be saints. Consequently, many young persons lost interest and left the movement.

PBI membership is open to anyone who contributes at least $5.00 annually. It is managed by a board of directors and has an editorial committee of five. Its annual volume of service work and its net assets since World War II have remained fairly constant, both over $20,000. Its primary purpose is to supervise the pilgrim work which teaches followers and the publication of *The Herald of Christ's Kingdom* (10,000 circulation in thirty countries) and related publications. A basic baptismal confession only is enforced for fellowship, and the organization sponsors teachers called pilgrims.

Leaders before the war included J.J. Blackburn, Isaac F. and John Hoskins, Dr. S.D. Bennett, and Dr. John G. Keuhn. PBI leaders at various times since World War II include Percy L. Read, W.J. Siekman, Paul E. Thomson, Horace E Hollister, James C. Jordan, John T. Read, Benjamin F. Hollister, Alex L. Muir, Fred A Esler, James Burpee

Webster, Alex Gonczewski, the Petrans, and others. Considerable emphasis has been placed on visiting Bible Students in isolated places and in the British Isles.

The Pastoral Bible Institute has also experienced several schisms since its founding. The literature of the early schisms is extremely rare, and there are few remaining adherents. Some of the more recent schisms are still operating, and thus literature can be obtained from the headquarters or members. Many of the schisms died out as they often involved only thirty to one-hundred or so members, and groups this small, unless they are aggressive proselytizers, usually later disband and their literature is lost or destroyed. In addition it is often difficult to recognize the literature of these schisms, and thus much of it was destroyed or will remain unknown and lost forever in the history of the Bible Student movement.

The PBI is one of the freest of the Bible Student groups in terms of the latitude of doctrine allowed and its use of material that is not strictly Russellite in origin. Advertised in the *Herald* are works by non-PBI Russellites and even by non-Russellite Bible students, such as Werner Keller's *The Bible as History*. The British-based *Bible Fellowship Union* works closely with the PBI, and H.O. Hudson's booklets are widely circulated by them (see under Bible Fellowship Union).

The two main writers of Institute-sponsored material are R.E. Streeter and Percy L. Read. The former was the author of several expository books which refigured Russell's chronology. Streeter based his chronology upon 588 B.C. fall of Jerusalem date instead of Russell's 606 B.C. date producing a different date for the return of Christ and the end of the world. Read was the single most influential member of the PBI until he died in 1983. He wrote a series of pamphlets which are the most advertised works among the members.

Magazine

The Herald of Christ's Kingdom (Ed. by R.E. Streeter until 1924). Vol. 1, No. 1, 1918 to date. Approximately 10,000 copies printed per issue.

Books

Russell, C.T. *The Divine Plan of the Ages.* Reprinted by the Pastoral Bible Institute in Brooklyn, NY, 1922, 354 pp. (Has an eight page preface by PBI).

Sadlack, Emil, and Otto Sadlack. *The Desolations of the Sanctuary.* Brooklyn, NY: Pastoral Bible Institute, 1930.

Streeter, R.E. *The Revelation of Jesus Christ: Volume I.* Brooklyn, NY: Pastoral Bible Institute, 1923, 571 pp. (Covers modern day fulfillment of prophesy and doctrine).

_____. *The Revelation of Jesus Christ, Volume II.* Brooklyn, NY: Pastoral Bible Institute, 1924, 638 pp. (Covers modern day fulfillment of prophesy and doctrine).

_____. *Daniel the Beloved of Jehovah.* Brooklyn, NY: Pastoral Bible Institute, 1928, 493 pp. (published posthumously). (Covers modern day fulfillment of prophesy).

Booklets

Anonymous. *Conversion in the After-life.* N.d., 16 pp.

_____. *A Message to the Watchers and All That Mourn.* N.d., 8 pp.

_____. *The Resurrection of the Dead.* N.d., 16 pp.

_____. *The Second Advent--Its Nature and Purpose.* N.d., 16 pp.

_____. *That Servant--"Faithful and Wise."* Brooklyn, NY, n.d., 9 pp.

_____. *World Conversion--When?* N.d., 16 pp.

Hollister, Horace Edward. *I Will Come Again.* Chicago: Society for Bible Research, 1950, 319 pp.

Jones, L.W. *God's Best Gift.* Chicago: Sacred Lyceum, 1927, 30 pp. A children's book.

Read, P.L. *The ABC of the Bible Prophecy.* N.d., 17 pp.

_____. *After Death Judgment.* N.d., 16 pp.
_____. *Are Wars to Cease?* N.d., 11 pp.
_____. *Beliefs That Matter.* N.d., 19 pp.
_____. *Do You Know What the Bible Foretells of Today and Tomorrow?*
_____. *Elias Shall First Come.* N.d., 20 pp. (condensed from original by C.T.
Russell).
_____. *Great World Changes Long Foretold.* N.d., 15 pp.
_____. *Has Judgment Day Begun?* N.d., 15 pp.
_____. *Heathendom's Hope.*
_____. *If a Man Die, Shall He Live Again?* N.d., 16 pp.
_____. *Is Israel Emerging from Hell?* N.d., 15 pp.
_____. *Israel and the Middle East.* N.d., 25 pp.
_____. *Is Israel Emerging from Hell?* N.d., 15 pp.
_____. *Our Lord's Return.* N.d., 31 pp.
_____. *Parables of the Kingdom.* N.d., 21 pp.
_____. *The Place of Israel in the Plan of God.* 1954.
_____. *What Is the Soul?* N.d., 15 pp.
_____. *What Say the Scriptures about Hell?* N.d., 36 pp. (condensed from an original
by C.T. Russell).
_____. *Why Does God Permit Evil?* N.d., 15 pp.
_____. *The World Tomorrow.*
_____. *Acceptable Sacrifices.*
_____. *The Antiquity of the Book of Moses.*
_____. *The Bible--The Book for Today.*
_____. *Everlasting Punishment.*
_____. *Helpful Literature.*
_____. *Immortality and the Resurrection of the Dead.*
_____. *Our Association Together in the Ministry.*
_____. *Paul to Philemon.*
_____. *The Personality of the Devil.*
_____. *What Is the Truth?*

Siekman, W.J. *The Coming World Potentate.* N.d., 16 pp.

D. The Stand Fast Bible Students

Most of the adherents of the PBI lived in the New York, New Jersey, and Pennsylvania areas. The Bible Students in the northwestern states that split from the Watchtower Society formed a group called the *Stand Fasters*, or *Standfasters*, formally called the *Stand Fast Bible Student Association.*

The Stand Fasters took this name from their determination to "stand fast on the war principles that our dear Pastor Russell announced." Charles E. Heard of Vancouver and many others concluded that Rutherford's recommendation in the spring of 1918 to buy war bonds was "cowardice" and a sacrilegious perpetuation of the harvest work. They felt that the Watchtower reneged on its earlier stand on Liberty Bonds bonds which went toward supporting the war and non-combatant service. The Stand Fasters also concluded that a Christian could not support the army in any way, either by buying Liberty Bonds or by involving himself in non-combatant service (combatant service was forbidden by both the Stand Fasters and the Watchtower).

The *Stand Fast Bible Students Association* was organized on December 1, 1918, at Portland, Oregon. It published *Old Corn Gems* (taken from Josh. 5:11-12) and organized conventions throughout the United States. Well-known members included Heard and W.B. Plamer, R.O. Hadley, William H. Wisdom (the author of the only book-length biography of Russell then), H.A. Livermore, Ian C. Edwards, Allen A. Yeres, and Finley McNercher. Many, mostly non-doctrinal divisions followed a Seattle convention held on July 25-27, 1919. Interestingly, the Stand Fasters accepted the Seventh Volume--one of the main reasons for many other contemporary splits (and in 1919 a split from the Stand Fasters occurred over the Seventh Volume). At first they were quite successful in attracting adherents who did not accept what they saw as compromises over the war issue.

They believed that everything taught by the Watchtower up to Easter of 1918 was scriptural, but after that date the "separation of Elija and Elisha" had begun and the Stand Fasters were the Elija class who "stood fast" on Pastor Russell's teachings. Of course, most of the schismatic groups, at first at least, claimed to be following Russell's wishes and therefore were the "true followers of Russell," but the Stand Fasters claimed to follow *only* his teachings and did not claim that they were legitimate messengers of his or "God's organization" as did some of the other splits. The Pastoral Bible Institute, for example, came to believe that the Watchtower apostatized from the "truth" and that only they, the Pastoral Bible Institute, taught the "primitive truth." The Stand Fasters, on the other hand, taught that leaders and organizations were relatively unimportant. They were organized primarily to help others learn about Russell's teachings. This belief and their loose organization was probably one of the main reasons that they were one of the first schismatic groups to disintegrate.

An interesting chapter of their history was the "westward movement," the encouragement that the Stand Fasters move to the west because the rapture (removal of people to heaven, an idea from the teaching that Christ ascended to heaven in a "twinkling of an eye") would take place in 1920, and only in the western states! Consequently, those not living in the correct state would not be part of the rapture.

In 1923 I.C. Edwards and C.E. Heard organized into the *Star Construction Company* in Victoria, B.C. Fearing "the time of trouble" (part of the sign of the end of the world) would start in 1924, Edwards took over three-hundred followers to Stookie and the Gordon River to live a communal existence which, according to P.S.L. Johnson, "degenerated into communism." Their business failed in 1927 and the commune was soon thereafter shut down by Alec McCarter and Oscar Kuenzi. From the original twelve hundred adherents in 1919 in the Northwest and near Wisconsin, this "Seventh Volume movement" soon dwindled to a few believers, and no formal organization exists today. Their experiment at communal living, often called the *Stookie Movement* because it was located at Stookie Harbor, British Columbia, ended in failure. The history of its development and disintegration would make an important sociological study.

Books, Booklets and Tracts

Temple Notes: A Helping Hand for the Royal Priesthood. Victoria, B.C., Canada, c. 1922, 142 pp., hb. (The meaning for today of the Israelite Temple).
The Temple of Beauty Foreshadowing Messiah's Kingdom in Earth. N.d., (c. 1920), 32 pp.
Heard, C.E. "The Ship's Acts 27th Chapter." Seattle WA, 1919, 11 pp. Stenographic report of an address at the Standfast Bible Students Convention, Jan. 12, 1919.
McKercher, F. *Letter and Charter of Stand Fast Bible Students Association*, Dec. 7, 1918.
_____. *Circular Letter.* Jan. 6, 1919, 1 p.

Magazine

Old Corn Gems. Ed. F. McKercher. Magazine published from Jan. 1919, semi-monthly. No. 1. 8 pp. mime. No. 2. 10 pp. mime. No. 3. Feb. 15, 1919, to. No. 13. July 15, 1919, 16 pp. typeset. No. 14 and 15. issued in 1919; no copies known.

E. Elijah Voice Society

In 1923, John A Hardersen, C.D. McCray, and about 300 persons from the *Stand Fast Bible Students* organized the *Elijah Voice Society* to effect an ambitious regathering and witness work. For several years they published the *Elijah Voice Monthly* and many tracts. This group became the most prominent Seventh Volume group; the group is discussed by Paul Johnson in his *Elijah and Elisha.*

They felt they were "called to smite Babylon," a teaching similar to the Stand Fasters, only they were more extreme--they refused to contribute to the Red Cross, buy Liberty Bonds, or salute the flag many years before the Jehovah's Witnesses prohibited their members from this act--all behavior which they felt clearly marked one "of Satan." Many tracts were written, but all are unknown to this researcher. Their known publications include the *Elijah Voice Monthly* and a journal (or series of tracts) entitled *The Bible Reflector*, published from Seattle, Washington; *The Present World Crisis*, *The Brighter Future Outlook*, 4 pp. c. 1947-1948, and *The United Nations--An Analysis and Prophetic Observation*, 2 pp. c. 1947-1948 (the latter talks of "two years or more since the origin of the United Nations).

F. Servants of Yah

One of the more unusual splinter groups is the *Servants of Yah* started in 1943 and led by C.H. Zook and headquartered in Brooklyn, NY, and later Levittown, NY. They also had a branch in Vienna, Austria. They taught that "Jehovah" is actually the name of Satan and the name of God is "Yah." From this they conclude that the Jehovah's Witnesses must actually be followers of Satan, although their doctrine is very similar to that of the Witnesses. Only the 144,000 are destined to discover the "hidden meaning of the scriptures" and enter heaven. The meaning is "hidden" partly because they believe that our Bible texts were altered. The Servants of Yah see the Bible as primarily a book of prophecy, most of which relates to the present century. They deny Bible Student and Watchtower doctrine about Armageddon, the Genesis Flood, water baptism, the ransom sacrifice, and the existence of Satan as a living person in the sense that most Bible Students believe. They are Universalists and believe all persons who ever existed (except the 144,000 who will live in heaven) will someday live forever on a perfected earth.

Most all of their publications were written by C.H. Zook. These include *Armageddon Is as False as Hell*. Brooklyn, NY, n.d., 2 pp.; *The Basis for the Correct Understanding of the Scriptures*. N.d., 6 pp.?, hb.; *The Glory of God's Character*. Levittown, NY, n.d., 1 p.; *The Name of Almighty God*. n.d., n.p., 2 p.;*Reincarnation*. Levittown, NY, n.d., 2 pp.; *The Resurrection of the Dead*. Brooklyn, NY, n.d., 2 pp. and *Goodrich-Fogh Hysteria*, 4 pp.

G. Watchers of the Morning

In the early 1930s due to the influence of Henninge and McPhail, some of the prominent members of the PBI began to believe that the "Church" (the PBI members) was now under the Mediator (Christ) and also under what they call the New Covenant (a new set of relationships between God and man) and that the "Church" had no part in the sin offering of Christ. Some also began to doubt the doctrine that Christ returned in 1874 and that the "sleeping saints" had already been raised from the dead. Others concluded that only those fully in harmony with "Present Truth" should engage in the official PBI ministry. Still others, who were in harmony with the PBI in other areas, came to believe that those who disagreed with PBI still continue in the work without limitation.

At the PBI annual meeting on June 6, 1936, the "liberal" directors P.L. Read, Dr. S.D. Bennett, J.J. Blackburn, J.C. Jordan, and P.E. Thomson were elected, together with their nominees, Chester A. Stiles of Washington, DC, and Benjamin Boulter of New Jersey. The "Present Truth" directors, I.F. Hoskins and B.A., Parkes, were not elected nor were their nominees, P.A. Gates of Memphis, TN, Dr. Kuehn of Toledo, OH, C.W. McCoy of Spokane, WA, S.N. McElvany of Pittsburgh, PA, and G.C. Stroke of Buffalo, NY.

At this time, Isaac F. Hoskins withdrew from the PBI and in April of 1937 began his own group which published *The Watchers of the Morning*. He emphasized the "Present Truth" as opposed to what he termed Russell's past truth. Among those Bible students that cooperated with Hoskins included H.H. Eddy of Providence, RI, C.W. McCoy of Spokane, WA, and Charles F. Moser of Toledo, OH. The journal *Watchers of the Morning* ceased publication when Hoskins died in August of 1957 (the last issue was June 1957).

H. Laymen's Home Missionary Movement

Shortly before Russell died in 1916, he had arranged for Paul S.L. Johnson to travel to England to mediate in some problems involving the Watchtower's British branch managers. In the meantime, Russell died and Rutherford became President of the Society. He and the other six Directors of the Society agreed to Johnson's trip to Britain as Russell planned.

The Watchtower officials reportedly gave Johnson the authority to do what was necessary to solve the problems in Britain. Among other actions, Johnson fired two of the managers at the London office. Evidently, Rutherford was intimidated by Johnson--he was probably one of the most intelligent and knowledgeable Bible Students. An ordained Lutheran minister who was born a Jew, Johnson graduated with high honors from Capital University in Columbus, OH, and had a good knowledge of Hebrew, Greek, and several other languages.

In 1917 Rutherford cabled to London, telling Johnson that he was "absolutely without authority" and told him to come home immediately. Rutherford later claimed that he was given full authority to make changes only to get a passport, a difficult task then during the war. The majority of the Board sided with Johnson but Rutherford ousted them on a legal technicality then forced Johnson out. After the 1918 election meeting in Pittsburgh, Johnson, Raymond Jolly, and others withdrew from the Watch Tower organization and formed the Pastoral Bible Institute. This group also experienced numerous differences, which resulted in Johnson and Jolly's forming another new group using a name Russell had once used, the Laymen's Home Missionary Movement (LHMM).

Johnson came to believe that although Pastor Russell was a Parousia messenger, he, Johnson, was a special "Epiphany messenger" with a commission to announce that the door to the "high calling" (heaven) was now closed. In later years it was taught that he was the last member of the Church. After he organized the LHMM in July of 1920 he began publishing *The Bible Standard.* He also wrote voluminously on the interpretation of "types," (prophecy parallels), the multi-meanings of scriptures and *shadows* (scriptures which have their major fulfillment in our day). Adherents believe that they constitute a class of "Youthful Worthies" or an Epiphany Company who will reign with the Ancient Worthies. Johnson's chief co-worker, Raymond G. Jolly, was his successor and became the leader of the movement when Johnson died in October of 1950. After Jolly's death in 1979, August Gohlke headed the movement until he died on Dec 18, 1985 and was replaced by Bernard W. Hedman.

The LHMM, like most of the Bible Student movements, still uses almost all of Russell's writings as its primary study material and is closer to Russell in doctrine than most Bible Student groups. The movement has grown, especially in Poland, where there are probably as many as 5,000 members and as many sympathizers. Worldwide the movement claims members in the ten's of thousands.

Of interest is the fact that Johnson adopted the *Bible Numerics* system of Ivan Panin and purchased the last 300 copies of his *Numeric Greek New Testament* for resale. Bible numerics is the belief that the Bible can be "proved" to be of divine origin by adding up the values of various words and sentences (a = 1pt., b = 2 pts., etc.) to come up with certain patterns which would be impossible by chance. This idea has been hotly debated but is nonetheless intriguing.

The LHMM movement strongly opposes the Watchtower, especially because they have left most of Russell's teachings. The LHMM also opposed the Watchtower ruling that it is wrong to salute the flag and receive blood transfusions, and especially the fact that they have set aside the Biblical scriptures which refer to the modern nation of Israel (the Watchtower teaches that "Israel" in the New Testament usually refers to *symbolic Israel*, i.e., themselves). They are largely, but not totally, loyal to Russell's theology. As Russell did, they spent much of their time looking for Biblical types in current events, both secular and related to their organization and its activities.

The LHMM has produced a set of sound and color film strips which are often shown in various churches, bible study classes, YMCA, YWCA, and similar groups. Members also often comb the obituaries then send personal letters and LHMM literature to relatives of the deceased. Shortly after Johnson set up his organization he began the publication of a series of books, based upon and supplemental to Russell's *Studies in the Scriptures.* He repudiated the Seventh Volume as a fraud and began his own completion of Russell's six volumes called the *Epiphany Studies in Scriptures.* This series ran to some 15 volumes by the time he died. Jolly also edited some materials of Johnson's after his death, adding several more volumes to the series.

Magazines

The Present Truth and Herald of Christ's Epiphany. Dec. 1918 to date, 62 years
(698 issues), 11, 168 pp., published monthly until 1952, then bimonthly
to date, each 16 pp. Bound volumes are as follows: Vol. 1, 1920-1926;
Vol. 2, 1927-31; Vol. 3, 1932-35; Vol. 4, 1936-39; Vol. 5, 1940-43; Vol.
6, 1944-47; Vol. 7, 1948-51; Vol. 8, 1952-59; Vol. 9, 1960-67; Vol. 10,
1968-1975.

The Herald of the Epiphany. July 15, 1920 to Dec. 15, 1951, 31 years (312
issues), 588 or 476 issues, total 3,800 pages. Bimonthly, each 8 pp.
Replaced by *The Bible Standard and Herald of Christ's Kingdom.*

The Bible Standard and Herald of Christ's Kingdom. Jan. 1952 to date, 28 years
(336 issues), 2,688 pp. Published monthly, each 8 pp. For the general
public.

The Herald of the Epiphany and the Bible Standard. Bound volumes: Vol. 1,
1920-29; Vol. 2, 1930-39; Vol. 3, 1940-51; Vol. 4, 1952-56; Vol. 5,
1957-61; Vol. 6, 1962-66; Vol. 7, 1967-71; Vol. 8, 1972-76. Indexes,
1920-1960; 1961-1970; 1971-1980.

Shortly after Johnson set up his organization he began the publication of a series of
books, based upon and supplemental to Russell's *Studies in the Scriptures.* He repudiated
the Seventh Volume as a fraud and began his own completion of Russell's six volumes
called the *Epiphany Studies in Scriptures.* This series ran to some 15 volumes by the time
he died. Jolly also edited some materials of Johnson's after his death, adding several
more volumes to the series.

Epiphany Studies in the Scriptures by Paul S. Johnson (Vols. 1-15), and
Raymond Jolly (vols. 16-17), all published in Chester Springs, PA. These volumes
are an excellent source of material found nowhere else on the early history of the
Watchtower and its many offshoots--the primary subject of most of these volumes.
Vol. 1. *God.* 1938, 547 pp. (Covers the classic proofs for His existence and His
character [as opposed to evolution]).
Vol. 2. *Creation.* 1938, 585 pp. (Covers both Biblical and scientific evidence for
creation).
Vol. 3. *Elijah and Elisha.* 1938, 477 pp. (A review of how their histories apply to
today; covers types and anti-types).
Vol. 4. *The Epiphany's Elect.* 1938, 469 pp. (On the various classes; youthful
worthies).
Vol. 5. *A Miscellany.* 1938, 542 pp. (Many topics covered; much on the Watchtower
splits).
Vol. 6. *Merariism.* 1938, 750 pp. (A critique of Rutherford and the Watchtower).
Vol. 7. *Gershonism.* 1938, 494 pp. (A critique of the PBI and other Russell groups).
Vol. 8. *Numbers.* 1938, 484 pp. (Applies Numbers 1-10; 26 to history and modern
events).
Vol. 9. *The Parousia Messenger.* 1938, 605 pp. (Much on early Watchtower history).
Vol. 10. *The Epiphany Messenger.* 1941, 829 pp. (Much on types and anti-types and
Bible student history; contains an index of the first ten volumes p. 674-829).
Vol. 11. *Exodus.* 1948, 716 pp. (The type and anti-type in Exodus and its relation to
modern Bible student movement).
Vol. 12. *The Bible.* 1949, 797 pp. (Its background , history, teachings, evidence for
inspiration).
Vol. 13. *Samuel, Kings, Chronicles.* 1949, 847 pp. (An anti-type type commentary).
Vol. 14. *The Parousia Messenger.* Vol. 2 (part 2 of Vol. 9), 1949, 573 pp. (Much on
early Bible student history and C.T. Russell).
Vol. 15. *Christ--Spirit--Covenants.* 1950, 736 pp. (On Christ, the Holy Spirit, and the
Covenants).
Vol. 16. *The Chart of God's Plan.* 1953, 351 pp. (God's purpose for humans
presented in a dispensational framework; much on the various Biblical Hells, p. 205-

298).
Vol. 17. *The Millennium.* 1956, 480 pp. (Christ's return, Satan, and Old and New
   Testament teaching on the millennium).

Other Books (all reprints, some revised)

Daily Heavenly Manna and Devotional Service. Revised by P.S.L. Johnson, 1937
   (original edition WtBTS, 1907), c. 350 pp. Revised again and enlarged, 1980, 400
   pp.

Hymns of the Millennial Dawn. Revised by P.S.L. Johnson, 1937, 346 pp.
   (republished from WtBTS edition of 1905).

Life-Death-Hereafter. 1st edition, 1920; 4th revised and enlarged by Raymond Jolly in
   1968, 216 pp. (Consists mostly of republished, revised C.T. Russell booklets).

Poems of Dawn. 1965, 318 pp. Republished from the WtBTS edition of 1912.

Tabernacle Shadows of the Better Sacrifices: A Helping Hand for the Royal Priesthood,
   by C.T. Russell, 1936, 168 pp. Republished from the WtBTS edition of 1881.

Studies in the Scriptures by C.T. Russell, 1937, 3,500 pp. Republished in 6 Vol, with
   120 pp. of appendix notes and questions. Republished again without appendix and
   notes, 1965, 3,380 pp.

Booklets (24 pp. each; contents from *The Bible Standard*, except as noted. All
   published at Chester Springs, PA.)

"Faith Healing:" Dangers in Hypnotism and Spirit Healing. c. 1970, 24 pp. (partly taken
   from Pastor Russell. Argues these practices are demonism).).
"Christian Science Examined." c. 1970, 24 pp. (A critique of Christian Science).
Present Day "Speaking in Tongues:" Is It of God? N.d. (see May 1954 *Bible Standard*).
The Kingdom of God--Heavenly and Earthly. N.d.
Mormonism--A Modern Delusion. 1970, 24 pp. (A history and critique of Mormonism).
Why We Believe in God's Existence. c. 1978, 24 pp. (About the creation-evolution
   controversy, supports creationism).
Jolly, Raymond. *Angola-Israelism--A Strong Delusion.* 1975, 80 pp.
The Gift of Tongues. 1975, 80 pp. (Argues against glossalalia).
Is There Hope for Any of the Unsaved Dead? 1975, 80 pp.
Satan, Satanism, Demonism and Exorcism. 1975, 80 pp. (Argues against most forms of
   parapsychology and demon involvement).
Born Again. 1975, 48 pp.
The Great Pyramid and the Bible. Reprinted with slight revisions from the original by Dr.
   John Edgar, n.d., 48 pp.
The Restoration of Israel. Reprinted from Vol. 3, of *Studies in the Scriptures.*
The Hell of the Bible. 1st ed. c. 1920, latest ed. 1972, 60 pp.
Spiritism, Ancient and Modern. 1st ed. c. 1926, latest ed. 1972, 67 pp.
Jewish Hopes and Prospects. Israel Commission, 1954, 50 pp.
The Revised Standard Version of the bible in the Light of True Doctrine. 1952, 32 pp.
The Teachings of Jehovah's Witnesses Examined in the Light of the Scriptures. 1954, 36
   pp. (From *The Bible Standard* March and April 1954).

Booklets Pertaining to the 1918 Split.

Johnson, Paul S. *Harvest Siftings Reviewed.* Brooklyn, NY, Nov. 1, 1917, 20 pp.
_____. *Another Harvest Siftings Reviewed.* Philadelphia, PA, Aug. 22, 1918, 12 pp.

In 1950 when Johnson died and his longtime associate Raymond G. Jolly headed the
group, the bimonthly *Herald* became the monthly *Bible Standard and Herald of Christ's
Kingdom.* A second periodical, primarily circulated among members, is *The Present
Truth and Herald of Christ's Epiphany,* also monthly and dating from 1920.

I. Offshoots of the Laymen's Home Missionary Movement

Epiphany Bible Students Association

After the death of a charismatic leader, a number of schisms usually occur. This was true of the Laymen's Home Missionary Movement. When Paul Johnson died in October of 1950 and Raymond Jolly became the leader of the organization, disagreement occurred between John J. Hoefle and Jolly. Hoefle was a prominent leader who had spoken at Johnson's funeral and had also been a Watchtower pilgrim in Johnson's day. Among other points, the two men disagreed about the time of Christ's 1,000--year reign and the nature and validity of John's baptism. Hoefle also disagreed with the LHMM on whether new converts can presently attain the spirit plane as can members of the Ancient Worthies. Hoefle was also charged with dishonesty in business, and he in turn, charged Jolly with slander and lying.

Hoefle was formally disfellowshipped on February 8, 1956, from the LHMM after which he began to publish a newsletter about his side of the issue called *A Message of Importance to the Epiphany Elect* which became a regular monthly publication by the end of 1957. In this newsletter he discussed his position and defended his doctrinal views. Actually, Hoefle agreed with most of the teachings of Russell and Johnson, although much of his newsletter is devoted to discussing the differences between him and the modern LHMM and other Bible Student groups including the Watchtower.

Hoefle's father was a Catholic and his mother Lutheran. Although he read the Bible, he felt he could not understand most of it. Later, while employed in a plumbing company in Dayton, OH, he began to associate with a fellow employee who was affiliated with the Watchtower. He soon began attending their meetings and devoured the *Studies in The Scriptures* written by C.T. Russell. Shortly thereafter, in spite of the fact that he was quite ill because of the 1913 Dayton, OH flood, he was drafted into the Army on May 29, 1918. He earned a conscientious objector status but experienced a great deal of antagonism in the Army. After his abilities as a stenographer were made known, he began working in the office for the Army. Upon leaving the Army, he again began attending IBSA meetings and later became a full-time colporteur (pioneer). When the seventh volume was published, he objected to it, and refused to place it in his assigned pilgrim territory. This caused problems and eventually the elders took his territory away from him.

He was told that his views were similar to P.S.L. Johnson's, and he soon got in touch with him. Thereafter, he then affiliated with the Layman's Home Missionary Movement and remained there until Johnson died in October of 1950. He was quite close to Johnson, traveling with him extensively and contributing thousands of dollars to his movement. Considered a "special assistant," he did a variety of work for the LHMM. while working at various jobs in Detroit and elsewhere to support himself. In 1947 he began to work full time for the writing department of LHMM., assisting with correspondence, etc. When Johnson died, Hoefle gave the funeral talk. Jolly was appointed executive trustee of the LHMM and Hoefle and Jolly immediately came into conflict. According to Hoefle, Jolly slowly changed the Johnson teachings, something which Hoefle strenuously objected to.

In 1955, both Hoefle and his wife were excommunicated, although they continued to attend the LHMM conventions for several years, and some LHMM adherents continued fellowship with them. He finally began his own organization which many dissonant LHMM persons as well as dissonant Witnesses, Dawnites, etc., and others in various ways affiliated with. John Hoefle died on April 16, 1989, and his work is now carried on by his wife, Emily Hoefle, and other co-workers. Their publications include a magazine titled *Epiphany Bible Students Assn. Journal* Ed. John H. Hoefle. June 1955 to date, published monthly, each 8 pp. The above title was formally first used in 1968. Also several newsletters were specially issued at various times and ten issues of *The Herald of the Epiphany* were published.

The Present Truth (Laodicean Home Missionary Movement)

Another offshoot was started by John W. Krewson of Levittown, PA, who was disfellowshipped from the LHMM in 1955 within months after Raymond Jolly took over the LHMM. He then began to publish his *The Present Truth of Apokalypsis* and several books and tracts. Sometimes Jolly and Krewson agreed with Hoefle, and sometimes Hoefle and Jolly united against Krewson. The arguments concerned what most outsiders felt were minor points, and most of the publications are directed toward those who are or were affiliated with the LHMM or EBSA movements (Hoefle's group) and not outsiders. They discuss mostly doctrinal points of concern to the three groups and very few to outsiders. Krewson published a magazine titled *The Present Truth of the Apokalypsis.* Vol. 1, No. 1, 1957 to date (July-Aug. 1980, No. 153). Issued bimonthly. Circulation is in the hundreds.

Books

Krewson, John W. *Apokalypsis Studies in the Scriptures.* 3 vol., hb.

   Vol. I. *Apokalypsis Disclosures.* Levittown, PA, 1947, 480 pp. (Covers doctrine and prophesy).
   Vol. II. *Laodicean Home Missionary Movement.* Levittown, PA, 1976, 516 pp. (Primarily a history of the various Watchtower offshoots, especially the LHMM).
   Vol. III. *Gospel Harvest Testimonies.* Levittown, PA, 1979, 601 pp. (Primarily modern day fulfillment of prophesy, anti-types).

_____. *Harvest Manna for Daily Worship.* Levittown, PA, 1972, c 460 pp

J. The Dawn Bible Students

In the early 1930s, an energetic effort began to reorganize the Bible Students outside the Watchtower Society and to again present Russell's message to the public. This work was spearheaded by the Brooklyn, NY, ecclesia but had support around the country. William Norman Woodworth and John E. Dawson left WBBR and the Society in 1929 and later formed the Brooklyn, NY, Radio Committee which began radio broadcasts in New York and then in Boston on April 12, 1931. The broadcasts were discontinued after three months due to shortage of funds but were later reinstated.

Listeners to the Watchtower Society's radio programs prior to the 1930s no doubt noticed that its message was often closer to the teachings of Russell than to those of Rutherford. William Norman Woodworth, who disagreed with many of Rutherford's "new' ideas, wrote most of the radio programs. Rutherford unsuccessfully tried to force Woodworth to conform to his new ideas: soon Woodworth left the Watchtower and associated himself with an independent Brooklyn ecclesia which in 1931 held a convention and elected a central committee that became the Dawn organization.

Woodworth originally had wanted to work with the Pastoral Bible Institute (PBI), but PBI had serious reservations about a radio ministry. George M. Wilson and Woodworth attempted in 1931 to displace the directors of the PBI over a disagreement about their "passive" method of preaching. The voters, however, reelected the former directors by a "large majority" and thus in October of 1932 Wilson, Woodworth and their supporters founded Dawn Incorporated of New York and almost immediately began publishing their own magazine. The Dawn Bible Students gradually expanded, in time becoming larger and more important than the Pastoral Bible Institute.

The Dawn resumed the "Frank and Ernest" radio broadcasts in about 1940. The broadcast increased in scope after the war, and in 1949 the ABC radio network of 174 stations began broadcasting "Frank and Ernest" throughout the United States and Canada. The initial rate of mail response was about 5,000 letters per month. "Frank and Ernest" is currently broadcasting from approximately 100 stations in America, Europe, Africa, and Australia. They later added a television show, "The Bible Answers."

The low cost and popularity of tape recorders during the 1950s led to the recording and mailing of discourses. Early in 1953 two Dawnites established the Dawn Tape-Recorded Lecture Service in Los Angeles, which prospered. It soon moved to the Dawn offices in New Jersey, where it has expanded into an international service. The exchange of tape recordings between Bible Students is widespread. Most of the talks at conventions are recorded and the tapes are widely distributed.

Over 1,000 *Dawn* subscriptions are supplied without cost to libraries, schools, hospitals, etc. The *Dawn Magazine* is an enlarged edition of the four-page weekly tract *The Radio Echo*, which was published in conjunction with the radio ministry of the Dawn. The *Dawn* which has a circulation of around 30,000 copies per month once grew at a rate of about 1,000 subscriptions per year. The Dawn also advertises in many secular magazines, as do the Laymen's Home Missionary Movement and other Watchtower splinter groups. They are especially active at local and state fairs and other places where large numbers of people gather. Members typically set up a booth, engage in discussion with whoever will listen to them, and hand out literature.

The Dawn also has produced a number of low-budget motion pictures which have been shown on television hundreds of times. Their television series "The Bible Answers" was regularly shown by hundreds of stations. *The Unknown God* movie has been especially popular in churches, clubs, and schools. Some estimate that these films have had a total attendance of hundreds of thousands. They also have a recorded lecture service and a pilgrim department which sends out speakers on request.

The Dawn corporation is composed of some 72 or so members managed by a board of 12 trustees to whom the office staff is responsible. Its annual volume of service work has grown from a post-war value of $25,000 to over $250,000 today. Its primary purpose has been to regather Bible Students with increasing emphasis on public witness. The Dawn Bible Students have always been zealous proselytizers, utilizing both radio and television. Because of this they are now the second largest extant movement in America that owes its existence to Russell. They are also the most active proselytizers. Doctrinally, the Dawn is very similar to Pastoral Bible Institute, but is more conservative, differing primarily in the matter of stricter adherence to Russell and less tolerance of nonconformity. The Dawn does not manifest the hatred toward other religions that some of the offshoots of the Witnesses and the Witnesses themselves express. Differences of opinion on doctrine are usually tolerated within the organization unless the ideas begin to create dissension. In recent years, the Dawn has introduced some changes and relaxed its strictness which has caused a number of groups to break away, most notably the Divine Plan Movement. A basic baptismal confession is sufficient for fellowship, but the organization will not sponsor or approve representatives who are not in harmony with their teachings.

Prime movers of the Dawn at various times since the second World War include William Woodworth, William J. Hollister, and Peter Kolliman. About one-quarter of the members and one-half of the Dawn trustees live in the New York area; the rest are spread around the United States, Canada, and England.

The individual and collective efforts of the Bible Students were somewhat reduced during the years of wartime economy. An unsuccessful attempt was made in 1946-47 to unite the Dawn and the PBI (most of the correspondence about this is published in the 1947 PBI *Herald*). Shortly before this, the very important booklet *When Pastor Russell Died* (1st ed. 1946, 65 pp.; 2nd ed. 1951, 48 pp.) was published. This booklet is the Dawn's statement of their *raison d'être* and is essential reading for researchers of the movement. It is significant that the work contains an attack on the ideas of R.E. Streeter, one of the PBI founders.

The Dawn's voluminous publications are frustrating to list due to their lack of dates. Therefore, an alphabetical arrangement is followed with dates and editions listed where possible. Prior to 1944, works were published at the Brooklyn headquarters, and later literature was published at East Rutherford, New Jersey. The Dawn offices, originally in Brooklyn (251 Washington St., then 136 Fullton St.), moved to East Rutherford, New Jersey, on January 1, 1944. At this time the name Dawn Bible Student's Association was adopted. The pre-1944 publications are listed where known. The Dawn is also an avid reprinter of Russell's major works and supplies them to many other groups. *Our Most Holy Faith* (1950, 720 pp.) a reprint of many of Russell's most popular articles and sermons, is the Dawn's most challenging publication to date.

Books

Anonymous. *"Behold Your King,"* A Herald of Christ's Presence. East Rutherford, NJ, 1948 (9th ed.), 144 pp., hb. (About Christ's plan for a new heaven and earth).

_____. *The Book of Books.* East Rutherford, NJ, 1962 (4th ed.), 320 pp.
_____. *The Creator's Grand Decision.* East Rutherford, NJ, 1969, 240 pp.
_____. *God's Promises Come True.* East Rutherford, NJ, 1954, 244 pp., hb. (An
  illustrated basic doctrine book for the young and adolescents).
_____. *Our Most Holy Faith.* 1948, 719 pp., hb. (A collection of Russell's writings).
_____. *Songs of the Night.* East Rutherford, NJ, c. 1950, 226 pp., hb.
_____. *Zionism in Prophecy: The Return of Israel to the Holy Land: A Fulfillment of
  Biblical Promises.* New York: Pro-Palestine Federation of America, 1936, 64
  pp., pb. (Argues that the formation of Israel is in fulfillment of Bible prophesy).
Hudgings, William. *Evolutionists at the Crossroads.* Brooklyn, NY: Dawn Publishers,
  Inc., 1935, 128 pp. p. 6. (Argues that science supports creationism; much on the
  problems of human evolution).
Russell, C.T. *Tabernacle Shadows of the "Better Sacrifices."* Reprint of the 1881
  WtBTS ed., 131 pp., bound with *Berean Questions*, 33 pp.; total 164 pp.
_____. Reprints of *Studies in the Scriptures* (originally written by C.T. Russell). All
  are reset.
  Vol. I. *The Divine Plan of the Ages.* Reprinted in 1975, 358 pp., hb., pb.
  Vol. II. *The Time Is at Hand.* Reprint in 1959, 371 pp., hb., pb.
  Vol. III. *Thy Kingdom Come.* Reprinted in 1949, 379 pp., hb., pb.
  Vol. IV. *The Battle of Armageddon*, n.d., 660 pp. hb., pb.
  Vol. V. *At-One-Ment Between God and Man.* N.d., 498 pp., hb., pb.
  Vol. VI. *The New Creation.* Reprinted in 1976, 738 pp., hb., pb.
Siebert, Gertrude and Hattie Woodward. *Daily Heavenly Manna.* Reprinted without
  birthday section; introduction, scriptural and topic indexes, and several
  commentary pages added, n.d., c. 200 pp.
_____. *Daily Heavenly manna.* Reprint of the 1907 WtBTS ed., c. 365 pp., hb.
Hymns of Dawn. Printed both with and without music, pb., hb.

Booklets

Archeology Proves the Bible. East Rutherford, NJ, n.d., 60 pp. (A review of the
  archeological evidence for validity and accuracy of the Bible record).
Armageddon, Then World Peace (2d ed., 1952), last ed. 1963, 31 pp. Discusses
  prophecies of our day.
As Angels of Light. East Rutherford, NJ, n.d., 48 pp.
The Bible and Its Message. East Rutherford, NJ, n.d., 16 pp.
The Bible, the Word of God. East Rutherford, NJ, n.d., 14 pp.
The Birth of a Nation. East Rutherford, NJ, 1951, 62 pp.
The Blood of Atonement. East Rutherford, NJ, 1953.
Born of the Spirit. East Rutherford, NJ, 1959, 32 pp.
Chosen People. 5th ed., 64 pp., 1951.
Christ's Thousand-Year Kingdom. East Rutherford, NJ, 1963, 64 pp.; also n.d., 32 pp.
The Church. West Rutherford, NJ, 4th ed. 1959; 5th ed. 1962, 32 pp.
"Created He Them." East Rutherford, NJ, 7th ed., 1952, 64 pp. (The biblical and
  scientific evidence for creationism).
Creation. East Rutherford, NJ, 1956, 56 pp. (A revision of the above; examines the
  Genesis Record, and the problems of evolution).
Creation. N.d., 112 pp. (Examines the Genesis Record).
The Day of Judgment. East Rutherford, NJ, 1962, 32 pp.
Divine Healing. East Rutherford, NJ, 2nd ed. 1952; also 1957, 32 pp.
Divine Intervention Near. N.d., 30 pp.
Does God Answer Prayer? East Rutherford, NJ, 2nd ed. 1962, 32 pp.
Early Christian View of War and Military Service. East Rutherford, NJ, 1967, 44 pp.
  (Argues that the early Christians were pacifists).
The Everlasting Gospel. N.d., 64 pp.
Evolution versus the Bible. East Rutherford, NJ, n.d., 14 pp.
Exceeding Great and Precious Promises. 1954. (A selection reprinted from C.T.
  Russell's writings).
Failure to Recognize God's Organization: A Fruitful Cause of Division Among Christians.
  Unpub. Assembly. Notes, 1933.
Faith of Our Fathers by Charles Redeker (?) N.d., 104 pp.

Father, Son and Holy Spirit. East Rutherford, NJ, 4th ed. 1950; also 1964, 32 pp.
The Further and Reason by Frank Fact Finder (William Norman Woodworth), Brooklyn,
    NY: Dawn Publishers, 1st ed., 1934, 124 pp.
God and Reason. 94 pp. Discusses how God will bring peace.
God and Reason. East Rutherford, NJ, n.d., 54 pp.
God Has a Plan. East Rutherford, NJ, n.d., 15 pp. (Outlines basic Dawn theology).
God's Assurance of Survival. N.d., 16 pp.
God's Hand in the Affairs of Men. N.d., 16 pp.
God's Kingdom Conquers. N.d.
God's Plan. East Rutherford, NJ, 9th ed., 1952, 1963, 48 pp. (Illustrated by charts).
God's Plan for Man. East Rutherford, NJ, n.d., 48 pp.
God's Remedy for a World Gone Mad. A Clear and Concise Presentation of the Doctrine
    of the Kingdom.
The Grace of Jehovah. 1st ed. 1954 (3rd ed. 1961), 64 pp. (God appeals through love).
Hope. 16 pp.
Hope Beyond the Grave. East Rutherford, NJ, 1963, 94 pp. (The Bible's teaching on
    the soul, spirit, heaven, hell and paradise).
Hope for a Fear-Filled World. East Rutherford, NJ, n.d., 32 pp.
How God Answers Prayer. East Rutherford, NJ, n.d., 30 pp.
How to Increase Faith. East Rutherford, NJ, n.d., 14 pp.
Israel in History and Prophecy. East Rutherford, NJ, 1961, 64 pp. (Significance of the
    present rebuilding of Palestine).
Jesus--The World's Savior. East Rutherford, NJ, n.d., 32 pp.
Job Sees God. East Rutherford, NJ, n.d., 16 pp.
The Kingdom of God by Charles F. Redeker. N.d., 61 pp. (Evidence that it is near).
The Language of the Bible. East Rutherford, NJ, n.d., 14 pp.
Life After Death. East Rutherford, NJ, 1964, 22 pp.
The Light of the World. East Rutherford, NJ, 1957, 32 pp. (Identifies the "true
    witnesses" of Jehovah and Jesus).
Man's Creation and the Final Destiny. N.d., 16 pp.
A New Manna Book. N.d.
Oh the Blessedness! East Rutherford, NJ, n.d., 26 pp.
Old Time Religion. East Rutherford, NJ, n.d., 15 pp.
Our Day in Prophecy. East Rutherford, NJ, n.d., 14 pp.
Our Lord's Return. East Rutherford, NJ, 1956, 48 pp. (The method and purpose).
Paradise Without Pollution (God's Solution to Man's Problems).
Paul' Letter to the Hebrews. Paul Counsels the Church.
Peace Through Christ's Kingdom. East Rutherford, NJ, 1962, 32 pp.
The People of the Bible. East Rutherford, NJ, n.d., 16 pp.
Reincarnation versus Resurrection. East Rutherford, NJ, 1956, 32 pp.
A Royal Nation. East Rutherford, NJ, 1959, 32 pp.
Science and Creation. East Rutherford, NJ, n.d., 32 pp. (Argues for the harmony of
    science and the Bible; covers the major events on each Genesis day).
Spiritualism. East Rutherford, NJ, n.d., 16 pp.
Three Keys to the Bible. East Rutherford, NJ, n.d., 24 pp.
The Truth About Hell. East Rutherford, NJ, n.d., 24 pp.
The Voice of God. East Rutherford, NJ, n.d., 14 pp.
What Can a Man Believe?
When a Man Dies. East Rutherford, NJ, 1950, 48 pp.
When Pastor Russell Died. East Rutherford, NJ, 1946 (revised end. n.d., 44 pp.), 63
    pp. (Argues that the Watchtower is not the followers of Russell, and who is).
Why God Permits Evil. East Rutherford, NJ, n.d., 20 pp. (Argues God has a purpose
    for evil).
"Your Adversary the Devil." East Rutherford, NJ, 1964, 32 pp.
Russell, C.T. *The Sin-Offering and the Covenants.* 1954, 32 pp. Reprint of 1907 ed.

Magazines

Bible Students News. Published from 1932 to 1939, and again from 1947 to 1950 (semi-
    yearly), Vol. I, No. 1 to Vol. IV, No. 2; Vol. III, No. 2 is 40 pp., Vol. IV, No. 2

is 32 pp.

Witness Bulletin. October 1931 to 1934.

Bible Student Radio Echo. Tracts issued from April 29, 1931 to Sept. 1932. Became *The Dawn.*

The Dawn. October 1932-1986. Published monthly, each about 64 pp. Index. Sent for only a token subscription cost.

Convention Reports *Bible Students News.* Vol. 3, No. 2. East Rutherford, NJ, 1949, 40 pp. *Bible Students News.* Vol. 4, No. 2. East Rutherford, NJ, 1950, 32 pp.

K. The Bible Student Examiner

Olin R. Moyle, one of the very few attorneys in the Watchtower movement, was the Society's attorney from about 1930 to 1939 and the author of several Watchtower legal publications. He later became increasingly disenchanted with the moral tone of Bethel, especially at the harsh and obscene language Rutherford used (often in print) and what he considered to be excessive drinking there. His personality was probably the opposite of the bombastic, jovial yet gruff Rutherford.

When he could no longer tolerate the situation, he wrote a letter to Rutherford with his complaints and was promptly expelled from Bethel. He intended to continue to associate with the congregation in his hometown of Milwaukee, Wisconsin, but by then Rutherford wanted Moyle out of the organization. He then instructed the local congregation to disfellowship him, which they did. Moyle later circulated a typeset set of letters which discussed some of his complaints. Included were his letter to Rutherford (dated July 21, 1939), his letter to the Milwaukee, Wisconsin congregation of Jehovah's Witnesses relative to his excommunication "under orders from the Society's president" (dated September 25, 1940), and an additional letter dated May 18, 1940, addressed to Judge Rutherford outlining his objections to certain Bethel practices. He charged Rutherford with "a glorification of alcohol," "filthy and vulgar language," "ill treatment of the Bethel family," as well as unscriptural practices such as "strong criticism of marriage," a practice discouraged until Knorr himself married.

The Watchtower's response to this tract was to print a short announcement in the *Watchtower* condemning Moyle (*Watchtower*, Sept. 1, 1939, p. 258) and another, even stronger condemnation which was printed in the October 15, 1939 issue (pp. 316-317). Moyle, in turn, sued the Watchtower Society and won (see *the Golden Age*, December 20, 1944, p. 21 and June 23, 1943, pp. 27-28, for the outcome of the trial and the appeal, at which damages were reduced from $30,000 to $15,000). According to a letter by Peter Moyle published on p. 382 of the 1939 *Watchtower*, he sided with the Watchtower against his father, but he later left the Society and still later left his father's group and converted to Judaism. He is now an agnostic.

Olin Moyle originally associated with the New Covenant Believers but because they still held to Russell's chronological system that taught Christ returned in 1874, then the date was changed to 1914, Moyle started his own group and began publishing his *Bible Student Inquirer*, which he later called the *Bible Student Examiner*. When Moyle died in 1959, Henry Wallis took over. The only publication that the group has produced is their magazine which ceased publication in 1982 when Wallis died.

Henry Wallis became involved with Russell in 1914 when he was 22. In response to a circular he read, he attended the Photodrama and as a result turned from "a skeptic attending a Presbyterian Church" to a follower of Pastor Russell. So enthusiastic was he that he claimed that he read the complete six volumes in only two months and soon began attending the Baltimore Ecclesia. A year later he was elected an elder and was viewed by the class as a very capable Bible Student. When Rutherford became President of the Society, Wallis became increasingly disenchanted but remained involved until about 1932.

After he had worked with Rutherford, Wallis concluded that Rutherford was a "proud, dictatorial autocrat." An example of his concern is Rutherford publicly stated that he had never said that the resurrection would take place in 1925, yet he had in print stated this in the *"Millions* Book," among others.

From 1932 to 1950 Wallis studied the Bible with a small group of friends, and in

1950 he was introduced to Moyle's work. He contributed articles for about four years and became an associate editor in 1954 a post he retained until 1959 when he became the editor, remaining in this position until he died in 1982.

Magazines

The Bible Student Inquirer. Ed. Olin R. Moyle. Published from about 1940 to 1959 at Baltimore, MD.

The Bible Student Examiner. Ed. Henry Wallis. Vol. 1, No. 1, 1959, to Vol. 22, Nos. 1 & 2, Jan. & Feb. 1982, Baltimore, MD, 16 pp., bimonthly.

L. Back to the Bible Way

The founder, Roy D. Goodrich, was a Watchtower pioneer from 1919 (his wife Maud, daughter of Dr. Hodgson, pioneered from 1914) until 1945 when both he and his wife were disfellowshipped. Evidently, in 1943 a friend told him that certain "demonistic practices" that he thought had stopped were still occurring at the Brooklyn headquarters (Raines, 1996). In an attempt to correct the matter, he sent letters to the directors of the Society, none of whom answered him. Further research by Goodrich uncovered what he concluded many "demonistic practices" that high-level Watchtower administrators and theorists practiced. The "demonistic practices" were centered around an medical treatment called "radio diagnosis" (a quack method of treating disease especially cancer by radio waves (Warner, 1941). At this time Goodrich was a company servant and because he was quite outspoken about these matters to his congregation, he was disfellowshipped.

Goodrich not only had a falling out with the Witnesses but later was alienated from the various Bible Student groups. Evidently he was a difficult person to get along with, insistent upon the correctness of his ideas and position and intolerant of others. His voluminous literature records the many confrontations he had had with virtually every Bible Student group, most of whom tried to ignore him.

Goodrich disagreed with the main body of Bible Students on three main points: he denied that Charles Taze Russell was the "wise and faithful servant" of Matthew 25: 45-47. He also rejected Russell's thinking relative to the ransom and to the significance of the year 1914. Goodrich, his wife, and others were very active passing out tracts at the large Witness and Bible Student assemblies, an action which often resulted in harsh treatment from not only Witnesses but from Bible Students as well. For example, he picketed the 1946 Witness convention in Cleveland and caused such a stir that *The Messenger*, the official Watchtower assembly report, was forced to discuss the situation.

In 1952 he began the *Back to Bible Way* magazine, which was published until his death in 1977. Goodrich was a prolific writer, and many of his writings display a good understanding of and insight into religious matters. He was one of the few college-educated Witnesses (Goodrich was a high school science teacher for many years). His research eventually caused him to reject a large number of Russell's ideas and accept many of George Storrs' beliefs, and even some of the teachings of the early Adventists.

In contrast to many of the splinter groups' leaders, he was a lively and energetic writer, and his works tend to be informative and useful to the student of Witness history. He includes a great deal of information about the history of the Watchtower Bible & Tract Society in his writings. When he and his wife died in 1977 (within months of each other) his movement, always fairly small, became even more so. Engineer Havilland W. Davis, of Albany, NY, carries on the work and prints a newsletter and still distributes some of Goodrich's publications.

Theologically, Goodrich held to the fundamentals advocated by Russell (denial of the trinity, immortality of the soul, hell, the idea that Christendom is apostate, etc.) but he disagreed strongly with the "invisible second presence theory," the belief that Christ's second coming is invisible. He also did not view Russell as the faithful and wise servant as do many Bible Student groups, nor did he view the ransom as merely a "curse," and rejected most of Russell's dates, such as 1914 and 1874.

Goodrich's involvement in the various Bible Student groups was his main source of converts, although many ex-Witnesses joined him. His mailing list was as large as 3,000. His publications included a magazine and 440 different brochures that vary from one-page mimeographed items to printed booklets to postcards. Many of these publications deal with the many problems in the Watchtower theology.

Magazine

Back to the Bible Way: A Journal of Faith, Love, Sincerity, and Present Truth. Vol. 1, No. 1, Jan. 1952, to the last issue Vol. 21, No. 23, Dec. 1973, Whole number, 145, Vol. 1, 500 pp; Vol. II, 492 pp; Vol. III, 512 pp; Vol. IV, 492 pp.

Brochures No. 1 to 444. (All by Roy D. Goodrich, published by author in Fort Lauderdale, FL).
1. *To N.H. Knorr.* Oct. 1944.
2. *To Fort Lauderdale "Sheep" (if any).* Nov. 1944, 2 pp.
3. *To "Dear Friends."* Nov. 1944, 2 pp.
9. (Nos. 1, 2, 3 revised and mimeographed.)
14. *An Open Letter to N.H. Knorr.* N.d., 2 pp.
15. *Tamp Assembly Highlights.* Feb. 1945.
19. *Something's Hot.* Feb. 1945.
20. *The Spook Cure.* March 1945, 2 pp.
21. *Notes from "The Grape Cure" Book.* March 1945.
22. *Stalks of the Ghost of Wm. Penn to Clayton J. Woodworth.* March 1945.
23. *Dare You Face the Facts?* April 1945.
25. "Radioclass" Reproductions. April 1945.
27. *Special Meetings.* West Palm Beach, FL, 1945, 5 pp.
30. *A Letter to a Brother Who Was Grossly Offended and Excommunicated, and with Whom I Disagree.* May 1945, 22 pp. About Moyle.
31. *Heavens and Earth--Which Are Now."* Jan. 1946, 3 pp.
32. *Jehovah of Hosts, the God of "Peace."* Sept. 1, 1945, 15 pp. (same as No. 133).
34. *Response of Hate.* Oct. 1945, 3 pp.
37. *An Open Letter to N.H. Knorr.* N.d., 2 pp. Reprint of No. 14.
38. *Bethel Rides the Broom.* Feb. 1946, 18 pp.
39. *An Open Letter to N.H. Knorr--Unanswered Yet.*
40. *To My Anointed Brethren.* Dec. 24, 1944, 4 pp. (same as No. 9).
41. *The "Murder" of a Pioneer.* Dec. 1945, 1 p.
42. *To My Brethren Whom It May Concern.* Jan. 1946, 3 pp.
43. *The Spook Cure as Advocated by Doctor Rollin Jones, Personal Physician to Judge.* N.d., 4 pp.
46a. *An Introduction to, and History of the Manuscript--"Theocratic Judgment" As Scorned, Unread by N.J. Knorr.* April 1947, 5 pp.
46b. *Dear "Evil Servant" and Brothers and Sisters to Whom This Shall Come.* Sept. 1946, 4 pp.
47a. *Thank God! After 30-odd Years Satan has Been Compelled to Allow Freedom of Communication among the Enlightened Members of Temple of the God Jehovah!* Revised 1976, 9 pp.
47b. *Shall the Elders of God's Free Church Remain Gagged and Bound by Fear?* June 1946, 12 pp.
48. *Lawrence E. Drew to Directors.* May 1946.
49. *Circular Letter to Miami Friends.* May 1946.
50. "We Think." June 1946, 1 p.
56. *Charter of the Watchtower Society of Pennsylvania.* 1945, 8 pp. (A reprint of the Society's charter to show how much they have now deviated from it).
57. *Tobacco.* Oct. 1946, 1 p.
59. *Together with God.* Nov. 1946, 7 pp.
60. *Voices, Thunderings, Lightnings, Earthquake.* Dec. 1946, 3 pp.
61. "Watch and Be Sober." Dec. 1946, 3 pp.
62. "Fogh Hysteria:" According to C.H. Zook, "The Instrument of Yah." Dec. 1946, 2 pp.

63. *Reprint of Letter to Mrs. J.H. Donovan.* March 10, 1945, 1 p.
64. *Ouija Boards, Small and Large.* Dec. 1947, 11 pp.
65. *Introduction to KIM.* Jan. 1947, 1 p.
66. *Crawford and Stoneman Letters.* Dec. 1946, 1 p.
67. *Form Letter "A."* N.d., 1 p.
68. *Spoken in Darkness, Heard in Light.* Jan. 1947, 9 pp.
69. *From Letters "B" and "C."* Jan. 1947, 4 pp.
70. *Jehovah's Witnesses.* N.d., 1 p.
71. *Shall We Study the Watchtower?* Jan. 1947, 4 pp.
72. *Character Development.* Feb. 1947, 7 pp.
73. *"Great Is Diana of the Ephesians:" A Goddess Falls Down from Heaven!.* March 1947, 1 p.
74. *Railing, Reviling, Evil Speaking, Scripturally Defined.* Feb. 1947, 2 pp.
75. *Men and Brethren, What Shall We Do When We See the Errors of "Organization."* Feb. 1947, 6 pp.
76. *A Watchtower Study: Remembrance of Jesus vs. "A Memorial of Integrity."* Feb. 15, 1947, 4 pp.
77. *The Memorial of Jesus.* March 1947 (5 pp. revised).
78. *Zion Repents, Do You?* March 1947, 10 pp.
79. *Moyle's Original Letters.* Feb. 1947, 6 pp.
80. *David and His Sin.* March 9, 1946, 5 pp.
81. *Postscript on Bible Chronology.* Nov. 1, 1945, 5 pp.
82. *Copyrights.* May 6, 1946, 3 pp.
83. *"Bethel:" The House of God, as Seen from the Inside.* Feb. 1947, 8 pp. By M.P. Fogh.
85. *To the Beloved of God Convention "Meat."* April 1947, 3 pp.
86. *As Sheep Having no Shepherd.* April 1947, 2 pp.
88. *Ridicule, Sarcasm, Derision and Reproach.* May 1947, 1 p.
89. *Answer to Miller's Tirade.* May 1947, 1 p.
91. *Betrayal.* July 6, 1947, 4 pp.
92. *"What Next?"* Aug. 1947, 2 pp.
94. *For Los Angeles Contacts* (printed post card). Aug. 1947.
95. (Postcard photo of defaced sandwich sign). Oct. 1946.
96. *The Wobbling "Channel."* Aug. 1947, 1 p.
97. *In the Temple Gate.* Sept. 1947, 11 pp.
98. *Love: What Is It? The Inspired Answer.* Oct. 1947, 4 pp.
99. *Advice.* Oct. 28, 1947, 1 p.
100. *To Jehovah's Witnesses, Dawn Readers and Others.* Nov. 5, 1947, 4 pp.
101. *Scriptures Please!* Nov. 1947, reprinted 1952, 2 pp.
102. *By What Authority?* Dec. 1947, 1 p.
103. *Parousia vs. Presence--Our First Inkling of the Truth on This Subject.* Dec. 1947, 10 pp.
104. *Brotherly Love at Philadelphia.* Jan. 1948, 1 p.
105. *"Ye Shall Know Them by Their Fruits."* Jan. 1948, 1 p.
106. *The Christian Controversy.* Jan. 1948, 19 pp.
107. *A Terrible Disturbance.* Feb. 1948, 1 p.
108. *A Flower Upon My Mother's Grave.* Feb. 1948, 3 pp.
108a. *To Relatives and Friends of My Mothers.* Feb. 1948, 1 p.
109. *Letter.* N.d., 1 p.
111. *Preaching the Word.* Nov. 1948, 1 p.
112. *The Atlanta Assembly of the Watchtower Witnesses of Jehovah.* March 1948, 2 pp.
113. *Preaching the Word, to My Fee Brethren.* April 15, 1948, 3 pp.
114. *Contradicting the Almighty--the Watchtower vs. God.* April 1948, 6 pp. (A list of Watchtower contradictions).
116. *"Freely Ye Have Received, Freely Give" the Gospel--Our Report from 1944 to 1948.* May 1948, 3 pp.
117. *No Going to Heaven, No Baptism, No Lord's Supper.* May 7, 1948, 1 p.
118. *An Answer to "Free" Bible Students.* May 1948, 5 pp.
119. *Contribution Acknowledgement.* N.d., 1 p.
120. *To Those Concerned as to Merwyn Fogh.* N.d., 1 p.
121. *He Stirith up the People."* May 21, 1948, 1 p.

122. *Finke Replies.* May 1948, 1 p.
123. *Preaching the Word.* N.d., 1 p.
124. *The Image of Jealousy.* May 1948, 3 pp.
125. *"That Servant--Faithful and Wise."* June 1, 1948 (enlarged in 1957), 8 pp.
126. *Earnestly Contend for the Faith.* June 3, 1948, 3 pp.
127. *Preaching the Word.* July 25, 1948, 1 p.
128. *Established by God's Grace.* N.d., 1 p.
129. *A Witness Among Wolves.* Oct. 1948, 7 pp.
130. *Postscript to Witness Among Wolves.* Oct. 1948, 3 pp.
131. *Judging.* Oct. 1948, 8 pp. (same as No. 130).
133. *Jehovah' of Hosts--The God of "Peace."* Oct. 1948, 8 pp.
134. *N.H. Knorr's Criticism of the Above "Peace" Manuscript.* Oct. 1948, 2 pp.
135. *To the P.B.I. Editors and Directors.* Nov. 1948, 1 p.
136. *"Are You Interested?"* (postcard). 1 p.
137. *Established by God's Grace, or Tossed To and Fro?* Nov. 1948, 8 pp.
138. *"We Wrestle Not...."* Nov. 1948, 1 p.
139. *In Whose Seat? Christ's or Caesar's?* Dec. 1978, 1 p.
140. *Contribution Acknowledgement.* Dec. 1948, 1 p.
141. *Crucify Him! Crucify Him! An Eye-Witness Account of the Scriptural Murder of Olin R. Moyle by 65,000 J.W.s at ST. Louis in 1941.* Dec. 1948, 2 pp.
142. *Financial Report for 1948.* Jan. 1949, 1 p.
143. *Freedom to Do God's Will in 1949.* Jan. 1949, 1 p.
144. *To Russellite and Watchtower Brethren.* Jan. 1949, 1 p.
145. *As to Adam.* Jan. 1949, 2 pp.
146. *"Self-Justification."* Feb. 1949, 2 pp.
147. *"Rather Reprove Them."* Feb. 1949, 1 p.
148. *"The Key to Studying the Bible."* may 1949, 1 p.
149. *God's (Not Man's) Co-Workers.* Feb. 1949, 1 p.
151. *To All Bible Students of the Miami Ecclesia.* April 23, 1949, 3 pp.
152. *Whom Will You Obey?* May 1949, 1 p.
153. *Proposed Assembly Witness* (letter). May 1949, 2 pp.
154. *Decency Commended.* May 1949, 1 p.
155. *What Would Happen to Jesus Christ If He Attended a "JW" Assembly?* June 11, 1949, 1 p.
156. *To Hayden C. Covington, et al.* May 1949, 1 p.
159. *It Happened in 1949, Visits to JW Assemblies Recounted.* Aug. 1949, 12 pp.
160. *In Welchem Recht?* 2 pp. (No. 102 above, in German).
161. *The Heavenly Call of Christianity, the "No Heaven" Challenge of Demonism Squarely Met.* Aug. 1949, 4 pp.
162. *Immortality, What Is It?* Aug. 1949, 2 pp.
163. *What Is the Hope of His Calling?* Aug. 1949, 4 pp.
164. *Is Your Heart Right With God?* Aug. 1949, 1 p.
165. *When? How? and Why? Was the Now Infamous "Goodrich" Thrown Out on His Face by Men Less Righteous Than He?* Sept. 1949, 4 pp.
166. *The Zooky Servants of Yah: A "Truth" Cult Denying Everything, Even the Existence of Jesus as a Man.* Dept. 1949, 1 p.
167. *"Berean Study" False and True.* Sept. 1949, 1 p.
168. *Does the Watchtower Answer Goodrich?* Sept. 1949, 1 p.
169. *Have the "Free Brethren" Answered Goodrich?* Sept. 1949, 1 p.
170. *The Kingdom of God Is at Hand.* Oct. 1949, 2 pp.
171. *From the Last Supper to the First Fruits of Them That Slept, in Type and Anti-type.* Oct. 1949, 17 pp.
172. *Present Truth on Parousia.* Nov. 1949, 2 pp.
173. *Chronoligitis, A Dread Disease.* Dec. 1949, 3 pp.
174. *Please.* Dec. 1949, 1 p.
175. *The Day of Atonement.* Dec. 1949, 4 pp.
176. *Christian Science.* Dec. 1949, 1 p.
176a. *Man Dying in Trailer, Unable to Get Word to Officers.* Dec. 1949, 1 p. (About Bible Student Merwyn Fogh's death).
177. *Lift Up Your Heads! 1950 Is Here!* Jan. 1950, 3 pp.
178a. *Jesus' Soul, the Sin Offering.* Jan. 1950, 2 pp.

179. *Do It Now* (An Interest Form). Jan. 1950, 1 p.
180. *Christian Baptism.* Jan. 1950, 26 pp.
181. *Whence Came Russell's "Secret Presence" Theory?* July 1961, 1 p.
182. *On Seeing Alike.* Jan. 1950, 1 p. On freedom of communication.
183. *Absurdity masquerading as the "Deep Things of God" Dies Hard.* Feb. 1950, 7 pp.
184. *Questions.* Feb. 15, 1950, 1 p.
185b. (Monthly and yearly summary forms). March 1950.
186. (Form letter for Britain). March 1950, 4 pp.
187. *Some Questions* (poem). April 1950, 1 p.
188. *Vice regency: The Great Mistake and Abomination of the Gospel Age.* April 1950,
        8 pp.
189. *General Letter of May 1950.* May 1950, 1 p.
190. *Octogenarian Asks Questions.* May 1950, 1 p.
191. *G. R. Pollock Visits Britain.* May 1950, 3 pp.
192. *My Purpose, My Work and Yours.* 1950 (revised Feb. 1958), 1 p.
193. *Second John Seven--Is Jesus Coming in the Flesh?* June 1950, 1 p.
194. *Comfort All tat Mourn in Zion.* June 1950.
195. *The Bible Student Soul-Searcher.* June 1950, 2 pp. Also Aug. 1950, *The bible
        Student Soul-Searcher* (no number).
196. *The Bible Student Soul-Searcher.* Supplement No. 1, June 1950, 1 p.
197. *The Bible Student Soul-Searcher.* Supplement No. 2, June 1950, 1 p.
198. *Dawn General Convention, Bowling Green, OH; Watchtower International
        Assembly, Yankee Stadium, New York City.* Aug. 16, 1950, 1 p.
199. *Love...in Work and in Truth.* June 16, 1950, 1 p.
200. *Letter.* July 1950, 1 p.
201. *It Happened at 124 Columbia Heights*, Brooklyn, NY, July 24, 1950, 1 p.
202. *It Happened at 177 Prospect Place.* July 25, 1950, 1950, 2 pp.
203. *"Dawn" at Bowling Green.* Aug. 26, 1950, 3 pp.
204. *Wresting Universal Salvation unto Destruction.* Sept. 8, 1950, 10 pp. (revised and
        enlarged Ed., 24 pp. (An attempt to refute A.E. Knoch universalism teachings).
205. *A Personal Letter.* Sept. 27, 1950, 1 p.
206. *"Theocracy's Increase" at Yankee Stadium in 1950: Is This the Kingdom of God?
        Or Merelyn a New Increasing Religion?* Sept. 27, 1950, 5 pp.
207. *Evil Speaking Defined--Its Creed Examined.* Oct. 1950, 2 pp.
208. *Patience, Her Work and Her Creed.* Oct. 1950, 3 pp.
209. (Index card checking form). Dec. 1950, 1 p.
210. *JHVH? YHWH? What Is the Creator's Name?* Dec. 1950, 5 pp
211. (Advertising slip for No. 204). Dec. 1950, 1 p.
212. *"For the Elect's Sake."* Dec. 21, 1950, 4 pp.
213. *Proclaiming Repentance (1950 report).* Jan. 1951, 2 pp.
214. *The Season's Greetings, 1951.* Jan. 1951, 2 pp.
215. *Jehovah's Memorial Name in the New Testament.* Jan. 21, 1951, 10 pp.
216. *"Let Us Know."* Jan. 1951, 1 p.
217. *The Great Multitude* (by Percy Sidney Pryer). Feb. 1951, 4 pp.
218. *Nekros-Thanatos: An Answer to This Religious Noise.* Feb. 1951, 1 p.
219. *Two Viewpoints* (from England). March 6, 1951, 2 pp.
220. *In Remberance of Whom?* March 12, 1951, 6 pp.
221. *Contributions Are Now Possible.* March 15, 1951, 1p.
222. *God's Organization.* March 29, 1951, 6 pp.
223. *To All Who Love His Appearing* (Britain). April 1, 1951, 1 p.
224. *What Shall We Do "Until ..." What.* April 20, 1951, 2 pp.
225. *God's Organization.* April 1951, 4 pp. (Oct. 1957 fourth printing, 8 pp).
226. (Invitation to circulate No. 225). April 26, 1951, 1 p.
227. *Honest with Yourself and with Your God.* April 29, 1951, 1 p.
228. *"Not Forsaking the Assembling of Ourselves Together."* May 19, 1951, 1 p.
229. "Destroyed for Lack of Knowledge." May 20, 1951, 1 p.
230. *"Proclaim Liberty Throughout All the Land."* May 24, 1951, 1p.
231. (Form letter). June 17, 1951, 1 p.
232. *The New Watchtower Translation of 1950: An Unbiased Evaluation.* June 18,
        1951, 4 pp.
233. *The Atlanta District Assembly of Watchtower Witnesses.* June 8-10, 4 pp.

234. *Atlantic District Assembly of 1951, Addenda.* June 28, 1951, 1 p.
235. *Modern Scribes and Pharisees: Hypocrites!* July 2, 1951, 3 pp.
236. *Opinion--Profanity.* July 1951, 1 p.
237. *Who Is My Brother? The Bible Answer Surprises Many.* 7 pp.
238. *List of Brochures for Bible Students.* July 20, 1951, 1 p.
239. *Complete List of Brochures in Stock.* July 20, 1951, 1 p.
240. *Dear Friends All, from Dan to Beer-Sheba.* Aug. 17, 1951, 1 p.
241. *Reports of Unity Convention.* Sept. 4, 1951, 1 p.
242. (Name and address form). Sept. 5, 1951, 1 p.
243. *Th e Present Truth o n Parousia.* Sept. 10, 1951, 2 pp.
244. *Questionnaire Form with University Convention Report.* Oct. 17, 1951, 1 p.
245. *1951 Unity Convention Report.* Oct. 20, 1951, 8 pp.
246. *Christian Cooperation.* Nov. 2, 1951, 4 pp.
247. *Brother Strongly Advised Against.* Nov. 12, 1951, 1 p.
248. *Fellowship.* Nov. 19, 1951, 3 pp.
249. *New Year's Greetings, 1952.* Jan. 1, 1952, 1 p.
250. *From Australia on Unity Convention Report and the Sin Offering.* Jan. 1952, 1 p.
251. *Have Fervent Love Among Yourselves: Let's Get Acquainted!* Jan. 1952, 3 pp.
252. *Brethren All, from Dan to Beersheba.* Feb. 7, 1952, 1 p.
253. *Form Inquiring as to Interest.* Feb. 1952, 1 p.
254. *Back to the Bible No. 1.* Feb. 2, 1952.
255. *Back to the Bible No. 2.* March 12, 1952.
256. *For Polite Discontinue Requesters* (a card for persons to send back who do not want
     to receive Goodrich's literature). March 20, 1952, 1 p.
256a. (Correspondence-answering form). March 26, 1952, 1 p.
256b. (Correspondence-answering form). May 4, 1952, 1 p.
256c. (Correspondence convalescence). June 5, 1952, 1 p.
256e. (Letterhead--back to the Bible). June 24, 1952, 1 p.
256f. (Ditto, plus home from hospital letter). July 28, 1952, 1 p.
256g. (Back to Health letter). Oct. 17, 1952, 1 p.
256h. (Back to Health letter). Jan. 12, 1953, 1 p.
257. *"The True Basis of Christian Fellowship."* June 8, 1952, 1 p.
258. *Unity Convention Bible Study on "The True Basis of Christian Fellowship."* June
     8, 1952, 4 pp.
258a. *"Petition" to Jehovah's Witness Assembly Here.* April 18, 1952, 1 p.
259. *Jehovah' Witnesses Assemblies--Opportunity of Service.* Aug. 13, 1952, 1p.
260. *4 Questions to 66 Dawn and PBI Pilgrims.* May 25, 1953.
261. (For distribution at Yankee Stadium). June 1, 1953.
262. *Have Faith in God, Inviting to Help.* June 7, 1953, 1 p.
263. *Letter Reporting Macatawa and Yankee Stadium.* Aug. 10, 1953, 2 pp.
264. *Answering cards, 261 sent in Aug. 1953.*
265. *N.H. Knorr Speaks at Stadium to "Scores of Thousands,"* Sept. 5, 1953, 12 pp.
266. *Half-Truth Versus the Whole Truth.* Sept. 20, 1953, 1 p.
267. (From letter). Oct. 20, 1053, 1 p.
268. *Letter to Fry List."* Nov. 2, 1953, 1 p.
269. *Love Your Enemies* (Sister Clark's letter). Dec. 4, 1953, 2 pp.
270. *Seasons Greetings--Back to the Bible.* Dec. 15, 1953, 2 pp.
270a. *Are Your Interested in the Back to the Bible Public?* Dec. 18, 1953.
272. *Demonism and the Watchtower* (enlarged ed.). Jan. 1, 1954, 16 pp. (revised 1969,
     36 pp). (Argues that the Society is involved in demonism).
273. *Blood Transfusion--Does It Violate God's Law?* Feb. 12, 1954, 4 pp.
274. *To Jehovah's Witnesses, Disfellowshipped by Man or Who Fear Their Turn Is
     Next.* Feb. 17, 1954, 4 pp. (A critique of the Watchtower practice of
     disfellowshipping).
276. *"Out of the Mouths of Babes."* March 11, 1954, 2 pp.
277. *Passover Questions--Raised by Our Readers.* May 1, 1954, 4 pp. (A review of the
     Passover history).
278. *"It's Better Never Late."* May 2, 1954, 1 p.
279. *Problem: To Complete ___ Copies.* May 3, 1954, 1 p.
280. (Form letter). May 6, 1954, 1 p.
281. *Jehovah's Witnesses Assembly* (double postcard). May 6, 1954, 1 p.

282. *Jehovah's Witnesses* (postcard). May 21, 1954, 1 p.
283. (Form letters, etc.), June 7, 1954.
284. *Mighty as Death Is Love.* Aug. 12, 1954, 2 pp.
285. *To 39 Fellow Elders.* Sept. 12, 1954, 1 p.
286. (Correspondence-Answering form letter). Sept. 12, 1954, 1 p.
287. *"By What Authority" Growled the Elders.* Sept. 12, 1954, 1 p.
288. *Have You Seen the Light? God's Great Covenants in Simple Language.* Oct. 19, 1954, 8 pp. (A review of the covenants, Abraham, Mosaic, and the New Covenant).
289. *Circular Letter on Informal Sessions.* Nov. 25, 1954, 1 p.
290. *Open Letter of Psalm 82.* Dec. 18, 1954, 4 pp.
291. *They Shall All Know Me, Jer. 31:31-34.* Dec. 20, 1954, 1 p.
292. *"Salvation" Seasons Greetings.* Dec. 12, 1954, 1 p.
293. *The Holy Spirit of the God Jehovah by Percy Sidney Pryer.* Jan. 20, 1955, 8 pp. (A discussion of the Holy Spirit).
294. (Correspondence "Prescript"). Jan. 20, 1955, 1 p.
295. *A Back to the Bible Answer.* Feb. 4, 1955, 1 p.
296. *Twelve Back to the Bible Answers, to an ex-JW.* Feb. 5, 1955, 5 pp.
297. *To Universalists--All Brands.* Feb. 13, 1955, 1 p.
298. *The Whips of Solomon Change to the Scorpions of Rehoboam.* March 6, 1955, 2 pp.
299. (Announcements). March 24, 1955, 1 p.
300. "They Parousia" Honesty vs. Dishonesty. March 31, 1955, 3 pp.
301. (Form letter). May 14, 1955, 1 p.
302. *Which Son Are Your? Harvest Is Great--Laborers Are Few.* June 1955, 1 p.
303. "Jehovah's Witnesses Win a Right." June 1955, 4 pp.
304. *"Planned Free Time" Finis.* June 28, 1955. 1 p.
305. *Penetrating the Iron Curtain.* Aug. 1955, 1 p.
306. *Win Recognition in the "World of Satan."* Aug. 10, 1955, 5 pp.
307. (Form to reply to requests for No. 303). Sept. 10, 1955, 1 p.
308. *Funeral Discourse.* Jan. 5, 1956, 6 pp.
309. *Unpardonable Sin.* Feb. 17, 1956, 8 pp. (The definition and identification of the unpardonable sin).
310. *Myth, Mercy and Martyrdom--or Does Blood Transfusion Break God's Law?* Feb. 1956, 2 pp.
311. (Charles Glass correspondence). March 15, 1956, 5 pp.
312. *The Christian Sabbath.* March 16, 1956, 4 pp.
313. *ABC's of Bible Study.* June 30, 1956, 78 pp.
314. *Cry of the Hungry.* June 4, 1956, 3 pp.
315. *Try the Spirits* (postcard). June 10, 1956, 1 p.
316. *The Ransom of the Bible versus the Ransom of Confusion.* June 12, 1956, 1 p.
317. (Steno for stencil for big envelopes). June 26, 1956, 1 p.
318. (Slips about advance copies of No. 313). June 30, 1956, 1 p.
· 319. *The Atonement of Christ versus Spiritual Gangrene.* July 8, 1956, 2 pp.
320. *Behind the Scenes at Green Castle, Indiana in 1956.* Sept. 24, 1956, 12 pp. (A history of the conflicts Goodrich had with the Bible Students).
321. *The Watchtower Succumbs to Occult Control.* Sept. 24, 1954, 1 p. (Discusses the 1954 Scottish trial testimony).
322. (Correspondence-answering form). Oct. 19, 1956, 1 p.
323. *What about W.J. Schnell's Book: 30 YEARS A WATCHTOWER SLAVE?* Dec. 7, 1956, 2 pp.
324. *Mailing list double* (postcard). Dec. 20, 1956, 2 pp.
325. *The Authority of the Watchtower Society Examined.* Jan. 1, 1957, 4 pp.
325a. (Auf Deutsch). Feb. 14, 1958.
326. *A Happy Back to the Bible Greetings New Year to You!* Dec. 27, 1956, 1 p.
327. *The Night Cometh When No Man Can Work.* Jan. 15, 1957, 1 p.
328. *How to Reach Jehovah's Witnesses and Why.* Feb. 18, 1957, 4 pp.
329. *Dear Back to the Bible Reader.* Feb. 20, 1957, 1 p.
329a. (Newsletter). April 6, 1957, 1 p.
330. *The New Covenant in the Book of Hebrews.* May 5, 1957, 16 pp. (later ed. 28 pp). (Contrasts Russell's views on the New Covenant with Paul's).

331. *Challenge of the Hour, Bible Week.* May 20, 1957, 1 p.
331. (Bible Week forms for Laura Bridge). June 21, 1957, 1 p.
332. *Bible Week Suggestions.* July 1, 1957, 1 p.
334. *Song Book.* July 10, 1957, 19 pp.
335. *"Home Again"--A Brief Outline of Our 1957 Missionary Journey.* Sept. 14, 1957, 1 p.
336. *New York Watchtower Charter.* Oct. 15, 1957, 8 pp.
337. *Parental Discipline.* Nov. 14, 1957, 4 pp. (A reprint of an article Goodrich wrote for the Watchtower, *Golden Age* March 29, 1922).
338. (Correspondence-answering form letter). Dec. 28, 1957, 1 p.
339. *The Rich Man and Lazarus.* Feb. 1958, 8 pp. (Argues that Hell is only the grave and that Luke 16:19-31 is a parable of which Goodrich interprets the meaning).
341. (Reply form letter). Feb. 13, 1958, 1 p.
341a. (Corporation receipt form). April 10, 1958, 1 p.
342. *"Auf Deutsch"* (form letter). March 10, 1958, 1 p.
343. *Parable of the Unjust Steward.* April 16, 1958, 8 pp. (Argues that Christianity has failed God).
344. (Bible Week reservation request card). May 10, 1958, 1 p.
345. *Trying to Serve "Other Lords" and Christ.* May 12, 1958, 4 pp. (A critique of Watchtower teaching).
346. *The "Canon" of Scripture Chopping Down the Ransom. Are Scholars Wrong? John 1:1.* May 28, 1958, 8 pp. (Discusses the Cannon, the ransom doctrines and why the Trinity is unscriptural).
347. *Charter of the Bible Way Publications, Inc.* June 6, 1958, 10 pp. (The charter Goodrich filed in circuit court, in Broward County, FL).
348. *"Trembling at Men, Is What Lays a Snare."* June 15, 1958, 2 pp.
349. (Form letter on convention trip). Aug. 15, 1958, 2 pp.
350. *"Bird"* (form). *"Are You Alive."* Oct. 15, 1958, 1 p.
351. (Corresponding-answering form). Jan. 27, 1959, 1 p.
352. *Invitation to Fort Lauderdale Memorial Assembly.* June 27, 1959, 1 p.
353. *Dear Modesto California Friends, and Others Everywhere.* Feb. 23, 1959, 1 p.
354. *Remember the Patience of Job.* March 15, 1959, 1 p.
355. *The Symphony of Parousia and Mello.* April 4, 1959, 8 pp.
356. *BTTBW Index 1952-1956.* April 4, 1959, 13 pp.
357. *BTTBW Index 1957, 1958.* April 4, 1959, 5 pp.
358. *"The Tabernacle of David."* April 6, 1959, 4 pp. (Questions for class study).
358a. (Chart on Revelation).
359. *Type and Antitype. The Law and the Faith.* April 6, 1959, 10 pp. (A discussion of the type and anti-type doctrine of the Watchtower and other similar groups).
359a. (As above with Scriptures printed in full). July 15, 1961, 12 pp.
360. *Dual Fulfillment.* June 22, 1959, 8 pp. (A study guide to the concept of dual fulfillment).
361. *"The Tabernacle of David."* Sept. 30, 1959, 8 pp. (Argues against the Zionist's world view).
362. *Our Lord's Last Days Chart Explained.* June 22, 1959, 2 pp.
363. *"Great Signs and Wonders" in the Parousia-Time.* Aug. 24, 1959, 1p.
364. *"House to House."* Sept. 1, 1959, 2 pp.
365. *As a Snare...Watch...Stand...*March 3, 1960, 8 pp.
366. (Envelope negative). March 5, 1960, 1 p.
367. *Letter.* N.d., 2 pp.
368. *The P.S.L. Johnson Affair of 1917.* June 5, 1960, 5 pp.
369. *"Thou Shalt Love Thy Neighbor as Thyself"* (A detailed account about Charles Archer, who was thrown out of the Ward County, Texas J.W. Assembly). 1960, 8 pp.
370. *"Finding Peace in This Troubled World"* (More details about Charles Archer, who was thrown out of a Witness Assembly). 1960, 4 pp.
371. *Auf Deutsch.* Sept. 17, 1960, 12 pp.
372. *Mission Accomplished* (1960 trip). Sept. 7, 1960, 5 pp.
373. *To All the Ministers and Others Who Attended the Recent Minister's Meeting, August 20, 1960, at Belleville, Illinois.* Sept. 5, 1960, 2 pp.
374. *The Promise of the Father* (German). Oct. 8, 1960.

375. *The Modern Gift of Tongues* (German). Oct. 8, 1960.
376. *To: Dear Theta Chi Alumnus.* March 15, 1961, 1 p.
377. *Bricht Bluttransfusion Gottes Gesetz?* (No. 310 in German). May 6, 1961, 4 pp.
378. *Not Discerning the"Body" and Worshiping Demons.* July 21, 1961, 4 pp.
    (Documents several major changes in Watchtower policy and practice).
379. *Divine Providence.* Aug. 24, 1961, 2 pp.
380. *1962 Memorial Assembly Notes.* 1962, 8 pp.
381. *The Inspired Answer.* May 1962, 2 pp. (A set of scriptures about love).
382. *Index* (page, date and vol. coordinator), June 1962, 1 p.
383. *Pastor Russell and the Ransom.* July 6, 1962, 4 pp.
384. *To Faith's "Endurers."* July 15, 1962, 4 pp.
385. *The Abomination of Desolation.* June 25, 1962, 16 pp.
386. *"I Morti Non Sanno Nulla."* July 1962, 4 pp. (Italian; Dead Know Not Anything).
387. *Spirito, Anima, E. Corpo.* N.d., 4 pp. (Italian; Spirit, Soul and Body).
388. *Retrenchment* (form letter). Sept. 22, 1962, 1 p.
389. (Form letter). Dec. 16, 1962, 1 p.
390. (Postcard for returned journals). Jan. 29, 1963, 1 p.
391. *Backwards, Turn Backward O Time.* Jan. 10, 1963, 1 p.
392. (Form letter for answering correspondence). Feb. 5, 1963, 1 p.
393. Letter about Memorial Assembly). April 17, 1963, 1 p.
394. (Form letter, work on cottage). May 9, 1963, 1 p.
395. (Form letter, Mrs. Goodrich's driver's license, etc.). July 9, 1963, 1 p.
396. (Mrs. Goodrich's vacation, etc.). Aug. 25, 1963, 1 p.
397. (Program preview). March 1, 1964, 1 p.
398. *Memorial Assembly--Fort Lauderdale, Florida: Sunday April 26, Thru May 2, 1964.* April 1, 1964, 8 pp.
399. *A Bible Study Outline--Three Great Recent Advances in Bible Knowledge.* Feb. 22, 1965, 10 pp. (A study on Parousia).
400. *A Christian's Attitude Toward War.* July 24, 1964, 2 pp.
401. *Hell, A Bible Teaching.* Oct. 1960, 4 pp.
402. *The Resurrection of Jesus Christ, When?* Oct. 1960, 4 pp.
403. *"The Dead Know Not Anything"--But "There Shall Be a Resurrection of the Dead."* Oct. 1960, 4 pp.
404. *Spirit and Soul and Body."* Oct. 1960, 4 pp.
405. *Modern Gift of Tongues.* March 24, 1961, 4 pp.
406. *'Lord,' 'God,' 'Jesus,' and 'Christ.'* March 24, 1961, 4 pp.
407. *Ten Year Index to Back to the Bible Way.* N.d., 88 pp.
408. *The Oracle Which Habakkuk the Prophet Did See.* July, Aug., 1961, 4 pp.
409. *After 20 Years--Is This the New World?* (reprint of Dec. 1, 1944 issue). 6 pp.
410. *The ABCs of Bible Study: Primary Information--Knowledge the Youngest Need But Few of the Oldest Have* (enlarged and revised). April 8, 1963, 77 pp. (An outline of the Bible and its teachings).
411. *The Symphony of "Parousia" and "Mello"* (typeset reprint of No. 355). Dec. 21, 1960, 5 pp.
412. *The Resurrection Appearances of Jesus Christ.* Dec. 21, 1960, 8 pp.
413. *The Great Counterfeit now being called The Establishment of God.* 1962, 34 pp. (A critique of Watchtower teaching on Christ's second coming).
414. *Welcome Jehovah's Witnesses by Mrs. Goodwill.* Aug. 5, 1963, 4 pp. (A dialogue between a Witness and a Bible Student).
415. *Watchtower Witness Writes to Jehovah's Witnesses.* Sept. 10, 1963, 4 pp.
416. *Excommunication--1944 by the Watchtower; Vindication--1962 by the Watchtower.* Dec. 1964, 12 pp. (A history of the Watchtower's use of medical quackery specifically of Abrams, which was exposed in the *Golden Age* of March 5, 1930).
417. *In Trouble from Nuisance Witnesses Mary Seeks Help from Pearl.* July 1964, 4 pp. (About why a Witness of twenty-five years left the Watchtower).
418. *"Judge Not"* (The disfellowshipping includes the committee's letter of Jagdeo and Suresh Madoo of Trinidad). Aug. 12, 1964, 4 pp
419. *The "False Anointed" "Prophets" and the "Harvest."* N.d., 24 pp. (A critique of the Watchtower teachings on eschatology and other topics).
420. *Christ-Mass, Commonly Called Christmas.* Dec. 1964, 24 pp. (Argues that Christians should not celebrate Christmas).

421. *The Olivet Prophecy.* Jan., 1965, 40 pp. (On the signs of the end and Christ's second coming).
422. *A Review of Otto Sadlack's Book.* May 25, 1964, 32 pp.
423. *The Nightmare* (double postcard). Aug. 7, 1965, 4 pp. (A set of Scriptures criticizing the Watchtower).
424. (Order blank postcard). Aug. 7, 1965, 2 pp.
425. (Exhortation letter). Aug. 7, 1965, 1 p.
426. *'Nightmare' and 'Sole Channel,' Large.* Oct. 2, 1965, 2 pp.
427. *What Has the Watchtower Kingdom Been Doing Since 1914?* Sept. 25, 1966, 8 pp. (A good discussion of the Watchtower's failed prophesy).
428. (Postcard order). Dec. 23, 1966, 1 p.
429. *The Key to Studying the Bible: As Recommended in February 1st 1949 Watchtower.* Feb. 1969, 2 pp.
430. *Letter* (delaying Memorial date). March 17, 1969, 1 p.
431. *Invitation Card.* April 12, 1969, 2 pp.
432. (Correspondence letterhead explanation). July 10, 1969, 1 p.
433. (Form letter for Jehovah's Witnesses' names). Sept. 5, 1969, 1 p.
434. *Three Historic Documents: Six Sermons: The Doctrine of Election; the "Seventh Sermon"* by George Storrs (a reprint of 1847 ed.). Sept. 10, 1969, 100 pp. (On the soul, the state of the dead and eschatology; an important document that Russell used to develop his theology).
435. *Letter to Interested Church of Christ Responders.* Sept. 27, 1969, 1 p.
436. *The Permission of Evil--Why?* June 26, 1972, 87 pp. (A reprint of articles in *Back to the Bible Way*, covers the purpose of evil and why God allows it).
437. *Pergamos Means Watchtower.* June 30, 1972, 1 p.
438. *Back to the Bible Way: Seventeen-Year Index 1952 to 1967.* April 1971, 76 pp.
439. *Back to the Bible Way Index, Vol. 16, to Vol. 19.* Oct. 30, 1972, 3 pp. (An index to Goodrich's magazine).
440. *Who Is the Antichrist?* Aug. 20, 1974, 1 p.
441. *Rejoice!* March 20, 1975, 1 p.
442. *Olivet Prophecy.* March 20, 1975, 40 pp.
443. *"God's Organization;" J.F.R. Speaks Again; the Hierarchies Compared.*
444. *N.H. Knorr Speaks;'Analyzing Yankee Stadium Speech on July 30, 1953.*
445. *Salvation.* N.d., 4 pp. (Argues salvation is by Grace).

M. General Bible Student Publications

Most of these are independent groups and many persons associated with the groups listed are discussed in the previous section. Most follow basic Russell teachings, and many feel they adhere more closely to Russell than do the larger Bible Student groups.

Associated Bible Students (Waterbury, CT)

Booklets

After the War--What? (Waterbury, CT)
The Bible Made Plain. (Waterbury, CT) N.d., 26 pp.
Distress of Nations Precedes Armageddon. (Waterbury, CT) N.d., 24 pp.
How to Study the Bible and Have It Make Sense. 1985 (Waterbury, CT) 32 pp. (Basic background on the science of Hermeneutics).
Do You Know? (Waterbury, CT) N.d., 12 pp.
The Kingdom of God. Wilmington, DE, n.d., 14 pp.
"The Divine Plan of the Ages Epitomized." (Paterson, NJ) 16 pp.
If You Are Gods. Paterson, NJ, n.d., 8 pp. (On the basis of salvation).
Rawson, Kenneth. *the Association of Bible Students, Background, History, Organization, Ministry.* 24 pp.
_____. *The Association of Bible Students, Its Historic Position Toward War.* 10 pp.
_____. *The Time to Favor Zion Is Come.* 14 pp.
_____. *Truth's Challenge.*

Berean Bible Students (Vancouver, WA)

Books

Edgar, John, and Morton Edgar. *Great Pyramid Passages* (a photo lithographic reprint of
        the 1923 (part 1, 409 pp.) and 1924 (part 2, 1,310 pp) eds. of *Great Pyramid
        Passages* and the 1924 ed. of *The Great Pyramid: Its Scientific Features*). 217 pp.
        Bound with *The Great Pyramid: Why Was It Built and Who Built It?* by Morton
        Edgar (retypeset). 38 pp. Republished in 1976 with publisher's foreword, hb.

Edgar, John, Morton Edgar, and Minna Edgar. *Faith's Foundations* (a retypeset reprint of
        all of John, Morton, and Minna Edgar's small booklets; see Edgar's works for a
        complete list). Republished in 1976 with publisher's foreword; 372 pp.

Miami Valley Bible Students Ecclesia

Newsletter

Bible Students Newsletter. Vol. 1, No. 1, 1972 to date, published quarterly in March,
        June, Sept. and Dec. (An excellent source of information on the current activities
        of the Bible Student movement.)

Booklets

Directory [of] Bible Students' Ecclesia Meetings, June 1979. Centerville, OH, 1979, 28
        pp.
The Lord Is Present Now. C. 1975, 8 pp. (Argues Christ returned when the "signs" were
        fulfilled in our day).
Israel! Born to Destiny. C. 1975, 12 pp. (Argues modern Israel fulfills the scriptural
        prophecy).

Chicago Bible Students (Chicago, IL)

Many other Watchtower splinter groups exist, most follow basic Russell
teachings, and many feel they adhere more closely to Russell than do the larger Bible
Student groups. The most active Bible Student publishers are the Chicago Bible Students.
Their book republishing committee has now reprinted all of Russell's known works.

The Chicago group has also been most creative and diverse in producing its own
publications while still relying heavily on the ideas and conclusions of Russell.   In
addition to a number of attractive tracts they have published such items as *The Time Is at
Hand*, a pocket-purse calendar booklet and *Food for Thinking Christians*, not to be
confused with Russell's work by the same name.

One group, the Christian Bible Students of Warren, Michigan which was
doctrinally similar to the Dawn, disbanded in 1978. They assumed some independence
from the Dawn Bible Students in the late 1960s but retained most of the Dawn beliefs, and
stressed the works of C.T. Russell. They also broadcasted a radio program, *The Harvest
Message Broadcast* out of Nashville, Chicago, and Detroit.The magazine *The Harvest
Youth* (now *Harvest Youth News*). Vol. 1, No. 1, 1960 to date.

Books (Reprints of Russell's works)

Bible Students Manual. Reprinted from the original Watchtower 1909 Edition, 482 pp.
        and appendix.
Convention Report Sermons: Pastor Russell's Convention Discourses. C. 1970, 515 pp.
        (A collection of sermons, testimony meetings and special service transcripts by

Pastor Charles T. Russell as found in the "Convention Reports" from 1906 to 1916, plus press coverage of the various conventions, interviews with Pastor Russell, and an exhaustive account of his 1912 world missionary tour).

Daily Heavenly Manna. N.d., c. 208 pp. (Contains the text of the original 1905 ed., *Watchtower* comments, but not the birthday record).

Harvest Gleanings. 3 Vols c. 1979, 780 pp. (A collection of Charles T. Russell's writings which have been typeset and with a Scripture Index added. The works included in the first volume are *The Three Worlds,* (actually this book is by Barbour) *The Russell vs. Eaton Debates, The Russell vs. White Debates, Old Theology Quarterly Tracts,* and *Bible Students Monthly Tracts*).

Pastor Russell's Sermons (reprint of Watchtower 100,000 ed. 1917). 803 pp.

Photodrama of Creation. 1976 (retypeset, minor corrections made, and many new illustrations added; originally published in 1914 by WtBTS), 110 pp., hb., pb.

Reprints of the Original Watchtower and Herald of Christ's Presence. Vol. 1, 1879-1887, pp. 1-996; Vol. 2, 1888-1895; Vol. 3, 1896-1901; Vol. 4, 1902-1906, pp. 2, 2929-3,912; Vol. 5, 1907-1911, Vol. 6, 1912-1916; Index (also republished loose-leaf, and also bound in a 12-volume ed. (These reprints are reprints of the original *Watchtower* reprints).

What Pastor Russell Said (Photo reprint of 1917 d., edited by Leslie W. Jones, M.D.). 894 pp., hb.

What Pastor Russell Taught on the Covenants, Mediator, Ransom, Sin Offering, Atonement (Photo reprint of 1919 ed , edited by Leslie W. Jones, M.D.), 398 pp., hb.

What Pastor Russell Wrote for the Overland Monthly. 456 pp., hb. (Also includes table of contents, scriptural index, and consecutive pagination. Contains photocopies of all articles which appeared from Feb. 1909 to his death in Oct. 1916).

Original Publications (Books)

Book Republishing Committee. *Expanded Biblical Comments 1879-1916 Old Testament.* 1982, 402 pp. (An index of Russell's words listed by Scripture; producing an extensive Bible commentary taken from Russell's published works similar to *The Bible Students Manual.* This index includes all unsigned articles and those by other writers that Russell used in his publications; the Committee felt that if Russell printed something, he agreed with it, thus all of these articles should be included).

_____. *Expanded Biblical Comments 1879-1916, new Testament.* Same as above, except on the new Testament, which the Committee expects to be complete by 1985.

Poole, Laura Kathleen. *Palestine, Israel's Inheritance.* Mimeographed, n.p., n.d., 91 pp.

_____. *Sons of the Highest.* C. 1942, 205 pp.

_____. *The Ten Camels.* Melbourne, Australia, 1940, 137 pp. (reprint ed. 1955), 144 pp., pb. (The Divine Plan presented in language for children six to ten years of age).

_____. *The Son of the Highest.* C. 1975, 384 pp. (A well illustrated, well written story of Christ which is woven around the conversations of a mother and daughter, a follow-up to the author's *The Ten Camels*).

Booklets

Comfort & Consolation. N.d., 28 pp.

"Exceeding Great and Precious Promises." 1954, 96 pp. (A collection of writings from the early *Watchtowers, Studies in the Scriptures* (Vols. 1, 5, 6), and *Tabernacle Shadows*).

Excerpts from the Divine Plan of the Ages. N.d., 16 pp.

In the Beginning God.... c. 1970, 8 pp. (About the hope of a new world).

Rejoice, O Israel! N.d., 15 pp.

This Land Is Mind! N.d., 16 pp. About Israel, ancient and modern.

Where Are the Dead? (reprint of original written in 1900, with footnotes added). N.d., 108 pp. Reprinted later with different cover and slightly larger.

Christian Bible Students (Warren, MI).

This group, which was doctrinally similar to the Dawn, disbanded in 1978. They assumed some independence from the Dawn Bible Students in the late 1960s, but retained most of the Dawn beliefs, and stressed the works of C.T. Russell. They also broadcasted a radio program, *The Harvest Message Broadcast* out of Nashville, Chicago, and Detroit. They published *Harvest Message "A Herald of Christ's Presence."* Monthly, about 36 pp.from 1969 to 1978.

Fort Worth Bible Students (Fort Worth, TX).

Journal: *The Divine Plan Journal* usually published bimonthly

Booklets (all reprints of Charles T. Russell's publications)

The Bible versus the Evolution Theory. Photolithographic reprint of Watchtower 1912
          ed., reprinted 1973, 47 pp. (A critique of evolution).
The Divine Plan of the Ages. Reprinted, retypeset from an early 1900 ed., c. 1973, 88
          pp.
A Ray of Hope on a Troubled Sea. c. 1970, 10 pp. (The contents are selected from
          Pastor Russell's writings as a consolation message).
Our Lord's Return: His Parousia, Apocalypses and Epiphania. Photolithographic reprint
          of Watchtower 1900 ed.; also reprinted with author's foreword from the book *The
          Time Is at Hand* (1916), reprinted 1972, 73 pp.
Studies in the Scriptures. Photolithographic reprint, 1970, 800 pp. (The six volumes and
          Tabernacle Shadows are here bound in one volume).
What Say the Scriptures about Spiritism? Photolithographic reprint of Watchtower 1897
          ed., reprinted 1972, 119 pp.
What Say the Scriptures Concerning Hell? Reprinted, reset; from Watchtower 1900 ed.,
          c. 1973, 23 pp. pb.

Jewish Bible Students
          Since Pastor Russell's positive response to Zionism shortly after the turn of the
century, various Bible Students have felt a need for a special ministry with Jews. A few
worked toward conversion but most simply gave their active support to Zionism, a
movement which they believed fulfilled Bible prophesy.

Magazines: *Jews in the News.* Grand Rapids, MI, Vol. 1, No. 1, 1942. In 1968
moved to Paradise, CA, and changed its name to *Israel Restoration News.* Also *Israel
Digest.* Published in Jerusalem.The only other publication known is a book by Shelam
Ben-Hanan titled *This Is the Millennium.* 96 pp.

Love Ministries, Inc. (Worthville, KY)

Founded by Richard Hickman, a former Witness.

Magazine: *Love Magazine*, monthly, 16 pp., Vol. No. 1, 1981 (June) Name changed to
          Lovespirit May 1984, (Vol. 3, No. 11). (Last issue was Dec. 1985, Vol. 5, No.
          5).

Booklets

Bergman, Jerry. *I Am My Brother's Keeper.* 1984, 8 pp. (A story about Christian
          responsibility).
Francis, Richard. *Prophets of Profits.* 1983, 16. pp. (A general discussion and critique
          of Witness beliefs).
Thunderson, Michael (trans.). *The Way of Virtue*, 1983, 24 pp.

Pastor Russell Memorial Association

The Pastor Russell memorial Association of San Francisco was founded by Guy Bolger, who parted with Rutherford shortly after Russell's death. For 14 years they published a magazine titled *Berean Bible Student*. Ed. Guy Bolger. 9 to 34 pp., monthly (c. 1926 to c. 1940). The only known book is *Berean Poems*. San Francisco, CA, 1941, 56 pp.

N. Bible Student Literature by Individuals (Both books and booklets)

Berean Bible Student. *"That Faithful and Wise Servant."* San Francisco, CA, 18 pp.

Bible Research Council. *The Time of the End*. Manitoba, Canada, 84 pp. (A summary of Bible Student eschatology).

Bible Student's Association. *If Jesus Had Not Been Born*. Petersham, New South Wales.

Bible Student's Council. *God's Plan for Human Redemption*. Cheshire, B.S.C.

Bible Studies Fellowship San Diego, CA) *The Manner of Christ's Return and Appearing*. N.d., 59 pp.

_____. *A Ransom For All*. 1984, 34 pp. (Discusses Christ's sacrifice, its purpose and history).

_____. *"The Son of Man "* 1985, 30 pp. (Covers Christ's person and his second coming).

Bible Student's Publications. *For This Cause*. Bensenville, IL, c. 1979, 47 pp.

Black, Margaret Harris. *Paradise in Eden--How Lost and How Redeemed*. San Antonio, TX: Naylor Company, 3rd ed., 1963, 109 pp.

Bradenton Bible Students. *Daniel and the End of the Days*. Cortez, FL, c. 1975, 4 pp. (On how we know we are in the end time).

_____. *World Peace Then Armageddon*. Cortez, FL, c. 1975, 6 pp. (On Thess. 5:1-3).

Bricker, R.H., and Samuel McComb. *Who Is That Wise and Faithful Steward?* Pittsburgh, PA, n.d., 29 pp.

Bundy, Walter H. *Evil, Its Origin, Purpose and End*. Los Angeles, CA: Concordant Assembly Concern.

_____. *Paul's Inspired Letter to the Romans*.

_____. *The Sacred Scrolls of the Scriptures*.

_____. *Studies in the Scriptures, Investigating Bible Statements Analytically*. Los Angeles, CA: Concordant Concern, c. 1928, 160 pp. (Bundy was a Watchtower Pilgrim who left the Society and accepted many of the concordant groups beliefs such as universalism; this booklet is about his disagreements with the Watchtower and the rationale and basis for his new beliefs).

Bunker, Laurence H. *The Book and the Chosen People*. London, England: Chosen Books.

Carrington, Arthur. *Bible Versus Bank Rate*. Leeds, England: pub. by author, 1969, 4 pp.

_____. *God and the Common Market*. Great Britain: John H. Hirst & Co., n.d., 8 pp.

_____. *Is God Helping Israel?* 1967, 4 pp.

_____. *Perfecting Holiness in the Fear of God*. Great Britain: Headley Brothers, n.d., 8 pp.

Christian Bible Students. *Souvenir Notes from the Reunion convention of Christian Bible Students*. 1929, 112 pp.

Christian Fellowship. *Christ's Second Coming "The Hope of the World."* Manchester, England.

Coshocton Ecclesia. *Timely Excerpts from the Harvest Message*. Coshocton, OH, n.d., 124 pp., pb. (Much information taken from Russell's works, primarily a review of Russell's basic teachings).

Eddington, W. Clark. *A Letter to the Watford International Bible Student Association Class*. April 13, 1916.

Falkner, Carl G. *A Review, God's Wisdom versus Man's Wisdom*. Christian Fellowship Associates, OH, Jan. 1968.

Flood, Robert L. *Our Lord's Second Coming--Return to Earth Due for Our Time.*
    Roseville, MI, 1962.

Gaunt, Bonnie. *Stonehenge ... A Closer Look.* Ann Arbor, MI: Braun-Brumfield, 1979,
    222 pp. Reprinted with corrections by Bell Publishing Co., NY, 1982.

Gilbert, J.W. *In God's Own Words: A Useful Handbook for a Subject Study of the*
    Bible. Philadelphia, PA: pub. by author, n.d., 36 pp. (A compilation of
    scriptures listed under topic headings as "New Heavens and New Earth," and "The
    Second Death." No commentary is included).

Goulden. W.O. *Palestine, The Home of the Jews.* Greenville, TX.

Gray, Julian T. *The Authorship and Message of the Great Pyramid.* Cincinnati, OH: E.
    Steinman and Co., 1953, 306 pp.

————. *Which Is the True Chronology?* Cincinnati, OH, 1934, 154 pp., hb.

Greaves, Arnold E. *Are Wars to Cease on Earth?* Brooklyn, NY, 1965, 14 pp.

————. *"That Servant."* New York, 1932, 22 pp.

Harris, C.J. *When Will Wars, Sickness, Pain and Death Cease?* Vancouver, BC,
    Canada: pub. by author, n.d., 28 pp.

Harry, C. *Justification to Life, When? and How?* Brooklyn, NY, n.d., 16 pp.

Hollister, Horace Edward. *After Thirty Years Pastor Russell Answers 20 Up-To-Date*
    Questions on the Chronology. Chicago: The Society for Bible Research.

————. *"I Will Come Again"--Jesus? The Five Successive Phases of the Advent.*
    Chicago: The Society for Bible Research, 1950, 95 pp. (An extensive study of
    Christ's second coming).

————. *The Chronology and Time-Prophecies and the Bible.* 400 pp.

Horwood, Andrew. *The Revelation.* St. John's Newfoundland, Canada: unpublished
    duplicated notes, 1973, 41 pp.

Hudgings, William F. *Introduction to Einstein and Universal Relativity.* Arrow Book
    Co., 1922, 64 pp. (Hodgings was the first secretary/treasurer for *Golden Age*
    magazine).

Jones. Dr. Leslie W. *Souvenir Notes from Reunion Convention of Christian Bible*
    Students. Pittsburgh, PA, 1929.

————. *Transcontinental Tour of Pastor Russell.*

————. *The Jubilee System of Volume Two of Studies in the Scriptures.* Unpublished
    duplicated notes, c. 1953.

Kuehm, J.G. *A Voice from Switzerland.* 1932, 94 pp. This is a translation of *Das Tier*,
    a book on Revelation 13 and 17 by Werner Hodler, a Swiss Bible Student.

Kuehn, Hugo F. *The Coming of the Lord Draweth Near.* Assembly. by author, West
    Virginia booklet, 32 pp.

Lenfast, Edna T. *A Helping Hand for Bible Students: The Minor Prophets.* Bible
    Students, Acton, ME, 1967, 390 pp. (A verse by verse commentary on Hosea to
    Malachi).

————. *Brief General Monograph of the Prophecies.* N.d., 9 pp. (booklet).

————. *Charles Taze Russell 1852-1916.* N.d., 8 pp. (booklet).

————. *Ezekiel.* Acton, Main, 1965, 142 pp.

————. *Fellows of the Order of Royal Priesthood.* N.d., 68 pp. (booklet).

————. *God Through Isaiah Speaks to Israel.* Bible Students, Acton, ME, 1976, 329
    pp. (A verse by verse detailed commentary on Isaiah).

————. *Hail to the Brightness of Zion's Glad Morning.* N.d., 12 pp. (booklet).

————. *Jeremiah.* 1967, 278 pp.

————. *Proofs and Evidences of Messiah's Second Presence.* 51 pp.

————. *Revelation for the End of the Gospel Age.* Sanford, MA, 1965, 132 pp.
    Revised edition Bible Students, Acton, ME, 1985, 634 pp. (A large 8.5 by 11.5
    inch commentary on Revelation and Ezekiel relying heavily on Russell's writings).

————. *The Minor Prophets: Hosea to Malachi.* 1967. 290 pp., pb. (book).

Mitchell, Martin C. *Little Foxes Coloring Book.* Rutherford, NJ, 1965, 44 pp.

————. *Poems of the Way.* Rutherford, NJ, c. 1975, 192 pp. A book of poems, many
    reprinted from early *Watchtower* literature, especially *Poems of Dawn.*

Moore, John H. *The Day of Vengeance.* Vancouver, BC, Canada, 59 pp.

————. *Elias Shall First Come.* N.d., 32 pp.

————. *Israel, Type and Antitype.* N.d., 32 pp.

————. *Jerusalem of the New Testament.* Vancouver, BC, Canada, 1967, 30 pp.

————. *The New Covenant--Made with Whom?* Vancouver, BC, Canada, 1968, 28 pp.

_____. *To the Jew First, Will It Always Be So?* 1966, 28 pp.

_____. *Which Things Are An Allegory?* 1967, 30 pp.

New Albany Bible Students. *"What on Earth Is a Kingdom?"* New Albany, IN, 1982, 24 pp. (A well-illustrated, introduction to *The Divine Plan*; mostly pictures).

New Brunswick Bible Students (Edison, NJ) *Glossolalia (Tongues-Speaking); What Are Its Implications?* C. 1976, 39 pp. (A well done study written to refute the tongues movement, quotes some scientific studies).

_____. *What Is This World Coming To?* C. 1975, 39 pp. (On eschatology; and the permission of evil doctrine).

_____. *Where Are the Dead?* C. 1970, 108 pp.Rawson, Kenneth. *The Time to Favor Zion Is Come!* 1971, 31 pp.

North London Ecclesia. *Elias Shall First Come.* N.d., 24 pp.

Norwood, H. Dorothy. *The Bible Tells It Like It Is: The Imminent Fifth Universal Empire.* New York: Vantage Press, 1972, 153 pp. (Critique of many contemporary social issues including the occult, ecology, and a history of Christianity and the author's conclusions on doctrine and prophesy).

Olson, Carl W. *The World to Come, A Dissertation on the Divine Plan of God as Found in the Bible.* Minneapolis, MN, c. 1918.

_____. *A Treatise on the Revelation.* Published by author, Minneapolis, MN, 1918, 368 pp. (An extensive commentary on Revelation, much on chronology and Russell's errors in this area).

Panin, Ivan. *Biblical Chronology.* In two volumes. 328 pp., 1920? Panin was not a Bible Student. An often used supplementary text, mentioned by Paul Johnson in *The Present Truth*, Sept. 1, 1924 (p. 140) and recently reprinted by Canadian Bible Students.

_____; A.B. King; et al. *Ivan Panin's Scientific Demonstration of the Inspiration of the Scriptures.* Revised ed. Toronto, n.p., 1924.

Parkinson, James B. *Bible Student Fragments.* N.d., 32 pp.

_____. *The Bible Student Movement in the Days of C.T. Russell.* Los Angeles, CA: the author, 1965, 72 pp.

_____. *Chapters of History.* Mimeo by author, n.d., 10 pp. Discusses the last-day prophecies found in Daniel and Revelation.

_____. *New Testament Manuscript and Translation Studies.* Los Angeles, CA, 1970, 31 pp. (An effort to identify the major copy errors in the New Testament).

_____. *The Bible Student Movement.* Glendale, CA: pub. by author, 1976, 30 pp.

_____. *Bible Students' Fragments in Brief.* Glendale, CA: pub by author, 1976, 30 pp.

Phoenixville Bible Students. *The Lord Our God Is One Lord.* Kimberton, PA, n.d., 39 pp. (A critique of the Trinity doctrine).

Piqua Bible Students. *The Biblical Flood; A Scientific Confirmation.* Piqua, Oh, Piqua Bible Students, 1986, 32 pp. (Reprinted from *Bible Student Monthly*).

Prosser, C.E. *Interesting Data on Biblical Subjects.* Los Gatos, CA: pub. by author, n.d., 30 pp. (Selections from many sources which support Bible Student teachings).

_____. *On World Wide Ministry of Some of God's Servants.* Vol. 1, 102 pp., Vol. III, 320 pp. (A selection of Bible Student writings, Vol. I is by Russell Pollock).

Rice, Gilbert. *Salvation Promised in God's Covenants.* San Diego, CA: pub. by author, 1984, 44 pp. (An extensive review of the covenants and salvation as related to the classes, heavenly, earthly).

_____. *"When I Shall Take Away Their Sins."* San Diego, CA: Pub. by author, 1982, 30 pp. (A detailed commentary on the 11 chapters of Romans).

Schroeder, Charles, Compiler. *Harvest Time and Harvest Work.* Chicago: mimeographed, 1920, 10 pp.

Scripture Study Publishing House. *Sunrise: The Scheme Scripture.* Manchester, England, 1918.

Shallieu, Frank. *God, Angels, and Men.* Southfield, MI: C.L. Thornton, n.d., 69 pp. (A response to the chariots of the god's theology, much material on the Great Pyramid).

Stacy, Phyllis. *Gems From the Mine; Biblical Comments of Zion's Watchtower 1908-1976.* C. 1980, 698 pp. N.p. (A verse by verse compilation of the Watchtower's comments on most Bible verses; extremely useful for research).

Sunbom, Chester A. *Trumpets and Seals of Revelation.* Unpublished, 22 pp.
_____. *Notes on the Beast and His Image.* 38 pp.
Towell, Herbert. *The Book of Revelation.* London, England, 1918.
Welch, Edgar, and Gladys Welch. *Ending the Confusion.* Vista, CA: New View
        Publishers, 1976, 292 pp.
Young, J.W. *The Time of the End.* Winnipeg, Manitoba, Canada: Bible Research
        Council, n.d., 83 pp.

NON-AMERICAN OFFSHOOTS

The many doctrinal and organizational problems in America also caused schisms in many of the Watchtower's larger branch offices, especially the English speaking nations including Canada and England.

BRITISH AND CANADIAN GROUPS

The problems after Russell died especially affected England. As in America, in Britain a committee was formed after Pastor Russell's death to carry on the work outside of what they now viewed as the apostate Watchtower. Unlike America, close to half of Russell's followers in England left the Society. Also unlike the United States, the British brethren seceded primarily in one solid body from 1917-1925, forming *The Bible Students Committee* in 1919.

A conference of brethren from all over the country met at East Ham Town Hall, London, August 2-5, 1919. Shearn was appointed to be the first secretary and delegates from 65 seceded U.K. classes were present with instructions and written suggestions from about 40 more seceded classes (Hudson, 1989, p. 98). The group of seven formed the Bible Students Committee and soon began working with the American Pastoral Bible Institute and exchanged publications. The Bible Students Committee operated as a united body for about twenty years. By 1940 the annual election of a committee of seven became meaningless when only seven persons were prepared to stand for these positions. By 1945 the Bible Students Committee was dissolved because of differences of persons viewpoint concerning doctrine and policy (see *Bible Student Monthly* Dec. 1945).

About 1922 when PSL Johnson organized the LHMM in the United States, a small group organized under that name in Britain. In 1924 William Crawford organized the "Old Paths" group to stress certain doctrines. Both he and his wife remained in close fellowship with the main body of Bible students until they died. After about 1940 an emerging difference of outlook regarding the present or future advent began to develop into a difference in doctrinal beliefs, but what is left of the entire movement remains intact as a group. The British Bible Students Committee produced the following publications:

Books

Barton, B.H. *God's Covenants.* England: Bible Students Committee, 1930, 48 pp.
Russell, CT. *Divine Plan of the Ages.* 1922, library edition, 350 pp.
Shearn, H.J. *The Plan of God in Brief.* 1922, 102 pp. (last English edition. 1938, Revised English edition. 1993).
_____. *A Review of the Doctrines.* 1924.

Booklets

Holmes, T. *Beauty of Holiness.* 60 pp., 1940
Russell, C.T. *Parables of the Kingdom.* 30 pp., 1939.
Hudson, Albert O. *Promise of His Presence.* Second Advent Theology.
_____. *Lucifer Prince of Evil.* 1939.

A. Bible Fellowship Union (London, England)

The modern Bible Fellowship Union was founded in 1945 to propagate Russellite doctrine, especially the pre-Millennial advent of Christ and the doctrine of future probation relative to the Millennial reign of Christ. Other formal goals include the upholding of the historical accuracy of the Bible and investigating matters of history, archaeology, prophecy, etc., as related to the Bible teaching. The Bible Fellowship Union is not formally connected with any other Christian group. The group was headed by Albert O. Hudson (born in 1899) until he died in about 1993. In 1995 Derrick Nadal became editor. Hudson along with P.L. Read was considered by many to be one of the leading Bible Student scholars. He was originally connected with the Watchtower Society but left soon after Russell's death and has been active in the British Bible Student movement ever since.

Hudson writes extensively not only about Biblical doctrine but also about archaeology, history, Biblical languages, and science and the Bible. The magazine *Bible Study Monthly* (founded in 1924) was started at the inception of the Bible Students Committee and continued by national vote as its chief publication when the group became the Bible Fellowship Union. The circulation of *The Bible Study Monthly* is about 1,000 copies per issue in Great Britain and about the same in America and the rest of the world. At their peak they claimed 246 classes with 4,500 members, but by 1996 were reduced to 7 organized classes with a total normal attendance of only 75. (See letter from Albert Hudson in *Herald of Christ's Kingdom*, March-April 1996, page 17).

Magazines

Bible Study Monthly. Ed. Ebenezer Housden 1924-1935, Albert O. Hudson 1936 to present. Vol. 1, No. 1, Jan. 1924 to date (Vol. 70, 1993). 24 pp. each issue. *The Bible Students Committee Monthly* was begun in 1924, changed to *Bible Students Monthly* in 1927 and later to *Bible Study Monthly* (now a bimonthly).
Bible Students Broadsheet. Nos. 1, 2, 3, 4. March 1965, 1966, 1967, 1968. A United Kingdom newsletter.
Millennial Message. Nos. 1, 2, 3, 4, 1947-1952. A "Present Truth" newspaper.
The Young Bible Students Messenger, edited by D. Nadal 1946 to about 1964?
Gainsborough Journal. A newsletter subtitled *News of Happenings at Gainsborough House* (the Bible Fellowship Eventide Trust retirement home first mooted in 1975) (Issue 25 was dated January 1997).

Books and Booklets (all published in Hounslow, Middlesex, England)

God's Fulfilling Purpose, An Outline of the Divine Plan. 1953, 20 pp.
In the Land of Beginning Again. 1953, 22 pp. Four stories of the Resurrection and the Millennial world.
Jacob's Trouble. 1st edition. 1942; 2nd edition., revised in 1968, 32 pp. (An exposition of Gog and Magog chapters in Ezek. 38-39).
Holmes, T. *From a Prison Cell.* 1945, 40 pp. (Reflections on the prison epistles of Paul).
Ford, G.A. *The Cup of Our Lord.* 1965. 16 pp. (About Christ's passion).
Hudson, Albert O. *Sixteen Scriptural Truths.* 1954, 30 pp.
_____. *The Tragedy of Samson.* 1960, 52 pp.
_____. *The Tower of Babel.* 1962, 52 pp. (The history of the tower of Babel).
_____. *The Christian Doctrine of Baptism.* 1964, 32 pp.
_____. *Obadiah, the Messenger of Judgment.* 1965, 52 pp. (An exposition of the prophecy of Obadiah).
_____. *The Spirit of Prophecy.* 1965, 52 pp. (The nature of Biblical prophecy and the principles of its interpretation).
_____. *The Coming of the King.* 1968, 64 pp. (On Christ's Second Advent).
_____. *Watcher in Gethsemane.* 1969, 16 pp. (About Christ in Gethsemane).
_____. *The Golden Future.* 1st edition. 1939; 4th edition. 1970, 36 pp. (Study of the future as discussed in the Bible).
_____. *The Mission of Jonah.* 1st edition. 1946, 2nd edition. 1970, 80 pp.
_____. *God of All Space.* 1971, 48 pp. (The impact of space science on Christian

belief).
_____. *The Virgin Birth of Christ.* 1972, 24 pp.
_____. *The Millennial Gospel of Jesus.* 1st edition. 1947; 2nd edition. 1974, 32 pp.
    (A study of the New Testament on the Millennium).
_____. *Future Probation in Christian Belief.* 1975, 88 pp. (The basis for salvation and
    how it is achieved).
_____. *Samuel--Greatest of the Judges.* 1975, 38 pp.
_____. *Bible Students in Britain.* 1989, 200 pp. (An illustrated history of the British
    movement. Available only to readers of the Bible Study Monthly).
_____. *The Almighty, The Eternal*, 40 pp. 1994.
_____. *Paradise on Earth*, 100 pp. 1995.
Musk, F. *A Glimpse of God's Plan.* 1948.
Nadal, D. *Shepherd of Salvation.* 1967, 24 pp. (discusses three incidents in the life of
    Jesus).
Reynolds, C.O. *A Material Paradise.* 1953 (About the blessings of the Millennium).

Booklets, Numbered Set: 31 *The Bible--The Book for Today.* N.d., 11 pp.; 32.
World Conversion--When? N.d., 15 pp.; 33 *The Divine Permission of Evil.* N.d. 11
pp.; 34. *Everlasting Punishment of Evil.* N.d.,11 pp.; 35. *Conversion in the After-life.*
N.d., 15 pp.; 36. *The Resurrection of the Dead.* N.d., 15 pp.; 37. *The Secoind Advent--
Its Nature and Purpose.* N.d. 15 pp.; 38. *The Call and Destiny of Israel.* N.d., 15 pp.;
39. *The Personality of the Devil.* N.d., 11 pp.; 40. *The Gifts of the Spirit.* N.d., 12 pp.;
41. *Man--The Image of God.* N.d. 12 pp.; 42. *The Call and Purpose of the Church.* N.d.
4 pp.; 43. *The Aniquity of the Books of Moses.* N.d. 4 pp.; 44. *The Reality of God.*; 45.
The Destiny of Man.

B. New Jerusalem Fellowship (Ormskirk, Lancashire, England)

The New Jerusalem Fellowship is the name of a loose group of the Bible Students
united by the writings of Dr. F.S. Edgell, one of the members of the original Bible
Students Committee. During World War I he began circulating a mimeographed
newsletter at irregular intervals. In 1922, this then-unnamed periodical was given the title
Fellowship, later changed to *New Jerusalem Fellowship*. Most of Dr. Edgell's works
appeared in the magazine until he died.
    After Dr. Edgells death, the New Jerusalem Fellowship was headed by
E.T.Springett Moxham until his death in the late 1980s. Moxham became acquainted with
Dr. Edgell in the early 1940s and they worked together until Dr. Edgell's death in the early
1950s. Dr. Edgell was also well acquainted with Charles Russell and was obviously
much influenced by him.
    The fellowship stresses "freedom from all parties, sects, and creeds" and "the man
Jesus Christ who gave himself a ransom for all." Their book-length works explain the
particular message of the New Jerusalem Fellowship, which could be labeled as a form of
Anglo-Israelism. The book-length works listed below explain the particular message of the
New Jerusalem Fellowship, which could be labeled a variety of Anglo-Israelism.

Magazine: *New Jerusalem Fellowship: The Church Without Walls.* Last Ed. by Mrs. J.
B. Lawson. Vol. 1, No. 1, 1922 to 1993, published monthly, each 14 pp. The
forerunner of this magazine was started in 1914 and was mimeographed and stapled.

Books, Booklets

Edgell, F.B. *Correspondence with Charles Taze Russell and Others, 1902-1937,* 1938.
A Nation's Inheritance, 1938; 2nd edition. 1960, 48 pp.; *Man's Destiny.* 1946, 200 pp.;
Tabernacle Types, 1952, 36 pp.; *Man's Dilemma.* 1961, 68 pp.

C. Old Paths Publications (Ilford, England)

This group was directed for years by William Crawford, who was more rigid regarding doctrine than most Bible Students and concluded that the last days harvest was essentially over in the 1920's. He did not support the future Advent view and fully accepted the second presence teaching of Russell. Crawford created the first division in the Bible Students Committee (he was one of the original seven) in 1925 and soon thereafter began to publish his views in a series of pamphlets. The two series published were: (1) an unnumbered and undated set and (2) a numbered series that evolved into a monthly magazine. This second series began in 1932 and continued until 1961. A polemic against Crawford is found in Paul S.L. Johnson's *Gershonism* (published by the Laymen's Home Missionary Movement). Crawford originally wanted his views published over the Bible Students committee imprint, but a national vote of the committee recommended they be published separately. This amicably settled the controversy, and Crawford remained in fellowship with the entire movement until his death in 1957 (Hudson, 1989, pp. 123-125). (See Obituary in Oct./Nov. 1957 *Bible Students Monthly*).

Magazine: *Old Paths.(*1932 to 1961) Ed. by William Crawford until his death in 1948.

Books (most by Crawford and his co-worker Arnold Dinsdale)

Symbols of Revelation: Their Interpretation. 1953, 131 pp. (A commentary on most of
    Revelation).
Old Paths Publications: Part I. N.d., bound copy of "The End of All Things," 48 pp.;
    "Supplement," 28 p.; "Sealing the Servants of God," 28 pp.; "War in Heaven,"
    72 pp.; and "Thy God Reigneth!," 40 pp.; total of 216 pp.

Booklets (mostly by Crawford and listed in approximate publication order)
Justification: The Fact and Philosophy. 16. pp. 1919.; *Thy God Reigneth!* N.d., 40 pp.
The Unsearchable Riches of Christ. N.d., 48 pp.; *Gleanings in Revelation I.* 1944, 94
pp.; *Gleanings in Revelation II.* 1948, 152 pp.;*I srael's Tabernacle: Shadow and
Substance.* 1951, 52 pp.; *Justification by Faith.* N.d.; *The Three Great Covenants.*N.d.;
The Ransom and Sin offering N.d.; *The Midnight Cry.* N.d.; *Watchman, What of the
Night?* N.d.;*The End of All Things.* N.d.;*The End of All Things.* N.d. (supplement);
Sealing the Servants of God. N.d.; *The New Covenant in the Book of Hebrews.* N.d.;
War in Heaven. N.d.; *Thy God Reigneth.* N.d.;

Booklets (updated but numbered; listed in publication order).1. *Day of Atonement--Type
and Antitype;* 2. *Justification and Consecration--Their Order;* 3. *The Saints in Glory--Who
Are They?;* 4. *Millions Who Will Never Die. Why?;* 5. *The Harvest, When and What
For?;* 6. *The Kingdom Witness, What and When?;* 7. *The "Channel" Doctrine Examined;*
8. *Sound Doctrine*; 9. *This He Did Once--When and How?;* 10. *Strong Delusions. Why
Permitted?;* 11. *The Ransom for All--Scripturally Defined;* 12. *Tabernacle Figures
Explained;* 13. *Things You Should Know*; 14. *Lamps That Are Going Out*; 15. *Three
Views of Atonement;*16. *Back to Babylon;* 17. *The Time of Harvest;* 18. *The Work of
Harvest;* 19. *The Harvest Home;* 20. *The Winter Time;* 21. *Questions on Justification;* 22.
Questions on the Covenants; 23. *Questions on the Ransom;* 24. *False Christs and False
Prophets;* 25. *Within the Holy Place;* 26. *The Work of God Today;* 27. *Our Gathering
Unto Him;* 28. *Ye Must Be Born Again;* 29. *The Witness Work;* 30. *Steadfast in the Faith*;
31. *War in Heaven--A Criticism Examined;* 32. *The Greater and More A Perfect
Tabernacle;* 33. *Who Is the Man Child?*

After pamphlet number 33, the *Old Paths Publications* series of booklets was a monthly
periodical which continued the numbering used in the above pamphlets, ultimately
producing over 350 issues. Issue 345-347 was a large pamphlet entitled *The Light of
Life.* No new material was produced after 1956, and all issues after 1956 were reprints.

D. Forest Gate Church (London, England)

At the time of Russell's death, Forest Gate was the second largest Watchtower class in England. William Crawford's father-in-law, F.G. Fuard, Sr., led the class to withdraw its support from Rutherford. But they were unable to tolerate the pressure of further divergent views from Russell and in 1939 began their own publication, *The Forest Gate Church Bible Monthly*. It was advertised in the United States by the Pastoral Bible Institute.

The group was 500 strong at the time of secession from the Watchtower, and by 1986 membership was down to 12. Soon thereafter they disbanded as a church and sold their church building. Only 9 members were alive in 1993, and most of these were in their nineties. *The Forest Gate Bible Monthly* ceased publication about 1985. The March/April 1985 issue contains a history of Forest Gate Church. The Forest Gate Church defined itself as an autonomous group of Christians who met regularly to worship God and study the Bible. The results of their deliberations were presented as a help to others through their *Bible Monthly* magazine. They believed that Christ died as a "ransom for all" and that He will return at the appointed time still in the future to collect His Bride--the Church-- and to set up His Kingdom here on earth. Also, prominently associated with the Forest Gate Church was S.H. French, who was an excellent writer.

Magazine

The Forest Gate Church Bible Monthly. Secretary: D. Sutcliffe began publishing in 1939; published bimonthly. Issues average 20 pp. Typeset until Jan. 1979.

Booklets

Our Lord's Return. C. 1951, 24 pp. (A critique of the 1874 date and Russell's second coming teachings; much on the term Parousia and the Olivet teachings). Reprinted by Charles Aldridge and Andrew Jarmola in 1991 of Watch and Pray, Collierville, TN.

French, S.H. *The Middle East in Bible Prophecy.* London, England: B.D.M. "Maranatha," n.d., 22 pp.

_____. *The Unsealed Book: An Exposition of the Book of Revelation.* London, England: Prophetic Light Publications, 1968, 113 pp.

Hart, Alf A. *Pamphlet on Forest Gate Elders Views.* Cardiff, England, 1923. Not an official publication.

"Bible Student" Series: *Do You Know?* 16 pp.; *Why Did God Give Us a Bible So Difficult to Understand?* 16 pp. (revised edition, 32 pp.); *The True Trinity; The Prince of Life; Does Death End All Probation? Is There a Second Chance?* 32 pp.; *The Parables of Our Lord; The I.B.S.A. or Russellites in Prophecy.* 129 pp. (revised edition, 192 pp.); *Biblical Figures of Speech; The Book of Hebrew; The Telescope of Faith; Miracles; The Book of Romans.*

E. Maran-atha Conference (London, England)

The Maran-atha (Greek for "Our Lord Cometh") Conference corresponds to the Grove City Berean Conference in the United States. In 1942, the Maran-atha fellowship was formed from a sizable secession from the Watchtower Society then chiefly in the Manchester area. They were distinguished by viewing the second advent as a future event (some claimed it would be physically visible) a thesis hitherto unknown in the fellowship except for the Forest Gate Church. The group has now entered into full fellowship with those from the original Watchtower secession.

Magazine: *Maran-atha: The Lord Cometh!* Began publishing in 1951 and ceased publication in 1985, usually published bimonthly, each issue 12 pp. S.H. French of

Forest Gate Church also published in this magazine and under their imprint.

Book: *The I.B.S.A. or Russellites in Prophecy.* 129 pp. (revised edition, 192 pp.).

F.   Goshen Fellowship

Jessie Hemery became a Bible Student in 1888, and in 1901 Russell appointed him London branch manager, a post he held until 1951. He was also the vice-president of *The International Bible Student Association* (a Watchtower corporation) until 1946. Hemery was one of the most prominent Bible Students (see 1938 Watchtower, pp 272 and 336), and he maintained his association with the Society for many years, although his relations in later years were strained until he finally left.

Hemery once idealized the early Bible Student movement and agreed with most all of Russell's early beliefs. While doing research for a *Watchtower* article though, he became convinced that the fulfillment of most of the Bible book of Revelation was still in the future (a position that is and was totally unacceptable to the Society) and that the 1914 invisible return of Christ was totally without foundation. He first published his ideas in *Revelations Unfolded* (Hilltop Publishing Company, 1951).

Because Hemery was a "Rutherford man" and not a "Knorr Man" his many disagreements with the Society finally caused him to be disfellowshipped in 1951. Hemery (who died in 1955) agreed with many of the pre-1909 Watchtower views on the covenants and other matters and resisted especially the changes brought about by the Knorr administration. To disseminate his views, he founded the Goshen Fellowship in 1951. The group is currently headed by Frank L. Brown.

Both Jesse Hemery and Frank Brown maintained until their death that they were appointed by God to dictate "what is divine truth" to the world, generally manifesting the very spirit which caused the original Bible Student secession in 1919. It is thus not surprising that they did not join with the existing Bible Students fellowship and organization. When they left in 1951, their ideas and beliefs as ex-JWs were so alien to the original Bible Student movement that many of the latter had difficulty in recognizing them as brethren "in the truth." They have shown little desire to associate with the mainline ex-Russellite movement, claiming rather to represent the whole truth themselves.

Books (all published at Bexleyheath, Kent, England)

Hemery, Jesse. *Revelations Unfolded.* London, England: Hilltop Publishing Co.,
    c. 1951.
_____. *The Book of Daniel Unfolded.* London, England: Hilltop Publishing Co.,
    c. 1951.
_____. *The Second Coming of Christ, Earth's New Ruler.* London, England: Hilltop
    Publishing Co., c. 1951.
_____. *Christ's Great Prophecy of the Coming Events.* London, England: Hilltop
    Publishing Co., 1951.
_____. *The Letters to the Seven Churches in Asia.* London, England: Hilltop
    Publishing Co., 1955.
_____. *Preaching Christ to the Samaritans, Ancient and Modern.* Nd.
_____. *Who is that "Evil Servant"?* Nd.

Magazine: *Zion's Herald Journal of the Goshen Fellowship.* Ed. Jessie Hemry until
    1955, then Frank L. Brown. Vol. 1, No. 1, July 1965 to date.

Booklets series called *Zion's Herald,* authored by Frank L. Brown).*Christ Jesus Warns His Disciples. 1967, 84 pp.; The Scripture of Truth: The Vision: Its Understanding.* 1967, 84 pp.; *The Prophecy of the Book of Esther. 1967, 83 pp.; The Double Song, the Spirit and Bride; God's Plan and Purpose of Things to Come. 1968, 172 pp.; The Rise of*

Babylon the Great: Its Time Appointed of God. 1968, 107 pp.; *The Judgment of Babylon the Great.* 1969, 87 pp.; *Laodicea: The Angel and the Church.* 1969, 100 pp.; *Unity of the Faith: Judgment of the House of God.* 1969, 96 pp.; *The End of Years.* 1969, 90 pp.; *The Revelation of Jesus Christ.* 1970, 52 pp.; *The Ordinances of Heaven.* 1970, 99 pp.; *The Prophecy of Joel.* 1970, 86 pp.; *Ministry of the Lamb.* 1970, 108 pp.; *Wisdom: Her Seven Pillars.* 1970, 110 pp.; *My Servant Job (Part I).* 1971, 216 pp.; *My Servant Job (Part 2).* 1971, pp. 223-421; *God's Purpose in Life of Samson.* 1971, 84 pp.;*Thine the Kingdom O Lord.* 1971, 96 pp.; *The Preacher and 'I.'* 1971, 163 pp.; *Jonah: "Read:" In the Light of the Unveiling of Jesus Christ.* 1973, 72 pp.; *The Revealer of Secrets: Joseph: God's Chosen Interpreter.* 1973, 102 pp.; *Zechariah and the Heavenly Messenger.* 1973, 95 pp.; *Elisha, A Change of Ministry: The House of Healing.* 1973, 95 pp.; *The Lord of the Harvest and the Daughter of Zion: A Message for the Jews.* 1973, 79 pp.; *Paradise: God's Blessing for the Meek.* 1873, 84 pp.; *The Kingdom Gospel, What Is It? Teaching: Preaching: Publishing: When? How? Why?* 1973, 72 pp.; *The Resurrection: Its Priorities, How? Where? When? Will the Dead Be Raised?* 1974, 86 pp.; *Behold, I Make All Things New. The New Creation. New Heavens. New Earth. Joy in Heaven. God's Footstool Made Glorious.* 1975, 100 pp.; *The Son of Man His Coming.* 1975, 97 pp.; *La Reunion Prochaine de la Chrétienté* (Approaching Reunion of Christendom). 30 pp.; *Thou Hast Left They First Love.* N.d., 23 pp.

G. The Institute of Pyramidology (Harpenden, Hertfordshire, England)

Pastor Russell in the *Watchtower* and the *Studies in the Scriptures* introduced much speculation on God's plan and the Great Pyramid of Egypt into his movement. His late contemporary Morton Edgar did much to advance this speculation. This enterprise has been picked up most noticeably in recent years by Adam Rutherford and the *Institute of Pyramidology.*

The Institute of Pyramidology was founded in London in 1940 by the late Dr. Adam Rutherford, who retired at that time from his work as an accountant to devote all his energies to the Institute. Raised in a strong Christian family, Dr. Rutherford first became interested in the Great Pyramid at the age of nine in 1903. It was an interest which was to last all his life, and his contributions to the subject are not small. His early professional life as a school teacher helped him impart his knowledge to others in such a way as to make the matter easily understandable, and this quality is evident in his most famous work, *Pyramidology*, a study of the subject in five volumes.

The goal of the Institute of Pyramidology was to advance knowledge and research in Pyramidology in all its branches--scientific, prophetic, and religious. In essence, the belief that the information contained in the Great Pyramid of Egypt is so profound and so revealing that no one apart from Almighty God could have designed this structure. They teach that the basic message of the Great Pyramid is the same as the basic message of the Bible (so much so, in fact, that the Great Pyramid is termed "The Bible in Stone" based on evidence in the Bible itself). Pyramidology, which its believers find in many ways easier to understand than the Bible, portrays divine truth in a simple, logical manner, bringing comfort to those seeking to understand "the great mysteries of God in this age of confusion."

This group constituted a special interest fellowship only; Dr. Rutherford was fully committed to the general Bible Student fellowship and was an assiduous distributor of their literature. A man of boundless enthusiasm and tremendous energy, he was said to be highly esteemed by all who knew him. Hudson introduced him to the Septuagent chronology in 1931 after which he discovered that the Pyramid proves its chronology rather than that of the Masoretic text which Russell and Bowen of 1826 supported, and his very valuable exhaustive work on Bible Chronology is based on this manuscript.

Magazine: *Pyramidology Magazine.* Published in 1941 as an untitled monthly letter from the president of the Institute. In 1953 it was published quarterly and renamed *Pyramidology Magazine.* About 20 pp. per issue. It ceased publication on the death of James Rutherford, about 1982.

Books

Rutherford, Adam. *Pyramidology.* In 4 vols. Various eds. from 1957 to 1986. All
    published Harpenden, Hertfordshire, England: The Institute of Pyramidology.
Vol I. *Elements of Pyramidology. Revealing the Divine Plan for Our Planet.*
    Dunstable, Bedfordshire: Institute of Pyramidology, 1957, 219 pp. 2nd edition,
    Harpenden, Hertfordshire, 1962.Vol II. *The Glory of Christ as Revealed by the
    Great Pyramid.* Dunstable, Bedfordshire: Institute of Pyramidology, 1962.
Vol III. *Co-ordination of the Great Pyramid's Chronograph Bible Chronology and
    Archaeology.* Harpenden, Hertfordshire: Institute of Pyramidology, 1966.
Vol IV. *The History of the Great Pyramid.* Harpenden, Hertfordshire: Institute of
    Pyramidology, 1939, 400 pp.
_____. *Armageddon Due to Begin in the Autumn of 1928.* Glasgow, 1928.
_____. *Bridegroom Has Come; The Saints Now Entering Into Glory.* London,
    England, 1928.
_____. *The Midnight Cry--Behold the Bridegroom Come Go Ye Out to Meet Him.*
    Glasgow, 1925 (predicted Armageddon for Pentacost of 1928).
_____. *The Great Pyramid: A Scientific Revelation.* London, England, 1939.
Vol 1. *The Great Pyramid.* London, England, 1952, 154 pp.
Vol 2. *A New Revelation in the Great Pyramid.* London, England, 1945.
Vol 3. *Armageddon in 1955-6.* London, England, 1950.
Vol 4. *The Savior of the World as Revealed by the Great Pyramid.* London, England,
    1953.
_____.*Hebrew Chronology.* London, England, 1939.
_____. *Iceland's Great Inheritance.* London, England, 1939, 48 pp. Published in both
    English and Icelandic. The third edition was published only in Icelandic by Top
    Stone Books in 1979.
_____. *Israel-Britain or Anglo-Saxon Israel.* London, England, 1934; 1939 edition,
    828 pp.
_____.*Outline of Pyramidology.* London, England, 1957, 96 pp.
_____.*Treatise on Bible Chronology.* Harpenden, Hertfordshire, 1957, 555 pp.
_____. *Chart of the Great Pyramid. A Color Chart of the Great Pyramid's Interior
    Passages and Chambers.* 1957.
_____. *The Institute of Pyramidology.* C. 1974, 2 pp.
_____. *What Pastor Russell Taught about the Great Pyramid. His Remarkable Forecast.*
    N.d., 8 pp.

H. Bible Student Publishing Company (Edinburgh, Scotland)

The *Bible Student,* edited by William Robertson, was issued quarterly, Vol. 1,
No. 1, March 1914 to Vol. 9, No. 1, march 1924 (48 pp. per issue). There were no
issues for the years 1919, 1922, and 1924. Many articles are critical of the IBSA and of
both C.T. Russell and Rutherford. The periodical also contains letters to and from various
Watchtower officials, the Edgar brothers, Crawford, Paton, Hemery, etc. Also, *New Era
Enterprise* was published in the 1920s, possibly in Glasgow.

Robison, William (Ed.). *The Bible Student.* Vol. No. 1, March, 1914, Issued Quarterly,
    published at least until 1925 (no issues published in 1925). Published by The Bible
    Student Publishing Co., in 1909.
_____. No. 1. *Do You Know?* 16 pp. (Outlines, in a series of questions, the Creator's
    plans with relation to the human race--the ideal conditions of 6,000 years ago, why
    and how they were lost, and on what conditions they can be recovered).
_____. No. 2. *Why Did God Give Us a Bible So Difficult to Understand?* 32 pp.
    (Discusses why God's Book is written in a mysterious a style, why men are
    permitted to place so many contradictory "interpretations" upon it, and why have so
    many millions have lived and died in ignorance of its teachings).
_____. No. 3. *The True Trinity.* (Discusses the expressions--"The Father," "The
    Son," and "The Holy Spirit." Every important relative passage is explained in
    detail).

_____. No. 4. *The Price of Life*. (Investigates the question as to what a human being is composed of; defines and explains the terms "Life" and "Death" and treats the law of heredity. Also defines pardonable and unpardonable sins, and shows how the person's identity is preserved after death. The author further defines the object and traces the effect of Christ's crucifixion, explains the Works and the Faith Covenants or Agreements between God and Men, and sketches out a chart of the future of the human race).

_____. No. 5. *Does Death End All Probation? Is There a Second Chance?* 32 pp. (Treats the question of Future Probation; takes the middle position between the two extremes of "Calvinism" and "The Final Salvation of All").

_____. No. 6. *The Parables of our Lord*. (Covers 24 parables; and gives a detailed explanation of Christ's principles).

_____. No. 7. *The I.B.S.A. or Russellites in Prophecy*. 1925, 192 pp. (Origin and Growth and destiny of Pastor Russell's Movement, and an exposition of its principle errors of doctrine and practice).

God Has a Plan for Mankind. 13-page book published by the Associated Bible Students of Ilford, Essex.

Stracy, Tom S. *The Revelation*. Yeovil, Somerset, England, 1942, 229 pp. Stracy preferred to remain anonymous, thus used the pseudonym "Patmos." While with the Watchtower he published a set of miniature booklets on the Minor Prophets, applying them to theWatchtower of 1800-1916. The impact of his work was largely lost when he and most of his associates later left the Watchtower.

Berean Bible Institute. *Foregleams of the Golden Age*. Australia, 304 pp.; *Divine Plan of the Ages*. 350 pp. (blue cloth); *Plan of God--In Brief*. 102 pp.; *Some of the Parables*. 90 pp. (the BBI of Australia).

Booklets include*Christ's Return*. 35 pp., *Hell, Death, Spiritism*. 26 pp.,*Where Are the Dead?*; Poems of Dawn; Times of Refreshing; and Christ's Return.

I. The Way of the Truth Bible Association (Walsall Staffs)

Journal or Tract Series
The Standard of Jehovah, 8 pp. issue 3--June 1961. Writer/publisher A.L. Noake.

Booklet: *Are You looking for the Sign of the Coming of Jesus?* 48 pp. 1972.

Tracts: *What Can God Do with Dry Bones?* 2 pp. 1966, reprinted 1972. *Watchtower Chronological Deception*, 4 pp. 1972.

J. Christian Fellowships International

Christian Fellowships International was founded in 1981 by M. James Penton, Ph.D., and John Poole, at Lethbridge, Alberta, Canada.

Magazines

The Bible Examiner. Ed. M. James Penton, Ph.D. Vol. 1, No. 1, July 1981 to Vol. 3, No. 1, Jan-Feb. 1983. Published monthly. About 18 pp. per issue.
The Christian Quest. Ed. M. James Penton, Ph.D. Vol. 1, No. 1., Winter 1988 to Vol. 3, No. 1., Spring 1990. (Scholarly articles about the Watchtower and theology).

Booklets

Bartley, Colom. *Searching for the Deep Things of God*. Lethbridge, Alberta, Canada, 1981, 28 pp.

Burganger, Karl. *The Watchtower Society and Absolute Chronology.* Lethbridge,
    Alberta, Canada, 1981, 28 pp. (An excellent review of the major Watchtower
    Chronology problems)
Butt, Steve. *A Christian Letter from Steve Butt.* N.d. [1982], 14 pp.

EUROPEAN GROUPS

In 1919 to 1924 Watchtower offshoots were formed in Denmark, Norway,
Sweden and Finland. The British group kept in touch with these by periodic "pilgrim"
visits, but the work in Norway and Finland, then later Sweden, ceased all formal
activities. Close touch with Denmark, though, remained until 1960 or so. Anders Karlen
in Sweden leads a community that still survives from the Russell era. Carl Luttichau,
formerly WTBTS manager in Denmark in Russell's time, directed the independent
brethren in Denmark until his death about 1960 and P.C. Donk and George Van Halewin
in Holland kept the work going in Holland until the 1939-1945 war.

A. The Philanthropic Assembly of the Friends of Man

F.L. Alexander Freytag (1870-1947) was an effective organizer and a prolific
writer, and for a number of years was the manager of the Swiss branch of the International
Bible Students Association (IBSA) which he joined in 1898.

In the early years of the Watchtower much more tolerance existed for individual
opinions than today. As early as 1917 Freytag criticized Russell's *Studies in the Scriptures*
in print. When Rutherford became the president, many including Freytag could not accept
his rule and left. As a result Freytag was taken to court around 1919 by Rutherford and
the Watchtower Society. In 1920 he published the *Message of Laodicea* (a well written
critique of the Society) and Judge Rutherford responded with *The Harp of God*, his first
major book, before the year was out.

After 1919, Freytag wrote the pamphlet *A Message of Love to Laodicea*,
addressing it to the Adventists and the International Bible Students Association. Many
persons agreed with Freytag and soon allied around him. In 1919 he wrote the *Divine
Revelation* , in 1922 *The Message to Humanity*, and early in 1930 he finished his third
book, *Eternal Life*. In 1921, Freytag set up *The Church of the Kingdom of God*, also
known as the *Philanthropic Assembly of the Friends of Man*, taking with him many
Swiss, German, and French Bible Students. The Geneva London Bible and Tract Society
was also formed at this time. During the course of his ministry he also wrote various
pamphlets and composed almost 380 hymns and tunes. From the beginning, he published
a weekly sermon entitled *The Paper for All*. The intimate members of the family make
daily use of his book *The Dew of Heaven*, a Bible text for each day of the year with a
scriptural commentary by Freytag.

Freytag's principle concern was the problem of death. He believed that he had
found the answer in an intimate relationship with the person of Christ. One overcomes
death by conforming to the form of Jesus. By eschewing sin and following Jesus, one
escapes the wages of sin. Freytag's message of "death conquered" was set within a
framework of Russell's theology. His major deviation from Russell was the doctrine of
Universalism: he taught that eternal happiness is God's goal for *all* of mankind, without
exception. The replacement of hell's torment with soul annihilation as taught by Russell
was not far enough for Freytag, who demanded the conquering of death itself. The idea is
further supported by allegiance to the Universal Law--"God is love." This characteristic,
he taught, is the supreme fact of creation.

The movement is today especially strong in Switzerland, France, Germany,
Austria, Belgium, Italy and to a small extent in the United States. Several periodicals are
currently published, the most important being *The Monitor of the Reign of Justice*
(published once a month in England and Spain, and twice a month in the other above-
mentioned countries). It has a circulation of some 120,000 copies. Freytag believed that
eternal happiness is God's goal for all of mankind, and his newspaper, although of a
religious nature, tends to discuss secular topics in considerable detail. He also reprints a
large number of articles from secular sources. The movement owns a number of
"communities" in different countries of Europe. Although the movement still accepts

much of Russell's theology, this is not readily apparent from their publications.

Books (all authored by Freytag)

The Message of Laaodicea (A critique of the Watchtower Society). 1920.
The Divine Revelation: The Seven Spirits of God. Vol. I. Geneva, Switzerland: Disciples
    of Christ, 1922, 271 pp., pb. (French Ed., *La Révélation Divine*, 1920). (A
    history of Christianity showing that we are close to the establishment of God's
    kingdom on earth; the Watchtower teachings are very evident in this work).
The New Earth: The Message to Humanity. Vol. II. Geneva, Switzerland: Bible and
    Tract Society, 1922 (French Ed., *La Nouvelle Terre.* Paris, France, 1922), 2nd
    Ed. 1923, reprinted in New York, 1944, 301 pp., hb., pb. (A review of Freytag's
    theology as it relates to the New Earth doctrine).
Eternal Life: The Restoration of All Things. Vol. III. Geneva, Switzerland: The
    Messenger of the Lord, 1933; 2nd edition. 1969), 350 pp., pb. French ed.,
    L'Ange de l' Eternal. Paris, France, 1947. (About how humans can live forever
    on earth; much information about biology; critiques evolution).
Resurrection: Hope for the Whole Human Race. Vol. IV. Geneva, Switzerland n.d.
The Dew of Heaven: A Daily Devotional Reading, A Biblical Text and Commentary. N.d.

Booklets: *The Establishment of the Reign of Justice.* West New York, NJ, 1943, 64
pp. (Shows how history is leading to the new world), *The Light in the Darkness.* North
Bergen, NJ, c. 1945, 32 pp. (An outline of God's plan for humanity and the new earth;
includes history of the message, includes C.T. Russell); *The Lord's Second Coming:
What It Really Means.* London, England, c. 1946, 31 pp. (An excellent history of the
second coming teaching and the Miller-Russell movement); *The Mystery of Hell Revealed.*
London, England, 1946, 23 pp. (also in Spanish); *The Triumph of Good over Evil.*
London, England, 1953, 32 pp; *Popularies de l'Eglise du Royaume de Dieu.* 1944;
Hymns of the Messenger. Complete edition in French, German, Italian, abridged edition
in English, 1967; *The Destiny of Man.* c. 1969. Spanish only;*Consolation.* 1976;
Spanish; *Beautiful Christmas Stories.* c. 1978. Also Published in French; *The Morning of
the Resurrection (Le Matin de le Resurrection)*; *The Lord's Second Coming (La Seconde
Venue du seigneur)*; *A Word of Consolation.* c. 1978. *(Un Mot de Consolation)*;
The Triumph of Good over Evil. c. 1979. *(Le Triomphe du Bien sur le Mal) Is There a
God?* C. 1980. *(Y'atil due Dieu?)*; *Public Salvation.* c. 1981. *(Le Salut Publique)*; *The
Mystery of Hell Revealed.* c. 1980. *(Le Mystere de l'Enfer Devoile)*; *Man's Destiny.* c.
1981 *(La Destinee de L'Homme)*; *Living Experiences of God's Kingdom.* c. 1982.
(Histoires Vecues due Royaume de Dieu).

B.   The Association of Free Bible Students of France
(L'Association Francaise des Libres Etudients de la Bible)

This group is a French counterpart of the American Dawn Bible Association. They
published the *Dawn, Aurore,* since about 1951. The *Journal de Sion* began near Lille,
France, in 1956 and republished C.T. Russell's writings and some current articles. Polish
immigrants constitute the largest proportion of Bible Students in France.

Magazine:*Le Journal de Sion et Messenger de la Présence de Christ (Zion's Journal and
the Messenger of Christ's Presence).* Vol. 1, No. 1, 1956, published bimonthly
in Wallers, France.

Books

Vol. I. *Des Etudes des Ecritures.* (Vol. 1. *Studies in the Scriptures).*
Vol. 6. *Des Etudes des Ecritures.* (Vol. 6. *Studies in the Scriptures).*

Special Numbers of Zion's Journal listed in order of publication. *Quel est donc le serviteur fidele et prudent? (Who Really Is the Faithful and Discreet Servant?); L'Ecumenisme et la Bible (Eccumenialism and the Bible); Lé retablissement d'Israel (The Reestablishment of Israel); Rapport de Pilate sur Jesus-Christ (Dialogue of Pilate about Jesus Christ); Signes de la Presence de Christ (Signs of Christ's Presence); Apropos de l'infaillibilité des Papes (The Purpose of Papal Infallibility); La "Manne Celeste" ou nourritures spirituelle pour chaque jour (The Heavenly Manna or Spiritual Food for Each Day).Le Verite Concernant les Mortes (The Truth about the Dead); Monde ou vas-tu? (World, Where Are You Going?).*

C. German Bible Students

An early German offshoot was led by Samuel Lauper who published *Herold des Königreiches Christi (Herald of Christ's Kingdom)* and a German translation of Streeter's volumes on the Bible book of Revelation. Conrad C. Binkele began publishing *Der Pilgrim* in the 1930s, a work that was suspended when Hitler's government was in power (the Binkele and Boehmer families moved to Los Angeles in 1934). After the war, many Bible Students again received *Watchtower* literature for the first time in a decade, and some left the Society because of the many changes that occurred during the war. At this time *Die Brennende Lampe (The Burning Lamp)*, a journal similar to the American *Herald* and *Dawn*, began publication. Another publication, *Christliche Warte (Christian Watchtower)*, began in 1949 which stresses a preharvest theology. The *Tagesanbruch* began in Berlin around 1950 and later moved to Freiburg, Germany. The German general convention began in 1955 and is typically the host to about 200 Bible students. Many Bible Students also lived in the former East Germany. The booklets they publish include:

Burmester, Wilhelm. *Geheimnisvolle Aussprüche oder Das 2. Kommen des Herrn.* Lüneburg, Germany, 1967, 32 pp. *(Mysterious Sayings of the Second Coming of Our Lord).* (On the signs and theology of the second coming); *Der Göttliche Liebesplan in den Sternbildern.* N.d., 30 pp. *(The Divine Plan of Love in the Consolations); Die Weisse Wolke.* Lüneburg, Germany, 1971 *(The White Cloud).* (On the Great Pyramid and Russell's teachings); *Der Göttliche Steinzeuge.* Lüneburg, Germany, 1949, 20 pp. *(God's Witness Stone).* (About the Great Pyramid); *Bibel in Stein.* Lüneburg, Germany, 1971, 22 pp. *(The Bible in Stone).* (Argues for Russell's ideas using the Great Pyramid as proof); *Das Tier.* Lüneburg, Germany, 1975, 16 pp. *(The Animal).* (On escatology); *Wache auf, meine Seele.* Lüneburg, Germany, 1965, 16 pp. *(Awaken My Soul).* (An exposition of Ps. 57); *Erhebt ein Panier?* N.d. *(Lift a Banner); Die Sonnenuhr Ahas.* N.d. *(The Sundial of Ahas); Geheimnisvolle Aussprüche.* Lüneburg, Germany;

D. Greek Bible Students (Athens, Greece) (Also called the
Free Christian Church of Greece; started by C.J. Sonstas)

Constas, Constantine J. *The Revelation of Jesus Christ.* New York: Carleton Press, n.d., 638 pp.
_____. *"Heaven and Earth Shall Pass Away" Luke 21:33.* C. 1954, 13 pp.
_____. *A New World under New Heavens and on a New Earth.* C. 1960, 27 pp.
_____. *The Part of Israel in the Plan of God in Christ.* C. 1964, 25 pp.
_____. Christ's Great Olivet Prophecy. Athens, 1967.
_____. *An Open Letter.* Athens: unpub. dupl. notes, c. 1970.
An Open Letter of General Interest. N.d., 5 pp.
The Kingdom of Heaven Taking Place in Four Stages. N.d., 10 pp.
Has the Book of Revelation Any Special value for the Student of God's Word? N.d., 2 pp.

E. South India Bible Students Committee (Bangalore, South India)

In India L.S.P. Devasahayam (Davey) and his associates all left the Watchtower Society at the time of Russell's death and formed the *India Bible Students Association.* They have held conventions annually ever since 1921. Currently these conventions last about three days, attract over a hundred persons, and rotate from year to year among a few cities in India. The Bible Students Press publishes a monthly magazine in the Tamil language. Literature is also available in Telugu, Kanada, Canarese, and several other dialects. The few hundred Bible Students in India are scattered throughout the country but live primarily in South India.

Correspondence between Sudnar Raj Gilbert and H.A. Livermore of Portland, OR, led to foreign support of the work in India in 1947. The Northwest India Committee, consisting of one member each from the Vancouver, Seattle, Portland, and Salem Classes, receives cooperation from several Classes and individuals in the United States and Canada. Other assistance comes directly from Germany, France, and Australia. The Indian Bible Students Press has a working arrangement with the *Dawn* in America, and the group is also formally associated with the Dawn Bible Students, East Rutherford, NJ.

Magazine: *The Indian Bible Students' Association Monthly Magazine.* 1971 to date (Vol. 2, No. 5, May 1974), published monthly, each 20 pp.

Booklets:*The Bible Answers on Israel and Palestine.* N.d., 34 pp.; *The Bible Questions and Answers.* 1972, 68 pp.; *Is There a Hope for the Fallen Mankind?* N.d., 4 pp.

F. Polish Bible Students

The Polish movement outside the Society began in 1930 when they started publishing the journals *Strasz (Watchman)* in 1923 and *Bzask Nowej Ery (Dawn of a New Era).* Many non-Watchtower Society Bible Student classes formed in Poland especially after 1934. The general convention in Poland is held every two years and attracts over two thousand persons. Roughly three thousand registered with the government as Bible Students before the fall of communism. *Na Straszy (The Watch)* began publication in Warsaw in 1948.

Another group led by a Mr. Kaspczykowski (who died around 1960) severed ties with the Laymen's Home Missionary Movement in the United States and in 1958 began publishing *Swit (Daybreak)* in Warsaw. Many Polish Bible Student Classes exist throughout the United States and central Canada, and the American Polish General Convention alternates between Chicago and Detroit. The American Polish group is headquartered in Chicago, IL, and much English literature is translated into Polish there.

AUSTRALIAN GROUPS

The Australian Berean Bible Institute was founded in 1918 by R.E.B. Nickolson, partially as a result of his rejection of the Seventh Volume. The Institute has published the *People's Paper* in Melbourne since 1918. They are very close to the doctrines and beliefs of the Dawn Bible Students and since 1918 they have represented both the PBI and the Dawn in Australia. Several associated Berean Bible Student classes (including a Polish class) exist in Australia and also a few in New Zealand. The term Berean has about the same connotation in Australia as it had in America before World War II. At the same time, a revival group headed by Henninges in Melbourne published the *New Covenant Advocate* for several decades.

Frederick Lardent, who founded the *Christian Truth Institute* of Melbourne, Australia, and London, England, also published a number of booklets, pamphlets, and a periodical, *Gleanings for Truth Seekers.* In the United States, the Laymen's Home Missionary Movement distributes Lardent's Literature (see below).

A. Berean Bible Institute (Melbourne, Australia)

Magazines

The Voice. Melbourne, Australia: Berean Bible Institute, published irregularly, usually 2-
     4 pp.
People's Paper and Herald of Christ's Kingdom. Melbourne, Victoria, Australia: Berean
     Bible Institute, began in 1917 to date, published bimonthly, each issue 8 pp.

Books

Main, C.F. *Foregleams of the Golden Age.* Melbourne, Australia: Temple Court, 1919.
_____. *Notes on "The Finished Mystery."* Melbourne, Australia: Bible Students Tract
     Society, 1919, 43 pp.

Booklets
Hart, A.A. Our Lord's Return "That blessed Hope."
_____. Published as "The Word Paramount" Series no. 1, 12 pp. nd, published in
     Sydney, New South Wales, Australia.
Smith, W.A. *The Search for Truth--A True Life Story.* N.d., 35 pp.

Booklets, no author given: *Watch Israel--God's Time Clock.* c. 1978, 28 pp.; *Times
of Refreshing and Christ's Return.* c. 1978, 34 pp.; *The Christian's Joy.* N.d., c. 1978,
28 pp.;*Knowing God.* C. 1978, 40 pp.; *Earth's New Ruler--Humanity's Only Hope!* c.
1978, 32 pp.; *The Greatest of These Is Love.* c. 1978, 32 pp.; *Where Are the Dead? Do
They Know Anything?* c. 1978, 39 pp. (earlier edition., 16 pp. mimeo); *The Lord Is My
Shepherd.* c. 1979, 34 pp.; *Some of the Parables.* c. 1979, 58 pp.; *The Mystery of
Christ.* c. 1979, 32 pp.; *Our Lord's Great Prophecy.* c. 1979, 50 pp.; *A Peace Desired--
War Continues: Can Christianity Save the World?* c. 1980, 22 pp.; *The Manner of
Christ's Return an Appearing.* c. 1980, 64 pp. (On the second coming); *Christ's Return:
His Revealing and Manifestation.* c. 1980, 37 pp.; *The Abrahamic Seed of Blessing.* c.
1981, 30 pp.; *God's Rest Is Yet to Come.* c. 1981, 33 pp.; *Armageddon--Then Peace on
Earth.* c. 1981, 22 pp.

B. New Covenant Fellowship

     In 1909 three prominent pilgrims, H.G. Henninges, M.L. McPhail, and A.E.
Williamson, broke away from Russell's group partly because they could not accept his
new teaching on Christ's ransom and the atonement. They felt that it elevated the church
to the level of Christ as the Redeemer and Mediator for humanity. They also rejected what
they felt was Russell's heavy handedness and the common belief among Bible Students
that Russell was "that servant" mentioned in Matthew 25:45-47. These men influenced a
large number of persons, both in Australia and America, to leave Russell and join their
fellowships.
     A.M. McPhail was one of the most respected and loved Bible Students, second
only to Russell (Rogerson, 1972, p. 147). McPhail was quite active in the movement,
both as a pilgrim and in taking charge of the music at conventions. He composed hymns
and published a hymn book used by the Society, *Zion's Glad Songs*, which was the basis
of the Society's later hymn books. Another reason McPhail (as well as James Hay) and
E.C. Henninges left the Society was over the debate on the New Covenant issue. In 1880
Russell formulated an interpretation of the New Covenant which restricted its application
to the Millennial Age. Later he changed this interpretation, producing endless discussion
in the movement. The real issue was probably mostly over the degree of authority
Russell's works held in the movement.
     Nonetheless, McPhail left and in 1909 published his well known booklet.
Henninges and his wife, Rose Ball (the girl whom Russell had taken into his house and

who was involved in a scandal at Russell's divorce trial) published several books and tracts and later founded a new group named *The New Covenant Fellowship* in Australia. In America, the group took the name of *Christian Believers Conference.* They published the *Kingdom's Scribe* and the *Berean* and since 1910 an annual conference has been held, in recent years at Grove City College in Grove City, PA.

Most of their publications, even though no author is listed, were written by Henninges and are published under the auspices of the Covenant Publishing Company in Melbourne. In the 1920s the imprint became the *New Covenant Fellowship.* The main periodical is *The New Covenant Advocate and Kingdom Herald*, a monthly. Many of their publications, especially the shorter ones, were published as part of the series *The New Covenant Quarterly*, but some of the individual issues do not specifically name this series, which is possibly a continuation of Russell's *Old Theology* series. Dates are listed where known and the relative publishing order is attempted for the others.

Magazines

The New Covenant Advocate and Kingdom Herald. Ed. E.C. Heninges. 8 Fink's
    Building, Elizabeth Street, Melbourne, Australia, published monthly; started in
    1909, published until at least 1951.
New Covenant Messenger. Ed. H.S. Winbush, Melbourne, Australia.

Books

Hay, James. *Rays of Light from the Cross.* London: The Backroom, 1909.
Henninges, E.C., and R.B. Henninges. *Everlasting Punishment: An Appeal Direct to the
    Word.* Melbourne, Australia, 1911, hb., pb. (No 7 of *New Covenant Quarterly*,
    15,000 edition.). (An excellent detailed study of the doctrine of hell, concludes
    that hell is the grave, and no other hell exists).
_____. *Bible Talks for Heart and Mind.* Melbourne, Australia, 1909, 354 pp., hb., pb.
_____. *Daniel the Prophet in the Latter Days.* 1920.
_____. *Comparisons and Contrasts.* 1930, c. 434 pp.
McPhail, M.L. *The Covenants: Their Mediators and the Sin-Offerings.* Chicago, 1909,
    117 pp. (A critique of the Watchtower teaching on the covenants).
_____. *Types and Antitypes Reviewed.* Chicago, 1919.
McPhail, Mrs. *Three Views of the Ransom.*
_____. *The Three Sprinklings of the Precious Blood of Christ.*

Books, no author given. *Bible Talks for Heart and Mind.* 1909, 354, pp., 2nd
edition. 1911; *Miracles of the Past and Future.* 1911, 32 pp.; *The Parables of Our Lord.*
C. 1912, 400 pp., hb., pb.; *Everlasting Punishments.* c. 1912, 112 pp.; *The Christian's
Comforter.* 1913, 82 pp., hb., pb.; *Armageddon.* 1914, 64 pp.; *The Church and Its
Ceremonies.* 1914, 151 pp., hb., pb.; *Sabbath Observance: An Answer to Seventh-Day
Adventism.* 31 pp.; *The Dead, Where Are They?* 1917, hb., pb.; *The New Era.* 1920,
80 pp.; *The Spirits in Person: An Expose of Spiritualism.* 1920.; *The Inspiration of the
Bible.* 1926, 40 pp.; *Daniel the Prophet in the Latter Days.* c. 1927; *Christ's Prophecy
on Olivet.* c. 1927, 127 pp.; *The Divine Healer.* c. 1927, 80 pp.; *Do the Dead
Communicate?* C. 1928, 48 pp.; *Modernism, Fundamentalism and the Bible.* c. 1929, 45
pp., hb.; *Christ's Promised Return.* 1929, 38 pp.; *God's Plan for Humanity.* c. 1930;
Peace or War: Our Great Day and Its Issues. c. 1932, 96 pp., hb., pb.; *What Say the
Scriptures About the Ransom, Sin Offering, Covenants, Mediator, Scapegoat?* 1920, 80
pp., pb., hb. (Covers the basis for salvation)

Tracts include: *Death Abolished.* 16 pp., *The Wilderness of God's Mercy.* 4 pp.,
    Making the World Better. 8 pp. Believe. 4 pp.

C. The Christian Truth Institute

Frederick Lardent, who founded the *Christian Truth Institute* of Melbourne, Australia, and London, England, published a number of booklets, pamphlets, and a periodical, *Gleanings for Truth Seekers* (1931 to c. 1941).   In the United States, the Laymen's Home Missionary Movement distributes Lardent's Literature.   His booklets, listed in order of publication, include:

Booklets: *The Call of the Bride.*   N.d., 48 pp.; *God's Oath-Bound Promise.*   N.d., 23 pp.; *An Instrument of Ten Strings.*   N.d., 47 pp.; *Pilate's Report.*   N.d., 32 pp.; *These Things Shall Be!*   N.d., 14 pp.; *Think on These Things*, 20 pp. 1944, London England.

Several of Lardent's works (including *Call of the Bride* and *Comforted of God* are largely reproductions of his motto cards over 200 of these were issued (Hudson claims "with a sublime disregard for copyright" and when Lardent died in 1970 he left his printing blocks to Hudson who dumped them!)

Booklets: *God's Wonderful Time Clock.*   London, England; *Hidden Meaning of Bible Colours.*   London, England; *The Life of Abraham.*   London, England; *The Story of God's Far Reaching Plan.*   London, England; *Comforted of God.*   London, England: Christian Truth; *Covenants of God.*   London, England; *Out of Egypt.*   London, England; *Our Annointing*. London, England; *Pilate's Report.*   London, England; *Significant Forty.* London, England; *Then I Understand*. London, England.

Tracts: A set of tracts was issued under the name *Grace and Truth Series*.   Each tract was numbered. The only one identified is *A Little Child Shall Lead Them*. 4 pp.

Name Index

About the Compiler

JERRY BERGMAN is a professor in the Department of General Studies at Northwest State College. He has been researching and writing about the Jehovah's Witness movement for nearly four decades.